UKQR 2007

UK & Ireland Civil Registers Quick Reference

Compiled by Pete Webber

Copyright © Air-Britain (Historians) Ltd 2007

Published by: Air-Britain (Historians) Ltd
www.air-britain.co.uk

Sales Department: 41 Penshurst Road, Leigh,
Tonbridge, Kent TN11 8HL

Membership Enquiries: 1 Rose Cottages, 179 Penn Road,
Hazlemere, Buckinghamshire HP15 7NE

ISBN: 0 85130 382 X   9780851 303826

PHOTO CAPTIONS:
Front: Silence Twisters G-TWST and G-TWSR displaying at the Microlight Fair, Popham 29.4.06.
(Kevin Parsons/ABPic)
Back: Beautifully-restored Chilton DW.1 G-AESZ visiting the PFA Flying for Fun rally at Kemble 20.8.06.
(Dave Partington)
Aurigny ATR-72 G-BXTN landing in brilliant sunshine at Bristol International 8.9.06. (Pete Webber/ABPic)
Merlin HC-3 ZJ122 participated in the display at RIAT, Fairford 14.7.06. (Pete Webber)

Printed by Bell & Bain Ltd, Glasgow

UKQR 2007

United Kingdom & Ireland Civil Registers
Quick Reference 2007

Welcome to the latest edition of the Quick Reference UK & Ireland registers. The data contained herein is corrected to 20th February 2007.

No new sections this year, new gliders continue to join the register but many have used out-of-sequence marks which has resulted in a few in-sequence allocations not being taken up.

As ever any publication such as this is the work of many. I must thank all those who have written since the last edition for the many notes, changes and suggestions passed on. May I also thank Barrie Womersley for his notes and help, and Dave Partington and Chris Chatfield for their production assistance. The overseas-registered aircraft data has been compiled by Paul Hewins. The UK Bases data continues to be maintained by Dave Reid.

Once again may I ask that if you have any further suggestions for changes, note any missing information, or can help out with future editions in any way, you should contact me at the addess below.

Pete Webber
20 Purbeck Close
Swindon
Wilts SN3 3RE
pete.webber@air-britain.co.uk

United Kingdom current civil aircraft

☐ G-EASD	Avro 504L
☐ G-EBHX	DH.53
☐ G-EBIA	SE-5A
☐ G-EBIR	DH.51
☐ G-EBJO	ANEC II
☐ G-EBKY	Sopwith Dove
☐ G-EBLV	DH.60
☐ G-EBNV	English Electric Wren
☐ G-EBQP	DH.53
☐ G-EBWD	DH.60
☐ G-EBZN	DH.60X Moth
☐ G-AADR	DH.60G Moth
☐ G-AAEG	DH.60G Moth
☐ G-AAHI	DH.60G Moth
☐ G-AAHY	DH.60M Moth
☐ G-AAIN	Parnall Elf II
☐ G-AAJT	DH.60G Moth
☐ G-AALY	DH.60G Moth
☐ G-AAMY	DH.60GM Moth
☐ G-AANG	Bleriot XI
☐ G-AANH	Deperdussin Mono
☐ G-AANI	Blackburn Monoplane
☐ G-AANL	DH.60M Moth
☐ G-AANM	Bristol F.2B
☐ G-AANO	DH.60GMW Moth
☐ G-AANV	DH.60M Moth
☐ G-AAOK	Curtiss-Wright Travel Air
☐ G-AAOR	DH.60G Moth
☐ G-AAPZ	Desoutter 1
☐ G-AAUP	Klemm L.25-Ia
☐ G-AAWO	DH.60G Moth
☐ G-AAYT	DH.60G Moth
☐ G-AAYX	Southern Martlet
☐ G-AAZG	DH.60G Moth
☐ G-AAZP	DH.80A Puss Moth
☐ G-ABAA	Avro 504K
☐ G-ABAG	DH.60G Moth
☐ G-ABBB	Bristol Bulldog
☐ G-ABDA	DH.60G Moth
☐ G-ABDX	DH.60G Moth
☐ G-ABEV	DH.60G Moth
☐ G-ABLM	Cierva C.24
☐ G-ABLS	DH.80A Puss Moth
☐ G-ABMR	Hawker Hart
☐ G-ABNT	Civilian Coupe
☐ G-ABNX	Robinson Redwing
☐ G-ABOX	Sopwith Pup
☐ G-ABSD	DH.60G Moth
☐ G-ABTC	Comper Swift
☐ G-ABUS	Comper Swift
☐ G-ABVE	Arrow Active 2
☐ G-ABWP	Spartan Arrow I
☐ G-ABXL	Granger Archaeopteryx
☐ G-ABYA	DH.60G Moth
☐ G-ABZB	DH.60G Moth
☐ G-ACCB	DH.83 Fox Moth
☐ G-ACDA	DH.82A Tiger Moth
☐ G-ACDC	DH.82A Tiger Moth
☐ G-ACDI	DH.82A Tiger Moth
☐ G-ACEJ	DH.83 Fox Moth
☐ G-ACET	DH.84 Dragon
☐ G-ACGR	Percival Gull Four
☐ G-ACGT	Avro Avian IIIA
☐ G-ACGZ	DH.60G Moth
☐ G-ACIT	DH.84 Dragon
☐ G-ACLL	DH.85 Leopard Moth
☐ G-ACMA	DH.85 Leopard Moth
☐ G-ACMD	DH.82A Tiger Moth
☐ G-ACMN	DH.85 Leopard Moth
☐ G-ACNS	DH.60G Moth
☐ G-ACOJ	DH.85 Leopard Moth
☐ G-ACSP	DH.88 Comet
☐ G-ACSS	DH.88 Comet
☐ G-ACTF	Comper Swift
☐ G-ACUS	DH.85 Leopard Moth
☐ G-ACUU	Cierva C.30A
☐ G-ACUX	Short Scion
☐ G-ACVA	Kay Gyroplane
☐ G-ACWM	Cierva C.30A
☐ G-ACWP	Cierva C.30A
☐ G-ACXB	DH.60G Moth
☐ G-ACYR	DH.89 Dragon Rapide
☐ G-ACZE	DH.89A Dragon Rapide
☐ G-ADAH	DH.89 Dragon Rapide
☐ G-ADEV	Avro 504K
☐ G-ADGP	Miles Hawk Speed Six
☐ G-ADGT	DH.82A Tiger Moth
☐ G-ADGV	DH.82A Tiger Moth
☐ G-ADHD	DH.60G Moth
☐ G-ADIA	DH.82A Tiger Moth
☐ G-ADJJ	DH.82A Tiger Moth
☐ G-ADKC	DH.87B Hornet Moth
☐ G-ADKK	DH.87B Hornet Moth
☐ G-ADKL	DH.87B Hornet Moth
☐ G-ADKM	DH.87B Hornet Moth
☐ G-ADLY	DH.87B Hornet Moth
☐ G-ADMT	DH.87B Hornet Moth
☐ G-ADMW	Miles Hawk Major
☐ G-ADND	DH.87B Hornet Moth
☐ G-ADNE	DH.87B Hornet Moth
☐ G-ADNL	Miles Sparrowhawk
☐ G-ADNZ	DH.82A Tiger Moth
☐ G-ADOT	DH.87B Hornet Moth
☐ G-ADPC	DH.82A Tiger Moth
☐ G-ADPS	BA Swallow II
☐ G-ADRA	Pietenpol Aircamper
☐ G-ADRH	DH.87A Hornet Moth
☐ G-ADUR	DH.87B Hornet Moth
☐ G-ADWJ	DH.82A Tiger Moth
☐ G-ADWO	DH.82A Tiger Moth
☐ G-ADWT	Miles M.2W Hawk Tr
☐ G-ADXS	Mignet HM.14
☐ G-ADXT	DH.82A Tiger Moth
☐ G-ADYS	Aeronca C.3
☐ G-AEBB	Mignet HM.14
☐ G-AEBJ	Blackburn B.2
☐ G-AEDB	B.A.C. Drone
☐ G-AEDU	DH.90 Dragonfly
☐ G-AEEG	Miles M.3A Falcon Major
☐ G-AEEH	Mignet HM.14
☐ G-AEFG	Mignet HM.14
☐ G-AEFT	Aeronca C.3
☐ G-AEGV	Mignet HM.14
☐ G-AEHM	Mignet HM.14
☐ G-AEJZ	Mignet HM.14
☐ G-AEKR	Mignet HM.14
☐ G-AEKV	B.A.C. Drone
☐ G-AEKW	Miles M.12 Mohawk
☐ G-AELO	DH.87B Hornet Moth
☐ G-AEML	DH.89 Dragon Rapide
☐ G-AENP	Hawker Hind
☐ G-AEOA	DH.80A Puss Moth
☐ G-AEOF	Rearwin 8500
☐ G-AEPH	Bristol F.2B
☐ G-AERV	Miles Whitney Straight
☐ G-AESB	Aeronca C.3
☐ G-AESE	DH.87B Hornet Moth
☐ G-AESZ	Chilton DW.1
☐ G-AETA	Caudron G.III
☐ G-AEUJ	Miles Whitney Straight
☐ G-AEVS	Aeronca 100
☐ G-AEXF	Percival Mew Gull
☐ G-AEXT	Dart Kitten II
☐ G-AEXZ	Piper J-2 Cub
☐ G-AEYY	Martin Monoplane
☐ G-AEZF	Short Scion 2
☐ G-AEZJ	Percival Vega Gull
☐ G-AFAX	BA Eagle 2
☐ G-AFBS	Miles Hawk Trainer
☐ G-AFCL	BA Swallow II
☐ G-AFDO	Piper J-3C-65 Cub
☐ G-AFEL	Monocoupe 90A
☐ G-AFFD	Percival Q Six
☐ G-AFFH	Piper J-2 Cub
☐ G-AFGC	BA Swallow II
☐ G-AFGD	BA Swallow II
☐ G-AFGE	BA Swallow II
☐ G-AFGH	Chilton DW.1
☐ G-AFGI	Chilton DW.1
☐ G-AFGM	Piper J-4A Cub Coupe
☐ G-AFGZ	DH.82A Tiger Moth
☐ G-AFHC	BA Swallow II
☐ G-AFIN	Chrislea Airguard
☐ G-AFIR	Luton Minor
☐ G-AFJA	Taylor-Watkinson Dingbat
☐ G-AFJB	Foster-WicknerWicko
☐ G-AFJU	Miles Monarch
☐ G-AFLW	Miles Monarch
☐ G-AFNG	DH.94 Moth Minor
☐ G-AFNI	DH.94 Moth Minor
☐ G-AFOB	DH.94 Moth Minor
☐ G-AFOJ	DH.94 Moth Minor
☐ G-AFPN	DH.94 Moth Minor
☐ G-AFRZ	Miles Monarch
☐ G-AFSC	Tipsy Trainer 1
☐ G-AFSV	Chilton DW.1A
☐ G-AFTA	Hawker Tomtit
☐ G-AFTN	Taylorcraft Plus C2
☐ G-AFUP	Luscombe 8A Silvaire
☐ G-AFVE	DH.82A Tiger Moth
☐ G-AFWH	Piper J-4A Cub Coupe
☐ G-AFWI	DH.82A Tiger Moth
☐ G-AFWT	Tipsy Trainer 1
☐ G-AFYD	Luscombe 8AF Silvaire
☐ G-AFYO	Stinson 105
☐ G-AFZA	Piper J-4A Cub Coupe
☐ G-AFZK	Luscombe 8A Silvaire
☐ G-AFZL	Porterfield CP-50
☐ G-AFZN	Luscombe 8A Silvaire
☐ G-AGAT	Piper J-3F-50 Cub
☐ G-AGBN	GAL.42 Cygnet 2
☐ G-AGEG	DH.82A Tiger Moth
☐ G-AGFT	Avia FL.3
☐ G-AGHY	DH.82A Tiger Moth
☐ G-AGIV	Piper J-3C-65 Cub
☐ G-AGJG	DH.89A Dragon Rapide
☐ G-AGLK	Auster 5D
☐ G-AGMI	Luscombe 8A Silvaire
☐ G-AGNJ	DH.82A Tiger Moth
☐ G-AGNV	Avro York
☐ G-AGOH	Auster J/1 Autocrat
☐ G-AGOS	RS4 Desford Trainer
☐ G-AGPG	Avro 652 Anson
☐ G-AGPK	DH.82A Tiger Moth
☐ G-AGRU	Vickers Viking
☐ G-AGSH	DH.89A Dragon Rapide
☐ G-AGTM	DH.89A Dragon Rapide
☐ G-AGTO	Auster J/1 Autocrat
☐ G-AGTT	Auster J/1 Autocrat
☐ G-AGVG	Auster J/1 Autocrat
☐ G-AGVN	Auster J/1 Autocrat
☐ G-AGVV	Piper J-3C-65 Cub

☐ G-AGXN	Auster J/1N Alpha	
☐ G-AGXU	Auster J/1N Alpha	
☐ G-AGXV	Auster J/1 Autocrat	
☐ G-AGYD	Auster J/1N Alpha	
☐ G-AGYK	Auster J/1 Autocrat	
☐ G-AGYN	Auster J/1N Alpha	
☐ G-AGYT	Auster J/1N Alpha	
☐ G-AGYU	DH.82A Tiger Moth	
☐ G-AGYY	Ryan ST3KR	
☐ G-AGZZ	DH.82A Tiger Moth	
☐ G-AHAG	DH.89A Dragon Rapide	
☐ G-AHAL	Auster J/1N Alpha	
☐ G-AHAM	Auster J/1 Autocrat	
☐ G-AHAN	DH.82A Tiger Moth	
☐ G-AHAP	Auster J/1 Autocrat	
☐ G-AHAT	Auster J/1N Alpha	
☐ G-AHAU	Auster J/1 Autocrat-160	
☐ G-AHAV	Auster J/1 Autocrat	
☐ G-AHBL	DH.87B Hornet Moth	
☐ G-AHBM	DH.87B Hornet Moth	
☐ G-AHCL	Auster J/1N Alpha	
☐ G-AHCN	Auster J/1N Alpha	
☐ G-AHCR	Taylorcraft Plus D	
☐ G-AHEC	Luscombe 8A Silvaire	
☐ G-AHED	DH.89A Dragon Rapide	
☐ G-AHGD	DH.89A Dragon Rapide	
☐ G-AHGW	Taylorcraft Plus D	
☐ G-AHGZ	Taylorcraft Plus D	
☐ G-AHHH	Auster J/1 Autocrat	
☐ G-AHHT	Auster J/1N Alpha	
☐ G-AHIP	Piper J-3C-65 Cub	
☐ G-AHIZ	DH.82A Tiger Moth	
☐ G-AHKX	Avro 652 Anson	
☐ G-AHKY	Miles M.18	
☐ G-AHLK	Auster III	
☐ G-AHLT	DH.82A Tiger Moth	
☐ G-AHMN	DH.82A Tiger Moth	
☐ G-AHNR	Taylorcraft BC12D	
☐ G-AHOO	DH.82A Tiger Moth	
☐ G-AHPZ	DH.82A Tiger Moth	
☐ G-AHRI	DH.104 Dove 1B	
☐ G-AHSA	Avro 621 Tutor	
☐ G-AHSD	Taylorcraft Plus D	
☐ G-AHSO	Auster J/1N Alpha	
☐ G-AHSP	Auster J/1 Autocrat	
☐ G-AHSS	Auster J/1N Alpha	
☐ G-AHTE	Percival Proctor	
☐ G-AHTW	Airspeed Oxford	
☐ G-AHUF	DH.82A Tiger Moth	
☐ G-AHUG	Taylorcraft Plus D	
☐ G-AHUJ	Miles Hawk Trainer	
☐ G-AHUN	Globe GC-1B Swift	
☐ G-AHUV	DH.82A Tiger Moth	
☐ G-AHVU	DH.82A Tiger Moth	
☐ G-AHVV	DH.82A Tiger Moth	
☐ G-AHWJ	Taylorcraft Plus D	
☐ G-AHXE	Taylorcraft Plus D	
☐ G-AIBE	Fairey Fulmar 2	
☐ G-AIBH	Auster J/1N Alpha	
☐ G-AIBM	Auster J/1 Autocrat	
☐ G-AIBR	Auster J/1 Autocrat	
☐ G-AIBW	Auster J/1N Alpha	
☐ G-AIBX	Auster J/1 Autocrat	
☐ G-AIBY	Auster J/1 Autocrat	
☐ G-AICX	Luscombe 8A Silvaire	
☐ G-AIDL	DH.89A Dragon Rapide	
☐ G-AIDS	DH.82A Tiger Moth	
☐ G-AIEK	Miles Messenger	
☐ G-AIFZ	Auster J/1N Alpha	
☐ G-AIGD	Auster J/1 Autocrat	
☐ G-AIGF	Auster J/1N Alpha	
☐ G-AIGP	Auster J/1 Autocrat	
☐ G-AIGT	Auster J/1N Alpha	
☐ G-AIGU	Auster J/1N Alpha	
☐ G-AIIH	Piper J-3C-65 Cub	
☐ G-AIJM	Auster J/4 Archer	
☐ G-AIJT	Auster J/4 Archer	
☐ G-AIPR	Auster J/4 Archer	
☐ G-AIPV	Auster J/1 Autocrat	
☐ G-AIRC	Auster J/1 Autocrat	
☐ G-AIRI	DH.82A Tiger Moth	
☐ G-AIRK	DH.82A Tiger Moth	
☐ G-AISA	Tipsy B	
☐ G-AISC	Tipsy B	
☐ G-AISD	Miles M.65 Gemini 1A	
☐ G-AISS	Piper J-3C-65 Cub	
☐ G-AIST	Spitfire 1A	
☐ G-AISU	Spitfire LF.VB	
☐ G-AISX	Piper J-3C-85 Cub	
☐ G-AITB	Airspeed Oxford	
☐ G-AIUA	Miles M.14A Hawk Trainer	
☐ G-AIXJ	DH.82A Tiger Moth	
☐ G-AIXN	Mraz M.1C Sokol	
☐ G-AIYG	Stampe SV-4B	
☐ G-AIYR	DH.89A Dragon Rapide	
☐ G-AIYS	DH.85 Leopard Moth	
☐ G-AIZE	Fairchild F.24W	
☐ G-AIZG	Walrus 1	
☐ G-AIZU	Auster J/1 Autocrat	
☐ G-AIZY	Auster J/1 Autocrat	
☐ G-AJAD	Piper J-3C-65 Cub	
☐ G-AJAE	Auster J/1N Alpha	
☐ G-AJAJ	Auster J/1N Alpha	
☐ G-AJAM	Auster J/2 Arrow	
☐ G-AJAP	Luscombe 8A Silvaire	
☐ G-AJAS	Auster J/1N Alpha	
☐ G-AJBJ	DH.89A Dragon Rapide	
☐ G-AJCP	Druine D.31	
☐ G-AJDW	Auster J/1 Autocrat	
☐ G-AJEB	Auster J/1N Alpha	
☐ G-AJEE	Auster J/1 Autocrat	
☐ G-AJEH	Auster J/1N Alpha	
☐ G-AJEI	Auster J/1N Alpha	
☐ G-AJEM	Auster J/1 Autocrat	
☐ G-AJES	Piper J-3C-65 Cub	
☐ G-AJGJ	Auster 5	
☐ G-AJHJ	Auster 5	
☐ G-AJHS	DH.82A Tiger Moth	
☐ G-AJIH	Auster J/1 Autocrat	
☐ G-AJIS	Auster J/1N Alpha	
☐ G-AJIT	Auster J/1 Autocrat	
☐ G-AJIU	Auster J/1 Autocrat	
☐ G-AJIW	Auster J/1N Alpha	
☐ G-AJJS	Cessna 120	
☐ G-AJJT	Cessna 120	
☐ G-AJJU	Luscombe 8E Silvaire	
☐ G-AJKB	Luscombe 8E Silvaire	
☐ G-AJOE	Miles Messenger	
☐ G-AJON	Aeronca 7AC Champion	
☐ G-AJOZ	Fairchild F.24W	
☐ G-AJPI	Fairchild F.24R	
☐ G-AJPZ	Auster J/1 Autocrat	
☐ G-AJRB	Auster J/1 Autocrat	
☐ G-AJRC	Auster J/1 Autocrat	
☐ G-AJRE	Auster J/1 Autocrat	
☐ G-AJRH	Auster J/1N Alpha	
☐ G-AJRS	Miles Hawk Trainer	
☐ G-AJTW	DH.82A Tiger Moth	
☐ G-AJUE	Auster J/1 Autocrat	
☐ G-AJUL	Auster J/1N Alpha	
☐ G-AJVE	DH.82A Tiger Moth	
☐ G-AJVH	Fairey Swordfish II	
☐ G-AJWB	Miles Messenger	
☐ G-AJXC	Auster 5	
☐ G-AJXV	Auster 4	
☐ G-AJXY	Auster 4	
☐ G-AJYB	Auster J/1N Alpha	
☐ G-AKAT	Miles Hawk Trainer	
☐ G-AKAZ	Piper J-3C-65 Cub	
☐ G-AKDN	DHC-1 Chipmunk	
☐ G-AKDW	DH.89A Dragon Rapide	
☐ G-AKEK	Miles M.65 Gemini 1A	
☐ G-AKGE	Miles M.65 Gemini 1A	
☐ G-AKHP	Miles M.65 Gemini 1A	
☐ G-AKIB	Piper J-3C-90 Cub	
☐ G-AKIF	DH.89A Dragon Rapide	
☐ G-AKIN	Miles Messenger	
☐ G-AKIU	Percival Proctor	
☐ G-AKKB	Miles M.65 Gemini 1A	
☐ G-AKKH	Miles M.65 Gemini 1A	
☐ G-AKKR	Miles Hawk Trainer	
☐ G-AKKY	Miles Hawk Trainer	
☐ G-AKOW	Auster 5	
☐ G-AKPF	Miles Hawk Trainer	
☐ G-AKRA	Piper J-3C-65 Cub	
☐ G-AKRP	DH.89A Dragon Rapide	
☐ G-AKSY	Auster 5D	
☐ G-AKSZ	Auster 5C	
☐ G-AKTH	Piper J-3C-65 Cub	
☐ G-AKTI	Luscombe 8A Silvaire	
☐ G-AKTK	Aeronca 11AC Chief	
☐ G-AKTN	Luscombe 8A Silvaire	
☐ G-AKTO	Aeronca 7BCM Champion	
☐ G-AKTP	Piper PA-17 Vagabond	
☐ G-AKTR	Aeronca 7AC Champion	
☐ G-AKTS	Cessna 120	
☐ G-AKTT	Luscombe 8A Silvaire	
☐ G-AKUE	DH.82A Tiger Moth	
☐ G-AKUF	Luscombe 8F Silvaire	
☐ G-AKUG	Luscombe 8A Silvaire	
☐ G-AKUH	Luscombe 8E Silvaire	
☐ G-AKUI	Luscombe 8E Silvaire	
☐ G-AKUJ	Luscombe 8E Silvaire	
☐ G-AKUK	Luscombe 8A Silvaire	
☐ G-AKUL	Luscombe 8A Silvaire	
☐ G-AKUM	Luscombe 8F Silvaire	
☐ G-AKUN	Piper J-3C-85 Cub	
☐ G-AKUO	Aeronca 11AC Chief	
☐ G-AKUP	Luscombe 8E Silvaire	
☐ G-AKUR	Cessna 140	
☐ G-AKUW	Chrislea Super Ace	
☐ G-AKVF	Chrislea Super Ace	
☐ G-AKVM	Cessna 120	
☐ G-AKVN	Aeronca 11AC Chief	
☐ G-AKVO	Taylorcraft BC12D	
☐ G-AKVP	Luscombe 8A Silvaire	
☐ G-AKVR	Chrislea Super Ace	
☐ G-AKVZ	Miles Messenger	
☐ G-AKWS	Auster 5A-160	
☐ G-AKXP	Auster 5	
☐ G-AKXS	DH.82A Tiger Moth	
☐ G-AKZN	Percival Proctor	
☐ G-ALBJ	Auster 5	
☐ G-ALBK	Auster 5	
☐ G-ALBN	Bristol B.173 Mk.1	
☐ G-ALCK	Percival Proctor	
☐ G-ALCU	DH.104 Dove 2B	
☐ G-ALDG	HP.81 Hermes 4	
☐ G-ALEH	Piper PA-17 Vagabond	
☐ G-ALFA	Auster 5	
☐ G-ALFT	DH.104 Dove 6	
☐ G-ALFU	DH.104 Dove 6	
☐ G-ALGA	Piper PA-15 Vagabond	
☐ G-ALGT	Spitfire F.Mk.XIVc	
☐ G-ALIJ	Piper PA-17 Vagabond	
☐ G-ALIW	DH.82A Tiger Moth	
☐ G-ALJF	Percival Proctor	
☐ G-ALJL	DH.82A Tiger Moth	
☐ G-ALLF	Slingsby T.30A	

☐ G-ALNA	DH.82A Tiger Moth
☐ G-ALND	DH.82A Tiger Moth
☐ G-ALOD	Cessna 140
☐ G-ALRI	DH.82A Tiger Moth
☐ G-ALSX	Bristol Sycamore
☐ G-ALTO	Cessna 140
☐ G-ALUC	DH.82A Tiger Moth
☐ G-ALWB	DHC-1 Chipmunk
☐ G-ALWF	Vickers Viscount
☐ G-ALWS	DH.82A Tiger Moth
☐ G-ALWW	DH.82A Tiger Moth
☐ G-ALXT	DH.89A Dragon Rapide
☐ G-ALXZ	Auster 5
☐ G-ALYB	Auster 5
☐ G-ALYW	DH.106 Comet 1
☐ G-ALZE	BN1F
☐ G-ALZO	Airspeed AS.57-2
☐ G-AMAW	Luton Minor
☐ G-AMBB	DH.82A Tiger Moth
☐ G-AMCK	DH.82A Tiger Moth
☐ G-AMDA	Avro 652 Anson 1
☐ G-AMEN	Piper PA-18-115
☐ G-AMHF	DH.82A Tiger Moth
☐ G-AMIV	DH.82A Tiger Moth
☐ G-AMKU	Auster J/1B Aiglet
☐ G-AMLZ	Percival Prince
☐ G-AMMS	Auster J/5K Aiglet Trainer
☐ G-AMNN	DH.82A Tiger Moth
☐ G-AMOG	Vickers Viscount
☐ G-AMPG	Piper PA-12 Super Cruiser
☐ G-AMPI	Stampe SV-4C
☐ G-AMPY	Douglas DC-3
☐ G-AMRA	Douglas DC-3
☐ G-AMRF	Auster J/5F Aiglet Trainer
☐ G-AMRK	Gloster Gladiator 1
☐ G-AMSG	SIPA 903
☐ G-AMSN	Douglas DC-3
☐ G-AMTA	Auster J/5F Aiglet Trainer
☐ G-AMTF	DH.82A Tiger Moth
☐ G-AMTK	DH.82A Tiger Moth
☐ G-AMTM	Auster J/1 Autocrat
☐ G-AMTV	DH.82A Tiger Moth
☐ G-AMUF	DHC-1 Chipmunk
☐ G-AMUI	Auster J/5F Aiglet Trainer
☐ G-AMVD	Auster 5
☐ G-AMVP	Tipsy Junior
☐ G-AMVS	DH.82A Tiger Moth
☐ G-AMYD	Auster J/5L Aiglet Trainer
☐ G-AMZI	Auster J/5F Aiglet Trainer
☐ G-AMZT	Auster J/5F Aiglet Trainer
☐ G-AMZU	Auster J/5F Aiglet Trainer
☐ G-ANAF	Douglas DC-3
☐ G-ANAP	DH.104 Dove 6
☐ G-ANCF	Bristol B.175-308F
☐ G-ANCS	DH.82A Tiger Moth
☐ G-ANCX	DH.82A Tiger Moth
☐ G-ANDE	DH.82A Tiger Moth
☐ G-ANDM	DH.82A Tiger Moth
☐ G-ANDP	DH.82A Tiger Moth
☐ G-ANEH	DH.82A Tiger Moth
☐ G-ANEL	DH.82A Tiger Moth
☐ G-ANEM	DH.82A Tiger Moth
☐ G-ANEN	DH.82A Tiger Moth
☐ G-ANEW	DH.82A Tiger Moth
☐ G-ANEZ	DH.82A Tiger Moth
☐ G-ANFC	DH.82A Tiger Moth
☐ G-ANFH	Westland Whirlwind
☐ G-ANFI	DH.82A Tiger Moth
☐ G-ANFL	DH.82A Tiger Moth
☐ G-ANFM	DH.82A Tiger Moth
☐ G-ANFP	DH.82A Tiger Moth
☐ G-ANFU	Auster 5
☐ G-ANFV	DH.82A Tiger Moth

☐ G-ANGK	Cessna 140A
☐ G-ANHK	DH.82A Tiger Moth
☐ G-ANHR	Auster 5
☐ G-ANHS	Auster 4
☐ G-ANHU	Auster 4
☐ G-ANIE	Auster 5
☐ G-ANIJ	Auster 5D
☐ G-ANIS	Auster 5
☐ G-ANJA	DH.82A Tiger Moth
☐ G-ANJD	DH.82A Tiger Moth
☐ G-ANJK	DH.82A Tiger Moth
☐ G-ANJV	Westland Whirlwind
☐ G-ANKK	DH.82A Tiger Moth
☐ G-ANKT	DH.82A Tiger Moth
☐ G-ANKV	DH.82A Tiger Moth
☐ G-ANKZ	DH.82A Tiger Moth
☐ G-ANLD	DH.82A Tiger Moth
☐ G-ANLS	DH.82A Tiger Moth
☐ G-ANMO	DH.82A Tiger Moth
☐ G-ANMY	DH.82A Tiger Moth
☐ G-ANNB	DH.82A Tiger Moth
☐ G-ANNE	DH.82A Tiger Moth
☐ G-ANNG	DH.82A Tiger Moth
☐ G-ANNI	DH.82A Tiger Moth
☐ G-ANNK	DH.82A Tiger Moth
☐ G-ANOH	DH.82A Tiger Moth
☐ G-ANON	DH.82A Tiger Moth
☐ G-ANOO	DH.82A Tiger Moth
☐ G-ANOV	DH.104 Dove 6
☐ G-ANPE	DH.82A Tiger Moth
☐ G-ANRF	DH.82A Tiger Moth
☐ G-ANRM	DH.82A Tiger Moth
☐ G-ANRN	DH.82A Tiger Moth
☐ G-ANRP	Auster 5
☐ G-ANRX	DH.82A Tiger Moth
☐ G-ANSM	DH.82A Tiger Moth
☐ G-ANTE	DH.82A Tiger Moth
☐ G-ANTK	Avro York C1
☐ G-ANUO	DH.114 Heron 2D
☐ G-ANUW	DH.104 Dove 6
☐ G-ANWB	DHC-1 Chipmunk
☐ G-ANWX	Auster J/5L Aiglet Trainer
☐ G-ANXB	DH.114 Heron 1B
☐ G-ANXC	Auster J/5R Alpine
☐ G-ANXR	Percival Proctor
☐ G-ANZT	Thruxton Jackaroo
☐ G-ANZU	DH.82A Tiger Moth
☐ G-ANZZ	DH.82A Tiger Moth
☐ G-AOAA	DH.82A Tiger Moth
☐ G-AOBG	Somers-Kendall SK-1
☐ G-AOBH	DH.82A Tiger Moth
☐ G-AOBO	DH.82A Tiger Moth
☐ G-AOBU	Jet Provost T1
☐ G-AOBX	DH.82A Tiger Moth
☐ G-AOCR	Auster 5D
☐ G-AOCU	Auster 5
☐ G-AODA	Westland Whirlwind
☐ G-AODR	DH.82A Tiger Moth
☐ G-AODT	DH.82A Tiger Moth
☐ G-AOEH	Aeronca 7AC Champion
☐ G-AOEI	DH.82A Tiger Moth
☐ G-AOEL	DH.82A Tiger Moth
☐ G-AOES	DH.82A Tiger Moth
☐ G-AOET	DH.82A Tiger Moth
☐ G-AOEX	Thruxton Jackaroo
☐ G-AOFE	DHC-1 Chipmunk
☐ G-AOFJ	Auster Alpha 5
☐ G-AOFS	Auster J/5L Aiglet Trainer
☐ G-AOGE	Percival Proctor 3
☐ G-AOGI	DH.82A Tiger Moth
☐ G-AOGR	DH.82A Tiger Moth
☐ G-AOGV	Auster J/5R Alpine
☐ G-AOHY	DH.82A Tiger Moth

☐ G-AOHZ	Auster J/5P Autocar
☐ G-AOIL	DH.82A Tiger Moth
☐ G-AOIM	DH.82A Tiger Moth
☐ G-AOIR	Thruxton Jackaroo
☐ G-AOIS	DH.82A Tiger Moth
☐ G-AOIY	Auster J/5V Autocar
☐ G-AOJH	DH.83C Fox Moth
☐ G-AOJJ	DH.82A Tiger Moth
☐ G-AOJK	DH.82A Tiger Moth
☐ G-AOJR	DHC-1 Chipmunk
☐ G-AOJT	DH.106 Comet 1XB
☐ G-AOKH	Percival Prentice
☐ G-AOKL	Percival Prentice
☐ G-AOKO	Percival Prentice
☐ G-AOKZ	Percival Prentice
☐ G-AOLK	Percival Prentice
☐ G-AOLU	Percival Prentice
☐ G-AORB	Cessna 170B
☐ G-AORG	DH.114 Heron 2
☐ G-AORW	DHC-1 Chipmunk
☐ G-AOSF	DHC-1 Chipmunk
☐ G-AOSK	DHC-1 Chipmunk
☐ G-AOSY	DHC-1 Chipmunk
☐ G-AOTD	DHC-1 Chipmunk
☐ G-AOTF	DHC-1 Chipmunk
☐ G-AOTI	DH.114 Heron 2D
☐ G-AOTK	Druine Turbi
☐ G-AOTR	DHC-1 Chipmunk
☐ G-AOTY	DHC-1 Chipmunk
☐ G-AOUJ	Fairey Ultralight
☐ G-AOUO	DHC-1 Chipmunk
☐ G-AOUP	DHC-1 Chipmunk
☐ G-AOUR	DH.82A Tiger Moth
☐ G-AOVF	Bristol B.175-312F
☐ G-AOVT	Bristol B.175-312
☐ G-AOVW	Auster 5
☐ G-AOXG	DH.82A Tiger Moth
☐ G-AOXN	DH.82A Tiger Moth
☐ G-AOZE	Westland Widgeon
☐ G-AOZH	DH.82A Tiger Moth
☐ G-AOZL	Auster J/5Q Alpine
☐ G-AOZP	DHC-1 Chipmunk
☐ G-APAF	Auster 5
☐ G-APAH	Auster 5
☐ G-APAJ	Thruxton Jackaroo
☐ G-APAL	DH.82A Tiger Moth
☐ G-APAM	DH.82A Tiger Moth
☐ G-APAO	DH.82A Tiger Moth
☐ G-APAP	DH.82A Tiger Moth
☐ G-APAS	DH.106 Comet 1A
☐ G-APBE	Auster 5
☐ G-APBI	DH.82A Tiger Moth
☐ G-APBO	Druine Turbi
☐ G-APBW	Auster 5A
☐ G-APCB	Auster J/5Q Alpine
☐ G-APCC	DH.82A Tiger Moth
☐ G-APDB	DH.106 Comet
☐ G-APEP	Vickers Vanguard
☐ G-APFA	Druine Turbi
☐ G-APFJ	Boeing 707-436
☐ G-APFU	DH.82A Tiger Moth
☐ G-APFV	Piper PA-23-160 Apache
☐ G-APGL	DH.82A Tiger Moth
☐ G-APHV	Avro 652 Anson 2
☐ G-APIE	Tipsy Belfair
☐ G-APIH	DH.82A Tiger Moth
☐ G-APIK	Auster J/1N Alpha
☐ G-APIM	Vickers Viscount
☐ G-APIT	Percival Prentice
☐ G-APIU	Percival Prentice
☐ G-APIY	Percival Prentice
☐ G-APIZ	Druine Turbulent
☐ G-APJB	Percival Prentice

Reg	Type	Reg	Type	Reg	Type
☐ G-APJJ	Fairey Ultralight	☐ G-ARAN	Piper PA-18-150	☐ G-ARJT	Piper PA-23-160 Apache G
☐ G-APJO	DH.82A Tiger Moth	☐ G-ARAO	Piper PA-18-95	☐ G-ARJU	Piper PA-23-160 Apache G
☐ G-APKN	Auster J/1N Alpha	☐ G-ARAP	Aeronca 7EC Traveler	☐ G-ARJV	Piper PA-23-160 Apache G
☐ G-APLG	Auster J/5L Aiglet Trainer	☐ G-ARAS	Aeronca 7FC Tri-Traveler	☐ G-ARJZ	Druine Turbulent
☐ G-APLO	DHC-1 Chipmunk	☐ G-ARAT	Cessna 180C	☐ G-ARKG	Auster J/5G Autocar
☐ G-APLU	DH.82A Tiger Moth	☐ G-ARAU	Cessna 150	☐ G-ARKJ	Beech 35N Bonanza
☐ G-APMB	DH.106 Comet 4B	☐ G-ARAW	Cessna 182C Skylane	☐ G-ARKK	Piper PA-22-108 Colt
☐ G-APMH	Auster J/1U Workmaster	☐ G-ARAX	Piper PA-22-150 Tri-Pacer	☐ G-ARKM	Piper PA-22-108 Colt
☐ G-APMX	DH.82A Tiger Moth	☐ G-ARAZ	DH.82A Tiger Moth	☐ G-ARKN	Piper PA-22-108 Colt
☐ G-APMY	Piper PA-22-160 Tri-Pacer	☐ G-ARBE	DH.104 Dove 8	☐ G-ARKP	Piper PA-22-108 Colt
☐ G-APNJ	Cessna 310	☐ G-ARBG	Tipsy Nipper T.66	☐ G-ARKS	Piper PA-22-108 Colt
☐ G-APNS	Bianchi Linnet	☐ G-ARBO	Piper PA-24-250 Comanche	☐ G-ARLB	Piper PA-24-250 Comanche
☐ G-APNT	Phoenix Currie Wot	☐ G-ARBP	Tipsy Nipper 2	☐ G-ARLG	Auster D4-180
☐ G-APNZ	Druine Turbulent	☐ G-ARBS	Piper PA-22-160 Tri-Pacer	☐ G-ARLK	Piper PA-24-250 Comanche
☐ G-APOI	Saro Skeeter 6	☐ G-ARBV	Piper PA-22-160 Tri-Pacer	☐ G-ARLP	Beagle A.61 Terrier
☐ G-APPA	DHC-1 Chipmunk	☐ G-ARBZ	Druine Turbulent	☐ G-ARLR	Beagle A.61 Terrier
☐ G-APPL	Percival Prentice	☐ G-ARCF	Piper PA-22-150 Tri-Pacer	☐ G-ARLX	Jodel D.140B
☐ G-APPM	DHC-1 Chipmunk	☐ G-ARCS	Auster D6-180	☐ G-ARLZ	Druine Turbulent
☐ G-APPN	DH.82A Tiger Moth	☐ G-ARCT	Piper PA-18 Super Cub 95	☐ G-ARMA	Piper PA-23-160 Apache G
☐ G-APRJ	Avro Lincoln	☐ G-ARCV	Cessna 175A Skylark	☐ G-ARMC	DHC-1 Chipmunk
☐ G-APRL	A.W. 650 Argosy	☐ G-ARCW	Piper PA-22-160 Tri-Pacer	☐ G-ARMD	DHC-1 Chipmunk
☐ G-APRR	Aero 45	☐ G-ARCX	Gloster Meteor NF14	☐ G-ARMF	DHC-1 Chipmunk
☐ G-APRS	Twin Pioneer	☐ G-ARDB	Piper PA-24-250 Comanche	☐ G-ARMG	DHC-1 Chipmunk
☐ G-APRT	Taylor Monoplane	☐ G-ARDD	Piel Emeraude	☐ G-ARML	Cessna 175B Skylark
☐ G-APSA	Douglas DC-6A	☐ G-ARDG	Lancashire EP-9	☐ G-ARMN	Cessna 175B Skylark
☐ G-APSR	Auster J/1U Workmaster	☐ G-ARDJ	Auster D6-180	☐ G-ARMO	Cessna 175B Skylark
☐ G-APSZ	Cessna 172	☐ G-ARDO	Jodel D.112	☐ G-ARMR	Cessna 175B Skylark
☐ G-APTR	Auster J/1N Alpha	☐ G-ARDS	Piper PA-22-150 Tri-Pacer	☐ G-ARMZ	Druine Turbulent
☐ G-APTU	Auster 5	☐ G-ARDT	Piper PA-22-160 Tri-Pacer	☐ G-ARNB	Auster J/5G Autocar
☐ G-APTW	Westland Widgeon	☐ G-ARDV	Piper PA-22-160 Tri-Pacer	☐ G-ARND	Piper PA-22-108 Colt
☐ G-APTY	Beech 35G Bonanza	☐ G-ARDY	Tipsy Nipper 2	☐ G-ARNE	Piper PA-22-108 Colt
☐ G-APTZ	Druine Turbulent	☐ G-ARDZ	Jodel D.140A	☐ G-ARNG	Piper PA-22-108 Colt
☐ G-APUD	Bensen B.7M	☐ G-AREA	DH.104 Dove 9	☐ G-ARNJ	Piper PA-22-108 Colt
☐ G-APUE	L-40 Meta-Sokol	☐ G-AREH	DH.82A Tiger Moth	☐ G-ARNK	Piper PA-22-108 Colt
☐ G-APUK	Auster J/1 Autocrat	☐ G-AREI	Auster III	☐ G-ARNL	Piper PA-22-108 Colt
☐ G-APUP	Sopwith Pup Rep	☐ G-AREL	Piper PA-22-150 Tri-Pacer	☐ G-ARNO	Beagle A.61 Terrier
☐ G-APUR	Piper PA-22-160 Tri-Pacer	☐ G-AREO	Piper PA-18-150	☐ G-ARNP	Beagle A.109 Airedale
☐ G-APUW	Auster J/5V-160 Autocar	☐ G-ARET	Piper PA-22-160 Tri-Pacer	☐ G-ARNY	Jodel D.117
☐ G-APUZ	Piper PA-24-250 Comanche	☐ G-AREV	Piper PA-22-160 Tri-Pacer	☐ G-ARNZ	Druine Turbulent
☐ G-APVF	Putzer Elster B	☐ G-AREX	Aeronca 15AC Sedan	☐ G-AROA	Cessna 172B Skyhawk
☐ G-APVG	Auster J/5L Aiglet Trainer	☐ G-ARFB	Piper PA-22-160 Tri-Pacer	☐ G-AROC	Cessna 175B Skylark
☐ G-APVL	Saunders-Roe P531-2	☐ G-ARFD	Piper PA-22-160 Tri-Pacer	☐ G-ARON	Piper PA-22-108 Colt
☐ G-APVN	Druine Turbulent	☐ G-ARFG	Cessna 175A Skylark	☐ G-AROO	Ercoupe F1A
☐ G-APVS	Cessna 170B	☐ G-ARFI	Cessna 150A	☐ G-AROW	Jodel D.140B
☐ G-APVU	L-40 Meta Sokol	☐ G-ARFO	Cessna 150A	☐ G-AROY	Boeing Stearman A75N1
☐ G-APVV	Mooney M.20A	☐ G-ARFV	Tipsy Nipper 2	☐ G-ARPH	DH.121 Trident 1C
☐ G-APVZ	Druine Turbulent	☐ G-ARGG	DHC-1 Chipmunk	☐ G-ARPK	DH.121 Trident 1C
☐ G-APWA	HPR7 Herald	☐ G-ARGO	Piper PA-22-108 Colt	☐ G-ARPO	DH.121 Trident 1C
☐ G-APWJ	HPR7 Herald	☐ G-ARGV	Piper PA-18-180	☐ G-ARRD	Jodel DR.1051
☐ G-APWL	EON 460 Olympia	☐ G-ARGY	Piper PA-22-150 Tri-Pacer	☐ G-ARRE	Jodel DR.1050
☐ G-APWN	Westland Whirlwind	☐ G-ARGZ	Druine Turbulent	☐ G-ARRI	Cessna 175B Skylark
☐ G-APWP	Druine Turbulent	☐ G-ARHB	Ercoupe F1A	☐ G-ARRL	Auster J/1N Alpha
☐ G-APWY	Piaggio P.166	☐ G-ARHC	Ercoupe F1A	☐ G-ARRM	Beagle B.206X
☐ G-APXJ	Piper PA-24-250 Comanche	☐ G-ARHF	Ercoupe F1A	☐ G-ARRO	Beagle A.109 Airedale
☐ G-APXR	Piper PA-22-160 Tri-Pacer	☐ G-ARHI	Piper PA-24-180 Comanche	☐ G-ARRS	Piel Emeraude
☐ G-APXT	Piper PA-22-150 Tri-Pacer	☐ G-ARHM	Auster 6A	☐ G-ARRT	Wallis WA-116Mc
☐ G-APXU	Piper PA-22-150 Tri-Pacer	☐ G-ARHN	Piper PA-22-150 Tri-Pacer	☐ G-ARRU	Druine Turbulent
☐ G-APXW	Lancashire EP.9	☐ G-ARHP	Piper PA-22-160 Tri-Pacer	☐ G-ARRX	Auster 6A
☐ G-APXX	DHA.3 Drover 2	☐ G-ARHR	Piper PA-22-150 Tri-Pacer	☐ G-ARRY	Jodel D.140B
☐ G-APXY	Cessna 150	☐ G-ARHW	DH.104 Dove 8	☐ G-ARRZ	Druine Turbulent
☐ G-APXZ	Knight Twister	☐ G-ARHX	DH.104 Dove 8	☐ G-ARSB	Cessna 150A
☐ G-APYB	Tipsy Nipper T.66	☐ G-ARHZ	Druine Condor	☐ G-ARSG	Roe Triplane Rep
☐ G-APYD	DH.106 Comet 4B	☐ G-ARID	Cessna 172B Skyhawk	☐ G-ARSL	Beagle A.61 Terrier
☐ G-APYG	DHC-1 Chipmunk	☐ G-ARIH	Auster 6A	☐ G-ARSU	Piper PA-22-108 Colt
☐ G-APYI	Piper PA-22-135 Tri-Pacer	☐ G-ARIK	Piper PA-22-150 Tri-Pacer	☐ G-ARTH	Piper PA-12 Super Cruiser
☐ G-APYN	Piper PA-22-160 Tri-Pacer	☐ G-ARIL	Piper PA-22-150 Tri-Pacer	☐ G-ARTL	DH.82A Tiger Moth
☐ G-APYT	Aeronca 7FC Tri-Traveler	☐ G-ARIM	Druine Turbulent	☐ G-ARTM	Beagle A.61 Terrier
☐ G-APYU	Aeronca 7FC Tri-Traveler	☐ G-ARJB	DH.104 Dove 8	☐ G-ARUG	Auster J/5G Autocar
☐ G-APZJ	Piper PA-18-150	☐ G-ARJE	Piper PA-22-108 Colt	☐ G-ARUI	Beagle A.61 Terrier
☐ G-APZL	Piper PA-22-160 Tri-Pacer	☐ G-ARJF	Piper PA-22-108 Colt	☐ G-ARUL	LeVier Cosmic Wind
☐ G-APZX	Piper PA-22-150 Tri-Pacer	☐ G-ARJH	Piper PA-22-108 Colt	☐ G-ARUO	Piper PA-24-180 Comanche
☐ G-ARAI	Piper PA-22-160 Tri-Pacer	☐ G-ARJR	Piper PA-23-160 Apache G	☐ G-ARUV	Piel Emeraude
☐ G-ARAM	Piper PA-18-150	☐ G-ARJS	Piper PA-23-160 Apache G	☐ G-ARUY	Auster J/1N Alpha

☐ G-ARUZ Cessna 175C Skylark	☐ G-ASII Piper PA-28-180 Cherokee	☐ G-ASUR Dornier Do. 28A1
☐ G-ARVM VC10-1101	☐ G-ASIJ Piper PA-28-180 Cherokee	☐ G-ASUS Jurca Tempete
☐ G-ARVO Piper PA-18-95	☐ G-ASIL Piper PA-28-180 Cherokee	☐ G-ASVG Piel Emeraude
☐ G-ARVT Piper PA-28-160 Cherokee	☐ G-ASIS Jodel D.112	☐ G-ASVM Reims F172E
☐ G-ARVU Piper PA-28-160 Cherokee	☐ G-ASIT Cessna 180	☐ G-ASVN Cessna 206
☐ G-ARVV Piper PA-28-160 Cherokee	☐ G-ASIY Piper PA-25-235 Pawnee	☐ G-ASVP Piper PA-25-235 Pawnee
☐ G-ARVZ Druine Condor	☐ G-ASJL Beech 35H Bonanza	☐ G-ASVZ Piper PA-28-140 Cherokee
☐ G-ARWB DHC-1 Chipmunk	☐ G-ASJV Spitfire LF.IXB	☐ G-ASWJ Beagle B.206 Srs.1
☐ G-ARWO Cessna 172C Skyhawk	☐ G-ASJY Gardan GY-80-160	☐ G-ASWL Reims F172F
☐ G-ARWR Cessna 172C Skyhawk	☐ G-ASKC DH.98 Mosquito	☐ G-ASWW Piper PA-30-160
☐ G-ARWS Cessna 175C Skylark	☐ G-ASKK HPR7 Herald	☐ G-ASWX Piper PA-28-180 Cherokee
☐ G-ARXB Beagle A.109 Airedale	☐ G-ASKL Jodel D.150 Mascaret	☐ G-ASXD Brantly B.2B
☐ G-ARXC Beagle A.109 Airedale	☐ G-ASKP DH.82A Tiger Moth	☐ G-ASXF Brantly 305
☐ G-ARXD Beagle A.109 Airedale	☐ G-ASKT Piper PA-28-180 Cherokee	☐ G-ASXI Tipsy Nipper 3
☐ G-ARXG Piper PA-24-250 Comanche	☐ G-ASLH Cessna 182F Skylane	☐ G-ASXJ Luton Minor
☐ G-ARXH Bell 47G	☐ G-ASLP Bensen B.7	☐ G-ASXR Cessna 210 Centurion
☐ G-ARXN Tipsy Nipper	☐ G-ASLV Piper PA-28-235 Cherokee	☐ G-ASXS Jodel DR.1050
☐ G-ARXT Jodel DR.1050	☐ G-ASLX Piel Emeraude	☐ G-ASXU Jodel D.120A Paris-Nice
☐ G-ARXU Auster 6A	☐ G-ASMA Piper PA-30-160	☐ G-ASXX Avro Lancaster B.VII
☐ G-ARXW MS.885 Super Rallye	☐ G-ASME Bensen B.8M	☐ G-ASXY Jodel D.117A
☐ G-ARYB BAe 125-1	☐ G-ASMF Beech 95-D55 Baron	☐ G-ASXZ Cessna 182G Skylane
☐ G-ARYC BAe 125-1	☐ G-ASMJ Reims F172E	☐ G-ASYD BAC 111-475AM
☐ G-ARYD Auster AOP.6	☐ G-ASML Luton Minor	☐ G-ASYG Beagle A.61 Terrier
☐ G-ARYF Piper PA-23-250 Aztec B	☐ G-ASMM Druine Turbulent	☐ G-ASYJ Beech 95-D55 Baron
☐ G-ARYH Piper PA-22-160 Tri-Pacer	☐ G-ASMO Piper PA-23-160 Apache G	☐ G-ASYN Beagle A.61 Terrier
☐ G-ARYI Cessna 172C Skyhawk	☐ G-ASMS Cessna 150A	☐ G-ASYP Cessna 150E
☐ G-ARYK Cessna 172C Skyhawk	☐ G-ASMT Fairtravel Linnet 2	☐ G-ASZB Cessna 150E
☐ G-ARYR Piper PA-28-180 Cherokee	☐ G-ASMU Cessna 150D	☐ G-ASZD Bolkow Bo.208A2 Junior
☐ G-ARYS Cessna 172C Skyhawk	☐ G-ASMW Cessna 150D	☐ G-ASZE Beagle A.61 Terrier
☐ G-ARYV Piper PA-24-250 Comanche	☐ G-ASMY Piper PA-23-160 Apache H	☐ G-ASZR Fairtravel Linnet 2
☐ G-ARYZ Beagle A.109 Airedale	☐ G-ASMZ Beagle A.61 Terrier	☐ G-ASZS Gardan GY-80-160
☐ G-ARZB Wallis WA-116-1	☐ G-ASNC Auster D5-180 Husky	☐ G-ASZU Cessna 150E
☐ G-ARZN Beech 35N Bonanza	☐ G-ASNI Piel Emeraude	☐ G-ASZV Tipsy Nipper 2
☐ G-ARZS Beagle A.109 Airedale	☐ G-ASNK Cessna 205	☐ G-ASZX Beagle A.61 Terrier
☐ G-ARZW Phoenix Currie Wot	☐ G-ASNN Cessna 182F Skylane	☐ G-ATAF Reims F172F
☐ G-ASAA Luton Minor	☐ G-ASNW Reims F172E	☐ G-ATAG Jodel DR.1050
☐ G-ASAI Beagle A.109 Airedale	☐ G-ASNY Bensen B.8M	☐ G-ATAH Cessna 336
☐ G-ASAJ Beagle A.61 Terrier	☐ G-ASOC Auster 6A	☐ G-ATAS Piper PA-28-180 Cherokee
☐ G-ASAL Scottish Aviation Bulldog	☐ G-ASOH Beech 95-B55 Baron	☐ G-ATAU Druine Condor
☐ G-ASAT MS.880B Rallye	☐ G-ASOI Beagle A.61 Terrier	☐ G-ATAV Druine Condor
☐ G-ASAU MS.880B Rallye	☐ G-ASOK Reims F172E	☐ G-ATBG Nord 1002 Pingouin
☐ G-ASAX Beagle A.61 Terrier	☐ G-ASOM Beagle A.61 Terrier	☐ G-ATBH Aero 145
☐ G-ASAZ Hiller UH-12 E-4	☐ G-ASOX Cessna 205A	☐ G-ATBI Beech A23
☐ G-ASBA Phoenix Currie Wot	☐ G-ASPF Jodel D.120 Paris-Nice	☐ G-ATBJ Sikorsky S-61N
☐ G-ASBH Beagle A.109 Airedale	☐ G-ASPP Bristol Boxkite Rep	☐ G-ATBL DH.60G Moth
☐ G-ASBY Beagle A.109 Airedale	☐ G-ASPS Piper J-3C-90 Cub	☐ G-ATBP Fournier RF3
☐ G-ASCC Auster AOP.11	☐ G-ASPV DH.82A Tiger Moth	☐ G-ATBS Druine Turbulent
☐ G-ASCD Beagle A.61 Terrier	☐ G-ASRB Druine Condor	☐ G-ATBU Beagle A.61 Terrier
☐ G-ASCM Isaacs Fury II	☐ G-ASRC Druine Condor	☐ G-ATBW Tipsy Nipper 2
☐ G-ASCU Piper PA-18A-150	☐ G-ASRK Beagle A.109 Airedale	☐ G-ATBX Piper PA-20-125 Pacer
☐ G-ASCZ Piel Emeraude	☐ G-ASRO Piper PA-30-160	☐ G-ATBZ Westland Wessex
☐ G-ASDB Druine Turbulent	☐ G-ASRT Jodel D.150 Mascaret	☐ G-ATCC Beagle A.109 Airedale
☐ G-ASDK Beagle A.61 Terrier	☐ G-ASRW Piper PA-28-180 Cherokee	☐ G-ATCD Auster D5-180 Husky
☐ G-ASDY Wallis WA-116F	☐ G-ASSF Cessna 182G Skylane	☐ G-ATCE Cessna U206
☐ G-ASEA Luton Minor	☐ G-ASSM BAe 125 1/522	☐ G-ATCJ Luton Minor
☐ G-ASEB Luton Minor	☐ G-ASSP Piper PA-30-160	☐ G-ATCL Airtourer 100
☐ G-ASEO Piper PA-24-250 Comanche	☐ G-ASSS Cessna 172E Skyhawk	☐ G-ATCX Cessna 182H Skylane
☐ G-ASEP Piper PA-23-235 Apache	☐ G-ASST Cessna 150D	☐ G-ATDA Piper PA-28-160 Cherokee
☐ G-ASEU Druine Condor	☐ G-ASSV Kensinger KF	☐ G-ATDB Nord 1101 Noralpha
☐ G-ASFA Cessna 172D Skyhawk	☐ G-ASSW Piper PA-28-140 Cherokee	☐ G-ATDN Beagle A.61 Terrier
☐ G-ASFD LET L-200A Morava	☐ G-ASSY Druine Turbulent	☐ G-ATDO Bolkow Bo.208C1 Junior
☐ G-ASFK Auster J/5G Autocar	☐ G-ASTA Druine Turbulent	☐ G-ATEF Cessna 150E
☐ G-ASFL Piper PA-28-180 Cherokee	☐ G-ASTG Nord 1002 Pingouin	☐ G-ATEM Piper PA-28-180 Cherokee
☐ G-ASFR Bolkow Bo.208C Junior	☐ G-ASTI Auster 6A	☐ G-ATEV Jodel DR.1050
☐ G-ASFX Druine Turbulent	☐ G-ASTL Fairey Firefly 1	☐ G-ATEX Airtourer 100
☐ G-ASGC VC10-1151	☐ G-ASTP Hiller UH-12C	☐ G-ATEZ Piper PA-28-140 Cherokee
☐ G-ASHD Brantly B.2A	☐ G-ASUB Mooney M.20E	☐ G-ATFD Jodel DR.1050
☐ G-ASHH Piper PA-23-250 Aztec	☐ G-ASUD Piper PA-28-180 Cherokee	☐ G-ATFF Piper PA-23-250 Aztec C
☐ G-ASHS Stampe SV-4C	☐ G-ASUE Cessna 150D	☐ G-ATFG Brantly B.2B
☐ G-ASHT Druine Turbulent	☐ G-ASUG Beech E18S	☐ G-ATFM Sikorsky S-61N
☐ G-ASHU Piper PA-15 Vagabond	☐ G-ASUH Reims F172E	☐ G-ATFR Piper PA-25-150 Pawnee
☐ G-ASHX Piper PA-28-180 Cherokee	☐ G-ASUI Beagle A.61 Terrier	☐ G-ATFV Agusta Bell 47 J-2A
☐ G-ASIB Reims F172D	☐ G-ASUP Reims F172E	

G-ATFW Luton Minor	G-ATRI Bolkow Bo.208C1 Junior	G-AVEM Reims F150G
G-ATFY Reims F172G	G-ATRK Reims F150F	G-AVEN Reims F150G
G-ATGE Jodel DR.1050	G-ATRM Reims F150F	G-AVEO Reims F150G
G-ATGO Reims F172G	G-ATRO Piper PA-28-140 Cherokee	G-AVER Reims F150G
G-ATGY Gardan GY-80-160	G-ATRR Piper PA-28-140 Cherokee	G-AVEU Wassmer WA.41
G-ATHD DHC-1 Chipmunk	G-ATRW Piper PA-32-260	G-AVEX Druine Condor
G-ATHK Aeronca 7AC Champion	G-ATRX Piper PA-32-260	G-AVEY Phoenix Currie Wot
G-ATHM Wallis WA-116F	G-ATSI Bolkow Bo.208 Junior	G-AVFB DH.121 Trident 2E
G-ATHN Nord 1101 Noralpha	G-ATSL Reims F172G	G-AVFP Piper PA-28-140 Cherokee
G-ATHR Piper PA-28-180 Cherokee	G-ATSR Beech 35H Bonanza	G-AVFR Piper PA-28-140 Cherokee
G-ATHT Airtourer 115	G-ATSX Bolkow Bo.208C1 Junior	G-AVFU Piper PA-32-300
G-ATHU Beagle A.61 Terrier	G-ATSY Wassmer WA.41	G-AVFX Piper PA-28-140 Cherokee
G-ATHV Cessna 150F	G-ATSZ Piper PA-30-160	G-AVFZ Piper PA-28-140 Cherokee
G-ATHZ Cessna 150F	G-ATTB Wallis WA-116F	G-AVGA Piper PA-24-260 Comanche
G-ATIA Piper PA-24-260 Comanche	G-ATTD Cessna 182J Skylane	G-AVGC Piper PA-28-140 Cherokee
G-ATIC Jodel DR.1050	G-ATTI Piper PA-28-140 Cherokee	G-AVGD Piper PA-28-140 Cherokee
G-ATIN Jodel D.117	G-ATTK Piper PA-28-140 Cherokee	G-AVGE Piper PA-28-140 Cherokee
G-ATIR Stampe SV-4C	G-ATTM Robin DR.250 160	G-AVGI Piper PA-28-140 Cherokee
G-ATIS Piper PA-28-180 Cherokee	G-ATTR Bolkow Bo.208C1 Junior	G-AVGJ Jodel DR.1050
G-ATIZ Jodel D.117	G-ATTV Piper PA-28-140 Cherokee	G-AVGK Piper PA-28-180 Cherokee
G-ATJA Jodel DR.1050	G-ATTX Piper PA-28-180 Cherokee	G-AVGU Reims F150G
G-ATJC Airtourer 100	G-ATUB Piper PA-28-140 Cherokee	G-AVGY Cessna 182K Skylane
G-ATJG Piper PA-28-140 Cherokee	G-ATUD Piper PA-28-140 Cherokee	G-AVGZ Jodel DR.1050
G-ATJL Piper PA-24-260 Comanche	G-ATUF Reims F150F	G-AVHH Reims F172H
G-ATJM Fokker Triplane Rep	G-ATUG Druine Condor	G-AVHL Jodel DR.105A
G-ATJN Jodel D.119	G-ATUH Tipsy Nipper 1	G-AVHM Reims F150G
G-ATJT Gardan GY-80-160	G-ATUI Bolkow Bo.208C1 Junior	G-AVHT Auster AOP.9
G-ATJV Piper PA-32-260	G-ATUL Piper PA-28-180 Cherokee	G-AVHY Fournier RF4D
G-ATKF Cessna 150F	G-ATVF DHC-1 Chipmunk	G-AVIA Reims F150G
G-ATKG Hiller UH-12B	G-ATVK Piper PA-28-140 Cherokee	G-AVIB Reims F150G
G-ATKH Luton Minor	G-ATVO Piper PA-28-140 Cherokee	G-AVIC Reims F172H
G-ATKI Piper J-3C-65 Cub	G-ATVP Vickers Gunbus Rep	G-AVID Cessna 182K Skylane
G-ATKT Reims F172G	G-ATVS Piper PA-28-180 Cherokee	G-AVII Agusta Bell 206A
G-ATKX Jodel D.140C	G-ATVW Druine Condor	G-AVIL Ercoupe A.2
G-ATLA Cessna 182J Skylane	G-ATVX Bolkow Bo.208 Junior	G-AVIN MS.880B Rallye
G-ATLB Jodel DR.1050M1	G-ATWA Jodel DR.1050	G-AVIP Brantly B.2B
G-ATLH Fewsdale Gyroplane	G-ATWB Jodel D.117	G-AVIS Reims F172H
G-ATLM Reims F172G	G-ATWJ Reims F172F	G-AVIT Reims F150G
G-ATLP Bensen B.8M	G-ATWS Luton Minor	G-AVIZ Scheibe SF25A
G-ATLT Cessna U206A	G-ATXA Piper PA-22-150 Tri-Pacer	G-AVJF Reims F172H
G-ATLV Jodel D.120 Paris-Nice	G-ATXD Piper PA-30-160 B	G-AVJH Druine Condor
G-ATMC Reims F150F	G-ATXM Piper PA-28-180 Cherokee	G-AVJJ Piper PA-30-160 B
G-ATMH Auster D5-180 Husky	G-ATXN Mitchell-Procter Kittiwake	G-AVJK Jodel DR.1050M1
G-ATMJ HS.748-2A	G-ATXO SIPA 903	G-AVJO Fokker E.III Rep
G-ATML Reims F150F	G-ATXX McCandless M.4	G-AVJV Wallis WA-117-1
G-ATMM Reims F150F	G-ATXZ Bolkow Bo.208C Junior	G-AVJW Wallis WA-118M
G-ATMT Piper PA-30-160	G-ATYM Reims F150G	G-AVKB Brochet MB.50
G-ATMW Piper PA-28-140 Cherokee	G-ATYS Piper PA-28-180 Cherokee	G-AVKD Fournier RF4D
G-ATMY Cessna 150F	G-ATZK Piper PA-28-180 Cherokee	G-AVKE Gadfly HDW-1
G-ATNB Piper PA-28-180 Cherokee	G-ATZM Piper J-3C-90 Cub	G-AVKG Reims F172H
G-ATNE Reims F150F	G-ATZS Wassmer WA.41	G-AVKI Tipsy T.66 Nipper
G-ATNL Reims F150F	G-ATZY Reims F150G	G-AVKK Slingsby Nipper 3
G-ATNV Piper PA-24-260 Comanche	G-AVAR Reims F150G	G-AVKL Piper PA-30-160 B
G-ATOA Piper PA-23-160 Apache G	G-AVAW Druine Condor	G-AVKN Cessna 401
G-ATOD Reims F150F	G-AVAX Piper PA-28-180 Cherokee	G-AVKP Beagle A.109 Airedale
G-ATOH Druine Condor	G-AVBG Piper PA-28-180 Cherokee	G-AVKR Bolkow Bo.208C1 Junior
G-ATOI Piper PA-28-140 Cherokee	G-AVBH Piper PA-28-180 Cherokee	G-AVKZ Piper PA-23-250 Aztec C
G-ATOJ Piper PA-28-140 Cherokee	G-AVBS Piper PA-28-180 Cherokee	G-AVLB Piper PA-28-140 Cherokee
G-ATOK Piper PA-28-140 Cherokee	G-AVBT Piper PA-28-180 Cherokee	G-AVLC Piper PA-28-140 Cherokee
G-ATOL Piper PA-28-140 Cherokee	G-AVCM Piper PA-24-260 Comanche	G-AVLE Piper PA-28-140 Cherokee
G-ATOM Piper PA-28-140 Cherokee	G-AVCN BN2A-8 Islander	G-AVLF Piper PA-28-140 Cherokee
G-ATON Piper PA-28-140 Cherokee	G-AVCS Beagle A.61 Terrier	G-AVLG Piper PA-28-140 Cherokee
G-ATOO Piper PA-28-140 Cherokee	G-AVCV Cessna 182J Skylane	G-AVLI Piper PA-28-140 Cherokee
G-ATOP Piper PA-28-140 Cherokee	G-AVDA Cessna 182K Skylane	G-AVLJ Piper PA-28-140 Cherokee
G-ATOR Piper PA-28-140 Cherokee	G-AVDF Beagle B.121 Pup	G-AVLM Beagle B.121 Pup
G-ATOT Piper PA-28-180 Cherokee	G-AVDG Wallis WA-116	G-AVLN Beagle B.121 Pup
G-ATOU Mooney M.20E	G-AVDT Aeronca 7AC Champion	G-AVLO Bolkow Bo.208C1 Junior
G-ATOY Piper PA-24-260 Comanche	G-AVDV Piper PA-22-150 Tri-Pacer	G-AVLT Piper PA-28-140 Cherokee
G-ATOZ Bensen B.8M	G-AVDY Luton Minor	G-AVLY Jodel D.120A Paris-Nice
G-ATPN Piper PA-28-140 Cherokee	G-AVEB Morane MS.230	G-AVMA Gardan GY-80-180
G-ATPT Cessna 182J Skylane	G-AVEC Reims F172H	G-AVMB Druine Condor
G-ATPV Barritault Minicab	G-AVEF Jodel D.150 Mascaret	G-AVMD Cessna 150G
G-ATRG Piper PA-18-180	G-AVEH SIAI-Marchetti S.205-20R	G-AVMF Reims F150G

Reg	Type
G-AVMO	BAC 111-510ED
G-AVNC	Reims F150G
G-AVNE	Westland Wessex
G-AVNN	Piper PA-28-180 Cherokee
G-AVNO	Piper PA-28-180 Cherokee
G-AVNS	Piper PA-28-180 Cherokee
G-AVNU	Piper PA-28-180 Cherokee
G-AVNW	Piper PA-28-180 Cherokee
G-AVNZ	Fournier RF4D
G-AVOA	Jodel DR.1050
G-AVOC	Robin DR.221 Dauphin
G-AVOD	Auster D5-180 Husky
G-AVOH	Druine Condor
G-AVOM	Robin DR.221 Dauphin
G-AVOO	Piper PA-18-150
G-AVOZ	Piper PA-28-140 Cherokee
G-AVPD	Jodel D.9 Bebe
G-AVPI	Reims F172H
G-AVPJ	DH.82A Tiger Moth
G-AVPM	Jodel D.117
G-AVPN	HPR7 Herald
G-AVPO	Hindustan Pushpak
G-AVPV	Piper PA-28-180 Cherokee
G-AVPY	Piper PA-25-235 Pawnee
G-AVRK	Piper PA-28-180 Cherokee
G-AVRP	Piper PA-28-140 Cherokee
G-AVRS	Gardan GY-80-180
G-AVRU	Piper PA-28-180 Cherokee
G-AVRW	Barritault Minicab
G-AVRY	Piper PA-28-180 Cherokee
G-AVRZ	Piper PA-28-180 Cherokee
G-AVSA	Piper PA-28-180 Cherokee
G-AVSB	Piper PA-28-180 Cherokee
G-AVSC	Piper PA-28-180 Cherokee
G-AVSD	Piper PA-28-180 Cherokee
G-AVSE	Piper PA-28-180 Cherokee
G-AVSF	Piper PA-28-180 Cherokee
G-AVSI	Piper PA-28-140 Cherokee
G-AVSP	Piper PA-28-180 Cherokee
G-AVSR	Auster D5-180 Husky
G-AVSZ	Agusta Bell 206B
G-AVTC	Slingsby Nipper T66
G-AVTP	Reims F172H
G-AVTV	MS.893A Commodore
G-AVUD	Piper PA-30-160 B
G-AVUG	Reims F150H
G-AVUH	Reims F150H
G-AVUS	Piper PA-28-140 Cherokee
G-AVUT	Piper PA-28-140 Cherokee
G-AVUU	Piper PA-28-140 Cherokee
G-AVUZ	Piper PA-32-300
G-AVVC	Reims F172H
G-AVVI	Piper PA-30-160 B
G-AVVJ	MS.893A Commodore
G-AVVL	Reims F150H
G-AVVO	Avro 652A Anson
G-AVWA	Piper PA-28-140 Cherokee
G-AVWD	Piper PA-28-140 Cherokee
G-AVWE	Piper PA-28-140 Cherokee
G-AVWG	Piper PA-28-140 Cherokee
G-AVWI	Piper PA-28-140 Cherokee
G-AVWJ	Piper PA-28-140 Cherokee
G-AVWL	Piper PA-28-140 Cherokee
G-AVWM	Piper PA-28-140 Cherokee
G-AVWN	Piper PA-28R-180
G-AVWO	Piper PA-28R-180
G-AVWR	Piper PA-28R-180
G-AVWT	Piper PA-28R-180
G-AVWU	Piper PA-28R-180
G-AVWY	Fournier RF4D
G-AVXA	Piper PA-25-235 Pawnee
G-AVXD	Slingsby Nipper T66
G-AVXF	Piper PA-28R-180
G-AVXW	Druine Condor
G-AVXY	Auster AOP.9
G-AVYE	DH.121 Trident 1E
G-AVYK	Beagle A.61 Terrier 3
G-AVYL	Piper PA-28-180 Cherokee
G-AVYM	Piper PA-28-180 Cherokee
G-AVYR	Piper PA-28-140 Cherokee
G-AVYS	Piper PA-28R-180
G-AVYT	Piper PA-28R-180
G-AVYV	Jodel D.120A Paris-Nice
G-AVZB	Aero Z.37
G-AVZI	Bolkow Bo.208C1 Junior
G-AVZN	Beagle B.121 Pup
G-AVZP	Beagle B.121 Pup
G-AVZR	Piper PA-28-180 Cherokee
G-AVZU	Reims F150H
G-AVZV	Reims F172H
G-AVZW	EAA Biplane
G-AVZX	MS.880B Rallye
G-AWAC	Gardan GY-80
G-AWAJ	Beech D55 Baron
G-AWAT	Druine Condor
G-AWAU	Vickers Vimy Rep
G-AWAW	Reims F150F
G-AWAX	Cessna 150D
G-AWAZ	Piper PA-28R-180
G-AWBA	Piper PA-28R-180
G-AWBB	Piper PA-28R-180
G-AWBC	Piper PA-28R-180
G-AWBE	Piper PA-28-140 Cherokee
G-AWBG	Piper PA-28-140 Cherokee
G-AWBH	Piper PA-28-140 Cherokee
G-AWBJ	Fournier RF4D
G-AWBM	Druine Turbulent
G-AWBN	Piper PA-30-160 B
G-AWBS	Piper PA-28-140 Cherokee
G-AWBT	Piper PA-30-160 B
G-AWBU	Morane Type N Rep
G-AWBX	Reims F150H
G-AWCN	Reims FR172E Rocket
G-AWCP	Reims F150H
G-AWDA	Slingsby Nipper T66
G-AWDI	Piper PA-23-250 Aztec C
G-AWDO	Druine Turbulent
G-AWDP	Piper PA-28-180 Cherokee
G-AWDR	Reims FR172E Rocket
G-AWDU	Brantly B.2B
G-AWDW	Campbell B.8MS
G-AWEF	Stampe SV-4C
G-AWEI	Druine Condor
G-AWEL	Fournier RF4D
G-AWEM	Fournier RF4D
G-AWEN	Jodel DR.1050
G-AWEO	Reims F150H
G-AWEP	Barritault Minicab
G-AWES	Cessna 150H
G-AWEV	Piper PA-28-140 Cherokee
G-AWEX	Piper PA-28-140 Cherokee
G-AWEZ	Piper PA-28R-180
G-AWFB	Piper PA-28R-180
G-AWFC	Piper PA-28R-180
G-AWFD	Piper PA-28R-180
G-AWFF	Reims F150H
G-AWFH	Reims F150H
G-AWFJ	Piper PA-28R-180
G-AWFN	Druine Condor
G-AWFO	Druine Condor
G-AWFP	Druine Condor
G-AWFT	Jodel D.9 Bebe
G-AWFW	Jodel D.117
G-AWFZ	Beech A23-19
G-AWGA	Beagle A.109 Airedale
G-AWGD	Reims F172H
G-AWGK	Reims F150H
G-AWGN	Fournier RF4D
G-AWGZ	Taylor Monoplane
G-AWHX	Rollason Beta B2
G-AWHY	Falconar F.11 3
G-AWIF	Brookland Mosquito
G-AWII	Spitfire LF.Vc
G-AWIO	Brantly B.2B
G-AWIP	Luton Minor
G-AWIR	Midget Mustang
G-AWIT	Piper PA-28-180 Cherokee
G-AWIV	Airmark TSR.3
G-AWIW	Stampe SV-4B
G-AWJE	Slingsby Nipper T66
G-AWJF	Slingsby Nipper T66
G-AWJV	DH.98 Mosquito
G-AWJX	Zlin Z.526
G-AWJY	Zlin Z.526
G-AWKD	Piper PA-17 Vagabond
G-AWKO	Beagle B.121 Pup
G-AWKT	MS.880B Rallye
G-AWKX	Beech 65-A80 Queen Air
G-AWLA	Reims F150H
G-AWLF	Reims F172H
G-AWLG	SIPA 903
G-AWLI	Piper PA-22-150 Tri-Pacer
G-AWLM	Campbell B.8MS
G-AWLO	Boeing Stearman E75
G-AWLP	Mooney M.20F
G-AWLR	Slingsby Nipper T66
G-AWLS	Slingsby Nipper T66
G-AWLX	Auster J/2 Arrow
G-AWLZ	Fournier RF4D
G-AWMD	Jodel D.11
G-AWMF	Piper PA-18-180
G-AWMI	Airtourer T2
G-AWMN	Luton Minor
G-AWMP	Reims F172H
G-AWMR	Druine Turbulent
G-AWMT	Reims F150H
G-AWNT	BN2A Islander
G-AWOA	MS.880B Rallye
G-AWOE	Rockwell 680E
G-AWOF	Piper PA-15 Vagabond
G-AWOH	Piper PA-17 Vagabond
G-AWOT	Reims F150H
G-AWOU	Cessna 170B
G-AWOX	Westland Wessex
G-AWPH	Percival Provost T1
G-AWPJ	Reims F150H
G-AWPN	Shield Xyla
G-AWPS	Piper PA-28-140 Cherokee
G-AWPU	Reims F150J
G-AWPW	Piper PA-12 Super Cruiser
G-AWPY	Campbell B.8M
G-AWPZ	Andreasson BA4B
G-AWRK	Reims F150J
G-AWRS	Avro C19/2 Anson
G-AWRY	Percival Provost T1
G-AWSH	Zlin Z.526
G-AWSL	Piper PA-28-180 Cherokee
G-AWSM	Piper PA-28-235 Cherokee
G-AWSN	Druine Condor
G-AWSP	Druine Condor
G-AWSS	Druine Condor
G-AWST	Druine Condor
G-AWSV	Saro Skeeter AOP12
G-AWSW	Auster D5-180 Husky
G-AWTJ	Reims F150J
G-AWTL	Piper PA-28-180 Cherokee
G-AWTS	Beech A23-19
G-AWTV	Beech A23-19

☐ G-AWTX	Reims F150J	
☐ G-AWUA	Cessna P206D	
☐ G-AWUB	GY-201 Minicab	
☐ G-AWUE	Jodel DR.1050	
☐ G-AWUG	Reims F150H	
☐ G-AWUJ	Reims F150H	
☐ G-AWUK	Reims F150H	
☐ G-AWUL	Reims F150H	
☐ G-AWUN	Reims F150H	
☐ G-AWUO	Reims F150H	
☐ G-AWUT	Reims F150J	
☐ G-AWUU	Reims F150J	
☐ G-AWUX	Reims F172H	
☐ G-AWUY	Reims F172H	
☐ G-AWUZ	Reims F172H	
☐ G-AWVA	Reims F172H	
☐ G-AWVB	Jodel D.117	
☐ G-AWVC	Beagle B.121 Pup	
☐ G-AWVE	Jodel DR.1050M1	
☐ G-AWVF	Percival Provost T1	
☐ G-AWVG	Airtourer T2	
☐ G-AWVN	Aeronca 7AC Champion	
☐ G-AWVZ	Jodel D.112	
☐ G-AWWE	Beagle B.121 Pup 2	
☐ G-AWWI	Jodel D.117	
☐ G-AWWM	GY-201 Minicab	
☐ G-AWWN	Jodel DR.1050	
☐ G-AWWP	Woody Pusher 3	
☐ G-AWWT	Druine Turbulent	
☐ G-AWWU	Reims FR172F Rocket	
☐ G-AWXR	Piper PA-28-180 Cherokee	
☐ G-AWXS	Piper PA-28-180 Cherokee	
☐ G-AWXZ	Stampe SV-4C	
☐ G-AWYB	Reims FR172F Rocket	
☐ G-AWYI	BE.2c Replica	
☐ G-AWYJ	Beagle B.121 Pup 2	
☐ G-AWYL	Robin DR.253 Regent	
☐ G-AWYO	Beagle B.121 Pup	
☐ G-AWYX	MS.880B Rallye	
☐ G-AWYY	Sopwith Camel Rep	
☐ G-AWZM	DH.121 Trident 3B	
☐ G-AXAB	Piper PA-28-140 Cherokee	
☐ G-AXAN	DH.82A Tiger Moth	
☐ G-AXAS	Wallis WA-116T	
☐ G-AXAT	Jodel D.117A	
☐ G-AXBF	Auster D5-180 Husky	
☐ G-AXBG	Bensen B.8M	
☐ G-AXBH	Reims F172H	
☐ G-AXBJ	Reims F172H	
☐ G-AXBW	DH.82A Tiger Moth	
☐ G-AXBZ	DH.82A Tiger Moth	
☐ G-AXCA	Piper PA-28R-200	
☐ G-AXCG	Jodel D.117	
☐ G-AXCI	Bensen B.8M	
☐ G-AXCM	MS.880B Rallye	
☐ G-AXCX	Beagle B.121 Pup 2	
☐ G-AXCY	Jodel D.117A	
☐ G-AXCZ	Stampe SV-4C	
☐ G-AXDC	Piper PA-23-250 Aztec D	
☐ G-AXDI	Reims F172H	
☐ G-AXDK	Robin DR.315	
☐ G-AXDN	BAC Concorde 100	
☐ G-AXDV	Beagle B.121 Pup	
☐ G-AXDW	Beagle B.121 Pup	
☐ G-AXDY	Falconar F.11	
☐ G-AXED	Piper PA-25-235 Pawnee	
☐ G-AXEH	Scottish Aviation Bulldog	
☐ G-AXEI	Ward Gnome	
☐ G-AXEO	Scheibe SF25B Falke	
☐ G-AXEV	Beagle B.121 Pup 2	
☐ G-AXFN	Jodel D.119	
☐ G-AXGA	Piper PA-18-95	
☐ G-AXGE	MS.880B Rallye	
☐ G-AXGG	Reims F150J	
☐ G-AXGP	Piper J-3C-90 Cub	
☐ G-AXGR	Luton Minor	
☐ G-AXGS	Druine Condor	
☐ G-AXGV	Druine Condor	
☐ G-AXGZ	Druine Condor	
☐ G-AXHA	Cessna 337A	
☐ G-AXHC	Stampe SV-4C	
☐ G-AXHO	Beagle B.121 Pup 2	
☐ G-AXHP	Piper J-3C-65 Cub	
☐ G-AXHR	Piper J-3C-65 Cub	
☐ G-AXHS	MS.880B Rallye	
☐ G-AXHT	MS.880B Rallye	
☐ G-AXHV	Jodel D.117A	
☐ G-AXIA	Beagle B.121 Pup	
☐ G-AXIE	Beagle B.121 Pup 2	
☐ G-AXIF	Beagle B.121 Pup	
☐ G-AXIG	Scottish Aviation Bulldog	
☐ G-AXIO	Piper PA-28-140 Cherokee	
☐ G-AXIR	Piper PA-28-140 Cherokee	
☐ G-AXIW	Scheibe SF25B Falke	
☐ G-AXIX	Airtourer T4	
☐ G-AXIY	Bird Gyrocopter	
☐ G-AXJB	Omega 84	
☐ G-AXJH	Beagle B.121 Pup 2	
☐ G-AXJI	Beagle B.121 Pup 2	
☐ G-AXJJ	Beagle B.121 Pup 2	
☐ G-AXJO	Beagle B.121 Pup 2	
☐ G-AXJR	Scheibe SF25B Falke	
☐ G-AXJV	Piper PA-28-140 Cherokee	
☐ G-AXJX	Piper PA-28-140 Cherokee	
☐ G-AXKH	Luton Minor	
☐ G-AXKJ	Jodel D.9 Bebe	
☐ G-AXKO	Westland Bell 47G-4A	
☐ G-AXKS	Westland Bell 47G-4A	
☐ G-AXKX	Westland Bell 47G-4A	
☐ G-AXKY	Westland Bell 47G-4A	
☐ G-AXLG	Cessna 310K	
☐ G-AXLI	Slingsby Nipper T66	
☐ G-AXLS	Robin D.105A	
☐ G-AXLZ	Piper PA-18-95	
☐ G-AXMA	Piper PA-24-180 Comanche	
☐ G-AXMB	Slingsby Motor Cadet	
☐ G-AXMN	Auster J/5B Autocar	
☐ G-AXMT	Bucker Bu.133C	
☐ G-AXMW	Beagle B.121 Pup	
☐ G-AXMX	Beagle B.121 Pup 2	
☐ G-AXNJ	Jodel D.120 Paris-Nice	
☐ G-AXNM	Beagle B.121 Pup	
☐ G-AXNN	Beagle B.121 Pup 2	
☐ G-AXNP	Beagle B.121 Pup 2	
☐ G-AXNR	Beagle B.121 Pup 2	
☐ G-AXNS	Beagle B.121 Pup 2	
☐ G-AXNW	Stampe SV-4C	
☐ G-AXNX	Cessna 182M Skylane	
☐ G-AXNZ	Pitts S-1C Special	
☐ G-AXOH	MS.894A Minerva	
☐ G-AXOJ	Beagle B.121 Pup 2	
☐ G-AXOS	MS.894A Minerva	
☐ G-AXOT	MS.893A Commodore	
☐ G-AXOZ	Beagle B.121 Pup	
☐ G-AXPA	Beagle B.121 Pup	
☐ G-AXPB	Beagle B.121 Pup	
☐ G-AXPC	Beagle B.121 Pup	
☐ G-AXPF	Reims F150K	
☐ G-AXPG	Mignet HM.293	
☐ G-AXPM	Beagle B.121 Pup	
☐ G-AXPN	Beagle B.121 Pup 2	
☐ G-AXPZ	Campbell Cricket	
☐ G-AXRC	Campbell Cricket	
☐ G-AXRK	Practavia Pilot Sprite	
☐ G-AXRP	Stampe SV-4A	
☐ G-AXRR	Auster AOP.9	
☐ G-AXRT	Reims FA150K Aerobat	
☐ G-AXRU	Reims FA150K Aerobat	
☐ G-AXSC	Beagle B.121 Pup	
☐ G-AXSD	Beagle B.121 Pup	
☐ G-AXSF	Nash Petrel	
☐ G-AXSG	Piper PA-28-180 Cherokee	
☐ G-AXSI	Reims F172H	
☐ G-AXSM	Jodel DR.1051	
☐ G-AXSW	Reims FA150K Aerobat	
☐ G-AXSZ	Piper PA-28-140 Cherokee	
☐ G-AXTA	Piper PA-28-140 Cherokee	
☐ G-AXTC	Piper PA-28-140 Cherokee	
☐ G-AXTJ	Piper PA-28-140 Cherokee	
☐ G-AXTL	Piper PA-28-140 Cherokee	
☐ G-AXTO	Piper PA-24-260 Comanche	
☐ G-AXTP	Piper PA-28-180 Cherokee	
☐ G-AXUA	Beagle B.121 Pup	
☐ G-AXUB	BN2A Islander	
☐ G-AXUC	Piper PA-12 Super Cruiser	
☐ G-AXUF	Reims FA150K Aerobat	
☐ G-AXUJ	Auster J/1 Autocrat	
☐ G-AXUK	Jodel DR.1050	
☐ G-AXVB	Reims F172H	
☐ G-AXVK	Campbell Cricket	
☐ G-AXVL	Campbell Cricket	
☐ G-AXVM	Campbell Cricket	
☐ G-AXVN	McCandless M.4	
☐ G-AXWA	Auster AOP.9	
☐ G-AXWT	Jodel D.11	
☐ G-AXWV	Robin DR.253 Regent	
☐ G-AXWZ	Piper PA-28R-200	
☐ G-AXXC	Piel Emeraude	
☐ G-AXXV	DH.82A Tiger Moth	
☐ G-AXXW	Jodel D.117	
☐ G-AXYK	Taylor Monoplane	
☐ G-AXYU	Jodel D.9 Bebe	
☐ G-AXZD	Piper PA-28-180 Cherokee	
☐ G-AXZF	Piper PA-28-180 Cherokee	
☐ G-AXZK	BN2A-26 Islander	
☐ G-AXZO	Cessna 180	
☐ G-AXZP	Piper PA-23-250 Aztec D	
☐ G-AXZT	Jodel D.117A	
☐ G-AXZU	Cessna 182N Skylane	
☐ G-AYAB	Piper PA-28-180 Cherokee	
☐ G-AYAC	Piper PA-28R-200	
☐ G-AYAF	Piper PA-30-160	
☐ G-AYAN	Slingsby Motor Cadet	
☐ G-AYAR	Piper PA-28-180 Cherokee	
☐ G-AYAT	Piper PA-28-180 Cherokee	
☐ G-AYAW	Piper PA-28-180 Cherokee	
☐ G-AYBD	Reims F150K	
☐ G-AYBG	Scheibe SF25B Falke	
☐ G-AYBO	Piper PA-23-250 Aztec D	
☐ G-AYBP	Jodel D.112	
☐ G-AYBR	Jodel D.112	
☐ G-AYCC	Campbell Cricket	
☐ G-AYCE	Piel Emeraude	
☐ G-AYCF	Reims FA150K Aerobat	
☐ G-AYCG	Stampe SV-4C	
☐ G-AYCJ	Cessna TP206D	
☐ G-AYCK	Stampe SV-4C	
☐ G-AYCN	Piper J-3C-65 Cub	
☐ G-AYCO	Robin DR.360	
☐ G-AYCP	Jodel D.112	
☐ G-AYCT	Reims F172H	
☐ G-AYDI	DH.82A Tiger Moth	
☐ G-AYDR	Stampe SV-4C	
☐ G-AYDV	Coates Swalesong SA.11	
☐ G-AYDW	Beagle A.61 Terrier	
☐ G-AYDX	Beagle A.61 Terrier	
☐ G-AYDY	Luton Minor	
☐ G-AYDZ	Jodel DR.200	
☐ G-AYEB	Jodel D.112	

☐ G-AYEC	Piel Emeraude	☐ G-AYPM	Piper PA-18-95	☐ G-AZCK	Beagle B.121 Pup 2
☐ G-AYEE	Piper PA-28-180 Cherokee	☐ G-AYPO	Piper PA-18-95	☐ G-AZCL	Beagle B.121 Pup 2
☐ G-AYEF	Piper PA-28-180 Cherokee	☐ G-AYPS	Piper PA-18-95	☐ G-AZCN	Beagle B.121 Pup 2
☐ G-AYEG	Falconar F-9	☐ G-AYPT	Piper PA-18-95	☐ G-AZCP	Beagle B.121 Pup
☐ G-AYEH	Jodel DR.1050	☐ G-AYPU	Piper PA-28R-200	☐ G-AZCT	Beagle B.121 Pup
☐ G-AYEJ	Jodel DR.1050	☐ G-AYPV	Piper PA-28-140 Cherokee	☐ G-AZCU	Beagle B.121 Pup
☐ G-AYEN	Piper J-3C-65 Cub	☐ G-AYPZ	Campbell Cricket	☐ G-AZCV	Beagle B.121 Pup 2
☐ G-AYEV	Jodel DR.1050	☐ G-AYRC	Campbell Cricket	☐ G-AZCZ	Beagle B.121 Pup 2
☐ G-AYEW	Jodel DR.1050	☐ G-AYRF	Reims F150L	☐ G-AZDA	Beagle B.121 Pup
☐ G-AYFC	Druine Condor	☐ G-AYRG	Reims F172K	☐ G-AZDD	Bolkow Bo.209-150FF
☐ G-AYFD	Druine Condor	☐ G-AYRH	MS.892A Commodore	☐ G-AZDE	Piper PA-28R-200
☐ G-AYFF	Druine Condor	☐ G-AYRI	Piper PA-28R-200	☐ G-AZDG	Beagle B.121 Pup 2
☐ G-AYFG	Druine Condor	☐ G-AYRM	Piper PA-28-140 Cherokee	☐ G-AZDJ	Piper PA-32-300 D
☐ G-AYFP	Jodel D.140	☐ G-AYRO	Reims FA150L Aerobat	☐ G-AZDX	Piper PA-28-180 Cherokee
☐ G-AYFV	Andreasson BA4B	☐ G-AYRS	Jodel D.120A Paris-Nice	☐ G-AZDY	DH.82A Tiger Moth
☐ G-AYFX	Grumman AA-1 Yankee	☐ G-AYRT	Reims F172K	☐ G-AZEE	MS.880B Rallye
☐ G-AYGA	Jodel D.117	☐ G-AYRU	BN2 Islander	☐ G-AZEF	Jodel D.120 Paris-Nice
☐ G-AYGB	Cessna 310Q	☐ G-AYSB	Piper PA-30-160 C	☐ G-AZEG	Piper PA-28-140 Cherokee
☐ G-AYGC	Reims F150K	☐ G-AYSD	Slingsby T.61A	☐ G-AZER	Cameron O-42
☐ G-AYGD	Jodel DR.1050	☐ G-AYSH	Taylor Monoplane	☐ G-AZET	Scottish Aviation Bulldog
☐ G-AYGE	Stampe SV-4C	☐ G-AYSX	Reims F177RG	☐ G-AZEV	Beagle B.121 Pup 2
☐ G-AYGG	Jodel D.120 Paris-Nice	☐ G-AYSY	Reims F177RG	☐ G-AZEW	Beagle B.121 Pup 2
☐ G-AYGX	Reims FR172G Rocket	☐ G-AYTA	MS.880B Rallye	☐ G-AZEY	Beagle B.121 Pup 2
☐ G-AYHA	Grumman AA-1 Yankee	☐ G-AYTR	Piel Emeraude	☐ G-AZFA	Beagle B.121 Pup 2
☐ G-AYHX	Jodel D.117A	☐ G-AYTT	Luton Duet PM-3	☐ G-AZFC	Piper PA-28-140 Cherokee
☐ G-AYIA	Hughes 369HS	☐ G-AYTV	Jurca Tempete	☐ G-AZFF	Jodel D.112
☐ G-AYIG	Piper PA-28-140 Cherokee	☐ G-AYUA	Auster AOP.9	☐ G-AZFI	Piper PA-28R-200
☐ G-AYII	Piper PA-28R-200	☐ G-AYUB	Robin DR.253 Regent	☐ G-AZFM	Piper PA-28R-200
☐ G-AYIJ	Stampe SV-4B	☐ G-AYUH	Piper PA-28-180 Cherokee	☐ G-AZFR	Cessna 401B
☐ G-AYIM	HS.748-2A	☐ G-AYUJ	Evans VP-1	☐ G-AZGA	Jodel D.120 Paris-Nice
☐ G-AYIT	DH.82A Tiger Moth	☐ G-AYUM	Slingsby T.61A	☐ G-AZGE	Stampe SV-4C
☐ G-AYJA	Jodel DR.1050	☐ G-AYUN	Slingsby T.61A	☐ G-AZGF	Beagle B.121 Pup 2
☐ G-AYJB	Stampe SV-4C	☐ G-AYUP	Slingsby T.61A	☐ G-AZGL	MS.894A Minerva
☐ G-AYJD	Fournier RF3	☐ G-AYUR	Slingsby T.61A	☐ G-AZGY	Piel Emeraude
☐ G-AYJP	Piper PA-28-140 Cherokee	☐ G-AYUS	Taylor Monoplane	☐ G-AZGZ	DH.82A Tiger Moth
☐ G-AYJR	Piper PA-28-140 Cherokee	☐ G-AYUT	Jodel DR.1050	☐ G-AZHB	Robin HR.100
☐ G-AYJW	Reims FR172G Rocket	☐ G-AYUV	Reims F172H	☐ G-AZHC	Jodel D.112
☐ G-AYJY	Isaacs Fury II	☐ G-AYVO	Wallis WA-120-1	☐ G-AZHD	Slingsby T.61A
☐ G-AYKA	Beech 95-A55 Baron	☐ G-AYVP	Woody Pusher	☐ G-AZHH	Cavalier SA.102
☐ G-AYKD	Jodel DR.1050	☐ G-AYWD	Cessna 182N Skylane	☐ G-AZHI	Airtourer 150
☐ G-AYKJ	Jodel D.117A	☐ G-AYWE	Piper PA-28-140 Cherokee	☐ G-AZHJ	Twin Pioneer 3
☐ G-AYKK	Jodel D.117	☐ G-AYWH	Jodel D.117A	☐ G-AZHK	Robin HR.100
☐ G-AYKL	Reims F150L	☐ G-AYWM	Airtourer 150	☐ G-AZHR	Piccard AX6
☐ G-AYKS	Leopoldoff L.7 Colibri	☐ G-AYWT	Stampe SV-4C	☐ G-AZHT	Airtourer T3
☐ G-AYKT	Jodel D.117	☐ G-AYXP	Jodel D.117A	☐ G-AZHU	Luton Minor
☐ G-AYKW	Piper PA-28-140 Cherokee	☐ G-AYXS	SIAI-Marchetti S.205-18R	☐ G-AZIB	Gardan ST-10 Diplomat
☐ G-AYKZ	SAI KZ-VIII	☐ G-AYXT	Westland Whirlwind	☐ G-AZID	Reims FA150L Aerobat
☐ G-AYLA	Airtourer 115	☐ G-AYXU	Aeronca 7KCAB Citabria	☐ G-AZII	Jodel D.117A
☐ G-AYLC	Jodel DR.1051	☐ G-AYYL	Slingsby T.61A	☐ G-AZIJ	Robin DR.360
☐ G-AYLF	Jodel DR.1051	☐ G-AYYO	Jodel D.1050M1	☐ G-AZIK	Piper PA-34-200 Seneca
☐ G-AYLL	Jodel DR.1050	☐ G-AYYT	Jodel D.1050M1	☐ G-AZIL	Slingsby T.61A
☐ G-AYLP	Grumman AA-1 Yankee	☐ G-AYYU	Beech C23 Sundowner	☐ G-AZIP	Cameron O-65
☐ G-AYLV	Jodel D.120 Paris-Nice	☐ G-AYYX	MS.880B Rallye	☐ G-AZJC	Fournier RF5
☐ G-AYLZ	Super Aero 45	☐ G-AYZE	Piper PA-39-160 CR	☐ G-AZJE	Barritault Minicab
☐ G-AYME	Fournier RF5	☐ G-AYZH	Taylor Titch	☐ G-AZJN	Robin DR300/140 Major
☐ G-AYMK	Piper PA-28-140 Cherokee	☐ G-AYZI	Stampe SV-4C	☐ G-AZJV	Reims F172L
☐ G-AYMO	Piper PA-23-250 Aztec C	☐ G-AYZK	Jodel DR.1050M1	☐ G-AZJY	Reims FRA150L Aerobat
☐ G-AYMP	Phoenix Currie Wot	☐ G-AYZS	Druine Condor	☐ G-AZKC	MS.880B Rallye
☐ G-AYMR	Lederlin 380L	☐ G-AYZU	Slingsby T.61A	☐ G-AZKE	MS.880B Rallye
☐ G-AYMU	Jodel D.112	☐ G-AYZW	Slingsby T.61A	☐ G-AZKK	Cameron O-56
☐ G-AYMV	Western 20	☐ G-AZAB	Piper PA-30-160 B	☐ G-AZKO	Cessna 337F
☐ G-AYNA	Phoenix Currie Wot	☐ G-AZAJ	Piper PA-28R-200	☐ G-AZKP	Jodel D.117
☐ G-AYND	Cessna 310Q	☐ G-AZAW	Gardan GY-80-160	☐ G-AZKR	Piper PA-24-180 Comanche
☐ G-AYNF	Piper PA-28-140 Cherokee	☐ G-AZBB	Bolkow Bo.209-160FV	☐ G-AZKS	Grumman AA-1A Trainer
☐ G-AYNJ	Piper PA-28-140 Cherokee	☐ G-AZBE	Airtourer T5	☐ G-AZKW	Reims F172L
☐ G-AYNN	Cessna 185B Skywagon	☐ G-AZBI	Jodel D.150 Mascaret	☐ G-AZKZ	Reims F172L
☐ G-AYOW	Cessna 182N Skylane	☐ G-AZBL	Jodel D.9 Bebe	☐ G-AZLE	Boeing Stearman E75
☐ G-AYOY	Sikorsky S-61N	☐ G-AZBN	Noorduyn Harvard	☐ G-AZLF	Jodel D.120 Paris-Nice
☐ G-AYOZ	Reims FA150L Aerobat	☐ G-AZBT	Western O-65	☐ G-AZLH	Reims F150L
☐ G-AYPE	Bolkow Bo.209-160RV	☐ G-AZBU	Auster AOP.9	☐ G-AZLN	Piper PA-28-180 Cherokee
☐ G-AYPG	Reims F177RG	☐ G-AZBY	Westland Wessex	☐ G-AZLV	Cessna 172K Skyhawk
☐ G-AYPH	Reims F177RG	☐ G-AZCB	Stampe SV-4C	☐ G-AZLY	Reims F150L
☐ G-AYPJ	Piper PA-28-180 Cherokee	☐ G-AZCE	Pitts S-1C Special	☐ G-AZMC	Slingsby T.61A

Reg	Type
G-AZMD	Slingsby T.61C
G-AZMF	BAC 111-530FX
G-AZMJ	Grumman AA-5 Traveler
G-AZMN	Airtourer T5
G-AZMZ	MS.893A Commodore
G-AZNK	Stampe SV-4A
G-AZNL	Piper PA-28R-200
G-AZNO	Cessna 182P Skylane
G-AZNT	Cameron O-84
G-AZOA	Bolkow Bo.209-150FF
G-AZOE	Airtourer T2
G-AZOF	Airtourer T5
G-AZOG	Piper PA-28R-200
G-AZOL	Piper PA-34-200 Seneca
G-AZOO	Western O-65
G-AZOT	Piper PA-34-200 Seneca
G-AZOU	Jodel DR.1050
G-AZOZ	Reims FRA150L Aerobat
G-AZPA	Piper PA-25-235 Pawnee
G-AZPC	Slingsby T.61C
G-AZPF	Fournier RF5
G-AZPV	Luton Minor
G-AZPX	Western O-31
G-AZRA	Bolkow Bo.209-150FF
G-AZRD	Cessna 401B
G-AZRH	Piper PA-28-140 Cherokee
G-AZRI	Payne Balloon
G-AZRK	Fournier RF5
G-AZRL	Piper PA-18-95
G-AZRM	Fournier RF5
G-AZRN	Cameron O-84
G-AZRP	Airtourer T2
G-AZRS	Piper PA-22-150 Tri-Pacer
G-AZRW	Cessna T337C
G-AZRZ	Cessna U206F
G-AZSA	Stampe SV-4B
G-AZSC	Noorduyn Harvard
G-AZSF	Piper PA-28R-200
G-AZSW	Beagle B.121 Pup
G-AZTA	Bolkow Bo.209-150FF
G-AZTF	Reims F177RG
G-AZTK	Reims F172F
G-AZTS	Reims F172L
G-AZTV	Stolp SA.500
G-AZTW	Reims F177RG
G-AZUM	Reims F172L
G-AZUP	Cameron O-65
G-AZUT	MS.893A Commodore
G-AZUY	Cessna 310L
G-AZUZ	Reims FRA150L Aerobat
G-AZVA	Bolkow Bo.209-150FF
G-AZVB	Bolkow Bo.209-150FF
G-AZVF	MS.894A Minerva
G-AZVG	Grumman AA-5 Traveler
G-AZVH	MS.894A Minerva
G-AZVI	MS.892A Commodore
G-AZVJ	Piper PA-34-200 Seneca
G-AZVL	Jodel D.119
G-AZVP	Reims F177RG
G-AZWB	Piper PA-28-140 Cherokee
G-AZWD	Piper PA-28-140 Cherokee
G-AZWF	Jodel DR.1050
G-AZWS	Piper PA-28R-180
G-AZWT	Westland Lysander
G-AZWY	Piper PA-24-260 Comanche
G-AZXB	Cameron O-65
G-AZXD	Reims F172L
G-AZYA	Gardan GY-80-160
G-AZYD	MS.893A Commodore
G-AZYF	Piper PA-28-180 Cherokee
G-AZYS	Piel Emeraude
G-AZYU	Piper PA-23-250 Aztec E
G-AZYY	Slingsby T.61A
G-AZYZ	Wassmer WA.51A
G-AZZH	Practavia Pilot Sprite
G-AZZO	Piper PA-28-140 Cherokee
G-AZZR	Reims F150L
G-AZZV	Reims F172L
G-AZZZ	DH.82A Tiger Moth
G-BAAD	Evans VP-1
G-BAAF	Manning Flanders MF.1
G-BAAI	MS.893A Commodore
G-BAAT	Cessna 182P Skylane
G-BAAW	Jodel D.119
G-BABC	Reims F150L
G-BABD	Reims FRA150L Aerobat
G-BABE	Taylor Titch
G-BABG	Piper PA-28-180 Cherokee
G-BABH	Reims F150L
G-BABK	Piper PA-34-200 Seneca
G-BACB	Piper PA-34-200 Seneca
G-BACE	Fournier RF5
G-BACJ	Jodel D.120 Paris-Nice
G-BACL	Jodel D.150 Mascaret
G-BACN	Reims FRA150L Aerobat
G-BACO	Reims FRA150L Aerobat
G-BACP	Reims FRA150L Aerobat
G-BADC	Luton Beta
G-BADH	Slingsby T.61A
G-BADJ	Piper PA-23-250 Aztec E
G-BADM	Druine Condor
G-BADU	Cameron O-56
G-BADV	Brochet Pipistrelle
G-BADW	Pitts S-2A Special
G-BAEB	Robin DR.400-160 Major
G-BAEE	Jodel DR.1050M1
G-BAEM	Robin DR.400-120
G-BAEN	Robin DR.400-180 Regent
G-BAEO	Reims F172M
G-BAEP	Reims FRA150L Aerobat
G-BAER	LeVier Cosmic Wind
G-BAET	Piper J-3C-65 Cub
G-BAEU	Reims F150L
G-BAEV	Reims FRA150L Aerobat
G-BAEW	Reims F172M
G-BAEY	Reims F172M
G-BAEZ	Reims FRA150L Aerobat
G-BAFA	Grumman AA-5 Traveler
G-BAFG	DH.82A Tiger Moth
G-BAFH	Evans VP-1
G-BAFL	Cessna 182P Skylane
G-BAFP	Robin DR.400-160 Major
G-BAFT	Piper PA-18-150
G-BAFU	Piper PA-28-140 Cherokee
G-BAFV	Piper PA-18-95
G-BAFW	Piper PA-28-140 Cherokee
G-BAFX	Robin DR.400-140 Earl
G-BAGB	SIAI-Marchetti SF.260
G-BAGC	Robin DR.400-140 Earl
G-BAGF	Jodel D.92 Bebe
G-BAGG	Piper PA-32-300
G-BAGN	Reims F177RG
G-BAGR	Robin DR.400-140 Earl
G-BAGS	Robin DR.400-100
G-BAGT	Helio H295
G-BAGV	Cessna U206F
G-BAGX	Piper PA-28-140 Cherokee
G-BAGY	Cameron O-84
G-BAHD	Cessna 182P Skylane
G-BAHE	Piper PA-28-140 Cherokee
G-BAHF	Piper PA-28-140 Cherokee
G-BAHH	Wallis WA-121Mc
G-BAHI	Reims F150H
G-BAHJ	Piper PA-24-250 Comanche
G-BAHL	Robin DR.400-160 Major
G-BAHO	Beech C23 Sundowner
G-BAHP	Volmer Sportsman
G-BAHS	Piper PA-28R-200
G-BAHX	Cessna 182P Skylane
G-BAIG	Piper PA-34-200 Seneca
G-BAIH	Piper PA-28R-200
G-BAII	Reims FRA150L Aerobat
G-BAIK	Reims F150L
G-BAIP	Reims F150L
G-BAIR	Thunder Ax7-77
G-BAIS	Reims F177RG
G-BAIW	Reims F172M
G-BAIX	Reims F172M
G-BAIZ	Slingsby T.61A
G-BAJA	Reims F177RG
G-BAJB	Reims F177RG
G-BAJC	Evans VP-1
G-BAJE	Cessna 177 Cardinal
G-BAJN	Grumman AA-5 Traveler
G-BAJO	Grumman AA-5 Traveler
G-BAJR	Piper PA-28-180 Cherokee
G-BAJY	Robin DR.400-180 Regent
G-BAJZ	Robin DR.400-125
G-BAKD	Piper PA-34-200 Seneca
G-BAKH	Piper PA-28-140 Cherokee
G-BAKJ	Piper PA-30-160 B
G-BAKM	Robin DR.400-140 Earl
G-BAKN	Stampe SV-4C
G-BAKR	Jodel D.117
G-BAKV	Piper PA-18-150
G-BAKW	Beagle B.121 Pup 2
G-BAKY	Slingsby T.61C
G-BALF	Robin DR.400-140 Earl
G-BALG	Robin DR.400-180 Regent
G-BALH	Robin DR.400-140 Earl
G-BALI	Robin DR.400 2+2
G-BALJ	Robin DR.400-180 Regent
G-BALK	Stampe SV-4C
G-BALN	Cessna 310Q
G-BALY	Practavia Pilot Sprite
G-BALZ	Bell 212
G-BAMB	Slingsby T.61C
G-BAMC	Reims F150L
G-BAMJ	Cessna 182P Skylane
G-BAMM	Piper PA-28-235 Cherokee
G-BAMR	Piper PA-16 Clipper
G-BAMS	Robin DR.400-160 Major
G-BAMT	Robin DR.400-160 Major
G-BAMU	Robin DR.400-160 Major
G-BAMV	Robin DR.400-180 Regent
G-BAMY	Piper PA-28R-200
G-BANA	Robin DR.221 Dauphin
G-BANB	Robin DR.400-180 Regent
G-BANC	GY-201 Minicab
G-BANF	Luton Minor
G-BANU	Jodel D.120 Paris-Nice
G-BANW	Piel Emeraude
G-BANX	Reims F172M
G-BAOB	Reims F172M
G-BAOH	MS.880B Rallye
G-BAOJ	MS.880B Rallye
G-BAOP	Reims FRA150L Aerobat
G-BAOS	Reims F172M
G-BAOU	Grumman AA-5 Traveler
G-BAPB	DHC-1 Chipmunk
G-BAPI	Reims FRA150L Aerobat
G-BAPJ	Reims FRA150L Aerobat
G-BAPL	Piper PA-23-250 Aztec E
G-BAPR	Jodel D.11
G-BAPS	Campbell Cougar
G-BAPV	Robin DR.400-160 Major
G-BAPW	Piper PA-28R-180
G-BAPX	Robin DR.400-160 Major
G-BAPY	Robin HR.100-210 Safari

☐ G-BARC	Reims FR172J Rocket	
☐ G-BARD	Cessna 337C	
☐ G-BARF	Jodel D.112	
☐ G-BARG	Cessna 310Q	
☐ G-BARH	Beech C23 Sundowner	
☐ G-BARN	Taylor Titch	
☐ G-BARP	Bell 206B Jet Ranger	
☐ G-BARS	DHC-1 Chipmunk	
☐ G-BARV	Cessna 310Q	
☐ G-BARZ	Scheibe SF28A Falke	
☐ G-BASH	Grumman AA-5 Traveler	
☐ G-BASJ	Piper PA-28-180 Cherokee	
☐ G-BASL	Piper PA-28-140 Cherokee	
☐ G-BASM	Piper PA-34-200 Seneca	
☐ G-BASN	Beech C23 Sundowner	
☐ G-BASO	Lake LA-4-180	
☐ G-BASP	Beagle B.121 Pup	
☐ G-BATC	MBB Bo.105D	
☐ G-BATJ	Jodel D.119	
☐ G-BATN	Piper PA-23-250 Aztec E	
☐ G-BATR	Piper PA-34-200 Seneca	
☐ G-BATV	Piper PA-28-180 Cherokee	
☐ G-BATW	Piper PA-28-140 Cherokee	
☐ G-BAUC	Piper PA-25-235 Pawnee	
☐ G-BAUH	Jodel D.112	
☐ G-BAUI	Piper PA-23-250 Aztec D	
☐ G-BAVB	Reims F172M	
☐ G-BAVH	DHC-1 Chipmunk	
☐ G-BAVL	Piper PA-23-250 Aztec E	
☐ G-BAVO	Boeing Stearman A75N1	
☐ G-BAVR	Grumman AA-5 Traveler	
☐ G-BAVS	Grumman AA-5 Traveler	
☐ G-BAWG	Piper PA-28R-200	
☐ G-BAWK	Piper PA-28-140 Cherokee	
☐ G-BAWR	Robin HR.100-120	
☐ G-BAWW	Thunder Ax7-77	
☐ G-BAXE	Hughes 269A	
☐ G-BAXJ	Piper PA-32-300 B	
☐ G-BAXS	Bell 47G-5	
☐ G-BAXU	Reims F150L	
☐ G-BAXV	Reims F150L	
☐ G-BAXY	Reims F172M	
☐ G-BAXZ	Piper PA-28-140 Cherokee	
☐ G-BAYL	Nord 1203 Norecrin	
☐ G-BAYO	Cessna 150L	
☐ G-BAYP	Cessna 150L	
☐ G-BAYR	Robin HR.100-210 Safari	
☐ G-BAZM	Jodel D.11	
☐ G-BAZS	Reims F150L	
☐ G-BAZT	Reims F172M	
☐ G-BBAW	Robin HR.100-210 Safari	
☐ G-BBAX	Robin DR.400-140 Earl	
☐ G-BBAY	Robin DR.400-140 Earl	
☐ G-BBBB	Taylor Monoplane	
☐ G-BBBC	Reims F150L	
☐ G-BBBI	Grumman AA-5 Traveler	
☐ G-BBBK	Piper PA-28-140 Cherokee	
☐ G-BBBL	Cessna 337B	
☐ G-BBBN	Piper PA-28-180 Cherokee	
☐ G-BBBO	SIPA 903	
☐ G-BBBW	Clutton FRED 2	
☐ G-BBBX	Cessna 310L	
☐ G-BBBY	Piper PA-28-140 Cherokee	
☐ G-BBCA	Bell 206B Jet Ranger	
☐ G-BBCB	Western O-65	
☐ G-BBCC	Piper PA-23-250 Aztec D	
☐ G-BBCH	Robin DR.400 2+2	
☐ G-BBCI	Cessna 150H	
☐ G-BBCK	Cameron O-77	
☐ G-BBCS	Robin DR.400-140 Earl	
☐ G-BBCY	Luton Minor	
☐ G-BBCZ	Grumman AA-5 Traveler	
☐ G-BBDC	Piper PA-28-140 Cherokee	
☐ G-BBDE	Piper PA-28R-200	
☐ G-BBDH	Reims F172M	
☐ G-BBDJ	Thunder Ax6-56	
☐ G-BBDL	Grumman AA-5 Traveler	
☐ G-BBDM	Grumman AA-5 Traveler	
☐ G-BBDO	Piper PA-23-250 Aztec E	
☐ G-BBDP	Robin DR.400-160 Major	
☐ G-BBDS	Piper PA-31-310 Navajo	
☐ G-BBDT	Cessna 150H	
☐ G-BBDV	SIPA 903	
☐ G-BBEA	Luton Minor	
☐ G-BBEB	Piper PA-28R-200	
☐ G-BBEC	Piper PA-28-180 Cherokee	
☐ G-BBED	MS.894A Minerva	
☐ G-BBEF	Piper PA-28-140 Cherokee	
☐ G-BBEN	Aeronca 7GCBC Citabria	
☐ G-BBEX	Cessna 185A Skywagon	
☐ G-BBFC	Grumman AA-1B Trainer	
☐ G-BBFD	Piper PA-28R-200	
☐ G-BBFL	GY-201 Minicab	
☐ G-BBFV	Piper PA-32-260	
☐ G-BBGC	MS.893E Commodore	
☐ G-BBGE	Piper PA-23-250 Aztec D	
☐ G-BBGI	Fuji FA.200-160	
☐ G-BBGL	Oldfield Baby Lakes	
☐ G-BBGR	Cameron O-65	
☐ G-BBGZ	Cambridge Balloon	
☐ G-BBHF	Piper PA-23-250 Aztec E	
☐ G-BBHG	Cessna 310Q	
☐ G-BBHI	Cessna 177RG Cardinal	
☐ G-BBHJ	Piper J-3C-85 Cub	
☐ G-BBHK	Noorduyn Harvard	
☐ G-BBHL	Sikorsky S-61N	
☐ G-BBHY	Piper PA-28-180 Cherokee	
☐ G-BBIA	Piper PA-28R-200	
☐ G-BBIF	Piper PA-23-250 Aztec E	
☐ G-BBIH	Enstrom F-28A	
☐ G-BBII	Fiat G.46-3B	
☐ G-BBIL	Piper PA-28-140 Cherokee	
☐ G-BBIN	Enstrom F-28A	
☐ G-BBIO	Robin HR.100-210 Safari	
☐ G-BBIX	Piper PA-28-140 Cherokee	
☐ G-BBJI	Isaacs Spitfire	
☐ G-BBJU	Robin DR.400-140 Earl	
☐ G-BBJV	Reims F177RG	
☐ G-BBJX	Reims F150L	
☐ G-BBJY	Reims F172M	
☐ G-BBJZ	Reims F172M	
☐ G-BBKA	Reims F150L	
☐ G-BBKB	Reims F150L	
☐ G-BBKE	Reims F150L	
☐ G-BBKG	Reims FR172J Rocket	
☐ G-BBKI	Reims F150L	
☐ G-BBKL	Piel Emeraude	
☐ G-BBKX	Piper PA-28-180 Cherokee	
☐ G-BBKY	Reims F150L	
☐ G-BBKZ	Cessna 172M Skyhawk	
☐ G-BBLH	Piper J-3C-65 Cub	
☐ G-BBLM	MS.880B Rallye	
☐ G-BBLS	Grumman AA-5 Traveler	
☐ G-BBLU	Piper PA-34-200 Seneca	
☐ G-BBMB	Robin DR.400-180 Regent	
☐ G-BBMH	EAA Biplane	
☐ G-BBMJ	Piper PA-23-250 Aztec E	
☐ G-BBMN	DHC-1 Chipmunk	
☐ G-BBMO	DHC-1 Chipmunk	
☐ G-BBMR	DHC-1 Chipmunk	
☐ G-BBMT	DHC-1 Chipmunk	
☐ G-BBMW	DHC-1 Chipmunk	
☐ G-BBMX	DHC-1 Chipmunk	
☐ G-BBMZ	DHC-1 Chipmunk	
☐ G-BBNA	DHC-1 Chipmunk	
☐ G-BBNC	DHC-1 Chipmunk	
☐ G-BBND	DHC-1 Chipmunk	
☐ G-BBNG	Bell 206B Jet Ranger	
☐ G-BBNH	Piper PA-34-200 Seneca	
☐ G-BBNI	Piper PA-34-200 Seneca	
☐ G-BBNJ	Reims F150L	
☐ G-BBNT	Piper PA-31-350 Chieftain	
☐ G-BBNZ	Reims F172M	
☐ G-BBOA	Reims F172M	
☐ G-BBOC	Cameron O-77	
☐ G-BBOE	Robin HR.200-100	
☐ G-BBOH	Pitts S-1S Special	
☐ G-BBOL	Piper PA-18-150	
☐ G-BBOO	Thunder Ax6-56	
☐ G-BBOR	Bell 206B Jet Ranger	
☐ G-BBOX	Thunder Ax7-77	
☐ G-BBPN	Enstrom F-28A	
☐ G-BBPO	Enstrom F-28A	
☐ G-BBPP	Piper PA-28-180 Cherokee	
☐ G-BBPS	Jodel D.117	
☐ G-BBPX	Piper PA-34-200 Seneca	
☐ G-BBPY	Piper PA-28-180 Cherokee	
☐ G-BBRA	Piper PA-23-250 Aztec E	
☐ G-BBRC	Fuji FA.200-180	
☐ G-BBRI	Bell 47G-5A	
☐ G-BBRN	Mitchell-Procter Kittiwake	
☐ G-BBRV	DHC-1 Chipmunk	
☐ G-BBRX	SIAI-Marchetti S.205-18F	
☐ G-BBRY	Cessna 210 Centurion	
☐ G-BBRZ	Grumman AA-5 Traveler	
☐ G-BBSA	Grumman AA-5 Traveler	
☐ G-BBSB	Beech C23 Sundowner	
☐ G-BBSM	Piper PA-32-300	
☐ G-BBSS	DHC-1 Chipmunk	
☐ G-BBSW	Pietenpol Aircamper	
☐ G-BBTB	Reims FRA150L Aerobat	
☐ G-BBTG	Reims F172M	
☐ G-BBTH	Reims F172M	
☐ G-BBTJ	Piper PA-23-250 Aztec E	
☐ G-BBTS	Beech V35B Bonanza	
☐ G-BBTY	Beech C23 Sundowner	
☐ G-BBTZ	Reims F150L	
☐ G-BBUE	Grumman AA-5 Traveler	
☐ G-BBUF	Grumman AA-5 Traveler	
☐ G-BBUG	Piper PA-16 Clipper	
☐ G-BBUJ	Cessna 421B	
☐ G-BBUT	Western O-65	
☐ G-BBUU	Piper J-3C-65 Cub	
☐ G-BBVA	Sikorsky S-61N	
☐ G-BBVF	Twin Pioneer 3	
☐ G-BBVG	Piper PA-23-250 Aztec C	
☐ G-BBVO	Isaacs Fury II	
☐ G-BBWZ	Grumman AA-1B Trainer	
☐ G-BBXB	Reims FRA150L Aerobat	
☐ G-BBXH	Reims FR172F Rocket	
☐ G-BBXK	Piper PA-34-200 Seneca	
☐ G-BBXL	Cessna 310Q	
☐ G-BBXS	Piper J-3C-90 Cub	
☐ G-BBXU	Beech B24R Sierra 200	
☐ G-BBXW	Piper PA-28-151 Warrior	
☐ G-BBXY	Aeronca 7GCBC Citabria	
☐ G-BBXZ	Evans VP-1	
☐ G-BBYB	Piper PA-18-95	
☐ G-BBYH	Cessna 182P Skylane	
☐ G-BBYL	Cameron O-77	
☐ G-BBYM	HP.137 Jetstream 200	
☐ G-BBYP	Piper PA-28-140 Cherokee	
☐ G-BBYR	Cameron O-65	
☐ G-BBYS	Cessna 182P Skylane	
☐ G-BBZF	Piper PA-28-140 Cherokee	
☐ G-BBZH	Piper PA-28R-200	
☐ G-BBZN	Fuji FA.200-180	
☐ G-BBZS	Enstrom F-28A	
☐ G-BBZV	Piper PA-28R-200	

☐ G-BCAH	DHC-1 Chipmunk
☐ G-BCAZ	Piper PA-12 Super Cruiser
☐ G-BCBG	Piper PA-23-250 Aztec E
☐ G-BCBH	Fairchild F.24R
☐ G-BCBJ	Piper PA-25-235 Pawnee
☐ G-BCBL	Fairchild F.24R
☐ G-BCBR	Wittman Tailwind
☐ G-BCBX	Reims F150L
☐ G-BCBZ	Cessna 337C
☐ G-BCCC	Reims F150L
☐ G-BCCD	Reims F172M
☐ G-BCCE	Piper PA-23-250 Aztec E
☐ G-BCCF	Piper PA-28-180 Cherokee
☐ G-BCCG	Thunder Ax7-65
☐ G-BCCJ	Grumman AA-5 Traveler
☐ G-BCCK	Grumman AA-5 Traveler
☐ G-BCCR	Piel Emeraude
☐ G-BCCX	DHC-1 Chipmunk
☐ G-BCCY	Robin HR.200-100
☐ G-BCDJ	Piper PA-28-140 Cherokee
☐ G-BCDK	Partenavia P.68B
☐ G-BCDL	Cameron O-42
☐ G-BCDY	Reims FRA150L Aerobat
☐ G-BCEA	Sikorsky S-61N
☐ G-BCEB	Sikorsky S-61N
☐ G-BCEE	Grumman AA-5 Traveler
☐ G-BCEF	Grumman AA-5 Traveler
☐ G-BCEN	BN2A-8 Islander
☐ G-BCEP	Grumman AA-5 Traveler
☐ G-BCER	GY-201 Minicab
☐ G-BCEX	Piper PA-23-250 Aztec E
☐ G-BCEY	DHC-1 Chipmunk
☐ G-BCEZ	Cameron O-84
☐ G-BCFF	Fuji FA.200-160
☐ G-BCFN	Cameron O-65
☐ G-BCFO	Piper PA-18-150
☐ G-BCFR	Reims FRA150L Aerobat
☐ G-BCFW	SAAB 91D
☐ G-BCFY	Luton Minor
☐ G-BCGB	Bensen B.8
☐ G-BCGC	DHC-1 Chipmunk
☐ G-BCGH	Nord NC.854S
☐ G-BCGI	Piper PA-28-140 Cherokee
☐ G-BCGJ	Piper PA-28-140 Cherokee
☐ G-BCGM	Jodel D.120 Paris-Nice
☐ G-BCGN	Piper PA-28-140 Cherokee
☐ G-BCGS	Piper PA-28R-200
☐ G-BCGW	Jodel D.11
☐ G-BCHK	Reims F172H
☐ G-BCHL	DHC-1 Chipmunk
☐ G-BCHM	Aerospatiale Gazelle
☐ G-BCHP	Super Emeraude
☐ G-BCHT	Schleicher ASK-16
☐ G-BCHV	DHC-1 Chipmunk
☐ G-BCID	Piper PA-34-200 Seneca
☐ G-BCIH	DHC-1 Chipmunk
☐ G-BCIJ	Grumman AA-5 Traveler
☐ G-BCIN	Thunder Ax7-77
☐ G-BCIR	Piper PA-28-151 Warrior
☐ G-BCJM	Piper PA-28-140 Cherokee
☐ G-BCJN	Piper PA-28-140 Cherokee
☐ G-BCJO	Piper PA-28R-200
☐ G-BCJP	Piper PA-28-140 Cherokee
☐ G-BCKN	DHC-1 Chipmunk
☐ G-BCKS	Fuji FA.200-180
☐ G-BCKT	Fuji FA.200-180
☐ G-BCKU	Reims FRA150L Aerobat
☐ G-BCKV	Reims FRA150L Aerobat
☐ G-BCLC	Sikorsky S-61N
☐ G-BCLD	Sikorsky S-61N
☐ G-BCLI	Grumman AA-5 Traveler
☐ G-BCLL	Piper PA-28-180 Cherokee
☐ G-BCLS	Cessna 170B
☐ G-BCLT	MS.894A Minerva
☐ G-BCLU	Jodel D.117
☐ G-BCLW	Grumman AA-1B Trainer
☐ G-BCMD	Piper PA-18-95
☐ G-BCMF	Levi Go-Plane
☐ G-BCMJ	Cavalier SA.102
☐ G-BCMT	Isaacs Fury II
☐ G-BCNC	GY-201 Minicab
☐ G-BCNP	Cameron O-77
☐ G-BCNR	Thunder Ax7-77A
☐ G-BCNX	Piper J-3C-65 Cub
☐ G-BCNZ	Fuji FA.200-160
☐ G-BCOB	Piper J-3C-65 Cub
☐ G-BCOI	DHC-1 Chipmunk
☐ G-BCOJ	Cameron O-56
☐ G-BCOL	Reims F172M
☐ G-BCOM	Piper J-3C-90 Cub
☐ G-BCOO	DHC-1 Chipmunk
☐ G-BCOR	MS.880B Rallye
☐ G-BCOU	DHC-1 Chipmunk
☐ G-BCOY	DHC-1 Chipmunk
☐ G-BCPD	GY-201 Minicab
☐ G-BCPG	Piper PA-28R-200
☐ G-BCPH	Piper J-3C-65 Cub
☐ G-BCPJ	Piper J-3C-65 Cub
☐ G-BCPK	Reims F172M
☐ G-BCPN	Grumman AA-5 Traveler
☐ G-BCPU	DHC-1 Chipmunk
☐ G-BCRB	Reims F172M
☐ G-BCRI	Cameron O-65
☐ G-BCRK	Cavalier SA.105
☐ G-BCRL	Piper PA-28-151 Warrior
☐ G-BCRP	Piper PA-23-250 Aztec E
☐ G-BCRR	Grumman AA-5B Tiger
☐ G-BCRT	Reims F150M
☐ G-BCRX	DHC-1 Chipmunk
☐ G-BCSA	DHC-1 Chipmunk
☐ G-BCSL	DHC-1 Chipmunk
☐ G-BCST	MS.893A Commodore
☐ G-BCSX	Thunder Ax7-77
☐ G-BCTF	Piper PA-28-151 Warrior
☐ G-BCTI	Schleicher ASK-16
☐ G-BCTK	Reims FR172J Rocket
☐ G-BCTT	Evans VP-1
☐ G-BCUB	Piper J-3C-65 Cub
☐ G-BCUF	Reims F172M
☐ G-BCUH	Reims F150M
☐ G-BCUJ	Reims F150M
☐ G-BCUO	Scottish Aviation Bulldog
☐ G-BCUS	Scottish Aviation Bulldog
☐ G-BCUV	Scottish Aviation Bulldog
☐ G-BCUY	Reims FRA150M Aerobat
☐ G-BCVB	Piper PA-17 Vagabond
☐ G-BCVC	MS.880B Rallye
☐ G-BCVF	Practavia Pilot Sprite
☐ G-BCVG	Reims FRA150L Aerobat
☐ G-BCVH	Reims FRA150L Aerobat
☐ G-BCVJ	Reims F172M
☐ G-BCVY	Piper PA-34-200T Seneca
☐ G-BCWB	Cessna 182P Skylane
☐ G-BCWH	Practavia Pilot Sprite
☐ G-BCWK	Fournier RF3
☐ G-BCXB	MS.880B Rallye
☐ G-BCXE	Robin DR.400 2+2
☐ G-BCXJ	Piper J-3C-65 Cub
☐ G-BCXN	DHC-1 Chipmunk
☐ G-BCXZ	Cameron O-56
☐ G-BCYH	Slingsby T.31M
☐ G-BCYM	DHC-1 Chipmunk
☐ G-BCYR	Reims F172M
☐ G-BCZM	Reims F172M
☐ G-BCZO	Cameron O-77
☐ G-BDAC	Cameron O-77
☐ G-BDAD	Taylor Monoplane
☐ G-BDAG	Taylor Monoplane
☐ G-BDAI	Reims FRA150M Aerobat
☐ G-BDAK	Rockwell 112
☐ G-BDAO	SIPA 91
☐ G-BDAP	Wittman Tailwind
☐ G-BDAR	Evans VP-1
☐ G-BDAY	Thunder Ax5-42A
☐ G-BDBD	Wittman Tailwind
☐ G-BDBF	Clutton FRED II
☐ G-BDBH	Aeronca 7GCBC Citabria
☐ G-BDBI	Cameron O-77
☐ G-BDBJ	Cessna 182P Skylane
☐ G-BDBU	Reims F150M
☐ G-BDBV	Jodel D.11A
☐ G-BDCD	Piper J-3C-90 Cub
☐ G-BDCI	Piel Emeraude
☐ G-BDCL	Grumman AA-5 Traveler
☐ G-BDCO	Beagle B.121 Pup
☐ G-BDDD	DHC-1 Chipmunk
☐ G-BDDF	Jodel D.120 Paris-Nice
☐ G-BDDG	Jodel D.112
☐ G-BDDS	Piper PA-25-260 Pawnee
☐ G-BDDX	Whittaker Excalibur
☐ G-BDDZ	Piel Emeraude
☐ G-BDEC	MS.880B Rallye
☐ G-BDEH	Jodel D.120A Paris-Nice
☐ G-BDEI	Jodel D.9 Bebe
☐ G-BDEU	DHC-1 Chipmunk
☐ G-BDEX	Reims FRA150M Aerobat
☐ G-BDEY	Piper J-3C-65 Cub
☐ G-BDEZ	Piper J-3C-65 Cub
☐ G-BDFB	Phoenix Currie Wot
☐ G-BDFH	Auster AOP.9
☐ G-BDFJ	Reims F150M
☐ G-BDFR	Fuji FA.200-160
☐ G-BDFU	Dragonfly MPA
☐ G-BDFW	Rockwell 112A
☐ G-BDFX	Auster 5
☐ G-BDFY	Grumman AA-5 Traveler
☐ G-BDFZ	Reims F150M
☐ G-BDGB	Barritault Minicab
☐ G-BDGH	Thunder Ax7-77
☐ G-BDGM	Piper PA-28-151 Warrior
☐ G-BDGY	Piper PA-28-140 Cherokee
☐ G-BDHK	Piper J-3C-65 Cub
☐ G-BDIE	Rockwell 112
☐ G-BDIG	Cessna 182P Skylane
☐ G-BDIH	Jodel D.117
☐ G-BDIJ	Sikorsky S-61N
☐ G-BDIN	Scottish Aviation Bulldog
☐ G-BDIX	DH.106 Comet 4
☐ G-BDJC	Wittman Tailwind
☐ G-BDJD	Jodel D.112
☐ G-BDJG	Luton Minor
☐ G-BDJP	Piper J-3C-65 Cub
☐ G-BDJR	Nord NC.858S
☐ G-BDJV	BN-2A-21 Islander
☐ G-BDKC	Cessna A185F
☐ G-BDKD	Enstrom F-28A
☐ G-BDKH	Piel Emeraude
☐ G-BDKJ	Cavalier SA.102.5
☐ G-BDKM	SIPA 903
☐ G-BDKW	Rockwell 112
☐ G-BDLO	Grumman AA-5A Cheetah
☐ G-BDLT	Rockwell 112
☐ G-BDLY	Cavalier SA.102.5
☐ G-BDMO	Thunder Ax7-77
☐ G-BDMS	Piper J-3C-65 Cub
☐ G-BDMW	Robin DR.100A
☐ G-BDNC	Taylor Monoplane
☐ G-BDNG	Taylor Monoplane
☐ G-BDNO	Taylor Monoplane

☐ G-BDNR	Reims FRA150M Aerobat
☐ G-BDNT	Jodel D.92 Bebe
☐ G-BDNU	Reims F172M
☐ G-BDNW	Grumman AA-1B Trainer
☐ G-BDNX	Grumman AA-1B Trainer
☐ G-BDOC	Sikorsky S-61N
☐ G-BDOD	Reims F150M
☐ G-BDOE	Reims FR172J Rocket
☐ G-BDOG	Scottish Aviation Bulldog
☐ G-BDOL	Piper J-3C-65 Cub
☐ G-BDON	Thunder Ax7-77A
☐ G-BDOT	BN2A-III Trislander
☐ G-BDOW	Reims FRA150M Aerobat
☐ G-BDPA	Piper PA-28-151 Warrior
☐ G-BDPJ	Piper PA-25-235 Pawnee
☐ G-BDPK	Cameron O-56
☐ G-BDPN	BN-2A-21 Islander
☐ G-BDRD	Reims FRA150M Aerobat
☐ G-BDRG	Taylor Titch
☐ G-BDRJ	DHC-1 Chipmunk
☐ G-BDRK	Cameron O-65
☐ G-BDSB	Piper PA-28-181 Archer
☐ G-BDSE	Cameron O-77
☐ G-BDSF	Cameron O-56
☐ G-BDSH	Piper PA-28-140 Cherokee
☐ G-BDSK	Cameron O-65
☐ G-BDSL	Reims F150M
☐ G-BDSM	Slingsby T.31M
☐ G-BDTB	Evans VP-1
☐ G-BDTL	Evans VP-1
☐ G-BDTO	BN2A-III Trislander
☐ G-BDTU	Van Den Bemden
☐ G-BDTV	Mooney M.20F
☐ G-BDTX	Reims F150M
☐ G-BDUI	Cameron V-56
☐ G-BDUL	Evans VP-1
☐ G-BDUM	Reims F150M
☐ G-BDUN	Piper PA-34-200T Seneca
☐ G-BDUO	Reims F150M
☐ G-BDUY	Robin DR.400-140 Earl
☐ G-BDUZ	Cameron O-56
☐ G-BDVA	Piper PA-17 Vagabond
☐ G-BDVB	Piper PA-15 Vagabond
☐ G-BDVC	Piper PA-17 Vagabond
☐ G-BDVG	Thunder Ax6-56A
☐ G-BDVX	BN-2A-21 Islander
☐ G-BDWA	MS.880B Rallye
☐ G-BDWE	Flaglor SkySkooter
☐ G-BDWH	MS.880B Rallye
☐ G-BDWJ	Replica Plans SE5A
☐ G-BDWM	Bonsall Mustang
☐ G-BDWO	Howes Ax6
☐ G-BDWP	Piper PA-32R-300
☐ G-BDWX	Jodel D.120A Paris-Nice
☐ G-BDWY	Piper PA-28-140 Cherokee
☐ G-BDXE	Boeing 747-236B
☐ G-BDXG	Boeing 747-236B
☐ G-BDXH	Boeing 747-236B
☐ G-BDXJ	Boeing 747-236B
☐ G-BDXX	Nord NC.858S
☐ G-BDYD	Rockwell 114
☐ G-BDYH	Cameron V-56
☐ G-BDZA	Scheibe SF25E Falke
☐ G-BDZC	Reims F150M
☐ G-BDZD	Reims F172M
☐ G-BDZI	BN-2A-21 Islander
☐ G-BDZU	Cessna 421C
☐ G-BEAB	Jodel DR.1051
☐ G-BEAC	Piper PA-28-140 Cherokee
☐ G-BEAG	Piper PA-34-200T Seneca
☐ G-BEAH	Auster J/2 Arrow
☐ G-BEBE	Grumman AA-5A Cheetah
☐ G-BEBG	PZL Ogar SZD45A
☐ G-BEBN	Cessna 177B Cardinal
☐ G-BEBR	GY-201 Minicab
☐ G-BEBS	Andreasson BA4B
☐ G-BEBU	Rockwell 112
☐ G-BEBZ	Piper PA-28-151 Warrior
☐ G-BECA	MS.880B Rallye
☐ G-BECB	MS.880B Rallye
☐ G-BECF	Scheibe SF25A
☐ G-BECK	Cameron V-56
☐ G-BECN	Piper J-3C-65 Cub
☐ G-BECS	Thunder Ax6-56A
☐ G-BECT	CASA I-131E
☐ G-BECW	CASA I-131E
☐ G-BECZ	Mudry CAP.10B
☐ G-BEDB	Nord 1203 Norecrin
☐ G-BEDD	Jodel D.117A
☐ G-BEDF	B.17 G-105-VE
☐ G-BEDG	Rockwell 112
☐ G-BEDJ	Piper J-3C-65 Cub
☐ G-BEDP	BN2A-III Trislander
☐ G-BEDV	Vickers Varsity
☐ G-BEDW	BN-2A-21 Islander
☐ G-BEEG	BN2A-26 Islander
☐ G-BEEH	Cameron V-56
☐ G-BEER	Isaacs Fury II
☐ G-BEEU	Piper PA-28-140 Cherokee
☐ G-BEEV	Piper PA-28-140 Cherokee
☐ G-BEFA	Piper PA-28-151 Warrior
☐ G-BEFF	Piper PA-28-140 Cherokee
☐ G-BEFI	BN-2A-21 Islander
☐ G-BEGG	Scheibe SF25E Falke
☐ G-BEHH	Piper PA-32R-300
☐ G-BEHM	Taylor Monoplane
☐ G-BEHU	Piper PA-34-200T Seneca
☐ G-BEHV	Reims F172N
☐ G-BEIA	Reims FRA150M Aerobat
☐ G-BEIF	Cameron O-65
☐ G-BEIG	Reims F150M
☐ G-BEII	Piper PA-25-235 Pawnee
☐ G-BEIL	MS.880B Rallye
☐ G-BEIP	Piper PA-28-181 Archer
☐ G-BEIS	Evans VP-1
☐ G-BEJD	HS.748-1
☐ G-BEJK	Cameron S-31
☐ G-BEJV	Piper PA-34-200T Seneca
☐ G-BEKL	Bede BD-4E
☐ G-BEKM	Evans VP-1
☐ G-BEKN	Reims FRA150M Aerobat
☐ G-BEKO	Reims F182Q Skylane
☐ G-BEKR	GY-201 Minicab
☐ G-BELF	BN2A-26 Islander
☐ G-BELP	Piper PA-28-151 Warrior
☐ G-BELT	Reims F150J
☐ G-BEMB	Reims F172M
☐ G-BEMM	Slingsby T.31M-III
☐ G-BEMU	Thunder AX5-42
☐ G-BEMW	Piper PA-28-181 Archer
☐ G-BEMY	Reims FRA150M Aerobat
☐ G-BEND	Cameron V-56
☐ G-BENJ	Rockwell 112B
☐ G-BENK	Reims F172M
☐ G-BENN	Cameron V-56
☐ G-BEOD	Cessna 180
☐ G-BEOE	Reims FRA150M Aerobat
☐ G-BEOH	Piper PA-28R-201T
☐ G-BEOI	Piper PA-18-180
☐ G-BEOK	Reims F150M
☐ G-BEOL	Short Skyvan
☐ G-BEOX	Hudson-IIIA
☐ G-BEOY	Reims FRA150L Aerobat
☐ G-BEOZ	A.W. 650 Argosy
☐ G-BEPC	Stampe SV-4C
☐ G-BEPF	Stampe SV-4C
☐ G-BEPV	Fokker S.11
☐ G-BEPY	Rockwell 112B
☐ G-BERA	MS.880B Rallye
☐ G-BERC	MS.880B Rallye
☐ G-BERD	Thunder AX6-56A
☐ G-BERI	Rockwell 114
☐ G-BERT	Cameron V-56
☐ G-BERW	Rockwell 114
☐ G-BERY	Grumman AA-1B Trainer
☐ G-BETD	Robin HR.200-100
☐ G-BETE	Rollason Beta B.2A
☐ G-BETF	Cameron 35SS
☐ G-BETG	Cessna 180K Skywagon
☐ G-BETH	Thunder AX6-56A
☐ G-BETI	Pitts S-1D Special
☐ G-BETL	Piper PA-25-235 Pawnee
☐ G-BETM	Piper PA-25-235 Pawnee
☐ G-BETW	Rand KR-2
☐ G-BEUA	Piper PA-18-180
☐ G-BEUD	Robin HR.100-285 Tiara
☐ G-BEUI	Piper J-3C-65 Cub
☐ G-BEUM	Taylor Monoplane
☐ G-BEUP	Robin DR.400-180 Regent
☐ G-BEUU	Piper PA-18-95
☐ G-BEUX	Reims F172N
☐ G-BEUY	Cameron N-31
☐ G-BEVB	MS.880B Rallye
☐ G-BEVC	MS.880B Rallye
☐ G-BEVG	Piper PA-34-200T Seneca
☐ G-BEVI	Thunder Ax7-77A
☐ G-BEVO	Fournier RF5
☐ G-BEVP	Evans VP-2
☐ G-BEVS	Taylor Monoplane
☐ G-BEVT	BN2A-III Trislander
☐ G-BEVW	MS.880B Rallye
☐ G-BEWN	DH.82A Tiger Moth
☐ G-BEWO	Zlin Z.326
☐ G-BEWP	Reims F150M
☐ G-BEWR	Reims F172N
☐ G-BEWX	Piper PA-28R-201
☐ G-BEWY	Bell 206B Jet Ranger
☐ G-BEXN	Grumman AA-1C Lynx
☐ G-BEXO	Piper PA-22-160 Tri-Pacer
☐ G-BEXW	Piper PA-28-181 Archer
☐ G-BEXX	Cameron V-56
☐ G-BEXZ	Cameron N-56
☐ G-BEYA	Enstrom 280C
☐ G-BEYB	Fairey Flycatcher Rep
☐ G-BEYL	Piper PA-28-180 Cherokee
☐ G-BEYO	Piper PA-28-140 Cherokee
☐ G-BEYT	Piper PA-28-140 Cherokee
☐ G-BEYV	Cessna T210M
☐ G-BEYW	Taylor Monoplane
☐ G-BEYZ	Jodel DR.1050M1
☐ G-BEZC	Grumman AA-5 Traveler
☐ G-BEZE	Rutan VariEze
☐ G-BEZF	Grumman AA-5 Traveler
☐ G-BEZG	Grumman AA-5 Traveler
☐ G-BEZH	Grumman AA-5 Traveler
☐ G-BEZI	Grumman AA-5 Traveler
☐ G-BEZK	Reims F172H
☐ G-BEZL	Piper PA-31-325 Navajo
☐ G-BEZO	Reims F172M
☐ G-BEZP	Piper PA-32-300
☐ G-BEZR	Reims F172M
☐ G-BEZV	Reims F172M
☐ G-BEZY	Rutan VariEze
☐ G-BEZZ	Jodel D.112
☐ G-BFAA	Gardan GY-80-160
☐ G-BFAB	Cameron N-56
☐ G-BFAF	Aeronca 7BCM Champion
☐ G-BFAH	Phoenix Currie Wot
☐ G-BFAI	Rockwell 114

G-BFAK	MS.892A Commodore
G-BFAP	SIAI-Marchetti S.205-20R
G-BFAS	Evans VP-1
G-BFAW	DHC-1 Chipmunk
G-BFAX	DHC-1 Chipmunk
G-BFBA	Robin DR.100A
G-BFBB	Piper PA-23-250 Aztec E
G-BFBC	Taylor Monoplane
G-BFBE	Robin HR.200-100
G-BFBR	Piper PA-28-161 Warrior
G-BFBU	Partenavia P.68B
C-BFBY	Piper J-3C-65 Cub
G-BFCT	Cessna TU206F
G-BFDC	DHC-1 Chipmunk
G-BFDE	Sopwith Tabloid Rep
G-BFDF	MS.893 Rallye 235GT
G-BFDI	Piper PA-28-181 Archer
G-BFDK	Piper PA-28-161 Warrior
G-BFDL	Piper J-3C-65 Cub
G-BFDO	Piper PA-28R-201T
G-BFDZ	Taylor Monoplane
G-BFEB	Jodel D.150 Mascaret
G-BFEF	Agusta Bell 47G-3B1
G-BFEH	Jodel D.117A
G-BFEK	Reims F152
G-BFER	Bell 212
G-BFEV	Piper PA-25-235 Pawnee
G-BFFB	Evans VP-2
G-BFFC	Reims F152
G-BFFE	Reims F152
G-BFFJ	Sikorsky S-61N
G-BFFP	Piper PA-18-150
G-BFFT	Cameron V-56
G-BFFW	Reims F152
G-BFFY	Reims F150M
G-BFGD	Reims F172N
G-BFGG	Reims FRA150M Aerobat
G-BFGH	Reims F337G
G-BFGK	Jodel D.117
G-BFGL	Reims FA152 Aerobat
G-BFGO	Fuji FA.200-160
G-BFGS	MS.880B Rallye
G-BFGX	Reims F150H
G-BFGZ	Reims FRA150M Aerobat
G-BFHH	DH.82A Tiger Moth
G-BFHI	Piper J-3C-65 Cub
G-BFHP	Aeronca 7GCAA Sky-Trac
G-BFHR	Robin DR.220 2+2
G-BFHT	Reims F152
G-BFHU	Reims F152
G-BFHV	Reims F152
G-BFIB	Piper PA-31-310 Navajo
G-BFID	Taylor Titch
G-BFIE	Reims FRA150M Aerobat
G-BFIG	Reims FR172K Hawk XP
G-BFIJ	Grumman AA-5A Cheetah
G-BFIN	Grumman AA-5A Cheetah
G-BFIT	Thunder AX6-56Z
G-BFIU	Reims FR172K Hawk XP
G-BFIV	Reims F177RG
G-BFIX	Thunder Ax7-77A
G-BFIY	Reims F150M
G-BFJJ	Evans VP-1
G-BFJR	Cessna 337F/G
G-BFJZ	Robin DR.400-140 Earl
G-BFKB	Reims F172N
G-BFKF	Reims FA152 Aerobat
G-BFKH	Reims F152
G-BFKL	Cameron N-56
G-BFLH	Piper PA-34-200T Seneca
G-BFLI	Piper PA-28R-201T
G-BFLM	Cessna 150M
G-BFLU	Reims F152
G-BFLX	Grumman AA-5A Cheetah
G-BFLZ	Beech 95-A55 Baron
G-BFMF	Cassutt Racer IIIM
G-BFMG	Piper PA-28-161 Warrior
G-BFMH	Cessna 177B Cardinal
G-BFMK	Reims FA152 Aerobat
G-BFMR	Piper PA-20-125 Pacer
G-BFMX	Reims F172N
G-BFMZ	Payne Ax6-62
G-BFNG	Jodel D.112
G-BFNI	Piper PA-28-161 Warrior
C-BFNK	Piper PA-28-161 Warrior
G-BFNM	Globe GC-1B Swift
G-BFNU	BN2B-21 Islander
G-BFOE	Reims F152
G-BFOF	Reims F152
G-BFOG	Cessna 150M
G-BFOJ	Grumman AA-1 Yankee
G-BFOM	Piper PA-31-310 Navajo
G-BFOP	Jodel D.120 Paris-Nice
G-BFOS	Thunder Ax6-56A
G-BFOU	Taylor Monoplane
G-BFOV	Reims F172N
G-BFPA	Scheibe SF25B Falke
G-BFPH	Reims F172K
G-BFPM	Reims F172M
G-BFPO	Rockwell 112B
G-BFPP	Bell 47J-2
G-BFPR	Piper PA-25-235 Pawnee
G-BFPS	Piper PA-25-235 Pawnee
G-BFPZ	Reims F177RG
G-BFRD	Bowers Fly Baby
G-BFRI	Sikorsky S-61N
G-BFRR	Reims FRA150M Aerobat
G-BFRS	Reims F172N
G-BFRV	Reims FA152 Aerobat
G-BFRY	Piper PA-25-235 Pawnee
G-BFSA	Reims F182Q Skylane
G-BFSC	Piper PA-25-235 Pawnee
G-BFSD	Piper PA-25-235 Pawnee
G-BFSR	Reims F150K
G-BFSS	Reims FR172G Rocket
G-BFSY	Piper PA-28-181 Archer
G-BFTC	Piper PA-28R-201T
G-BFTF	Grumman AA-5B Tiger
G-BFTG	Grumman AA-5B Tiger
G-BFTH	Reims F172N
G-BFTT	Cessna 421C
G-BFTX	Reims F172N
G-BFTZ	MS.880B Rallye
G-BFUB	Piper PA-32RT-300
G-BFUD	Scheibe SF25E Falke
G-BFUZ	Cameron V-77
G-BFVG	Piper PA-28-181 Archer
G-BFVH	Airco DH.2 Rep
G-BFVM	Westland Bell 47G-3B1
G-BFVS	Grumman AA-5B Tiger
G-BFVU	Cessna 150L
G-BFWB	Piper PA-28-161 Warrior
G-BFWD	Phoenix Currie Wot
G-BFWE	Piper PA-23-250 Aztec E
G-BFXF	Andreasson BA4B
G-BFXG	Druine Turbulent
G-BFXK	Piper PA-28-140 Cherokee
G-BFXL	Albatros D.Va Rep
G-BFXR	Jodel D.112
G-BFXS	Rockwell 114
G-BFXW	Grumman AA-5B Tiger
G-BFXX	Grumman AA-5B Tiger
G-BFYA	MBB Bo.105DB
G-BFYC	Piper PA-32RT-300
G-BFYI	Westland Bell 47G-3B1
G-BFYK	Cameron V-77
G-BFYL	Evans VP-2
G-BFYM	Piper PA-28-161 Warrior
G-BFYO	SPAD XIII Rep
G-BFZA	Fournier RF3
G-BFZB	Piper J-3C-65 Cub
G-BFZD	Reims FR182RG Skylane
G-BFZH	Piper PA-28R-200
G-BFZM	Rockwell 112TCA
G-BFZN	Reims FA152 Aerobat
G-BFZO	Grumman AA-5A Cheetah
G-BFZT	Reims FA152 Aerobat
G-BFZU	Reims FA152 Aerobat
G-BFZV	Reims F172M
G-BGAA	Cessna 152
G-BGAB	Reims F152
G-BGAE	Reims F152
G-BGAF	Reims FA152 Aerobat
G-BGAG	Reims F172N
G-BGAJ	Reims F182Q Skylane
G-BGAU	Rearwin 9000L
G-BGAX	Piper PA-28-140 Cherokee
G-BGAZ	Cameron V-77
G-BGBA	Robin R.2100A
G-BGBE	Jodel DR.1050
G-BGBF	Druine Turbulent
G-BGBG	Piper PA-28-181 Archer
G-BGBI	Reims F150L
G-BGBK	Piper PA-38-112 Tomahawk
G-BGBN	Piper PA-38-112 Tomahawk
G-BGBR	Reims F172N
G-BGBU	Auster AOP.9
G-BGBW	Piper PA-38-112 Tomahawk
G-BGBZ	Rockwell 114
G-BGCG	Douglas DC-3
G-BGCM	Grumman AA-5A Cheetah
G-BGCO	Piper PA-44-180 Seminole
G-BGCY	Taylor Monoplane
G-BGEF	Jodel D.112
G-BGEH	Monnett Sonerai II
G-BGEI	Baby Great Lakes
G-BGEW	Nord NC.854S
G-BGEX	Brookland Mosquito
G-BGFC	Evans VP-2
G-BGFF	Clutton FRED II
G-BGFG	Grumman AA-5A Cheetah
G-BGFH	Reims F182Q Skylane
G-BGFI	Grumman AA-5A Cheetah
G-BGFJ	Jodel D.9 Bebe
G-BGFT	Piper PA-34-200T Seneca
G-BGFX	Reims F152
G-BGGA	Aeronca 7GCBC Citabria
G-BGGB	Aeronca 7GCBC Citabria
G-BGGC	Aeronca 7GCBC Citabria
G-BGGD	Bellanca 8GCBC Scout
G-BGGE	Piper PA-38-112 Tomahawk
G-BGGI	Piper PA-38-112 Tomahawk
G-BGGL	Piper PA-38-112 Tomahawk
G-BGGM	Piper PA-38-112 Tomahawk
G-BGGN	Piper PA-38-112 Tomahawk
G-BGGO	Reims F152
G-BGGP	Reims F152
G-BGGU	Wallis WA-116RR
G-BGGV	Wallis WA-120
G-BGGW	Wallis WA-122
G-BGHF	Westland WG.30
G-BGHI	Reims F152
G-BGHJ	Reims F152
G-BGHM	Robin R.1180T Aiglon
G-BGHP	Beech 76 Duchess
G-BGHS	Cameron N-31
G-BGHT	Falconar F.12
G-BGHU	North American AT-6
G-BGHV	Cameron V-77

G-BGHY	Taylor Monoplane	
G-BGHZ	Clutton FRED II	
G-BGIB	Cessna 152	
G-BGIG	Piper PA-38-112 Tomahawk	
G-BGIO	Bensen B.8MR	
G-BGIU	Reims F172H	
G-BGIX	Helio H295	
G-BGIY	Reims F172N	
G-BGJB	Piper PA-44-180 Seminole	
G-BGJU	Cameron V-65	
G-BGKC	MS.880B Rallye	
G-BGKO	GY-20 Minicab	
G-BGKS	Piper PA-28-161 Warrior	
G-BGKT	Auster AOP.9	
G-BGKU	Piper PA-28R-201	
G-BGKV	Piper PA-28R-201	
G-BGKY	Piper PA-38-112 Tomahawk	
G-BGKZ	Auster J/5F Aiglet Trainer	
G-BGLA	Piper PA-38-112 Tomahawk	
G-BGLB	Bede BD-5B	
G-BGLF	Evans VP-1	
G-BGLG	Cessna 152	
G-BGLK	Monnett Sonerai IIL	
G-BGLN	Reims FA152 Aerobat	
G-BGLO	Reims F172N	
G-BGLS	Oldfield Baby Lakes	
G-BGLZ	Stitts SA-3A Playboy	
G-BGMJ	GY-201 Minicab	
G-BGMN	HS.748-2A	
G-BGMO	HS.748-2A	
G-BGMP	Reims F172G	
G-BGMR	Barritault Minicab	
G-BGMS	Taylor Titch	
G-BGMT	MS.893 Rallye 235E	
G-BGMV	Scheibe SF25B Falke	
G-BGND	Reims F172N	
G-BGNH	Short SD.330-200	
G-BGNT	Reims F152	
G-BGNV	Grumman GA-7 Cougar	
G-BGOD	Colt 77A	
G-BGOG	Piper PA-28-161 Warrior	
G-BGOI	Cameron O-56	
G-BGOJ	Reims F150L	
G-BGOL	Piper PA-28R-201T	
G-BGON	Grumman GA-7 Cougar	
G-BGOO	Colt 56SS	
G-BGOR	North American AT-6D	
G-BGPA	Cessna 182Q Skylane	
G-BGPB	CCF Harvard 4	
G-BGPD	Piper J-3C-65 Cub	
G-BGPF	Thunder Ax6-56Z	
G-BGPH	Grumman AA-5B Tiger	
G-BGPI	Plumb Biplane	
G-BGPJ	Piper PA-28-161 Warrior	
G-BGPL	Piper PA-28-161 Warrior	
G-BGPM	Evans VP-2	
G-BGPN	Piper PA-18-150	
G-BGPU	Piper PA-28-140 Cherokee	
G-BGRC	Piper PA-28-140 Cherokee	
G-BGRE	Beech 200 Super King Air	
G-BGRG	Beech 76 Duchess	
G-BGRH	Robin DR.400 2+2	
G-BGRI	Jodel DR.1050	
G-BGRM	Piper PA-38-112 Tomahawk	
G-BGRO	Reims F172M	
G-BGRR	Piper PA-38-112 Tomahawk	
G-BGRS	Thunder Ax7-77Z	
G-BGRT	Steen Skybolt	
G-BGRX	Piper PA-38-112 Tomahawk	
G-BGSA	MS.880B Rallye	
G-BGSH	Piper PA-38-112 Tomahawk	
G-BGSJ	Piper J-3C-65 Cub	
G-BGSV	Reims F172N	
G-BGSW	Beech F33 Bonanza	
G-BGSY	Grumman GA-7 Cougar	
G-BGTC	Auster AOP.9	
G-BGTF	Piper PA-44-180 Seminole	
G-BGTG	Piper PA-23-250 Aztec F	
G-BGTI	Piper J-3C-65 Cub	
G-BGTJ	Piper PA-28-180 Cherokee	
G-BGTT	Cessna 310R	
G-BGTX	Jodel D.117	
G-BGUB	Piper PA-32-300	
G-BGVB	Robin DR.315	
G-BGVE	Super Emeraude	
G-BGVH	Beech 76 Duchess	
G-BGVK	Piper PA-28-161 Warrior	
G-BGVN	Piper PA-28RT-201	
G-BGVS	Reims F172M	
G-BGVV	Grumman AA-5A Cheetah	
G-BGVY	Grumman AA-5B Tiger	
G-BGVZ	Piper PA-28-181 Archer	
G-BGWC	Robin DR.400-180 Regent	
G-BGWH	Piper PA-18-150	
G-BGWJ	Sikorsky S-61N	
G-BGWK	Sikorsky S-61N	
G-BGWM	Piper PA-28-181 Archer	
G-BGWN	Piper PA-38-112 Tomahawk	
G-BGWO	Jodel D.112	
G-BGWR	Cessna U206A	
G-BGWU	Piper PA-38-112 Tomahawk	
G-BGWV	Aeronca 7AC Champion	
G-BGWZ	Eclipse Super Eagle	
G-BGXA	Piper J-3C-65 Cub	
G-BGXB	Piper PA-38-112 Tomahawk	
G-BGXC	SOCATA TB-10 Tobago	
G-BGXD	SOCATA TB-10 Tobago	
G-BGXO	Piper PA-38-112 Tomahawk	
G-BGXR	Robin HR.200-100	
G-BGXS	Piper PA-28-236 Dakota	
G-BGXT	SOCATA TB-10 Tobago	
G-BGYH	Piper PA-28-161 Warrior	
G-BGYN	Piper PA-18-150	
G-BGZF	Piper PA-38-112 Tomahawk	
G-BGZJ	Piper PA-38-112 Tomahawk	
G-BGZO	MS.880B Rallye	
G-BGZZ	Thunder Ax5-56	
G-BHAA	Cessna 152	
G-BHAC	Cessna A152 Aerobat	
G-BHAD	Cessna A152 Aerobat	
G-BHAI	Reims F152	
G-BHAJ	Robin DR.400-160 Major	
G-BHAR	Westland Bell 47G-3B1	
G-BHAT	Thunder Ax7-77	
G-BHAV	Reims F152	
G-BHAW	Reims F172N	
G-BHAX	Enstrom F-28C2 UK	
G-BHAY	Piper PA-28RT-201	
G-BHBA	Campbell Cricket	
G-BHBE	Westland Bell 47G-3B1	
G-BHBF	Sikorsky S-76A+	
G-BHBG	Piper PA-32R-300	
G-BHBI	Mooney M.20J	
G-BHBT	Marquart Charger	
G-BHBZ	Partenavia P.68B	
G-BHCC	Cessna 172M Skyhawk	
G-BHCE	Jodel D.117A	
G-BHCM	Reims F172H	
G-BHCP	Reims F152	
G-BHCZ	Piper PA-38-112 Tomahawk	
G-BHDD	Vickers Varsity	
G-BHDE	SOCATA TB-10 Tobago	
G-BHDK	Boeing B.29	
G-BHDM	Reims F152	
G-BHDP	Reims F182Q Skylane	
G-BHDR	Reims F152	
G-BHDS	Reims F152	
G-BHDU	Reims F152	
G-BHDV	Cameron V-77	
G-BHDW	Reims F152	
G-BHDX	Reims F172N	
G-BHDZ	Reims F172N	
G-BHEC	Reims F152	
G-BHED	Reims FA152 Aerobat	
G-BHEG	Jodel D.150 Mascaret	
G-BHEK	Super Emeraude	
G-BHEL	Jodel D.117	
G-BHEM	Bensen B.8M	
G-BHEN	Reims FA152 Aerobat	
G-BHEU	Thunder Ax7-65	
G-BHEV	Piper PA-28R-200	
G-BHEX	Colt 56A	
G-BHEZ	Jodel D.150 Mascaret	
G-BHFC	Reims F152	
G-BHFE	Piper PA-44-180 Seminole	
G-BHFF	Jodel D.112	
G-BHFG	Stampe SV-4C	
G-BHFH	Piper PA-34-200T Seneca	
G-BHFI	Reims F152	
G-BHFJ	Piper PA-28R-201T	
G-BHFK	Piper PA-28-151 Warrior	
G-BHFR	Eiri PIK-20E	
G-BHGC	Piper PA-18-150	
G-BHGF	Cameron V-56	
G-BHGJ	Jodel D.120 Paris-Nice	
G-BHGO	Piper PA-32-260	
G-BHGP	SOCATA TB-10 Tobago	
G-BHGY	Piper PA-28R-200	
G-BHHB	Cameron V-77	
G-BHHE	Jodel DR.1051M1	
G-BHHG	Reims F152	
G-BHHH	Thunder Ax7-65	
G-BHHK	Cameron N-77	
G-BHHN	Cameron V-77	
G-BHHX	Jodel D.112	
G-BHIB	Reims F182Q Skylane	
G-BHIC	Reims F182Q Skylane	
G-BHIG	Colt 31A	
G-BHII	Cameron V-77	
G-BHIJ	Eiri PIK-20E	
G-BHIK	Adam RA14 Loisirs	
G-BHIN	Reims F152	
G-BHIS	Thunder Ax7-65	
G-BHIT	SOCATA TB-9 Tampico	
G-BHIY	Reims F150K	
G-BHJF	SOCATA TB-10 Tobago	
G-BHJI	Mooney M.20J	
G-BHJK	Maule M-5-235C	
G-BHJN	Fournier RF4D	
G-BHJO	Piper PA-28-161 Warrior	
G-BHJS	Partenavia P.68B	
G-BHJU	Robin DR.400 2+2	
G-BHKH	Cameron O-65	
G-BHKJ	Cessna 421C	
G-BHKT	Jodel D.112	
G-BHKV	Grumman AA-5A Cheetah	
G-BHLE	Robin DR.400-180 Regent	
G-BHLH	Robin DR.400-180 Regent	
G-BHLT	DH.82A Tiger Moth	
G-BHLU	Fournier RF3	
G-BHLW	Cessna 120	
G-BHLX	Grumman AA-5B Tiger	
G-BHMA	SIPA 903	
G-BHMG	Reims FA152 Aerobat	
G-BHMI	Reims F172N	
G-BHMR	Stinson 108-3 Voyager	
G-BHMT	Evans VP-1	
G-BHNA	Reims F152	
G-BHNC	Cameron O-65	

☐ G-BHND	Cameron N-65	
☐ G-BHNK	Jodel D.120A Paris-Nice	
☐ G-BHNL	Jodel D.112	
☐ G-BHNO	Piper PA-28-181 Archer	
☐ G-BHNP	Eiri PIK-20E	
☐ G-BHNV	Westland Bell 47G-3B-1	
☐ G-BHNX	Jodel D.117	
☐ G-BHOA	Robin DR.400-160 Major	
☐ G-BHOG	Sikorsky S-61N	
☐ G-BHOH	Sikorsky S-61N	
☐ G-BHOJ	Colt 14A	
☐ G-BHOL	Jodel DR.1050	
☐ G-BHOM	Piper PA-18-95	
☐ G-BHOO	Thunder Ax7-65	
☐ G-BHOR	Piper PA-28-161 Warrior	
☐ G-BHOT	Cameron V-65	
☐ G-BHOZ	SOCATA TB-9 Tampico	
☐ G-BHPK	Piper J-3C-65 Cub	
☐ G-BHPL	CASA I-131E	
☐ G-BHPS	Jodel D.120A Paris-Nice	
☐ G-BHPY	Cessna 152	
☐ G-BHPZ	Cessna 172N Skyhawk	
☐ G-BHRB	Reims F152	
☐ G-BHRC	Piper PA-28-161 Warrior	
☐ G-BHRH	Reims FA150K Aerobat	
☐ G-BHRM	Reims F152	
☐ G-BHRN	Reims F152	
☐ G-BHRO	Rockwell 112	
☐ G-BHRP	Piper PA-44-180 Seminole	
☐ G-BHRR	Piel Emeraude	
☐ G-BHRW	Robin DR.221 Dauphin	
☐ G-BHRY	Colt 56A	
☐ G-BHSB	Cessna 172N Skyhawk	
☐ G-BHSD	Scheibe SF25E Falke	
☐ G-BHSE	Rockwell 114	
☐ G-BHSN	Cameron N-56	
☐ G-BHSP	Thunder Ax7-77Z	
☐ G-BHSS	Pitts S-1C Special	
☐ G-BHSY	Jodel DR.1050	
☐ G-BHTA	Piper PA-28-236 Dakota	
☐ G-BHTC	Jodel DR.1051M1	
☐ G-BHTG	Thunder Ax6-56	
☐ G-BHUB	Douglas DC-3	
☐ G-BHUE	Jodel DR.1050	
☐ G-BHUG	Cessna 172N Skyhawk	
☐ G-BHUI	Cessna 152	
☐ G-BHUJ	Cessna 172N Skyhawk	
☐ G-BHUM	DH.82A Tiger Moth	
☐ G-BHUP	Reims F152	
☐ G-BHUR	Thunder Ax3	
☐ G-BHUU	Piper PA-25-260 Pawnee	
☐ G-BHVB	Piper PA-28-161 Warrior	
☐ G-BHVC	Cessna 172RG Cutlass	
☐ G-BHVF	Jodel D.150A Mascaret	
☐ G-BHVP	Cessna 182Q Skylane	
☐ G-BHVR	Cessna 172N Skyhawk	
☐ G-BHVV	Piper J-3C-65 Cub	
☐ G-BHWA	Reims F152	
☐ G-BHWB	Reims F152	
☐ G-BHWH	Weedhopper JC-24C	
☐ G-BHWK	MS.880B Rallye	
☐ G-BHWY	Piper PA-28R-200	
☐ G-BHWZ	Piper PA-28-181 Archer	
☐ G-BHXA	Scottish Aviation Bulldog	
☐ G-BHXD	Jodel D.120 Paris-Nice	
☐ G-BHXJ	Nord 1203 Norecrin	
☐ G-BHXK	Piper PA-28-140 Cherokee	
☐ G-BHXS	Jodel D.120 Paris-Nice	
☐ G-BHXT	Thunder Ax6-56Z	
☐ G-BHXY	Piper J-3C-65 Cub	
☐ G-BHYA	Cessna R182 Skylane RG	
☐ G-BHYC	Cessna 172RG Cutlass	
☐ G-BHYD	Cessna R172K Hawk XP	
☐ G-BHYG	Piper PA-34-200T Seneca	
☐ G-BHYI	Stampe SV-4A	
☐ G-BHYO	Cameron N-77	
☐ G-BHYP	Reims F172M	
☐ G-BHYR	Reims F172M	
☐ G-BHYV	Evans VP-1	
☐ G-BHYX	Cessna 152	
☐ G-BHZE	Piper PA-28-181 Archer	
☐ G-BHZH	Reims F152	
☐ G-BHZK	Grumman AA-5B Tiger	
☐ G-BHZO	Grumman AA-5A Cheetah	
☐ G-BHZR	Scottish Aviation Bulldog	
☐ G-BHZS	Scottish Aviation Bulldog	
☐ G-BHZT	Scottish Aviation Bulldog	
☐ G-BHZU	Piper J-3C-65 Cub	
☐ G-BHZV	Jodel D.120A Paris-Nice	
☐ G-BHZX	Thunder Ax7-69A	
☐ G-BIAC	MS.893 Rallye 235E	
☐ G-BIAH	Jodel D.112	
☐ G-BIAP	Piper PA-16 Clipper	
☐ G-BIAU	Sopwith Pup Rep	
☐ G-BIAX	Taylor Titch	
☐ G-BIAY	Grumman AA-5 Traveler	
☐ G-BIBA	SOCATA TB-9 Tampico	
☐ G-BIBB	Mooney M.20C	
☐ G-BIBG	Sikorsky S-76A II+	
☐ G-BIBJ	Enstrom 280C-UK	
☐ G-BIBN	Reims FA150K Aerobat	
☐ G-BIBO	Cameron V-65	
☐ G-BIBS	Cameron P20	
☐ G-BIBT	Grumman AA-5B Tiger	
☐ G-BIBW	Reims F172N	
☐ G-BICD	Auster 5	
☐ G-BICE	North American AT-6C	
☐ G-BICG	Reims F152	
☐ G-BICJ	Monnett Sonerai II	
☐ G-BICM	Colt 56A	
☐ G-BICP	Robin DR.360	
☐ G-BICR	Jodel D.120A Paris-Nice	
☐ G-BICS	Robin R.2100A	
☐ G-BICU	Cameron V-56	
☐ G-BICW	Piper PA-28-161 Warrior	
☐ G-BICX	Maule M-5-235C	
☐ G-BIDD	Evans VP-1	
☐ G-BIDF	Reims F172P	
☐ G-BIDG	Jodel D.150A Mascaret	
☐ G-BIDH	Cessna 152	
☐ G-BIDI	Piper PA-28R-201	
☐ G-BIDJ	Piper PA-18A-150	
☐ G-BIDK	Piper PA-18-150	
☐ G-BIDO	Piel Emeraude	
☐ G-BIDW	Sopwith 1 1/2 Rep	
☐ G-BIDX	Jodel D.112	
☐ G-BIEF	Cameron V-77	
☐ G-BIEJ	Sikorsky S-76A+	
☐ G-BIEN	Jodel D.120A Paris-Nice	
☐ G-BIEO	Jodel D.112	
☐ G-BIES	Maule M-5-235C	
☐ G-BIET	Cameron O-77	
☐ G-BIEY	Piper PA-28-151 Warrior	
☐ G-BIFA	Cessna 310R	
☐ G-BIFB	Piper PA-28-150 Cherokee	
☐ G-BIFO	Evans VP-1	
☐ G-BIFY	Reims F150L	
☐ G-BIGJ	Reims F172M	
☐ G-BIGK	Taylorcraft BC12D	
☐ G-BIGL	Cameron O-65	
☐ G-BIGP	Bensen B.8M	
☐ G-BIGZ	Scheibe SF25B Falke	
☐ G-BIHD	Robin DR.400-160 Major	
☐ G-BIHF	Replica Plans SE5A	
☐ G-BIHI	Cessna 172M Skyhawk	
☐ G-BIHO	DHC-6-300	
☐ G-BIHT	Piper PA-17 Vagabond	
☐ G-BIHX	Bensen B.8M	
☐ G-BIIA	Fournier RF3	
☐ G-BIIB	Reims F172M	
☐ G-BIID	Piper PA-18-95	
☐ G-BIIE	Reims F172P	
☐ G-BIIK	MS.883 Rallye	
☐ G-BIIL	Thunder Ax6-56	
☐ G-BIIP	BN2B-26 Islander	
☐ G-BIIT	Piper PA-28-161 Warrior	
☐ G-BIIV	Piper PA-28-181 Archer	
☐ G-BIIZ	Great Lakes 2T-1A	
☐ G-BIJB	Piper PA-18-150	
☐ G-BIJD	Bolkow Bo.208C Junior	
☐ G-BIJE	Piper J-3C-65 Cub	
☐ G-BIJS	Luton Minor	
☐ G-BIJU	Piel Emeraude	
☐ G-BIJV	Reims F152	
☐ G-BIJW	Reims F152	
☐ G-BIKC	Boeing 757-236	
☐ G-BIKE	Piper PA-28R-200	
☐ G-BIKF	Boeing 757-236	
☐ G-BIKG	Boeing 757-236	
☐ G-BIKI	Boeing 757-236	
☐ G-BIKJ	Boeing 757-236	
☐ G-BIKK	Boeing 757-236	
☐ G-BIKM	Boeing 757-236	
☐ G-BIKN	Boeing 757-236	
☐ G-BIKO	Boeing 757-236	
☐ G-BIKP	Boeing 757-236	
☐ G-BIKS	Boeing 757-236	
☐ G-BIKU	Boeing 757-236	
☐ G-BIKV	Boeing 757-236	
☐ G-BIKZ	Boeing 757-236	
☐ G-BILA	Dalotel Viking	
☐ G-BILI	Piper J-3C-65 Cub	
☐ G-BILJ	Reims FA152 Aerobat	
☐ G-BILL	Piper PA-25-260 Pawnee	
☐ G-BILR	Cessna 152	
☐ G-BILS	Cessna 152	
☐ G-BILU	Cessna 172RG Cutlass	
☐ G-BILZ	Taylor Monoplane	
☐ G-BIMM	Piper PA-18-135	
☐ G-BIMN	Steen Skybolt	
☐ G-BIMO	Stampe SV-4C	
☐ G-BIMT	Reims FA152 Aerobat	
☐ G-BIMU	Sikorsky S-61N	
☐ G-BIMX	Rutan VariEze	
☐ G-BIMZ	Beech 76 Duchess	
☐ G-BIOA	Hughes 369D	
☐ G-BIOB	Reims F172P	
☐ G-BIOC	Reims F150L	
☐ G-BIOI	Jodel DR.1050M	
☐ G-BIOJ	Rockwell 112TCA	
☐ G-BIOK	Reims F152	
☐ G-BIOU	Jodel D.117A	
☐ G-BIOW	Slingsby T.67A	
☐ G-BIPA	Grumman AA-5B Tiger	
☐ G-BIPI	Everett Gyroplane	
☐ G-BIPN	Fournier RF3	
☐ G-BIPO	Mudry CAP.20	
☐ G-BIPT	Jodel D.112	
☐ G-BIPV	Grumman AA-5B Tiger	
☐ G-BIPY	Bensen B.8	
☐ G-BIRD	Pitts S-1D Special	
☐ G-BIRE	Colt Bottle SS	
☐ G-BIRH	Piper PA-18-180	
☐ G-BIRI	CASA I-131E	
☐ G-BIRT	Robin R.1180TD Aiglon	
☐ G-BIRW	Morane MS.505	
☐ G-BISG	Clutton FRED III	
☐ G-BISH	Cameron O-42	
☐ G-BISX	Colt 56A	

Reg	Type
G-BISZ	Sikorsky S-76A+
G-BITA	Piper PA-18-150
G-BITE	SOCATA TB-10 Tobago
G-BITF	Reims F152
G-BITH	Reims F152
G-BITK	Clutton FRED II
G-BITM	Reims F172P
G-BITO	Jodel D.112D
G-BITS	Drayton B-56
G-BIUM	Reims F152
G-BIUP	Nord NC.858S
G-BIUV	HS.748-2A
G-BIUW	Piper PA-28-161 Warrior
G-BIUY	Piper PA-28-181 Archer
G-BIVA	Robin R.2112 Alpha
G-BIVB	Jodel D.112
G-BIVC	Jodel D.112
G-BIVF	Piel Emeraude
G-BIVK	Bensen B.8V
G-BIVL	Bensen B.8M
G-BIVW	Grumman AA-5A Cheetah
G-BIWK	Cameron V-65
G-BIWL	Piper PA-32-301
G-BIWN	Jodel D.112
G-BIWR	Mooney M.20F
G-BIWU	Cameron V-65
G-BIWW	Grumman AA-5 Traveler
G-BIWY	Westland WG.30
G-BIXA	SOCATA TB-9 Tampico
G-BIXB	SOCATA TB-9 Tampico
G-BIXH	Reims F152
G-BIXL	North American P-51D
G-BIXN	Boeing Stearman A75N1
G-BIXV	Bell 212
G-BIXW	Colt 56B
G-BIXZ	Grob 109
G-BIYI	Cameron V-65
G-BIYJ	Piper PA-18-95
G-BIYK	Isaacs Fury II
G-BIYP	Piper PA-20-125 Pacer
G-BIYR	Piper PA-18-150
G-BIYT	Colt 17A
G-BIYU	Fokker S.11-1
G-BIYW	Jodel D.112
G-BIYX	Piper PA-28-140 Cherokee
G-BIYY	Piper PA-18-95
G-BIZE	SOCATA TB-9 Tampico
G-BIZF	Reims F172P
G-BIZG	Reims F152
G-BIZI	Robin DR.400-120
G-BIZK	Nord 3202B1
G-BIZM	Nord 3202B
G-BIZO	Piper PA-28R-200
G-BIZR	SOCATA TB-9 Tampico
G-BIZU	Thunder Ax6-56Z
G-BIZV	Piper PA-18-95
G-BIZV	Aeronca 7GCBC Citabria
G-BIZY	Jodel D.112
G-BJAD	Clutton FRED 2
G-BJAE	Starck AS.80 Holiday
G-BJAF	Piper J-3C-65 Cub
G-BJAG	Piper PA-28-181 Archer
G-BJAJ	Grumman AA-5B Tiger
G-BJAL	CASA I-131E
G-BJAO	Bensen B.8M
G-BJAP	DH.82A Tiger Moth
G-BJAV	Gardan GY-80-160
G-BJAW	Cameron V-65
G-BJAY	Piper J-3C-65 Cub
G-BJBK	Piper PA-18-95
G-BJBM	Monnett Sonerai I
G-BJBO	Robin DR.250-160
G-BJBW	Piper PA-28-161 Warrior
G-BJBX	Piper PA-28-161 Warrior
G-BJCA	Piper PA-28-161 Warrior
G-BJCF	Piel Emeraude
G-BJCI	Piper PA-18-180
G-BJCW	Piper PA-32R-301 SP
G-BJDE	Reims F172M
G-BJDF	MS.880B Rallye
G-BJDO	Grumman AA-5A Cheetah
G-BJDW	Reims F172M
G-BJEE	BN2T Islander
G-BJEF	BN2T Islander
G-BJEI	Piper PA-18
G-BJEJ	BN2T Islander
G-BJEL	Nord NC.858S
G-BJEV	Aeronca 11AC Chief
G-BJEX	Bolkow Bo.208C Junior
G-BJFE	Piper PA-18-95
G-BJFL	Sikorsky S-76A+
G-BJFM	Jodel D.120 Paris-Nice
G-BJGE	Thunder Ax3
G-BJGK	Cameron V-77
G-BJGX	Sikorsky S-76A+
G-BJGY	Reims F172P
G-BJHB	Mooney M.20J
G-BJHK	EAA Acrosport I
G-BJHV	Voisin Scale Rep
G-BJIG	Slingsby T.67A
G-BJIV	Piper PA-18-180
G-BJKF	SOCATA TB-9 Tampico
G-BJKW	Wills Aera II
G-BJKY	Reims F152
G-BJLB	Nord NC.858S
G-BJLC	Monnett Sonerai
G-BJML	Cessna 120
G-BJMO	Taylor Monoplane
G-BJMR	Cessna 310R
G-BJMW	Thunder Ax8-105
G-BJNF	Reims F152
G-BJNG	Slingsby T.67A
G-BJNN	Piper PA-38-112 Tomahawk
G-BJNY	Aeronca 11CC Super Chief
G-BJNZ	Piper PA-23-250 Aztec F
G-BJOA	Piper PA-28-181 Archer
G-BJOB	Jodel D.140C
G-BJOE	Jodel D.120A Paris-Nice
G-BJOP	BN2B-26 Islander
G-BJOT	Jodel D.117
G-BJOV	Reims F150K
G-BJPI	Bede BD-5B
G-BJST	CCF Harvard 4
G-BJSV	Piper PA-28-161 Warrior
G-BJSW	Thunder Ax7-65Z
G-BJSZ	Piper J-3C-65 Cub
G-BJTB	Cessna A150M Aerobat
G-BJTO	Piper J-3C-65 Cub
G-BJTP	Piper PA-18-95
G-BJUC	Robinson R22HP
G-BJUD	Robin DR.400-180 Regent
G-BJUR	Piper PA-38-112 Tomahawk
G-BJUS	Piper PA-38-112 Tomahawk
G-BJUV	Cameron V-20
G-BJVC	Evans VP-2
G-BJVH	Reims F182Q Skylane
G-BJVJ	Reims F152
G-BJVK	Grob 109
G-BJVM	Cessna 172N Skyhawk
G-BJVS	Piel Emeraude
G-BJVT	Reims F152
G-BJVU	Thunder Ax6-56
G-BJVV	Robin R.1180TD Aiglon
G-BJWC	Saro Skeeter AOP10
G-BJWH	Reims F152
G-BJWI	Reims F172P
G-BJWJ	Cameron V-65
G-BJWO	BN2A-26 Islander
G-BJWT	Wittman Tailwind
G-BJWV	Colt 17A
G-BJWW	Reims F172P
G-BJWX	Piper PA-18-95
G-BJWZ	Piper PA-18-95
G-BJXA	Slingsby T.67A
G-BJXB	Slingsby T.67A
G-BJXK	Fournier RF5
G-BJXP	Colt 56B
G-BJXR	Auster AOP.9
G-BJXX	Piper PA-23-250 Aztec E
G-BJXZ	Cessna 172N Skyhawk
G-BJYD	Reims F152
G-BJYF	Colt 56A
G-BJYK	Jodel D.120A Paris-Nice
G-BJYN	Piper PA-38-112 Tomahawk
G-BJZA	Cameron N-65
G-BJZB	Evans VP-2
G-BJZF	DH.82A Tiger Moth
G-BJZN	Slingsby T.67A
G-BJZR	Colt 42A
G-BKAE	Jodel D.120 Paris-Nice
G-BKAF	Clutton FRED II
G-BKAM	Slingsby T.67M
G-BKAO	Jodel D.112
G-BKAS	Piper PA-38-112 Tomahawk
G-BKAY	Rockwell 114
G-BKAZ	Cessna 152
G-BKBB	Hawker Fury Rep
G-BKBD	Thunder Ax3
G-BKBF	MS.894A Minerva
G-BKBN	SOCATA TB-10 Tobago
G-BKBO	Colt 17A
G-BKBS	Bensen B.8MV
G-BKBV	SOCATA TB-10 Tobago
G-BKBW	SOCATA TB-10 Tobago
G-BKCC	Piper PA-28-180 Cherokee
G-BKCE	Reims F172P
G-BKCI	Brugger Colibri
G-BKCL	Piper PA-30-160 C
G-BKCN	Phoenix Currie Wot
G-BKCR	SOCATA TB-9 Tampico
G-BKCV	EAA Acrosport II
G-BKCW	Jodel D.120 Paris-Nice
G-BKCX	Mudry CAP.10B
G-BKCZ	Jodel D.120A Paris-Nice
G-BKDC	Monnett Sonerai
G-BKDH	Robin DR.400-120
G-BKDI	Robin DR.400-120
G-BKDJ	Robin DR.400-120
G-BKDK	Thunder Ax7-77Z
G-BKDP	Clutton FRED II
G-BKDR	Pitts S-1S Special
G-BKDS	Colt 14A Cloudhopper
G-BKDT	Replica Plans SE5A
G-BKDX	Jodel DR.1050
G-BKEK	Piper PA-32-300
G-BKEP	Reims F172M
G-BKER	Replica Plans SE5A
G-BKET	Piper PA-18-95
G-BKEU	Taylor Monoplane
G-BKEV	Reims F172M
G-BKEW	Bell 206B Jet Ranger
G-BKEY	Clutton FRED II
G-BKFA	Monnett Sonerai II
G-BKFC	Reims F152
G-BKFI	Evans VP-1
G-BKFK	Isaacs Fury II
G-BKFL	Aerosport Scamp
G-BKFM	QAC Quickie Q2
G-BKFN	Bell 214ST

G-BKFR	Piel Emeraude
G-BKFW	Percival Provost T1
G-BKFY	Beech C90 King Air
G-BKFZ	Piper PA-28R-200
G-BKGA	MS.892A Commodore
G-BKGB	Jodel D.120 Paris-Nice
G-BKGC	Maule M-6-235C
G-BKGL	Beech D18S
G-BKGM	Beech D18S
G-BKGR	Cameron O-85
G-BKGT	MS.880B Rallye
G-BKGW	Reims F152
G-BKHA	Westland Whirlwind
G-BKHD	Baby Great Lakes
G-BKHG	Piper J-3C-65 Cub
G-BKHJ	Cessna 182P Skylane
G-BKHW	Glasair IIRG
G-BKHY	Taylor Monoplane
G-BKIB	SOCATA TB-9 Tampico
G-BKIF	Fournier RF6B
G-BKII	Reims F172M
G-BKIJ	Reims F172M
G-BKIR	Jodel D.117
G-BKIS	SOCATA TB-10 Tobago
G-BKIT	SOCATA TB-9 Tampico
G-BKJB	Piper PA-18-135
G-BKJF	MS.880B Rallye
G-BKJS	Jodel D.120A Paris-Nice
G-BKJW	Piper PA-23-250 Aztec E
G-BKKN	Cessna 182R Skylane
G-BKKO	Cessna 182R Skylane
G-BKKZ	Pitts S-1S Special
G-BKLO	Reims F172M
G-BKMA	Mooney M.20J
G-BKMB	Mooney M.20J
G-BKMG	HP 0/400 Rep
G-BKMI	Spitfire HF.VIIIc
G-BKMT	Piper PA-32R-301 SP
G-BKMX	Short SD.360-100
G-BKNA	Cessna 421
G-BKNI	Gardan GY-80
G-BKNO	Monnett Sonerai IIL
G-BKNP	Cameron V-77
G-BKNZ	Piel Emeraude
G-BKOA	MS.893A Commodore
G-BKOB	Zlin Z.326
G-BKOT	Wassmer WA.81
G-BKOU	Jet Provost T.3
G-BKPA	Diamond H.36
G-BKPB	Aerosport Scamp
G-BKPC	Cessna A185F
G-BKPD	Viking Dragonfly
G-BKPE	Robin DR.250-160
G-BKPN	Cameron N-77
G-BKPS	Grumman AA-5B Tiger
G-BKPX	Jodel D.120A Paris-Nice
G-BKPZ	Pitts S-1 Special
G-BKRA	North American T-6G
G-BKRF	Piper PA-18-95
G-BKRH	Brugger Colibri
G-BKRK	Stampe SV-4C
G-BKRN	Beech D18S
G-BKRS	Cameron V-56
G-BKSD	Colt 56A
G-BKSE	QAC Quickie Q2
G-BKSP	Schleicher ASK14
G-BKST	Rutan VariEze
G-BKSX	Stampe SV-4C
G-BKTA	Piper PA-18-95
G-BKTH	Sea Hurricane IB
G-BKTM	PZL Ogar SZD45A
G-BKTR	Cameron V-77
G-BKTV	Reims F152

G-BKTZ	Slingsby T.67M
G-BKUE	SOCATA TB-9 Tampico
G-BKUL	Aerospatiale AS.355F1
G-BKUR	Piel Emeraude
G-BKUU	Thunder Ax7-77
G-BKVA	MS.893E Rallye 180GT
G-BKVB	MS.880B Rallye
G-BKVC	SOCATA TB-9 Tampico
G-BKVF	Clutton FRED III
G-BKVG	Scheibe SF25E Falke
G-BKVK	Auster AOP.9
G-BKVL	Robin DR.400-160 Major
G-BKVM	Piper PA-18-150
G-BKVO	Pietenpol Aircamper
G-BKVP	Pitts S-1 Special
G-BKVS	Campbell Cricket
G-BKVT	Piper PA-23-250 Aztec E
G-BKVW	Airtour AH-56
G-BKVX	Airtour AH-56C
G-BKVY	Airtour B-31
G-BKWD	Taylor Titch
G-BKWR	Cameron V-65
G-BKWW	Cameron O-77
G-BKWY	Reims F152
G-BKXA	Robin R.2100A
G-BKXD	Aerospatiale AS.365N
G-BKXF	Piper PA-28R-200
G-BKXM	Colt 17A
G-BKXN	IAR IS.28M2A
G-BKXO	Rutan LongEz
G-BKXP	Auster AOP.6
G-BKXR	Druine Turbulent
G-BKZB	Cameron V-77
G-BKZE	Aerospatiale AS.332L
G-BKZF	Cameron V-56
G-BKZG	Aerospatiale AS.332L
G-BKZT	Clutton FRED II
G-BKZV	Bede BD-4
G-BLAC	Reims FA152 Aerobat
G-BLAF	Stolp SA.900
G-BLAG	Pitts S-1D Special
G-BLAH	Thunder Ax7-77
G-BLAI	Monnett Sonerai
G-BLAM	Robin DR.360
G-BLAT	Jodel D.150 Mascaret
G-BLAX	Reims FA152 Aerobat
G-BLCC	Thunder Ax7-77
G-BLCG	SOCATA TB-10 Tobago
G-BLCH	Colt 56D
G-BLCI	EAA Acrosport P
G-BLCM	SOCATA TB-9 Tampico
G-BLCT	Jodel DR.220
G-BLCU	Scheibe SF25B Falke
G-BLCV	Diamond H.36
G-BLCW	Evans VP-1
G-BLCY	Thunder Ax7-65Z
G-BLDB	Taylor Monoplane
G-BLDD	Acro Trainer
G-BLDG	Piper PA-25-260 Pawnee
G-BLDK	Robinson R22
G-BLDN	Rand KR-2
G-BLDV	BN2B-26 Islander
G-BLEB	Colt 69A
G-BLEP	Cameron V-65
G-BLES	Stolp SA.750
G-BLET	Thunder Ax7-77
G-BLEZ	Aerospatiale AS.365N
G-BLFI	Piper PA-28-181 Archer
G-BLFW	Grumman AA-5 Traveler
G-BLFY	Cameron V-77
G-BLFZ	Piper PA-31-310 Navajo
G-BLGH	Robin DR.300-180
G-BLGS	MS.880B Rallye

G-BLGV	Bell 206B Jet Ranger
G-BLHH	Robin DR.315
G-BLHI	Colt 17A
G-BLHJ	Reims F172P
G-BLHK	Colt 105A
G-BLHM	Piper PA-18-95
G-BLHN	Robin HR.100-285 Tiara
G-BLHR	Grumman GA-7 Cougar
G-BLHS	Aeronca 7ECA Citabria
G-BLHW	Varga Kachina
G-BLID	DH.112 Venom FB50
G-BLIH	Piper PA-18-135
G-BLIK	Wallis WA-116F/S
G-BLIT	Thorp T.18CW
G-BLIW	Percival Provost T1
G-BLIX	Saro Skeeter
G-BLIY	MS.892A Commodore
G-BLJD	Glaser-Dirks DG-400
G-BLJH	Cameron N-77
G-BLJM	Beech 95-B55 Baron
G-BLJO	Reims F152
G-BLKM	Jodel DR.1051
G-BLKY	Beech 58 Baron
G-BLKZ	Pilatus P.2
G-BLLA	Bensen B.8M
G-BLLB	Bensen B.8M
G-BLLD	Cameron O-77
G-BLLH	Robin DR.220 2+2
G-BLLN	Piper PA-18-95
G-BLLO	Piper PA-18-95
G-BLLP	Slingsby T.67B
G-BLLR	Slingsby T.67B
G-BLLS	Slingsby T.67B
G-BLLW	Colt 56B
G-BLLZ	Rutan LongEz
G-BLMA	Zlin Z.526A
G-BLMC	Avro Vulcan B.2A
G-BLME	Robinson R22HP
G-BLMG	Grob 109B
G-BLMI	Piper PA-18-95
G-BLMN	Rutan LongEz
G-BLMP	Piper PA-17 Vagabond
G-BLMR	Piper PA-18-150
G-BLMT	Piper PA-18-135
G-BLMW	Tipsy Nipper 3
G-BLMZ	Colt 105A
G-BLNJ	BN2B-26 Islander
G-BLNO	Clutton FRED III
G-BLOR	Piper PA-30-160
G-BLOS	Cessna 185A Skywagon
G-BLOT	Colt 56B
G-BLOV	Thunder Ax5-42
G-BLPA	Piper J-3C-65 Cub
G-BLPB	Turner TSW
G-BLPE	Piper PA-18-95
G-BLPF	Reims FR172G Rocket
G-BLPG	Auster J/1N Alpha
G-BLPH	Reims FA150L Aerobat
G-BLPI	Slingsby T.67B
G-BLPM	Aerospatiale AS.332L
G-BLPP	Cameron V-77
G-BLRA	BAe 146-100
G-BLRC	Piper PA-18-135
G-BLRF	Slingsby T.67C
G-BLRG	Slingsby T.67B
G-BLRL	Piel Emeraude
G-BLRM	Glaser-Dirks DG-400
G-BLST	Cessna 421C
G-BLTA	Colt 77A
G-BLTC	Druine Turbulent
G-BLTF	Robinson R22
G-BLTK	Rockwell 112TCA
G-BLTM	Robin HR.200-160

☐ G-BLTN	Thunder Ax7-65	
☐ G-BLTR	Scheibe SF25B Falke	
☐ G-BLTS	Rutan LongEz	
☐ G-BLTW	Slingsby T.67B	
☐ G-BLTY	Westland WG.30	
☐ G-BLUI	Thunder Ax7-65	
☐ G-BLUL	Jodel DR.1051M1	
☐ G-BLUM	Aerospatiale AS.365N	
☐ G-BLUN	Aerospatiale AS.365N	
☐ G-BLUV	Grob 109B	
☐ G-BLUX	Slingsby T.67M	
☐ G-BLUY	Colt 69A	
☐ G-BLUZ	DH.82B	
☐ G-BLVA	Airtour AH-31	
☐ G-BLVB	Airtour AH-56	
☐ G-BLVI	Slingsby T.67M	
☐ G-BLVK	Mudry CAP.10B	
☐ G-BLVL	Piper PA-28-161 Warrior	
☐ G-BLVS	Cessna 150M	
☐ G-BLVW	Reims F172H	
☐ G-BLWD	Piper PA-34-200T Seneca	
☐ G-BLWF	Robin HR.100-210 Safari	
☐ G-BLWH	Fournier RF6B	
☐ G-BLWM	Bristol M.1C Rep	
☐ G-BLWP	Piper PA-38-112 Tomahawk	
☐ G-BLWT	Evans VP-1	
☐ G-BLWV	Reims F152	
☐ G-BLWY	Robin R.2160D	
☐ G-BLXA	SOCATA TB-20 Trinidad	
☐ G-BLXG	Colt 21A	
☐ G-BLXH	Fournier RF3	
☐ G-BLXI	Piel Emeraude	
☐ G-BLXO	Jodel D.150 Mascaret	
☐ G-BLXP	Piper PA-28R-200	
☐ G-BLXR	Aerospatiale AS.332L	
☐ G-BLYD	SOCATA TB-20 Trinidad	
☐ G-BLYE	SOCATA TB-10 Tobago	
☐ G-BLYK	Piper PA-34-220T Seneca	
☐ G-BLYP	Robin R.3000-120	
☐ G-BLYT	Airtour AH-77	
☐ G-BLZA	Scheibe SF25B Falke	
☐ G-BLZE	Reims F152	
☐ G-BLZF	Thunder Ax7-77	
☐ G-BLZH	Reims F152	
☐ G-BLZN	Bell 206B Jet Ranger	
☐ G-BLZP	Reims F152	
☐ G-BLZS	Cameron O-77	
☐ G-BMAD	Cameron V-77	
☐ G-BMAL	Sikorsky S-76A+	
☐ G-BMAO	Taylor Monoplane	
☐ G-BMAV	Aerospatiale AS.350B	
☐ G-BMAX	Clutton FRED II	
☐ G-BMAY	Piper PA-18-135	
☐ G-BMBB	Reims F150L	
☐ G-BMBJ	Janus CM	
☐ G-BMBS	Colt 105A	
☐ G-BMBW	Bensen B.8MR	
☐ G-BMBZ	Scheibe SF25E Falke	
☐ G-BMCC	Thunder Ax7-77	
☐ G-BMCD	Cameron V-65	
☐ G-BMCG	Grob 109B	
☐ G-BMCI	Reims F172H	
☐ G-BMCN	Reims F152	
☐ G-BMCS	Piper PA-22-135 Tri-Pacer	
☐ G-BMCV	Reims F152	
☐ G-BMCW	Aerospatiale AS.332L	
☐ G-BMCX	Aerospatiale AS.332L	
☐ G-BMDB	Replica Plans SE5A	
☐ G-BMDC	Piper PA-32-301	
☐ G-BMDE	Pietenpol Aircamper	
☐ G-BMDJ	Price Ax7-77S	
☐ G-BMDK	Piper PA-34-220T Seneca	
☐ G-BMDP	Partenavia P.64B	
☐ G-BMDS	Jodel D.120 Paris-Nice	
☐ G-BMEA	Piper PA-18-95	
☐ G-BMEE	Cameron O-105	
☐ G-BMEG	SOCATA TB-10 Tobago	
☐ G-BMEH	Jodel D.150 Mascaret	
☐ G-BMET	Taylor Monoplane	
☐ G-BMEU	Isaacs Fury II	
☐ G-BMEX	Cessna A150K Aerobat	
☐ G-BMFD	Piper PA-23-250 Aztec F	
☐ G-BMFG	Dornier Do.27A1	
☐ G-BMFI	PZL Ogar SZD45A	
☐ G-BMFP	Piper PA-28-161 Warrior	
☐ G-BMFU	Cameron N-90	
☐ G-BMFY	Grob 109B	
☐ G-BMFZ	Reims F152	
☐ G-BMGB	Piper PA-28R-200	
☐ G-BMGC	Fairey Swordfish	
☐ G-BMGG	Cessna 152	
☐ G-BMGR	Grob 109B	
☐ G-BMHA	Rutan LongEz	
☐ G-BMHC	Cessna U206F	
☐ G-BMHJ	Thunder Ax7-65	
☐ G-BMHL	Wittman Tailwind	
☐ G-BMHS	Reims F172M	
☐ G-BMHT	Piper PA-28RT-201T	
☐ G-BMID	Jodel D.120 Paris-Nice	
☐ G-BMIG	Cessna 172N Skyhawk	
☐ G-BMIM	Rutan LongEz	
☐ G-BMIO	Glasair	
☐ G-BMIP	Jodel D.112	
☐ G-BMIR	Westland Wasp	
☐ G-BMIS	Monnett Sonerai	
☐ G-BMIV	Piper PA-28R-201T	
☐ G-BMIW	Piper PA-28-181 Archer	
☐ G-BMIX	SOCATA TB-20 Trinidad	
☐ G-BMIY	Baby Great Lakes	
☐ G-BMJA	Piper PA-32R-301 SP	
☐ G-BMJC	Cessna 152	
☐ G-BMJD	Cessna 152	
☐ G-BMJG	Piper PA-28R-200	
☐ G-BMJL	Rockwell 114	
☐ G-BMJM	Evans VP-1	
☐ G-BMJN	Cameron O-65	
☐ G-BMJO	Piper PA-34-220T Seneca	
☐ G-BMJR	Cessna T337H	
☐ G-BMJW	North American T-6	
☐ G-BMJX	Wallis WA-116X	
☐ G-BMJY	Yakovlev Yak-18A	
☐ G-BMJZ	Cameron N-90	
☐ G-BMKB	Piper PA-18-135	
☐ G-BMKC	Piper J-3C-90 Cub	
☐ G-BMKD	Beech 65-90 King Air	
☐ G-BMKF	Robin DR.221 Dauphin	
☐ G-BMKG	Piper PA-38-112 Tomahawk	
☐ G-BMKI	Colt 21A	
☐ G-BMKJ	Cameron V-77	
☐ G-BMKK	Piper PA-28R-200	
☐ G-BMKP	Cameron V-77	
☐ G-BMKR	Piper PA-28-161 Warrior	
☐ G-BMKW	Cameron V-77	
☐ G-BMKY	Cameron O-65	
☐ G-BMLB	Jodel D.120A Paris-Nice	
☐ G-BMLC	Short SD.360-200	
☐ G-BMLJ	Cameron N-77	
☐ G-BMLK	Grob 109B	
☐ G-BMLL	Grob 109B	
☐ G-BMLM	Beech 58 Baron	
☐ G-BMLS	Piper PA-28-201	
☐ G-BMLT	Pietenpol Aircamper	
☐ G-BMLW	Cameron V-65	
☐ G-BMLX	Reims F150L	
☐ G-BMMF	Clutton FRED II	
☐ G-BMMI	Pazmany PL-4	
☐ G-BMMK	Cessna 182P Skylane
☐ G-BMMM	Cessna 152
☐ G-BMMP	Grob 109B
☐ G-BMMV	IAR IS.28M2A
☐ G-BMMW	Thunder Ax7-77
☐ G-BMMY	Thunder Ax7-77
☐ G-BMNL	Piper PA-28R-200
☐ G-BMNV	Stampe SV-4C
☐ G-BMOE	Piper PA-28R-200
☐ G-BMOF	Cessna U206G
☐ G-BMOG	Thunder Ax7-77
☐ G-BMOH	Cameron N-77
☐ G-BMOI	Partenavia P.68B
☐ G-BMOK	ARV Super 2
☐ G-BMOM	IAR IS.28M2A
☐ G-BMOT	Bensen B.8M
☐ G-BMOV	Cameron O-105
☐ G-BMPC	Piper PA-28-181 Archer
☐ G-BMPD	Cameron V-65
☐ G-BMPL	Optica OA.7
☐ G-BMPP	Cameron N-77
☐ G-BMPR	Piper PA-28R-201
☐ G-BMPS	Strojnik S-2A
☐ G-BMPY	DH.82A Tiger Moth
☐ G-BMRA	Boeing 757-236
☐ G-BMRB	Boeing 757-236
☐ G-BMRC	Boeing 757-236
☐ G-BMRD	Boeing 757-236
☐ G-BMRE	Boeing 757-236
☐ G-BMRF	Boeing 757-236
☐ G-BMRH	Boeing 757-236
☐ G-BMRJ	Boeing 757-236
☐ G-BMSA	Stinson HW-75
☐ G-BMSB	Spitfire XI
☐ G-BMSC	Evans VP-2
☐ G-BMSD	Piper PA-28-181 Archer
☐ G-BMSE	Taifun 17E
☐ G-BMSF	Piper PA-38-112 Tomahawk
☐ G-BMSG	SAAB Lansen
☐ G-BMSL	Clutton FRED III
☐ G-BMSU	Cessna 152
☐ G-BMTA	Cessna 152
☐ G-BMTB	Cessna 152
☐ G-BMTC	Aerospatiale AS.355F1
☐ G-BMTJ	Cessna 152
☐ G-BMTN	Cameron O-77
☐ G-BMTO	Piper PA-38-112 Tomahawk
☐ G-BMTR	Piper PA-28-161 Warrior
☐ G-BMTS	Cessna 172N Skyhawk
☐ G-BMTU	Pitts S-1E Special
☐ G-BMTX	Cameron V-77
☐ G-BMUD	Cessna 182P Skylane
☐ G-BMUG	Rutan LongEz
☐ G-BMUO	Cessna A152 Aerobat
☐ G-BMUT	Piper PA-34-200T Seneca
☐ G-BMUU	Thunder Ax7-77
☐ G-BMUZ	Piper PA-28-161 Warrior
☐ G-BMVA	Scheibe SF25B Falke
☐ G-BMVB	Reims F152
☐ G-BMVG	QAC Quickie Q1
☐ G-BMVL	Piper PA-38-112 Tomahawk
☐ G-BMVM	Piper PA-38-112 Tomahawk
☐ G-BMVS	Cameron Benihana 70SS
☐ G-BMVT	Thunder Ax7-77A
☐ G-BMVU	Monnett Moni
☐ G-BMVW	Cameron O-65
☐ G-BMWA	Hughes 269C
☐ G-BMWE	ARV Super 2
☐ G-BMWF	ARV Super 2
☐ G-BMWM	ARV Super 2
☐ G-BMWR	Rockwell 112
☐ G-BMWU	Cameron N-42
☐ G-BMWV	Putzer Elster B

Registration	Type		Registration	Type		Registration	Type
☐ G-BMXA	Cessna 152		☐ G-BNGJ	Cameron V-77		☐ G-BNME	Cessna 152
☐ G-BMXB	Cessna 152		☐ G-BNGN	Cameron V-77		☐ G-BNMF	Cessna 152
☐ G-BMXC	Cessna 152		☐ G-BNGO	Thunder Ax7-77		☐ G-BNMG	Cameron O-77
☐ G-BMXD	Fokker F.27-500		☐ G-BNGR	Piper PA-38-112 Tomahawk		☐ G-BNMH	Pietenpol Aircamper
☐ G-BMXJ	Reims F150L		☐ G-BNGT	Piper PA-28-181 Archer		☐ G-BNMK	Dornier Do.27A-1
☐ G-BMXM	Colt 180A		☐ G-BNGV	ARV Super 2		☐ G-BNML	Rand KR-2
☐ G-BMXX	Cessna 152		☐ G-BNGY	ARV Super 2		☐ G-BNMO	Cessna R182 Skylane RG
☐ G-BMYC	SOCATA TB-10 Tobago		☐ G-BNHB	ARV Super 2		☐ G-BNMX	Thunder Ax7-77
☐ G-BMYD	Beech A36 Bonanza		☐ G-BNHG	Piper PA-38-112 Tomahawk		☐ G-BNNA	Stolp Starduster 2
☐ G-BMYF	Bensen B.7M		☐ G-BNHI	Cameron V-77		☐ G-BNNE	Cameron N-77
☐ G-BMYG	Reims FA152 Aerobat		☐ G-BNHJ	Cessna 152		☐ G-BNNO	Piper PA-28-161 Warrior
☐ G-BMYI	Grumman AA-5 Traveler		☐ G-BNHK	Cessna 152		☐ G-BNNR	Cessna 152
☐ G-BMYJ	Cameron V-65		☐ G-BNHT	Fournier RF3		☐ G-BNNS	Piper PA-28-161 Warrior
☐ G-BMYN	Colt 77A		☐ G-BNID	Cessna 152		☐ G-BNNT	Piper PA-28-151 Warrior
☐ G-BMYP	Fairey Gannet AEW.3		☐ G-BNII	Cameron N-90		☐ G-BNNU	Piper PA-38-112 Tomahawk
☐ G-BMYS	Thunder Ax7-77Z		☐ G-BNIK	Robin HR.200-120		☐ G-BNNX	Piper PA-28R-201T
☐ G-BMYU	Jodel D.120 Paris-Nice		☐ G-BNIM	Piper PA-38-112 Tomahawk		☐ G-BNNY	Piper PA-28-161 Warrior
☐ G-BMZB	Cameron N-77		☐ G-BNIN	Cameron V-77		☐ G-BNNZ	Piper PA-28-161 Warrior
☐ G-BMZF	WSK LIM-2		☐ G-BNIO	Luscombe 8AC Silvaire		☐ G-BNOB	Wittman Tailwind
☐ G-BMZN	Everett Gyroplane		☐ G-BNIP	Luscombe 8A Silvaire		☐ G-BNOE	Piper PA-28-161 Warrior
☐ G-BMZP	Everett Gyroplane		☐ G-BNIU	Cameron O-77		☐ G-BNOF	Piper PA-28-161 Warrior
☐ G-BMZS	Everett Gyroplane		☐ G-BNIV	Cessna 152		☐ G-BNOH	Piper PA-28-161 Warrior
☐ G-BMZW	Bensen B.8M		☐ G-BNIW	Boeing Stearman A75N1		☐ G-BNOJ	Piper PA-28-161 Warrior
☐ G-BMZX	Wolf Boredom Fighter		☐ G-BNJB	Cessna 152		☐ G-BNOM	Piper PA-28-161 Warrior
☐ G-BNAG	Colt 105A		☐ G-BNJC	Cessna 152		☐ G-BNON	Piper PA-28-161 Warrior
☐ G-BNAI	Wolf Boredom Fighter		☐ G-BNJD	Cessna 152		☐ G-BNOP	Piper PA-28-161 Warrior
☐ G-BNAJ	Cessna 152		☐ G-BNJG	Cameron O-77		☐ G-BNOZ	Cessna 152
☐ G-BNAN	Cameron V-65		☐ G-BNJH	Cessna 152		☐ G-BNPE	Cameron N-77
☐ G-BNAU	Cameron V-65		☐ G-BNJL	Bensen B.8		☐ G-BNPF	Slingsby T.31M
☐ G-BNAW	Cameron V-65		☐ G-BNJO	QAC Quickie Q2		☐ G-BNPH	Percival Pembroke
☐ G-BNBL	Thunder Ax7-77		☐ G-BNJR	Piper PA-28R-201T		☐ G-BNPM	Piper PA-38-112 Tomahawk
☐ G-BNBP	Colt Snowflake SS		☐ G-BNJT	Piper PA-28-161 Warrior		☐ G-BNPO	Piper PA-28-181 Archer
☐ G-BNBV	Thunder Ax7-77		☐ G-BNJV	Cessna 152		☐ G-BNPU	Percival Pembroke
☐ G-BNBW	Thunder Ax7-77		☐ G-BNJZ	Cassutt Racer 3M		☐ G-BNPV	Bowers Fly Baby 1A
☐ G-BNBY	Beech 95-A55 Baron		☐ G-BNKC	Cessna 152		☐ G-BNPY	Cessna 152
☐ G-BNCB	Cameron V-77		☐ G-BNKD	Cessna 172N Skyhawk		☐ G-BNPZ	Cessna 152
☐ G-BNCC	Thunder Ax7-77		☐ G-BNKE	Cessna 172N Skyhawk		☐ G-BNRA	SOCATA TB-10 Tobago
☐ G-BNCJ	Cameron V-77		☐ G-BNKH	Piper PA-38-112 Tomahawk		☐ G-BNRG	Piper PA-28-161 Warrior
☐ G-BNCO	Piper PA-38-112 Tomahawk		☐ G-BNKI	Cessna 152		☐ G-BNRK	Cessna 152
☐ G-BNCR	Piper PA-28-161 Warrior		☐ G-BNKP	Cessna 152		☐ G-BNRL	Cessna 152
☐ G-BNCS	Cessna 180		☐ G-BNKR	Cessna 152		☐ G-BNRP	Piper PA-28-181 Archer
☐ G-BNCU	Thunder Ax7-77		☐ G-BNKS	Cessna 152		☐ G-BNRR	Cessna 172P Skyhawk
☐ G-BNCX	Hawker Hunter T.7		☐ G-BNKT	Cameron O-77		☐ G-BNRX	Piper PA-34-200T Seneca
☐ G-BNCZ	Rutan LongEz		☐ G-BNKV	Cessna 152		☐ G-BNRY	Cessna 182Q Skylane
☐ G-BNDE	Piper PA-38-112 Tomahawk		☐ G-BNLA	Boeing 747-436		☐ G-BNSG	Piper PA-28R-201
☐ G-BNDG	Wallis WA-201R		☐ G-BNLB	Boeing 747-436		☐ G-BNSI	Cessna 152
☐ G-BNDN	Cameron V-77		☐ G-BNLC	Boeing 747-436		☐ G-BNSL	Piper PA-38-112 Tomahawk
☐ G-BNDO	Cessna 152		☐ G-BNLD	Boeing 747-436		☐ G-BNSM	Cessna 152
☐ G-BNDP	Brugger Colibri		☐ G-BNLE	Boeing 747-436		☐ G-BNSN	Cessna 152
☐ G-BNDR	SOCATA TB-10 Tobago		☐ G-BNLF	Boeing 747-436		☐ G-BNSO	Slingsby T.67M
☐ G-BNDT	Brugger Colibri		☐ G-BNLG	Boeing 747-436		☐ G-BNSP	Slingsby T.67M
☐ G-BNDV	Cameron N-77		☐ G-BNLH	Boeing 747-436		☐ G-BNSR	Slingsby T.67M
☐ G-BNDW	DH.82A Tiger Moth		☐ G-BNLI	Boeing 747-436		☐ G-BNST	Cessna 172N Skyhawk
☐ G-BNED	Piper PA-22-135 Tri-Pacer		☐ G-BNLJ	Boeing 747-436		☐ G-BNSU	Cessna 152
☐ G-BNEE	Piper PA-28R-201		☐ G-BNLK	Boeing 747-436		☐ G-BNSV	Cessna 152
☐ G-BNEK	Piper PA-38-112 Tomahawk		☐ G-BNLL	Boeing 747-436		☐ G-BNSY	Piper PA-28-161 Warrior
☐ G-BNEL	Piper PA-28-161 Warrior		☐ G-BNLM	Boeing 747-436		☐ G-BNSZ	Piper PA-28-161 Warrior
☐ G-BNEN	Piper PA-34-200T Seneca		☐ G-BNLN	Boeing 747-436		☐ G-BNTC	Piper PA-28R-201T
☐ G-BNEO	Cameron V-77		☐ G-BNLO	Boeing 747-436		☐ G-BNTD	Piper PA-28-161 Warrior
☐ G-BNES	Cameron V-77		☐ G-BNLP	Boeing 747-436		☐ G-BNTP	Cessna 172N Skyhawk
☐ G-BNET	Cameron O-84		☐ G-BNLR	Boeing 747-436		☐ G-BNTS	Piper PA-28R-201T
☐ G-BNEV	Viking Dragonfly		☐ G-BNLS	Boeing 747-436		☐ G-BNTT	Beech 76 Duchess
☐ G-BNEX	Cameron O-120		☐ G-BNLT	Boeing 747-436		☐ G-BNTW	Cameron V-77
☐ G-BNFG	Cameron O-77		☐ G-BNLU	Boeing 747-436		☐ G-BNTZ	Cameron N-77
☐ G-BNFI	Cessna 150J		☐ G-BNLV	Boeing 747-436		☐ G-BNUC	Cameron O-77
☐ G-BNFM	Colt 21A		☐ G-BNLW	Boeing 747-436		☐ G-BNUL	Cessna 152
☐ G-BNFN	Cameron N-105		☐ G-BNLX	Boeing 747-436		☐ G-BNUN	Beech 58PA Baron
☐ G-BNFO	Cameron V-77		☐ G-BNLY	Boeing 747-436		☐ G-BNUO	Beech 76 Duchess
☐ G-BNFP	Cameron O-84		☐ G-BNLZ	Boeing 747-436		☐ G-BNUS	Cessna 152
☐ G-BNFR	Cessna 152		☐ G-BNMA	Cameron O-77		☐ G-BNUT	Cessna 152
☐ G-BNFS	Cessna 152		☐ G-BNMB	Piper PA-28-151 Warrior		☐ G-BNUV	Piper PA-23-250 Aztec F
☐ G-BNFV	Robin DR.400-120		☐ G-BNMC	Cessna 152		☐ G-BNUX	Diamond H.36
☐ G-BNGE	Auster AOP.6		☐ G-BNMD	Cessna 152		☐ G-BNUY	Piper PA-38-112 Tomahawk

Reg	Type
G-BNVB	Grumman AA-5A Cheetah
G-BNVD	Piper PA-38-112 Tomahawk
G-BNVE	Piper PA-28-181 Archer
G-BNVT	Piper PA-28R-201T
G-BNVZ	Beech 95-B55 Baron
G-BNWA	Boeing 767-336ER
G-BNWB	Boeing 767-336ER
G-BNWC	Boeing 767-336ER
G-BNWD	Boeing 767-336ER
G-BNWH	Boeing 767-336ER
G-BNWI	Boeing 767-336ER
G-BNWM	Boeing 767-336ER
G-BNWN	Boeing 767-336ER
G-BNWO	Boeing 767-336ER
G-BNWR	Boeing 767-336ER
G-BNWS	Boeing 767-336ER
G-BNWT	Boeing 767-336ER
G-BNWU	Boeing 767-336ER
G-BNWV	Boeing 767-336ER
G-BNWW	Boeing 767-336ER
G-BNWX	Boeing 767-336ER
G-BNWY	Boeing 767-336ER
G-BNWZ	Boeing 767-336ER
G-BNXD	Cessna 172N Skyhawk
G-BNXE	Piper PA-28-161 Warrior
G-BNXI	Robin DR.400-180 Regent
G-BNXL	Glaser-Dirks DG-400
G-BNXM	Piper PA-18-95
G-BNXR	Cameron O-84
G-BNXT	Piper PA-28-161 Warrior
G-BNXU	Piper PA-28-161 Warrior
G-BNXV	Piper PA-38-112 Tomahawk
G-BNXX	SOCATA TB-20 Trinidad
G-BNXZ	Thunder Ax7-77
G-BNYB	Piper PA-28-201T
G-BNYD	Bell 206B Jet Ranger
G-BNYK	Piper PA-38-112 Tomahawk
G-BNYL	Cessna 152
G-BNYM	Cessna 172N Skyhawk
G-BNYN	Cessna 152
G-BNYO	Beech 76 Duchess
G-BNYP	Piper PA-28-181 Archer
G-BNYS	Boeing 767-204ER
G-BNYX	Denney Kitfox
G-BNYZ	Stampe SV-4E
G-BNZB	Piper PA-28-161 Warrior
G-BNZC	DHC-1 Chipmunk
G-BNZK	Thunder Ax7-77
G-BNZM	Cessna T210N
G-BNZN	Cameron N-56
G-BNZO	Rotorway Exec 90
G-BNZR	Clutton FRED II
G-BNZV	Piper PA-25-235 Pawnee
G-BNZZ	Piper PA-28-161 WarriorG-
G-BOAA	BAC Concorde 102
G-BOAB	BAC Concorde 102
G-BOAC	BAC Concorde 102
G-BOAF	BAC Concorde 102
G-BOAH	Piper PA-28-161 Warrior
G-BOAI	Cessna 152
G-BOAL	Cameron V-65
G-BOAO	Thunder Ax7-77
G-BOAS	Air Command 503
G-BOAU	Cameron V-77
G-BOBA	Piper PA-28R-201
G-BOBH	Airtour AH-77B
G-BOBR	Cameron N-77
G-BOBT	Stolp SA.500
G-BOBV	Reims F150M
G-BOBY	Monnett Sonerai
G-BOCG	Piper PA-34-200T Seneca
G-BOCI	Cessna 140A
G-BOCK	Sopwith Triplane Rep
G-BOCL	Slingsby T.67C
G-BOCM	Slingsby T.67C
G-BOCN	Robinson R22B
G-BODB	Piper PA-28-161 Warrior
G-BODC	Piper PA-28-161 Warrior
G-BODD	Piper PA-28-161 Warrior
G-BODE	Piper PA-28-161 Warrior
G-BODI	Glasair SH-2H
G-BODM	Piper PA-28-180 Cherokee
G-BODO	Cessna 152
G-BODP	Piper PA-38-112 Tomahawk
G-BODR	Piper PA-28-161 Warrior
G-BODS	Piper PA-38-112 Tomahawk
G-BODT	Jodel D.18
G-BODU	Scheibe SF25C-2000
G-BODX	Beech 76 Duchess
G-BODY	Cessna 310R
G-BODZ	Robinson R22B
G-BOEC	Piper PA-38-112 Tomahawk
G-BOEE	Piper PA-28-181 Archer
G-BOEH	Robin DR.340 Major
G-BOEK	Cameron V-77
G-BOEN	Cessna 172M Skyhawk
G-BOER	Piper PA-28-161 Warrior
G-BOET	Piper PA-28RT-201
G-BOEW	Robinson R22B
G-BOFC	Beech 76 Duchess
G-BOFD	Cessna U206G
G-BOFE	Piper PA-34-200T Seneca
G-BOFF	Cameron N-77
G-BOFL	Cessna 152
G-BOFM	Cessna 152
G-BOFW	Cessna A150M Aerobat
G-BOFX	Cessna A150M Aerobat
G-BOFY	Piper PA-28-140 Cherokee
G-BOFZ	Piper PA-28-161 Warrior
G-BOGC	Cessna 152
G-BOGG	Cessna 152
G-BOGI	Robin DR.400-180 Regent
G-BOGK	ARV Super 2
G-BOGM	Piper PA-28R-201T
G-BOGO	Piper PA-32R-301 SP
G-BOGP	Cameron V-77
G-BOGV	Air Command 532 Elite
G-BOGY	Cameron V-77
G-BOHA	Piper PA-28-161 Warrior
G-BOHD	Colt 77A
G-BOHF	Thunder Ax8-84
G-BOHH	Cessna 172N Skyhawk
G-BOHI	Cessna 152
G-BOHJ	Cessna 152
G-BOHL	Cameron A-120
G-BOHM	Piper PA-28-180 Cherokee
G-BOHO	Piper PA-28-161 Warrior
G-BOHR	Piper PA-28-151 Warrior
G-BOHS	Piper PA-38-112 Tomahawk
G-BOHT	Piper PA-38-112 Tomahawk
G-BOHU	Piper PA-38-112 Tomahawk
G-BOHV	Wittman Tailwind
G-BOHW	Van's RV-4
G-BOIA	Cessna 180K Skywagon
G-BOIB	Wittman Tailwind
G-BOIC	Piper PA-28R-201T
G-BOID	Aeronca 7ECA Citabria
G-BOIG	Piper PA-28-161 Warrior
G-BOIJ	Thunder Ax7-77
G-BOIK	Air Command 503
G-BOIL	Cessna 172N Skyhawk
G-BOIO	Cessna 152
G-BOIR	Cessna 152
G-BOIT	SOCATA TB-10 Tobago
G-BOIV	Cessna 150M
G-BOIX	Cessna 172N Skyhawk
G-BOIY	Cessna 172N Skyhawk
G-BOIZ	Piper PA-34-200T Seneca
G-BOJB	Cameron V-77
G-BOJI	Piper PA-28RT-201
G-BOJK	Piper PA-34-220T Seneca
G-BOJM	Piper PA-28-181 Archer
G-BOJO	Colt 120A
G-BOJR	Cessna 172P Skyhawk
G-BOJS	Cessna 172P Skyhawk
G-BOJU	Cameron N-77
G-BOJW	Piper PA-28-161 Warrior
G-BOJZ	Piper PA-28-161 Warrior
G-BOKA	Piper PA-28-201T
G-BOKB	Piper PA-28-161 Warrior
G-BOKF	Air Command 532 Elite
G-BOKH	Whittaker MW-7
G-BOKK	Piper PA-28-161 Warrior
G-BOKW	Bolkow Bo.208C Junior
G-BOKX	Piper PA-28-161 Warrior
G-BOKY	Cessna 152
G-BOLB	Taylorcraft BC-12
G-BOLC	Fournier RF6B
G-BOLD	Piper PA-38-112 Tomahawk
G-BOLE	Piper PA-38-112 Tomahawk
G-BOLF	Piper PA-38-112 Tomahawk
G-BOLG	Aeronca 7KCAB Citabria
G-BOLI	Cessna 172P Skyhawk
G-BOLL	Lake LA-4-200
G-BOLN	Colt 21A
G-BOLO	Bell 206B Jet Ranger
G-BOLP	Colt 31A
G-BOLR	Colt 21A
G-BOLS	Clutton FRED II
G-BOLT	Rockwell 114
G-BOLU	Robin R.3000-120
G-BOLV	Cessna 152
G-BOLW	Cessna 152
G-BOLY	Cessna 172N Skyhawk
G-BOLZ	Rand KR-2
G-BOMB	Cassutt Racer 3M
G-BOMN	Cessna 150F
G-BOMO	Piper PA-38-112 Tomahawk
G-BOMP	Piper PA-28-181 Archer
G-BOMS	Cessna 172N Skyhawk
G-BOMU	Piper PA-28-181 Archer
G-BOMY	Piper PA-28-161 Warrior
G-BOMZ	Piper PA-38-112 Tomahawk
G-BONC	Piper PA-28RT-201
G-BONG	Enstrom F-28A
G-BONO	Cessna 172N Skyhawk
G-BONP	CFM Shadow SA
G-BONR	Cessna 172N Skyhawk
G-BONS	Cessna 172N Skyhawk
G-BONT	Slingsby T.67M
G-BONU	Slingsby T.67B
G-BONW	Cessna 152
G-BONY	Denney Kitfox
G-BONZ	Beech V35B Bonanza
G-BOOB	Cameron N-65
G-BOOC	Piper PA-18-150
G-BOOD	Slingsby T.31M
G-BOOE	Grumman GA-7 Cougar
G-BOOF	Piper PA-28-181 Archer
G-BOOG	Piper PA-28RT-201
G-BOOH	Jodel D.112
G-BOOI	Cessna 152
G-BOOJ	Air Command 532 Elite
G-BOOL	Cessna 172N Skyhawk
G-BOOW	Aerosport Scamp
G-BOOX	Rutan LongEz
G-BOOZ	Cameron N-77
G-BOPA	Piper PA-28-181 Archer
G-BOPB	Boeing 767-204ER

☐ G-BOPC Piper PA-28-161 Warrior	☐ G-BOWZ Bensen B.8OV	☐ G-BPEE Boeing 757-236ER
☐ G-BOPD Bede BD-4	☐ G-BOXA Piper PA-28-161 Warrior	☐ G-BPEI Boeing 757-236ER
☐ G-BOPH Cessna TR182	☐ G-BOXC Piper PA-28-161 Warrior	☐ G-BPEJ Boeing 757-236ER
☐ G-BOPO Optica OA.7	☐ G-BOXG Cameron O-77	☐ G-BPEK Boeing 757-236ER
☐ G-BOPR Optica OA.7	☐ G-BOXH Pitts S-1S Special	☐ G-BPEM Cessna 150K
☐ G-BOPT Grob 115	☐ G-BOXJ Piper J-3C-90 Cub	☐ G-BPEO Cessna 152
☐ G-BOPU Grob 115	☐ G-BOXR Grumman GA-7 Cougar	☐ G-BPES Piper PA-38-112 Tomahawk
☐ G-BOPX Cessna A152 Aerobat	☐ G-BOXT Hughes 269C	☐ G-BPEZ Colt 77A
☐ G-BORA Colt 77A	☐ G-BOXU Grumman AA-5B Tiger	☐ G-BPFB Colt 77A
☐ G-BORB Cameron V-77	☐ G-BOXV Pitts S-1D Special	☐ G-BPFC Mooney M.20C
☐ G-BORD Thunder Ax7-77	☐ G-BOXW Cassutt Racer 3M	☐ G-BPFD Jodel D.112
☐ G-BORG Campbell Cricket	☐ G-BOYB Cessna A152 Aerobat	☐ G-BPFF Cameron DP-70
☐ G-BORH Piper PA-34-200T Seneca	☐ G-BOYC Robinson R22B	☐ G-BPFH Piper PA-28-161 Warrior
☐ G-BORI Cessna 152	☐ G-BOYF Sikorsky S-76B	☐ G-BPFI Piper PA-28-181 Archer
☐ G-BORJ Cessna 152	☐ G-BOYH Piper PA-28-151 Warrior	☐ G-BPFL Davis DA-2A
☐ G-BORK Piper PA-28-161 Warrior	☐ G-BOYI Piper PA-28-161 Warrior	☐ G-BPFM Aeronca 7AC
☐ G-BORL Piper PA-28-161 Warrior	☐ G-BOYL Cessna 152	☐ G-BPFN Short SD.360-300
☐ G-BORN Cameron N-77	☐ G-BOYM Cameron O-84	☐ G-BPFZ Cessna 152
☐ G-BORO Cessna 152	☐ G-BOYO Cameron V-20	☐ G-BPGC Air Command 532 Elite
☐ G-BORR Thunder Ax8-90	☐ G-BOYP Cessna 172N Skyhawk	☐ G-BPGD Cameron V-65
☐ G-BORS Piper PA-28-181 Archer	☐ G-BOYR Reims F337G	☐ G-BPGE Cessna U206C
☐ G-BORT Colt 77A	☐ G-BOYS Cameron N-77	☐ G-BPGF Thunder Ax7-77
☐ G-BORW Cessna 172P Skyhawk	☐ G-BOYU Cessna A150L Aerobat	☐ G-BPGH EAA Acrosport
☐ G-BORY Cessna 150L	☐ G-BOYV Piper PA-28R-201T	☐ G-BPGK Aeronca 7AC Champion
☐ G-BOSB Thunder Ax7-77	☐ G-BOYX Robinson R22B	☐ G-BPGT Colt AS-80 II
☐ G-BOSD Piper PA-34-200T Seneca	☐ G-BOZI Piper PA-28-161 Warrior	☐ G-BPGU Piper PA-28-181 Archer
☐ G-BOSE Piper PA-28-181 Archer	☐ G-BOZN Cameron N-77	☐ G-BPGV Robinson R22B
☐ G-BOSJ Nord 3400	☐ G-BOZO Grumman AA-5B Tiger	☐ G-BPGZ Cessna 150G
☐ G-BOSM Robin DR.253 Regent	☐ G-BOZR Cessna 152	☐ G-BPHD Cameron N-42
☐ G-BOSN Aerospatiale AS.355F2	☐ G-BOZS Pitts S-1C Special	☐ G-BPHG Robin DR.400-180 Regent
☐ G-BOSO Cessna A152 Aerobat	☐ G-BOZU Sparrow Hawk	☐ G-BPHH Cameron V-77
☐ G-BOSR Piper PA-28-140 Cherokee	☐ G-BOZV Robin DR.340 Major	☐ G-BPHI Piper PA-38-112 Tomahawk
☐ G-BOSU Piper PA-28-140 Cherokee	☐ G-BOZW Bensen B.8M	☐ G-BPHJ Cameron V-77
☐ G-BOTD Cameron O-105	☐ G-BOZY Cameron RTW-120	☐ G-BPHK Whittaker MW-7
☐ G-BOTF Piper PA-28-151 Warrior	☐ G-BOZZ Grumman AA-5B Tiger	☐ G-BPHL Piper PA-28-161 Warrior
☐ G-BOTG Cessna 152	☐ G-BPAA Acro Advanced	☐ G-BPHO Taylorcraft BC12D
☐ G-BOTH Cessna 182Q Skylane	☐ G-BPAB Cessna 150M	☐ G-BPHP Taylorcraft BC-12
☐ G-BOTI Piper PA-28-151 Warrior	☐ G-BPAF Piper PA-28-161 Warrior	☐ G-BPHR DH.82A Tiger Moth
☐ G-BOTK Cameron O-105	☐ G-BPAI Bell 47G-3B-1	☐ G-BPHT Cessna 152
☐ G-BOTN Piper PA-28-161 Warrior	☐ G-BPAJ DH.82A Tiger Moth	☐ G-BPHU Thunder Ax7-77
☐ G-BOTO Aeronca 7ECA Citabria	☐ G-BPAL DHC-1 Chipmunk	☐ G-BPHW Cessna 140
☐ G-BOTP Cessna 150J	☐ G-BPAS SOCATA TB-20 Trinidad	☐ G-BPHX Cessna 140
☐ G-BOTU Piper J-3C-75 Cub	☐ G-BPAW Cessna 150M	☐ G-BPHZ Morane MS.505
☐ G-BOTV Piper PA-32RT-300	☐ G-BPAX Cessna 150M	☐ G-BPIF Bensen Two Place
☐ G-BOTW Cameron V-77	☐ G-BPAY Piper PA-28-181 Archer	☐ G-BPII Denney Kitfox
☐ G-BOUE Cessna 172N Skyhawk	☐ G-BPBA Bensen B.8MR	☐ G-BPIJ Brantly B.2B
☐ G-BOUF Cessna 172N Skyhawk	☐ G-BPBB Evans VP-2	☐ G-BPIK Piper PA-38-112 Tomahawk
☐ G-BOUJ Cessna 150M	☐ G-BPBG Cessna 152	☐ G-BPIL Cessna 310B
☐ G-BOUK Piper PA-34-200T Seneca	☐ G-BPBJ Cessna 152	☐ G-BPIN Glaser-Dirks DG-400
☐ G-BOUL Piper PA-34-200T Seneca	☐ G-BPBK Cessna 152	☐ G-BPIP Slingsby T.31M
☐ G-BOUM Piper PA-34-200T Seneca	☐ G-BPBM Piper PA-28-161 Warrior	☐ G-BPIR Scheibe SF25E Falke
☐ G-BOUN Rand KR-2	☐ G-BPBO Piper PA-28R-201T	☐ G-BPIT Robinson R22B
☐ G-BOUP Piper PA-28-161 Warrior	☐ G-BPBP Brugger Colibri	☐ G-BPIU Piper PA-28-161 Warrior
☐ G-BOUT Colomban MC-15 Cri-Cri	☐ G-BPBV Cameron V-77	☐ G-BPIV Bristol Blenheim
☐ G-BOUV Bensen B.8MR	☐ G-BPBW Cameron O-105	☐ G-BPIZ Grumman AA-5B Tiger
☐ G-BOUZ Cessna 150G	☐ G-BPBY Cameron V-77	☐ G-BPJB Schweizer 269C
☐ G-BOVB Piper PA-15 Vagabond	☐ G-BPCA BN2B-26 Islander	☐ G-BPJD MS.880B Rallye
☐ G-BOVK Piper PA-28-161 Warrior	☐ G-BPCF Piper J-3C-65 Cub	☐ G-BPJE Cameron A-105
☐ G-BOVT Cessna 150M	☐ G-BPCG Colt AS-80	☐ G-BPJG Piper PA-18-150
☐ G-BOVU Glasair III	☐ G-BPCI Cessna R172K Hawk XP	☐ G-BPJH Piper PA-18-95
☐ G-BOVV Cameron V-77	☐ G-BPCK Piper PA-28-161 Warrior	☐ G-BPJK Colt 77A
☐ G-BOVW Colt 69A	☐ G-BPCL Scottish Aviation Bulldog	☐ G-BPJO Piper PA-28-161 Warrior
☐ G-BOVX Hughes 269C	☐ G-BPCM Rotorway Exec 152	☐ G-BPJP Piper PA-28-161 Warrior
☐ G-BOWB Cameron V-77	☐ G-BPCR Mooney M.20K	☐ G-BPJR Piper PA-28-161 Warrior
☐ G-BOWE Piper PA-34-200T Seneca	☐ G-BPCV Bensen B.8MR	☐ G-BPJS Piper PA-28-161 Warrior
☐ G-BOWL Cameron V-77	☐ G-BPCX Piper PA-28-236 Dakota	☐ G-BPJU Piper PA-28-161 Warrior
☐ G-BOWM Cameron V-56	☐ G-BPDG Cameron V-77	☐ G-BPJV Taylorcraft F-21
☐ G-BOWN Piper PA-12 Super Cruiser	☐ G-BPDJ Mini Coupe	☐ G-BPJW Cessna A150K Aerobat
☐ G-BOWO Cessna R182 Skylane RG	☐ G-BPDM CASA I-131E	☐ G-BPKF Grob 115
☐ G-BOWP Jodel D.120A Paris-Nice	☐ G-BPDT Piper PA-28-161 Warrior	☐ G-BPKK Denney Kitfox
☐ G-BOWU Cameron O-84	☐ G-BPDV Pitts S-1S Special	☐ G-BPKM Piper PA-28-161 Warrior
☐ G-BOWV Cameron V-65	☐ G-BPEC Boeing 757-236ER	☐ G-BPKO Cessna 140
☐ G-BOWY Piper PA-28R-201T	☐ G-BPED Boeing 757-236ER	☐ G-BPKR Piper PA-28-151 Warrior

Registration	Type	Registration	Type	Registration	Type
G-BPLH	Jodel DR.1051	G-BPUG	Air Command 532 Elite	G-BRBG	Piper PA-28-180 Cherokee
G-BPLM	Stampe SV-4C	G-BPUJ	Cameron N-90	G-BRBH	Cessna 150H
G-BPLV	Cameron V-77	G-BPUL	Piper PA-18-150	G-BRBI	Cessna 172N Skyhawk
G-BPLY	Pitts S-2B Special	G-BPUM	Cessna R182 Skylane RG	G-BRBJ	Cessna 172M Skyhawk
G-BPLZ	Hughes 369S	G-BPUP	Whittaker MW-7	G-BRBK	Robin DR.400-180 Regent
G-BPMB	Maule M-5-235C	G-BPUR	Piper J-3L-65 Cub	G-BRBL	Robin DR.400-180 Regent
G-BPME	Cessna 152	G-BPUU	Cessna 140	G-BRBM	Robin DR.400-180 Regent
G-BPMF	Piper PA-28-151 Warrior	G-BPUW	Colt 90A	G-BRBN	Pitts S-1S Special
G-BPML	Cessna 172M Skyhawk	G-BPVA	Cessna 172F Skyhawk	G-BRBO	Cameron V-77
G-BPMR	Piper PA-28-161 Warrior	G-BPVC	Cameron V-77	G-BRBP	Cessna 152
G-BPMU	Nord 3202B	G-BPVE	Bleriot XI Rep	G-BRBS	Bensen B.8M
G-BPMW	QAC Quickie Q2	G-BPVH	Piper J-3C-85 Cub	G-BRBT	Trotter Ax3-20
G-BPMX	ARV Super 2	G-BPVI	Piper PA-32R-301 SP	G-BRBV	Piper J-4A Cub Coupe
G-BPNA	Cessna 150L	G-BPVK	Varga Kachina	G-BRBW	Piper PA-28-140 Cherokee
G-BPNI	Robinson R22B	G-BPVM	Cameron V-77	G-BRBX	Piper PA-28-181 Archer
G-BPNJ	HS.748 2A	G-BPVN	Piper PA-32R-301 SP	G-BRBY	Robinson R22B
G-BPNN	Bensen B.8MR	G-BPVO	Cassutt Racer 3M	G-BRCA	Jodel D.112
G-BPNO	Zlin Z.526	G-BPVU	Thunder Ax7-77	G-BRCE	Pitts S-1C Special
G-BPNT	BAe 146-300	G-BPVW	CASA I-131E	G-BRCF	Bensen B.8
G-BPNU	Thunder Ax7-77	G-BPVY	Cessna 172D Skyhawk	G-BRCI	Pitts S-1C Special
G-BPOA	Gloster Meteor T.7	G-BPVZ	Luscombe 8E Silvaire	G-BRCJ	Cameron H-20
G-BPOB	Sopwith Camel Rep	G-BPWB	Sikorsky S-61N	G-BRCM	Cessna 172L Skyhawk
G-BPOM	Piper PA-28-161 Warrior	G-BPWC	Cameron V-77	G-BRCO	Cameron H-20
G-BPON	Piper PA-34-200T Seneca	G-BPWD	Cessna 120	G-BRCT	Denney Kitfox
G-BPOO	Bensen B.8MR	G-BPWE	Piper PA-28-161 Warrior	G-BRCV	Aeronca 7AC Champion
G-BPOS	Cessna 150M	G-BPWG	Cessna 150M	G-BRCW	Aeronca 11AC Chief
G-BPOT	Piper PA-28-181 Archer	G-BPWI	Bell 206B Jet Ranger	G-BRDB	Zenair CH.701
G-BPOU	Luscombe 8A Silvaire	G-BPWK	Fournier RF5B	G-BRDD	Mudry CAP.10B
G-BPPA	Cameron O-65	G-BPWL	Piper PA-25-235 Pawnee	G-BRDE	Thunder Ax7-77
G-BPPE	Piper PA-38-112 Tomahawk	G-BPWM	Cessna 150L	G-BRDF	Piper PA-28-161 Warrior
G-BPPF	Piper PA-38-112 Tomahawk	G-BPWN	Cessna 150L	G-BRDG	Piper PA-28-161 Warrior
G-BPPK	Piper PA-28-151 Warrior	G-BPWP	Rutan LongEz	G-BRDJ	Luscombe 8A Silvaire
G-BPPM	Beech B200 Super King Air	G-BPWR	Cessna R172K Hawk XP	G-BRDM	Piper PA-28-161 Warrior
G-BPPO	Luscombe 8A Silvaire	G-BPWS	Cessna 172P Skyhawk	G-BRDN	MS.880B Rallye
G-BPPP	Cameron N-77	G-BPXA	Piper PA-28-181 Archer	G-BRDO	Cessna 177B Cardinal
G-BPPS	Mudry CAP.21	G-BPXB	Glaser-Dirks DG-400	G-BRDT	Cameron DP-70
G-BPPU	Air Command 532 Elite	G-BPXE	Enstrom 280C	G-BRDW	Piper PA-24-180 Comanche
G-BPPY	Hughes 269B	G-BPXF	Cameron V-65	G-BREB	Piper J-3C-65 Cub
G-BPPZ	Taylorcraft BC12D	G-BPXG	Colt 42A	G-BREE	Whittaker MW-7
G-BPRA	Aeronca 11AC Chief	G-BPXH	Colt 17A	G-BREH	Cameron V-65
G-BPRC	Cameron Elephant	G-BPXJ	Piper PA-28R-201T	G-BREP	Piper PA-28RT-201
G-BPRD	Pitts S-1C Special	G-BPXX	Piper PA-34-200T Seneca	G-BRER	Aeronca 7AC Champion
G-BPRI	Aerospatiale AS.355F1	G-BPXY	Aeronca 11AC Chief	G-BREU	Bensen B.8
G-BPRJ	Aerospatiale AS.355F1	G-BPYJ	Wittman Tailwind	G-BREY	Taylorcraft BC12D
G-BPRL	Aerospatiale AS.355F	G-BPYK	Thunder Ax7-77	G-BRFB	Rutan LongEz
G-BPRM	Reims F172L	G-BPYL	Hughes 369D	G-BRFC	Percival Sea Prince
G-BPRN	Piper PA-28-161 Warrior	G-BPYN	Piper J-3C-65 Cub	G-BRFE	Cameron V-77
G-BPRR	Rand KR-2	G-BPYO	Piper PA-28-181 Archer	G-BRFI	Aeronca 7DC Champion
G-BPRX	Aeronca 11AC Chief	G-BPYR	Piper PA-31-310 Navajo	G-BRFJ	Aeronca 11AC Chief
G-BPRY	Piper PA-28-161 Warrior	G-BPYS	Cameron O-77	G-BRFL	Piper PA-38-112 Tomahawk
G-BPSH	Cameron V-77	G-BPYT	Cameron V-77	G-BRFM	Piper PA-28-161 Warrior
G-BPSJ	Thunder Ax6-56	G-BPYV	Cameron V-77	G-BRFO	Cameron V-77
G-BPSK	Bensen B.8M	G-BPYZ	Thunder Ax7-77	G-BRFW	Bensen B.8
G-BPSL	Cessna 177 Cardinal	G-BPZA	Luscombe 8A Silvaire	G-BRFX	Pazmany PL-4A
G-BPSO	Cameron N-90	G-BPZB	Cessna 120	G-BRGD	Cameron O-84
G-BPSR	Cameron V-77	G-BPZD	Nord NC.858S	G-BRGF	Luscombe 8E Silvaire
G-BPSS	Cameron A-120	G-BPZE	Luscombe 8E Silvaire	G-BRGG	Luscombe 8A Silvaire
G-BPTA	Stinson 108-2	G-BPZK	Cameron O-120	G-BRGI	Piper PA-28-180 Cherokee
G-BPTC	Taylorcraft BC12D	G-BPZM	Piper PA-28RT-201	G-BRGO	Air Command 532 Elite
G-BPTD	Cameron V-77	G-BPZP	Robin DR.400-180 Regent	G-BRGT	Piper PA-32-260
G-BPTE	Piper PA-28-181 Archer	G-BPZS	Colt 105A	G-BRGW	Barritault Minicab
G-BPTG	Rockwell 112TC	G-BPZU	Scheibe SF25C-2000	G-BRHA	Piper PA-32RT-300
G-BPTI	SOCATA TB-20 Trinidad	G-BPZY	Pitts S-1C Special	G-BRHG	Colt 90A
G-BPTL	Cessna 172N Skyhawk	G-BPZZ	Thunder Ax8-105	G-BRHL	Bensen B.8M
G-BPTS	CASA I-131E	G-BRAF	Spitfire FR.XVIIIe	G-BRHO	Piper PA-34-200 Seneca
G-BPTU	Cessna 152	G-BRAK	Cessna 172N Skyhawk	G-BRHP	Aeronca O-58B
G-BPTV	Bensen B.8	G-BRAR	Aeronca 7AC Champion	G-BRHR	Piper PA-38-112 Tomahawk
G-BPTX	Cameron O-120	G-BRAX	Knight Twister	G-BRHT	Piper PA-38-112 Tomahawk
G-BPTZ	Robinson R22B	G-BRBA	Piper PA-28-161 Warrior	G-BRHW	DH.82A Tiger Moth
G-BPUA	EAA Biplane	G-BRBB	Piper PA-28-161 Warrior	G-BRHX	Luscombe 8E Silvaire
G-BPUB	Cameron V-31	G-BRBC	North American T-6G	G-BRHY	Luscombe 8E Silvaire
G-BPUE	Air Command 532 Elite	G-BRBD	Piper PA-28-151 Warrior	G-BRIA	Cessna 310L
G-BPUF	Thunder Ax6-56Z	G-BRBE	Piper PA-28-161 Warrior	G-BRIE	Cameron N-77

☐ G-BRIF	Boeing 767-204ER
☐ G-BRIG	Boeing 767-204ER
☐ G-BRIH	Taylorcraft BC12D
☐ G-BRII	Zenair CH.600
☐ G-BRIJ	Taylorcraft F-19
☐ G-BRIK	Tipsy Nipper 2
☐ G-BRIL	Piper J-5A Cub Cruiser
☐ G-BRIO	Turner T-40 Super
☐ G-BRIR	Cameron V-56
☐ G-BRIV	SOCATA TB-9 Tampico
☐ G-BRIY	Taylorcraft DF-65
☐ G-BRJA	Luscombe 8A Silvaire
☐ G-BRJB	Zenair CH.600
☐ G-BRJC	Cessna 120
☐ G-BRJK	Luscombe 8A Silvaire
☐ G-BRJL	Piper PA-15 Vagabond
☐ G-BRJN	Pitts S-1C Special
☐ G-BRJR	Piper PA-38-112 Tomahawk
☐ G-BRJT	Cessna 150H
☐ G-BRJV	Piper PA-28-161 Warrior
☐ G-BRJW	Aeronca 7GCBC Citabria
☐ G-BRJX	Rand KR-2
☐ G-BRJY	Rand KR-2
☐ G-BRKC	Auster J/1 Autocrat
☐ G-BRKH	Piper PA-28-236 Dakota
☐ G-BRKL	Cameron H-34
☐ G-BRKR	Cessna 182R Skylane
☐ G-BRKW	Cameron V-77
☐ G-BRKY	Viking Dragonfly II
☐ G-BRLB	Air Command 532 Elite
☐ G-BRLF	Campbell Cricket
☐ G-BRLG	Piper PA-28R-201T
☐ G-BRLI	Piper J-5A Cub Cruiser
☐ G-BRLL	Cameron A-105
☐ G-BRLO	Piper PA-38-112 Tomahawk
☐ G-BRLP	Piper PA-38-112 Tomahawk
☐ G-BRLR	Cessna 150F
☐ G-BRLS	Thunder Ax7-77
☐ G-BRLT	Colt 77B
☐ G-BRLV	CCF Harvard 4
☐ G-BRMA	Westland WS.51
☐ G-BRMB	Bristol Belvedere
☐ G-BRME	Piper PA-28-181 Archer
☐ G-BRMI	Cameron V-65
☐ G-BRMT	Cameron V-31
☐ G-BRMU	Cameron V-77
☐ G-BRMV	Cameron O-77
☐ G-BRMW	Whittaker MW-7
☐ G-BRNC	Cessna 150M
☐ G-BRND	Cessna 152
☐ G-BRNE	Cessna 152
☐ G-BRNK	Cessna 152
☐ G-BRNN	Cessna 152
☐ G-BRNT	Robin DR.400-180 Regent
☐ G-BRNU	Robin DR.400-180 Regent
☐ G-BRNV	Piper PA-28-181 Archer
☐ G-BRNW	Cameron V-77
☐ G-BRNX	Piper PA-22-150 Tri-Pacer
☐ G-BRNZ	Piper PA-32-300 B
☐ G-BROB	Cameron V-77
☐ G-BROE	Cameron N-65
☐ G-BROG	Cameron V-65
☐ G-BROH	Cameron O-90
☐ G-BROI	CFM Shadow SA
☐ G-BROJ	Colt 31A
☐ G-BROO	Luscombe 8E Silvaire
☐ G-BROP	Van's RV-4
☐ G-BROR	Piper J-3C-65 Cub
☐ G-BROX	Robinson R22B
☐ G-BROY	Cameron V-77
☐ G-BROZ	Piper PA-18-150
☐ G-BRPE	Cessna 120
☐ G-BRPF	Cessna 120

☐ G-BRPG	Cessna 120
☐ G-BRPH	Cessna 120
☐ G-BRPJ	Cameron N-90
☐ G-BRPK	Piper PA-28-140 Cherokee
☐ G-BRPM	Tipsy Nipper 3
☐ G-BRPP	Brookland Hornet
☐ G-BRPR	Aeronca O-58B
☐ G-BRPS	Cessna 177B Cardinal
☐ G-BRPT	Rans S10 Sakota
☐ G-BRPU	Beech 76 Duchess
☐ G-BRPV	Cessna 152
☐ G-BRPX	Taylorcraft BC-12
☐ G-BRPY	Piper PA-15 Vagabond
☐ G-BRPZ	Luscombe 8A Silvaire
☐ G-BRRB	Luscombe 8E Silvaire
☐ G-BRRD	Scheibe SF25B Falke
☐ G-BRRF	Cameron O-77
☐ G-BRRG	Glaser-Dirks DG-500M
☐ G-BRRJ	Piper PA-28R-201T
☐ G-BRRK	Cessna 182Q Skylane
☐ G-BRRL	Piper PA-18-95
☐ G-BRRR	Cameron V-77
☐ G-BRRU	Colt 90A
☐ G-BRRY	Robinson R22B
☐ G-BRSA	Cameron N-56
☐ G-BRSD	Cameron V-77
☐ G-BRSE	Piper PA-28-161 Warrior
☐ G-BRSF	Spitfire HF.IXc
☐ G-BRSK	Boeing Stearman B75N1
☐ G-BRSN	Rand KR-2
☐ G-BRSO	CFM Shadow SA
☐ G-BRSP	Air Command 532 Elite
☐ G-BRSW	Luscombe 8AC Silvaire
☐ G-BRSX	Piper PA-15 Vagabond
☐ G-BRSY	Hatz CB-1
☐ G-BRTD	Cessna 152
☐ G-BRTJ	Cessna 150F
☐ G-BRTK	Boeing Stearman E75
☐ G-BRTL	Hughes 369E
☐ G-BRTP	Cessna 152
☐ G-BRTT	Schweizer 269C
☐ G-BRTV	Cameron O-77
☐ G-BRTW	Glaser-Dirks DG-400
☐ G-BRTX	Piper PA-28-151 Warrior
☐ G-BRUB	Piper PA-28-161 Warrior
☐ G-BRUD	Piper PA-28-181 Archer
☐ G-BRUG	Luscombe 8E Silvaire
☐ G-BRUH	Colt 105A
☐ G-BRUI	Piper PA-44-180 Seminole
☐ G-BRUJ	Boeing Stearman A75N1
☐ G-BRUM	Cessna A152 Aerobat
☐ G-BRUN	Cessna 120
☐ G-BRUO	Taylor Monoplane
☐ G-BRUV	Cameron V-77
☐ G-BRUX	Piper PA-44-180 Seminole
☐ G-BRVB	Stolp SA.300
☐ G-BRVE	Beech D17S Staggerwing
☐ G-BRVF	Colt 77A
☐ G-BRVG	North American T-6
☐ G-BRVI	Robinson R22B
☐ G-BRVJ	Slingsby T.31M
☐ G-BRVL	Pitts S-1C Special
☐ G-BRVN	Thunder Ax7-77
☐ G-BRVO	Aerospatiale AS.350B
☐ G-BRVR	Barnett Rotorcraft
☐ G-BRVS	Barnett Rotorcraft
☐ G-BRVT	Pitts S-2B Special
☐ G-BRVU	Colt 77A
☐ G-BRVZ	Jodel D.117
☐ G-BRWA	Aeronca 7AC Champion
☐ G-BRWD	Robinson R22B
☐ G-BRWO	Piper PA-28-140 Cherokee
☐ G-BRWP	CFM Shadow SA

☐ G-BRWR	Aeronca 11AC Chief
☐ G-BRWT	Scheibe SF25C-2000
☐ G-BRWU	Luton Minor
☐ G-BRWV	Brugger Colibri
☐ G-BRWX	Cessna 172P Skyhawk
☐ G-BRWZ	Cameron Macaw SS
☐ G-BRXA	Cameron O-120
☐ G-BRXB	Thunder Ax7-77
☐ G-BRXD	Piper PA-28-181 Archer
☐ G-BRXE	Taylorcraft BC12D
☐ G-BRXF	Aeronca 11AC Chief
☐ G-BRXG	Aeronca 7AC Champion
☐ G-BRXH	Cessna 120
☐ G-BRXL	Aeronca 11AC Chief
☐ G-BRXN	Bensen B.8MR
☐ G-BRXO	Piper PA-34-200T Seneca
☐ G-BRXP	Stampe SV-4C
☐ G-BRXS	Howard Special T
☐ G-BRXV	Robinson R22B
☐ G-BRXW	Piper PA-24-260 Comanche
☐ G-BRXY	Pietenpol Aircamper
☐ G-BRYU	DHC-8-311A
☐ G-BRYV	DHC-8-311A
☐ G-BRYW	DHC-8-311A
☐ G-BRYX	DHC-8-311A
☐ G-BRYY	DHC-8-311A
☐ G-BRYZ	DHC-8-311A
☐ G-BRZA	Cameron O-77
☐ G-BRZD	Hapi Cygnet SF-2A
☐ G-BRZE	Thunder Ax7-77
☐ G-BRZG	Enstrom F-28A
☐ G-BRZI	Cameron N-180
☐ G-BRZK	Stinson 108-2
☐ G-BRZL	Pitts S-1D Special
☐ G-BRZS	Cessna 172P Skyhawk
☐ G-BRZT	Cameron V-77
☐ G-BRZV	Colt Apple SS
☐ G-BRZW	Rans S10 Sakota
☐ G-BRZX	Pitts S-1S Special
☐ G-BRZZ	CFM Shadow SA
☐ G-BSAI	Glasair III
☐ G-BSAJ	CASA I-131E
☐ G-BSAK	Colt 21A
☐ G-BSAS	Cameron V-65
☐ G-BSAV	Thunder Ax7-77
☐ G-BSAW	Piper PA-28-161 Warrior
☐ G-BSAZ	Denney Kitfox
☐ G-BSBA	Piper PA-28-161 Warrior
☐ G-BSBG	CCF Harvard 4
☐ G-BSBI	Cameron O-77
☐ G-BSBN	Thunder Ax7-77
☐ G-BSBR	Cameron V-77
☐ G-BSBT	Piper J-3C-65 Cub
☐ G-BSBV	Rans S10 Sakota
☐ G-BSBW	Bell 206B Jet Ranger
☐ G-BSBX	Bensen B.8MR
☐ G-BSBZ	Cessna 150M
☐ G-BSCA	Cameron N-90
☐ G-BSCC	Colt 105A
☐ G-BSCE	Robinson R22B
☐ G-BSCF	Thunder Ax7-77
☐ G-BSCG	Denney Kitfox
☐ G-BSCH	Denney Kitfox
☐ G-BSCI	Colt 77A
☐ G-BSCK	Cameron H-24
☐ G-BSCN	SOCATA TB-20 Trinidad
☐ G-BSCO	Thunder Ax7-77
☐ G-BSCP	Cessna 152
☐ G-BSCS	Piper PA-28-181 Archer
☐ G-BSCV	Piper PA-28-161 Warrior
☐ G-BSCW	Taylorcraft BC-65
☐ G-BSCX	Thunder Ax8-105
☐ G-BSCY	Piper PA-28-151 Warrior

G-BSCZ	Cessna 152	
G-BSDA	Taylorcraft BC12D	
G-BSDD	Denney Kitfox	
G-BSDH	Robin DR.400-180 Regent	
G-BSDI	Corben Junior Ace	
G-BSDJ	Piper J-4A Cub Coupe	
G-BSDK	Piper J-5A Cub Cruiser	
G-BSDL	SOCATA TB-10 Tobago	
G-BSDN	Piper PA-34-200T Seneca	
G-BSDO	Cessna 152	
G-BSDP	Cessna 152	
G-BSDS	Boeing Stearman E75	
G-BSDV	Colt 31A	
G-BSDW	Cessna 182P Skylane	
G-BSDX	Cameron V-77	
G-BSDZ	Enstrom 280FX	
G-BSED	Piper PA-22-160 Tri-Pacer	
G-BSEE	Rans S9 Chaos	
G-BSEF	Piper PA-28-180 Cherokee	
G-BSEG	Ken Brock KB-2	
G-BSEJ	Cessna 150M	
G-BSEK	Robinson R22	
G-BSEL	Slingsby T.61G	
G-BSEP	Cessna 172	
G-BSER	Piper PA-28-160 Cherokee	
G-BSEU	Piper PA-28-181 Archer	
G-BSEV	Cameron O-77	
G-BSEY	Beech 36 Bonanza	
G-BSFA	Aero Designs Pulsar	
G-BSFB	CASA I-131E	
G-BSFD	Piper J-3C-65 Cub	
G-BSFE	Piper PA-38-112 Tomahawk	
G-BSFF	Robin DR.400-180 Regent	
G-BSFP	Cessna 152	
G-BSFR	Cessna 152	
G-BSFV	Woody Pusher	
G-BSFW	Piper PA-15 Vagabond	
G-BSFX	Denney Kitfox	
G-BSFY	Denney Kitfox	
G-BSGB	Gaertner Ax4	
G-BSGD	Piper PA-28-180 Cherokee	
G-BSGF	Robinson R22B	
G-BSGG	Denney Kitfox	
G-BSGH	Airtour AH-56B	
G-BSGJ	Monnett Sonerai	
G-BSGK	Piper PA-34-200T Seneca	
G-BSGL	Piper PA-28-161 Warrior	
G-BSGP	Cameron N-65	
G-BSGS	Rans S10 Sakota	
G-BSGT	Cessna T210N	
G-BSHA	Piper PA-34-200T Seneca	
G-BSHC	Colt 69A	
G-BSHD	Colt 69A	
G-BSHH	Luscombe 8E Silvaire	
G-BSHI	Luscombe 8DF Silvaire	
G-BSHK	Denney Kitfox	
G-BSHO	Cameron V-77	
G-BSHP	Piper PA-28-161 Warrior	
G-BSHS	Colt 105A	
G-BSHT	Cameron V-77	
G-BSHV	Piper PA-18-135	
G-BSHY	EAA Acrosport	
G-BSIC	Cameron V-77	
G-BSIF	Denney Kitfox	
G-BSIG	Colt 21A	
G-BSIH	Rutan LongEz	
G-BSII	Piper PA-34-200T Seneca	
G-BSIJ	Cameron V-77	
G-BSIK	Denney Kitfox	
G-BSIM	Piper PA-28-181 Archer	
G-BSIO	Cameron House SS	
G-BSIU	Colt 90A	
G-BSIY	Schleicher ASK14	
G-BSIZ	Piper PA-28-181 Archer	
G-BSJB	Bensen B.8	
G-BSJU	Cessna 150M	
G-BSJX	Piper PA-28-161 Warrior	
G-BSJZ	Cessna 150J	
G-BSKA	Cessna 150M	
G-BSKD	Cameron V-77	
G-BSKE	Cameron O-84	
G-BSKG	Maule MX-7-180	
G-BSKI	Thunder Ax8-90	
G-BSKK	Piper PA-38-112 Tomahawk	
G-BSKL	Piper PA-38-112 Tomahawk	
G-BSKP	Spitfire F.XIVe	
G-BSKU	Cameron O-84	
G-BSKW	Piper PA-28-181 Archer	
G-BSLA	Robin DR.400-180 Regent	
G-BSLH	CASA I-131E	
G-BSLI	Piper PA-28-161 Warrior	
G-BSLM	Piper PA-28-160 Cherokee	
G-BSLT	Piper PA-28-161 Warrior	
G-BSLU	Piper PA-28-140 Cherokee	
G-BSLV	Enstrom 280FX	
G-BSLW	Aeronca 7ECA Citabria	
G-BSLX	WAR Focke-Wulf FW191	
G-BSMD	Nord 1101 Noralpha	
G-BSME	Bolkow Bo.208 Junior	
G-BSMG	Bensen B.8M	
G-BSMK	Cameron O-84	
G-BSML	Schweizer 269C	
G-BSMM	Colt 31A	
G-BSMN	CFM Shadow	
G-BSMO	Denney Kitfox	
G-BSMS	Cameron V-77	
G-BSMT	Rans S10 Sakota	
G-BSMU	Rans S6 Coyote II (N)	
G-BSMV	Piper PA-17 Vagabond	
G-BSMX	Bensen B.8MR	
G-BSND	Air Command 532 Elite	
G-BSNE	Luscombe 8E Silvaire	
G-BSNF	Piper J-3C-65 Cub	
G-BSNG	Cessna 172N Skyhawk	
G-BSNJ	Cameron N-90	
G-BSNL	Bensen B.8MR	
G-BSNN	Rans S10 Sakota	
G-BSNP	Piper PA-28R-201T	
G-BSNT	Luscombe 8A Silvaire	
G-BSNU	Colt 105A	
G-BSNX	Piper PA-28-181 Archer	
G-BSNY	Bensen B.8M	
G-BSNZ	Cameron O-105	
G-BSOE	Luscombe 8A Silvaire	
G-BSOF	Colt 25A	
G-BSOG	Cessna 172M Skyhawk	
G-BSOJ	Thunder Ax7-77	
G-BSOK	Piper PA-28-161 Warrior	
G-BSOM	Glaser-Dirks DG-400	
G-BSON	Green S-25	
G-BSOO	Cessna 172F Skyhawk	
G-BSOR	CFM Shadow SA	
G-BSOT	Piper PA-38-112 Tomahawk	
G-BSOU	Piper PA-38-112 Tomahawk	
G-BSOX	Luscombe 8AE Silvaire	
G-BSOZ	Piper PA-28-161 Warrior	
G-BSPA	QAC Quickie Q2	
G-BSPB	Thunder Ax8-84	
G-BSPE	Reims F172P	
G-BSPG	Piper PA-34-200T Seneca	
G-BSPI	Piper PA-28-161 Warrior	
G-BSPJ	Bensen B.8	
G-BSPK	Cessna 195A	
G-BSPL	CFM Shadow SA-II	
G-BSPM	Piper PA-28-161 Warrior	
G-BSPN	Piper PA-28R-201T	
G-BSPT	BN-2B-26 Islander	
G-BSPW	Avid Speed Wing	
G-BSRD	Cameron N-105	
G-BSRH	Pitts S-1C Special	
G-BSRI	Neico Lancair 235	
G-BSRK	ARV Super 2	
G-BSRL	Campbell Cricket	
G-BSRP	Rotorway Exec	
G-BSRR	Cessna 182Q Skylane	
G-BSRT	Denney Kitfox	
G-BSRX	CFM Shadow SA	
G-BSSA	Luscombe 8E Silvaire	
G-BSSB	Cessna 150L	
G-BSSC	Piper PA-28-161 Warrior	
G-BSSE	Piper PA-28-140 Cherokee	
G-BSSF	Denney Kitfox	
G-BSSI	Rans S6 Coyote II (N)	
G-BSSK	QAC Quickie Q2	
G-BSSP	Robin DR.400-180 Regent	
G-BSST	BAC Concorde	
G-BSSV	CFM Shadow SA	
G-BSSW	Piper PA-28-161 Warrior	
G-BSSX	Piper PA-28-161 Warrior	
G-BSTC	Aeronca 11AC Chief	
G-BSTE	Aerospatiale AS.355F2	
G-BSTH	Piper PA-25-235 Pawnee	
G-BSTI	Piper J-3C-85 Cub	
G-BSTK	Thunder Ax8-90	
G-BSTL	Rand KR-2	
G-BSTM	Cessna 172L Skyhawk	
G-BSTO	Cessna 152	
G-BSTP	Cessna 152	
G-BSTR	Grumman AA-5 Traveler	
G-BSTT	Rans S6 Coyote II (N)	
G-BSTV	Piper PA-32-300	
G-BSTX	Luscombe 8A Silvaire	
G-BSTY	Thunder Ax8-90	
G-BSTZ	Piper PA-28-140 Cherokee	
G-BSUA	Rans S6 Coyote II	
G-BSUB	Colt 77A	
G-BSUD	Luscombe 8A Silvaire	
G-BSUE	Cessna U206G	
G-BSUF	Piper PA-32RT-300	
G-BSUK	Colt 77A	
G-BSUO	Scheibe SF25C-2000	
G-BSUT	Rans S6 Coyote II (N)	
G-BSUV	Cameron O-77	
G-BSUW	Piper PA-34-200T Seneca	
G-BSUX	Carlson Sparrow	
G-BSUZ	Denney Kitfox	
G-BSVB	Piper PA-28-181 Archer	
G-BSVE	Binder Smaragd	
G-BSVG	Piper PA-28-161 Warrior	
G-BSVH	Piper J-3C-70 Cub	
G-BSVI	Piper PA-16 Clipper	
G-BSVK	Denney Kitfox	
G-BSVM	Piper PA-28-161 Warrior	
G-BSVN	Thorp T.18	
G-BSVR	Schweizer 269C	
G-BSVS	Robin DR.400-100	
G-BSWB	Rans S10 Sakota	
G-BSWC	Boeing Stearman E75	
G-BSWF	Piper PA-16 Clipper	
G-BSWG	Piper PA-15 Vagabond	
G-BSWH	Cessna 152	
G-BSWL	Slingsby T.61F	
G-BSWM	Slingsby T.61F	
G-BSWR	BN2T Islander	
G-BSWV	Cameron N-77	
G-BSWX	Cameron V-90	
G-BSWY	Cameron N-77	
G-BSWZ	Cameron A-180	
G-BSXA	Piper PA-28-161 Warrior	

☐	G-BSXB	Piper PA-28-161 Warrior	☐	G-BTDF	Luscombe 8AF Silvaire
☐	G-BSXC	Piper PA-28-161 Warrior	☐	G-BTDI	Robinson R22
☐	G-BSXD	Soko P2 Kraguj	☐	G-BTDN	Denney Kitfox
☐	G-BSXI	Mooney M.20E	☐	G-BTDR	Aero Designs Pulsar XP
☐	G-BSXM	Cameron V-77	☐	G-BTDS	Colt 77A
☐	G-BSXS	Piper PA-28-181 Archer	☐	G-BTDT	CASA I-131E
☐	G-BSXT	Piper J-5A Cub Cruiser	☐	G-BTDV	Piper PA-28-161 Warrior
☐	G-BSXX	Whittaker MW-7	☐	G-BTDW	Cessna 152
☐	G-BSYA	Jodel D.18	☐	G-BTDZ	CASA I-131E
☐	G-BSYB	Cameron N-120	☐	G-BTEA	Cameron N-105
☐	G-BSYC	Piper PA-32R-300	☐	G-BTEE	Cameron O-120
☐	G-BSYD	Cameron A-180	☐	G-BTEL	CFM Shadow SA
☐	G-BSYG	Piper PA-12 Super Cruiser	☐	G-BTES	Cessna 150H
☐	G-BSYH	Luscombe 8A Silvaire	☐	G-BTET	Piper J-3C-65 Cub
☐	G-BSYI	Aerospatiale AS.355F1	☐	G-BTEU	Aerospatiale AS.365N2
☐	G-BSYO	Piper J-3C-90 Cub	☐	G-BTEW	Cessna 120
☐	G-BSYU	Robin DR.400-180 Regent	☐	G-BTEX	Piper PA-28-140 Cherokee
☐	G-BSYV	Cessna 150M	☐	G-BTFC	Reims F152
☐	G-BSYW	Cessna 150M	☐	G-BTFE	Parsons Gyroplane
☐	G-BSYY	Piper PA-28-161 Warrior	☐	G-BTFF	Cessna T310R
☐	G-BSYZ	Piper PA-28-161 Warrior	☐	G-BTFG	Boeing Stearman A75N1
☐	G-BSZB	Stolp SA.300	☐	G-BTFJ	Piper PA-15 Vagabond
☐	G-BSZC	Beech C45H	☐	G-BTFK	Taylorcraft BC12D
☐	G-BSZD	Robin DR.400-180 Regent	☐	G-BTFL	Aeronca 11AC Chief
☐	G-BSZF	Robin DR.250-160	☐	G-BTFM	Cameron O-105
☐	G-BSZG	Stolp SA.100	☐	G-BTFO	Piper PA-28-161 Warrior
☐	G-BSZH	Thunder Ax7-77	☐	G-BTFS	Cessna A150M Aerobat
☐	G-BSZI	Cessna 152	☐	G-BTFT	Beech 58 Baron
☐	G-BSZJ	Piper PA-28-181 Archer	☐	G-BTFU	Cameron N-90
☐	G-BSZM	Bensen B.8	☐	G-BTFV	Whittaker MW-7
☐	G-BSZO	Cessna 152	☐	G-BTFX	Bell 206B Jet Ranger
☐	G-BSZT	Piper PA-28-161 Warrior	☐	G-BTGD	Rand KR-2
☐	G-BSZU	Cessna 150F	☐	G-BTGG	Rans S10 Sakota
☐	G-BSZV	Cessna 150F	☐	G-BTGH	Cessna 152
☐	G-BSZW	Cessna 152	☐	G-BTGI	Rearwin 175
☐	G-BTAG	Cameron O-77	☐	G-BTGJ	Smith Miniplane
☐	G-BTAL	Reims F152	☐	G-BTGL	Avid Flyer
☐	G-BTAM	Piper PA-28-181 Archer	☐	G-BTGM	Aeronca 7AC Champion
☐	G-BTAN	Thunder Ax7-65Z	☐	G-BTGO	Piper PA-28-140 Cherokee
☐	G-BTAS	Piper PA-38-112 Tomahawk	☐	G-BTGP	Cessna 150M
☐	G-BTAT	Denney Kitfox	☐	G-BTGR	Cessna 152
☐	G-BTAU	Thunder Ax7-77	☐	G-BTGS	Stolp SA.300
☐	G-BTAW	Piper PA-28-161 Warrior	☐	G-BTGT	CFM Shadow SA
☐	G-BTAZ	Evans VP-2	☐	G-BTGU	Piper PA-34-220T Seneca
☐	G-BTBA	Robinson R22B	☐	G-BTGV	Piper PA-34-200T Seneca
☐	G-BTBB	Thunder Ax8-105	☐	G-BTGW	Cessna 152
☐	G-BTBC	Piper PA-28-161 Warrior	☐	G-BTGX	Cessna 152
☐	G-BTBF	Fisher Super Koala	☐	G-BTGY	Piper PA-28-161 Warrior
☐	G-BTBG	Denney Kitfox	☐	G-BTGZ	Piper PA-28-181 Archer
☐	G-BTBH	Ryan ST3KR	☐	G-BTHA	Cessna 182P Skylane
☐	G-BTBI	WAR P.47 Rep	☐	G-BTHE	Cessna 150L
☐	G-BTBL	Bensen B.8MR	☐	G-BTHF	Cameron V-90
☐	G-BTBP	Cameron N-90	☐	G-BTHH	Robin DR.100A
☐	G-BTBU	Piper PA-18-150	☐	G-BTHI	Robinson R22B
☐	G-BTBW	Cessna 120	☐	G-BTHJ	Evans VP-2
☐	G-BTBX	Piper J-3C-65 Cub	☐	G-BTHK	Thunder Ax7-77
☐	G-BTBY	Piper PA-17 Vagabond	☐	G-BTHM	Thunder Ax8-105
☐	G-BTCA	Piper PA-32R-300	☐	G-BTHN	Renegade Spirit UK
☐	G-BTCB	Air Command 582	☐	G-BTHP	Thorp T.211
☐	G-BTCC	Grumman Hellcat	☐	G-BTHU	Avid Flyer
☐	G-BTCD	North American P-51D	☐	G-BTHV	MBB Bo.105S
☐	G-BTCE	Cessna 152	☐	G-BTHW	Beech F33C Bonanza
☐	G-BTCH	Luscombe 8E Silvaire	☐	G-BTHX	Colt 105A
☐	G-BTCI	Piper PA-17 Vagabond	☐	G-BTHY	Bell 206B Jet Ranger
☐	G-BTCJ	Luscombe 8AE Silvaire	☐	G-BTHZ	Cameron V-56
☐	G-BTCM	Cameron N-90	☐	G-BTID	Piper PA-28-161 Warrior
☐	G-BTCR	Rans S10 Sakota	☐	G-BTIE	SOCATA TB-10 Tobago
☐	G-BTCS	Colt 90A	☐	G-BTIF	Denney Kitfox
☐	G-BTCZ	Cameron Chateau SS	☐	G-BTII	Grumman AA-5B Tiger
☐	G-BTDA	Slingsby T.61F	☐	G-BTIJ	Luscombe 8E Silvaire
☐	G-BTDC	Denney Kitfox	☐	G-BTIK	Cessna 152
☐	G-BTDD	CFM Shadow SA-I	☐	G-BTIL	Piper PA-38-112 Tomahawk
☐	G-BTDE	Cessna C-165 Airmaster	☐	G-BTIM	Piper PA-28-161 Warrior

☐	G-BTIO	Stampe SV-4C
☐	G-BTIR	Denney Kitfox
☐	G-BTIU	MS.892A Commodore
☐	G-BTIV	Piper PA-28-161 Warrior
☐	G-BTIW	Jodel DR.1050M1
☐	G-BTIZ	Cameron A-105
☐	G-BTJA	Luscombe 8E Silvaire
☐	G-BTJB	Luscombe 8E Silvaire
☐	G-BTJC	Luscombe 8F Silvaire
☐	G-BTJD	Thunder Ax8-90
☐	G-BTJH	Cameron O-77
☐	G-BTJK	Piper PA-38-112 Tomahawk
☐	G-BTJL	Piper PA-38-112 Tomahawk
☐	G-BTJN	Bensen B.8MR
☐	G-BTJO	Thunder Ax9-140
☐	G-BTJS	Bensen B.8M
☐	G-BTJU	Cameron V-90
☐	G-BTJX	Rans S10 Sakota
☐	G-BTKA	Piper J-5A Cub Cruiser
☐	G-BTKB	Murphy Renegade
☐	G-BTKC	BAe 146-200
☐	G-BTKD	Denney Kitfox
☐	G-BTKG	Avid Flyer
☐	G-BTKL	MBB Bo.105DBS/4
☐	G-BTKN	Cameron O-120
☐	G-BTKP	CFM Shadow SA-I
☐	G-BTKT	Piper PA-28-161 Warrior
☐	G-BTKV	Piper PA-22-160 Tri-Pacer
☐	G-BTKW	Cameron O-105
☐	G-BTKX	Piper PA-28-181 Archer
☐	G-BTKZ	Cameron O-77
☐	G-BTLB	Wassmer WA.52
☐	G-BTLG	Piper PA-28R-200
☐	G-BTLL	Pilatus P.3-03
☐	G-BTLM	Piper PA-22-160 Tri-Pacer
☐	G-BTLP	Grumman AA-1C Lynx
☐	G-BTMA	Cessna 172N Skyhawk
☐	G-BTMK	Cessna R172K Hawk XP
☐	G-BTMN	Thunder Ax9-120
☐	G-BTMO	Colt 69A
☐	G-BTMP	Campbell Cricket
☐	G-BTMR	Cessna 172M Skyhawk
☐	G-BTMS	Avid Speed Wing
☐	G-BTMT	Denney Kitfox
☐	G-BTMV	Everett Gyroplane
☐	G-BTMW	Zenair CH.701
☐	G-BTMY	Cameron Train SS
☐	G-BTNA	Robinson R22B
☐	G-BTNC	Aerospatiale AS.365N2
☐	G-BTND	Piper PA-38-112 Tomahawk
☐	G-BTNE	Piper PA-28-161 Warrior
☐	G-BTNH	Piper PA-28-161 Warrior
☐	G-BTNO	Aeronca 7AC Champion
☐	G-BTNR	Denney Kitfox
☐	G-BTNT	Piper PA-28-151 Warrior
☐	G-BTNV	Piper PA-28-161 Warrior
☐	G-BTNW	Rans S6 Coyote II (N)
☐	G-BTOC	Robinson R22B
☐	G-BTOG	DH.82A Tiger Moth
☐	G-BTOL	Denney Kitfox
☐	G-BTON	Piper PA-28-140 Cherokee
☐	G-BTOO	Pitts S-1C Special
☐	G-BTOP	Cameron V-77
☐	G-BTOS	Cessna 140
☐	G-BTOT	Piper PA-15 Vagabond
☐	G-BTOU	Cameron O-120
☐	G-BTOW	MS.893E Rallye 180GT
☐	G-BTOZ	Thunder Ax9-120
☐	G-BTPA	BAe ATP
☐	G-BTPC	BAe ATP
☐	G-BTPD	BAe ATP
☐	G-BTPE	BAe ATP
☐	G-BTPF	BAe ATP

Reg	Type	Reg	Type	Reg	Type
☐ G-BTPG	BAe ATP	☐ G-BTWF	DHC-1 Chipmunk	☐ G-BUCM	Sea Fury FB.11
☐ G-BTPH	BAe ATP	☐ G-BTWI	EAA Acrosport	☐ G-BUCO	Pietenpol Aircamper
☐ G-BTPJ	BAe ATP	☐ G-BTWJ	Cameron V-77	☐ G-BUCS	Cessna 150F
☐ G-BTPL	BAe ATP	☐ G-BTWL	Wag-Aero CUBy Trainer	☐ G-BUCT	Cessna 150L
☐ G-BTPN	BAe ATP	☐ G-BTWM	Cameron V-77	☐ G-BUDA	Slingsby T.61F
☐ G-BTPT	Cameron N-77	☐ G-BTWV	Cameron O-90	☐ G-BUDB	Slingsby T.61F
☐ G-BTPV	Colt 90A	☐ G-BTWX	SOCATA TB-9 Tampico	☐ G-BUDC	Slingsby T.61F
☐ G-BTPX	Thunder Ax8-90	☐ G-BTWY	Aero Designs Pulsar	☐ G-BUDE	Piper PA-22-135 Tri-Pacer
☐ G-BTRB	Colt Micky SS	☐ G-BTWZ	Rans S10 Sakota	☐ G-BUDF	Rand KR-2
☐ G-BTRC	Avid Speed Wing	☐ G-BTXB	Colt 77A	☐ G-BUDI	Aero Designs Pulsar XP
☐ G-BTRF	Aero Designs Pulsar XP	☐ G-BTXD	Rans S6 Coyote II (T)	☐ G-BUDK	Thunder Ax7-77
☐ G-BTRG	Aeronca 65C	☐ G-BTXF	Cameron V-90	☐ G-BUDL	Auster III
☐ G-BTRI	Aeronca 11CC Super Chief	☐ G-BTXG	BAe Jetstream 31	☐ G-BUDN	Cameron Shoe SS
☐ G-BTRK	Piper PA-28-161 Warrior	☐ G-BTXH	Colt AS-56	☐ G-BUDO	PZL Koliber 150
☐ G-BTRL	Cameron N-105	☐ G-BTXI	Noorduyn Harvard	☐ G-BUDR	Denney Kitfox
☐ G-BTRN	Thunder Ax9-120	☐ G-BTXK	Thunder Ax7-65	☐ G-BUDS	Rand KR-2
☐ G-BTRO	Thunder Ax8-90	☐ G-BTXM	Colt 21A Cloudhopper	☐ G-BUDT	Slingsby T.61F
☐ G-BTRP	Hughes 369E	☐ G-BTXS	Cameron O-120	☐ G-BUDU	Cameron V-77
☐ G-BTRR	Thunder Ax7-77	☐ G-BTXT	Maule MXT-7-180	☐ G-BUDW	Brugger Colibri
☐ G-BTRS	Piper PA-28-161 Warrior	☐ G-BTXW	Cameron V-77	☐ G-BUEC	Van's RV-6
☐ G-BTRT	Piper PA-28R-200	☐ G-BTXX	Bellanca 8KCAB Decathlon	☐ G-BUED	Slingsby T.61F
☐ G-BTRU	Robin DR.400-180 Regent	☐ G-BTXZ	Zenair CH.250	☐ G-BUEF	Cessna 152
☐ G-BTRW	Slingsby T.61F	☐ G-BTYC	Cessna 150L	☐ G-BUEG	Cessna 152
☐ G-BTRX	Cameron V-77	☐ G-BTYE	Cameron A-180	☐ G-BUEI	Thunder Ax8-105
☐ G-BTRY	Piper PA-28-161 Warrior	☐ G-BTYF	Thunder Ax10-180	☐ G-BUEK	Slingsby T.61F
☐ G-BTRZ	Jodel D.18	☐ G-BTYH	Pottier P.80S	☐ G-BUEN	VPM M-14 Scout
☐ G-BTSB	Corben Baby Ace	☐ G-BTYI	Piper PA-28-181 Archer	☐ G-BUEP	Maule MXT-7-180
☐ G-BTSJ	Piper PA-28-161 Warrior	☐ G-BTYK	Cessna 310R	☐ G-BUEV	Cameron O-77
☐ G-BTSL	Cameron Beer SS	☐ G-BTYT	Cessna 152	☐ G-BUEW	Rans S6 Coyote II
☐ G-BTSM	Cessna 180A	☐ G-BTYW	Cessna 120	☐ G-BUEX	Schweizer 269C
☐ G-BTSN	Cessna 150G	☐ G-BTYY	Curtiss Robin C-2	☐ G-BUFA	Cameron R-77
☐ G-BTSP	Piper J-3C-65 Cub	☐ G-BTYZ	Colt 210A	☐ G-BUFC	Cameron R-77
☐ G-BTSR	Aeronca 11AC Chief	☐ G-BTZA	Beech 23A Bonanza	☐ G-BUFE	Cameron R-77
☐ G-BTSV	Denney Kitfox	☐ G-BTZB	Yakovlev Yak-50	☐ G-BUFG	Slingsby T.61F
☐ G-BTSW	Colt AS-105GD	☐ G-BTZD	Yakovlev Yak-1	☐ G-BUFH	Piper PA-28-161 Warrior
☐ G-BTSX	Thunder Ax7-77	☐ G-BTZE	Yakovlev Yak-11	☐ G-BUFJ	Cameron V-90
☐ G-BTSY	Lightning F.6	☐ G-BTZG	BAe ATP	☐ G-BUFN	Slingsby T.61F
☐ G-BTSZ	Cessna 177A Cardinal	☐ G-BTZH	BAe ATP	☐ G-BUFR	Slingsby T.61F
☐ G-BTTB	Cameron V-90	☐ G-BTZK	BAe ATP	☐ G-BUFT	Cameron O-120
☐ G-BTTD	Bensen B.8MR	☐ G-BTZL	Oldfield Baby Lakes	☐ G-BUFV	Avid Speed Wing
☐ G-BTTE	Cessna 150L	☐ G-BTZO	SOCATA TB-20 Trinidad	☐ G-BUFW	Aerospatiale AS.355F1
☐ G-BTTL	Cameron V-90	☐ G-BTZP	SOCATA TB-9 Tampico	☐ G-BUFY	Piper PA-28-161 Warrior
☐ G-BTTO	BAe ATP	☐ G-BTZS	Colt 77B	☐ G-BUGB	Stolp SA.750
☐ G-BTTR	Pitts S-2A Special	☐ G-BTZU	Cameron C-60	☐ G-BUGD	Cameron V-77
☐ G-BTTS	Colt 77A	☐ G-BTZV	Cameron V-77	☐ G-BUGE	Aeronca 7GCAA Sky-Trac
☐ G-BTTW	Thunder Ax7-77	☐ G-BTZX	Piper J-3C-65 Cub	☐ G-BUGG	Cessna 150F
☐ G-BTTY	Denney Kitfox	☐ G-BTZY	Colt 56A	☐ G-BUGJ	Robin DR.400-180 Regent
☐ G-BTTZ	Slingsby T.61F	☐ G-BTZZ	CFM Shadow SA	☐ G-BUGL	Slingsby T.61F
☐ G-BTUA	Slingsby T.61F	☐ G-BUAA	Corben Baby Ace	☐ G-BUGM	CFM Shadow SA
☐ G-BTUB	Yakovlev Yak-11	☐ G-BUAB	Aeronca 11AC Chief	☐ G-BUGO	Colt 56B
☐ G-BTUG	MS.893E Rallye 180GT	☐ G-BUAC	Slingsby Motor Cadet	☐ G-BUGP	Cameron V-77
☐ G-BTUH	Cameron N-65	☐ G-BUAF	Cameron N-77	☐ G-BUGS	Cameron V-77
☐ G-BTUJ	Thunder Ax9-120	☐ G-BUAG	Jodel D.18	☐ G-BUGT	Slingsby T.61F
☐ G-BTUK	Pitts S-2A Special	☐ G-BUAI	Everett Gyroplane	☐ G-BUGV	Slingsby T.61F
☐ G-BTUL	Pitts S-2A Special	☐ G-BUAJ	Cameron N-90	☐ G-BUGW	Slingsby T.61F
☐ G-BTUM	Piper J-3C-65 Cub	☐ G-BUAM	Cameron V-77	☐ G-BUGY	Cameron V-65
☐ G-BTUR	Piper PA-18-95	☐ G-BUAO	Luscombe 8A Silvaire	☐ G-BUGZ	Slingsby T.61F
☐ G-BTUS	Whittaker MW-7	☐ G-BUAT	Thunder Ax9-120	☐ G-BUHA	Slingsby T.61F
☐ G-BTUU	Cameron O-120	☐ G-BUAV	Cameron O-105	☐ G-BUHM	Cameron V-77
☐ G-BTUV	Aeronca 65TAC	☐ G-BUAX	Rans S-10 Sakota	☐ G-BUHO	Cessna 140
☐ G-BTUW	Piper PA-28-151 Warrior	☐ G-BUBJ	BN-2B-20 Islander	☐ G-BUHR	Slingsby T.61F
☐ G-BTUZ	American General AG-5B	☐ G-BUBN	BN-2B-26 Islander	☐ G-BUHS	Glasair I TD
☐ G-BTVA	Thunder Ax7-77	☐ G-BUBS	Lindstrand LBL-77B	☐ G-BUHZ	Cessna 120
☐ G-BTVB	Everett Gyroplane	☐ G-BUBT	Glasair IISRG	☐ G-BUIE	Cameron N-90
☐ G-BTVC	Denney Kitfox	☐ G-BUBU	Piper PA-34-220T Seneca	☐ G-BUIF	Piper PA-28-161 Warrior
☐ G-BTVE	Hawker Demon	☐ G-BUBW	Robinson R22B	☐ G-BUIG	Campbell Cricket
☐ G-BTVV	Reims F337G	☐ G-BUBY	Thunder Ax8-105	☐ G-BUIH	Slingsby T.61F
☐ G-BTVW	Cessna 152	☐ G-BUCA	Cessna A150K Aerobat	☐ G-BUIJ	Piper PA-28-161 Warrior
☐ G-BTVX	Cessna 152	☐ G-BUCB	Cameron H-34	☐ G-BUIK	Piper PA-28-161 Warrior
☐ G-BTWB	Denney Kitfox	☐ G-BUCC	CASA I-131E	☐ G-BUIL	CFM Shadow SA
☐ G-BTWC	Slingsby T.61F	☐ G-BUCG	Schleicher ASW 20	☐ G-BUIN	Thunder Ax7-77
☐ G-BTWD	Slingsby T.61F	☐ G-BUCH	Stinson V-77	☐ G-BUIP	Denney Kitfox
☐ G-BTWE	Slingsby T.61F	☐ G-BUCK	CASA I-131E	☐ G-BUIR	Avid Speed Wing

G-BUIU	Cameron V-90
G-BUIZ	Cameron N-90
G-BUJA	Slingsby T.61F
G-BUJB	Slingsby T.61F
G-BUJE	Cessna 177B Cardinal
G-BUJH	Colt 77B
G-BUJI	Slingsby T.61F
G-BUJJ	Avid Speed Wing
G-BUJK	Montgomerie B.8MR
G-BUJL	Aero Designs Pulsar
G-BUJM	Cessna 120
G-BUJN	Cessna 172N Skyhawk
G-BUJO	Piper PA-28-161 Warrior
G-BUJP	Piper PA-28-161 Warrior
G-BUJR	Cameron A-180
G-BUJV	Avid Speed Wing
G-BUJW	Thunder Ax8-90
G-BUJX	Slingsby T.61F
G-BUJZ	Rotorway Exec 90
G-BUKB	Rans S10 Sakota
G-BUKF	Denney Kitfox
G-BUKH	Druine Turbulent
G-BUKI	Thunder Ax7-77
G-BUKJ	BAe ATP
G-BUKK	Bucker Bu.133D
G-BUKN	Piper PA-15 Vagabond
G-BUKO	Cessna 120
G-BUKP	Denney Kitfox
G-BUKR	MS.880B Rallye
G-BUKS	Colt 77B
G-BUKT	Luscombe 8E Silvaire
G-BUKU	Luscombe 8E Silvaire
G-BUKX	Piper PA-28-161 Warrior
G-BUKZ	Evans VP-2
G-BULB	Thunder Ax7-77
G-BULC	Avid Flyer
G-BULD	Cameron N-105
G-BULF	Colt 77A
G-BULG	Van's RV-4
G-BULH	Cessna 172N Skyhawk
G-BULJ	CFM Shadow SA
G-BULK	Thunder Ax9-120
G-BULL	Scottish Aviation Bulldog
G-BULM	Aero Designs Pulsar XP
G-BULN	Colt 210A
G-BULO	Luscombe 8A Silvaire
G-BULR	Piper PA-28-140 Cherokee
G-BULT	Campbell Cricket
G-BULY	Avid Flyer
G-BULZ	Denney Kitfox
G-BUMP	Piper PA-28-181 Archer
G-BUNB	Slingsby T.61F
G-BUNC	PZL Wilga 35A
G-BUND	Piper PA-28-201T
G-BUNG	Cameron N-77
G-BUNH	Piper PA-28-201T
G-BUNJ	Cavalier SA.102
G-BUNM	Denney Kitfox
G-BUNO	Neico Lancair 320
G-BUNV	Thunder Ax7-77
G-BUNZ	Thunder Ax10-180
G-BUOA	Whittaker MW-6S
G-BUOB	CFM Shadow SA
G-BUOD	Replica Plans SE5A
G-BUOE	Cameron V-90
G-BUOF	Druine Condor
G-BUOI	Piper PA-20-125 Pacer
G-BUOJ	Cessna 172N Skyhawk
G-BUOK	Rans S6 Coyote II
G-BUOL	Denney Kitfox
G-BUON	Avid Aerobat
G-BUOR	CASA I-131E
G-BUOS	Spitfire FR.XVIIIe
G-BUOW	Aero Designs Pulsar XP
G-BUOX	Cameron V-77
G-BUOZ	Thunder Ax10-180
G-BUPA	Rutan LongEz
G-BUPB	Stolp SA.300
G-BUPC	Rollason Beta B2
G-BUPF	Bensen B.8R
G-BUPG	Cessna 180K Skywagon
G-BUPH	Colt 25A
G-BUPI	Cameron V-77
G-BUPJ	Fournier RF4D
G-BUPK	Aerospatiale AS350B
G-BUPM	VPM M16 Tandem
G-BUPP	Cameron V-42
G-BUPR	Jodel D.18
G-BUPU	Thunder Ax7-77
G-BUPV	Great Lakes 2T-1A
G-BUPW	Denney Kitfox
G-BURD	Reims F172N
G-BURE	Jodel D.9 Bebe
G-BURG	Colt 77A
G-BURH	Cessna 150E
G-BURI	Enstrom F-28C
G-BURL	Colt 105A
G-BURN	Cameron O-120
G-BURP	Rotorway Exec 90
G-BURS	Sikorsky S-76A
G-BURT	Piper PA-28-161 Warrior
G-BURU	BAe Jetstream 31
G-BURX	Cameron N-105
G-BURZ	Hawker Nimrod II
G-BUSB	Airbus A320-111
G-BUSC	Airbus A320-111
G-BUSE	Airbus A320-111
G-BUSF	Airbus A320-111
G-BUSG	Airbus A320-211
G-BUSH	Airbus A320-211
G-BUSI	Airbus A320-211
G-BUSJ	Airbus A320-211
G-BUSK	Airbus A320-211
G-BUSR	Aero Designs Pulsar
G-BUSS	Cameron Bus SS
G-BUSV	Colt 105A
G-BUSW	Rockwell 114
G-BUSY	Thunder Ax6-56A
G-BUTB	CFM Shadow SA-I
G-BUTD	Van's RV-6
G-BUTE	Anderson Kingfisher
G-BUTF	Aeronca 11AC Chief
G-BUTG	Zenair CH.601HD
G-BUTH	Robin DR.220 2+2
G-BUTJ	Cameron O-77
G-BUTK	Murphy Renegade
G-BUTM	Rans S6 Coyote II (T)
G-BUTW	BAe Jetstream 31
G-BUTX	Bucker Bu.133C
G-BUTY	Brugger Colibri
G-BUTZ	Piper PA-28-180 Cherokee
G-BUUA	Slingsby T.67M
G-BUUB	Slingsby T.67M
G-BUUC	Slingsby T.67M
G-BUUD	Slingsby T.67M
G-BUUE	Slingsby T.67M
G-BUUF	Slingsby T.67M
G-BUUI	Slingsby T.67M
G-BUUJ	Slingsby T.67M
G-BUUK	Slingsby T.67M
G-BUUL	Slingsby T.67M
G-BUUM	Piper PA-28RT-201
G-BUUO	Cameron N-90
G-BUUP	BAe ATP
G-BUUR	BAe ATP
G-BUUT	Interavia 70TA
G-BUUX	Piper PA-28-180 Cherokee
G-BUUZ	BAe Jetstream 31
G-BUVA	Piper PA-22-135 Tri-Pacer
G-BUVC	BAe Jetstream 31
G-BUVD	BAe Jetstream 31
G-BUVE	Colt 77B
G-BUVL	Fisher Super Koala
G-BUVM	Robin DR.250-160
G-BUVN	CASA I-131E
G-BUVO	Reims F182P Skylane
G-BUVR	Aviat A-1 Husky
G-BUVS	Colt 77A
G-BUVT	Colt 77A
G-BUVW	Cameron N-90
G-BUVX	CFM Shadow SA
G-BUVZ	Thunder Ax10-180
G-BUWE	Replica Plans SE5A
G-BUWF	Cameron N-105
G-BUWH	Parsons Gyroplane
G-BUWI	Lindstrand LBL-77A
G-BUWJ	Pitts S-1C
G-BUWK	Rans S6 Coyote II (N)
G-BUWL	Piper J-4A Cub Coupe
G-BUWM	BAe ATP
G-BUWR	CFM Shadow SA-I
G-BUWS	Denney Kitfox
G-BUWT	Rand KR-2
G-BUWU	Cameron V-77
G-BUXC	CFM Shadow SA
G-BUXD	Maule MXT-7-160
G-BUXI	Steen Skybolt
G-BUXJ	Slingsby T.61F
G-BUXK	Pietenpol Aircamper
G-BUXL	Taylor Monoplane
G-BUXN	Beech C23 Sundowner
G-BUXO	Pober P-9 Pixie
G-BUXR	Cameron A-250
G-BUXS	MBB Bo.105DBS/4
G-BUXV	Piper PA-22-160 Tri-Pacer
G-BUXW	Thunder Ax8-90
G-BUXX	Piper PA-17 Vagabond
G-BUXY	Piper PA-25-235 Pawnee
G-BUYB	Aero Designs Pulsar
G-BUYC	Cameron C-80
G-BUYD	Thunder Ax8-90
G-BUYF	Falcon XP
G-BUYJ	Lindstrand LBL-105A
G-BUYK	Denney Kitfox
G-BUYL	RAF 2000
G-BUYO	Colt 77A
G-BUYR	Mooney M.20C
G-BUYS	Robin DR.400-180 Regent
G-BUYU	Bowers Fly Baby
G-BUYY	Piper PA-28-180 Cherokee
G-BUZA	Denney Kitfox
G-BUZB	Aero Designs Pulsar XP
G-BUZC	Everett Gyroplane
G-BUZD	Aerospatiale AS.332L
G-BUZE	Avid Speed Wing
G-BUZF	Colt 77B
G-BUZG	Zenair CH.601HD
G-BUZH	Starlite SL-1
G-BUZJ	Lindstrand LBL-105A
G-BUZK	Cameron V-77
G-BUZL	VPM M16 Tandem
G-BUZM	Avid Flyer
G-BUZN	Cessna 172H Skyhawk
G-BUZO	Pietenpol Aircamper
G-BUZR	Lindstrand LBL-77A
G-BUZS	Colt Pig SS
G-BUZT	Kolb Twinstar Mk.3
G-BUZV	Ken Brock KB.2
G-BUZZ	Agusta Bell 206B

Reg	Type	Reg	Type	Reg	Type
G-BVAB	Zenair CH.601HDS	G-BVGH	Hawker Hunter T.7	G-BVLZ	Lindstrand LBL-120A
G-BVAC	Zenair CH.601HD	G-BVGI	Pereira Osprey 2	G-BVMA	Beech 200 Super King Air
G-BVAF	Piper J-3C-65 Cub	G-BVGJ	Cameron C-80	G-BVMC	Robinson R44
G-BVAG	Lindstrand LBL-90A	G-BVGK	Lindstrand Newspaper SS	G-BVMF	Cameron V-77
G-BVAH	Denney Kitfox	G-BVGO	Denney Kitfox	G-BVMH	Wag-Aero CUBy
G-BVAI	PZL Koliber 150	G-BVGP	Bucker Bu.133C	G-BVMI	Piper PA-18-150
G-BVAM	Evans VP-1	G-BVGS	Robinson R22B	G-BVNY	Cameron Eagle SS
G-BVAO	Colt 25A	G-BVGT	Auster J/1 Mod	G-BVML	Lindstrand LBL-210A
G-BVAW	Staaken Flitzer	G-BVGW	Luscombe 8A Silvaire	G-BVMM	Robin HR.200-100
G-BVAX	Colt 77A	G-BVGY	Luscombe 8E Silvaire	G-BVMN	Ken Brock KB.2
G-BVAY	Rutan VariEze	G-BVGZ	Fokker Triplane Rep	G-BVMP	BAe 146-200
G-BVAZ	Bensen B.8	G-BVHC	Grob 115D2	G-BVMR	Cameron V-90
G-BVBP	Avro Lancaster	G-BVHD	Grob 115D2	G-BVMT	BAe 146-200
G-BVBR	Avid Speed Wing	G-BVHE	Grob 115D2	G-BVMU	Yakovlev Yak-52
G-BVBS	Cameron N-77	G-BVHF	Grob 115D2	G-BVNG	DH.60G Moth
G-BVBU	Cameron V-77	G-BVHG	Grob 115D2	G-BVNI	Taylor Titch
G-BVBV	Avid Speed Wing	G-BVHI	Rans S10 Sakota	G-BVNR	Cameron N-105
G-BVCA	Cameron N-105	G-BVHK	Cameron V-77	G-BVNS	Piper PA-28-181 Archer
G-BVCC	Monnett Sonerai	G-BVHL	Nicollier HN700 Menestrel	G-BVNU	FLS Sprint
G-BVCG	Van's RV-6	G-BVHM	Piper PA-38-112 Tomahawk	G-BVNY	Rans S7 Courier
G-BVCL	Rans S6 Coyote II (N)	G-BVHO	Cameron V-90	G-BVOA	Piper PA-28-181 Archer
G-BVCM	Cessna 525 CitationJet	G-BVHP	Colt 42A	G-BVOB	Fokker F.27-500
G-BVCO	Clutton FRED II	G-BVHR	Cameron V-90	G-BVOC	Cameron V-90
G-BVCP	Piper Metisse	G-BVHS	Murphy Rebel	G-BVOH	Campbell Cricket
G-BVCS	Aeronca 7AC Champion	G-BVHT	Avid Speed Wing	G-BVOI	Rans S6 Coyote II
G-BVCT	Denney Kitfox	G-BVHV	Cameron N-105	G-BVOK	Yakovlev Yak-52
G-BVCX	Sikorsky S-76A	G-BVIA	Rand KR-2	G-BVON	Lindstrand LBL-105A
G-BVCY	Cameron H-24	G-BVIE	Piper PA-18-95	G-BVOO	Lindstrand LBL-105A
G-BVDB	Thunder Ax7-77	G-BVIF	Bensen B.8MR	G-BVOP	Cameron N-90
G-BVDC	Van's RV-3	G-BVIK	Maule MXT-7-180	G-BVOR	CFM Shadow SA
G-BVDD	Colt 69A	G-BVIL	Maule MXT-7-180	G-BVOS	Europa
G-BVDH	Piper PA-28RT-201	G-BVIN	Rans S6 Coyote II (N)	G-BVOU	HS.748-2A
G-BVDI	Van's RV-4	G-BVIR	Lindstrand LBL-69A	G-BVOV	HS.748-2A
G-BVDJ	Campbell Cricket	G-BVIS	Brugger Colibri	G-BVOW	Europa
G-BVDM	Cameron C-60	G-BVIT	Campbell Cricket	G-BVOX	Taylorcraft F-22
G-BVDO	Lindstrand LBL-105A	G-BVIV	Avid Aerobat	G-BVOY	Rotorway Exec 90
G-BVDP	Sequoia F.8L Falco	G-BVIW	Piper PA-18-150	G-BVOZ	Colt 56A
G-BVDR	Cameron O-77	G-BVIX	Lindstrand LBL-180A	G-BVPA	Thunder Ax8-105
G-BVDS	Lindstrand LBL-69A	G-BVIZ	Europa	G-BVPD	CASA I-131E
G-BVDT	CFM Shadow SA-I	G-BVJE	Aerospatiale AS.350B1	G-BVPK	Cameron O-90
G-BVDW	Thunder Ax8-90	G-BVJF	Bensen B.8MR	G-BVPL	Zenair CH.601HD
G-BVDX	Cameron V-90	G-BVJG	Cyclone AX3	G-BVPM	Evans VP-2
G-BVDY	Cameron C-60	G-BVJK	Glaser-Dirks DG-800A	G-BVPN	Piper J-3C-65 Cub
G-BVDZ	Taylorcraft BC12D	G-BVJN	Europa	G-BVPP	Folland Gnat T1
G-BVEA	Nostalgair N.3 Pup	G-BVJT	Reims F406	G-BVPR	Robinson R22B
G-BVEH	Jodel D.112	G-BVJU	Evans VP-1	G-BVPS	Jodel D.112
G-BVEK	Cameron C-80	G-BVJX	Marquart Charger	G-BVPV	Lindstrand LBL-77B
G-BVEL	Evans VP-1	G-BVJZ	Piper PA-28-161 Warrior	G-BVPW	Rans S6 Coyote II (N)
G-BVEN	Cameron C-80	G-BVKB	Boeing 737-59D	G-BVPX	Bensen B.8
G-BVEP	Luscombe 8A Silvaire	G-BVKD	Boeing 737-59D	G-BVPY	CFM Shadow SA
G-BVER	DHC-2 Beaver	G-BVKF	Europa	G-BVRA	Europa
G-BVES	Cessna 340A	G-BVKH	Thunder Ax8-90	G-BVRH	Taylorcraft BL-65
G-BVEU	Cameron O-105	G-BVKK	Slingsby T.61F	G-BVRI	Thunder Ax6-56
G-BVEV	Piper PA-34-200 Seneca	G-BVKL	Cameron A-180	G-BVRK	Rans S6 Coyote II
G-BVEW	Lindstrand LBL-150A	G-BVKM	Rutan VariEze	G-BVRL	Lindstrand LBL-21A
G-BVEY	Denney Kitfox	G-BVKR	Sikorsky S-76A+	G-BVRR	Lindstrand LBL-77A
G-BVEZ	Jet Provost T.3A	G-BVKU	Slingsby T.61F	G-BVRU	Lindstrand LBL-105A
G-BVFA	Rans S10 Sakota	G-BVKX	Colt 14A	G-BVRV	Van's RV-4
G-BVFB	Cameron N-31	G-BVKZ	Thunder Ax9-120	G-BVRZ	Piper PA-18-95
G-BVFF	Cameron V-77	G-BVLD	Campbell Cricket	G-BVSB	TEAM Minimax
G-BVFM	Rans S6 Coyote II (N)	G-BVLE	McCandless M.4	G-BVSD	Aerospatiale Alouette II
G-BVFO	Avid Speed Wing	G-BVLF	CFM Shadow SS-D	G-BVSF	Aero Designs Pulsar
G-BVFP	Cameron V-90	G-BVLG	Aerospatiale AS.355F1	G-BVSM	RAF 2000
G-BVFR	CFM Shadow SA	G-BVLI	Cameron V-77	G-BVSN	Avid Speed Wing
G-BVFT	Maule M-5-235C	G-BVLL	Lindstrand LBL-210A	G-BVSO	Cameron A-120
G-BVFU	Cameron Sphere	G-BVLN	Aero Designs Pulsar XP	G-BVSP	Jet Provost T.3A
G-BVFY	Colt 240A	G-BVLP	Piper PA-38-112 Tomahawk	G-BVSS	Jodel D.150 Mascaret
G-BVFZ	Maule M-5-180C	G-BVLR	Van's RV-4	G-BVST	Jodel D.150 Mascaret
G-BVGA	Bell 206B Jet Ranger	G-BVLT	Aeronca 7GCBC Citabria	G-BVSX	TEAM Minimax
G-BVGB	Thunder Ax8-105	G-BVLU	Druine Turbulent	G-BVSZ	Pitts S-1E Special
G-BVGE	Westland Whirlwind	G-BVLV	Europa	G-BVTA	Tri-R-Kis
G-BVGF	Europa	G-BVLW	Avid Hauler	G-BVTC	Jet Provost T.5A
G-BVGG	Lindstrand LBL-69A	G-BVLX	Slingsby T.61F	G-BVTD	CFM Shadow SA

☐	G-BVTL	Colt 31A	☐	G-BVZX	Cameron H-34	☐ G-BWFR	Hawker Hunter F.58
☐	G-BVTM	Reims F152	☐	G-BVZZ	DHC-1 Chipmunk	☐ G-BWFT	Hawker Hunter T.8M
☐	G-BVTN	Cameron N-90	☐	G-BWAA	Cameron N-133	☐ G-BWFV	Diamond Katana
☐	G-BVTO	Piper PA-28-151 Warrior	☐	G-BWAB	Jodel D.14	☐ G-BWFX	Europa
☐	G-BVTV	Rotorway Exec 90	☐	G-BWAC	Waco YKS-7	☐ G-BWFZ	Murphy Rebel
☐	G-BVTW	Aero Designs Pulsar	☐	G-BWAD	RAF 2000	☐ G-BWGA	Lindstrand LBL-105A
☐	G-BVTX	DHC-1 Chipmunk	☐	G-BWAF	Hawker Hunter F.6A	☐ G-BWGF	Jet Provost T.5A
☐	G-BVUA	Cameron O-105	☐	G-BWAG	Cameron O-120	☐ G-BWGG	Max Holste 1521C1
☐	G-BVUC	Colt 56A	☐	G-BWAH	Bensen B.8MR	☐ G-BWGJ	Chilton DW1A Rep
☐	G-BVUG	Betts TB.1	☐	G-BWAI	CFM Shadow SA	☐ G-BWGK	Hawker Hunter GA.11
☐	G-BVUH	Thunder Ax6-65B	☐	G-BWAJ	Cameron V-77	☐ G-BWGL	Hawker Hunter T.8C
☐	G-BVUI	Lindstrand LBL-25A	☐	G-BWAN	Cameron N-77	☐ G-BWGM	Hawker Hunter T.8C
☐	G-BVUJ	Ken Brock KB.2	☐	G-BWAO	Cameron C-80	☐ G-BWGN	Hawker Hunter T.8C
☐	G-BVUK	Cameron V-77	☐	G-BWAP	Clutton FRED III	☐ G-BWGO	Slingsby T.67
☐	G-BVUM	Rans S6 Coyote II	☐	G-BWAR	Denney Kitfox	☐ G-BWGP	Cameron C-80
☐	G-BVUN	Van's RV-4	☐	G-BWAT	Pietenpol Aircamper	☐ G-BWGS	Jet Provost T.5A
☐	G-BVUT	Evans VP-2	☐	G-BWAU	Cameron V-90	☐ G-BWGT	Jet Provost T.4
☐	G-BVUU	Cameron C-80	☐	G-BWAV	Schweizer 269C	☐ G-BWGY	Diamond Katana
☐	G-BVUV	Europa	☐	G-BWAW	Lindstrand LBL-77A	☐ G-BWHC	Cameron N-77
☐	G-BVUZ	Cessna 140	☐	G-BWBA	Cameron V-65	☐ G-BWHD	Lindstrand LBL-31A
☐	G-BVVA	Yakovlev Yak-52	☐	G-BWBB	Lindstrand LBL-14A	☐ G-BWHF	Piper PA-31-325 Navajo
☐	G-BVVB	Carlson Sparrow II	☐	G-BWBE	Colt Ice Cream SS	☐ G-BWHG	Cameron N-65
☐	G-BVVE	Jodel D.112	☐	G-BWBF	Colt Ice Cream SS	☐ G-BWHI	DHC-1 Chipmunk
☐	G-BVVG	Nanchang CJ-6A	☐	G-BWBI	Taylorcraft F-22A	☐ G-BWHK	Rans S6 Coyote II (N)
☐	G-BVVH	Europa	☐	G-BWBJ	Colt 21A	☐ G-BWHP	CASA I-131E
☐	G-BVVI	Hawker Audax I	☐	G-BWBO	Lindstrand LBL-77A	☐ G-BWHR	Tipsy Nipper
☐	G-BVVK	DHC-6-300	☐	G-BWBT	Lindstrand LBL-77A	☐ G-BWHS	RAF 2000
☐	G-BVVL	EAA Acrosport 2	☐	G-BWBY	Schleicher ASH 26E	☐ G-BWHU	Westland Scout
☐	G-BVVM	Zenair CH.601HD	☐	G-BWBZ	ARV Super 2	☐ G-BWHV	Denney Kitfox
☐	G-BVVN	Brugger Colibri	☐	G-BWCA	CFM Shadow SA	☐ G-BWHY	Robinson R22
☐	G-BVVP	Europa	☐	G-BWCC	Van Den Bemden	☐ G-BWIA	Rans S10 Sakota
☐	G-BVVR	Stitts SA-3A Playboy	☐	G-BWCG	Lindstrand LBL-42A	☐ G-BWIB	Scottish Aviation Bulldog
☐	G-BVVS	Van's RV-4	☐	G-BWCK	Everett Gyroplane	☐ G-BWID	Druine Turbulent
☐	G-BVVU	Lindstrand Four SS	☐	G-BWCO	Dornier Do.28D2	☐ G-BWII	Cessna 150G
☐	G-BVVW	Yakovlev Yak-52	☐	G-BWCS	Jet Provost T.5	☐ G-BWIJ	Europa
☐	G-BVVZ	Corby CJ-1 Starlet	☐	G-BWCT	Tipsy Nipper	☐ G-BWIK	DH.82A Tiger Moth
☐	G-BVWB	Thunder Ax8-90	☐	G-BWCV	Europa	☐ G-BWIL	Rans S10 Sakota
☐	G-BVWC	Canberra B.2	☐	G-BWCY	Murphy Rebel	☐ G-BWIP	Cameron N-90
☐	G-BVWI	Cameron Light Bulb SS	☐	G-BWDA	ATR 72-202	☐ G-BWIR	Dornier Do.328-110
☐	G-BVWM	Europa	☐	G-BWDB	ATR 72-202	☐ G-BWIV	Europa
☐	G-BVWW	Lindstrand LBL-90A	☐	G-BWDF	PZL Wilga 35A	☐ G-BWIW	Sky 180-24
☐	G-BVWY	Porterfield CP.65	☐	G-BWDH	Cameron N-105	☐ G-BWIX	Sky 120-24
☐	G-BVWZ	Piper PA-32-301	☐	G-BWDM	Lindstrand LBL-120A	☐ G-BWIZ	Quickie Tri-Q-200
☐	G-BVXA	Cameron N-105	☐	G-BWDO	Sikorsky S-76B	☐ G-BWJG	Mooney M.20J
☐	G-BVXB	Cameron V-77	☐	G-BWDP	Europa	☐ G-BWJH	Europa
☐	G-BVXE	Steen Skybolt	☐	G-BWDR	Jet Provost T.3A	☐ G-BWJI	Cameron V-90
☐	G-BVXF	Cameron O-120	☐	G-BWDS	Jet Provost T.3	☐ G-BWJM	Bristol M.1C Rep
☐	G-BVXJ	Bucker Bu.133	☐	G-BWDT	Piper PA-34-220T Seneca	☐ G-BWJN	Bensen B.8
☐	G-BVXK	Yakovlev Yak-52	☐	G-BWDU	Cameron V-90	☐ G-BWJR	Sky 120-24
☐	G-BVXM	Aerospatiale AS.350B	☐	G-BWDV	Schweizer 269C	☐ G-BWJW	Westland Scout
☐	G-BVXR	DH.104 Devon C.2	☐	G-BWDX	Europa	☐ G-BWJY	DHC-1 Chipmunk
☐	G-BVXS	Taylorcraft BC12D	☐	G-BWDZ	Sky 105-24	☐ G-BWKD	Cameron O-120
☐	G-BVYF	Piper PA-31-350 Chieftain	☐	G-BWEA	Lindstrand LBL-120A	☐ G-BWKE	Cameron AS-105GD
☐	G-BVYG	Robin DR.300-120	☐	G-BWEB	Jet Provost T.5A	☐ G-BWKF	Cameron N-105
☐	G-BVYK	TEAM Minimax	☐	G-BWEE	Cameron V-42	☐ G-BWKG	Europa
☐	G-BVYM	Robin DR.300-180	☐	G-BWEF	Stampe SV-4C	☐ G-BWKJ	Rans S7 Courier
☐	G-BVYO	Robin R.2160	☐	G-BWEG	Europa	☐ G-BWKK	Auster AOP.9
☐	G-BVYP	Piper PA-25-235 Pawnee	☐	G-BWEM	Seafire L.III	☐ G-BWKR	Sky 90-24
☐	G-BVYU	Cameron A-140	☐	G-BWEN	Macair Merlin GT	☐ G-BWKT	Akro Laser
☐	G-BVYX	Avid Speed Wing	☐	G-BWEU	Reims F152	☐ G-BWKU	Cameron A-250
☐	G-BVYY	Pietenpol Aircamper	☐	G-BWEV	Cessna 152	☐ G-BWKV	Cameron V-77
☐	G-BVYZ	Stemme S-10V	☐	G-BWEW	Cameron N-105	☐ G-BWKW	Thunder Ax8-90
☐	G-BVZD	Tri-Kis	☐	G-BWEY	Bensen B.8M	☐ G-BWKX	Cameron A-250
☐	G-BVZE	Boeing 737-59D	☐	G-BWEZ	Piper J-3C-85 Cub	☐ G-BWKZ	Lindstrand LBL-77A
☐	G-BVZG	Boeing 737-5Q8	☐	G-BWFG	Robin HR.200-120	☐ G-BWLA	Lindstrand LBL-69A
☐	G-BVZH	Boeing 737-5Q8	☐	G-BWFH	Europa	☐ G-BWLD	Cameron O-120
☐	G-BVZI	Boeing 737-5Q8	☐	G-BWFI	Diamond Katana	☐ G-BWLF	Cessna 404
☐	G-BVZJ	Rand KR-2	☐	G-BWFJ	Evans VP-1	☐ G-BWLJ	Taylorcraft DCO-65
☐	G-BVZN	Cameron C-80	☐	G-BWFK	Lindstrand LBL-77A	☐ G-BWLL	Murphy Rebel
☐	G-BVZO	Rans S6 Coyote II (N)	☐	G-BWFM	Yakovlev Yak-50	☐ G-BWLN	Cameron O-84
☐	G-BVZR	Zenair CH.601HD	☐	G-BWFN	Hapi Cygnet SF-2A	☐ G-BWLP	Diamond Katana
☐	G-BVZT	Lindstrand LBL-90A	☐	G-BWFO	Colomban MC-15 Cri-Cri	☐ G-BWLR	Max Holste 1521C1
☐	G-BVZV	Rans S6 Coyote II (N)	☐	G-BWFP	Yakovlev Yak-52	☐ G-BWLS	Diamond Katana

G-BWLY	Rotorway Exec 90
G-BWLZ	Wombat
G-BWMA	Colt 105A
G-BWMB	Jodel D.119
G-BWMC	Cessna 182P Skylane
G-BWMF	Gloster Meteor T.7
G-BWMH	Lindstrand LBL-77B
G-BWMI	Piper PA-28R-201T
G-BWMJ	Nieuport Scout Rep
G-BWMK	DH.82A Tiger Moth
G-BWML	Cameron A-275
G-BWMN	Rans S7 Courier
G-BWMO	Oldfield Baby Lakes
G-BWMS	DH.82A Tiger Moth
G-BWMU	Cameron 105SS
G-BWMV	Colt AS-105
G-BWMX	DHC-1 Chipmunk
G-BWMY	Cameron B+B SS
G-BWNB	Cessna 152
G-BWNC	Cessna 152
G-BWND	Cessna 152
G-BWNI	Piper PA-24-180 Comanche
G-BWNJ	Hughes 269C
G-BWNK	DHC-1 Chipmunk
G-BWNM	Piper PA-28R-180
G-BWNO	Cameron O-90
G-BWNP	Cameron 90SS
G-BWNS	Cameron O-90
G-BWNT	DHC-1 Chipmunk
G-BWNU	Piper PA-38-112 Tomahawk
G-BWNY	Aeromot AMT-200
G-BWNZ	Agusta 109C
G-BWOA	Sky 105-24
G-BWOB	Luscombe 8F Silvaire
G-BWOF	Jet Provost T.5
G-BWOH	Piper PA-28-161 Cadet
G-BWOI	Piper PA-28-161 Cadet
G-BWOJ	Piper PA-28-161 Cadet
G-BWON	Europa
G-BWOR	Piper PA-18-135
G-BWOT	Jet Provost T.3A
G-BWOU	Hawker Hunter F.58A
G-BWOV	Enstrom F-28A
G-BWOW	Cameron N-105
G-BWOX	DHC-1 Chipmunk
G-BWOY	Sky 31-24
G-BWOZ	CFM Shadow SA
G-BWPB	Cameron V-77
G-BWPC	Cameron V-77
G-BWPE	Renegade Spirit UK
G-BWPF	Sky 120-24
G-BWPH	Piper PA-28-181 Archer
G-BWPJ	Steen Skybolt
G-BWPP	Sky 105-24
G-BWPS	CFM Shadow SA
G-BWPT	Cameron N-90
G-BWPX	BN2T-4S Defender 4000
G-BWPZ	Cameron N-105
G-BWRA	Sopwith Triplane Rep
G-BWRC	Avid Speed Wing
G-BWRM	Colt 105A
G-BWRO	Europa
G-BWRR	Cessna 182Q Skylane
G-BWRS	Stampe SV-4C
G-BWRT	Cameron C-60
G-BWRY	Cameron N-105
G-BWRZ	Lindstrand LBL-105A
G-BWSB	Lindstrand LBL-105A
G-BWSC	Piper PA-38-112 Tomahawk
G-BWSD	Campbell Cricket
G-BWSG	Jet Provost T.5
G-BWSH	Jet Provost T.3A
G-BWSI	Cavalier SA.102
G-BWSJ	Denney Kitfox
G-BWSL	Sky 77-24
G-BWSN	Denney Kitfox
G-BWSO	Cameron Apple SS
G-BWSP	Cameron Carrot SS
G-BWST	Sky 200-24
G-BWSU	Cameron N-105
G-BWSV	Yakovlev Yak-52
G-BWSW	Yakovlev Yak-52
G-BWSZ	Bensen B.8MR
G-BWTB	Lindstrand LBL-105A
G-BWTC	Zlin Z.242L
G-BWTD	Zlin Z.242L
G-BWTE	Cameron O-140
G-BWTG	DHC-1 Chipmunk
G-BWTH	Robinson R22B
G-BWTJ	Cameron V-77
G-BWTK	RAF 2000 GTX-SE
G-BWTN	Lindstrand LBL-90A
G-BWTO	DHC-1 Chipmunk
G-BWTR	Slingsby T.61F
G-BWTW	Mooney M.20C
G-BWTZ	QAC Quickie Q200
G-BWUA	Campbell Cricket
G-BWUB	Piper PA-18-135S
G-BWUE	Hispano HA-1112
G-BWUH	Piper PA-28-181 Archer
G-BWUJ	Rotorway Exec
G-BWUK	Sky 160-24
G-BWUL	Noorduyn Harvard
G-BWUM	Sky 105-24
G-BWUN	DHC-1 Chipmunk
G-BWUP	Europa
G-BWUR	Thunder Ax10-210
G-BWUS	Sky 65-24
G-BWUT	DHC-1 Chipmunk
G-BWUU	Cameron N-90
G-BWUV	DHC-1 Chipmunk
G-BWUZ	Campbell Cricket
G-BWVB	Pietenpol Aircamper
G-BWVC	Jodel D.18
G-BWVH	Robinson R44
G-BWVI	Stern ST.80 Balade
G-BWVN	Whittaker MW-7
G-BWVP	Sky 160-24
G-BWVR	Yakovlev Yak-52
G-BWVS	Europa
G-BWVT	DH.82A Tiger Moth
G-BWVU	Cameron O-90
G-BWVV	Jodel D.18
G-BWVY	DHC-1 Chipmunk
G-BWVZ	DHC-1 Chipmunk
G-BWWA	Pelican Club GS
G-BWWB	Europa
G-BWWC	DH.104 7
G-BWWE	Lindstrand LBL-90A
G-BWWF	Cessna 185A Skywagon
G-BWWG	MS.893 Rallye 235E
G-BWWI	Aerospatiale AS.332L
G-BWWK	Hawker Nimrod I
G-BWWL	Colt Egg SS
G-BWWN	Isaacs Fury II
G-BWWP	Rans S6 Coyote II (T)
G-BWWT	Dornier Do.328-100
G-BWWU	Piper PA-22-150 Tri-Pacer
G-BWWW	BAe Jetstream 31
G-BWWX	Yakovlev Yak-50
G-BWWY	Lindstrand LBL-105A
G-BWWZ	Denney Kitfox
G-BWXA	Slingsby T.67M
G-BWXB	Slingsby T.67M
G-BWXC	Slingsby T.67M
G-BWXD	Slingsby T.67M
G-BWXE	Slingsby T.67M
G-BWXF	Slingsby T.67M
G-BWXG	Slingsby T.67M
G-BWXH	Slingsby T.67M
G-BWXI	Slingsby T.67M
G-BWXJ	Slingsby T.67M
G-BWXK	Slingsby T.67M
G-BWXL	Slingsby T.67M
G-BWXM	Slingsby T.67M
G-BWXN	Slingsby T.67M
G-BWXO	Slingsby T.67M
G-BWXP	Slingsby T.67M
G-BWXR	Slingsby T.67M
G-BWXS	Slingsby T.67M
G-BWXT	Slingsby T.67M
G-BWXU	Slingsby T.67M
G-BWXV	Slingsby T.67M
G-BWXW	Slingsby T.67M
G-BWXX	Slingsby T.67M
G-BWXY	Slingsby T.67M
G-BWXZ	Slingsby T.67M
G-BWYB	Piper PA-28-160 Cherokee
G-BWYD	Europa
G-BWYE	Cessna 310R
G-BWYG	Cessna 310R
G-BWYH	Cessna 310R
G-BWYI	Denney Kitfox
G-BWYK	Yakovlev Yak-50
G-BWYM	Diamond Katana
G-BWYN	Cameron O-77
G-BWYO	Sequoia F.8L Falco
G-BWYP	Sky 56-24
G-BWYR	Rans S6 Coyote II (T)
G-BWYS	Cameron O-120
G-BWYU	Sky 120-24
G-BWZA	Europa
G-BWZG	Robin R.2160
G-BWZJ	Cameron A-250
G-BWZK	Cameron A-210
G-BWZN	Beech F33A Bonanza
G-BWZU	Lindstrand LBL-90B
G-BWZX	Aerospatiale AS.332L
G-BWZY	Hughes 269A
G-BXAB	Piper PA-28-161 Warrior
G-BXAC	RAF 2000 GTX-SE
G-BXAD	Thunder Ax11-225
G-BXAF	Pitts S-1D Special
G-BXAH	Piel Emeraude
G-BXAJ	Lindstrand LBL-14A
G-BXAK	Yakovlev Yak-52
G-BXAL	Cameron 90SS
G-BXAM	Cameron N-90
G-BXAN	Scheibe SF25C Falke
G-BXAO	Jabiru SK
G-BXAR	BAe 146-RJ100
G-BXAS	BAe 146-RJ100
G-BXAU	Pitts S-1 Special
G-BXAV	Yakovlev Yak-52
G-BXAY	Bell 206B Jet Ranger
G-BXBA	Cameron A-210
G-BXBC	Kingfisher EA.1
G-BXBG	Cameron A-210
G-BXBK	Mudry CAP.10B
G-BXBL	Lindstrand LBL-240A
G-BXBM	Cameron O-105
G-BXBP	Denney Kitfox
G-BXBR	Cameron A-120
G-BXBU	Mudry CAP.10B
G-BXBY	Cameron A-105
G-BXBZ	PZL Wilga 80
G-BXCA	Hapi Cygnet SF-2A
G-BXCC	Piper PA-28-201T

Registration	Type	Registration	Type	Registration	Type
G-BXCD	TEAM Minimax	G-BXHJ	Hapi Cygnet SF-2A	G-BXNA	Avid Flyer
G-BXCG	Robin DR.250-160	G-BXHL	Sky 77-24	G-BXNC	Europa
G-BXCH	Europa	G-BXHN	Lindstrand Pop Can SS	G-BXNN	DHC-1 Chipmunk
G-BXCJ	Campbell Cricket	G-BXHO	Lindstrand Sphere SS	G-BXNS	Bell 206B Jet Ranger
G-BXCL	Bensen B.8MR	G-BXHR	Stemme S-10V	G-BXNT	Bell 206B Jet Ranger
G-BXCM	Lindstrand LBL-150A	G-BXHT	Bushby-Long Midget	G-BXNV	Cameron AS-105
G-BXCN	Sky 105-24	G-BXHU	Campbell Cricket	G-BXNX	Lindstrand LBL-210A
G-BXCO	Colt 120A	G-BXHY	Europa	G-BXOA	Robinson R22B
G-BXCP	DHC-1 Chipmunk	G-BXIA	DHC-1 Chipmunk	G-BXOC	Evans VP-2
G-BXCT	DHC-1 Chipmunk	G-BXIC	Cameron A-275	G-BXOF	Diamond Katana
G-BXCU	Rans S6 Coyote II (N)	G-BXID	Yakovlev Yak-52	G-BXOI	Cessna 172R Skyhawk
G-BXCV	DHC-1 Chipmunk	G-BXIE	Cameron Colt 77B	G-BXOJ	Piper PA-28-161 Warrior
G-BXCW	Denney Kifox	G-BXIF	Piper PA-28-181 Archer	G-BXOM	Isaacs Spitfire
G-BXDA	DHC-1 Chipmunk	G-BXIG	Zenair CH.701	G-BXON	Auster AOP.9
G-BXDB	Cessna U206F	G-BXIH	Sky 200-24	G-BXOR	Robin HR.200-120
G-BXDD	RAF 2000 GTX-SE	G-BXII	Europa	G-BXOS	Cameron A-200
G-BXDE	RAF 2000 GTX-SE	G-BXIJ	Europa	G-BXOT	Cameron C-70
G-BXDF	Beech 95-B55 Baron	G-BXIM	DHC-1 Chipmunk	G-BXOU	Robin DR.360
G-BXDG	DHC-1 Chipmunk	G-BXIO	Jodel DR.1050M	G-BXOW	Colt 105A
G-BXDH	DHC-1 Chipmunk	G-BXIT	Zebedee V-31	G-BXOX	Grumman AA-5A Cheetah
G-BXDI	DHC-1 Chipmunk	G-BXIW	Sky 105-24	G-BXOY	QAC Quickie Q200
G-BXDM	DHC-1 Chipmunk	G-BXIX	VPM M16 Tandem	G-BXOZ	Piper PA-28-181 Archer
G-BXDN	DHC-1 Chipmunk	G-BXIY	Blake Bluetit	G-BXPC	Diamond Katana
G-BXDO	Rutan Cozy	G-BXIZ	Lindstrand LBL-31A	G-BXPD	Diamond Katana
G-BXDP	DHC-1 Chipmunk	G-BXJA	Cessna 402B	G-BXPE	Diamond Katana
G-BXDR	Lindstrand LBL-77A	G-BXJB	Yakovlev Yak-52	G-BXPI	Van's RV-4
G-BXDT	Robin HR.200-120	G-BXJC	Cameron A-210	G-BXPK	Cameron A-250
G-BXDU	Aero Designs Pulsar	G-BXJD	Piper PA-28-180 Cherokee	G-BXPL	Piper PA-28-140 Cherokee
G-BXDV	Sky 105-24	G-BXJG	Lindstrand LBL-105B	G-BXPM	Beech 58 Baron
G-BXDY	Europa	G-BXJH	Cameron N-42	G-BXPP	Sky 90-24
G-BXDZ	Lindstrand LBL-105A	G-BXJJ	Piper PA-28-161 Cadet	G-BXPR	Cameron Can SS
G-BXEA	RAF 2000 GTX-SE	G-BXJM	Cessna 152	G-BXPT	UltraMagic H-77
G-BXEB	RAF 2000 GTX-SE	G-BXJO	Cameron O-90	G-BXPY	Robinson R44
G-BXEC	DHC-1 Chipmunk	G-BXJP	Cameron C-80	G-BXRA	Mudry CAP.10B
G-BXEJ	VPM M16 Tandem	G-BXJS	Janus CM	G-BXRB	Mudry CAP.10B
G-BXEN	Cameron N-105	G-BXJT	Sky 90-24	G-BXRC	Mudry CAP.10B
G-BXES	Percival Pembroke	G-BXJV	Diamond Katana	G-BXRD	Enstrom 280FX
G-BXET	Piper PA-38-112 Tomahawk	G-BXJW	Diamond Katana	G-BXRF	Super Emeraude
G-BXEX	Piper PA-28-181 Archer	G-BXJY	Van's RV-6	G-BXRG	Piper PA-28-181 Archer
G-BXEY	Colt AS-105GD	G-BXJZ	Cameron C-60	G-BXRH	Cessna 185 Skywagon
G-BXEZ	Cessna 182P Skylane	G-BXKA	Airbus A320-214	G-BXRM	Cameron A-210
G-BXFB	Pitts S-1 Special	G-BXKB	Airbus A320-214	G-BXRO	Cessna U206G
G-BXFC	Jodel D.18	G-BXKC	Airbus A320-214	G-BXRP	Schweizer 269C
G-BXFD	Enstrom 280C	G-BXKD	Airbus A320-214	G-BXRR	Westland Scout
G-BXFE	Mudry CAP.10B	G-BXKF	Hawker Hunter T.7	G-BXRS	Westland Scout
G-BXFG	Europa	G-BXKH	Cameron Box SS	G-BXRT	Robin DR.400-180 Regent
G-BXFI	Hawker Hunter T.7	G-BXKL	Bell 206B Jet Ranger	G-BXRV	Van's RV-4
G-BXFK	CFM Shadow SA	G-BXKM	RAF 2000 GTX-SE	G-BXRY	Bell 206B Jet Ranger
G-BXFN	Cameron Colt 77A	G-BXKO	Sky 65-24	G-BXRZ	Rans S6 Coyote II
G-BXFU	Strikemaster Mk.83	G-BXKU	Cameron AS-120	G-BXSC	Cameron C-80
G-BXFV	Strikemaster Mk.83	G-BXKW	Slingsby T.67M	G-BXSD	Cessna 172R Skyhawk
G-BXFY	Cameron Beerkeg SS	G-BXKX	Auster 5	G-BXSE	Cessna 172R Skyhawk
G-BXGA	Aerospatiale AS.350B2	G-BXLC	Sky 120-24	G-BXSG	Robinson R22B
G-BXGC	Cameron N-105	G-BXLF	Lindstrand LBL-90A	G-BXSH	DG-808B
G-BXGD	Sky 90-24	G-BXLG	Cameron C-80	G-BXSI	Jabiru SK
G-BXGG	Europa	G-BXLK	Europa	G-BXSJ	Cameron C-80
G-BXGH	Diamond Katana	G-BXLN	Fournier RF4D	G-BXSP	Grob 109B
G-BXGL	DHC-1 Chipmunk	G-BXLO	Jet Provost T.4	G-BXSR	Reims F172N
G-BXGM	DHC-1 Chipmunk	G-BXLP	Sky 90-24	G-BXST	Piper PA-25-235 Pawnee
G-BXGO	DHC-1 Chipmunk	G-BXLR	PZL Koliber 150	G-BXSU	TEAM Minimax
G-BXGP	DHC-1 Chipmunk	G-BXLS	PZL Koliber 150	G-BXSV	Stampe SV-4C
G-BXGS	RAF 2000	G-BXLT	SOCATA TB-20 Trinidad XL	G-BXSX	Cameron V-77
G-BXGT	III Sky Arrow 650T	G-BXLW	Enstrom F-28F	G-BXSY	Robinson R22B
G-BXGV	Cessna 172R Skyhawk	G-BXLY	Piper PA-28-151 Warrior	G-BXTB	Cessna 152
G-BXGW	Robin HR.200-120	G-BXMF	Cassutt Racer 3M	G-BXTD	Europa
G-BXGX	DHC-1 Chipmunk	G-BXMG	RAF 2000 GTX	G-BXTE	Cameron A-275
G-BXGY	Cameron V-65	G-BXMH	Beech 76 Duchess	G-BXTF	Cameron N-105
G-BXGZ	Stemme S-10V	G-BXML	Mooney M.20A	G-BXTG	Cameron N-42
G-BXHA	DHC-1 Chipmunk	G-BXMM	Cameron A-180	G-BXTH	Aerospatiale Gazelle
G-BXHD	Beech 76 Duchess	G-BXMV	Scheibe SF25C Falke	G-BXTI	Pitts S-1S Special
G-BXHE	Lindstrand LBL-105A	G-BXMX	Phoenix Currie Wot	G-BXTJ	Cameron N-77
G-BXHF	DHC-1 Chipmunk	G-BXMY	Hughes 269C	G-BXTL	Schweizer 269C-1
G-BXHH	Grumman AA-5A Cheetah	G-BXMZ	Diamond Katana	G-BXTN	ATR 72-202

Registration	Type	Registration	Type	Registration	Type
G-BXTO	Hindustan Pushpak	G-BXYF	Colt AS-105	G-BYCJ	CFM Shadow DD
G-BXTP	Diamond Katana	G-BXYG	Cessna 310D	G-BYCL	Raj Hamsa X'Air
G-BXTS	Diamond Katana	G-BXYH	Cameron N-105	G-BYCM	Rans S6 Coyote II
G-BXTT	Grumman AA-5B Tiger	G-BXYI	Cameron H-34	G-BYCN	Rans S6 Coyote II
G-BXTV	Bug	G-BXYJ	Jodel DR.1050	G-BYCP	Beech B200 Super King Air
G-BXTW	Piper PA-28-181 Archer	G-BXYK	Robinson R22B	G-BYCS	Jodel DR.1051
G-BXTY	Piper PA-28-161 Cadet	G-BXYM	Piper PA-28-235 Cherokee	G-BYCT	Aero L.29A
G-BXTZ	Piper PA-28-161 Cadet	G-BXYO	Piper PA-28R-201T	G-BYCV	Murphy Maverick
G-BXUA	Campbell Cricket	G-BXYP	Piper PA-28R-201T	G-BYCW	Mainair Blade
G-BXUC	Robinson R22B	G-BXYR	Piper PA-28RT-201	G-BYCX	Westland Wasp
G-BXUE	Sky 240-24	G-BXYT	Piper PA-28RT-201	G-BYCY	III Sky Arrow 650T
G-BXUF	Agusta Bell 206B	G-BXYX	Van's RV-6	G-BYCZ	Jabiru SK
G-BXUG	Lindstrand Baby Bel SS	G-BXZA	Piper PA-38-112 Tomahawk	G-BYDB	Grob 115B
G-BXUH	Lindstrand LBL-31A	G-BXZB	Nanchang CJ-6A	G-BYDE	Spitfire IX
G-BXUI	Glaser-Dirks DG-800B	G-BXZF	Lindstrand LBL-90A	G-BYDF	Sikorsky S-76A
G-BXUM	Europa	G-BXZI	Lindstrand LBL-90A	G-BYDG	Beech C24R Sierra
G-BXUS	Sky 65-24	G-BXZK	MD.900 Explorer	G-BYDJ	Colt 120A
G-BXUU	Cameron V-65	G-BXZM	Cessna 182S Skylane	G-BYDK	Stampe SV-4C
G-BXUW	Colt 90A	G-BXZO	Pietenpol Aircamper	G-BYDL	Hawker Hurricane IIB
G-BXUX	Brugger Cherry	G-BXZS	Sikorsky S-76A	G-BYDT	Cameron N-90
G-BXUY	Cessna 310Q	G-BXZT	MS.880B Rallye	G-BYDU	Cameron Cart SS
G-BXVA	SOCATA TB-200XL Tobago	G-BXZU	Bantam B.22S	G-BYDV	Van's RV-6
G-BXVB	Cessna 152	G-BXZY	CFM Shadow DD	G-BYDY	Beech 58 Baron
G-BXVD	CFM Shadow SA	G-BXZZ	Sky 160-24	G-BYDZ	Pegasus Quantum
G-BXVE	Lindstrand LBL-330A	G-BYAA	Boeing 767-204ER	G-BYEA	Cessna 172P Skyhawk
G-BXVG	Sky 77-24	G-BYAB	Boeing 767-204ER	G-BYEC	Glaser-Dirks DG-800B
G-BXVI	Spitfire LF.XVIe	G-BYAD	Boeing 757-204ER	G-BYEE	Mooney M.20K
G-BXVJ	Cameron O-120	G-BYAE	Boeing 757-204ER	G-BYEH	Robin DR.250-160
G-BXVK	Robin HR.200-120	G-BYAF	Boeing 757-204ER	G-BYEI	Cameron Chick SS
G-BXVL	Sky 180-24	G-BYAH	Boeing 757-204ER	G-BYEJ	Scheibe SF28A Falke
G-BXVM	Van's RV-6A	G-BYAI	Boeing 757-204	G-BYEK	GlaStar
G-BXVO	Van's RV-6A	G-BYAJ	Boeing 757-204	G-BYEL	Van's RV-6
G-BXVP	Sky 31-24	G-BYAK	Boeing 757-204	G-BYEM	Cessna R182 Skylane RG
G-BXVR	Sky 90-24	G-BYAL	Boeing 757-204	G-BYEO	Zenair CH.601HDS
G-BXVS	Brugger Colibri	G-BYAN	Boeing 757-204	G-BYEP	Lindstrand LBL-90B
G-BXVT	Cameron O-77	G-BYAO	Boeing 757-204	G-BYER	Cameron C-80
G-BXVU	Piper PA-28-161 Warrior	G-BYAP	Boeing 757-204	G-BYES	Cessna 172P Skyhawk
G-BXVV	Cameron V-90	G-BYAR	Boeing 757-204	G-BYET	Cessna 172P Skyhawk
G-BXVW	Colt Piggy SS	G-BYAS	Boeing 757-204	G-BYEW	Pegasus Quantum
G-BXVX	Rutan Cozy	G-BYAT	Boeing 757-204	G-BYEX	Sky 120-24
G-BXVY	Cessna 152	G-BYAU	Boeing 757-204	G-BYEY	Lindstrand LBL-21
G-BXVZ	PZL TS-11 Iskra	G-BYAV	Taylor Monoplane	G-BYEZ	Dyn'Aero MCR-01
G-BXWA	Beech 76 Duchess	G-BYAW	Boeing 757-204	G-BYFA	Reims F152
G-BXWB	Robin HR.100-200	G-BYAX	Boeing 757-204	G-BYFC	Jabiru SK
G-BXWC	Cessna 152	G-BYAY	Boeing 757-204	G-BYFD	Grob 115A
G-BXWG	Sky 120-24	G-BYAZ	CFM Shadow SA	G-BYFE	Pegasus Quantum
G-BXWH	Denney Kitfox	G-BYBA	Agusta Bell 206B	G-BYFF	Pegasus Quantum
G-BXWK	Rans S6 Coyote II (N)	G-BYBC	Agusta Bell 206B	G-BYFG	Europa XS
G-BXWL	Sky 90-24	G-BYBD	Reims F172H	G-BYFI	CFM Shadow SA
G-BXWO	Piper PA-28-181 Archer	G-BYBE	Jodel D.120A Paris-Nice	G-BYFJ	Cameron N-105
G-BXWP	Piper PA-32-300	G-BYBF	Robin R.2160i	G-BYFL	Diamond H.36TTS
G-BXWR	CFM Shadow SA	G-BYBH	Piper PA-34-200T Seneca	G-BYFM	Jodel DR.1050M1
G-BXWT	Van's RV-6	G-BYBI	Bell 206B Jet Ranger	G-BYFR	Piper PA-32R-301
G-BXWU	FLS Sprint 160	G-BYBJ	Hybred 44XLR	G-BYFT	Pietenpol Aircamper
G-BXWV	FLS Sprint 160	G-BYBK	Murphy Rebel	G-BYFU	Lindstrand LBL-105B
G-BXWX	Sky 25-16	G-BYBL	Gardan GY-80	G-BYFV	TEAM Minimax
G-BXXG	Cameron N-105	G-BYBM	Jabiru SK	G-BYFX	Colt 77A
G-BXXH	Hatz CB-1	G-BYBN	Cameron N-77	G-BYFY	Mudry CAP.10B
G-BXXI	Grob 109B	G-BYBO	Eclipser 44XLR	G-BYGA	Boeing 747-436
G-BXXJ	Colt Yacht SS	G-BYBP	Cessna A185F	G-BYGB	Boeing 747-436
G-BXXK	Reims F172N	G-BYBR	Rans S6 Coyote II (N)	G-BYGC	Boeing 747-436
G-BXXL	Cameron N-105	G-BYBS	Sky 80-16	G-BYGD	Boeing 747-436
G-BXXN	Robinson R22B	G-BYBU	Renegade Spirit UK	G-BYGE	Boeing 747-436
G-BXXO	Lindstrand LBL-90B	G-BYBV	Mainair Rapier	G-BYGF	Boeing 747-436
G-BXXP	Sky 77-24	G-BYBW	TEAM Minimax	G-BYGG	Boeing 747-436
G-BXXR	Lovegrove Gyroplane	G-BYBX	Slingsby T.67M	G-BYHC	Cameron Z-90
G-BXXS	Sky 105-24	G-BYBY	Thorp T.18C	G-BYHE	Robinson R22B
G-BXXT	Beech 76 Duchess	G-BYBZ	Jabiru SK	G-BYHG	Dornier Do.328-110
G-BXXU	Colt 31A	G-BYCA	Piper PA-28-140 Cherokee	G-BYHH	Piper PA-28-161 Warrior
G-BXXW	Enstrom F-28F	G-BYCB	Sky 21-15	G-BYHI	Piper PA-28-161 Warrior
G-BXYC	Schweizer 269C	G-BYCD	Cessna 140	G-BYHJ	Piper PA-28R-201
G-BXYD	Eurocopter EC120B	G-BYCE	Robinson R44	G-BYHK	Piper PA-28-181 Archer
G-BXYE	Piel Emeraude	G-BYCF	Robinson R22B	G-BYHL	DHC-1 Chipmunk

Reg	Type	Reg	Type	Reg	Type
G-BYHM	BAe 125-800	G-BYKX	Cameron N-90	G-BYOT	Rans S6 Coyote II (N)
G-BYHN	Mainair Blade	G-BYKZ	Sky 140-24	G-BYOU	Rans S6 Coyote II (N)
G-BYHO	Mainair Blade	G-BYLB	DH.82A Tiger Moth	G-BYOV	Pegasus Quantum
G-BYHP	Robin DR.253 Regent	G-BYLC	Pegasus Quantum	G-BYOW	Mainair Blade
G-BYHR	Pegasus Quantum	G-BYLD	Pietenpol Aircamper	G-BYOX	Cameron Z-90
G-BYHS	Mainair Blade	G-BYLF	Zenair CH.601HDS	G-BYOZ	Mainair Rapier
G-BYHT	Robin DR.400-180 Regent	G-BYLH	Robin HR.200-120	G-BYPA	Aerospatiale AS.355F2
G-BYHU	Cameron N-105	G-BYLI	Nova Vertex 22	G-BYPB	Pegasus Quantum
G-BYHV	Raj Hamsa X'Air	G-BYLJ	Letov Sluka LK2M	G-BYPD	Cameron A-105
G-BYHX	Cameron AS-250	G-BYLL	Sequoia F.8L Falco	G-BYPE	Gardan GY-80-160
G-BYHY	Cameron V-77	G-BYLO	Tipsy Nipper	G-BYPF	Thruster T600N
G-BYIA	Jabiru SK	G-DYLP	Rand KR-2	G-BYPG	Thruster T600N
G-BYIB	Rans S6 Coyote II (T)	G-BYLR	Cessna 404	G-BYPH	Thruster T600N
G-BYIC	Cessna U206G	G-BYLS	Bede BD-4	G-BYPJ	Pegasus Quantum
G-BYID	Rans S6 Coyote II (N)	G-BYLT	Raj Hamsa X'Air	G-BYPL	Pegasus Quantum
G-BYIE	Robinson R22B	G-BYLV	Thunder Ax8-105	G-BYPM	Europa XS
G-BYII	TEAM Minimax	G-BYLW	Lindstrand LBL-77A	G-BYPN	MS.880B Rallye
G-BYIJ	CASA I-131E	G-BYLX	Lindstrand LBL-105A	G-BYPO	Raj Hamsa X'Air
G-BYIK	Europa	G-BYLY	Cameron V-77	G-BYPP	Medway Rebel SS
G-BYIL	Cameron N-105	G-BYLZ	Rutan Cozy	G-BYPR	Zenair CH.601HD
G-BYIM	Jabiru UL	G-BYMB	Diamond Katana	G-BYPT	Rans S6 Coyote II (N)
G-BYIN	RAF 2000 GTX-SE	G-BYMC	Piper PA-38-112 Tomahawk	G-BYPU	Piper PA-32R-301 HP
G-BYIO	Colt 105A	G-BYMD	Piper PA-38-112 Tomahawk	G-BYPW	Raj Hamsa X'Air
G-BYIP	Pitts S-2A Special	G-BYME	Gardan GY-80	G-BYPY	Ryan ST3KR
G-BYIR	Pitts S-1S Special	G-BYMF	Pegasus Quantum	G-BYPZ	Rans S6 Coyote II (N)
G-BYIS	Pegasus Quantum	G-BYMG	Cameron A-210	G-BYRC	Westland Wessex
G-BYIT	Robin DR.500	G-BYMH	Cessna 152	G-BYRG	Rans S6 Coyote II (N)
G-BYIU	Cameron V-90	G-BYMI	Pegasus Quantum	G-BYRH	Hybred 44XLR
G-BYIV	Cameron PM-80	G-BYMJ	Cessna 152	G-BYRJ	Pegasus Quantum
G-BYIX	Cameron PM-80	G-BYMK	Dornier Do.328-110	G-BYRK	Cameron V-42
G-BYIY	Lindstrand LBL-105B	G-BYML	Dornier Do.328-110	G-BYRO	Mainair Blade
G-BYIZ	Pegasus Quantum	G-BYMN	Rans S6 Coyote II (N)	G-BYRP	Mainair Blade
G-BYJB	Mainair Blade	G-BYMO	Campbell Cricket	G-BYRR	Mainair Blade
G-BYJC	Cameron N-90	G-BYMP	Campbell Cricket	G-BYRS	Rans S6 Coyote II (N)
G-BYJD	Jabiru UL	G-BYMR	Raj Hamsa X'Air	G-BYRU	Pegasus Quantum
G-BYJE	TEAM Minimax	G-BYMT	Pegasus Quantum	G-BYRV	Raj Hamsa X'Air
G-BYJF	Thorp T.211	G-BYMU	Rans S6 Coyote II (N)	G-BYRX	Westland Scout
G-BYJG	Lindstrand LBL-77A	G-BYMV	Rans S6 Coyote II (N)	G-BYRY	Slingsby T.67M
G-BYJH	Grob 109B	G-BYMW	Boland 52-12	G-BYRZ	Lindstrand LBL-77M
G-BYJI	Europa	G-BYMX	Cameron A-105	G-BYSA	Europa XS
G-BYJJ	Cameron C-80	G-BYMY	Cameron N-90	G-BYSE	Agusta Bell 206B
G-BYJK	Pegasus Quantum	G-BYNA	Reims F172H	G-BYSF	Jabiru SK
G-BYJL	Aero Designs Pulsar	G-BYND	Pegasus Quantum	G-BYSG	Robin HR.200-120
G-BYJM	Pegasus AX2000	G-BYNE	Pilatus PC-6 B2-H4	G-BYSI	PZL Koliber 160A
G-BYJN	Lindstrand LBL-105A	G-BYNF	North American Yale	G-BYSJ	DHC-1 Chipmunk
G-BYJO	Rans S6 Coyote II (T)	G-BYNH	Rotorway Exec 162F	G-BYSK	Cameron A-275
G-BYJP	Pitts S-1S Special	G-BYNI	Rotorway Exec 90	G-BYSM	Cameron A-210
G-BYJR	Lindstrand LBL-77B	G-BYNJ	Cameron N-77	G-BYSN	Rans S6 Coyote II (N)
G-BYJS	SOCATA TB-20 Trinidad	G-BYNK	Robin HR.200-160	G-BYSP	Piper PA-28-181 Archer
G-BYJT	Zenair CH.601HD	G-BYNM	Mainair Blade	G-BYSR	Pegasus Quantum
G-BYJU	Raj Hamsa X'Air	G-BYNN	Cameron V-90	G-BYSS	Medway Rebel SS
G-BYJW	Cameron Sphere SS	G-BYNO	Pegasus Quantum	G-BYSV	Cameron N-120
G-BYJX	Cameron C-70	G-BYNP	Rans S6 Coyote II	G-BYSW	Enstrom 280FX
G-BYJZ	Lindstrand LBL-105A	G-BYNR	Jabiru UL	G-BYSX	Pegasus Quantum
G-BYKA	Lindstrand LBL-69A	G-BYNS	Jabiru SK	G-BYSY	Raj Hamsa X'Air
G-BYKB	Rockwell 114	G-BYNT	Raj Hamsa X'Air	G-BYTA	Kolb Twinstar Mk.3
G-BYKC	Mainair Blade	G-BYNU	Cameron Ax7-77	G-BYTB	SOCATA TB-20 Trinidad
G-BYKD	Mainair Blade	G-BYNV	Sky 105-24	G-BYTC	Pegasus Quantum
G-BYKE	Rans S6 Coyote II (N)	G-BYNW	Cameron H-34	G-BYTE	Robinson R22B
G-BYKF	Enstrom F-28F	G-BYNX	Cameron RX-105	G-BYTG	Glaser-Dirks DG-400
G-BYKG	Pietenpol Aircamper	G-BYNY	Beech 76 Duchess	G-BYTH	Airbus A320-231
G-BYKI	Cameron N-105	G-BYOB	Slingsby T.67M	G-BYTI	Piper PA-24-250 Comanche
G-BYKJ	Westland Scout	G-BYOD	Slingsby T.67C	G-BYTJ	Cameron C-80
G-BYKK	Robinson R44	G-BYOG	Pegasus Quantum	G-BYTK	Jabiru UL
G-BYKL	Piper PA-28-181 Archer	G-BYOH	Raj Hamsa X'Air	G-BYTL	Mainair Blade
G-BYKN	Piper PA-28-161 Warrior	G-BYOI	Sky 80-16	G-BYTM	Dyn'Aero MCR-01
G-BYKO	Piper PA-28-161 Warrior	G-BYOJ	Raj Hamsa X'Air	G-BYTN	DH.82A Tiger Moth
G-BYKP	Piper PA-28R-201T	G-BYOK	Cameron F-90	G-BYTR	Raj Hamsa X'Air
G-BYKR	Piper PA-28-161 Warrior	G-BYOM	Sikorsky S-76C	G-BYTS	Bensen B.8MR
G-BYKS	Leopoldoff Colibri	G-BYON	Mainair Blade	G-BYTT	Raj Hamsa X'Air
G-BYKT	Pegasus Quantum	G-BYOO	CFM Shadow SA	G-BYTU	Mainair Blade
G-BYKU	Quad City Challenger	G-BYOR	Raj Hamsa X'Air	G-BYTV	Jabiru UL
G-BYKW	Lindstrand LBL-77B	G-BYOS	Mainair Blade	G-BYTW	Cameron O-90

Registration	Type	Registration	Type	Registration	Type
G-BYTX	Whittaker MW-6S	G-BYWW	Grob 115E	G-BZAL	Mainair Blade
G-BYTZ	Raj Hamsa X'Air	G-BYWX	Grob 115E	G-BZAM	Europa
G-BYUA	Grob 115E	G-BYWY	Grob 115E	G-BZAO	Rans S12-XL Airaile
G-BYUB	Grob 115E	G-BYWZ	Grob 115E	G-BZAP	Jabiru UL
G-BYUC	Grob 115E	G-BYXA	Grob 115E	G-BZAR	Denney Kitfox
G-BYUD	Grob 115E	G-BYXB	Grob 115E	G-BZAS	Isaacs Fury II
G-BYUE	Grob 115E	G-BYXC	Grob 115E	G-BZAT	BAe 146-RJ100
G-BYUF	Grob 115E	G-BYXD	Grob 115E	G-BZAU	BAe 146-RJ100
G-BYUH	Grob 115E	G-BYXE	Grob 115E	G-BZAV	BAe 146-RJ100
G-BYUI	Grob 115E	G-BYXF	Grob 115E	G-BZAW	BAe 146-RJ100
G-BYUJ	Grob 115E	G-BYXG	Grob 115E	G-BZAX	BAe 146-RJ100
G-BYUK	Grob 115E	G-BYXH	Grob 115E	G-BZAY	BAe 146-RJ100
G-BYUL	Grob 115E	G-BYXI	Grob 115E	G-BZAZ	BAe 146-RJ100
G-BYUM	Grob 115E	G-BYXJ	Grob 115E	G-BZBC	Rans S6 Coyote II (N)
G-BYUN	Grob 115E	G-BYXK	Grob 115E	G-BZBE	Cameron A-210
G-BYUO	Grob 115E	G-BYXL	Grob 115E	G-BZBF	Cessna 172M Skyhawk
G-BYUP	Grob 115E	G-BYXM	Thunder Ax7-65	G-BZBH	Thunder Ax7-65
G-BYUR	Grob 115E	G-BYXN	Grob 115E	G-BZBI	Cameron V-77
G-BYUS	Grob 115E	G-BYXO	Grob 115E	G-BZBJ	Lindstrand LBL-77A
G-BYUT	Grob 115E	G-BYXP	Grob 115E	G-BZBL	Lindstrand LBL-120A
G-BYUU	Grob 115E	G-BYXR	Grob 115E	G-BZBM	Cameron A-315
G-BYUV	Grob 115E	G-BYXS	Grob 115E	G-BZBN	Thunder Ax9-120
G-BYUW	Grob 115E	G-BYXT	Grob 115E	G-BZBO	Glasair III
G-BYUX	Grob 115E	G-BYXV	Medway EclipseR	G-BZBP	Raj Hamsa X'Air
G-BYUY	Grob 115E	G-BYXW	Medway EclipseR	G-BZBR	Pegasus Quantum
G-BYUZ	Grob 115E	G-BYXX	Grob 115E	G-BZBS	Piper PA-28-161 Warrior
G-BYVA	Grob 115E	G-BYXY	Cameron H-34	G-BZBT	Cameron H-34
G-BYVB	Grob 115E	G-BYXZ	Grob 115E	G-BZBU	Robinson R22
G-BYVC	Grob 115E	G-BYYA	Grob 115E	G-BZBW	Rotorway Exec 162F
G-BYVD	Grob 115E	G-BYYB	Grob 115E	G-BZBX	Rans S6 Coyote II (N)
G-BYVE	Grob 115E	G-BYYC	Hapi Cygnet SF2A	G-BZBZ	Jodel D.9 Bebe
G-BYVF	Grob 115E	G-BYYD	Cameron A-250	G-BZDA	Piper PA-28-161 Warrior
G-BYVG	Grob 115E	G-BYYE	Lindstrand LBL-77A	G-BZDB	Thruster T600T
G-BYVH	Grob 115E	G-BYYG	Slingsby T.67C	G-BZDC	Mainair Blade
G-BYVI	Grob 115E	G-BYYJ	Lindstrand LBL-25A	G-BZDD	Mainair Blade
G-BYVJ	Grob 115E	G-BYYL	Jabiru UL	G-BZDE	Lindstrand LBL-210A
G-BYVK	Grob 115E	G-BYYM	Raj Hamsa X'Air	G-BZDF	CFM Shadow SA
G-BYVL	Grob 115E	G-BYYN	Pegasus Quantum	G-BZDH	Piper PA-28R-200
G-BYVM	Grob 115E	G-BYYO	Piper PA-28R-201	G-BZDI	Aero L.39C
G-BYVN	Grob 115E	G-BYYP	Pegasus Quantum	G-BZDJ	Cameron Z-105
G-BYVO	Grob 115E	G-BYYR	Raj Hamsa X'Air	G-BZDK	Raj Hamsa X'Air
G-BYVP	Grob 115E	G-BYYT	Jabiru UL	G-BZDL	Pegasus Quantum
G-BYVR	Grob 115E	G-BYYX	TEAM Minimax	G-BZDM	GlaStar
G-BYVS	Grob 115E	G-BYYY	Pegasus Quantum	G-BZDN	Cameron N-105
G-BYVT	Grob 115E	G-BYYZ	Staaken Flitzer	G-BZDP	Scottish Aviation Bulldog
G-BYVU	Grob 115E	G-BYZA	Aerospatiale AS.355F2	G-BZDR	Tri-Kis R
G-BYVV	Grob 115E	G-BYZB	Mainair Blade	G-BZDS	Pegasus Quantum
G-BYVW	Grob 115E	G-BYZD	Kis Cruiser	G-BZDU	DHC-1 Chipmunk
G-BYVX	Grob 115E	G-BYZF	Raj Hamsa X'Air	G-BZDV	Aerospatiale Gazelle
G-BYVY	Grob 115E	G-BYZG	Cameron A-275	G-BZDX	Cameron Sugarbox
G-BYVZ	Grob 115E	G-BYZJ	Boeing 737-3Q8	G-BZDY	Cameron Sugarbox
G-BYWA	Grob 115E	G-BYZL	Cameron GP-65	G-BZDZ	Jabiru SP
G-BYWB	Grob 115E	G-BYZM	Piper PA-28-161 Warrior	G-BZEA	Cessna A152 Aerobat
G-BYWC	Grob 115E	G-BYZO	Rans S6 Coyote II (N)	G-BZEB	Cessna 152
G-BYWD	Grob 115E	G-BYZP	Robinson R22B	G-BZEC	Cessna 152
G-BYWE	Grob 115E	G-BYZR	III Sky Arrow 650TC	G-BZED	Pegasus Quantum
G-BYWF	Grob 115E	G-BYZS	Jabiru UL-450	G-BZEE	Agusta Bell 206B
G-BYWG	Grob 115E	G-BYZT	Nova Vertex 26	G-BZEG	Mainair Blade
G-BYWH	Grob 115E	G-BYZU	Pegasus Quantum	G-BZEH	Piper PA-28-235 Cherokee
G-BYWI	Grob 115E	G-BYZV	Sky 90-24	G-BZEJ	Raj Hamsa X'Air
G-BYWJ	Grob 115E	G-BYZW	Raj Hamsa X'Air	G-BZEK	Cameron C-70
G-BYWK	Grob 115E	G-BYZX	Cameron R-90	G-BZEL	Mainair Blade
G-BYWL	Grob 115E	G-BYZY	Pietenpol Aircamper	G-BZEM	Glaser-Dirks DG-800B
G-BYWM	Grob 115E	G-BYZZ	Robinson R22B	G-BZEN	Jabiru UL-450
G-BYWN	Grob 115E	G-BZAA	Mainair Blade	G-BZEP	Scottish Aviation Bulldog
G-BYWO	Grob 115E	G-BZAB	Mainair Rapier	G-BZER	Raj Hamsa X'Air
G-BYWP	Grob 115E	G-BZAD	Cessna 152	G-BZES	Rotorway Exec 90
G-BYWR	Grob 115E	G-BZAE	Cessna 152	G-BZET	Robin HR.200-120
G-BYWS	Grob 115E	G-BZAF	Raj Hamsa X'Air	G-BZEU	Raj Hamsa X'Air
G-BYWT	Grob 115E	G-BZAG	Lindstrand LBL-105A	G-BZEV	Semicopter 1
G-BYWU	Grob 115E	G-BZAH	Cessna 208B	G-BZEW	Rans S6 Coyote II (N)
G-BYWV	Grob 115E	G-BZAI	Pegasus Quantum	G-BZEX	Raj Hamsa X'Air
		G-BZAK	Raj Hamsa X'Air	G-BZEY	Cameron N-90

G-BZEZ	CFM Streak Shadow
G-BZFB	Robin R.2112 Alpha
G-BZFC	Pegasus Quantum
G-BZFD	Cameron N-90
G-BZFF	Raj Hamsa X'Air
G-BZFH	Pegasus Quantum
G-BZFI	Jabiru UL
G-BZFK	TEAM Minimax
G-BZFN	Scottish Aviation Bulldog
G-BZFO	Mainair Blade
G-BZFP	DHC-6-310
G-BZFR	Extra EA300/L
G-BZFS	Mainair Blade
G-BZFT	Murphy Rebel
G-BZFU	Lindstrand LBL HS-110
G-BZFV	Zenair CH.601UL
G-BZGA	DHC-1 Chipmunk
G-BZGB	DHC-1 Chipmunk
G-BZGC	Aerospatiale AS.355F1
G-BZGD	Piper PA-18-150
G-BZGF	Rans S6 Coyote II (N)
G-BZGG	Alouette II
G-BZGH	Reims F172N
G-BZGI	UltraMagic M-145
G-BZGJ	Thunder Ax10-180
G-BZGK	Rockwell OV-10B
G-BZGL	Rockwell OV-10B
G-BZGM	Mainair Blade
G-BZGN	Raj Hamsa X'Air
G-BZGO	Robinson R44
G-BZGP	Thruster T600N
G-BZGR	Rans S6 Coyote II (N)
G-BZGS	Mainair Blade
G-BZGT	Jabiru UL-450
G-BZGU	Raj Hamsa X'Air
G-BZGV	Lindstrand LBL-77A
G-BZGW	Mainair Blade
G-BZGX	Raj Hamsa X'Air
G-BZGY	Dyn'Aero CR100
G-BZGZ	Pegasus Quantum
G-BZHA	Boeing 767-336ER
G-BZHB	Boeing 767-336ER
G-BZHC	Boeing 767-336ER
G-BZHE	Cessna 152
G-BZHF	Cessna 152
G-BZHG	Tecnam P92 Echo
G-BZHI	Enstrom F-28A-UK
G-BZHJ	Raj Hamsa X'Air
G-BZHK	Piper PA-28-181 Archer
G-BZHL	Noorduyn Harvard
G-BZHN	Pegasus Quantum
G-BZHO	Pegasus Quantum
G-BZHP	Quad City Challenger
G-BZHR	Jabiru UL-450
G-BZHS	Europa
G-BZHT	Piper PA-28A-150
G-BZHU	Wag-Aero CUBy
G-BZHV	Piper PA-28-181 Archer
G-BZHW	Piper PA-28-181 Archer
G-BZHX	Thunder Ax11-250
G-BZHY	Mainair Blade
G-BZIA	Raj Hamsa X'Air
G-BZIC	Lindstrand Sun SS
G-BZID	Bensen B.8MR
G-BZIG	Thruster T600N
G-BZIH	Lindstrand LBL 31A
G-BZII	Extra EA300/L
G-BZIJ	Robin DR.500
G-BZIK	Cameron A-250
G-BZIL	Colt 120A
G-BZIM	Pegasus Quantum
G-BZIO	Piper PA-28-161 Warrior
G-BZIP	Bensen B.8MR
G-BZIS	Raj Hamsa X'Air
G-BZIT	Beech 95-B55 Baron
G-BZIV	Jabiru UL
G-BZIW	Pegasus Quantum
G-BZIX	Cameron N-90
G-BZIY	Raj Hamsa X'Air
G-BZIZ	UltraMagic H-31
G-BZJA	Cameron Fire SS
G-BZJB	Yakovlev Yak-52
G-BZJC	Thruster T600N
G-BZJD	Thruster T600T
G-BZJF	Pegasus Quantum
G-BZJH	Cameron Z-90
G-BZJI	Nova X-Large 37
G-BZJJ	Robinson R22B
G-BZJL	Mainair Blade
G-BZJM	VPM M16 Tandem
G-BZJN	Mainair Blade
G-BZJO	Pegasus Quantum
G-BZJP	Zenair CH.701
G-BZJS	Taylor Titch
G-BZJU	Cameron A-200
G-BZJV	CASA I-131E
G-BZJW	Cessna 150F
G-BZJX	UltraMagic N-250
G-BZJZ	Pegasus Quantum
G-BZKC	Raj Hamsa X'Air
G-BZKD	Stolp Starduster
G-BZKE	Lindstrand LBL-77B
G-BZKF	Rans S6 Coyote II
G-BZKG	Extreme Silex
G-BZKH	Doodle Bug Target
G-BZKI	Doodle Bug Target
G-BZKJ	Doodle Bug Target
G-BZKK	Cameron V-56
G-BZKL	Piper PA-28R-201
G-BZKN	Campbell Cricket
G-BZKO	Rans S6 Coyote II (N)
G-BZKR	Cameron Sugarbox
G-BZKS	Ercoupe 415CD
G-BZKT	Pegasus Quantum
G-BZKU	Cameron Z-105
G-BZKV	Cameron Sky 90-24
G-BZKW	UltraMagic M-77
G-BZKX	Cameron V-90
G-BZKY	Fw.189A1
G-BZLA	Aerospatiale Gazelle
G-BZLC	PZL Koliber 160A
G-BZLE	Rans S6 Coyote II
G-BZLF	CFM Shadow CD
G-BZLG	Robin HR.200-120
G-BZLH	Piper PA-28-161 Warrior
G-BZLI	SOCATA TB-21 Trinidad TC
G-BZLK	Slingsby T.31M
G-BZLL	Pegasus Quantum
G-BZLP	Robinson R44
G-BZLS	Cameron Sky 77-24
G-BZLT	Raj Hamsa X'Air
G-BZLU	Lindstrand LBL-90A
G-BZLV	Jabiru UL
G-BZLX	Pegasus Quantum
G-BZLY	Grob 109B
G-BZLZ	Pegasus Quantum
G-BZMB	Piper PA-28R-201
G-BZMC	Jabiru UL
G-BZMD	Scottish Aviation Bulldog
G-BZME	Scottish Aviation Bulldog
G-BZMF	Rutan LongEz
G-BZMG	Robinson R44
G-BZMH	Scottish Aviation Bulldog
G-BZMI	Pegasus Quantum
G-BZMJ	Rans S6 Coyote II (N)
G-BZML	Scottish Aviation Bulldog
G-BZMM	Robin DR.400-180 Regent
G-BZMO	Robinson R22B
G-BZMR	Raj Hamsa X'Air
G-BZMS	Mainair Blade
G-BZMT	Piper PA-28-161 Warrior
G-BZMV	Cameron C-80
G-BZMW	Pegasus Quantum
G-BZMY	Yakovlev Yak-11C
G-BZMZ	CFM Shadow SA
G-BZNB	Pegasus Quantum
G-BZNC	Pegasus Quantum
G-BZND	Sopwith Pup Rep
G-BZNE	Beech King Air 350
G-BZNF	Cameron Colt 120A
G-BZNG	Raj Hamsa X'Air
G-BZNH	Rans S6 Coyote II (N)
G-BZNI	Bell 206B Jet Ranger
G-BZNJ	Rans S6 Coyote II (T)
G-BZNK	Morane MS.315E
G-BZNM	Pegasus Quantum
G-BZNN	Beech 76 Duchess
G-BZNO	Ercoupe 415C
G-BZNP	Thruster T600N
G-BZNS	Mainair Blade
G-BZNT	Aero L.29
G-BZNU	Cameron A-300
G-BZNV	Lindstrand LBL-31A
G-BZNW	Isaacs Fury II
G-BZNX	MS.880B Rallye
G-BZNY	Europa XS
G-BZNZ	Lindstrand Cake SS
G-BZOB	Slepcev Storch
G-BZOD	Pegasus Quantum
G-BZOE	Pegasus Quantum
G-BZOF	Bensen B.8MR
G-BZOG	Dornier Do.328-100
G-BZOI	Nicollier HN700 Menestrel
G-BZOM	Rotorway Exec 162F
G-BZON	Scottish Aviation Bulldog
G-BZOO	Pegasus Quantum
G-BZOP	Robinson R44
G-BZOR	TEAM Minimax
G-BZOU	Pegasus Quantum
G-BZOV	Pegasus Quantum
G-BZOW	Whittaker MW-7
G-BZOX	Cameron Colt 90B
G-BZOY	Beech 76 Duchess
G-BZOZ	Van's RV-6
G-BZPA	Mainair Blade
G-BZPB	Hawker Hunter GA.11
G-BZPC	Hawker Hunter GA.11
G-BZPD	Cameron V-65
G-BZPE	Lindstrand LBL-310A
G-BZPF	Scheibe SF24B
G-BZPG	Beech C24R Sierra
G-BZPH	Van's RV-4
G-BZPI	SOCATA TB-20 Trinidad
G-BZPJ	Beech 76 Duchess
G-BZPK	Cameron C-80
G-BZPL	Robinson R44
G-BZPM	Cessna 172S Skyhawk
G-BZPN	Mainair Blade
G-BZPP	Westland Wasp
G-BZPR	UltraMagic N-210
G-BZPS	Scottish Aviation Bulldog
G-BZPT	UltraMagic N-210
G-BZPV	Lindstrand LBL-90B
G-BZPW	Cameron V-77
G-BZPX	UltraMagic S-105
G-BZPY	UltraMagic H-31
G-BZPZ	Mainair Blade
G-BZRA	Rans S6 Coyote II

☐ G-BZRB	Mainair Blade	
☐ G-BZRG	Hunt Wing Avon	
☐ G-BZRJ	Pegasus Quantum	
☐ G-BZRO	Piper PA-30-160 C	
☐ G-BZRP	Pegasus Quantum	
☐ G-BZRR	Pegasus Quantum	
☐ G-BZRS	Eurocopter EC135T1	
☐ G-BZRT	Beech 76 Duchess	
☐ G-BZRU	Cameron V-90	
☐ G-BZRV	Van's RV-6	
☐ G-BZRW	Mainair Blade	
☐ G-BZRX	UltraMagic M-105	
☐ G-BZRY	Rans S6 Coyote II (N)	
☐ G-BZRZ	Thunder Ax11-250	
☐ G-BZSA	Pegasus Quantum	
☐ G-BZSB	Pitts S-1S Special	
☐ G-BZSC	Sopwith Camel Rep	
☐ G-BZSD	Piper PA-46-310P Malibu	
☐ G-BZSE	Hawker Hunter T.8B	
☐ G-BZSF	Hawker Hunter T.8B	
☐ G-BZSG	Pegasus Quantum	
☐ G-BZSH	UltraMagic H-77	
☐ G-BZSI	Pegasus Quantum	
☐ G-BZSL	Sky 25-16	
☐ G-BZSM	Pegasus Quantum	
☐ G-BZSO	UltraMagic M-77C	
☐ G-BZSP	Stemme S-10	
☐ G-BZSS	Pegasus Quantum	
☐ G-BZST	Jabiru UL	
☐ G-BZSU	Cameron A-315	
☐ G-BZSV	Barracuda	
☐ G-BZSX	Pegasus Quantum	
☐ G-BZSY	Stampe SV-4A	
☐ G-BZSZ	Jabiru UL	
☐ G-BZTA	Robinson R44	
☐ G-BZTC	TEAM Minimax	
☐ G-BZTD	Thruster T600T	
☐ G-BZTF	Yakovlev Yak-52	
☐ G-BZTG	Piper PA-34-220T Seneca	
☐ G-BZTH	Europa	
☐ G-BZTI	Europa XS	
☐ G-BZTJ	CASA Bu.133C	
☐ G-BZTK	Cameron V-90	
☐ G-BZTL	Colt Ice Cream SS	
☐ G-BZTM	Mainair Blade	
☐ G-BZTN	Europa XS	
☐ G-BZTR	Mainair Blade	
☐ G-BZTS	Cameron Bertie SS	
☐ G-BZTT	Cameron A-275	
☐ G-BZTV	Mainair Blade	
☐ G-BZTW	Hunt Wing Avon	
☐ G-BZTX	Mainair Blade	
☐ G-BZTY	Jabiru UL	
☐ G-BZUB	Mainair Blade	
☐ G-BZUC	Pegasus Quantum	
☐ G-BZUD	Lindstrand LBL-105A	
☐ G-BZUE	Pegasus Quantum	
☐ G-BZUF	Mainair Rapier	
☐ G-BZUG	Sherwood Ranger	
☐ G-BZUH	Rans S6 Coyote II (N)	
☐ G-BZUI	Pegasus Quantum	
☐ G-BZUK	Lindstrand LBL-31A	
☐ G-BZUL	Jabiru UL	
☐ G-BZUN	Mainair Blade	
☐ G-BZUO	Cameron A-340HL	
☐ G-BZUP	Raj Hamsa X'Air	
☐ G-BZUU	Cameron O-90	
☐ G-BZUV	Cameron H-24	
☐ G-BZUX	Pegasus Quantum	
☐ G-BZUY	Van's RV-6	
☐ G-BZUZ	Hunt Avon Blade	
☐ G-BZVA	Zenair CH.701UL	
☐ G-BZVB	Reims FR172H Rocket	
☐ G-BZVC	Mickleburgh L107	
☐ G-BZVD	Colt Forklift 105SS	
☐ G-BZVE	Cameron N-133	
☐ G-BZVG	Aerospatiale AS.350B3	
☐ G-BZVH	Raj Hamsa X'Air	
☐ G-BZVI	Nova Vertex 24	
☐ G-BZVJ	Pegasus Quantum	
☐ G-BZVK	Raj Hamsa X'Air	
☐ G-BZVM	Rans S6 Coyote II	
☐ G-BZVN	Van's RV-6	
☐ G-BZVO	Cessna TR182	
☐ G-BZVR	Raj Hamsa X'Air	
☐ G-BZVS	CASA I-131E	
☐ G-BZVT	III Sky Arrow 650 TC	
☐ G-BZVU	Cameron Z-105	
☐ G-BZVV	Pegasus Quantum	
☐ G-BZVW	Ilyushin Il-2	
☐ G-BZVX	Ilyushin Il-2	
☐ G-BZWB	Mainair Blade	
☐ G-BZWC	Raj Hamsa X'Air	
☐ G-BZWG	Piper PA-28-140 Cherokee	
☐ G-BZWH	Cessna 152	
☐ G-BZWI	Medway EclipseR	
☐ G-BZWJ	CFM Streak Shadow	
☐ G-BZWK	Jabiru SK	
☐ G-BZWM	Pegasus XL-Q	
☐ G-BZWN	Van's RV-8	
☐ G-BZWS	Pegasus Quantum	
☐ G-BZWT	Tecnam P92 Echo	
☐ G-BZWU	Pegasus Quantum	
☐ G-BZWV	Steen Skybolt	
☐ G-BZWX	Whittaker MW-5D	
☐ G-BZWY	CFM Streak Shadow	
☐ G-BZWZ	Van's RV-6	
☐ G-BZXA	Raj Hamsa X'Air	
☐ G-BZXB	Van's RV-6	
☐ G-BZXC	Scottish Aviation Bulldog	
☐ G-BZXD	Rotorway Exec 162	
☐ G-BZXE	DHC-1 Chipmunk	
☐ G-BZXF	Cameron A-210	
☐ G-BZXG	Dyn'Aero MCR-01	
☐ G-BZXI	Nova Philou 26	
☐ G-BZXJ	Schweizer 269C-1	
☐ G-BZXK	Robin HR.200-120B	
☐ G-BZXL	Whittaker MW5D	
☐ G-BZXM	Mainair Blade	
☐ G-BZXN	Jabiru UL-450	
☐ G-BZXO	Cameron Z-105	
☐ G-BZXP	Air Creation Kiss 400	
☐ G-BZXR	Cameron N-90	
☐ G-BZXS	Scottish Aviation Bulldog	
☐ G-BZXT	Mainair Blade	
☐ G-BZXV	Pegasus Quantum	
☐ G-BZXW	VPM M16 Tandem	
☐ G-BZXX	Pegasus Quantum	
☐ G-BZXY	Robinson R44	
☐ G-BZXZ	Scottish Aviation Bulldog	
☐ G-BZYA	Rans S6 Coyote II	
☐ G-BZYD	Aerospatiale Gazelle	
☐ G-BZYE	Robinson R22	
☐ G-BZYG	Glaser-Dirks DG-500	
☐ G-BZYI	Nova Phocus 123	
☐ G-BZYK	Jabiru UL	
☐ G-BZYL	Rans S6 Coyote II (N)	
☐ G-BZYM	Raj Hamsa X'Air	
☐ G-BZYN	Pegasus Quantum	
☐ G-BZYO	Colt 210A	
☐ G-BZYR	Cameron N-31	
☐ G-BZYS	Bantam B.22S	
☐ G-BZYT	Interavia 80TA	
☐ G-BZYU	Whittaker MW-6	
☐ G-BZYV	Snowbird Mk.V	
☐ G-BZYW	Cameron N-90	
☐ G-BZYX	Raj Hamsa X'Air	
☐ G-BZYY	Cameron N-90	
☐ G-BZZD	Reims F172M	
☐ G-CAHA	Piper PA-34-200T Seneca	
☐ G-CAIN	CFM Shadow CD	
☐ G-CALL	Piper PA-23-250 Aztec F	
☐ G-CAMB	Aerospatiale AS.355F2	
☐ G-CAMM	Hawker Cygnet Rep	
☐ G-CAMP	Cameron N-105	
☐ G-CAMR	Quad City Challenger	
☐ G-CAPI	Mudry CAP.10B	
☐ G-CAPX	Mudry CAP.10B	
☐ G-CBAB	Scottish Aviation Bulldog	
☐ G-CBAD	Mainair Blade	
☐ G-CBAE	BAe 146-200	
☐ G-CBAF	Neico Lancair 320	
☐ G-CBAH	Raj Hamsa X'Air	
☐ G-CBAI	Flight Design CT2K	
☐ G-CBAK	Robinson R44	
☐ G-CBAL	Piper PA-28-161 Warrior	
☐ G-CBAN	Scottish Aviation Bulldog	
☐ G-CBAP	Zenair CH.601UL	
☐ G-CBAR	GlaStar	
☐ G-CBAS	Rans S6 Coyote II	
☐ G-CBAT	Cameron Z-90	
☐ G-CBAU	Rand KR-2	
☐ G-CBAV	Raj Hamsa X'Air	
☐ G-CBAW	Cameron A-300	
☐ G-CBAX	Tecnam P92 Echo	
☐ G-CBAY	Pegasus Quantum	
☐ G-CBAZ	Rans S-6ES Coyote II	
☐ G-CBBA	Robin DR.400-180R	
☐ G-CBBB	Pegasus Quantum	
☐ G-CBBC	Scottish Aviation Bulldog	
☐ G-CBBF	Beech 76 Duchess	
☐ G-CBBG	Mainair Blade	
☐ G-CBBH	Raj Hamsa X'Air	
☐ G-CBBK	Robinson R22B	
☐ G-CBBL	Scottish Aviation Bulldog	
☐ G-CBBM	ICP MXP-740 Savannah	
☐ G-CBBN	Pegasus Quantum	
☐ G-CBBO	Whittaker MW-5D	
☐ G-CBBP	Pegasus Quantum	
☐ G-CBBS	Scottish Aviation Bulldog	
☐ G-CBBT	Scottish Aviation Bulldog	
☐ G-CBBU	Scottish Aviation Bulldog	
☐ G-CBBV	Aerospatiale Gazelle	
☐ G-CBBW	Scottish Aviation Bulldog	
☐ G-CBBX	Lindstrand LBL-69A	
☐ G-CBBZ	Pegasus Quantum	
☐ G-CBCA	Piper PA-32R-301T	
☐ G-CBCB	Scottish Aviation Bulldog	
☐ G-CBCD	Pegasus Quantum	
☐ G-CBCF	Pegasus Quantum	
☐ G-CBCH	Zenair CH.701UL	
☐ G-CBCI	Raj Hamsa X'Air	
☐ G-CBCJ	RAF 2000 GTX-SE	
☐ G-CBCK	Slingsby Nipper 3	
☐ G-CBCL	GlaStar	
☐ G-CBCM	Raj Hamsa X'Air	
☐ G-CBCN	Schweizer 269C-1	
☐ G-CBCP	Van's RV-6A	
☐ G-CBCR	Scottish Aviation Bulldog	
☐ G-CBCV	Scottish Aviation Bulldog	
☐ G-CBCX	Pegasus Quantum	
☐ G-CBCY	Beech C24R Sierra	
☐ G-CBCZ	CFM Streak Shadow	
☐ G-CBDC	Thruster T600N	
☐ G-CBDD	Mainair Blade	
☐ G-CBDG	Zenair CH.601HD	
☐ G-CBDH	Flight Design CT2K	
☐ G-CBDI	Denney Kitfox	

G-CBDJ	Flight Design CT2K
G-CBDK	Scottish Aviation Bulldog
G-CBDL	Mainair Blade
G-CBDM	Tecnam P92 Echo
G-CBDN	Mainair Blade
G-CBDO	Raj Hamsa X'Air
G-CBDP	Mainair Blade
G-CBDS	Scottish Aviation Bulldog
G-CBDT	Zenair CH.601HD
G-CBDU	Quad City Challenger
G-CBDV	Raj Hamsa X'Air
G-CBDW	Raj Hamsa X'Air
G-CBDX	Pegasus Quantum
G-CBDY	Raj Hamsa X'Air
G-CBDZ	Pegasus Quantum
G-CBEB	Air Creation Kiss 400
G-CBEC	Cameron Z-105
G-CBED	Cameron Z-90
G-CBEE	Piper PA-28R-200
G-CBEF	Scottish Aviation Bulldog
G-CBEG	Robinson R44
G-CBEH	Scottish Aviation Bulldog
G-CBEI	Piper PA-22-108 Colt
G-CBEJ	Colt 120A
G-CBEK	Scottish Aviation Bulldog
G-CBEL	Hawker Sea Fury
G-CBEM	Mainair Blade
G-CBEN	Pegasus Quantum
G-CBEO	BAe Jetstream 31
G-CBES	Europa XS
G-CBET	Mainair Blade
G-CBEU	Pegasus Quantum
G-CBEV	Pegasus Quantum
G-CBEW	Flight Design CT2K
G-CBEX	Flight Design CT2K
G-CBEY	Cameron C-80
G-CBEZ	Robin DR.400-180 Regent
G-CBFA	Diamond DA.40 Star
G-CBFE	Raj Hamsa X'Air
G-CBFF	Cameron O-120
G-CBFH	Thunder AX8-105
G-CBFJ	Robinson R44
G-CBFK	Murphy Rebel
G-CBFM	SOCATA TB-21 Trinidad
G-CBFN	Robin HR.100-200B
G-CBFO	Cessna 172S Skyhawk
G-CBFP	Scottish Aviation Bulldog
G-CBFT	Raj Hamsa X'Air
G-CBFU	Scottish Aviation Bulldog
G-CBFV	Ikarus C42 Cyclone
G-CBFW	Bensen B.8
G-CBFX	Rans S6 Coyote II (N)
G-CBFY	Cameron Z-250
G-CBFZ	Jabiru UL-450
G-CBGA	PZL Koliber 160A
G-CBGB	Zenair CH.601UL
G-CBGC	SOCATA TB-10 Tobago
G-CBGD	Zenair CH.701UL
G-CBGE	Tecnam P92 Echo
G-CBGG	Pegasus Quantum
G-CBGH	Teverson Bisport
G-CBGI	CFM Streak Shadow
G-CBGJ	Aeroprakt A22 Foxbat
G-CBGL	Max Holste 1521
G-CBGN	Van's RV-4
G-CBGO	Maverick 430
G-CBGP	Ikarus C42 Cyclone
G-CBGR	Jabiru UL
G-CBGS	Cyclone AX2000
G-CBGU	Thruster T600N
G-CBGV	Thruster T600N
G-CBGW	Thruster T600N
G-CBGX	Scottish Aviation Bulldog
G-CBGZ	Aerospatiale Gazelle
G-CBHA	SOCATA TB-10 Tobago
G-CBHB	Raj Hamsa X'Air
G-CBHC	RAF 2000 GTX-SE
G-CBHD	Cameron Z-160
G-CBHG	Mainair Blade
G-CBHI	Europa XS
G-CBHJ	Mainair Blade
G-CBHK	Pegasus Quantum
G-CBHL	Aerospatiale AS.350B2
G-CBHM	Mainair Blade
G-CBHN	Pegasus Quantum
G-CBHO	Gloster Gladiator
G-CBHP	Corby CJ-1 Starlet
G-CBHR	Stephens Akro Z
G-CBHT	Dassault Falcon 900EX
G-CBHU	Sherwood Ranger
G-CBHV	Raj Hamsa X'Air
G-CBHW	Cameron Z-105
G-CBHX	Cameron V-77
G-CBHY	Pegasus Quantum
G-CBHZ	RAF 2000 GTX-SE
G-CBIB	Flight Design CT2K
G-CBIC	Raj Hamsa X'Air
G-CBID	Scottish Aviation Bulldog
G-CBIE	Flight Design CT2K
G-CBIF	Jabiru UL-450
G-CBIG	Mainair Blade
G-CBIH	Cameron Z-31
G-CBII	Raj Hamsa X'Air
G-CBIJ	Ikarus C42 Cyclone
G-CBIK	Rotorway Exec
G-CBIL	Cessna 182K Skylane
G-CBIM	Lindstrand LBL-90A
G-CBIN	TEAM Minimax
G-CBIO	Thruster T600N
G-CBIP	Thruster T600N
G-CBIR	Thruster T600N
G-CBIS	Raj Hamsa X'Air
G-CBIT	RAF 2000 GTX-SE
G-CBIU	Cameron Flame 90SS
G-CBIV	Best Off Sky Ranger
G-CBIW	Lindstrand LBL-310A
G-CBIX	Zenair CH.601UL
G-CBIY	EV-97 Eurostar
G-CBIZ	Pegasus Quantum
G-CBJA	Air Creation Kiss 400
G-CBJD	GlaStar
G-CBJE	RAF 2000 GTX-SE
G-CBJG	DHC-1 Chipmunk
G-CBJH	Aeroprakt A22 Foxbat
G-CBJJ	Scottish Aviation Bulldog
G-CBJK	Scottish Aviation Bulldog
G-CBJL	Air Creation Kiss 400
G-CBJM	Jabiru SP-470
G-CBJN	RAF 2000 GTX-SE
G-CBJO	Pegasus Quantum
G-CBJP	Zenair CH.601UL
G-CBJR	EV-97 Eurostar
G-CBJS	Cameron C-60
G-CBJT	Mainair Blade
G-CBJU	Van's RV-7A
G-CBJV	Rotorway Exec 162F
G-CBJW	Ikarus C42 Cyclone
G-CBJX	Raj Hamsa X'Air
G-CBJY	Jabiru UL-450
G-CBJZ	Aerospatiale Gazelle
G-CBKA	Aerospatiale Gazelle
G-CBKB	Bucker Bu.181C
G-CBKC	Aerospatiale Gazelle
G-CBKD	Aerospatiale Gazelle
G-CBKE	Air Creation Kiss 400
G-CBKF	Easy Rider
G-CBKG	Thruster T600N
G-CBKI	Cameron Z-90
G-CBKJ	Cameron Z-90
G-CBKK	UltraMagic S-130
G-CBKL	Raj Hamsa X'Air
G-CBKM	Mainair Blade
G-CBKN	Mainair Blade
G-CBKO	Mainair Blade
G-CBKR	Piper PA-28-161 Warrior
G-CBKS	Air Creation Kiss 400
G-CBKU	Ikarus C42 Cyclone
C-CBKV	Cameron Z-77
G-CBKW	Pegasus Quantum
G-CBKY	Jabiru SP-470
G-CBLA	Aero Designs Pulsar XP
G-CBLB	Tecnam P92 Echo
G-CBLD	Mainair Blade
G-CBLE	Robin R.2120U
G-CBLF	Raj Hamsa X'Air
G-CBLH	Raj Hamsa X'Air
G-CBLJ	Yakovlev Yak-52
G-CBLK	Hawker Hind
G-CBLL	Pegasus Quantum
G-CBLM	Mainair Blade
G-CBLN	Cameron Z-31
G-CBLO	Lindstrand LBL-42A
G-CBLP	Raj Hamsa X'Air
G-CBLS	Fiat CR.42 Falco
G-CBLT	Mainair Blade
G-CBLU	Cameron C-80
G-CBLV	Flight Design CT2K
G-CBLW	Raj Hamsa X'Air
G-CBLX	Air Creation Kiss 400
G-CBLY	Grob 109B
G-CBLZ	Rutan LongEz
G-CBMA	Raj Hamsa X'Air
G-CBMB	Cyclone AX2000
G-CBMC	Cameron Z-105
G-CBMD	Yakovlev Yak-52
G-CBME	Reims F172M
G-CBMI	Yakovlev Yak-52
G-CBMJ	RAF 2000 GTX-SE
G-CBMK	Cameron Z-120
G-CBML	DHC-6-310
G-CBMM	Mainair Blade
G-CBMO	Piper PA-28-180 Cherokee
G-CBMP	Cessna R182 Skylane RG
G-CBMR	Medway EclipseR
G-CBMS	Medway EclipseR
G-CBMT	Robin DR.400-180 Regent
G-CBMU	Cameron C-90
G-CBMV	Pegasus Quantum
G-CBMW	Zenair CH.701UL
G-CBMX	Air Creation Kiss 400
G-CBMY	
G-CBMZ	EV-97 Eurostar
G-CBNA	Flight Design CT2K
G-CBNB	Eurocopter EC120B
G-CBNC	Mainair Blade
G-CBNF	Rans S7 Courier
G-CBNG	Robin R.2112 Alpha
G-CBNI	Lindstrand LBL-90A
G-CBNJ	Raj Hamsa X'Air
G-CBNL	Dyn'Aero MCR-01
G-CBNM	North American P-51D
G-CBNN	
G-CBNO	CFM Streak Shadow
G-CBNT	Pegasus Quantum
G-CBNU	Spitfire LF.IX
G-CBNV	Rans S6 Coyote II (N)
G-CBNW	Cameron N-105
G-CBNX	Bensen B.8MR
G-CBNY	Air Creation Kiss 400

☐ G-CBNZ	TEAM Himax 1700R	
☐ G-CBOA	Auster B8 Agricola	
☐ G-CBOC	Raj Hamsa X'Air	
☐ G-CBOE	Hawker Hurricane IIB	
☐ G-CBOF	Europa XS	
☐ G-CBOG	Mainair Blade	
☐ G-CBOK	Rans S6 Coyote II	
☐ G-CBOM	Mainair Blade	
☐ G-CBON	Cameron Bull 110SS	
☐ G-CBOO	Mainair Blade	
☐ G-CBOP	Jabiru UL-450	
☐ G-CBOR	Reims F172N	
☐ G-CBOS	Rans S6 Coyote II	
☐ G-CBOT	Robinson R44	
☐ G-CBOU	Parsons Two Place Gyro	
☐ G-CBOV	Mainair Blade	
☐ G-CBOW	Cameron Z-120	
☐ G-CBOX		
☐ G-CBOY	Pegasus Quantum	
☐ G-CBOZ	Yakovlev Yak-52	
☐ G-CBPA		
☐ G-CBPC	Sportavia-Putzer RF-5B	
☐ G-CBPD	Ikarus C42 Cyclone	
☐ G-CBPE	SOCATA TB-10 Tobago	
☐ G-CBPF		
☐ G-CBPG	Balloon Works Firefly 7	
☐ G-CBPH	Lindstrand LBL-105A	
☐ G-CBPI	Piper PA-28R-201	
☐ G-CBPJ		
☐ G-CBPK	Rand KR-2	
☐ G-CBPL	TEAM Minimax	
☐ G-CBPM	Yakovlev Yak-50	
☐ G-CBPN	Thruster T600N	
☐ G-CBPO	Yakovlev Yak-50	
☐ G-CBPP	Jabiru UL-450	
☐ G-CBPR	Jabiru UL-450	
☐ G-CBPS		
☐ G-CBPU	Raj Hamsa X'Air	
☐ G-CBPV	Zenair CH.601UL	
☐ G-CBPW	Lindstrand LBL-105A	
☐ G-CBPY	Yakovlev Yak-52	
☐ G-CBPZ	UltraMagic N-300	
☐ G-CBRB	UltraMagic S-105	
☐ G-CBRC	Jodel D.18	
☐ G-CBRD	Jodel D.18	
☐ G-CBRE	Mainair Blade	
☐ G-CBRF	Ikarus C42 Cyclone	
☐ G-CBRG	Cessna 560 Citation XL	
☐ G-CBRH	Yakovlev Yak-52	
☐ G-CBRJ	Mainair Blade	
☐ G-CBRK	UltraMagic M-77	
☐ G-CBRL	Yakovlev Yak-52	
☐ G-CBRM	Mainair Blade	
☐ G-CBRN		
☐ G-CBRO	Robinson R44	
☐ G-CBRP	Yakovlev Yak-52	
☐ G-CBRR	EV-97 Eurostar	
☐ G-CBRT	Murphy Elite	
☐ G-CBRU	Yakovlev Yak-52	
☐ G-CBRV	Cameron C-90	
☐ G-CBRW	Yakovlev Yak-52	
☐ G-CBRX	Zenair CH.601UL	
☐ G-CBRY	P & M Quik	
☐ G-CBRZ	Air Creation Kiss 400	
☐ G-CBSD	Piper PA-28-236 Dakota	
☐ G-CBSF	Aerospatiale Gazelle	
☐ G-CBSH	Aerospatiale Gazelle	
☐ G-CBSI	Aerospatiale Gazelle	
☐ G-CBSK	Aerospatiale Gazelle	
☐ G-CBSL	Yakovlev Yak-52	
☐ G-CBSM	Mainair Blade	
☐ G-CBSN	Yakovlev Yak-52	
☐ G-CBSO	Piper PA-28-181 Archer	
☐ G-CBSP	Pegasus Quantum	
☐ G-CBSR	Yakovlev Yak-52	
☐ G-CBSS	Yakovlev Yak-52	
☐ G-CBSU	Jabiru UL	
☐ G-CBSV	Bensen B.8MR	
☐ G-CBSW		
☐ G-CBSX	Air Creation Kiss 400	
☐ G-CBSZ	Mainair Blade	
☐ G-CBTA		
☐ G-CBTB	III Sky Arrow 650TS	
☐ G-CBTC		
☐ G-CBTD	Pegasus Quantum	
☐ G-CBTE	Mainair Blade	
☐ G-CBTF		
☐ G-CBTG	Ikarus C42 Cyclone	
☐ G-CBTK	Raj Hamsa X'Air	
☐ G-CBTL	Monnett Moni	
☐ G-CBTM	Mainair Blade	
☐ G-CBTN	Piper PA-31 Navajo	
☐ G-CBTO	Rans S6 Coyote II (N)	
☐ G-CBTR	Lindstrand LBL-120A	
☐ G-CBTS	Gloster Gamecock Rep	
☐ G-CBTT	Piper PA-28-181 Archer	
☐ G-CBTW	Mainair Blade	
☐ G-CBTX	Denney Kitfox	
☐ G-CBTZ	Pegasus Quantum	
☐ G-CBUA	Extra EA230	
☐ G-CBUC	Raj Hamsa X'Air	
☐ G-CBUD	Pegasus Quantum	
☐ G-CBUE	UltraMagic N-250	
☐ G-CBUF	Flight Design CT2K	
☐ G-CBUG	Tecnam P92 Echo	
☐ G-CBUH	Westland Scout	
☐ G-CBUI	Westland Wasp	
☐ G-CBUJ	Raj Hamsa X'Air	
☐ G-CBUK	Van's RV-6A	
☐ G-CBUL		
☐ G-CBUM		
☐ G-CBUN	Barker Charade	
☐ G-CBUO	Cameron O-90	
☐ G-CBUP	VPM M16 Gyro	
☐ G-CBUR	Zenair CH.601UL	
☐ G-CBUS	Pegasus Quantum	
☐ G-CBUU	Pegasus Quantum	
☐ G-CBUV		
☐ G-CBUW	Cameron Z-133	
☐ G-CBUX	Cyclone AX2000	
☐ G-CBUY	Rans S6 Coyote II (N)	
☐ G-CBUZ	Pegasus Quantum	
☐ G-CBVA	Thruster T600N	
☐ G-CBVB	Robin R.2120U	
☐ G-CBVC	Raj Hamsa X'Air	
☐ G-CBVD	Cameron C-60	
☐ G-CBVE	Raj Hamsa X'Air	
☐ G-CBVF	Murphy Maverick	
☐ G-CBVG	Mainair Blade	
☐ G-CBVH	Lindstrand LBL-120A	
☐ G-CBVI	Robinson R44	
☐ G-CBVK	Fire Balloons G	
☐ G-CBVL	Robinson R22B	
☐ G-CBVM	EV-97 Eurostar	
☐ G-CBVN	P & M Quik	
☐ G-CBVO	Raj Hamsa X'Air	
☐ G-CBVR	Best Off Sky Ranger	
☐ G-CBVS	Best Off Skyranger	
☐ G-CBVT	Yakovlev Yak-52	
☐ G-CBVU	Piper PA-28R-200	
☐ G-CBVV	Cameron N-120	
☐ G-CBVX	Cessna 182P Skylane	
☐ G-CBVY	Ikarus C42 Cyclone	
☐ G-CBVZ	Flight Design CT2K	
☐ G-CBWA	Flight Design CT2K	
☐ G-CBWB	Piper PA-34-200T Seneca	
☐ G-CBWD	Piper PA-28-161 Warrior	
☐ G-CBWE	EV-97 Eurostar	
☐ G-CBWG	EV-97 Eurostar	
☐ G-CBWI	Thruster T600N	
☐ G-CBWJ	Thruster T600N	
☐ G-CBWK	UltraMagic H-77	
☐ G-CBWM	Mainair Blade	
☐ G-CBWN	Campbell Cricket Mk6	
☐ G-CBWO	Rotorway Exec 162F	
☐ G-CBWP	Europa	
☐ G-CBWS	Whittaker MW-6	
☐ G-CBWU	Rotorway Exec 162F	
☐ G-CBWV	Falconair F-12A	
☐ G-CBWW	Best Off Skyranger	
☐ G-CBWX	Slingsby T.67M	
☐ G-CBWY	Raj Hamsa X'Air	
☐ G-CBWZ	Robinson R22B	
☐ G-CBXA	Raj Hamsa X'Air	
☐ G-CBXC	Ikarus C42 Cyclone	
☐ G-CBXD	Bell 206L Long Ranger	
☐ G-CBXE	Easy Raider	
☐ G-CBXF	Easy Raider	
☐ G-CBXG	Thruster T600N	
☐ G-CBXH	Thruster T600N	
☐ G-CBXI		
☐ G-CBXJ	Cessna 172S Skyhawk	
☐ G-CBXK	Robinson R22M	
☐ G-CBXM	Mainair Blade	
☐ G-CBXN	Robinson R22B	
☐ G-CBXR	Raj Hamsa X'Air	
☐ G-CBXS	Best Off Sky Ranger	
☐ G-CBXT	Aerospatiale Gazelle	
☐ G-CBXU	TEAM Minimax	
☐ G-CBXV	Mainair Blade	
☐ G-CBXW	Europa XS	
☐ G-CBXZ	Rans S6 Coyote II (N)	
☐ G-CBYB	Rotorway Exec 162F	
☐ G-CBYC	Cameron Z-275	
☐ G-CBYD	Rans S6 Coyote II	
☐ G-CBYE	P & M Quik	
☐ G-CBYF	Mainair Blade	
☐ G-CBYH	Aeroprakt A22 Foxbat	
☐ G-CBYI	Pegasus Quantum	
☐ G-CBYJ	Steen Skybolt	
☐ G-CBYM	Mainair Blade	
☐ G-CBYN	Europa XS	
☐ G-CBYO	P & M Quik	
☐ G-CBYP	Whittaker MW-6S	
☐ G-CBYS	Lindstrand LBL-21A	
☐ G-CBYT	Thruster T600N	
☐ G-CBYU	Piper PA-28-161 Warrior	
☐ G-CBYV	Pegasus Quantum	
☐ G-CBYW	Hatz CB-1	
☐ G-CBYX	Bell 206B Jet Ranger	
☐ G-CBYY	Robinson R44	
☐ G-CBYZ	Tecnam P92 Echo	
☐ G-CBZA	Mainair Blade	
☐ G-CBZB	Mainair Blade	
☐ G-CBZC		
☐ G-CBZD	Mainair Blade	
☐ G-CBZE	Robinson R44	
☐ G-CBZF	Robinson R22B	
☐ G-CBZG	Rans S6 Coyote II	
☐ G-CBZH	P & M Quik	
☐ G-CBZI	Rotorway Exec 162F	
☐ G-CBZJ	Lindstrand LBL-25A	
☐ G-CBZK	Robin DR.400-180 Regent	
☐ G-CBZL	Aerospatiale Gazelle	
☐ G-CBZM	Jabiru SPL-450	
☐ G-CBZN	Rans S6 Coyote II (N)	
☐ G-CBZP	Hawker Fury I	
☐ G-CBZR	Piper PA-28R-201	
☐ G-CBZS	Lynden Aurora	

Reg	Type		Reg	Type		Reg	Type
G-CBZT	P & M Quik		G-CCDF	P & M Quik		G-CCGI	P & M Quik
G-CBZU	Lindstrand LBL-180A		G-CCDG	Best Off Sky Ranger		G-CCGK	Mainair Blade
G-CBZV	UltraMagic S-130		G-CCDH	Best Off Sky Ranger		G-CCGL	SOCATA TB-20 Trinidad
G-CBZW	Zenair CH.701UL		G-CCDJ	Raj Hamsa X'Air		G-CCGM	Air Creation Kiss 450
G-CBZX	Dyn'Aero MCR-01		G-CCDK	Pegasus Quantum		G-CCGO	Medway AV8R
G-CBZY	Doodle Bug/Target		G-CCDL	Raj Hamsa X'Air		G-CCGP	Bristol 200
G-CBZZ	Cameron Z-275		G-CCDM	Mainair Blade		G-CCGR	Raj Hamsa X'Air
G-CCAB	Mainair Blade		G-CCDN	Piper PA-28-181 Archer		G-CCGS	Dornier Do.328-100
G-CCAC	EV-97 Eurostar		G-CCDO	P & M Quik		G-CCGT	Cameron Z-425
G-CCAD	P & M Quik		G-CCDP	Raj Hamsa X'Air		G-CCGU	Van's RV-9A
G-CCAE	Jabiru UL-450		G-CCDR	Raj Hamsa X'Air		G-CCGV	Lindstrand LBL-150A
G-CCAF	Best Off Sky Ranger		G-CCDS	Nicollier HN700 Menestrel		G-CCGW	Europa
G-CCAG	Mainair Blade		G-CCDT	Rockwell 114		G-CCGX	
G-CCAH	M16 Tandem Trainer		G-CCDU	Tecnam P92 Echo		G-CCGY	Cameron Z-105
G-CCAK	Zenair CH.601HD		G-CCDV	Thruster T600N 450		G-CCGZ	Cameron Z-250
G-CCAL	Tecnam P92 Echo		G-CCDW	Best Off Sky Ranger		G-CCHA	Diamond DA.40D Star
G-CCAM	Mainair Blade		G-CCDX	EV-97 Eurostar		G-CCHB	Diamond DA.40D Star
G-CCAN	Cessna 182P Skylane		G-CCDY	Best Off Skyranger		G-CCHC	Diamond DA.40D Star
G-CCAP	Robinson R22B		G-CCDZ	Pegasus Quantum		G-CCHD	Diamond DA.40D Star
G-CCAR	Cameron N-77		G-CCEA	P & M Quik		G-CCHE	Diamond DA.40D Star
G-CCAS	P & M Quik		G-CCEB	Thruster T600N 450		G-CCHF	Diamond DA.40D Star
G-CCAT	Grumman AA-5A Cheetah		G-CCEC	Evans VP-1		G-CCHG	Diamond DA.40D Star
G-CCAU	Eurocopter EC135T1		G-CCED	Zenair CH.601UL		G-CCHH	P & M Quik
G-CCAV	Piper PA-28-181 Archer		G-CCEE	Piper PA-15 Vagabond		G-CCHI	P & M Quik
G-CCAW	Mainair Blade		G-CCEF	Europa		G-CCHJ	Air Creation Kiss 400
G-CCAY	Cameron Z-42		G-CCEG	Rans S6 Coyote II		G-CCHK	Diamond DA.40D Star
G-CCAZ	P & M Quik		G-CCEH	Best Off Sky Ranger		G-CCHL	Piper PA-28-181 Archer
G-CCBA	Best Off Sky Ranger		G-CCEI	Evans VP-2		G-CCHM	Air Creation Kiss 450
G-CCBB	Cameron N-90		G-CCEJ	EV-97 Eurostar		G-CCHN	Corby CJ-1 Starlet
G-CCBC	Thruster T600N 450		G-CCEK	Air Creation Kiss 400		G-CCHO	P & M Quik
G-CCBF	Maule M-5-235C		G-CCEL	Jabiru UL		G-CCHP	Cameron Z-31
G-CCBG	Best Off Sky Ranger		G-CCEM	EV-97 Eurostar		G-CCHR	Easy Raider
G-CCBH	Piper PA-28-235 Cherokee		G-CCEN	Cameron Z-120		G-CCHS	Raj Hamsa X'Air
G-CCBI	Raj Hamsa X'Air		G-CCEO	Thunder Ax10-180		G-CCHT	Cessna 152
G-CCBJ	Best Off Sky Ranger		G-CCEP	Raj Hamsa X'Air		G-CCHV	Mainair Rapier
G-CCBK	EV-97 Eurostar		G-CCER	Gemini Flash 2A		G-CCHW	Cameron Z-77
G-CCBL	Agusta Bell 206B		G-CCES	Raj Hamsa X'Air		G-CCHX	Scheibe SF25C Falke
G-CCBM	EV-97 Eurostar		G-CCET	Nova Vertex 28		G-CCHY	Bucker Bu.131
G-CCBN	Replica Plans SE5A		G-CCEU	RAF 2000 GTX-SE		G-CCIC	Thruster T600N
G-CCBO			G-CCEW	P & M Quik		G-CCID	Jabiru J400
G-CCBP	Lindstrand LBL-60X		G-CCEY	Raj Hamsa X'Air		G-CCIE	Colt 315A
G-CCBR	Jodel D.120 Paris-Nice		G-CCEZ	Easy Raider		G-CCIF	Mainair Blade
G-CCBS			G-CCFA	Air Creation Kiss 400		G-CCIG	Aero Designs Pulsar
G-CCBT	Cameron Z-90		G-CCFB	P & M Quik		G-CCIH	Pegasus Quantum
G-CCBU	Raj Hamsa X'Air		G-CCFC	Robinson R44		G-CCII	ICP MXP-740 Savannah
G-CCBV	Cameron Z-225		G-CCFD	Quad City Challenger		G-CCIJ	Piper PA-28R-180
G-CCBW	Sherwood Ranger		G-CCFE	Tipsy Nipper		G-CCIK	Best Off Sky Ranger
G-CCBX	Raj Hamsa X'Air		G-CCFF	Lindstrand LBL-150A		G-CCIO	Best Off Sky Ranger
G-CCBY	Jabiru UL-450		G-CCFG	Dyn'Aero MCR-01		G-CCIR	Van's RV-8
G-CCBZ	Aero Designs Pulsar		G-CCFH			G-CCIS	Scheibe SF28A Falke
G-CCCA	Spitfire Tr.IX		G-CCFI	Piper PA-32-260		G-CCIT	Zenair CH.701UL
G-CCCB	Thruster T600N 450		G-CCFJ	Kolb Twinstar Mk.3		G-CCIU	Cameron N-105
G-CCCD	Pegasus Quantum		G-CCFK	Europa XS		G-CCIV	P & M Quik
G-CCCE	Aeroprakt A22 Foxbat		G-CCFL	P & M Quik		G-CCIW	Raj Hamsa X'Air
G-CCCF	Thruster T600N 450		G-CCFM	Mainair Blade		G-CCIY	Best Off Sky Ranger
G-CCCG	P & M Quik		G-CCFN	Cameron N-105		G-CCIZ	PZL Koliber 160A
G-CCCI	Medway EclipseR		G-CCFO	Pitts S-1S Special		G-CCJA	Best Off Sky Ranger
G-CCCJ	Nicollier HN700 Menestrel		G-CCFP	Diamond DA.40D Star		G-CCJB	Zenair CH.701 STOL
G-CCCK	Best Off Sky Ranger		G-CCFR	Diamond DA.40D Star		G-CCJD	Pegasus Quantum
G-CCCM	Best Off Skyranger		G-CCFS	Diamond DA.40D Star		G-CCJE	Schweizer 269C-1
G-CCCN	Robin R.3000/160		G-CCFT	Pegasus Quantum		G-CCJF	Cameron C-90
G-CCCO	EV-97 Eurostar		G-CCFU	Diamond DA.40D Star		G-CCJG	Cameron A-200
G-CCCP	Yakovlev Yak-52		G-CCFV	Lindstrand LBL-77A		G-CCJH	Lindstrand LBL-90A
G-CCCR	Best Off Sky Ranger		G-CCFW	WAR Focke-Wulf FW190		G-CCJI	Van's RV-6
G-CCCT	Ikarus C42 Cyclone		G-CCFX	EAA Acrosport 2		G-CCJJ	Medway Pirana
G-CCCU	Thruster T600N 450		G-CCFY	Rotorway Exec 162F		G-CCJK	Yakovlev Yak-52
G-CCCV	Raj Hamsa X'Air		G-CCFZ	Ikarus C42 Cyclone		G-CCJL	ST Aviation Spitfire 26
G-CCCW	Pereira Osprey 2		G-CCGB	TEAM Minimax		G-CCJM	P & M Quik
G-CCCY	Best Off Sky Ranger		G-CCGC	P & M Quik		G-CCJN	Rans S6 Coyote II
G-CCDB	P & M Quik		G-CCGE	Robinson R22B		G-CCJO	ICP MXP-740 Savannah
G-CCDC	Rans S6 Coyote II		G-CCGF	Robinson R22B		G-CCJS	Easy Raider
G-CCDD	P & M Quik		G-CCGG	Jabiru J400		G-CCJT	Best Off Sky Ranger
G-CCDE	Robinson R22B		G-CCGH	ST Aviation Spitfire 26		G-CCJU	ICP MXP-740 Savannah

☐ G-CCJV	Aeroprakt A22 Foxbat	
☐ G-CCJW	Best Off Sky Ranger	
☐ G-CCJX	Europa XS	
☐ G-CCJY	Cameron Z-42	
☐ G-CCJZ		
☐ G-CCKF	Best Off Sky Ranger	
☐ G-CCKG	Best Off Skyranger	
☐ G-CCKH	Diamond DA.40D Star	
☐ G-CCKI	Diamond DA.40D Star	
☐ G-CCKJ	Raj Hamsa X'Air	
☐ G-CCKK	EV-97 Eurostar	
☐ G-CCKL	EV-97 Eurostar	
☐ G-CCKM	P & M Quik	
☐ G-CCKN	Nicollier HN700 Menestrel	
☐ G-CCKO	P & M Quik	
☐ G-CCKP	Robin DR.400-120	
☐ G-CCKR	Pietenpol Aircamper	
☐ G-CCKS	Hughes 369E	
☐ G-CCKT	Hapi Cygnet SF-2A	
☐ G-CCKU	Canadian Home Rotors	
☐ G-CCKV	Isaacs Fury II	
☐ G-CCKW	Piper PA-18-135	
☐ G-CCKX	Lindstrand LBL-210A	
☐ G-CCKY	Lindstrand LBL-240A	
☐ G-CCKZ	Customcraft A25	
☐ G-CCLA		
☐ G-CCLB	Diamond DA.40D Star	
☐ G-CCLC	Diamond DA.40D Star	
☐ G-CCLE	EV-97 Eurostar	
☐ G-CCLF	Best Off Sky Ranger	
☐ G-CCLH	Rans S6 Coyote II	
☐ G-CCLJ	Piper PA-28-140 Cherokee	
☐ G-CCLL	Zenair CH.601XL	
☐ G-CCLM	P & M Quik	
☐ G-CCLO	UltraMagic H-77	
☐ G-CCLP	ICP MXP-740 Savannah	
☐ G-CCLR	Schleicher ASH 26E	
☐ G-CCLS	Ikarus C42 Cyclone	
☐ G-CCLU	Best Off Sky Ranger	
☐ G-CCLV	Diamond DA.40D Star	
☐ G-CCLW	Diamond DA.40D Star	
☐ G-CCLX	P & M Quik	
☐ G-CCMC	Jabiru UL-450	
☐ G-CCMD	P & M Quik	
☐ G-CCME	P & M Quik	
☐ G-CCMF	Diamond DA.40D Star	
☐ G-CCMG		
☐ G-CCMH	Miles M.2H Hawk Major	
☐ G-CCMI	Scottish Aviation Bulldog	
☐ G-CCMJ	Easy Raider	
☐ G-CCMK	Raj Hamsa X'Air	
☐ G-CCML	P & M Quik	
☐ G-CCMM	Dyn'Aero MCR-01	
☐ G-CCMN	Cameron C-90	
☐ G-CCMO	EV-97 Eurostar	
☐ G-CCMP	EV-97 Eurostar	
☐ G-CCMR	Robinson R22B	
☐ G-CCMS	P & M Quik	
☐ G-CCMT	Thruster T600N	
☐ G-CCMU	Rotorway Exec 162F	
☐ G-CCMW	CFM Shadow DD	
☐ G-CCMX	Best Off Skyranger	
☐ G-CCMZ	Best Off Sky Ranger	
☐ G-CCNA	Robin DR.100A	
☐ G-CCNB	Rans S6 Coyote II	
☐ G-CCNC	Cameron Z-275	
☐ G-CCND	Van's RV-9A	
☐ G-CCNE	Pegasus Quantum	
☐ G-CCNF	Raj Hamsa X'Air	
☐ G-CCNG	Flight Design CT2K	
☐ G-CCNH	Rans S6 Coyote II (N)	
☐ G-CCNJ	Best Off Sky Ranger	
☐ G-CCNM	P & M Quik	
☐ G-CCNN	Cameron Z-90	
☐ G-CCNP	Flight Design CT2K	
☐ G-CCNR	Best Off Sky Ranger	
☐ G-CCNS	Best Off Sky Ranger	
☐ G-CCNT	Ikarus C42 Cyclone	
☐ G-CCNU	Best Off Sky Ranger	
☐ G-CCNV	Cameron Z-210	
☐ G-CCNW	Pegasus Quantum	
☐ G-CCNX	Mudry CAP.10B	
☐ G-CCNY	Robinson R44	
☐ G-CCNZ	Raj Hamsa X'Air	
☐ G-CCOB	Aero C-104	
☐ G-CCOC	Pegasus Quantum	
☐ G-CCOF	Rans S6 Coyote II	
☐ G-CCOG	P & M Quik	
☐ G-CCOH	Raj Hamsa X'Air	
☐ G-CCOI	Lindstrand LBL-90A	
☐ G-CCOJ		
☐ G-CCOK	P & M Quik	
☐ G-CCOM	Westland Lysander IIIA	
☐ G-CCOO	Raj Hamsa X'Air	
☐ G-CCOP	UltraMagic M-105	
☐ G-CCOR	Sequoia F.8L Falco	
☐ G-CCOS	Cameron Z-350	
☐ G-CCOT	Cameron Z-105	
☐ G-CCOU	P & M Quik	
☐ G-CCOV	Europa XS	
☐ G-CCOW	P & M Quik	
☐ G-CCOX	Piper J-3C-65 Cub	
☐ G-CCOY	North American AT-6D	
☐ G-CCOZ	Monnett Sonerai	
☐ G-CCPA	Air Creation Kiss 400	
☐ G-CCPC	P & M Quik	
☐ G-CCPD	Campbell Cricket Mk.4	
☐ G-CCPE	Steen Skybolt	
☐ G-CCPF	Best Off Sky Ranger	
☐ G-CCPG	P & M Quik	
☐ G-CCPH	EV-97 Eurostar	
☐ G-CCPJ	EV-97 Eurostar	
☐ G-CCPK	Murphy Rebel	
☐ G-CCPL	Best Off Sky Ranger	
☐ G-CCPM	Mainair Blade	
☐ G-CCPN	Dyn'Aero MCR-01	
☐ G-CCPO	Cameron N-77	
☐ G-CCPP	Cameron C-70	
☐ G-CCPS	Ikarus C42 Cyclone	
☐ G-CCPT	Cameron Z-90	
☐ G-CCPV	Jabiru J400	
☐ G-CCPW	BAe Jetstream 31	
☐ G-CCPX	Diamond DA.40D Star	
☐ G-CCPY	Hughes 369D	
☐ G-CCPZ	Cameron Z-225	
☐ G-CCRA	Glaser-Dirks DG-800B	
☐ G-CCRB	Kolb Twinstar Mk.3	
☐ G-CCRC	Cessna TU206G	
☐ G-CCRD	Robinson R44	
☐ G-CCRF	Pegasus Quantum	
☐ G-CCRG	UltraMagic M-77	
☐ G-CCRH	Cameron Z-315	
☐ G-CCRI	Raj Hamsa X'Air	
☐ G-CCRJ	Europa	
☐ G-CCRK	Luscombe 8A Silvaire	
☐ G-CCRN	Thruster T600N	
☐ G-CCRR	Best Off Sky Ranger	
☐ G-CCRS	Lindstrand LBL-210A	
☐ G-CCRT	Pegasus Quantum	
☐ G-CCRU		
☐ G-CCRV	Best Off Sky Ranger	
☐ G-CCRW	P & M Quik	
☐ G-CCRX	Jabiru UL-450	
☐ G-CCSA	Cameron Z-350	
☐ G-CCSD	P & M Quik	
☐ G-CCSE	P & M Quik	
☐ G-CCSF	P & M Quik	
☐ G-CCSG	Cameron Z-275	
☐ G-CCSH	P & M Quik	
☐ G-CCSI	Cameron Z-42	
☐ G-CCSJ	Cameron A-275	
☐ G-CCSK	Zenair CH.701	
☐ G-CCSL	P & M Quik	
☐ G-CCSM	Lindstrand LBL-105A	
☐ G-CCSN	Cessna U206G	
☐ G-CCSO	Raj Hamsa X'Air	
☐ G-CCSP	Cameron N-77	
☐ G-CCSR	EV-97 Eurostar	
☐ G-CCSS	Lindstrand LBL-90A	
☐ G-CCST	Piper PA-32R-301	
☐ G-CCSU	Yakovlev Yak-52	
☐ G-CCSV	ICP MXP-740 Savannah	
☐ G-CCSW	Nott PA HAFB	
☐ G-CCSX	Best Off Sky Ranger	
☐ G-CCSY	P & M Quik	
☐ G-CCTA	Zenair CH.601UL	
☐ G-CCTC	P & M Quik	
☐ G-CCTD	P & M Quik	
☐ G-CCTE	Dyn'Aero MCR-01	
☐ G-CCTF	Pitts S-2A Special	
☐ G-CCTG	Van's RV-3B	
☐ G-CCTH	EV-97 Eurostar	
☐ G-CCTI	EV-97 Eurostar	
☐ G-CCTK	Glaser-Dirks DG-800B	
☐ G-CCTL	Robinson R44	
☐ G-CCTM	Mainair Blade	
☐ G-CCTN	UltraMagic T-180	
☐ G-CCTO	EV-97 Eurostar	
☐ G-CCTP	EV-97 Eurostar	
☐ G-CCTR	Best Off Sky Ranger	
☐ G-CCTS	Cameron Z-120	
☐ G-CCTT	Cessna 172S Skyhawk	
☐ G-CCTU	P & M Quik	
☐ G-CCTV	Rans S6 Coyote II	
☐ G-CCTW	Cessna 152	
☐ G-CCTX	Rans S6 Coyote II	
☐ G-CCTZ	P & M Quik	
☐ G-CCUA	P & M Quik	
☐ G-CCUB	Piper J-3C-65 Cub	
☐ G-CCUD	Best Off Sky Ranger	
☐ G-CCUE	UltraMagic T-180	
☐ G-CCUF	Best Off Sky Ranger	
☐ G-CCUH	RAF 2000 GTX-SE	
☐ G-CCUI	Dyn'Aero MCR-01	
☐ G-CCUJ	Cameron C-90	
☐ G-CCUK	Agusta 109	
☐ G-CCUL	Europa XS	
☐ G-CCUN	Hughes 369D	
☐ G-CCUO	Hughes 369D	
☐ G-CCUP	Westland Wessex	
☐ G-CCUR	Pegasus Quantum	
☐ G-CCUS	Diamond DA.40D Star	
☐ G-CCUT	EV-97 Eurostar	
☐ G-CCUU	Shiraz Gyroplane	
☐ G-CCUV	Piper PA-25-260 Pawnee	
☐ G-CCUY	Europa	
☐ G-CCUZ	Thruster T600N	
☐ G-CCVA	EV-97 Eurostar	
☐ G-CCVB	P & M Quik	
☐ G-CCVD	Cameron Z-105	
☐ G-CCVE	Raj Hamsa X'Air	
☐ G-CCVF	Lindstrand LBL-105A	
☐ G-CCVG	Schweizer 269C-1	
☐ G-CCVH	Curtiss H75A-1	
☐ G-CCVI	Zenair CH.701 SP	
☐ G-CCVJ	Raj Hamsa X'Air	
☐ G-CCVK	EV-97 Eurostar	
☐ G-CCVL	Zenair CH.601XL	
☐ G-CCVM	Van's RV-7A	

☐ G-CCVN	Jabiru SP-470	
☐ G-CCVO	Bell 206B Jet Ranger	
☐ G-CCVP	Beech 58 Baron	
☐ G-CCVR	Best Off Sky Ranger	
☐ G-CCVS	Van's RV-6A	
☐ G-CCVT	Zenair CH.601UL	
☐ G-CCVU	Robinson R22B	
☐ G-CCVW	Nicollier HN700 Menestrel	
☐ G-CCVX	Mainair Tri-Flyer	
☐ G-CCVY	Robinson R22B	
☐ G-CCVZ	Cameron O-120	
☐ G-CCWA	Piper PA-28-181 Archer	
☐ G-CCWB	Aero L.39ZA	
☐ G-CCWC	Best Off Sky Ranger	
☐ G-CCWD	Robinson R44	
☐ G-CCWE	Lindstrand LBL-330A	
☐ G-CCWF	Raj Hamsa X'Air	
☐ G-CCWG	Whittaker MW-6	
☐ G-CCWH	Dyn'Aero MCR-01	
☐ G-CCWI	Robinson R44	
☐ G-CCWJ	Robinson R44	
☐ G-CCWK	Aerospatiale AS.355F2	
☐ G-CCWL	Mainair Blade	
☐ G-CCWM	Robin DR.400-180R	
☐ G-CCWN	Pegasus Quantum	
☐ G-CCWO	Pegasus Quantum	
☐ G-CCWP	EV-97 Eurostar	
☐ G-CCWR	P & M Quik	
☐ G-CCWT	Kubicek BB20GP	
☐ G-CCWU	Best Off Sky Ranger	
☐ G-CCWV	P & M Quik	
☐ G-CCWW	Pegasus Quantum	
☐ G-CCWX		
☐ G-CCWY	Pilatus PC-12	
☐ G-CCWZ	Raj Hamsa X'Air	
☐ G-CCXA	Boeing Stearman A75N1	
☐ G-CCXB	Boeing Stearman B75N1	
☐ G-CCXC	Mudry CAP.10B	
☐ G-CCXD	Lindstrand LBL-105B	
☐ G-CCXE	Cameron Z-120	
☐ G-CCXF	Cameron Z-90	
☐ G-CCXG	Replica Plans SE5A	
☐ G-CCXH	Best Off Sky Ranger	
☐ G-CCXI	Thorp T.211	
☐ G-CCXJ	Cessna 340A	
☐ G-CCXK	Pitts S-1S Special	
☐ G-CCXL	Best Off Sky Ranger	
☐ G-CCXM	Best Off Sky Ranger	
☐ G-CCXN	Best Off Sky Ranger	
☐ G-CCXO	Corby CJ-1 Starlet	
☐ G-CCXP	ICP MXP-740 Savannah	
☐ G-CCXR	Mainair Blade	
☐ G-CCXS	Bensen B.8MR	
☐ G-CCXT	P & M Quik	
☐ G-CCXU	Diamond DA.40D Star	
☐ G-CCXV	Thruster T600N	
☐ G-CCXW	Thruster T600N	
☐ G-CCXX	American General AG-5B	
☐ G-CCXZ	P & M Quik	
☐ G-CCYA	Jabiru J450	
☐ G-CCYB	Reality Escapade	
☐ G-CCYC	Robinson R44	
☐ G-CCYE	P & M Quik	
☐ G-CCYF	Aerophile 5500 Tethered	
☐ G-CCYG	Robinson R44	
☐ G-CCYH	Embraer EMB-145EP	
☐ G-CCYI	Cameron O-105	
☐ G-CCYJ	P & M Quik	
☐ G-CCYK	Cessna 180	
☐ G-CCYL	Pegasus Quantum	
☐ G-CCYM	Best Off Sky Ranger	
☐ G-CCYN	Cameron C-80	
☐ G-CCYO	Christen Eagle II	
☐ G-CCYP	Colt 56A	
☐ G-CCYR	Ikarus C42 Cyclone	
☐ G-CCYS	Reims F182Q Skylane	
☐ G-CCYT	Robinson R44	
☐ G-CCYU	UltraMagic S-90	
☐ G-CCYV		
☐ G-CCYX	Bell 412	
☐ G-CCYY	Piper PA-28-161 Warrior	
☐ G-CCYZ	Dornier EKW C3605	
☐ G-CCZA	MS.894A Minerva	
☐ G-CCZB	Pegasus Quantum	
☐ G-CCZC		
☐ G-CCZD	Van's RV-7	
☐ G-CCZG	Robinson R44	
☐ G-CCZH	Robinson R44	
☐ G-CCZI	Cameron A-275	
☐ G-CCZJ	Raj Hamsa X'Air	
☐ G-CCZK	Zenair CH.601UL	
☐ G-CCZL	Ikarus C42 Cyclone	
☐ G-CCZM	Best Off Sky Ranger	
☐ G-CCZN	Rans S6 Coyote II	
☐ G-CCZO	P & M Quik	
☐ G-CCZP	ST Aviation Spitfire 26	
☐ G-CCZR	Medway Raven Eclipse	
☐ G-CCZS	Raj Hamsa X'Air	
☐ G-CCZT	Van's RV-9A	
☐ G-CCZU	Diamond DA.40D Star	
☐ G-CCZV	Piper PA-28-151 Warrior	
☐ G-CCZW	Mainair Blade	
☐ G-CCZX	Robin DR.400-180 Regent	
☐ G-CCZY	Van's RV-9A	
☐ G-CCZZ	EV-97 Eurostar	
☐ G-CDAA	Pegasus Quantum	
☐ G-CDAB	Glasair IIS RG	
☐ G-CDAC	EV-97 Eurostar	
☐ G-CDAD	Lindstrand LBL-25A	
☐ G-CDAE	Van's RV-6A	
☐ G-CDAF	Bell 412	
☐ G-CDAG	Mainair Blade	
☐ G-CDAI	Robin DR.400-140B	
☐ G-CDAK	Zenair CH.601UL	
☐ G-CDAL	Zenair CH.601UL	
☐ G-CDAM	Sky 77-24	
☐ G-CDAO	Pegasus Quantum	
☐ G-CDAP	EV-97 Eurostar	
☐ G-CDAR	P & M Quik	
☐ G-CDAS		
☐ G-CDAT	ICP MXP-740 Savannah	
☐ G-CDAW	Robinson R22	
☐ G-CDAX	P & M Quik	
☐ G-CDAY	Best Off Sky Ranger	
☐ G-CDAZ	EV-97 Eurostar	
☐ G-CDBA	Best Off Sky Ranger	
☐ G-CDBB	P & M Quik	
☐ G-CDBC	Aviation Enterprises	
☐ G-CDBD	Jabiru J400	
☐ G-CDBE	Bensen B.8M	
☐ G-CDBF	Robinson R22	
☐ G-CDBG	Robinson R22	
☐ G-CDBJ		
☐ G-CDBK	Rotorway Exec 162F	
☐ G-CDBM	Robin DR.400-180 Regent	
☐ G-CDBO	Best Off Sky Ranger	
☐ G-CDBR	Stolp SA.300 Starduster Too	
☐ G-CDBS	MBB Bo.105DBS/4	
☐ G-CDBU	Ikarus C42 Cyclone	
☐ G-CDBV	Best Off Sky Ranger	
☐ G-CDBX	Europa XS	
☐ G-CDBY	Dyn'Aero MCR-01	
☐ G-CDBZ	Thruster T600N	
☐ G-CDCA	Robinson R44	
☐ G-CDCB	Robinson R44	
☐ G-CDCC	EV-97 Eurostar	
☐ G-CDCD	Van's RV-9A	
☐ G-CDCE	Mudry CAP.10B	
☐ G-CDCF	P & M Quik	
☐ G-CDCG	Ikarus C42 Cyclone	
☐ G-CDCH	Best Off Sky Ranger	
☐ G-CDCI	P & M Quik	
☐ G-CDCK	P & M Quik	
☐ G-CDCM	Ikarus C42 Cyclone	
☐ G-CDCO	Ikarus C42 Cyclone	
☐ G-CDCP	Jabiru J400	
☐ G-CDCR	ICP MXP-740 Savannah	
☐ G-CDCS	Piper PA-12 Super Cruiser	
☐ G-CDCT	EV-97 Eurostar	
☐ G-CDCU	Mainair Blade	
☐ G-CDCV	Robinson R44	
☐ G-CDCW	Reality Excapade	
☐ G-CDCX	Cessna 750 Citation X	
☐ G-CDCY	Pegasus Quantum	
☐ G-CDDA	SOCATA TB-20 Trinidad	
☐ G-CDDB	Schempp-Hirth Cirrus	
☐ G-CDDC	Cameron A-275	
☐ G-CDDD	Robinson R22B	
☐ G-CDDE	PZL Koliber 160A	
☐ G-CDDF	Pegasus Quantum	
☐ G-CDDG	Piper PA-28-161 Warrior	
☐ G-CDDH	Raj Hamsa X'Air	
☐ G-CDDI	Thruster T600N	
☐ G-CDDK	Cessna 172M Skyhawk	
☐ G-CDDL	Cameron Z-350	
☐ G-CDDM	Lindstrand LBL-90A	
☐ G-CDDN	Lindstrand LBL-90A	
☐ G-CDDO	Raj Hamsa X'Air	
☐ G-CDDP	Lazer Z.230	
☐ G-CDDR	Best Off Sky Ranger	
☐ G-CDDS	Zenair CH.601HD	
☐ G-CDDU	Best Off Sky Ranger	
☐ G-CDDV	Cameron Z-250	
☐ G-CDDW	Aeroprakt A22 Foxbat	
☐ G-CDDX	Thruster T600N	
☐ G-CDDY	Van's RV-8	
☐ G-CDEA	SAAB 2000	
☐ G-CDEB	SAAB 2000	
☐ G-CDEC	P & M Quik	
☐ G-CDED	Robinson R22B	
☐ G-CDEF	Piper PA-28-161 Cadet	
☐ G-CDEG	Boeing 737-8BK	
☐ G-CDEH	ICP MXP-740 Savannah	
☐ G-CDEI		
☐ G-CDEJ	Diamond DA.40D Star	
☐ G-CDEK	Diamond DA.40D Star	
☐ G-CDEL	Diamond DA.40D Star	
☐ G-CDEM	Raj Hamsa X'Air	
☐ G-CDEN	Pegasus Quantum	
☐ G-CDEO	Piper PA-28-180 Cherokee	
☐ G-CDEP	EV-97 Eurostar	
☐ G-CDER	Piper PA-28-161 Warrior	
☐ G-CDET	Culver Cadet	
☐ G-CDEU	Lindstrand LBL-90B	
☐ G-CDEV	Reality Escapade	
☐ G-CDEW	P & M Quik	
☐ G-CDEX	Europa	
☐ G-CDFA	Kolb Twinstar Mk.3	
☐ G-CDFC	UltraMagic S-160	
☐ G-CDFD	Scheibe SF25C Falke	
☐ G-CDFE	Yakovlev Yak-52	
☐ G-CDFF	ATR 42-300	
☐ G-CDFG	P & M Quik	
☐ G-CDFI	Cameron Colt 31A	
☐ G-CDFJ	Best Off Sky Ranger	
☐ G-CDFK	Jabiru SPL-450	
☐ G-CDFL	Zenair CH.601UL	
☐ G-CDFM	Raj Hamsa X'Air	
☐ G-CDFN	Thunder Ax7-77	

☐ G-CDFO	P & M Quik	
☐ G-CDFP	Best Off Sky Ranger	
☐ G-CDFR	Pegasus Quantum	
☐ G-CDFS	Embraer EMB-135ER	
☐ G-CDFU	Rans S6 Coyote II	
☐ G-CDFW	Sheffy Gyroplane	
☐ G-CDFY	Beech B200 Super King Air	
☐ G-CDGA	Taylor Monoplane	
☐ G-CDGB	Rans S6 Coyote II	
☐ G-CDGC	P & M Quik	
☐ G-CDGD	P & M Quik	
☐ G-CDGE	AirBourne XT912-B	
☐ G-CDGF	UltraMagic S-105	
☐ G-CDGG	Dyn'Aero MCR-01	
☐ G-CDGH	Rans S6 Coyote II	
☐ G-CDGI	Thruster T600N	
☐ G-CDGJ	Champion 7ECA	
☐ G-CDGN	Cameron C-90	
☐ G-CDGO	P & M Quik	
☐ G-CDGP	Zenair CH.601XL	
☐ G-CDGR	Zenair CH.701UL	
☐ G-CDGS	American General AG-5B	
☐ G-CDGT	Montgomerie Two Place	
☐ G-CDGU	Spitfire Mk.I	
☐ G-CDGW	Piper PA-28-181 Archer	
☐ G-CDGX	Pegasus Quantum	
☐ G-CDGY	Spitfire Mk.Vc	
☐ G-CDHA	Best Off Skyranger	
☐ G-CDHB	Strikemaster Mk.80A	
☐ G-CDHC	Slingsby T.67C	
☐ G-CDHD	Kubicek BB42	
☐ G-CDHE	Best Off Sky Ranger	
☐ G-CDHF	Piper PA-30-160	
☐ G-CDHG	P & M Quik	
☐ G-CDHH	Robinson R44	
☐ G-CDHI	North American P-51D	
☐ G-CDHK	Lindstrand LBL-330A	
☐ G-CDHL	Lindstrand LBL-330A	
☐ G-CDHM	Pegasus Quantum	
☐ G-CDHN	Lindstrand LBL-317A	
☐ G-CDHO	Raj Hamsa X'Air	
☐ G-CDHP	Lindstrand LBL-150A	
☐ G-CDHR	Ikarus C42 Cyclone	
☐ G-CDHS	Cameron N-90	
☐ G-CDHU	Best Off Sky Ranger	
☐ G-CDHX	Aeroprakt A22 Foxbat	
☐ G-CDHY	Cameron Z-90	
☐ G-CDHZ	Nicollier HN700 Menestrel	
☐ G-CDIA	Thruster T600N	
☐ G-CDIB	Cameron Z-350	
☐ G-CDIC		
☐ G-CDIE		
☐ G-CDIF	Mudry CAP.10B	
☐ G-CDIG	EV-97 Eurostar	
☐ G-CDIH	Cameron Z-275	
☐ G-CDIJ	Best Off Sky Ranger	
☐ G-CDIK	Cameron Z-120	
☐ G-CDIL	Pegasus Quantum	
☐ G-CDIM	Robin DR.400-180 Regent	
☐ G-CDIO	Cameron Z-90	
☐ G-CDIP	Best Off Sky Ranger	
☐ G-CDIR	Pegasus Quantum	
☐ G-CDIS	Cessna 150F	
☐ G-CDIT	Cameron Z-105	
☐ G-CDIU	Best Off Sky Ranger	
☐ G-CDIV	Lindstrand LBL-90A	
☐ G-CDIW	Lindstrand LBL-35A	
☐ G-CDIX	Ikarus C42 Cyclone	
☐ G-CDIY	EV-97 Eurostar	
☐ G-CDIZ	Reality Escapade	
☐ G-CDJA		
☐ G-CDJC	Best Off Sky Ranger	
☐ G-CDJD	ICP MXP-740 Savannah	
☐ G-CDJE	Thruster T600N	
☐ G-CDJF	Flight Design CT2K	
☐ G-CDJG	Zenair CH.601UL	
☐ G-CDJI	UltraMagic M-120	
☐ G-CDJJ	Yakovlev Yak-52	
☐ G-CDJK	Ikarus C42 Cyclone	
☐ G-CDJL	Jabiru J400	
☐ G-CDJM	Zenair CH.601XL	
☐ G-CDJN	RAF 2000 GTX-SE	
☐ G-CDJO	DH.82A Tiger Moth	
☐ G-CDJP	Best Off Sky Ranger	
☐ G-CDJR	EV-97 Eurostar	
☐ G-CDJS		
☐ G-CDJT	Aerospatiale Gazelle	
☐ G-CDJU	CASA I-131E	
☐ G-CDJV	Beech A36 Bonanza	
☐ G-CDJW	Van's RV-7	
☐ G-CDJX	Cameron N-56	
☐ G-CDJY	Cameron C-80	
☐ G-CDJZ	Robinson R44	
☐ G-CDKA	SAAB 2000	
☐ G-CDKB	SAAB 2000	
☐ G-CDKC	Raj Hamsa X'Air	
☐ G-CDKD	Boeing 737-683	
☐ G-CDKE	Rans S6 Coyote II	
☐ G-CDKF	Reality Escapade	
☐ G-CDKH	Best Off Sky Ranger	
☐ G-CDKI	Best Off Sky Ranger	
☐ G-CDKJ	Silence Twister	
☐ G-CDKK	P & M Quik	
☐ G-CDKL	Reality Escapade	
☐ G-CDKM	P & M Quik	
☐ G-CDKN	ICP MXP-740 Savannah	
☐ G-CDKO	ICP MXP-740 Savannah	
☐ G-CDKP	Jabiru UL-D	
☐ G-CDKR	Diamond DA42 Twin Star	
☐ G-CDKT	Boeing 737-683	
☐ G-CDKU	Robinson R44	
☐ G-CDKV		
☐ G-CDKX	Best Off Sky Ranger	
☐ G-CDKY	Robinson R44	
☐ G-CDKZ	Thunder Ax10-160	
☐ G-CDLA	P & M Quik	
☐ G-CDLB	Cameron Z-120	
☐ G-CDLC	CASA I-131E	
☐ G-CDLD	P & M Quik	
☐ G-CDLE	Reality Escapade	
☐ G-CDLF		
☐ G-CDLG	Best Off Sky Ranger	
☐ G-CDLH		
☐ G-CDLI	Airco DH.9	
☐ G-CDLJ	P & M Quik	
☐ G-CDLK	Best Off Sky Ranger	
☐ G-CDLL	Dyn'Aero MCR-01	
☐ G-CDLN		
☐ G-CDLO		
☐ G-CDLP	Aerospatiale AS.355F	
☐ G-CDLR	ICP MXP-740 Savannah	
☐ G-CDLS	Jabiru J400	
☐ G-CDLT	BAe 125-800XP	
☐ G-CDLU		
☐ G-CDLV	Lindstrand LBL-105A	
☐ G-CDLW	Zenair CH.601UL	
☐ G-CDLX	Robinson R44	
☐ G-CDLY	Cirrus SR20	
☐ G-CDLZ	Pegasus Quantum	
☐ G-CDMA	Piper PA-28-151 Warrior	
☐ G-CDMC	Cameron Z-105	
☐ G-CDMD	Robin DR.500 President	
☐ G-CDME	Van's RV-7	
☐ G-CDMF	Van's RV-9A	
☐ G-CDMG	Robinson R22	
☐ G-CDMH	Cessna P210N Centurion	
☐ G-CDMI	Robinson R44	
☐ G-CDMJ	P & M Quik	
☐ G-CDMK	Bensen B.8MR	
☐ G-CDML	P & M Quik	
☐ G-CDMM	Cessna 172P Skyhawk	
☐ G-CDMN	Van's RV-9	
☐ G-CDMO	Cameron Can SS	
☐ G-CDMP	Best Off Sky Ranger	
☐ G-CDMS	Ikarus C42 Cyclone	
☐ G-CDMT	Zenair CH.601XL	
☐ G-CDMU	P & M Quik	
☐ G-CDMV	Best Off Sky Ranger	
☐ G-CDMX	Piper PA-28-161 Warrior	
☐ G-CDMY	Piper PA-28-161 Warrior	
☐ G-CDMZ	P & M Quik	
☐ G-CDNA	Grob 109A	
☐ G-CDNB	BAe 146-RJ70	
☐ G-CDNC	BAe 146-RJ70	
☐ G-CDND	Grumman GA-7 Cougar	
☐ G-CDNE	Best Off Sky Ranger	
☐ G-CDNF	Aero Designs Pulsar	
☐ G-CDNG	EV-97 Eurostar	
☐ G-CDNH	P & M Quik	
☐ G-CDNI	EV-97 Eurostar	
☐ G-CDNJ	Colomban MC-15 Cri-Cri	
☐ G-CDNK	Learjet 45	
☐ G-CDNM	EV-97 Eurostar	
☐ G-CDNN		
☐ G-CDNO	Aerospatiale Gazelle	
☐ G-CDNP	EV-97 Eurostar	
☐ G-CDNR	Ikarus C42 Cyclone	
☐ G-CDNS	Aerospatiale Gazelle	
☐ G-CDNT	Zenair CH.601XL	
☐ G-CDNU	Ultralair AX3-16	
☐ G-CDNW	Ikarus C42 Cyclone	
☐ G-CDNY	Jabiru SP-470	
☐ G-CDNZ	UltraMagic M-120	
☐ G-CDOA	EV-97 Eurostar	
☐ G-CDOB	Cameron C-90	
☐ G-CDOC	P & M Quik	
☐ G-CDOD	Aviat A-1B Husky	
☐ G-CDOG	Lindstrand Dog SS	
☐ G-CDOH	Bell 206B Jet Ranger	
☐ G-CDOI	Cameron Z-90	
☐ G-CDOJ	Schweizer 269C-1	
☐ G-CDOK	Ikarus C42 Cyclone	
☐ G-CDOM	P & M Quik	
☐ G-CDON	Piper PA-28-161 Warrior	
☐ G-CDOO	Pegasus Quantum	
☐ G-CDOP	P & M Quik	
☐ G-CDOR	Mainair Blade	
☐ G-CDOT	Ikarus C42 Cyclone	
☐ G-CDOV	Best Off Sky Ranger	
☐ G-CDOW	P & M Quik	
☐ G-CDOY	Robin DR.400-180R	
☐ G-CDOZ	EV-97 Eurostar	
☐ G-CDPA	Alpi Pioneer 300	
☐ G-CDPB	Best Off Sky Ranger	
☐ G-CDPC		
☐ G-CDPD	P & M Quik	
☐ G-CDPE	Best Off Sky Ranger	
☐ G-CDPF	BAe 146-300	
☐ G-CDPG	Crofton Auster J/1A	
☐ G-CDPH	Sherwood Ranger	
☐ G-CDPI	Zenair CH.601UL	
☐ G-CDPJ	Van's RV-8	
☐ G-CDPK		
☐ G-CDPL	EV-97 Eurostar	
☐ G-CDPM	Jurca Spitfire	
☐ G-CDPN	UltraMagic S-105	
☐ G-CDPO	Aerochute Dual	
☐ G-CDPP	Ikarus C42 Cyclone	
☐ G-CDPR	Piper PA-18-95	

Registration	Type	Registration	Type	Registration	Type
G-CDPS	Raj Hamsa X'Air	G-CDTT	ICP MXP-740 Savannah	G-CDWZ	P & M Quik GT450
G-CDPT	Boeing 767-319ER	G-CDTU	EV-97 Eurostar	G-CDXA	Robinson R44
G-CDPU		G-CDTV	Tecnam P2002	G-CDXB	Robinson R44
G-CDPV	Piper PA-34-200T Seneca	G-CDTW	Schweizer 269C-1	G-CDXD	Medway SLA100 Exec
G-CDPW	Pegasus Quantum	G-CDTX	Reims F152 Aerobat	G-CDXE	Aerospatiale Gazelle
G-CDPX	Schleicher ASH 25M1	G-CDTY	ICP MXP-740 Savannah	G-CDXF	Lindstrand LBL-31A
G-CDPY	Europa	G-CDTZ	Aeroprakt A22 Foxbat	G-CDXG	Pegasus Quantum
G-CDPZ	Flight Design CT2K	G-CDUA		G-CDXH	BAe 146 RJ100
G-CDRA	Boeing 737-683	G-CDUB		G-CDXI	Cessna 182P
G-CDRB	Boeing 737-683	G-CDUC		G-CDXJ	Jabiru J400
G-CDRC	Cessna 182Q Skylane	G-CDUD		G-CDXK	Diamond DA42 Twin Star
G-CDRD	AirBourne XT912-B	G-CDUE	Robinson R44	G-CDXL	Flight Design CTSW
G-CDRE	Robinson R44	G-CDUF		G-CDXM	P & M Quik
G-CDRF	Cameron Z-90	G-CDUH	P & M Quik GT450	G-CDXN	P & M Quik
G-CDRG	P & M Quik	G-CDUI	BAe 146 RJ100	G-CDXO	Zenair CH.601UL
G-CDRH	Thruster T600N	G-CDUJ	Lindstrand LBL-31A	G-CDXP	EV-97 Eurostar
G-CDRI	Cameron O-105	G-CDUK	Ikarus C42 Cyclone	G-CDXR	Fokker DR.1 Replica
G-CDRJ	Tanarg iXess 15	G-CDUL	Best Off Sky Ranger	G-CDXS	EV-97 Eurostar
G-CDRK	BAe 146-RJ100	G-CDUM		G-CDXT	Van's RV-9
G-CDRL		G-CDUS	Best Off Sky Ranger	G-CDXU	Chilton DW.1A
G-CDRM	Van's RV-7A	G-CDUT	Jabiru J400	G-CDXV	Campbell Cricket Mk.6A
G-CDRN	Cameron Z-225	G-CDUU	P & M Quik	G-CDXW	Cameron Orange SS
G-CDRO	Ikarus C42 Cyclone	G-CDUV	ICP MXP-740 Savannah	G-CDXX	Robinson R44
G-CDRP	Ikarus C42 Cyclone	G-CDUW	Aeronca C3	G-CDXY	Kitfox Mk.7
G-CDRR	Pegasus Quantum	G-CDUX	Piper PA-32-300	G-CDXZ	
G-CDRS	Rotorway Exec 162F	G-CDUY	Thunder 77A	G-CDYA	Gippsland GA-8 Airvan
G-CDRT	P & M Quik	G-CDUZ		G-CDYB	Rans S-6ES Coyote II
G-CDRU	CASA I-131E	G-CDVA	Best Off Sky Ranger	G-CDYC	Piper PA-28RT-201
G-CDRV	Van's RV-9A	G-CDVB	Agusta A109E Power	G-CDYD	Ikarus C42 Cyclone
G-CDRW	P & M Quik	G-CDVC	Agusta A109E Power	G-CDYF	Rotorsport UK MT-03
G-CDRX	Cameron Z-275	G-CDVD	EV-97 Eurostar	G-CDYG	Cameron Z-105
G-CDRY	Ikarus C42 Cyclone	G-CDVE	Agusta A109E Power	G-CDYH	BAe Jetstream 41
G-CDRZ	Kubicek BB22	G-CDVF	P & M Quik GT450	G-CDYI	BAe Jetstream 41
G-CDSA	P & M Quik	G-CDVG	P & M Quik	G-CDYJ	Best Off Sky Ranger
G-CDSB	Alpi Pioneer 300	G-CDVH	Pegasus Quantum	G-CDYK	BAe 146 RJ85
G-CDSC	Scheibe SF25C Falke	G-CDVI	Ikarus C42 Cyclone	G-CDYL	Lindstrand LBL 77A
G-CDSD	Alpi Pioneer 300	G-CDVJ	Bensen B.8MR	G-CDYM	Murphy Maverick
G-CDSF	Diamond DA.40D Star	G-CDVK	ICP MXP-740 Savannah	G-CDYN	Extra EA.300/L
G-CDSG	Aerospatiale Alouette III	G-CDVL	Alpi Pioneer 300	G-CDYO	Ikarus C42 Cyclone
G-CDSH	ICP MXP-740 Savannah	G-CDVN	P & M Quik	G-CDYP	EV-97 Eurostar
G-CDSI	Jabiru J400	G-CDVO	P & M Quik	G-CDYR	
G-CDSJ	Aerospatiale Alouette III	G-CDVP	EV-97 Eurostar	G-CDYS	Bell 206B Jet Ranger
G-CDSK	Reality Escapade	G-CDVR	P & M Quik GT450	G-CDYT	Ikarus C42 Cyclone
G-CDSL	Cessna 182R Skylane	G-CDVS	Europa XS	G-CDYU	Zenair CH.701UL
G-CDSM	P & M Quik	G-CDVT	Van's RV-6	G-CDYV	
G-CDSN	Raj Hamsa X'Air	G-CDVU	EV-97 Eurostar	G-CDYW	Schweizer 269C-1
G-CDSO	Thruster T600N	G-CDVV	Bulldog T.1	G-CDYX	Lindstrand LBL 77B
G-CDSR	LearJet 45	G-CDVX	P47G Thunderbolt	G-CDYY	Alpi Pioneer 300
G-CDSS	P & M Quik	G-CDVY		G-CDYZ	Van's RV-7
G-CDST	UltraMagic N-250	G-CDVZ	P & M Quik GT450	G-CDZA	Alpi Pioneer 300
G-CDSU	Robinson R22B	G-CDWA	Kubicek BB37	G-CDZB	Zenair CH.601UL
G-CDSV	Aerospatiale AS332L	G-CDWB	Best Off Sky Ranger	G-CDZC	
G-CDSW	Ikarus C42 Cyclone	G-CDWC		G-CDZD	Van's RV-9A
G-CDSX	Canberra T Mk.4	G-CDWD	Cameron Z-105	G-CDZE	
G-CDSY	Robinson R44	G-CDWE	Nord NC.856 Norvigie	G-CDZF	
G-CDSZ	Diamond DA-42 Twin Star	G-CDWF	DHC-1 Chipmunk	G-CDZG	Ikarus C42 Cyclone
G-CDTA	EV-97 Eurostar	G-CDWG	Dyn'Aero MCR-01	G-CDZH	Boeing 737-804
G-CDTB	Pegasus Quantum	G-CDWI	Ikarus C42 Cyclone	G-CDZI	Boeing 737-804
G-CDTC	Pegasus Quantum	G-CDWJ	Flight Design CTSW	G-CDZJ	Tecnam P.92
G-CDTD	Eurocopter AS350 B2	G-CDWK	Robinson R44	G-CDZK	Tecnam P92 Echo
G-CDTE	Tecnam P2002	G-CDWL	Raj Hamsa X'Air	G-CDZL	Boeing 737-804
G-CDTF	Whittaker MW-5D	G-CDWM	Best Off Sky Ranger	G-CDZM	Boeing 737-804
G-CDTG	Diamond DA42 Twin Star	G-CDWN	UltraMagic N-210	G-CDZO	Lindstrand LBL 60X
G-CDTH	Schempp-Hirth Nimbus	G-CDWO	P & M Quik	G-CDZP	
G-CDTI	Messerschmitt Bf.109E	G-CDWP	P & M Quik	G-CDZR	Nicollier HN700 Menestrel
G-CDTJ	Reality Escapade	G-CDWR	P & M Quik	G-CDZS	Kolb Twinstar Mk.3
G-CDTK	Schweizer 269C-1	G-CDWS	P & M Quik	G-CDZT	Beech 200 Super King Air
G-CDTL	Jabiru J400	G-CDWT	Flight Design CTSW	G-CDZU	ICP MXP-740 Savannah
G-CDTM	Seafire MK.XVII	G-CDWU	Zenair CH.601UL	G-CDZV	
G-CDTN	Aerospatiale AS332L	G-CDWV	Lindstrand House SS	G-CDZW	Cameron N-105
G-CDTO	P & M Quik GT450	G-CDWW	P & M Quik GT450	G-CDZY	Medway SLA100 Exec
G-CDTP	Best Off Sky Ranger	G-CDWX	Lindstrand LBL-77A	G-CDZZ	Rotorsport UK MT-03
G-CDTR	P & M Quik GT450	G-CDWY	Agusta A109S Grand	G-CEAE	Boeing 737-229

☐ G-CEAF	Boeing 737-229	
☐ G-CEAG	Boeing 737-229	
☐ G-CEAH	Boeing 737-229	
☐ G-CEAK	Ikarus C42 Cyclone	
☐ G-CEAM	EV-97 Eurostar	
☐ G-CEAN	Ikarus C42 Cyclone	
☐ G-CEAO	Jurca MJ.5 Sirocco	
☐ G-CEAR	Alpi Pioneer 300	
☐ G-CEAT	Zenair CH.601HDS	
☐ G-CEAU	Robinson R44	
☐ G-CEAV	UltraMagic M-105	
☐ G-CEAW	Schweizer 269C-1	
☐ G-CEAX	UltraMagic S-130	
☐ G-CEAY	UltraMagic H-42	
☐ G-CEAZ		
☐ G-CEBA	Zenair CH.601XL Zodiac	
☐ G-CEBC	ICP MXP-740 Savannah	
☐ G-CEBD	P & M Quik	
☐ G-CEBE	Schweizer 269C-1	
☐ G-CEBF	EV-97A Eurostar	
☐ G-CEBG	Kubicek BB26	
☐ G-CEBH	Tanarg iXess 15	
☐ G-CEBI	Kolb Twinstar Mk.3	
☐ G-CEBJ		
☐ G-CEBK	Piper PA-31-350 Chieftain	
☐ G-CEBL	Kubicek BB20GP	
☐ G-CEBM	P & M Quik	
☐ G-CEBN	BAe 146-300	
☐ G-CEBO	UltraMagic M-65C	
☐ G-CEBP	EV-97 Eurostar	
☐ G-CEBR	BAe 146-200	
☐ G-CEBS	BAe 146-RJ85	
☐ G-CEBT	P & M Quik	
☐ G-CEBU	BAe 146-RJ85	
☐ G-CEBV	Europa XS	
☐ G-CEBW	North American P-51D	
☐ G-CEBX		
☐ G-CEBY	Tanarg iXess 15	
☐ G-CEBZ	Zenair CH.601UL	
☐ G-CECA	P & M Quik GT450	
☐ G-CECB	ELA Aviacion ELA 07S	
☐ G-CECC	Ikarus C42 Cyclone	
☐ G-CECD	Cameron C-90	
☐ G-CECE	Jabiru UL-D	
☐ G-CECF	Reality Escapade	
☐ G-CECG	Jabiru UL-D	
☐ G-CECH	Jodel D.150	
☐ G-CECI	Pilatus PC-6 B2-H4	
☐ G-CECJ	Super Ximango	
☐ G-CECK	ICP MXP-740 Savannah	
☐ G-CECL	Ikarus C42 Cyclone	
☐ G-CECM	P & M Quik GT450	
☐ G-CECN		
☐ G-CECO	Hughes 269C	
☐ G-CECP	Best Off Sky Ranger	
☐ G-CECR	Bilsam Sky Cruiser	
☐ G-CECS	Lindstrand LBL 105A	
☐ G-CECT	Eurocopter EC135T2	
☐ G-CECU	Boeing 767-222	
☐ G-CECV	Van's RV-7A	
☐ G-CECW	Robinson R44	
☐ G-CECX	Robinson R44	
☐ G-CECY	EV-97 Eurostar	
☐ G-CECZ	Zenair CH.601XL	
☐ G-CEDA	Cameron Z-105	
☐ G-CEDB	Reality Escapade	
☐ G-CEDC	Ikarus C42 Cyclone	
☐ G-CEDD	Piper PA-28RT-201	
☐ G-CEDE	Flight Design CTSW	
☐ G-CEDF	Cameron N-105	
☐ G-CEDG	Robinson R44	
☐ G-CEDI	Best Off Sky Ranger	
☐ G-CEDJ	Aero Designs Pulsar XP	
☐ G-CEDK		
☐ G-CEDL	TEAM Minimax 91	
☐ G-CEDM	Flight Design CTSW	
☐ G-CEDN	P & M Quik	
☐ G-CEDO	Raj Hamsa X'Air	
☐ G-CEDP	ELA Aviacion ELA 07R	
☐ G-CEDR	Ikarus C42 Cyclone	
☐ G-CEDT	Tanarg iXess 15	
☐ G-CEDV	EV-97 Eurostar	
☐ G-CEDW	TEAM Minimax 91	
☐ G-CEDX	EV-97 Eurostar	
☐ G-CEDZ	Best Off Sky Ranger	
☐ G-CEEA	ELA Aviacion ELA 07R	
☐ G-CEEB	Cameron C-80	
☐ G-CEEC	Raj Hamsa X'Air Hawk	
☐ G-CEED	ICP MXP-740 Savannah	
☐ G-CEEE	Robinson R44	
☐ G-CEEF	ELA Aviacion ELA 07R	
☐ G-CEEG	Alpi Pioneer 300	
☐ G-CEEH		
☐ G-CEEI	P & M Quik	
☐ G-CEEJ	Rans S-7 Courier	
☐ G-CEEK	Cameron Z-105	
☐ G-CEEL	UltraMagic S-90	
☐ G-CEEM	P & M Quik GT450	
☐ G-CEEN	Piper PA-28-161 Cadet	
☐ G-CEEO	Flight Design CTSW	
☐ G-CEEP	Van's RV-9A	
☐ G-CEER	ELA Aviacion ELA 07R	
☐ G-CEES	Cameron C-90	
☐ G-CEEU	Piper PA-28-161 Cadet	
☐ G-CEEV	Piper PA-28-161 Warrior	
☐ G-CEEW	Ikarus C42 Cyclone	
☐ G-CEEX	ICP MXP-740 Savannah	
☐ G-CEEY	Piper PA-28-161 Warrior	
☐ G-CEEZ	Piper PA-28-161 Warrior	
☐ G-CEFA	Ikarus C42 Cyclone	
☐ G-CEFB	Ultramagic H-31	
☐ G-CEFC	Super Marine Spitfire 26	
☐ G-CEFF	Boeing 747-422	
☐ G-CEFG	Boeing 767-319ER	
☐ G-CEFH	ELA Aviacion ELA 07S	
☐ G-CEFI	BAe Jetstream 41	
☐ G-CEFJ	Sonex	
☐ G-CEFK	EV-97 Eurostar	
☐ G-CEFL	BAe 146-RJ85	
☐ G-CEFM	Cessna 152	
☐ G-CEFN	BAe 146-RJ85	
☐ G-CEFO		
☐ G-CEFP	Jabiru J420	
☐ G-CEFR	Robinson R44	
☐ G-CEFS	Cameron C-100	
☐ G-CEFT	Whittaker MW-5D	
☐ G-CEFU		
☐ G-CEFV	Cessna 182T Skylane	
☐ G-CEFW	BAe 146 RJ100	
☐ G-CEFX	Diamond DA42 Twin Star	
☐ G-CEFY	ICP MXP-740 Savannah	
☐ G-CEFZ	EV-97 Eurostar	
☐ G-CEGC	Cameron Z-105	
☐ G-CEGD		
☐ G-CEGE		
☐ G-CEGF	Eurocopter EC135T2	
☐ G-CEGG	Lindstrand LBL 25A	
☐ G-CEGH	Van's RV-9A	
☐ G-CEGI	Van's RV-8	
☐ G-CEGJ	P & M Quik GT450	
☐ G-CEGK	ICP MXP-740 Savannah	
☐ G-CEGL	Ikarus C42 Cyclone	
☐ G-CEGM		
☐ G-CEGN		
☐ G-CEGO	EV-97A Eurostar	
☐ G-CEGP	Beech 200 Super King Air	
☐ G-CEGR	Beech 200 Super King Air	
☐ G-CEGS	Piper PA-28-161 Warrior	
☐ G-CEGT	P & M Quik GT450	
☐ G-CEGU	Piper PA-28-151 Warrior	
☐ G-CEGV	P & M Quik GT450	
☐ G-CEGW	P & M Quik GT450	
☐ G-CEGX		
☐ G-CEGY	ELA Aviacion ELA 07R	
☐ G-CEGZ	Ikarus C42 Cyclone	
☐ G-CEHA		
☐ G-CEHB		
☐ G-CEHC	P & M Quik GT450	
☐ G-CEHD	Best Off Sky Ranger	
☐ G-CEHE		
☐ G-CEHF		
☐ G-CEHG	Ikarus C42 Cyclone	
☐ G-CEHH	Edge XT912-B Streak	
☐ G-CEHI	P & M Quik GT450	
☐ G-CEHJ	Short Tucano T.1	
☐ G-CEHK	Robinson R44	
☐ G-CEHL	EV-97 Eurostar	
☐ G-CEHM	Rotorsport UK MT-03	
☐ G-CEHN	Rotorsport UK MT-03	
☐ G-CEHO	ELA Aviacion ELA 07R	
☐ G-CEHP		
☐ G-CEHR	Auster AOP.9	
☐ G-CEHS		
☐ G-CEHT	Rand-Robinson KR-2	
☐ G-CEHU	Cameron Z-105	
☐ G-CEHV	Ikarus C42 Cyclone	
☐ G-CEHW	P & M Quik GT450	
☐ G-CEHX	Lindstrand LBL 9A	
☐ G-CEHY		
☐ G-CEHZ	Edge XT912-B Streak	
☐ G-CEIA	Rotorsport UK MT-03	
☐ G-CEIB		
☐ G-CEIC		
☐ G-CEID	Van's RV-7A	
☐ G-CEIE	Flight Design CTSW	
☐ G-CEIF		
☐ G-CEIG	Van's RV-7	
☐ G-CEIH		
☐ G-CEII		
☐ G-CEIJ	BAe 146-200	
☐ G-CEIK	UltraMagic M-90	
☐ G-CEIL	Reality Escapade	
☐ G-CEIM	Robinson R44	
☐ G-CEIN	Cameron Z-105	
☐ G-CEIO	BN-2T-4S Islander	
☐ G-CEIP	BN-2T-4S Islander	
☐ G-CEIR	BN-2T-4S Islander	
☐ G-CEIS	Jodel DR1050	
☐ G-CEIT	Van's RV-7A	
☐ G-CEIU		
☐ G-CEIV	Tanarg iXess 15	
☐ G-CEIW	Europa	
☐ G-CEIX		
☐ G-CEIY		
☐ G-CEIZ	Piper PA-28-161 Archer	
☐ G-CEJA	Cameron V-77	
☐ G-CEJB	Piper PA-46-500TP	
☐ G-CEJC	Cameron N-77	
☐ G-CEJD	Piper PA-28-161 Warrior	
☐ G-CEJE	Wittman W10 Tailwind	
☐ G-CEJF		
☐ G-CEJG		
☐ G-CEJH	ELA Aviacion ELA 07S	
☐ G-CEJI	Lindstrand LBL 105A	
☐ G-CEJJ	P & M Quik GT450	
☐ G-CEJK		
☐ G-CEJL		
☐ G-CEJM		
☐ G-CEJN	Mooney M.20F	

☐ G-CEJO		
☐ G-CEJP		
☐ G-CEJR	Cameron Z-90	
☐ G-CEJS	Agusta A109E Power	
☐ G-CEJT	Cameron Z-31	
☐ G-CEJU	Bell P-39 Airacobra	
☐ G-CEJV	Piper PA-282-161 Cadet	
☐ G-CEJW	Ikarus C42 Cyclone	
☐ G-CEJX		
☐ G-CEJY		
☐ G-CEJZ		
☐ G-CEKA		
☐ G-CEKB	Taylor Monoplane	
☐ G-CEKC		
☐ G-CEKD		
☐ G-CEKE		
☐ G-CEKF		
☐ G-CEKG		
☐ G-CEKH		
☐ G-CEKI		
☐ G-CEKJ	EV-97A Eurostar	
☐ G-CEKK	Best Off Sky Ranger	
☐ G-CEKL		
☐ G-CEKM	Jabiru UL450	
☐ G-CEKN		
☐ G-CEKO		
☐ G-CEKP		
☐ G-CEKR		
☐ G-CEKS		
☐ G-CEKT		
☐ G-CEKU		
☐ G-CEKV		
☐ G-CEKW	Jabiru J430	
☐ G-CEKX		
☐ G-CEKY		
☐ G-CEKZ		
☐ G-CELA	Boeing 737-377	
☐ G-CELB	Boeing 737-377	
☐ G-CELC	Boeing 737-33A	
☐ G-CELD	Boeing 737-33A	
☐ G-CELE	Boeing 737-33A	
☐ G-CELF	Boeing 737-377	
☐ G-CELG	Boeing 737-377	
☐ G-CELH	Boeing 737-330	
☐ G-CELI	Boeing 737-330	
☐ G-CELJ	Boeing 737-330	
☐ G-CELK	Boeing 737-330	
☐ G-CELO	Boeing 737-33A	
☐ G-CELP	Boeing 737-330QC	
☐ G-CELR	Boeing 737-330QC	
☐ G-CELS	Boeing 737-377	
☐ G-CELU	Boeing 737-377	
☐ G-CELV	Boeing 737-377	
☐ G-CELW	Boeing 737-377	
☐ G-CELX	Boeing 737-377	
☐ G-CELY	Boeing 737-377	
☐ G-CELZ	Boeing 737-377	
☐ G-CEMA		
☐ G-CEMB		
☐ G-CEMC		
☐ G-CEMD		
☐ G-CEME	EV-97 Eurostar	
☐ G-CEMF		
☐ G-CEMG		
☐ G-CEMH		
☐ G-CEMI		
☐ G-CEMJ		
☐ G-CEMK		
☐ G-CEML		
☐ G-CEMM		
☐ G-CEMN		
☐ G-CEMO		
☐ G-CEMP		

☐ G-CEMR	
☐ G-CEMS	
☐ G-CEMT	
☐ G-CEMU	
☐ G-CEMV	
☐ G-CEMW	
☐ G-CEMX	
☐ G-CEMY	
☐ G-CEMZ	
☐ G-CENA	
☐ G-CENB	
☐ G-CENC	
☐ G-CEND	
☐ G-CENE	
☐ G-CENF	
☐ G-CENG	
☐ G-CENH	
☐ G-CENI	
☐ G-CENJ	
☐ G-CENK	
☐ G-CENL	
☐ G-CENM	
☐ G-CENN	
☐ G-CENO	
☐ G-CENP	
☐ G-CENR	
☐ G-CENS	
☐ G-CENU	
☐ G-CENV	
☐ G-CENW	
☐ G-CENX	
☐ G-CENY	
☐ G-CENZ	
☐ G-CEOA	
☐ G-CEOB	
☐ G-CEOC	
☐ G-CEOD	
☐ G-CEOE	
☐ G-CEOF	
☐ G-CEOG	
☐ G-CEOH	
☐ G-CEOI	
☐ G-CEOJ	
☐ G-CEOK	
☐ G-CEOL	
☐ G-CEOM	
☐ G-CEON	
☐ G-CEOO	
☐ G-CEOP	
☐ G-CEOR	
☐ G-CEOS	
☐ G-CEOT	
☐ G-CEOU	
☐ G-CEOV	
☐ G-CEOW	
☐ G-CEOX	
☐ G-CEOY	
☐ G-CEOZ	
☐ G-CEPA	
☐ G-CEPB	
☐ G-CEPC	
☐ G-CEPD	
☐ G-CEPE	
☐ G-CEPF	
☐ G-CEPG	
☐ G-CEPH	
☐ G-CEPI	
☐ G-CEPJ	
☐ G-CEPK	
☐ G-CEPL	
☐ G-CEPM	
☐ G-CEPN	
☐ G-CEPO	

☐ G-CEPP	
☐ G-CEPR	
☐ G-CEPS	
☐ G-CEPT	SOCATA TB-20 Trinidad
☐ G-CEPU	
☐ G-CEPV	
☐ G-CEPW	
☐ G-CEPX	
☐ G-CEPY	
☐ G-CEPZ	
☐ G-CERA	
☐ G-CERB	
☐ G-CERC	
☐ G-CERD	
☐ G-CERE	
☐ G-CERF	
☐ G-CERG	
☐ G-CERH	
☐ G-CERI	Europa XS
☐ G-CERJ	
☐ G-CERK	
☐ G-CERL	
☐ G-CERM	
☐ G-CERN	
☐ G-CERO	
☐ G-CERP	
☐ G-CERR	
☐ G-CERS	
☐ G-CERT	Mooney M.20K
☐ G-CERU	
☐ G-CERV	
☐ G-CERW	
☐ G-CERX	
☐ G-CERY	
☐ G-CERZ	
☐ G-CESA	
☐ G-CESB	
☐ G-CESC	
☐ G-CESD	
☐ G-CESE	
☐ G-CESF	
☐ G-CESG	
☐ G-CESH	
☐ G-CESI	
☐ G-CESJ	
☐ G-CESK	
☐ G-CESL	
☐ G-CESM	
☐ G-CESN	
☐ G-CESO	
☐ G-CESP	
☐ G-CESR	
☐ G-CESS	
☐ G-CEST	
☐ G-CESU	
☐ G-CESV	
☐ G-CESW	
☐ G-CESX	
☐ G-CESY	
☐ G-CESZ	
☐ G-CEYE	Piper PA-32R-300
☐ G-CFAA	BAe 146-RJ100
☐ G-CFBI	Colt 56A
☐ G-CFME	SOCATA TB-10 Tobago
☐ G-CFOG	Ikarus C42 Cyclone
☐ G-CFRY	Zenair CH.601UL Zodiac
☐ G-CFSA	Piper PA-44-180 Seminole
☐ G-CFTJ	EV-97 Eurostar
☐ G-CFWR	Best Off Sky Ranger
☐ G-CFWW	Schleicher ASH 25E
☐ G-CGDJ	Piper PA-28-161 Warrior
☐ G-CGHM	Piper PA-28-140 Cherokee
☐ G-CGOD	Cameron N-77

Reg.	Type	Reg.	Type	Reg.	Type
G-CGRD	Cirrus SR.22	G-CIVR	Boeing 747-436	G-CKJM	Schempp-Hirth Ventus
G-CGRI	Agusta 109S Grand	G-CIVS	Boeing 747-436	G-CKJN	Schleicher ASW 20
G-CHAD	Aeroprakt A22 Foxbat	G-CIVT	Boeing 747-436	G-CKJP	Schleicher ASK 21
G-CHAH	Europa	G-CIVU	Boeing 747-436	G-CKJS	Schleicher ASW 28
G-CHAM	Cameron 90SS	G-CIVV	Boeing 747-436	G-CKJV	Schleicher ASW 28
G-CHAN	Robinson R22B	G-CIVW	Boeing 747-436	G-CKJY	
G-CHAP	Robinson R44	G-CIVX	Boeing 747-436	G-CKJZ	Schempp-Hirth Discus
G-CHAR	Grob 109B	G-CIVY	Boeing 747-436	G-CKKB	Centrair 101A Pegase
G-CHAS	Piper PA-28-181 Archer	G-CIVZ	Boeing 747-436	G-CKKC	DG Flugzeugbau DG-300
G-CHAV	Europa	G-CJAB	Dornier Do.328 Jet	G-CKKD	Schleicher ASW 28
G-CHCD	Sikorsky S-76A	G-CJAD	Cessna 525 CitationJet	G-CKKE	Schempp-Hirth Duo Discus
G-CHCF	Aerospatiale AS.332L2	G-CJAG	Beech 390 Premier 1	G-CKKF	Schempp-Hirth Ventus
G-CHCG	Aerospatiale AS.332L2	G-CJAH	Beech 390 Premier 1	G-CKKH	Schleicher ASW 27B
G-CHCH	Aerospatiale AS.332L2	G-CJAY	P & M Quik	G-CKKK	AB Sportine Aviacija LAK17
G-CHCI	Aerospatiale AS.332L2	G-CJBC	Piper PA-28-180 Cherokee	G-CKKM	Schleicher ASW 28
G-CHCK	Sikorsky S-92A	G-CJCI	Pilatus P.2-05	G-CKKN	Schempp-Hirth Duo Discus
G-CHCP	Agusta AW139	G-CJUD	Denney Kitfox	G-CKKP	Schleicher ASK 21
G-CHCT	Agusta AW139	G-CKCK	Enstrom 280FX	G-CKKR	Schleicher ASK 13
G-CHEB	Europa	G-CKEM	Robinson R44	G-CKKV	Schempp-Hirth Duscus
G-CHEL	Colt 77B	G-CKEY	Piper PA-28-161 Warrior	G-CKKW	
G-CHEM	Piper PA-34-200T Seneca	G-CKFY	Schleicher ASK 21	G-CKKX	Rollenden-Schneider LS4
G-CHER	Piper PA-38-112 Tomahawk	G-CKFZ		G-CKKY	Schempp-Hirth Duo Discus
G-CHET	Europa	G-CKGA	Schempp-Hirth Ventus	G-CKLA	Schleicher ASK 13
G-CHEY	Piper PA-31T Cheyenne	G-CKGB	Schempp-Hirth Ventus	G-CKLB	Schleicher ASW 27B
G-CHEZ	BN2 Islander	G-CKGC	Schempp-Hirth Ventus	G-CKLC	Glasflugel H206 Hornet
G-CHGL	Bell 206B Jet Ranger	G-CKGD	Schempp-Hirth Ventus	G-CKLD	Schempp-Hirth Discus
G-CHIK	Reims F152	G-CKGE		G-CKLE	
G-CHIP	Piper PA-28-181 Archer	G-CKGF	Schempp-Hirth Duo Discus	G-CKLF	Schempp-Hirth Janus
G-CHIS	Robinson R22B	G-CKGG		G-CKLG	Rolladen-Schneider LS4
G-CHIX	Robin DR.500i	G-CKGH	Grob G102 Club Astir	G-CKLK	
G-CHKN	Air Creation Kiss 400	G-CKGJ		G-CKLL	
G-CHLL	Lindstrand LBL 90A	G-CKGK	Schleicher ASK 21	G-CKLN	Rolladen-Schneider LS4
G-CHOK	Cameron V-77	G-CKGL	Schempp-Hirth Ventus	G-CKLP	Schleicher ASW 28
G-CHOP	Westland Bell 47G-3B1	G-CKGM		G-CKLR	Pezetel SZD-55
G-CHOX	Europa XS	G-CKGN	Schleicher ASW 28	G-CKLS	Rolladen-Schneider LS4
G-CHPR	Robinson R22B	G-CKGP		G-CKLT	Schempp-Hirth Nimbus
G-CHPY	DHC-1 Chipmunk	G-CKGS		G-CKLV	Schempp-Hirth Discus
G-CHSU	Eurocopter EC135T1	G-CKGT	Schempp-Hirth Cirrus	G-CKLW	Schleicher ASK 21
G-CHTA	Grumman AA-5A Cheetah	G-CKGU	Schleicher ASW 19B	G-CKLX	
G-CHTG	Rotorway Exec 90	G-CKGV	Schleicher ASW 28	G-CKLY	Glaser-Dirks DG-100T
G-CHUG	Europa	G-CKGW		G-CKMA	Glaser-Dirks LS8-ST
G-CHUK	Cameron O-77	G-CKGX	Schleicher ASK 21	G-CKMB	
G-CHUM	Robinson R44	G-CKGY	Scheibe Bergfalke	G-CKMC	Grob 102 Astir CS77
G-CHYL	Robinson R22B	G-CKHA	PZL SZD-51-1 Junior	G-CKMD	Schempp-Hirth Cirrus
G-CHZN	Robinson R22B	G-CKHB	Rolladen-Schneider LS3	G-CKME	Glaser-Dirks LS8-ST
G-CIAO	III Sky Arrow 1450L	G-CKHC	Glaser-Dirks DG-505	G-CKMF	Centrair 101A Pegase
G-CIAS	BN2B-21 Islander	G-CKHD	Schleicher ASW 27B	G-CKMG	Glaser-Dirks DG-101G Elan
G-CIBO	Cessna 180K Skywagon	G-CKHE	AB Sportine Aviacija LAK17	G-CKMI	Schleicher K8C
G-CICI	Cameron R-15	G-CKHF	Schleicher ASW 20	G-CKMJ	Schleicher Ka 6CR
G-CIDA	Robinson R44	G-CKHG	Schleicher ASW 27B	G-CKML	Schempp-Hirth Duo Discus
G-CIDD	Aeronca 7ECA Citabria	G-CKHH	Schleicher ASK 13	G-CKMM	Schliecher ASW 28
G-CIEL	Cessna 560 Citation XL	G-CKHK	Schempp-Hirth Duo Discus	G-CKMO	Rolladen-Schneider LS7WL
G-CIFR	Piper PA-28-181 Archer	G-CKHL		G-CKMP	Sportine Aviacija LAK-17A
G-CIGY	Westland Bell 47G-3B1	G-CKHM	Centrair 101A Pegase 90	G-CKMR	Letov LF-107 Lunak
G-CITJ	Cessnsa 525	G-CKHN	PZL SZD-51-1 Junior	G-CKMT	Grob G.103 Twin Acro
G-CITR	Cameron Z-105	G-CKHP	Rollenden-Schneider LS8	G-CKMV	Rolladen-Schneider LS3-17
G-CITY	Piper PA-31-350 Chieftain	G-CKHR	PZL SZD-51-1 Junior	G-CKMW	Schleicher ASK 21
G-CIVA	Boeing 747-436	G-CKHS	Rolladen-Schneider LS7WL	G-CKMX	
G-CIVB	Boeing 747-436	G-CKHT		G-CKMY	Schleicher ASW 20
G-CIVC	Boeing 747-436	G-CKHV		G-CKMZ	Schleicher ASW 28
G-CIVD	Boeing 747-436	G-CKHW		G-CKNA	
G-CIVE	Boeing 747-436	G-CKHX	Schleicher ASW 28	G-CKNB	Schempp-Hirth Std Cirrus
G-CIVF	Boeing 747-436	G-CKJA	Schleicher ASW 28	G-CKNC	Caproni Calif A21S
G-CIVG	Boeing 747-436	G-CKJB	Schempp-Hirth Ventus	G-CKND	DG Flugzeugbau DG-100T
G-CIVH	Boeing 747-436	G-CKJC	Schempp-Hirth Nimbus	G-CKNE	Schempp-Hirth Cirrus
G-CIVI	Boeing 747-436	G-CKJD		G-CKNF	DG Flugzeugbau DG-100T
G-CIVJ	Boeing 747-436	G-CKJE	DG Flugzeugbau LS8-18	G-CKNG	Schleicher ASW 28
G-CIVK	Boeing 747-436	G-CKJF	Schempp-Hirth Cirrus	G-CKNH	
G-CIVL	Boeing 747-436	G-CKJG	Schempp-Hirth Cirrus	G-CKNI	
G-CIVM	Boeing 747-436	G-CKJH	Glaser-Dirks DG-303	G-CKNJ	Schempp-Hirth Duo Discus
G-CIVN	Boeing 747-436	G-CKJJ	DG Flugzeugbau DG-505	G-CKNK	Glaser-Dirks DG-500
G-CIVO	Boeing 747-436	G-CKJK	Schempp-Hirth Janus	G-CKNL	Schleicher ASK 21
G-CIVP	Boeing 747-436	G-CKJL	Schleicher ASK 13	G-CKNM	Schleicher ASK 18

Reg	Type		Reg	Type		Reg	Type
G-CKNN	Slingsby T21B Sedbergh		G-CKRL			G-COVA	Piper PA-28-161 Warrior
G-CKNO	Schempp-Hirth Ventus		G-CKRM			G-COVB	Piper PA-28-161 Warrior
G-CKNP			G-CKRN			G-COVD	Robin R.2160i
G-CKNR	Schempp-Hirth Ventus		G-CKRO			G-COVE	Jabiru UL
G-CKNS	Rolladen-Schneider LS4		G-CKRP			G-COXS	Aeroprakt A22 Foxbat
G-CKNT			G-CKRR			G-COXY	Air Creation Buggy Kiss
G-CKNU			G-CKRS			G-COZI	Rutan Cozy III
G-CKNV	Schleicher ASW 28		G-CKRT			G-CPCD	Robin DR.221 Dauphin
G-CKNW			G-CKRU			G-CPDA	DH.106 Comet 4C
G-CKNX			G-CKRV			G-CPEL	Boeing 757-236
G-CKNY			G-CKRW			G-CPEM	Boeing 757-236
G-CKNZ			G-CKRX			G-CPEN	Boeing 757-236
G-CKOA			G-CKRY			G-CPEO	Boeing 757-236
G-CKOB			G-CKRZ			G-CPEP	Boeing 757-2YO
G-CKOC			G-CLAC	Piper PA-28-161 Warrior		G-CPER	Boeing 757-236
G-CKOD	Schempp-Hirth Discus bT		G-CLAS	Short SD.360		G-CPES	Boeing 757-236
G-CKOE			G-CLAV	Europa		G-CPET	Boeing 757-236
G-CKOF			G-CLAX	Jurca Sirocco		G-CPFC	Reims F152
G-CKOG			G-CLAY	Bell 206B Jet Ranger		G-CPMK	DHC-1 Chipmunk
G-CKOH	DG Flugzeugbau DG-100T		G-CLCG	Beech B200 Super King Air		G-CPMS	SOCATA TB-20 Trinidad
G-CKOI	Sportine Aviacija LAK-17AT		G-CLEA	Piper PA-28-161 Warrior		G-CPOL	Aerospatiale AS.355F1
G-CKOJ	Schempp-Hirth Duo Discus		G-CLEE	Rans S6 Coyote II (N)		G-CPSF	Cameron N-90
G-CKOK			G-CLEM	Bolkow Bo.208A2 Junior		G-CPSH	Eurocopter EC135T1
G-CKOL			G-CLEO	Zenair CH.601HD		G-CPTM	Piper PA-28-161 Warrior
G-CKOM			G-CLFC	Mainair Blade		G-CPTS	Agusta Bell 206B
G-CKON			G-CLHD	BAe 146-200		G-CPXC	Mudry CAP.10C
G-CKOO			G-CLIC	Cameron N-105		G-CRAB	Best Off Sky Ranger
G-CKOP			G-CLIF	Ikarus C42 Cyclone		G-CRAY	Robinson R22B
G-CKOR	DG Flugzeugbau DG-300		G-CLKE	Robinson R44		G-CRBV	Kubicek BB26
G-CKOS			G-CLOE	Sky 90-24		G-CRDY	Agusta Bell 206A
G-CKOT			G-CLOP	Piper PA-32R-301T		G-CRES	Denney Kitfox
G-CKOU			G-CLOS	Piper PA-34-200T Seneca		G-CRIB	Robinson R44
G-CKOV			G-CLOW	Beech 200 Super King Air		G-CRIC	Colomban MC-15 Cri-Cri
G-CKOW			G-CLRK	Sky 77-24		G-CRIK	Colomban MC-15 Cri-Cri
G-CKOX			G-CLUB	Reims FRA150M Aerobat		G-CRIL	Rockwell 112B
G-CKOY			G-CLUE	Piper PA-34-200T Seneca		G-CRIS	Taylor Monoplane
G-CKOZ			G-CLUX	Reims F172N		G-CRLH	Bell 206B Jet Ranger
G-CKPA	Sportine Aviacija LAK-19T		G-CMBS	MD.900 Explorer		G-CROB	Europa XS
G-CKPB	Schempp-Hirth Discus B		G-CMED	SOCATA TB-9 Tampico		G-CROL	Maule MXT-7-180
G-CKPC			G-CMGC	Piper PA-25-235 Pawnee		G-CROW	Robinson R44
G-CKPD			G-CMOR	Best Off Sky Ranger		G-CROY	Europa
G-CKPE			G-CMOS	Cessna T303 Crusader		G-CRPH	Airbus A320-231
G-CKPF			G-CMSN	Robinson R22B		G-CRUM	Westland Scout
G-CKPG			G-CMXX	Robinson R44		G-CRUZ	Cessna T303 Crusader
G-CKPH			G-CNAB	Jabiru UL		G-CSAV	Thruster T600N
G-CKPI			G-CNCN	Rockwell 112TCA		G-CSBD	Piper PA-28-236 Dakota
G-CKPJ			G-COAI	Cranfield A.1		G-CSBM	Reims F150M
G-CKPK			G-COCO	Reims F172M		G-CSCS	Reims F172N
G-CKPL			G-CODE	Bell 206B Jet Ranger		G-CSDJ	Jabiru UL
G-CKPM			G-CODY	Kolb Twinstar		G-CSFC	Cessna 150L
G-CKPN			G-COIN	Bell 206B Jet Ranger		G-CSFD	UltraMagic M-90
G-CKPO			G-COLA	Beech F33C Bonanza		G-CSGT	Piper PA-28-161 Warrior
G-CKPP			G-COLH	Piper PA-28-140 Cherokee		G-CSIX	Piper PA-32-300
G-CKPR			G-COLL	Enstrom 280C-UK		G-CSMK	EV-97 Eurostar
G-CKPS			G-COLS	Van's RV-7A		G-CSNA	Cessna 421C
G-CKPT			G-COMB	Piper PA-30-160 B		G-CSSE	Cessna 172S Skyhawk
G-CKPU			G-COMU	Flight Design CT2K		G-CSUE	ICP MXP-740 Savannah
G-CKPV			G-CONB	Robin DR.400-180 Regent		G-CSWH	Piper PA-28R-180
G-CKPW			G-CONC	Cameron N-90		G-CSWL	Bell 206L Long Ranger
G-CKPX			G-CONI	Lockheed L- 749A		G-CSZM	Zenair CH.601XL
G-CKPY			G-CONL	SOCATA TB-10 Tobago		G-CTAA	Schempp-Hirth Janus
G-CKPZ			G-CONR	Champion 7GCBC Scout		G-CTAV	EV-97 Eurostar
G-CKRA			G-COOT	Taylor Coot A		G-CTCD	Diamond DA42 Twin Star
G-CKRB			G-COPS	Piper J-3C-65 Cub		G-CTCE	Diamond DA42 Twin Star
G-CKRC			G-COPZ	Van's RV-7		G-CTCF	Diamond DA42 Twin Star
G-CKRD			G-CORA	Europa XS		G-CTCG	Diamond DA42 Twin Star
G-CKRE			G-CORB	SOCATA TB-20 Trinidad		G-CTCL	SOCATA TB-10 Tobago
G-CKRF			G-CORD	Slingsby Nipper T66		G-CTDH	Flight Design CT2K
G-CKRG			G-CORN	Bell 206B Jet Ranger		G-CTEC	GlaStar
G-CKRH			G-CORP	BAe ATP		G-CTEL	Cameron N-90
G-CKRI			G-COSY	Lindstrand LBL-56A		G-CTFF	Cessna T206H
G-CKRJ			G-COTT	Cameron Cottage		G-CTGR	Cameron N-77
G-CKRK			G-COUP	Ercoupe 415C		G-CTIO	SOCATA TB-20 Trinidad

G-CTIX	Spitfire T.IX	
G-CTKL	Noorduyn Harvard	
G-CTOY	Denney Kitfox	
G-CTRL	Robinson R22B	
G-CTSW	Flight Design CTSW	
G-CTUG	Piper PA-25-235 Pawnee	
G-CTWW	Piper PA-34-200T Seneca	
G-CTZO	SOCATA TB-20 Trinidad	
G-CUBB	Piper PA-18-180	
G-CUBE	Best Off Sky Ranger	
G-CUBI	Piper PA-18-135	
G-CUBJ	Piper PA-18-150	
G-CUBN	Piper PA-18-150	
G-CUBP	Piper PA-18-150	
G-CUBS	Piper J-3C-65 Cub	
G-CUBW	Wag-Aero Acro Trainer	
G-CUBY	Piper J-3C-65 Cub	
G-CUCU	Colt 180A	
G-CUIK	QAC Quickie Q200	
G-CUPS	Yakovlev Yak-52	
G-CURR	Cessna 172R Skyhawk	
G-CURV	Avid Speed Wing	
G-CUTE	Dyn'Aero MCR-01	
G-CUTY	Europa	
G-CVAL	Ikarus C42 Cyclone	
G-CVBF	Cameron A-210	
G-CVCV	Rotorway Exec 162F	
G-CVII	DR.107 One Design	
G-CVIP	Bell 206B Jet Ranger	
G-CVIX	DH Sea Vixen D3	
G-CVLH	Piper PA-34-200T Seneca	
G-CVMI	Piper PA-18-150	
G-CVPM	VPM M16 Tandem	
G-CVST	Jodel D.140	
G-CWAG	Sequoia F.8L Falco	
G-CWAL	Raj Hamsa X'Air	
G-CWBM	Phoenix Currie Wot	
G-CWFA	Piper PA-38-112 Tomahawk	
G-CWFB	Piper PA-38-112 Tomahawk	
G-CWFD	Piper PA-38-112 Tomahawk	
G-CWIC	P & M Quik	
G-CWIK	P & M Quik	
G-CWMC	P & M Quik GT450	
G-CWMT	Dyn'Aero MCR-01	
G-CWOT	Phoenix Currie Wot	
G-CWTD	Aeroprakt A22 Foxbat	
G-CWVY	P & M Quik	
G-CXCX	Cameron N-90	
G-CXDZ	Cassutt Speed Two	
G-CXHK	Cameron N-77	
G-CXIP	Thruster T600N	
G-CXSM	Cessna 172R Skyhawk	
G-CYLL	Sequoia F.8L Falco	
G-CYLS	Cessna T303 Crusader	
G-CYMA	Grumman GA-7 Cougar	
G-CYRA	Kolb Twinstar Mk.3	
G-CYRS	Bell 206L Long Ranger	
G-CZAC	Zenair CH.601XL	
G-CZAG	Sky 90-24	
G-CZAW	CZAW Sportcruiser	
G-CZBE	CFM Shadow SA-M	
G-CZCZ	Mudry CAP.10B	
G-CZMI	Best Off Sky Ranger	
G-CZNE	BN2B-20 Islander	
G-DAAH	Piper PA-28R-201T	
G-DAAM	Robinson R22M	
G-DAAT	Eurocopter EC135T2	
G-DAAZ	Piper PA-28RT-201T	
G-DABS	Robinson R22B	
G-DACA	Percival Sea Prince	
G-DACC	Cessna 401B	
G-DACF	Cessna 152	
G-DACN	Agusta 109S Grand	
G-DADG	Piper PA-18-150	
G-DAEX	Dassault Falcon 900EX	
G-DAFY	Beech 58 Baron	
G-DAGJ	Zenair CH.601XL	
G-DAIR	Luscombe 8A Silvaire	
G-DAIV	UltraMagic H-77	
G-DAJB	Boeing 757-2T7ER	
G-DAJC	Boeing 767-31K	
G-DAKK	Douglas DC-3	
G-DAKM	Diamond DA.40 Star	
G-DAKO	Piper PA-28-236 Dakota	
G-DAMY	Europa	
G-DANA	Jodel DR.1050M1	
G-DAND	SOCATA TB-10 Tobago	
G-DANT	Rockwell 114	
G-DANY	Jabiru UL	
G-DANZ	Aerospatiale AS.355N	
G-DAPH	Cessna 180K Skywagon	
G-DARA	Piper PA-34-220T Seneca	
G-DARK	CFM Shadow DD	
G-DASH	Rockwell 112	
G-DASS	Ikarus C42 Cyclone	
G-DATG	Reims F182P Skylane	
G-DATH	EV-97 Eurostar	
G-DAUF	Aerospatiale AS.365N2	
G-DAVD	Reims FR172K Hawk XP	
G-DAVE	Jodel D.112	
G-DAVG	Robinson R44	
G-DAVO	Grumman AA-5B Tiger	
G-DAVS	AB Sportine Aviacija LAK17	
G-DAVV	Robinson R44	
G-DAWG	Scottish Aviation Bulldog	
G-DAWZ	Glasflugel 304	
G-DAYS	Europa	
G-DAYZ	Pietenpol Aircamper	
G-DAZY	Piper PA-34-200T Seneca	
G-DAZZ	Van's RV-8	
G-DBAT	Lindstrand LBL-56A	
G-DBCA	Airbus A319-131	
G-DBCB	Airbus A319-131	
G-DBCC	Airbus A319-131	
G-DBCD	Airbus A319-131	
G-DBCE	Airbus A319-131	
G-DBCF	Airbus A319-131	
G-DBCG	Airbus A319-131	
G-DBCH	Airbus A319-131	
G-DBCI	Airbus A319-131	
G-DBCJ	Airbus A319-131	
G-DBCK	Airbus A319-131	
G-DBDB	VPM M16 Tandem	
G-DBLA	Boeing 767-35EER	
G-DBOY	Agusta 109C	
G-DBUG	Robinson R44	
G-DBYE	Mooney M.20M	
G-DCEA	Piper PA-34-200T Seneca	
G-DCKK	Reims F172N	
G-DCMI	P & M Quik	
G-DCON	Robinson R44	
G-DCPA	MBB BK.117C-1C	
G-DCSE	Robinson R44	
G-DCSG	Robinson R44	
G-DCTA	BAe 125-800	
G-DCXL	Jodel D.140C	
G-DDAY	Piper PA-28R-201T	
G-DDBD	Europa	
G-DDIG	Rockwell 114	
G-DDJF	Schempp-Hirth Duo Discus	
G-DDMV	North American T-6G	
G-DDOG	Scottish Aviation Bulldog	
G-DEAN	Pegasus XL-Q	
G-DEBR	Europa	
G-DEBT	Alpi Pioneer 300	
G-DECK	Cessna T210N	
G-DECO	Dyn'Aero MCR-01	
G-DEER	Robinson R22B	
G-DEFM	BAe 146-200	
G-DEFY	Robinson R22B	
G-DEKA	Cameron Z-90	
G-DELF	Aero L.29A	
G-DELT	Robinson R22B	
G-DEMH	Reims F172M	
G-DEMM	Aerospatiale AS.350B	
G-DENB	Reims F150G	
G-DENC	Reims F150G	
G-DEND	Reims F150M	
G-DENE	Piper PA-28-140 Cherokee	
G-DENI	Piper PA-32-300	
G-DENS	Binder Smaragd	
G-DENZ	Piper PA-44-180 Seminole	
G-DERB	Robinson R22B	
G-DERI	Piper PA-46-500TP	
G-DERK	Piper PA-46-500TP	
G-DERV	Cameron Truck SS	
G-DEST	Mooney M.20J	
G-DEUX	Aerospatiale AS.355F2	
G-DEVL	Eurocopter EC120B	
G-DEVS	Piper PA-28-180 Cherokee	
G-DEXP	ARV Super 2	
G-DFKI	Aerospatiale Gazelle	
G-DFLY	Piper PA-38-112 Tomahawk	
G-DFOX	Aerospatiale AS.355F1	
G-DFUN	Van's RV-6	
G-DGCL	Glaser-Dirks DG-800B	
G-DGET	CL604 Challenger	
G-DGHD	Robinson R44	
G-DGHI	Dyn'Aero MCR-01	
G-DGIK	Glaser-Dirks DG-100S	
G-DGIV	Glaser-Dirks DG-800B	
G-DGOD	Robinson R22B	
G-DGWW	Rand KR-2	
G-DHAH	Aeronca 7AC Champion	
G-DHCC	DHC-1 Chipmunk	
G-DHCZ	DHC-2 Beaver	
G-DHDV	DH.104 Dove 8	
G-DHJH	Airbus A321-211	
G-DHLB	Cameron N-90	
G-DHLI	Colt World SS	
G-DHPM	DHC-1 Chipmunk	
G-DHSS	DH.112 Venom FB50	
G-DHTM	DH.82A Tiger Moth Rep	
G-DHTT	DH.112 Venom FB50	
G-DHUU	DH.112 Venom FB50	
G-DHVM	DH.112 Venom FB50	
G-DHVV	DH.115 Vampire T.55	
G-DHWW	DH.115 Vampire T.55	
G-DHXX	DH.100 Vampire FB.6	
G-DHZF	DH.82A Tiger Moth	
G-DHZZ	DH.115 Vampire T.55	
G-DIAL	Cameron N-90	
G-DIAM	Diamond DA 40D Star	
G-DIAT	Piper PA-28-140 Cherokee	
G-DICK	Thunder Ax6-56Z	
G-DIDY	Thruster T600T	
G-DIGI	Piper PA-32-300	
G-DIKY	Murphy Rebel	
G-DIMB	Boeing 767-31KER	
G-DIME	Rockwell 114	
G-DINA	Grumman AA-5B Tiger	
G-DING	Colt 77A	
G-DINK	Lindstrand Bulb SS	
G-DINO	Pegasus Quantum	
G-DINT	Bristol Beaufighter	
G-DIPI	Cameron Tub SS	
G-DIPM	Piper PA-46-310P Malibu	
G-DIRK	Glaser-Dirks DG-400	
G-DISA	Scottish Aviation Bulldog	

Registration	Type	Registration	Type	Registration	Type
☐ G-DISK	Piper PA-24-250 Comanche	☐ G-DONT	Zenair CH.601XL	☐ G-DYCE	Robinson R44
☐ G-DISO	Jodel D.150 Mascaret	☐ G-DOOM	Cameron Z-105	☐ G-DYKE	Dyke Delta
☐ G-DIWY	Piper PA-32-300	☐ G-DOOZ	Aerospatiale AS.355F2	☐ G-DYNA	Dynamic WT9
☐ G-DIXY	Piper PA-28-181 Archer	☐ G-DORA	Focke-Wulf Fw190-D9	☐ G-DYNE	Cessna 414
☐ G-DIZI	Reality Escapade	☐ G-DORN	Dornier C-3605	☐ G-DYNG	Colt 105A
☐ G-DIZO	Jodel D.120A Paris-Nice	☐ G-DORS	Eurocopter EC135T2	☐ G-EAGA	Sopwith Dove Rep
☐ G-DIZY	Piper PA-28-201T	☐ G-DOTT	CFM Streak Shadow	☐ G-EAVX	Sopwith Pup Rep
☐ G-DIZZ	Hughes 369E	☐ G-DOVE	Cessna 182Q Skylane	☐ G-EBJI	Hawker Cygnet Rep
☐ G-DJAE	Cessna 500 Citation	☐ G-DOWN	Colt 31A	☐ G-ECAN	DH.84 Dragon
☐ G-DJAY	Jabiru UL	☐ G-DOZI	Ikarus C42 Cyclone	☐ G-ECBH	Reims F150K
☐ G-DJCR	Varga Kachina	☐ G-DPHN	Aerospatiale AS.365N1	☐ G-ECDX	DH.71 Rep
☐ G-DJET	Diamond DA42 Twin Star	☐ G-DPPF	Agusta 109E Power	☐ G-ECGC	Reims F172N
☐ G-DJJA	Piper PA-28-181 Archer	☐ G-DPYE	Robin DR400/500i	☐ G-ECGO	Bolkow Bo.208C Junior
☐ G-DJMM	Cessna 172S Skyhawk	☐ G-DRAG	Cessna 152	☐ G-ECIL	Robinson R44
☐ G-DJNH	Denney Kitfox	☐ G-DRAM	Reims FR172F Rocket	☐ G-ECJI	Dassault Falcon 10
☐ G-DJST	Air Creation iXess	☐ G-DRAW	Colt 77A	☐ G-ECJM	Piper PA-28R-201T
☐ G-DKDP	Grob 109	☐ G-DRAY	Taylor Monoplane	☐ G-ECLI	Schweizer 269C
☐ G-DKEY	Piper PA-28-161 Warrior	☐ G-DRBG	Cessna 172M Skyhawk	☐ G-ECON	Cessna 172M Skyhawk
☐ G-DKMK	Robinson R44	☐ G-DREX	Cameron Saturn SS	☐ G-ECOX	Pietenpol Aircamper
☐ G-DLCB	Europa	☐ G-DRFC	ATR 72-300	☐ G-ECUB	Piper PA-18-150
☐ G-DLCH	Boeing 737-8Q8	☐ G-DRGN	Cameron N-105	☐ G-ECVB	Pietenpol Aircamper
☐ G-DLDL	Robinson R22B	☐ G-DRGS	Cessna 182S Skylane	☐ G-EDAV	Scottish Aviation Bulldog
☐ G-DLEE	SOCATA TB-9 Tampico	☐ G-DRID	Reims FR172J Rocket	☐ G-EDCJ	Cessna 525 CitationJet
☐ G-DLOM	SOCATA TB-20 Trinidad	☐ G-DRIV	Robinson R44	☐ G-EDCK	Cessna 525 CitationJet
☐ G-DLTR	Piper PA-28-180 Cherokee	☐ G-DRMM	Europa	☐ G-EDCS	Raytheon 400XP
☐ G-DMAC	Jabiru UL	☐ G-DRNT	Sikorsky S-76	☐ G-EDEE	Ikarus C42 Cyclone
☐ G-DMAH	SOCATA TB-20 Trinidad	☐ G-DROP	Cessna U206C	☐ G-EDEN	SOCATA TB-10 Tobago
☐ G-DMCD	Robinson R22B	☐ G-DRSV	Robin DR.315 Mod	☐ G-EDES	Robinson R44
☐ G-DMCS	Piper PA-28R-200	☐ G-DRYI	Cameron N-77	☐ G-EDFS	Pietenpol Aircamper
☐ G-DMCT	Flight Design CT	☐ G-DRYS	Cameron N-90	☐ G-EDGA	Piper PA-28-161 Warrior
☐ G-DMND	Diamond DA42 Twin Star	☐ G-DRZF	Robin DR.360	☐ G-EDGE	Jodel D.150 Mascaret
☐ G-DMRS	Robinson R44	☐ G-DSFT	Piper PA-28R-200	☐ G-EDGI	Piper PA-28-161 Warrior
☐ G-DMSS	Aerospatiale Gazelle	☐ G-DSGC	Piper PA-25-260 Pawnee	☐ G-EDLY	AirBourne XT912-B
☐ G-DMWW	CFM Shadow DD	☐ G-DSID	Piper PA-34-220T Seneca	☐ G-EDMC	Pegasus Quantum
☐ G-DNCS	Piper PA-28R-201T	☐ G-DSKI	EV-97 Eurostar	☐ G-EDNA	Piper PA-38-112 Tomahawk
☐ G-DNGA	Kubicek BB20	☐ G-DSLL	Pegasus Quantum	☐ G-EDRE	Lindstrand LBL-90A
☐ G-DNGR	Colt 31A	☐ G-DSPI	Robinson R44	☐ G-EDRV	Van's RV-6A
☐ G-DNHI	Agusta 109A	☐ G-DSPK	Cameron Z-140	☐ G-EDTO	Reims FR172F Rocket
☐ G-DNKS	Ikarus C42 Cyclone	☐ G-DSPZ	Robinson R44	☐ G-EDVL	Piper PA-28R-200
☐ G-DNOP	Piper PA-46-310P Malibu	☐ G-DTFF	Cessna T182T	☐ G-EECO	Lindstrand LBL-25A
☐ G-DOCA	Boeing 737-436	☐ G-DTOY	Ikarus C42 Cyclone	☐ G-EEEK	Extra EA.300/200
☐ G-DOCB	Boeing 737-436	☐ G-DTUG	Wag-Aero Super Sport	☐ G-EEGL	Christen Eagle II
☐ G-DOCE	Boeing 737-436	☐ G-DTWO	Schempp-Hirth Discus	☐ G-EEGU	Piper PA-28-161 Warrior
☐ G-DOCF	Boeing 737-436	☐ G-DUAL	Cirrus SR22	☐ G-EEJE	Piper PA-31 Navajo
☐ G-DOCG	Boeing 737-436	☐ G-DUBI	Lindstrand LBL 120A	☐ G-EEKY	Piper PA-28-140 Cherokee
☐ G-DOCH	Boeing 737-436	☐ G-DUDE	Van's RV-8	☐ G-EELS	Cessna 208B
☐ G-DOCL	Boeing 737-436	☐ G-DUDZ	Robin DR.400-180 Regent	☐ G-EENA	Piper PA-32R-301 SP
☐ G-DOCN	Boeing 737-436	☐ G-DUGE	Ikarus C42 Cyclone	☐ G-EENI	Europa
☐ G-DOCO	Boeing 737-436	☐ G-DUGI	Lindstrand LBL-90A	☐ G-EENY	Grumman GA-7 Cougar
☐ G-DOCS	Boeing 737-436	☐ G-DUKK	Extra EA300/L	☐ G-EERH	Ruschmeyer RG90RG
☐ G-DOCT	Boeing 737-436	☐ G-DUKY	Robinson R44	☐ G-EERV	Van's RV-6
☐ G-DOCU	Boeing 737-436	☐ G-DUMP	Customcraft A25	☐ G-EESA	Europa
☐ G-DOCV	Boeing 737-436	☐ G-DUOA	Canadair CRJ-200	☐ G-EEST	BAe Jetstream 31
☐ G-DOCW	Boeing 737-436	☐ G-DUOC	Canadair CRJ-200	☐ G-EETG	Cessna 172Q Cutlass
☐ G-DOCX	Boeing 737-436	☐ G-DUOD	Canadair CRJ-700	☐ G-EEUP	Stampe SV-4C
☐ G-DOCY	Boeing 737-436	☐ G-DUOT	Schempp-Hirth Duo Discus	☐ G-EEWZ	P & M Quik
☐ G-DOCZ	Boeing 737-436	☐ G-DUOX	Schempp-Hirth Duo Discus	☐ G-EEYE	Mainair Blade
☐ G-DODB	Robinson R22B	☐ G-DURO	Europa	☐ G-EEZA	Robinson R44
☐ G-DODD	Reims F172P	☐ G-DURX	Colt 77A	☐ G-EEZR	Robinson R44
☐ G-DODG	EV-97 Eurostar	☐ G-DUSK	DH.115 Vampire T.11	☐ G-EEZS	Cessna 182P Skylane
☐ G-DODR	Robinson R22B	☐ G-DUST	Stolp SA.300	☐ G-EEZZ	Zenair CH.601XL
☐ G-DOEA	Grumman AA-5A Cheetah	☐ G-DUVL	Reims F172N	☐ G-EFAM	Cessna 182S Skylane
☐ G-DOFY	Bell 206B Jet Ranger	☐ G-DVBF	Lindstrand LBL-210A	☐ G-EFBP	Reims FR172K
☐ G-DOGE	Scottish Aviation Bulldog	☐ G-DVON	DH.104 Devon C.2	☐ G-EFFI	Rotorway Exec 162F
☐ G-DOGG	Scottish Aviation Bulldog	☐ G-DWCE	Robinson R44	☐ G-EFGH	Robinson R22B
☐ G-DOGZ	Horizon 1	☐ G-DWEL	SIPA 903	☐ G-EFIR	Piper PA-28-181 Archer
☐ G-DOIN	Best Off Sky Ranger	☐ G-DWIA	Chilton DW.1A	☐ G-EFOF	Robinson R22B
☐ G-DOIT	Aerospatiale AS.350B1	☐ G-DWIB	Chilton DW.1B	☐ G-EFRY	Avid Aerobat
☐ G-DOLY	Cessna T303 Crusader	☐ G-DWJM	Cessna 550 Citation II	☐ G-EFSM	Slingsby T.67M
☐ G-DOME	Piper PA-28-161 Warrior	☐ G-DWMS	Jabiru UL-450	☐ G-EFTE	Bolkow Bo.207
☐ G-DOMS	EV-97 Eurostar	☐ G-DWPF	Tecnam P92 Echo	☐ G-EFTF	Aerospatiale AS.350B
☐ G-DONI	Grumman AA-5B Tiger	☐ G-DWPH	UltraMagic M-77	☐ G-EGAG	SOCATA TB-20 Trinidad
☐ G-DONS	Piper PA-28R-201T	☐ G-DXCC	UltraMagic M-77	☐ G-EGAL	Christen Eagle II

☐ G-EGAN	Enstrom F-28A-UK	
☐ G-EGBS	Van's RV-9A	
☐ G-EGEE	Cessna 310Q	
☐ G-EGEG	Cessna 172R Skyhawk	
☐ G-EGEL	Christen Eagle II	
☐ G-EGGI	Ikarus C42 Cyclone	
☐ G-EGGS	Robin DR.400-180 Regent	
☐ G-EGGY	Robinson R22B	
☐ G-EGHB	Ercoupe 415D	
☐ G-EGHH	Hawker Hunter F.58	
☐ G-EGJA	SOCATA TB-20 Trinidad	
☐ G-EGLE	Christen Eagle II	
☐ G-EGLG	Piper PA-31 Navajo	
☐ G-EGLL	Piper PA-28-161 Warrior	
☐ G-EGLS	Piper PA-28-181 Archer	
☐ G-EGLT	Cessna 310R	
☐ G-EGNA	Diamond DA42 Twin Star	
☐ G-EGNR	Piper PA-38-112 Tomahawk	
☐ G-EGPG	Piper PA-18-135 Super Cub	
☐ G-EGTB	Piper PA-28-161 Warrior	
☐ G-EGTC	Robinson R44	
☐ G-EGTR	Piper PA-28-161 Warrior	
☐ G-EGUL	Christen Eagle II	
☐ G-EGUR	Jodel D.140B	
☐ G-EHBJ	CASA I-131E	
☐ G-EHDS	CASA I-131E	
☐ G-EHGF	Piper PA-28-181 Archer	
☐ G-EHIC	Jodel D.140B	
☐ G-EHLX	Piper PA-28-181 Archer	
☐ G-EHMF	Isaacs Fury II	
☐ G-EHMJ	Beech 35S Bonanza	
☐ G-EHMM	Robin DR.400-180 Regent	
☐ G-EHMS	MD.900 Explorer	
☐ G-EHUP	Aerospatiale Gazelle	
☐ G-EHXP	Rockwell 112	
☐ G-EIBM	Robinson R22B	
☐ G-EIII	Extra EA300	
☐ G-EIKY	Europa	
☐ G-EIRE	Cessna T182T	
☐ G-EISO	MS.892A Commodore	
☐ G-EITE	Luscombe 8E Silvaire	
☐ G-EIWT	Reims FR182RG Skylane	
☐ G-EIZO	Eurocopter EC120B	
☐ G-EJAR	Airbus A319-111	
☐ G-EJEL	Cessna 550 Citation II	
☐ G-EJGO	Zlin Z.226	
☐ G-EJJB	Airbus A319-111	
☐ G-EJMG	Reims F150H	
☐ G-EJOC	Aerospatiale AS.350B	
☐ G-EJRS	Piper PA-28-161 Warrior	
☐ G-EJTC	Robinson R44	
☐ G-EKIM	Alpi Pioneer 300	
☐ G-EKIR	Piper PA-28-161 Warrior	
☐ G-EKKC	Reims FR172G Rocket	
☐ G-EKKL	Piper PA-28-161 Warrior	
☐ G-EKKO	Robinson R44	
☐ G-EKMN	Zlin Z.242L	
☐ G-EKOS	Reims FR182RG Skylane	
☐ G-EKWS	Cessna 550 Citation II	
☐ G-EKYD	Robinson R44	
☐ G-ELAM	Piper PA-30-160	
☐ G-ELDR	Piper PA-32-260	
☐ G-ELEE	Cameron Z-105	
☐ G-ELEN	Robin DR.400-180 Regent	
☐ G-ELIS	Piper PA-34-200T Seneca	
☐ G-ELIT	Bell 206L Long Ranger	
☐ G-ELIZ	Denney Kitfox	
☐ G-ELKA	Christen Eagle II	
☐ G-ELKS	Avid Speed Wing	
☐ G-ELLA	Piper PA-32R-301	
☐ G-ELLE	Cameron N-90	
☐ G-ELLI	Bell 206B Jet Ranger	
☐ G-ELMH	North American T-6	
☐ G-ELMO	Robinson R44	
☐ G-ELNX	Canadair RJ.200ER	
☐ G-ELSE	Diamond DA42 Twin Star	
☐ G-ELSI	Air Creation iXess	
☐ G-ELTE	Agusta 109A	
☐ G-ELUN	Robin DR.400-180R	
☐ G-ELUT	Piper PA-28R-200	
☐ G-ELZN	Piper PA-28-161 Warrior	
☐ G-ELZY	Piper PA-28-161 Warrior	
☐ G-EMAA	Eurocopter EC135T2	
☐ G-EMAS	Eurocopter EC135T1	
☐ G-EMAX	Piper PA-31-350 Chieftain	
☐ G-EMBC	Embraer EMB-145EU	
☐ G-EMBD	Embraer EMB-145EU	
☐ G-EMBE	Embraer EMB-145EU	
☐ G-EMBF	Embraer EMB-145EU	
☐ G-EMBG	Embraer EMB-145EU	
☐ G-EMBH	Embraer EMB-145EU	
☐ G-EMBI	Embraer EMB-145EU	
☐ G-EMBJ	Embraer EMB-145EU	
☐ G-EMBK	Embraer EMB-145EU	
☐ G-EMBL	Embraer EMB-145EU	
☐ G-EMBM	Embraer EMB-145EU	
☐ G-EMBN	Embraer EMB-145EU	
☐ G-EMBO	Embraer EMB-145EU	
☐ G-EMBP	Embraer EMB-145EU	
☐ G-EMBS	Embraer EMB-145EU	
☐ G-EMBT	Embraer EMB-145EU	
☐ G-EMBU	Embraer EMB-145EU	
☐ G-EMBV	Embraer EMB-145EU	
☐ G-EMBW	Embraer EMB-145EU	
☐ G-EMBX	Embraer EMB-145EU	
☐ G-EMBY	Embraer EMB-145EU	
☐ G-EMCA	Rockwell 114B	
☐ G-EMDM	Diamond DA.40 Star	
☐ G-EMER	Piper PA-34-200 Seneca	
☐ G-EMHB	Agusta 109E Power	
☐ G-EMHH	Aerospatiale AS.355F2	
☐ G-EMHK	Bolkow Bo.209-150FV	
☐ G-EMID	Eurocopter EC135P2	
☐ G-EMIN	Europa	
☐ G-EMJA	CASA I-131E	
☐ G-EMLE	EV-97 Eurostar	
☐ G-EMLY	Pegasus Quantum	
☐ G-EMMI	Robinson R44	
☐ G-EMMS	Piper PA-38-112 Tomahawk	
☐ G-EMMY	Rutan VariEze	
☐ G-EMSB	Piper PA-22-160 Tri-Pacer	
☐ G-EMSI	Europa	
☐ G-EMSL	Piper PA-28-161 Warrior	
☐ G-EMSY	DH.82A Tiger Moth	
☐ G-ENCE	Partenavia P.68B	
☐ G-ENEE	CFM Shadow SA	
☐ G-ENES	Bell 206B Jet Ranger	
☐ G-ENGL	Piper PA-28-140 Cherokee	
☐ G-ENGO	Steen Skybolt	
☐ G-ENHB	Enstrom 480B	
☐ G-ENIE	Tipsy Nipper T.66	
☐ G-ENII	Reims F172M	
☐ G-ENNI	Robin R.3000-180	
☐ G-ENNK	Cessna 172S Skyhawk	
☐ G-ENNY	Cameron V-77	
☐ G-ENOA	Reims F172F	
☐ G-ENRE	Jabiru UL	
☐ G-ENRI	Lindstrand LBL-105A	
☐ G-ENRM	Cessna 182L Skylane	
☐ G-ENRY	Cameron N-105	
☐ G-ENTS	Van's RV-9A	
☐ G-ENTT	Reims F152	
☐ G-ENTW	Reims F152	
☐ G-ENVY	Mainair Blade	
☐ G-ENYA	Robinson R44	
☐ G-ENZO	Cameron Z-105	
☐ G-EODE	Piper PA-46-350P Malibu	
☐ G-EOFF	Taylor Titch	
☐ G-EOFS	Europa	
☐ G-EOFW	Pegasus Quantum	
☐ G-EOHL	Cessna 182L Skylane	
☐ G-EOIN	Zenair CH.701UL	
☐ G-EOLD	Piper PA-28-161 Warrior	
☐ G-EOLX	Cessna 172N Skyhawk	
☐ G-EOMA	Airbus A330-242	
☐ G-EORG	Piper PA-38-112 Tomahawk	
☐ G-EORJ	Europa	
☐ G-EPAR	Robinson R22B	
☐ G-EPDI	Cameron N-77	
☐ G-EPED	Piper PA-31-350 Chieftain	
☐ G-EPIC	Jabiru UL-450	
☐ G-EPOC	Jabiru UL-450	
☐ G-EPOX	Aero Designs Pulsar XP	
☐ G-EPPO	Robinson R44	
☐ G-EPTR	Piper PA-28R-200	
☐ G-ERBL	Robinson R22B	
☐ G-ERCO	Ercoupe 415D	
☐ G-ERDA	Staaken Flitzer	
☐ G-ERDS	DH.82A Tiger Moth	
☐ G-ERFS	Piper PA-28-161 Warrior	
☐ G-ERIC	Rockwell 112TC	
☐ G-ERIK	Cameron N-77	
☐ G-ERIS	Hughes 369D	
☐ G-ERIW	Staaken Flitzer	
☐ G-ERJA	Embraer EMB-145EU	
☐ G-ERJB	Embraer EMB-145EU	
☐ G-ERJC	Embraer EMB-145EU	
☐ G-ERJD	Embraer EMB-145EU	
☐ G-ERJE	Embraer EMB-145EU	
☐ G-ERJF	Embraer EMB-145EU	
☐ G-ERJG	Embraer EMB-145EU	
☐ G-ERMO	ARV Super 2	
☐ G-ERMS	Thunder Ax3	
☐ G-ERNI	Piper PA-28-181 Archer	
☐ G-EROL	Aerospatiale Gazelle	
☐ G-EROM	Robinson R22B	
☐ G-EROS	Cameron H-34	
☐ G-ERRI	Lindstrand LBL-77A	
☐ G-ERRY	Grumman AA-5B Tiger	
☐ G-ERTE	Best Off Sky Ranger	
☐ G-ERTI	Staaken Flitzer	
☐ G-ESCA	Reality Escapade	
☐ G-ESCC	Reality Escapade	
☐ G-ESCP	Reality Escapade	
☐ G-ESEX	Eurocopter EC135T2	
☐ G-ESFT	Piper PA-28-161 Warrior	
☐ G-ESKA	Reality Escapade	
☐ G-ESKY	Piper PA-23-250 Aztec D	
☐ G-ESLH	Agusta 109E Power	
☐ G-ESME	Cessna R182 Skylane RG	
☐ G-ESSL	Cessna 182R Skylane	
☐ G-ESSY	Robinson R44	
☐ G-ESTA	Cessna 550 Citation II	
☐ G-ESTR	Van's RV-6	
☐ G-ESUS	Rotorway Exec	
☐ G-ETAT	Cessna 172S Skyhawk	
☐ G-ETBY	Piper PA-32-260	
☐ G-ETCW	GlaStar	
☐ G-ETDC	Cessna 172P Skyhawk	
☐ G-ETHI	Yakovlev Yak-52	
☐ G-ETHY	Cessna 208	
☐ G-ETIM	Eurocopter EC120B	
☐ G-ETIN	Robinson R22B	
☐ G-ETIV	Robin DR.400-180 Regent	
☐ G-ETME	Nord 1002 Pingouin	
☐ G-ETNT	Robinson R44	
☐ G-ETOU	Agusta 109S	
☐ G-ETPS	Hawker Hunter FGA.9	
☐ G-EUOA	Airbus A319-131	

☐ G-EUOB	Airbus A319-131	
☐ G-EUOC	Airbus A319-131	
☐ G-EUOD	Airbus A319-131	
☐ G-EUOE	Airbus A319-131	
☐ G-EUOF	Airbus A319-131	
☐ G-EUOG	Airbus A319-131	
☐ G-EUOH	Airbus A319-131	
☐ G-EUOI	Airbus A319-131	
☐ G-EUPA	Airbus A319-131	
☐ G-EUPB	Airbus A319-131	
☐ G-EUPC	Airbus A319-131	
☐ G-EUPD	Airbus A319-131	
☐ G-EUPE	Airbus A319-131	
☐ G-EUPF	Airbus A319-131	
☐ G-EUPG	Airbus A319-131	
☐ G-EUPH	Airbus A319-131	
☐ G-EUPJ	Airbus A319-131	
☐ G-EUPK	Airbus A319-131	
☐ G-EUPL	Airbus A319-131	
☐ G-EUPM	Airbus A319-131	
☐ G-EUPN	Airbus A319-131	
☐ G-EUPO	Airbus A319-131	
☐ G-EUPP	Airbus A319-131	
☐ G-EUPR	Airbus A319-131	
☐ G-EUPS	Airbus A319-131	
☐ G-EUPT	Airbus A319-131	
☐ G-EUPU	Airbus A319-131	
☐ G-EUPV	Airbus A319-131	
☐ G-EUPW	Airbus A319-131	
☐ G-EUPX	Airbus A319-131	
☐ G-EUPY	Airbus A319-131	
☐ G-EUPZ	Airbus A319-131	
☐ G-EURX	Europa XS	
☐ G-EUSO	Robin DR.400-140 Earl	
☐ G-EUUA	Airbus A320-232	
☐ G-EUUB	Airbus A320-232	
☐ G-EUUC	Airbus A320-232	
☐ G-EUUD	Airbus A320-232	
☐ G-EUUE	Airbus A320-232	
☐ G-EUUF	Airbus A320-232	
☐ G-EUUG	Airbus A320-232	
☐ G-EUUH	Airbus A320-232	
☐ G-EUUI	Airbus A320-232	
☐ G-EUUJ	Airbus A320-232	
☐ G-EUUK	Airbus A320-232	
☐ G-EUUL	Airbus A320-232	
☐ G-EUUM	Airbus A320-232	
☐ G-EUUN	Airbus A320-232	
☐ G-EUUO	Airbus A320-232	
☐ G-EUUP	Airbus A320-232	
☐ G-EUUR	Airbus A320-232	
☐ G-EUUS	Airbus A320-232	
☐ G-EUUT	Airbus A320-232	
☐ G-EUUU	Airbus A320-232	
☐ G-EUXC	Airbus A321-231	
☐ G-EUXD	Airbus A321-231	
☐ G-EUXE	Airbus A321-231	
☐ G-EUXF	Airbus A321-231	
☐ G-EUXG	Airbus A321-231	
☐ G-EUXH	Airbus A321-231	
☐ G-EUXI	Airbus A321-231	
☐ G-EVBF	Cameron Z-350	
☐ G-EVET	Cameron C-80	
☐ G-EVEY	Thruster T600N	
☐ G-EVIE	Piper PA-28-161 Warrior	
☐ G-EVLE	Rearwin Cloudster	
☐ G-EVLN	Gulfstream 4	
☐ G-EVPI	Evans VP-1	
☐ G-EVRO	EV-97 Eurostar	
☐ G-EVTO	Piper PA-28-161 Warrior	
☐ G-EWAN	Protech PT-2C	
☐ G-EWAW	Bell 206B Jet Ranger	
☐ G-EWBC	Jabiru SK	

☐ G-EWES	Alpi Pioneer 300	
☐ G-EWHT	Robin R.2112 Alpha	
☐ G-EWIZ	Pitts S-2SE Special	
☐ G-EWME	Piper PA-28-235 Cherokee	
☐ G-EWRT	Eurocopter EC135T2	
☐ G-EXAM	Piper PA-28RT-201T	
☐ G-EXEA	Extra EA300/L	
☐ G-EXEC	Piper PA-34-200 Seneca	
☐ G-EXES	Europa XS	
☐ G-EXEX	Cessna 404	
☐ G-EXIT	MS.893E Rallye 180GT	
☐ G-EXLL	Zenair CH.601XL	
☐ G-EXON	Piper PA-28-161 Warrior	
☐ G-EXPD	Stemme S10-VT	
☐ G-EXPL	Aeronca 7GCBC Citabria	
☐ G-EXTR	Extra EA260	
☐ G-EXXO	Piper PA-28-161 Warrior	
☐ G-EYAK	Yakovlev Yak-50	
☐ G-EYAS	Denney Kitfox	
☐ G-EYCO	Robin DR.400-180 Regent	
☐ G-EYES	Cessna 402C	
☐ G-EYNL	MBB Bo.105DBS5	
☐ G-EYOR	Van's RV-6	
☐ G-EYRE	Bell 206L Long Ranger	
☐ G-EZAA	Airbus A319-111	
☐ G-EZAB	Airbus A319-111	
☐ G-EZAC	Airbus A319-111	
☐ G-EZAD	Airbus A319-111	
☐ G-EZAE	Airbus A319-111	
☐ G-EZAF	Airbus A319-111	
☐ G-EZAG	Airbus A319-111	
☐ G-EZAH	Airbus A319-111	
☐ G-EZAI	Airbus A319-111	
☐ G-EZAJ	Airbus A319-111	
☐ G-EZAK	Airbus A319-111	
☐ G-EZAL	Airbus A319-111	
☐ G-EZAM	Airbus A319-111	
☐ G-EZAN	Airbus A319-111	
☐ G-EZAO	Airbus A319-111	
☐ G-EZAP	Airbus A319-111	
☐ G-EZAR	P & M Quik	
☐ G-EZAS	Airbus A319-111	
☐ G-EZAT	Airbus A319-111	
☐ G-EZAU	Airbus A319-111	
☐ G-EZAV	Airbus A319-111	
☐ G-EZAW	Airbus A319-111	
☐ G-EZAX	Airbus A319-111	
☐ G-EZAY	Airbus A319-111	
☐ G-EZAZ	Airbus A319-111	
☐ G-EZBA	Airbus A319-111	
☐ G-EZBB	Airbus A319-111	
☐ G-EZBC	Airbus A319-111	
☐ G-EZBD	Airbus A319-111	
☐ G-EZBE	Airbus A319-111	
☐ G-EZBF	Airbus A319-111	
☐ G-EZBG	Airbus A319-111	
☐ G-EZBH	Airbus A319-111	
☐ G-EZBI	Airbus A319-111	
☐ G-EZBJ	Airbus A319-111	
☐ G-EZBK	Airbus A319-111	
☐ G-EZBL	Airbus A319-111	
☐ G-EZBM	Airbus A319-111	
☐ G-EZBN	Airbus A319-111	
☐ G-EZBO	Airbus A319-111	
☐ G-EZBP	Airbus A319-111	
☐ G-EZBR	Airbus A319-111	
☐ G-EZBT	Airbus A319-111	
☐ G-EZBU	Airbus A319-111	
☐ G-EZBV	Airbus A319-111	
☐ G-EZBW	Airbus A319-111	
☐ G-EZBX	Airbus A319-111	
☐ G-EZBY	Airbus A319-111	
☐ G-EZBZ	Airbus A319-111	

☐ G-EZDC	Airbus A319-111	
☐ G-EZDG	Rutan VariEze	
☐ G-EZEA	Airbus A319-111	
☐ G-EZEB	Airbus A319-111	
☐ G-EZEC	Airbus A319-111	
☐ G-EZED	Airbus A319-111	
☐ G-EZEF	Airbus A319-111	
☐ G-EZEG	Airbus A319-111	
☐ G-EZEJ	Airbus A319-111	
☐ G-EZEK	Airbus A319-111	
☐ G-EZEL	Aerospatiale Gazelle	
☐ G-EZEO	Airbus A319-111	
☐ G-EZEP	Airbus A319-111	
☐ G-EZER	Cameron H-34	
☐ G-EZET	Airbus A319-111	
☐ G-EZEV	Airbus A319-111	
☐ G-EZEW	Airbus A319-111	
☐ G-EZEZ	Airbus A319-111	
☐ G-EZIA	Airbus A319-111	
☐ G-EZIC	Airbus A319-111	
☐ G-EZID	Airbus A319-111	
☐ G-EZIE	Airbus A319-111	
☐ G-EZIF	Airbus A319-111	
☐ G-EZIG	Airbus A319-111	
☐ G-EZIH	Airbus A319-111	
☐ G-EZII	Airbus A319-111	
☐ G-EZIJ	Airbus A319-111	
☐ G-EZIK	Airbus A319-111	
☐ G-EZIL	Airbus A319-111	
☐ G-EZIM	Airbus A319-111	
☐ G-EZIN	Airbus A319-111	
☐ G-EZIO	Airbus A319-111	
☐ G-EZIP	Airbus A319-111	
☐ G-EZIR	Airbus A319-111	
☐ G-EZIR	Airbus A319-111	
☐ G-EZIS	Airbus A319-111	
☐ G-EZIT	Airbus A319-111	
☐ G-EZIU	Airbus A319-111	
☐ G-EZIV	Airbus A319-111	
☐ G-EZIW	Airbus A319-111	
☐ G-EZIX	Airbus A319-111	
☐ G-EZIY	Airbus A319-111	
☐ G-EZIZ	Airbus A319-111	
☐ G-EZJA	Boeing 737-73V	
☐ G-EZJB	Boeing 737-73V	
☐ G-EZJC	Boeing 737-73V	
☐ G-EZJF	Boeing 737-73V	
☐ G-EZJG	Boeing 737-73V	
☐ G-EZJH	Boeing 737-73V	
☐ G-EZJI	Boeing 737-73V	
☐ G-EZJJ	Boeing 737-73V	
☐ G-EZJK	Boeing 737-73V	
☐ G-EZJL	Boeing 737-73V	
☐ G-EZJM	Boeing 737-73V	
☐ G-EZJN	Boeing 737-73V	
☐ G-EZJO	Boeing 737-73V	
☐ G-EZJP	Boeing 737-73V	
☐ G-EZJR	Boeing 737-73V	
☐ G-EZJS	Boeing 737-73V	
☐ G-EZJT	Boeing 737-73V	
☐ G-EZJU	Boeing 737-73V	
☐ G-EZJV	Boeing 737-73V	
☐ G-EZJW	Boeing 737-73V	
☐ G-EZJX	Boeing 737-73V	
☐ G-EZJY	Boeing 737-73V	
☐ G-EZJZ	Boeing 737-73V	
☐ G-EZKA	Boeing 737-73V	
☐ G-EZKB	Boeing 737-73V	
☐ G-EZKC	Boeing 737-73V	
☐ G-EZKD	Boeing 737-73V	
☐ G-EZKE	Boeing 737-73V	
☐ G-EZKF	Boeing 737-73V	
☐ G-EZKG	Boeing 737-73V	

G-EZMH	Airbus A319-111	
G-EZMS	Airbus A319-111	
G-EZNC	Airbus A319-111	
G-EZNM	Airbus A319-111	
G-EZPG	Airbus A319-111	
G-EZPZ	Champion 8KCAB	
G-EZSM	Airbus A319-111	
G-EZUB	Zenair CH.601HD	
G-EZVS	Colt 77B	
G-EZXO	Colt 56A	
G-EZYU	Piper PA-34-200 Seneca	
G-EZZA	Europa XS	
G-EZZY	EV-97 Eurostar	
G-FABB	Cameron V-77	
G-FABI	Robinson R44	
G-FABM	Beech 95-A55 Baron	
G-FABS	Thunder Ax9-120	
G-FACE	Cessna 172S Skyhawk	
G-FAIR	SOCATA TB-10 Tobago	
G-FAKE	Robinson R44	
G-FALC	Sequoia F.8L Falco	
G-FALO	Sequoia F.8L Falco	
G-FAME	CFM Shadow SA-II	
G-FAMH	Zenair CH.701	
G-FANL	Cessna R172K Hawk XP	
G-FANY	Bell 206L Long Ranger	
G-FARE	Robinson R44	
G-FARL	Pitts S-1E Special	
G-FARM	MS.894E Minerva	
G-FARO	Starlite SL-1	
G-FARR	Jodel D.150 Mascaret	
G-FARY	QAC Quickie Tri-Q	
G-FATB	Rockwell 114B	
G-FAUX	Cessna 182S Skylane	
G-FAVC	DH.80A Puss Moth	
G-FBAT	Aeroprakt A22 Foxbat	
G-FBEA	Embraer ERJ-195	
G-FBEB	Embraer ERJ-195	
G-FBEC	Embraer ERJ-195	
G-FBED	Embraer ERJ-195	
G-FBEE	Embraer ERJ-195	
G-FBEF	Embraer ERJ-195	
G-FBEG	Embraer ERJ-195	
G-FBEH	Embraer ERJ-195	
G-FBEI	Embraer ERJ-195	
G-FBFI	Canadair CL-601	
G-FBII	Ikarus C42 Cyclone	
G-FBMW	Cameron N-90	
G-FBPI	ANEC IV MisselThrush	
G-FBRN	Piper PA-28-181 Archer	
G-FBWH	Piper PA-28R-180	
G-FCAB	Diamond DA42 Twin Star	
G-FCDB	Cessna 550 Citation II	
G-FCED	Piper PA-31T Cheyenne	
G-FCKD	Eurocopter EC120B	
G-FCLA	Boeing 757-28A	
G-FCLB	Boeing 757-28A	
G-FCLC	Boeing 757-28A	
G-FCLD	Boeing 757-25F	
G-FCLE	Boeing 757-2Q8	
G-FCLF	Boeing 757-28A	
G-FCLG	Boeing 757-28A	
G-FCLH	Boeing 757-28A	
G-FCLI	Boeing 757-2Q8	
G-FCLJ	Boeing 757-2Y0	
G-FCLK	Boeing 757-2Y0	
G-FCSP	Robin DR.400-180 Regent	
G-FCUK	Pitts S-1C Special	
G-FDPS	Pitts S-2C Special	
G-FDZA	Boeing 737-8K5	
G-FEAB	Piper PA-28-181 Archer	
G-FEBE	Cessna 340A	
G-FEBY	Robinson R22B	
G-FEDA	Eurocopter EC120B	
G-FEES	Eurocopter EC135T2	
G-FEET	P & M Quik	
G-FEFE	Scheibe SF25B Falke	
G-FELL	Europa	
G-FELT	Cameron N-77	
G-FERN	Mainair Blade	
G-FEWG	Fuji FA.200-160	
G-FEZZ	Agusta Bell 206B	
G-FFAB	Cameron N-105	
G-FFAF	Reims F150L	
G-FFEN	Reims F150M	
G-FFFT	Lindstrand LBL-31A	
G-FFIT	P & M Quik	
G-FFOX	Hawker Hunter T.7B	
G-FFRA	Dassault Falcon 20EW	
G-FFRI	Aerospatiale AS.355F1	
G-FFTI	SOCATA TB-20 Trinidad	
G-FFTT	Lindstrand FT SS	
G-FFUN	Pegasus Quantum	
G-FFWD	Cessna 310R	
G-FGID	Vought FG-1D	
G-FGSK	Cameron Beer Crate SS	
G-FHAS	Scheibe SF25E Falke	
G-FIAT	Piper PA-28-140 Cherokee	
G-FIBS	Aerospatiale AS.350B	
G-FIFE	Reims FA152 Aerobat	
G-FIFI	SOCATA TB-20 Trinidad	
G-FIFT	Ikarus C42 Cyclone	
G-FIGA	Cessna 152	
G-FIGB	Cessna 152	
G-FIGP	Boeing 737-2E7	
G-FIII	Extra EA300/L	
G-FIJJ	Reims F177RG	
G-FIJR	Lockheed L-188 Electra	
G-FIJV	Lockheed L-188 Electra	
G-FILE	Piper PA-34-200T Seneca	
G-FILL	Piper PA-31-310 Navajo	
G-FINA	Reims F150L	
G-FIND	Reims F406	
G-FINK	BAe 125-1000B	
G-FINZ	III Sky Arrow 650 T	
G-FIRM	Cessna 550 Citation II	
G-FIRS	Robinson R22B	
G-FIRZ	Renegade Spirit UK	
G-FISH	Cessna 310R	
G-FISK	Pazmany PL-4	
G-FITZ	Cessna 335	
G-FIXX	Van's RV-7	
G-FIZU	Lockheed L-188 Electra	
G-FIZY	Europa	
G-FIZZ	Piper PA-28-161 Warrior	
G-FJCE	Thruster T600T	
G-FJEA	Boeing 757-23A	
G-FJEB	Boeing 757-23A	
G-FJET	Cessna 550 Citation II	
G-FJMS	Partenavia P.68B	
G-FJTH	Aeroprakt A22 Foxbat	
G-FKNH	Piper PA-15 Vagabond	
G-FLAG	Colt 77A	
G-FLAK	Beech E55 Baron	
G-FLAV	Piper PA-28-161 Warrior	
G-FLBI	Robinson R44	
G-FLCA	Fleet 80 Canuck	
G-FLCT	Hallam Fleche	
G-FLDG	Best Off Sky Ranger	
G-FLEA	SOCATA TB-10 Tobago	
G-FLEW	Lindstrand LBL-90A	
G-FLEX	P & M Quik	
G-FLGT	Lindstrand LBL-105A	
G-FLIK	Pitts S-1S Special	
G-FLIP	Reims FA152 Aerobat	
G-FLIT	Rotorway Exec 162F	
G-FLIZ	Staaken Flitzer	
G-FLKE	Scheibe SF25C Falke	
G-FLKS	Scheibe SF25C Falke	
G-FLOA	Cameron O-120	
G-FLOP	Cessna 152	
G-FLOR	Europa	
G-FLOW	Cessna 172S Skyhawk	
G-FLOX	Europa	
G-FLPI	Rockwell 112A	
G-FLSH	Yakovlev Yak-52	
G-FLTA	BAe 146-200	
G-FLTC	BAe 146-300	
G-FLTD	BAe 146-200	
G-FLTG	Cameron A-140	
G-FLTL	MD83	
G-FLTZ	Beech 58 Baron	
G-FLUF	Lindstrand Bunny SS	
G-FLUX	Piper PA-28-181 Archer	
G-FLYA	Mooney M.20J	
G-FLYB	Ikarus C42 Cyclone	
G-FLYC	Ikarus C42 Cyclone	
G-FLYE	Cameron A-210	
G-FLYF	Mainair Blade	
G-FLYG	Slingsby T.67C	
G-FLYH	Robinson R22B	
G-FLYI	Piper PA-34-200 Seneca	
G-FLYP	Beagle B.206	
G-FLYS	Robinson R44	
G-FLYT	Europa	
G-FLYY	Strikemaster Mk.80	
G-FLZR	Staaken Flitzer	
G-FMAH	Fokker F.28-100	
G-FMAM	Piper PA-28-151 Warrior	
G-FMGG	Maule M-5-235C	
G-FMKA	Diamond H.36TC	
G-FMSG	Reims FA150K Aerobat	
G-FNEY	Reims F177RG	
G-FNLD	Cessna 172N Skyhawk	
G-FNLY	Reims F172M	
G-FNPT	Piper PA-28-161 Warrior	
G-FOFO	Robinson R44	
G-FOGG	Cameron N-90	
G-FOGI	Europa XS	
G-FOGY	Robinson R22B	
G-FOKK	Fokker DR1 Replica	
G-FOLI	Robinson R22B	
G-FOLY	Pitts S-2A Special	
G-FONZ	Best Off Sky Ranger	
G-FOPP	Neico Lancair 320	
G-FORC	Stampe SV-4C	
G-FORR	Piper PA-28-181 Archer	
G-FORZ	Pitts S-1S Special	
G-FOSY	MS.880B Rallye	
G-FOWL	Cameron 90A	
G-FOWS	Cameron N-105	
G-FOXA	Piper PA-28-161 Warrior	
G-FOXB	Aeroprakt A22 Foxbat	
G-FOXC	Denney Kitfox	
G-FOXD	Denney Kitfox	
G-FOXF	Denney Kitfox	
G-FOXG	Denney Kitfox	
G-FOXI	Denney Kitfox	
G-FOXL	Zenair CH.601XL	
G-FOXM	Bell 206B Jet Ranger	
G-FOXS	Denney Kitfox	
G-FOXX	Denney Kitfox	
G-FOXZ	Denney Kitfox	
G-FOZZ	Beech A36 Bonanza	
G-FPIG	Piper PA-28-151 Warrior	
G-FPLA	Beech B200 Super King Air	
G-FPLB	Beech B200 Super King Air	
G-FPLD	Beech 200 Super King Air	
G-FPLE	Beech B200 Super King Air	

Reg	Type	Reg	Type	Reg	Type
G-FPSA	Piper PA-28-161 Warrior	G-GASS	Thunder Ax7-77	G-GFFF	Boeing 737-53A
G-FRAD	Dassault Falcon 20EW	G-GATE	Robinson R44	G-GFFG	Boeing 737-505
G-FRAF	Dassault Falcon 20EW	G-GATT	Robinson R44	G-GFFH	Boeing 737-5H6
G-FRAG	Piper PA-32-300	G-GAZA	Aerospatiale Gazelle	G-GFFI	Boeing 737-528
G-FRAH	Dassault Falcon 20EW	G-GAZI	Aerospatiale Gazelle	G-GFFJ	Boeing 737-5H6
G-FRAI	Dassault Falcon 20EW	G-GAZZ	Aerospatiale Gazelle	G-GFIA	Cessna 152
G-FRAJ	Dassault Falcon 20EW	G-GBAB	Piper PA-28-161 Warrior	G-GFIB	Reims F152
G-FRAK	Dassault Falcon 20EW	G-GBAO	Robin R.1180TD Aiglon	G-GFKY	Zenair CH.250
G-FRAL	Dassault Falcon 20EW	G-GBEE	P & M Quik	G-GFLY	Reims F150L
G-FRAN	Piper J-3C-90 Cub	G-GBFF	Reims F172N	G-GFMT	Cessna 172S Skyhawk
G-FRAO	Dassault Falcon 20EW	G-GBFR	Reims F177RG	G-GFNO	Robin ATL
G-FRAP	Dassault Falcon 20EW	G-GBGA	Scheibe SF25C Falke	G-GFOX	Aeroprakt A22 Foxbat
G-FRAR	Dassault Falcon 20EW	G-GBGB	UltraMagic M-105	G-GFPA	Piper PA-28-181 Archer
G-FRAS	Dassault Falcon 20EW	G-GBHI	SOCATA TB-10 Tobago	G-GFRD	Robin ATL
G-FRAT	Dassault Falcon 20EW	G-GBJP	Pegasus Quantum	G-GFRO	Robin ATL
G-FRAU	Dassault Falcon 20EW	G-GBJS	Robin HR200/100	G-GFSA	Cessna 172R
G-FRAW	Dassault Falcon 20EW	G-GBLP	Reims F172M	G-GFTA	Piper PA-28-161 Warrior
G-FRAY	Cassutt Racer 3M	G-GBLR	Reims F150L	G-GFTB	Piper PA-28-161 Warrior
G-FRBA	Dassault Falcon 20EW	G-GBMR	Beech B200 Super King Air	G-GGCT	Flight Design CT2K
G-FRCE	Folland Gnat	G-GBRB	Piper PA-28-180 Cherokee	G-GGGG	Thunder Ax7-77
G-FRGN	Piper PA-28-236 Dakota	G-GBRU	Bell 206B Jet Ranger	G-GGHZ	Robin ATL
G-FRIL	Lindstrand LBL 105A	G-GBSL	Beech 76 Duchess	G-GGJK	Robin DR.400-140B
G-FRNK	Best Off Sky Ranger	G-GBTA	Boeing 737-436	G-GGLE	Piper PA-22-108 Colt
G-FROH	Aerospatiale AS.350B2	G-GBTB	Boeing 737-436	G-GGNG	Robinson R44
G-FROM	Ikarus C42 Cyclone	G-GBTL	Cessna 172S Skyhawk	G-GGOW	Colt 77A
G-FROS	Piper PA-28R-201 Arrow	G-GBUE	Robin DR.400-120A	G-GGRH	Robinson R44
G-FRYI	Beech 200 Super King Air	G-GBUN	Cessna 182T Skylane	G-GGRR	Scottish Aviation Bulldog
G-FRYL	Beech 390 Premier	G-GBVX	Robin DR400/120A	G-GGTT	Agusta Bell 47G-4A
G-FSEU	Beech 200 Super King Air	G-GBXF	Robin HR.200/120	G-GHDC	Robinson R44
G-FSHA	Denney Kitfox	G-GBXS	Europa XS	G-GHEE	EV-97 Eurostar
G-FTIL	Robin DR.400-180R	G-GCAC	Europa XS	G-GHIA	Cameron N-120
G-FTIM	Robin DR.400-100	G-GCAT	Piper PA-28-140 Cherokee	G-GHIN	Thunder Ax7-77
G-FTIN	Robin DR.400-100	G-GCBC	Champion 7GCBC Citabria	G-GHKX	Piper PA-28-161 Warrior
G-FTSE	BN2A-III Trislander	G-GCCL	Beech 76 Duchess	G-GHOW	Reims F182Q Skylane
G-FTSL	Canadair CL-604	G-GCEA	P & M Quik	G-GHPG	Cessna 550 Citation II
G-FTUO	Van's RV-4	G-GCKI	Mooney M.20K	G-GHRW	Piper PA-28RT-201
G-FUEL	Robin DR.400-180R	G-GCUF	Robin DR400/160	G-GHSI	Piper PA-44-180 Seminole
G-FUKM	Aerospatiale Gazelle	G-GCYC	Reims F182Q Skylane	G-GHZJ	SOCATA TB-9 Tampico
G-FULL	Piper PA-28R-200	G-GDAV	Robinson R44	G-GIDY	Europa XS
G-FULM	Sikorsky S-76C	G-GDER	Robin R.1180T Aiglon	G-GIGI	MS.893A Commodore
G-FUND	Thunder Ax7-65Z	G-GDJF	Robinson R44	G-GILI	Robinson R44
G-FUNK	Yakovlev Yak-50	G-GDKR	Robin DR400/140D	G-GILT	Cessna 421C
G-FUNN	Plumb Biplane	G-GDMW	Beech 76 Duchess	G-GIRY	American General AG-5B
G-FUNY	Robinson R44	G-GDOG	Piper PA-28R-200	G-GIWT	Europa XS
G-FURI	Issacs Fury	G-GDOV	Robinson R44	G-GJCD	Robinson R22B
G-FUSE	Cameron N-105	G-GDRV	Van's RV-6	G-GJKK	Mooney M.20K
G-FUZY	Cameron N-77	G-GDSG	Agusta 109E Power	G-GKAT	Enstrom 280C
G-FUZZ	Piper PA-18-95	G-GDTU	Mudry CAP.10B	G-GKFC	Sherwood Ranger
G-FVBF	Lindstrand LBL-210A	G-GEDY	Dassault Falcon 2000	G-GKKI	CAP 231EX
G-FVEL	Cameron Z-90	G-GEEP	Robin R.1180T Aiglon	G-GKUE	SOCATA TB-9 Tampico
G-FVRY	Colt 105A	G-GEES	Cameron N-77	G-GLAD	Gloster Gladiator II
G-FWAY	Lindstrand LBL-90A	G-GEEZ	Cameron N-77	G-GLAW	Cameron N-90
G-FWPW	Piper PA-28-236 Dakota	G-GEHL	Cessna 172S Skyhawk	G-GLED	Cessna 150M
G-FXBT	Aeroprakt A22 Foxbat	G-GEHP	Piper PA-28RT-201	G-GLHI	Best Off Sky Ranger
G-FZZA	General Avia F.22A	G-GEMM	Cirrus SR20	G-GLIB	Robinson R44
G-FZZI	Cameron H-34	G-GEMS	Thunder Ax8-90	G-GLID	Schleicher ASW 27
G-GACA	Percival Sea Prince	G-GENI	Robinson R44	G-GLST	Great Lakes Sport
G-GACB	Robinson R44	G-GENN	Grumman GA-7 Cougar	G-GLSU	Bucker Bu.181B
G-GAFA	Piper PA-34-200T Seneca	G-GEOF	Pereira Osprey II	G-GLTT	Piper PA-31-350 Chieftain
G-GAFT	Piper PA-44-180 Seminole	G-GEOS	Diamond HK36 TTC	G-GLUC	Van's RV-6
G-GAII	Hawker Hunter GA.11	G-GERT	Van's RV-7	G-GLUE	Cameron N-65
G-GAJB	Grumman AA-5B Tiger	G-GERY	GlaStar	G-GLUG	Piper PA-31-350 Chieftain
G-GALA	Piper PA-28-140 Cherokee	G-GEST	Robinson R44	G-GMAA	Learjet 45
G-GALB	Piper PA-28-161 Warrior	G-GEZZ	Bell 206B Jet Ranger	G-GMAB	BAe 125-1000A
G-GALL	Piper PA-38-112 Tomahawk	G-GFCA	Piper PA-28-161 Warrior	G-GMAX	Stampe SV-4C
G-GALX	Dassault Falcon 900EX	G-GFCB	Piper PA-28-161 Warrior	G-GMKD	Robin HR200/120B
G-GAME	Cessna T303 Crusader	G-GFCD	Piper PA-34-220T Seneca	G-GMPB	BN2T-4S Defender
G-GAND	Agusta Bell 206B	G-GFEA	Cessna 172S Skyhawk	G-GMPS	MD.900 Explorer
G-GANE	Sequoia F.8L Falco	G-GFEY	Piper PA-34-200T Seneca	G-GMSI	SOCATA TB-9 Tampico
G-GAOH	Robin DR.400 2+2	G-GFFA	Boeing 737-59D	G-GNAA	MD.900 Explorer
G-GAOM	Robin DR.400-2+2	G-GFFB	Boeing 737-505	G-GNJW	Ikarus C42 Cyclone
G-GASC	Hughes 369HS	G-GFFD	Boeing 737-59D	G-GNMG	Cessna U206F
G-GASP	Piper PA-28-181 Archer	G-GFFE	Boeing 737-528	G-GNRV	Van's RV-9A

☐ G-GNTB	SF.340A	
☐ G-GNTF	SF.340B	
☐ G-GNTZ	BAe 146-200	
☐ G-GOAC	Piper PA-34-200T Seneca	
☐ G-GOAL	Lindstrand LBL-105A	
☐ G-GOBD	Piper PA-32R-301 HP	
☐ G-GOBT	Colt 77A	
☐ G-GOCX	Cameron N-90	
☐ G-GOGB	Lindstrand LBL-90A	
☐ G-GOGS	Piper PA-34-200T Seneca	
☐ G-GOGW	Cameron N-90	
☐ G-GOJP	Piper PA-46-310P Malibu	
☐ G-GOLF	SOCATA TB-10 Tobago	
☐ G-GOMO	Learjet 45	
☐ G-GOOD	SOCATA TB-20 Trinidad	
☐ G-GOSL	Robin DR.400-180R	
☐ G-GOTC	Grumman GA-7 Cougar	
☐ G-GOTF	Cessna 208B Caravan	
☐ G-GOTH	Piper PA-28-161 Warrior	
☐ G-GOTO	Piper PA-32R-301T	
☐ G-GOUP	Robinson R22B	
☐ G-GPAG	Van's RV-6	
☐ G-GPAS	Jabiru UL-450	
☐ G-GPEG	Sky 90-24	
☐ G-GPFI	Boeing 737-229	
☐ G-GPMW	Piper PA-28R-201T	
☐ G-GPPN	Cameron TR-70	
☐ G-GPSF	Jabiru J430	
☐ G-GPST	Phillips ST.1 Speedtwin	
☐ G-GREY	Piper PA-46-310P Malibu	
☐ G-GRIN	Van's RV-6	
☐ G-GRMN	Aerospool Dynamic WT9	
☐ G-GRND	Agusta 109S Grand	
☐ G-GROE	Grob 115A	
☐ G-GROL	Maule MXT-7-180	
☐ G-GRPA	Ikarus C42 Cyclone	
☐ G-GRRC	Piper PA-28-161 Warrior	
☐ G-GRRR	Scottish Aviation Bulldog	
☐ G-GRWL	Lilliput Type 4	
☐ G-GRWW	Robinson R44	
☐ G-GRYZ	Beech F33A Bonanza	
☐ G-GSCV	Ikarus C42 Cyclone	
☐ G-GSIL	Aerospatiale AS.355N	
☐ G-GSJH	Bell 206B Jet Ranger	
☐ G-GSPG	Hughes 369HS	
☐ G-GSPN	Boeing 737-31S	
☐ G-GSPY	Robinson R44	
☐ G-GSSA	Boeing 747-47UF	
☐ G-GSSB	Boeing 747-47UF	
☐ G-GSSC	Boeing 747-47UF	
☐ G-GSSO	Gulfstream G550	
☐ G-GSYJ	Diamond DA42 Twin Star	
☐ G-GTDL	Airbus A320-231	
☐ G-GTFC	P & M Quik	
☐ G-GTGT	P & M Quik GT450	
☐ G-GTHM	Piper PA-38-112 Tomahawk	
☐ G-GTJD	P & M Quik GT450	
☐ G-GTJM	Eurocopter EC120B	
☐ G-GTSO	P & M Quik	
☐ G-GTTP	P & M Quik GT450	
☐ G-GUCK	Beech C23 Sundowner	
☐ G-GUFO	Cameron Saucer SS	
☐ G-GULF	Lindstrand LBL-105A	
☐ G-GULP	III Sky Arrow 650T	
☐ G-GUMS	Cessna 182P Skylane	
☐ G-GUNS	Cameron V-77	
☐ G-GURL	Cameron A-210	
☐ G-GURN	Piper PA-31 Navajo	
☐ G-GURU	Piper PA-28-161 Warrior	
☐ G-GUSS	Piper PA-28-151 Warrior	
☐ G-GUST	Agusta Bell 206B	
☐ G-GUYS	Piper PA-34-200T Seneca	

☐ G-GVPI	Evans VP-1
☐ G-GWIZ	Colt Clown SS
☐ G-GWYN	Reims F172M
☐ G-GYAK	Yakovlev Yak-50
☐ G-GYAT	Gardan GY-80-160
☐ G-GYAV	Cessna 172N Skyhawk
☐ G-GYBO	Gardan GY-80
☐ G-GYMM	Piper PA-28R-200
☐ G-GYRO	Campbell Cricket
☐ G-GYTO	Piper PA-28-161 Warrior
☐ G-GZDO	Cessna 172N Skyhawk
☐ G-GZLE	Aerospatiale Gazelle
☐ G-GZRP	Piper PA-42-720
☐ G-HAAM	Dassault Falcon 900
☐ G-HABT	Super Marine Spitfire 26
☐ G-HACE	Van's RV-6A
☐ G-HACK	Piper PA-18-150
☐ G-HADA	Enstrom 480
☐ G-HAEC	CAC-18 Mustang
☐ G-HAFG	Cessna 340A
☐ G-HAFT	Diamond DA42 Twin Star
☐ G-HAIB	Aviat A-1B Husky
☐ G-HAIG	Rutan LongEz
☐ G-HAIR	Robin DR.400-180 Regent
☐ G-HAJJ	Glaser-Dirks DG-400
☐ G-HALC	Piper PA-28R-200
☐ G-HALJ	Cessna 140
☐ G-HALL	Piper PA-22-160 Tri-Pacer
☐ G-HALP	SOCATA TB-10 Tobago
☐ G-HALT	P & M Quik
☐ G-HAMI	Fuji FA.200-180
☐ G-HAMM	Yakovlev Yak-50
☐ G-HAMP	Aeronca 7ACA Champ
☐ G-HAMR	Piper PA-28-161 Warrior
☐ G-HAMS	P & M Quik
☐ G-HAMY	Van's RV-6
☐ G-HANG	Diamond DA42 Twin Star
☐ G-HANS	Robin DR.400 2+2
☐ G-HANY	Agusta Bell 206B
☐ G-HAPI	Lindstrand LBL-105A
☐ G-HAPR	Bristol Sycamore
☐ G-HAPY	DHC-1 Chipmunk
☐ G-HARD	Dyn'Aero MCR-01 Banbi
☐ G-HARE	Cameron N-77
☐ G-HARI	Raj Hamsa X'Air
☐ G-HARK	CL604 Challenger
☐ G-HARN	Piper PA-28-181 Archer
☐ G-HARR	Robinson R22B
☐ G-HART	Cessna 152
☐ G-HARY	Ercoupe A-2
☐ G-HASO	Diamond DA.40D Star
☐ G-HATF	Thorp T.18CW
☐ G-HATZ	Hatz CB-1
☐ G-HAUL	Westland WG.30
☐ G-HAUS	Hughes 369HM
☐ G-HAZE	Thunder Ax8-90
☐ G-HBBC	DH.104 Dove 8
☐ G-HBBH	Ikarus C42 Cyclone
☐ G-HBEK	Agusta 109C
☐ G-HBMW	Robinson R22
☐ G-HBOS	Scheibe SF25C Falke
☐ G-HBUG	Cameron N-90
☐ G-HCBI	Schweizer 269C-1
☐ G-HCSA	Cessna 525A CitationJet 2
☐ G-HCSL	Piper PA-34-220T Seneca
☐ G-HDAE	DHC-1 Chipmunk
☐ G-HDEW	Piper PA-32R-301 SP
☐ G-HDIX	Enstrom 280FX
☐ G-HDTV	Agusta 109A
☐ G-HEBE	Bell 206B Jet Ranger
☐ G-HECB	Fuji FA.200-160
☐ G-HEDI	Cessna 182T Skylane
☐ G-HELA	SOCATA TB-10 Tobago

☐ G-HELE	Bell 206B Jet Ranger
☐ G-HELN	Piper PA-18-95
☐ G-HELP	Colt 17A
☐ G-HELV	DH.115 Vampire T.55
☐ G-HEMS	Aerospatiale AS.365N
☐ G-HENT	MS.880B Rallye
☐ G-HENY	Cameron V-77
☐ G-HERB	Piper PA-28R-201
☐ G-HERC	Cessna 172S Skyhawk
☐ G-HERD	Lindstrand LBL-77B
☐ G-HERM	ATR 72-201
☐ G-HEVN	SOCATA TB-200XL Tobago
☐ G-HEWI	Piper J-3C-90 Cub
☐ G-HEXE	Colt 17A
☐ G-HEYY	Cameron 72SS
☐ G-HFBM	Curtiss Robin C-2
☐ G-HFCA	Cessna A150L Aerobat
☐ G-HFCB	Reims F150L
☐ G-HFCI	Reims F150L
☐ G-HFCL	Reims F152
☐ G-HFCT	Reims F152
☐ G-HGPI	SOCATA TB-20 Trinidad
☐ G-HGRB	Robinson R44
☐ G-HHAA	Buccaneer S2B
☐ G-HHAB	Hawker Hunter F.58
☐ G-HHAC	Hawker Hunter F.58
☐ G-HHAF	Hawker Hunter F.58
☐ G-HHOG	Robinson R44
☐ G-HIBM	Cameron N-145
☐ G-HIEL	Robinson R22B
☐ G-HIJK	Cessna 421C
☐ G-HIJN	Ikarus C42 Cyclone
☐ G-HILO	Rockwell 114
☐ G-HILS	Reims F172H
☐ G-HILT	SOCATA TB-10 Tobago
☐ G-HILZ	Van's RV-8
☐ G-HIND	Maule MT-7-235
☐ G-HINZ	Jabiru SK
☐ G-HIPE	Sorrell SNS-7 Hiperbipe
☐ G-HIPO	Robinson R22B
☐ G-HIRE	Grumman GA-7 Cougar
☐ G-HITM	Raj Hamsa X'Air
☐ G-HIUP	Cameron A-250
☐ G-HIVA	Cessna 337A
☐ G-HIVE	Reims F150M
☐ G-HIYA	Best Off Sky Ranger
☐ G-HIZZ	Robinson R22B
☐ G-HJSM	Nimbus 4DM
☐ G-HJSS	Stampe SV-4C
☐ G-HKHM	Hughes 369D
☐ G-HLCF	CFM Shadow SA
☐ G-HLIX	Cameron Oilcan SS
☐ G-HMBJ	Rockwell 114B
☐ G-HMED	Piper PA-28-161 Warrior
☐ G-HMEI	Dassault Falcon 900
☐ G-HMEV	Dassault Falcon 900
☐ G-HMJB	Piper PA-34-220T Seneca
☐ G-HMMV	Cessna 525 CitationJet
☐ G-HMPF	Robinson R44
☐ G-HMPH	Bell 206B Jet Ranger
☐ G-HMPT	Agusta Bell 206B
☐ G-HMSS	Bell 206B Jet Ranger
☐ G-HNGE	Ikarus C42 Cyclone
☐ G-HNTR	Hawker Hunter T.7
☐ G-HOBO	Denney Kitfox
☐ G-HOCK	Piper PA-28-180 Cherokee
☐ G-HOFC	Europa
☐ G-HOFM	Cameron N-56
☐ G-HOGS	Cameron Pig SS
☐ G-HOHO	Colt Santa SS
☐ G-HOIL	Learjet 60
☐ G-HOLY	Gardan ST-10
☐ G-HOLZ	Agusta Bell 206B

Reg	Type
G-HONG	Slingsby T.67M
G-HONI	Robinson R22B
G-HONK	Cameron O-105
G-HONY	Lilliput Type 1
G-HOOD	SOCATA TB-20 Trinidad
G-HOPA	Lindstrand LBL-35A
G-HOPE	Beech F33A Bonanza
G-HOPI	Cameron N-42
G-HOPR	Lindstrand LBL-25A
G-HOPY	Van's RV-6A
G-HORN	Cameron N-77
G-HOSS	Beech F33A Bonanza
G-HOTI	Colt 77A
G-HOTT	Cameron O-120
G-HOTZ	Colt 77B
G-HOUS	Colt 31A Air Chair
G-HOWE	Thunder Ax7-77
G-HOWL	RAF 2000 GTX-SE
G-HOXN	Van's RV-9A
G-HPAD	Bell 206B Jet Ranger
G-HPOL	MD.900 Explorer
G-HPSB	Rockwell 114B
G-HPSE	Rockwell 114B
G-HPSF	Rockwell 114B
G-HPSL	Rockwell 114B
G-HPUX	Hawker Hunter T.7
G-HRAK	Aerospatiale AS.350B
G-HRBS	Robinson R22B
G-HRCC	Robin HR200/100
G-HRDS	Gulfstream 550
G-HRHE	Robinson R22B
G-HRHI	Beagle B.206 Srs.1
G-HRHS	Robinson R44
G-HRIO	Robin HR.100-210 Safari
G-HRLI	Hawker Hurricane
G-HRLK	SAAB 91D
G-HRLM	Brugger Colibri
G-HRLO	Hawker Hurricane Mk.X
G-HRNT	Cessna 182S Skylane
G-HROI	Rockwell 112
G-HRPN	Robinson R44
G-HRVD	CCF Harvard 4
G-HRYZ	Piper PA-28-180 Cherokee
G-HSDW	Bell 206B Jet Ranger
G-HSKI	Aviat A-1B Husky
G-HSLA	Robinson R22B
G-HSOO	Hughes 369HE
G-HSTH	Lindstrand LBL HS-110
G-HTEL	Robinson R44
G-HTRL	Piper PA-34-220T Seneca
G-HUBB	Partenavia P.68B
G-HUCH	Cameron 80SS
G-HUEW	Europa XS
G-HUEY	Bell UH-1H
G-HUFF	Cessna 182P Skylane
G-HUGO	Colt 260A
G-HUGS	Robinson R22B
G-HUKA	Hughes 369E
G-HULK	Best Off Sky Ranger
G-HULL	Reims F150M
G-HUMH	Van's RV-9A
G-HUNI	Aeronca 7GCBC Citabria
G-HUPW	Hawker Hurricane
G-HURI	Hawker Hurricane
G-HURN	Robinson R22B
G-HURR	Hawker Hurricane
G-HUSK	Aviat A-1B Husky
G-HUTT	Denney Kitfox
G-HUTY	Van's RV-7
G-HVAN	Sherwood Ranger
G-HVBF	Lindstrand LBL-210A
G-HVIP	Hawker Hunter T.68
G-HVRD	Piper PA-31-350 Chieftain
G-HVRZ	Eurocopter EC120B
G-HXTD	Robin DR.400-180 Regent
G-HYAK	Yakovlev Yak-52
G-HYLT	Piper PA-32R-301 SP
G-HYST	Enstrom 280FX
G-IAGD	Robinson R22B
G-IAJS	Ikarus C42 Cyclone
G-IAMP	Cameron H-34
G-IANB	Glaser-Dirks DG-800B
G-IANC	SOCATA TB-10 Tobago
G-IANH	SOCATA TB-10 Tobago
G-IANI	Europa XS
G-IANJ	Reims F150K
G-IANN	Kolb Twinstar Mk.3
G-IANV	Diamond DA42 Twin Star
G-IANW	Aerospatiale AS.350B3
G-IARC	GlaStar
G-IASL	Beech 60 Duke
G-IATU	Cessna 182P Skylane
G-IBAZ	Ikarus C42 Cyclone
G-IBBC	Cameron BBC World
G-IBBS	Europa
G-IBED	Robinson R22A
G-IBET	Cameron Can SS
G-IBEV	Cameron C-90
G-IBFC	Quad City Challenger
G-IBFP	VPM M16 Tandem
G-IBFW	Piper PA-28R-201
G-IBHH	Hughes 269C
G-IBIG	Bell 206B Jet Ranger
G-IBLU	Cameron Z-90
G-IBMS	Robinson R44
G-IBZS	Cessna 182S Skylane
G-ICAB	Robinson R44
G-ICAS	Pitts S-2B Special
G-ICBM	Glasair III
G-ICCL	Robinson R22B
G-ICKY	Lindstrand LBL-77A
G-ICMT	EV-97 Eurostar
G-ICOI	Lindstrand LBL-105A
G-ICOM	Reims F172M
G-ICON	Rutan LongEz
G-ICRS	Ikarus C42 Cyclone
G-ICSG	Aerospatiale AS.355F1
G-ICWT	Pegasus Quantum
G-IDAB	Cessna 550 Citation II
G-IDAY	Skyfox Gazelle
G-IDDI	Cameron N-77
G-IDII	DR.107 One Design
G-IDOL	EV-97 Eurostar
G-IDPH	Piper PA-28-181 Archer
G-IDSL	Flight Design CT2K
G-IDUP	Enstrom 280C
G-IDWR	Hughes 369HS
G-IEIO	Piper PA-34-200T Seneca
G-IEJH	Jodel D.150A Mascaret
G-IEYE	Robin DR.400-180 Regent
G-IFAB	Reims F182Q Skylane
G-IFBP	Aerospatiale AS.350B
G-IFDM	Robinson R44
G-IFFR	Piper PA-32-300
G-IFIF	Cameron TR-60
G-IFIT	Piper PA-31-350 Chieftain
G-IFLE	EV-97 Eurostar
G-IFLI	Grumman AA-5A Cheetah
G-IFLP	Piper PA-34-200T Seneca
G-IFTE	BAe 125-700B
G-IFTS	Robinson R44
G-IGGL	SOCATA TB-10 Tobago
G-IGHH	Enstrom 480
G-IGIE	SIAI-Marchetti SF.260
G-IGII	Europa
G-IGLA	Colt 240A
G-IGLE	Cameron V-90
G-IGLZ	Champion 8KCAB
G-IGNL	Robinson R44
G-IGPW	Eurocopter EC120B
G-IHOP	Cameron Z-31
G-IHOT	EV-97 Eurostar
G-IIAC	Aeronca 11AC Chief
G-IIAN	Aero Designs Pulsar
G-IICI	Pitts S-2C Special
G-IICX	Schempp-Hirth Ventus
G-IIDI	Extra EA300/L
G-IIDY	Pitts S-2B Special
G-IIEI	Extra EA300/S
G-IIEX	Extra EA300/L
G-IIFR	Robinson R22B
G-IIGI	Van's RV-4
G-IIID	DR.107 One Design
G-IIIE	Pitts S-2B Special
G-IIIG	Boeing Stearman A75N1
G-IIII	Pitts S-2B Special
G-IIIL	Pitts S-1T Special
G-IIIM	Stolp SA.100 Starduster
G-IIIO	Schempp-Hirth Ventus
G-IIIR	Pitts S-1S Special
G-IIIS	Sukhoi Su-26M2
G-IIIT	Pitts S-2A Special
G-IIIV	Pitts Super Stinker
G-IIIX	Pitts S-1S Special
G-IIIZ	Sukhoi Su-26
G-IIMI	Extra EA300/L
G-IIMT	Bushby-Long Midget
G-IINI	Van's RV-9A
G-IIPT	Robinson R22B
G-IIRG	Glasair IIRGS
G-IIUI	Extra EA300/S
G-IIVI	Mudry CAP.232
G-IIXI	Extra EA300/L
G-IIXX	Parsons Gyroplane
G-IIYK	Yakovlev Yak-50
G-IIZI	Extra EA300
G-IJAC	Avid Speed Wing
G-IJAG	Cessna 182T Skylane
G-IJBB	Enstrom 480
G-IJMC	VPM M16 Tandem
G-IJMI	Extra EA300/L
G-IJOE	Piper PA-28R-201T
G-IJYS	BAe Jetstream 31
G-IKAP	Cessna T303 Crusader
G-IKAT	Diamond Katana
G-IKBP	Piper PA-28-161 Warrior
G-IKEA	Cameron IKEA 120 SS
G-IKES	GlaStar
G-IKEV	Jabiru UL-450
G-IKON	Van's RV-4
G-IKOS	Cessna 550 Citation II
G-IKRK	Europa
G-IKRS	Ikarus C42 Cyclone
G-IKUS	Ikarus C42 Cyclone
G-ILDA	Spitfire HF.IX
G-ILEE	Colt 56A
G-ILET	Robinson R44
G-ILLE	Boeing Stearman E75
G-ILLG	Robinson R44
G-ILLY	Piper PA-28-181 Archer
G-ILMD	Pilatus PC-12/45
G-ILRS	Ikarus C42 Cyclone
G-ILSE	Corby CJ-1 Starlet
G-ILTS	Piper PA-32-300
G-IMAB	Europa
G-IMAC	Canadair CL-601
G-IMAN	Colt 31A
G-IMBI	QAC Quickie Q1
G-IMBY	Pietenpol Aircamper

☐ G-IMCD Van's RV-7	☐ G-ISPH Bell 206B Jet Ranger	☐ G-JAME Zenair CH.601UL Zodiac
☐ G-IMEA Beech 200 Super King Air	☐ G-ISSV Eurocopter EC155B1	☐ G-JAMP Piper PA-28-151 Warrior
☐ G-IMGL Beech B200 Super King Air	☐ G-ISSW Eurocopter EC155B1	☐ G-JAMY Europa XS
☐ G-IMIC Yakovlev Yak-52	☐ G-ISSY Eurocopter EC120B	☐ G-JANA Piper PA-28-181 Archer
☐ G-IMLI Cessna 310Q	☐ G-ISTT Thunder Ax8-84	☐ G-JANI Robinson R44
☐ G-IMME Zenair CH.701 STOL	☐ G-ITIH Dassault Falcon 50	☐ G-JANN Piper PA-34-220T Seneca
☐ G-IMNY Reality Escapade	☐ G-ITII Pitts S-2A Special	☐ G-JANO Piper PA-28R-201T
☐ G-IMOK Diamond H.36R	☐ G-ITOI Cameron N-90	☐ G-JANS Reims FR172J Rocket
☐ G-IMPX Rockwell 112B	☐ G-ITON Maule MX-7-235	☐ G-JANT Piper PA-28-181 Archer
☐ G-IMPY Avid Flyer	☐ G-ITTI Pitts S-1S Special	☐ G-JARA Robinson R22B
☐ G-IMUP Air Creation iXess	☐ G-ITUG Piper PA-28-180 Cherokee	☐ G-JASE Piper PA-28-161 Warrior
☐ G-INAV Europa	☐ G-ITVM Lindstrand LBL-105A	☐ G-JAST Mooney M.20J
☐ G-INCA Glaser-Dirks DG-400	☐ G-ITWB DHC-1 Chipmunk	☐ G-JATD Robinson R22B
☐ G-INCE Best Off Skyranger	☐ G-IUAN Cessna 525 CitationJet	☐ G-JAVO Piper PA-28-161 Warrior
☐ G-INDC Cessna T303 Crusader	☐ G-IUII Yakovlev Yak-52	☐ G-JAWC Pegasus Quantum
☐ G-INDX Robinson R44	☐ G-IVAC Airtour AH-77B	☐ G-JAWZ Pitts S-1S Special
☐ G-INGA Thunder Ax8-84	☐ G-IVAL Mudry CAP.10C	☐ G-JAXS Jabiru UL
☐ G-INGE Thruster T600N	☐ G-IVAN Shaw Twin-Eze	☐ G-JAYI Auster J/1 Autocrat
☐ G-INIT SOCATA TB-9 Tampico	☐ G-IVAR Yakovlev Yak-50	☐ G-JAYS Best Off Sky Ranger
☐ G-INJA Ikarus C42 Cyclone	☐ G-IVAS Bell 206B Jet Ranger	☐ G-JAZZ Grumman AA-5A Cheetah
☐ G-INKY Robinson R22B	☐ G-IVDM Nimbus 4DM	☐ G-JBAS Neico Lancair 200
☐ G-INNI Jodel D.112	☐ G-IVEL Fournier RF4D	☐ G-JBBZ Aerospatiale AS.350B3
☐ G-INNY Replica Plans SE5A	☐ G-IVEN Robinson R44	☐ G-JBDB Agusta Bell 206B
☐ G-INOW Monnett Moni	☐ G-IVER Europa XS	☐ G-JBDH Robin DR.400-180 Regent
☐ G-INSR Cameron N-90	☐ G-IVET Europa	☐ G-JBEK Agusta A109C
☐ G-INTO Pilatus PC-12/45	☐ G-IVII Van's RV-7	☐ G-JBEN Mainair Blade
☐ G-INTS Van's RV-4	☐ G-IVIV Robinson R44	☐ G-JBHH Bell 206B Jet Ranger
☐ G-IOCO Beech 58 Baron	☐ G-IVOR Aeronca 11AC Chief	☐ G-JBII Robinson R22B
☐ G-IOFR Lindstrand LBL-105A	☐ G-IVYS Parsons Gyroplane	☐ G-JBIS Cessna 550 Citation II
☐ G-IOIA III Sky Arrow 650XP	☐ G-IWDB Hawker 800XP	☐ G-JBIZ Cessna 550 Citation II
☐ G-IOOI Robin DR.400-160 Major	☐ G-IWON Cameron V-90	☐ G-JBJB Colt 69A
☐ G-IOOX Learjet 45	☐ G-IWRB Agusta A109A-II	☐ G-JBKA Robinson R44
☐ G-IOPT Cessna 182P Skylane	☐ G-IWRC Eurocopter EC135T1	☐ G-JBMC SOCATA TB-10 Tobago
☐ G-IORG Robinson R22B	☐ G-IXES Air Creation iXess	☐ G-JBRN Cessna 182S Skylane
☐ G-IOSI Jodel DR.1050	☐ G-IXII Christen Eagle II	☐ G-JBSP Jabiru SP-470
☐ G-IOSO Jodel DR.1050	☐ G-IXIX III Sky Arrow 650T	☐ G-JBTR Van's RV-8A
☐ G-IOWA BN2A-21 Islander	☐ G-IYAK Yakovlev Yak-11C	☐ G-JBUZ Robin DR.400-180R
☐ G-IOWE Europa XS	☐ G-IYCO Robin DR.500	☐ G-JCAP Robinson R22B
☐ G-IPAL Cessna 550 Citation II	☐ G-IZII Marganski Swift S-1	☐ G-JCAR Piper PA-46-310P Malibu
☐ G-IPAT Jabiru SP	☐ G-IZIT Rans S6 Coyote II (N)	☐ G-JCAS Piper PA-28-181 Archer
☐ G-IPAX Cessna 560 Citation XL	☐ G-IZOD Cessna T182T	☐ G-JCBB Sikorsky S-76B
☐ G-IPFM Bensen B.8MR	☐ G-IZZI Cessna 172S Skyhawk	☐ G-JCBC Gulfstream 550
☐ G-IPKA Alpi Pioneer 300	☐ G-IZZS Cessna 172S Skyhawk	☐ G-JCBJ Sikorsky S-76C
☐ G-IPSI Grob 109B	☐ G-IZZY Cessna 172R Skyhawk	☐ G-JCIT Cessna 208B
☐ G-IPSY Rutan VariEze	☐ G-IZZZ Champion 8KCAB	☐ G-JCKT Stemme S-10VT
☐ G-IPUP Beagle B.121 Pup 2	☐ G-JAAB Jabiru UL	☐ G-JCMW Rand KR-2
☐ G-IRAF RAF 2000 GTX-SE	☐ G-JABB Jabiru UL	☐ G-JCUB Piper PA-18-135
☐ G-IRAL Thruster T600N 450	☐ G-JABE Jabiru UL-D	☐ G-JDBC Piper PA-34-200 Seneca
☐ G-IRAN Cessna 152	☐ G-JABI Jabiru J400	☐ G-JDEE SOCATA TB-20 Trinidad
☐ G-IRIS Grumman AA-5B Tiger	☐ G-JABJ Jabiru J400	☐ G-JDEL Jodel D.150 Mascaret
☐ G-IRJX Avro RJX-100	☐ G-JABO Focke Wulf FW190Rep	☐ G-JDIX Mooney M.20B
☐ G-IRKB Piper PA-28R-201	☐ G-JABS Jabiru UL-450	☐ G-JDJM Piper PA-28-140 Cherokee
☐ G-IRLY Colt 90A	☐ G-JABU Jabiru J400	☐ G-JEAJ BAe 146-200
☐ G-IRLZ Lindstrand LBL 60X	☐ G-JABY Jabiru SPL-450	☐ G-JEAK BAe 146-200
☐ G-IRON Europa XS	☐ G-JABZ Jabiru UL-450	☐ G-JEAM BAe 146-300
☐ G-IRPC Cessna 182Q Skylane	☐ G-JACA Piper PA-28-161 Warrior	☐ G-JEAO BAe 146-100
☐ G-IRTH Lindstrand LBL-150A	☐ G-JACB Piper PA-28-181 Archer	☐ G-JEAS BAe 146-100
☐ G-IRYC Schweizer 269C-1	☐ G-JACC Piper PA-28-181 Archer	☐ G-JEAU BAe 146-100
☐ G-ISAX Piper PA-28-181 Archer	☐ G-JACK Cessna 421C	☐ G-JEAV BAe 146-200
☐ G-ISCA Piper PA-28RT-201	☐ G-JACO Jabiru UL	☐ G-JEAW BAe 146-200
☐ G-ISDB Piper PA-28-161 Warrior	☐ G-JACS Piper PA-28-181 Archer	☐ G-JEAY BAe 146-300
☐ G-ISDN Boeing Stearman A75N1	☐ G-JADJ Piper PA-28-181 Archer	☐ G-JEBA Mainair Blade
☐ G-ISEH Cessna 182R Skylane	☐ G-JAEE Van's RV-6A	☐ G-JEBB BAe 146-300
☐ G-ISEL Best Off Sky Ranger	☐ G-JAES Bell 206B Jet Ranger	☐ G-JEBC BAe 146-300
☐ G-ISEW P & M Quik	☐ G-JAGS Reims FRA150L Aerobat	☐ G-JEBD BAe 146-300
☐ G-ISFC Piper PA-31-310 Navajo	☐ G-JAIR Mainair Blade	☐ G-JEBE BAe 146-300
☐ G-ISHA Piper PA-28-161 Warrior	☐ G-JAJB Grumman AA-5A Cheetah	☐ G-JEBF BAe 146-300
☐ G-ISHK Cessna 172S Skyhawk	☐ G-JAJK Piper PA-31-350 Chieftain	☐ G-JEBG BAe 146-300
☐ G-ISKA PZL TS-11 Iskra	☐ G-JAJP Jabiru UL	☐ G-JEBV BAe 146 RJ100
☐ G-ISLB BAe Jetstream 31	☐ G-JAKF Robinson R44	☐ G-JECE DHC-8-402Q
☐ G-ISLC BAe Jetstream 31	☐ G-JAKI Mooney M.20R	☐ G-JECF DHC-8-402Q
☐ G-ISLD BAe Jetstream 31	☐ G-JAKS Piper PA-28-160 Cherokee	☐ G-JECG DHC-8-402Q
☐ G-ISMO Robinson R22B	☐ G-JAMA Schweizer 269C-1	☐ G-JECH DHC-8-402Q

☐ G-JECI	DHC-8-402Q	
☐ G-JECJ	DHC-8-402Q	
☐ G-JECK	DHC-8-402Q	
☐ G-JECL	DHC-8-402Q	
☐ G-JECM	DHC-8-402Q	
☐ G-JECN	DHC-8-402Q	
☐ G-JECO	DHC-8-402Q	
☐ G-JECP	DHC-8-402Q	
☐ G-JECR	DHC-8-402Q	
☐ G-JECS	DHC-8-402Q	
☐ G-JECT	DHC-8-402Q	
☐ G-JECU	DHC-8-402Q	
☐ G-JEDG	DHC-8-402Q	
☐ G-JEDH	Robin DR.400-180R	
☐ G-JEDI	DHC-8-402Q	
☐ G-JEDJ	DHC-8-402Q	
☐ G-JEDK	DHC-8-402Q	
☐ G-JEDL	DHC-8-402Q	
☐ G-JEDM	DHC-8-402Q	
☐ G-JEDN	DHC-8-402Q	
☐ G-JEDO	DHC-8-402Q	
☐ G-JEDP	DHC-8-402Q	
☐ G-JEDR	DHC-8-402Q	
☐ G-JEDS	Andreasson BA4B	
☐ G-JEDT	DHC-8-402Q	
☐ G-JEDU	DHC-8-402Q	
☐ G-JEDV	DHC-8-402Q	
☐ G-JEDW	DHC-8-402Q	
☐ G-JEEP	EV-97A Eurostar	
☐ G-JEET	Reims FA152 Aerobat	
☐ G-JEFA	Robinson R44	
☐ G-JEJE	RAF 2000 GTX-SE	
☐ G-JEMA	BAe ATP	
☐ G-JEMB	BAe ATP	
☐ G-JEMC	BAe ATP	
☐ G-JEMD	BAe ATP	
☐ G-JEME	BAe ATP	
☐ G-JEMH	Aerospatiale AS355F2	
☐ G-JEMX	Short SD.360-200	
☐ G-JEMY	Lindstrand LBL-90A	
☐ G-JENA	Mooney M.20J	
☐ G-JENI	Cessna R182 Skylane RG	
☐ G-JENN	Grumman AA-5B Tiger	
☐ G-JENO	Lindstrand LBL-105A	
☐ G-JERO	Europa XS	
☐ G-JERS	Robinson R22B	
☐ G-JESA	Gemini Raven	
☐ G-JESG	Robinson R44	
☐ G-JESI	Aerospatiale AS.350B	
☐ G-JESS	Piper PA-28R-201T	
☐ G-JETC	Cessna 550 Citation II	
☐ G-JETF	Dassault Falcon 2000EX	
☐ G-JETH	Sea Hawk FGA.6	
☐ G-JETI	BAe 125-800B	
☐ G-JETJ	Cessna 550 Citation II	
☐ G-JETM	Gloster Meteor T.7	
☐ G-JETO	Cessna 550 Citation II	
☐ G-JETU	Aerospatiale AS.355F2	
☐ G-JETX	Bell 206B Jet Ranger	
☐ G-JETZ	Hughes 369E	
☐ G-JEZZ	Best Off Skyranger	
☐ G-JFMK	Zenair CH.701SP	
☐ G-JFRV	Van's RV-7A	
☐ G-JFWI	Reims F172N	
☐ G-JGBI	Bell 206L Long Ranger	
☐ G-JGMN	CASA I-131E	
☐ G-JGSI	Pegasus Quantum	
☐ G-JHAC	Reims FRA150L Aerobat	
☐ G-JHEW	Robinson R22B	
☐ G-JHKP	Europa XS	
☐ G-JHNY	Cameron A-210	
☐ G-JHYS	Europa	
☐ G-JIFI	Schempp-Hirth Duo Discus	

☐ G-JIII	Stolp SA.300	
☐ G-JILL	Rockwell 112TCA	
☐ G-JILS	Van's RV-8	
☐ G-JILY	Robinson R44	
☐ G-JIMB	Beagle B.121 Pup	
☐ G-JIMH	Reims F152	
☐ G-JIMM	Europa XS	
☐ G-JIMZ	Van's RV-4	
☐ G-JIVE	Hughes 369E	
☐ G-JJAB	Jabiru J400	
☐ G-JJAN	Piper PA-28-181 Archer	
☐ G-JJDC	Aviat A-1B Husky	
☐ G-JJEN	Piper PA-28-181 Archer	
☐ G-JJMX	Dassault Falcon 900EX	
☐ G-JJPJ	Reims F172N Skyhawk	
☐ G-JJSI	BAe 125-800B	
☐ G-JKAY	Robinson R44	
☐ G-JKMF	Diamond DA.40D Star	
☐ G-JKMG	Diamond DA.40D Star	
☐ G-JKMH	Diamond DA42 Twin Star	
☐ G-JKMJ	Diamond DA42 Twin Star	
☐ G-JLAT	EV-97 Eurostar	
☐ G-JLCA	Piper PA-34-200T Seneca	
☐ G-JLEE	Agusta Bell 206B	
☐ G-JLHS	Beech A36 Bonanza	
☐ G-JLIN	Piper PA-28-161 Warrior	
☐ G-JLMW	Cameron V-77	
☐ G-JLRW	Beech 76 Duchess	
☐ G-JMAA	Boeing 757-3CQ	
☐ G-JMAB	Boeing 757-3CQ	
☐ G-JMAC	BAe Jetstream 41	
☐ G-JMAN	Mainair Blade	
☐ G-JMAX	BAe 125-800XP	
☐ G-JMCD	Boeing 757-25F	
☐ G-JMCG	Boeing 757-2G5	
☐ G-JMDI	Schweizer 269C	
☐ G-JMDW	Cessna 550 Citation II	
☐ G-JMJR	Cameron Z-90	
☐ G-JMKE	Cessna 172S Skyhawk	
☐ G-JMON	Agusta A109A-II	
☐ G-JMTS	Robin DR.400-180 Regent	
☐ G-JMTT	Piper PA-28R-201T	
☐ G-JMXA	Agusta 109E Power	
☐ G-JNAS	Grumman AA-5A Cheetah	
☐ G-JNNB	Colt 90A	
☐ G-JOAL	Beech B200	
☐ G-JOBA	P & M Quik	
☐ G-JODI	Agusta 109A	
☐ G-JODL	Jodel DR.1050M	
☐ G-JOEM	Airbus A320-231	
☐ G-JOEY	BN2A-III Trislander	
☐ G-JOIE	Champion 7GCAA	
☐ G-JOJO	Cameron A-210	
☐ G-JOLY	Cessna 120	
☐ G-JONB	Robinson R22B	
☐ G-JONG	Rotorway Exec 162F	
☐ G-JONH	Robinson R22B	
☐ G-JONI	Reims FA152 Aerobat	
☐ G-JONO	Colt 77A	
☐ G-JONY	Pegasus AX2000	
☐ G-JONZ	Cessna 172P Skyhawk	
☐ G-JOOL	Mainair Blade	
☐ G-JOON	Cessna 182D Skylane	
☐ G-JOPT	Cessna 560 Citation V	
☐ G-JOSH	Cameron N-105	
☐ G-JOST	Europa	
☐ G-JOYD	Robinson R22B	
☐ G-JOYT	Piper PA-28-181 Archer	
☐ G-JOYZ	Piper PA-28-181 Archer	
☐ G-JPAL	Aerospatiale AS.355N	
☐ G-JPAT	Robin HR.200-100	
☐ G-JPJR	Robinson R44	
☐ G-JPMA	Jabiru UL	

☐ G-JPOT	Piper PA-32R-301 SP	
☐ G-JPRO	Jet Provost T.5A	
☐ G-JPSX	Dassault Falcon 900EX	
☐ G-JPTT	Enstrom 480	
☐ G-JPTV	Jet Provost T.5	
☐ G-JPVA	Jet Provost T.5A	
☐ G-JPWM	Best Off Sky Ranger	
☐ G-JRED	Robinson R44	
☐ G-JREE	Maule MX-7-180	
☐ G-JRKD	Jodel D.18	
☐ G-JRME	Jodel D.140E	
☐ G-JSAK	Robinson R22B	
☐ G-JSAR	Aerospatiale AS.332L2	
☐ G-JSAT	BN2T Islander	
☐ G-JSON	Cameron O-105	
☐ G-JSPC	BN2T Islander	
☐ G-JSPL	Jabiru SPL-450	
☐ G-JSRV	Van's RV-6	
☐ G-JSSD	HP.137 Jetstream	
☐ G-JTCA	Piper PA-23-250 Aztec E	
☐ G-JTEM	Van's RV-7	
☐ G-JTNC	Cessna 500 Citation	
☐ G-JTPC	Aeromot AMT-200	
☐ G-JTWO	Piper J-2 Cub	
☐ G-JUDD	Jabiru UL	
☐ G-JUDE	Robin DR.400-180 Regent	
☐ G-JUDI	North American AT-6D	
☐ G-JUDY	Grumman AA-5A Cheetah	
☐ G-JUGE	EV-97 Eurostar	
☐ G-JUIN	Cessna T303 Crusader	
☐ G-JULE	P & M Quik	
☐ G-JULL	Stemme S-10VT	
☐ G-JULU	Cameron V-90	
☐ G-JULZ	Europa	
☐ G-JUNG	CASA I-131E	
☐ G-JUPP	Piper PA-32RT-300	
☐ G-JURA	BAe Jetstream 31	
☐ G-JURE	SOCATA TB-10 Tobago	
☐ G-JURG	Rockwell 114A GT	
☐ G-JUST	Beech F33A Bonanza	
☐ G-JVBF	Lindstrand LBL-210A	
☐ G-JVBP	EV-97 Eurostar	
☐ G-JWBI	Agusta Bell 206B	
☐ G-JWCM	Scottish Aviation Bulldog	
☐ G-JWDB	Ikarus C42 Cyclone	
☐ G-JWDS	Reims F150G	
☐ G-JWEB	Robinson R44	
☐ G-JWFT	Robinson R22B	
☐ G-JWIV	Jodel DR.1051	
☐ G-JWJW	CASA I-131E	
☐ G-JXTA	BAe Jetstream 31	
☐ G-JXTC	BAe Jetstream 31	
☐ G-JYAK	Yakovlev Yak-50	
☐ G-JYRO	Rotorsport UK MT-03	
☐ G-KAAT	MD.900 Explorer	
☐ G-KADY	Rutan LongEz	
☐ G-KAEW	Gannet AEW.3	
☐ G-KAFE	Cameron N-65	
☐ G-KAFT	Diamond DA.40D Star	
☐ G-KAIR	Piper PA-28-181 Archer	
☐ G-KALS	Challenger 300	
☐ G-KAMM	Hawker Hurricane XIIA	
☐ G-KAMP	Piper PA-18-135	
☐ G-KANZ	Westland Wasp	
☐ G-KAOM	Scheibe SF25C Falke	
☐ G-KAOS	Van's RV-7	
☐ G-KAPW	Percival Provost T1	
☐ G-KARA	Brugger Colibri	
☐ G-KARI	Fuji FA.200-160	
☐ G-KARK	Dyn'Aero MCR-01	
☐ G-KART	Piper PA-28-161 Warrior	
☐ G-KASX	Seafire F.XVII	
☐ G-KATI	Rans S7 Courier	

☐ G-KATS	Piper PA-28-140 Cherokee
☐ G-KATT	Cessna 152
☐ G-KAWA	Denney Kitfox
☐ G-KAXF	Hawker Hunter F.6A
☐ G-KAXT	Westland Wasp
☐ G-KAYH	Extra EA300/L
☐ G-KAYI	Cameron Z-90
☐ G-KAZA	Sikorsky S-76C+
☐ G-KAZB	Sikorsky S-76C+
☐ G-KAZI	Pegasus Quantum
☐ G-KBKB	Thunder Ax8-90
☐ G-KBPI	Piper PA-28-161 Warrior
☐ G-KCHG	Schempp-Hirth Ventus
☐ G-KCIG	Fournier RF5B
☐ G-KCIN	Piper PA-28-161 Cadet
☐ G-KDCC	Europa XS
☐ G-KDCD	Thruster T600N
☐ G-KDET	Piper PA-28-161 Cadet
☐ G-KDEY	Scheibe SF25E Falke
☐ G-KDIX	Jodel D.9 Bebe
☐ G-KDMA	Cessna 560 Citation V
☐ G-KDOG	Scottish Aviation Bulldog
☐ G-KEAM	Schleicher ASH 26E
☐ G-KEEF	Rockwell 114B
☐ G-KEEN	Stolp SA.300
☐ G-KEES	Piper PA-28-180 Cherokee
☐ G-KEJY	EV-97 Eurostar
☐ G-KELI	Robinson R44
☐ G-KELL	Van's RV-6
☐ G-KELS	Van's RV-7
☐ G-KELV	Diamond DA42 Twin Star
☐ G-KELZ	Van's RV-8
☐ G-KEMC	Grob 109
☐ G-KEMI	Piper PA-28-181 Archer
☐ G-KEMY	Cessna 182T Skylane
☐ G-KENB	Air Command 503
☐ G-KENG	Rotorsport UK MT-03
☐ G-KENI	Rotorway Exec 152
☐ G-KENM	Luscombe 8EF Silvaire
☐ G-KENW	Robin DR.400-500
☐ G-KENZ	Rutan VariEze
☐ G-KEPE	Schempp-Hirth Nimbus
☐ G-KEPP	Rans S6 Coyote II
☐ G-KESS	Glaser-Dirks DG-400
☐ G-KEST	Steen Skybolt
☐ G-KETH	Agusta Bell 206B
☐ G-KEVB	Piper PA-28-181 Archer
☐ G-KEVI	Jabiru J400
☐ G-KEWT	UltraMagic M-90
☐ G-KEYS	Piper PA-23-250 Aztec F
☐ G-KEYY	Cameron N-77
☐ G-KFAN	Scheibe SF25B Falke
☐ G-KFOX	Denney Kitfox
☐ G-KFRA	Piper PA-32-300
☐ G-KFZI	KFZ-1 Tigerfalk
☐ G-KGAO	Scheibe SF25C Falke
☐ G-KGED	Campbell Cricket
☐ G-KHCC	Schempp-Hirth Ventus
☐ G-KHOM	Aeromot AMT-200
☐ G-KHOP	Zenair CH.601HDS
☐ G-KHRE	MS.880B Rallye
☐ G-KICK	Pegasus Quantum
☐ G-KIDD	Jabiru J430
☐ G-KIII	Extra EA300/L
☐ G-KIMA	Zenair CH.601XL
☐ G-KIMB	Robin DR.300-140
☐ G-KIMK	Partenavia P.68
☐ G-KIMM	Europa XS
☐ G-KIMY	Robin DR.400-140B
☐ G-KINE	Grumman AA-5A Cheetah
☐ G-KIPP	Thruster T600N
☐ G-KIRB	Europa XS
☐ G-KIRC	Pietenpol Aircamper

☐ G-KIRK	Piper J-3C-65 Cub
☐ G-KISS	Rand KR-2
☐ G-KITE	Piper PA-28-181 Archer
☐ G-KITF	Denney Kitfox
☐ G-KITH	Alpi Pioneer 300
☐ G-KITI	Pitts S-2E Special
☐ G-KITS	Europa Tri-Gear
☐ G-KITT	Curtiss P-40M
☐ G-KITY	Denney Kitfox
☐ G-KIZZ	Air Creation Kiss
☐ G-KKCW	Flight Design CT2K
☐ G-KKER	Jabiru UL
☐ G-KKES	SOCATA TB-20 Trinidad
☐ G-KLAS	Robinson R44
☐ G-KMRV	Van's RV-9A
☐ G-KNAP	Piper PA-28-161 Warrior
☐ G-KNEE	UltraMagic M-77C
☐ G-KNEK	Grob 109B
☐ G-KNIB	Robinson R22B
☐ G-KNIX	Cameron Z-315
☐ G-KNOB	Lindstrand LBL-180A
☐ G-KNOT	Jet Provost T.3A
☐ G-KNOW	Piper PA-32-300
☐ G-KNOX	Robinson R22B
☐ G-KNYT	Robinson R44
☐ G-KOBH	Schempp-Hirth Discus bT
☐ G-KODA	Cameron O-77
☐ G-KOFM	DG-600-18M
☐ G-KOHF	Schleicher ASK 14
☐ G-KOKL	Diamond H.36
☐ G-KOLB	Kolb Twinstar Mk.3
☐ G-KOLI	PZL Koliber-150
☐ G-KONG	Slingsby T.67M
☐ G-KOOL	DH.104 Sea Devon
☐ G-KORN	Cameron Bottle SS
☐ G-KOTA	Piper PA-28-236 Dakota
☐ G-KOYY	Schempp-Hirth Nimbus
☐ G-KPAO	Robinson R44
☐ G-KPTT	SOCATA TB-20 Trinidad
☐ G-KRES	Glasair IIRG
☐ G-KRII	Rand KR-2
☐ G-KRMA	Cessna 425 Corsair
☐ G-KRNW	Eurocopter EC135T1
☐ G-KSIR	Glasair IIS RG
☐ G-KSKS	Cameron N-105
☐ G-KSKY	Sky 77-24
☐ G-KSPB	Robinson R44
☐ G-KSVB	Piper PA-24-260 Comanche
☐ G-KTEE	Cameron V-77
☐ G-KTKT	Sky 260-24
☐ G-KTOL	Robinson R44
☐ G-KTTY	Denney Kitfox
☐ G-KTWO	Cessna 182T Skylane
☐ G-KUBB	SOCATA TB-20 Trinidad
☐ G-KUIK	P & M Quik
☐ G-KUKI	Robinson R22B
☐ G-KULA	Best Off Sky Ranger
☐ G-KUPP	Flight Design CTSW
☐ G-KUUI	Piper J-3C-65 Cub
☐ G-KVBF	Cameron A-340HL
☐ G-KVIP	Beech 200 Super King Air
☐ G-KWAK	Scheibe SF25C Falke
☐ G-KWAX	Cessna 182E Skylane
☐ G-KWIC	P & M Quik
☐ G-KWIK	Partenavia P.68B
☐ G-KWIN	Dassault Falcon 2000EX
☐ G-KWKI	QAC Quickie Q200
☐ G-KWLI	Cessna 421C
☐ G-KYAK	Yakovlev Yak-11
☐ G-KYLE	Thruster T600N 450
☐ G-KYTE	Piper PA-28-161 Warrior
☐ G-LAAC	Cameron C-90
☐ G-LABS	Europa

☐ G-LACA	Piper PA-28-161 Warrior
☐ G-LACB	Piper PA-28-161 Warrior
☐ G-LACD	Piper PA-28-181 Archer
☐ G-LACE	Europa
☐ G-LACI	Cessna 172S Skyhawk
☐ G-LACR	Denney Kitfox
☐ G-LADD	Enstrom 480
☐ G-LADI	Piper PA-30-160
☐ G-LADS	Rockwell 114
☐ G-LADZ	Enstrom 480
☐ G-LAGR	Cameron N-90
☐ G-LAID	Robinson R44
☐ G-LAIN	Robinson R22B
☐ G-LAIR	Glasair IIS
☐ G-LAJT	Beech D17S Staggerwing
☐ G-LAKE	Lake LA-250
☐ G-LAMA	Aerospatiale Lama
☐ G-LAMM	Europa
☐ G-LAMP	Cameron Bulb SS
☐ G-LAMS	Reims F152
☐ G-LANC	Avro Lancaster B.X
☐ G-LANE	Reims F172N
☐ G-LAOK	Yakovlev Yak-52
☐ G-LAOL	Piper PA-28RT-201
☐ G-LAOR	BAe 125-800XP
☐ G-LAPN	Avid Aerobat
☐ G-LARA	Robin DR.400-180 Regent
☐ G-LARE	Piper PA-39-160CR
☐ G-LARK	Helton Lark 95
☐ G-LARR	Aerospatiale AS.350B3
☐ G-LARS	Dyn'Aero MCR-01
☐ G-LARY	Robinson R44
☐ G-LASN	Best Off Sky Ranger
☐ G-LASR	Glasair II
☐ G-LASS	Rutan VariEze
☐ G-LAST	Diamond DA.40D Star
☐ G-LASU	Eurocopter EC135T1
☐ G-LAVE	Cessna 172R Skyhawk
☐ G-LAXY	Everett Gyroplane
☐ G-LAZA	Lazer Z.200
☐ G-LAZL	Piper PA-28-161 Warrior
☐ G-LAZR	Cameron O-77
☐ G-LAZY	Lindstrand Chair SS
☐ G-LAZZ	GlaStar
☐ G-LBDC	Bell 206B Jet Ranger
☐ G-LBLI	Lindstrand LBL-69A
☐ G-LBMM	Piper PA-28-161 Warrior
☐ G-LBRC	Piper PA-28RT-201
☐ G-LBUK	Lindstrand LBL-77A
☐ G-LBUZ	EV-97 Eurostar
☐ G-LCGL	Comper Swift Rep
☐ G-LCOC	BN2A-III Trislander
☐ G-LCPL	Aerospatiale AS.365N2
☐ G-LCUB	Piper PA-18-95
☐ G-LCYA	Dassault Falcon 900EX
☐ G-LDAH	Best Off Skyranger
☐ G-LDFM	Cessna 560XL
☐ G-LDWS	Jodel D.150 Mascaret
☐ G-LDYS	Thunder Ax6-56Z
☐ G-LEAF	Reims F406
☐ G-LEAH	Alpi Pioneer 300
☐ G-LEAM	Piper PA-28-236 Dakota
☐ G-LEAP	BN2 Islander
☐ G-LEAS	Sky 90-24
☐ G-LEAU	Cameron N-31
☐ G-LEBE	Europa
☐ G-LECA	Aerospatiale AS.355F1
☐ G-LEDR	Aerospatiale Gazelle
☐ G-LEED	Denney Kitfox
☐ G-LEEE	Jabiru UL
☐ G-LEEH	UltraMagic M-90
☐ G-LEEN	Aero Designs Pulsar XP
☐ G-LEES	Glaser-Dirks DG-400

☐ G-LEEZ	Bell 206L Long Ranger	☐ G-LINC	Hughes 369HS	☐ G-LRBW	Lindstrand LBL HS-110
☐ G-LEGG	Reims F182Q Skylane	☐ G-LINE	Aerospatiale AS.355N	☐ G-LRGE	Lindstrand LBL-330A
☐ G-LEGO	Cameron O-77	☐ G-LINN	Europa XS	☐ G-LRSN	Robinson R44
☐ G-LEIC	Reims FA152 Aerobat	☐ G-LINX	Schweizer 269C-1	☐ G-LSAA	Boeing 757-236
☐ G-LEKT	Robin DR.400-180 Regent	☐ G-LIOA	Lockheed L-10A	☐ G-LSAB	Boeing 757-27B
☐ G-LELE	Lindstrand LBL-31A	☐ G-LION	Piper PA-18-135	☐ G-LSAC	Boeing 757-23A
☐ G-LEMO	Cessna U206G	☐ G-LIOT	Cameron O-77	☐ G-LSAD	Boeing 757-236
☐ G-LENA	Yakovlev Yak-52	☐ G-LIPA	Cessna U206G	☐ G-LSAE	Boeing 757-27B
☐ G-LENF	Mainair Blade	☐ G-LIPE	Robinson R22B	☐ G-LSAG	Boeing 757-21B
☐ G-LENI	Aerospatiale AS.355F2	☐ G-LIPS	Cameron Lips SS	☐ G-LSAH	Boeing 757-21B
☐ G-LENN	Cameron V-65	☐ G-LISO	SIAI Marchetti SM.1019	☐ G-LSAI	Boeing 757-21B
☐ G-LENS	Thunder Ax7-77Z	☐ G-LITE	Rockwell 112A	☐ G-LSCM	Cessna 172S Skyhawk
☐ G-LENX	Cessna 172N Skyhawk	☐ G-LITZ	Pitts S-1E Special	☐ G-LSFI	Grumman AA-5A Cheetah
☐ G-LENY	Piper PA-34-220T Seneca	☐ G-LIVH	Piper J-3C-65 Cub	☐ G-LSFT	Piper PA-28-161 Warrior
☐ G-LEOD	Pietenpol Aircamper	☐ G-LIVS	Schleicher ASH 26E	☐ G-LSGM	Rollanden-Schneider LS3
☐ G-LEOS	Robin DR.400-120	☐ G-LIZA	Cessna 340A	☐ G-LSHI	Colt 77A
☐ G-LESZ	Denney Kitfox	☐ G-LIZI	Piper PA-28-161 Warrior	☐ G-LSKY	Reims F152
☐ G-LEVI	Aeronca 7AC Champion	☐ G-LIZY	Westland Lysander	☐ G-LSMI	Reims F152
☐ G-LEVO	Robinson R44	☐ G-LIZZ	Piper PA-23-250 Aztec E	☐ G-LSPA	Agusta Bell 206B
☐ G-LEXI	Cameron N-77	☐ G-LJCC	Murphy Rebel	☐ G-LSTR	GlaStar
☐ G-LEXX	Van's RV-8	☐ G-LJRM	Sikorsky S-76C	☐ G-LSWL	Robinson R22B
☐ G-LEZZ	GlaStar	☐ G-LKET	Cameron Kindernet Dog	☐ G-LTFB	Piper PA-28-140 Cherokee
☐ G-LFIX	Spitfire Trainer 9	☐ G-LKTB	Piper PA-28-181 Archer	☐ G-LTFC	Piper PA-28-140 Cherokee
☐ G-LFLY	Flight Design CTSW	☐ G-LLAN	Grob 109B	☐ G-LTRF	Fournier RF7
☐ G-LFSA	Piper PA-38-112 Tomahawk	☐ G-LLEW	Aeromot AMT-200S	☐ G-LTSB	Cameron LTSB-90
☐ G-LFSB	Piper PA-38-112 Tomahawk	☐ G-LLMC	Cessna T310Q	☐ G-LUBE	Cameron N-77
☐ G-LFSC	Piper PA-28-140 Cherokee	☐ G-LLMW	Diamond DA42 Twin Star	☐ G-LUBY	Jabiru J430
☐ G-LFSD	Piper PA-38-112 Tomahawk	☐ G-LLOY	Alpi Pioneer 300	☐ G-LUCK	Reims F150M
☐ G-LFSG	Piper PA-28-180 Cherokee	☐ G-LMAX	Sequoia F.8L Falco	☐ G-LUDM	Van's RV-8
☐ G-LFSH	Piper PA-38-112 Tomahawk	☐ G-LMCG	Robinson R44	☐ G-LUED	Aero Designs Pulsar
☐ G-LFSI	Piper PA-28-140 Cherokee	☐ G-LMLV	Dyn'Aero MCR-01	☐ G-LUFT	Putzer Elster C
☐ G-LFSJ	Piper PA-28-161 Warrior	☐ G-LNAA	MD.900 Explorer	☐ G-LUKE	Rutan LongEz
☐ G-LFSK	Piper PA-28-161 Warrior	☐ G-LNTY	Aerospatiale AS.355F1	☐ G-LUKI	Robinson R44
☐ G-LFSM	Piper PA-38-112 Tomahawk	☐ G-LNYS	Reims F177RG	☐ G-LUKY	Robinson R44
☐ G-LFSN	Piper PA-38-112 Tomahawk	☐ G-LOAD	DR.107 One Design	☐ G-LULA	Cameron C-90
☐ G-LFVB	Spitfire LF.VB	☐ G-LOAN	Cameron N-77	☐ G-LULU	Grob 109
☐ G-LFVC	Spitfire LF.Vc	☐ G-LOBO	Cameron O-120	☐ G-LUMB	Best Off Sky Ranger
☐ G-LGAR	Learjet 60	☐ G-LOCH	Piper J-3C-90 Cub	☐ G-LUNA	Piper PA-32R-300T
☐ G-LGCA	Robin DR.400-180R	☐ G-LOCO	Robinson R44	☐ G-LUND	Cessna 340
☐ G-LGCB	Robin DR.400-180R	☐ G-LOFB	Lockheed L-188 Electra	☐ G-LUNE	P & M Quik
☐ G-LGEZ	Rutan LongEz	☐ G-LOFC	Lockheed L-188 Electra	☐ G-LUSC	Luscombe 8E Silvaire
☐ G-LGKO	Canadair CL-604	☐ G-LOFD	Lockheed L-188 Electra	☐ G-LUSH	Piper PA-28-151 Warrior
☐ G-LGNA	SF.340B	☐ G-LOFE	Lockheed L-188 Electra	☐ G-LUSI	Luscombe 8F Silvaire
☐ G-LGNB	SF.340B	☐ G-LOFF	Lockheed L-188 Electra	☐ G-LUST	Luscombe 8E Silvaire
☐ G-LGNC	SF.340B	☐ G-LOFM	Maule MX-7-180A	☐ G-LUVY	Aerospatiale AS.355F1
☐ G-LGND	SF.340B	☐ G-LOFT	Cessna 500 Citation	☐ G-LUXE	BAe 146-300
☐ G-LGNE	SF.340B	☐ G-LOGO	Hughes 369E	☐ G-LUXY	Cessna 551 Citation
☐ G-LGNF	SF.340B	☐ G-LOIS	Jabiru UL	☐ G-LVBF	Lindstrand LBL-330A
☐ G-LGNG	SF.340B	☐ G-LOKI	UltraMagic M-77C	☐ G-LVES	Cessna 182S Skylane
☐ G-LGNH	SF.340B	☐ G-LOKM	PZL Koliber-160A	☐ G-LVLV	Canadair CL-604
☐ G-LGNI	SF.340B	☐ G-LOKO	Cameron Loco 105 SS	☐ G-LVPL	Edge XT912-B Streak
☐ G-LGNJ	SF.340B	☐ G-LOLA	Beech A36 Bonanza	☐ G-LWAY	Robinson R44
☐ G-LGNK	SF.340B	☐ G-LOLL	Cameron V-77	☐ G-LWNG	Aero Designs Pulsar XP
☐ G-LGTE	Boeing 737-3Y0	☐ G-LONE	Bell 206L Long Ranger	☐ G-LWUK	Robinson R44
☐ G-LGTF	Boeing 737-382	☐ G-LOOP	Pitts S-1C Special	☐ G-LXRS	BD700 Global Express
☐ G-LGTG	Boeing 737-3Q8	☐ G-LORC	Piper PA-28-161 Warrior	☐ G-LXUS	Alpi Pioneer 300
☐ G-LGTH	Boeing 737-3Y0	☐ G-LORD	Piper PA-34-200T Seneca	☐ G-LYAK	Yakovlev Yak-52
☐ G-LGTI	Boeing 737-3Y0	☐ G-LORN	Mudry CAP.10B	☐ G-LYDA	Diamond H.36
☐ G-LHCA	Robinson R22B	☐ G-LORR	Piper PA-28-181 Archer	☐ G-LYDB	Piper PA-31-350 Chieftain
☐ G-LHCB	Robinson R22B	☐ G-LORT	Avid Speed Wing	☐ G-LYDC	Piper PA-31-350 Chieftain
☐ G-LHCC	Eurocopter EC120B	☐ G-LORY	Thunder Ax4-31Z	☐ G-LYDF	Piper PA-31-350 Chieftain
☐ G-LHEL	Aerospatiale AS.355F2	☐ G-LOSI	Cameron Z-105	0 G-LYDR	Schempp-Hirth Discus
☐ G-LIBB	Cameron V-77	☐ G-LOSM	Gloster Meteor NF.11	☐ G-LYFA	Yakovlev Yak-52
☐ G-LIBS	Hughes 369HS	☐ G-LOST	Denney Kitfox	☐ G-LYNC	Robinson R22B
☐ G-LICK	Cessna 172N Skyhawk	☐ G-LOSY	EV-97 Eurostar	☐ G-LYND	Piper PA-25-235 Pawnee
☐ G-LIDA	Diamond H.36R	☐ G-LOTA	Robinson R44	☐ G-LYNI	EV-97 Eurostar
☐ G-LIDE	Piper PA-31-350 Chieftain	☐ G-LOTI	Bleriot XI Replica	☐ G-LYNK	CFM Shadow DD
☐ G-LIFE	Thunder Ax6-56Z	☐ G-LOVB	BAe Jetstream 31	☐ G-LYPG	Jabiru UL-450
☐ G-LILA	Bell 206L Long Ranger	☐ G-LOWS	Sky 77-24	☐ G-LYTB	P & M Quik GT450
☐ G-LILP	Europa XS	☐ G-LOYA	Reims FR172J Rocket	☐ G-LYTE	Thunder Ax7-77
☐ G-LILY	Bell 206B Jet Ranger	☐ G-LOYD	Aerospatiale Gazelle	☐ G-LZZY	Piper PA-28R-201T
☐ G-LIMO	Bell 206L Long Ranger	☐ G-LOYN	Robinson R44	☐ G-MAAN	Europa XS
☐ G-LIMP	Cameron C-80	☐ G-LPAD	Lindstrand LBL-105A	☐ G-MAAV	Aerospatiale AS.350B3

G-MAAX	Bell 206L Long Ranger
G-MABE	Reims F150L
G-MABH	Fokker F.28-100
G-MABR	BAe 146-100
G-MACA	Robinson R22B
G-MACE	Hughes 369E
G-MACH	SIAI-Marchetti SF.260
G-MACK	Piper PA-28R-200
G-MAFA	Reims F406
G-MAFB	Reims F406
G-MAFE	Dornier Do.228
G-MAFF	BN2T Islander
G-MAFI	Dornier Do.228-200
G-MAFT	Diamond DA.40D Star
G-MAGC	Cameron Illusion SS
G-MAGG	Pitts S-1SE Special
G-MAGL	Sky 77-24
G-MAGZ	Robin DR.500
G-MAIE	Piper PA-32R-301T
G-MAIK	Piper PA-34-220T Seneca
G-MAIN	Mainair Blade
G-MAIR	Piper PA-34-200T Seneca
G-MAJA	BAe Jetstream 41
G-MAJB	BAe Jetstream 41
G-MAJC	BAe Jetstream 41
G-MAJD	BAe Jetstream 41
G-MAJE	BAe Jetstream 41
G-MAJF	BAe Jetstream 41
G-MAJG	BAe Jetstream 41
G-MAJH	BAe Jetstream 41
G-MAJI	BAe Jetstream 41
G-MAJJ	BAe Jetstream 41
G-MAJK	BAe Jetstream 41
G-MAJL	BAe Jetstream 41
G-MAJM	BAe Jetstream 41
G-MAJN	BAe Jetstream 41
G-MAJO	BAe Jetstream 41
G-MAJP	BAe Jetstream 41
G-MAJR	DHC-1 Chipmunk
G-MAJS	Airbus A300B4-605R
G-MAJT	BAe Jetstream 41
G-MAJU	BAe Jetstream 41
G-MAJV	BAe Jetstream 41
G-MAJW	BAe Jetstream 41
G-MAJX	BAe Jetstream 41
G-MAJY	BAe Jetstream 41
G-MAJZ	BAe Jetstream 41
G-MALA	Piper PA-28-181 Archer
G-MALC	Grumman AA-5 Traveler
G-MALS	Mooney M.20K
G-MALT	Colt Hop SS
G-MAMC	Rotorway Exec 90
G-MAMD	Beech 200 Super King Air
G-MAMH	Fokker F.28-100
G-MAMO	Cameron V-77
G-MANE	BAe ATP
G-MANF	BAe ATP
G-MANG	BAe ATP
G-MANH	BAe ATP
G-MANL	BAe ATP
G-MANM	BAe ATP
G-MANN	Aerospatiale Gazelle
G-MANO	BAe ATP
G-MANS	BAe 146-200
G-MANW	Tri-R Kis
G-MANX	Clutton FRED II
G-MAPL	Robinson R44
G-MAPP	Cessna 402B
G-MAPR	Beech A36 Bonanza
G-MARA	Airbus A321-231
G-MARE	Schweizer 269C
G-MARO	Best Off Sky Ranger
G-MARX	Van's RV-4
G-MARZ	Thruster T600N
G-MASC	Jodel D.150A Mascaret
G-MASF	Piper PA-28-181 Archer
G-MASH	Westland Bell 47G-4A
G-MASI	P & M Quik GT450
G-MASS	Cessna 152
G-MASZ	Mosquito M.58
G-MATE	Zlin Z. 50LX
G-MATS	Colt GA-42 Airship
G-MATT	Robin R.2160
G-MATX	Pilatus PC-12/45
G-MATY	Robinson R22
G-MATZ	Piper PA-28-140 Cherokee
G-MAUK	Colt 77A
G-MAUS	Europa
G-MAVI	Robinson R22B
G-MAXG	Pitts S-1S Special
G-MAXI	Piper PA-34-200T Seneca
G-MAXR	UltraMagic S-90
G-MAXS	P & M Quik
G-MAXV	Van's RV-4
G-MAYB	Robinson R44
G-MAYE	Bell 407
G-MAYO	Piper PA-28-161 Warrior
G-MBAA	Skytrike Excalibur
G-MBAB	Hovey Whing-Ding
G-MBAW	Pterodactyl Ptraveler
G-MBBB	Wheeler Scout II
G-MBBM	Eipper Quicksilver MX
G-MBCJ	Tri-Flyer Typhoon
G-MBCK	Eipper Quicksilver MX
G-MBCL	Skytrike Typhoon
G-MBCU	Eagle Amphibian
G-MBCX	Hornet Nimrod
G-MBDG	Eurowing Goldwing
G-MBDM	Southdown Sigma
G-MBET	MEA Mistral Trainer
G-MBEU	Chargus Demon
G-MBFK	Skytrike Demon
G-MBFO	Eipper Quicksilver MX
G-MBFZ	Eurowing Goldwing
G-MBGF	Twamley Cherokee
G-MBGS	Rotec Rally 2B
G-MBGX	Southdown Lightning
G-MBHE	American Eagle 430B
G-MBHK	Tri-Flyer Striker
G-MBHZ	Pterodactyl Ptraveler
G-MBIA	Flexiform Sealander
G-MBIO	American Eagle 215B
G-MBIT	Skytrike Demon
G-MBIY	Tripacer Lightning
G-MBIZ	Tri-Flyer Vulcan
G-MBJD	Eagle 215B
G-MBJF	Skytrike Vulcan
G-MBJG	Chargus Nimrod
G-MBJK	American Eagle 430B
G-MBJL	Hornet Nimrod
G-MBJM	Striplin Lone Ranger
G-MBKY	American Eagle 215B
G-MBKZ	Skytrike Super Scorpion
G-MBLU	Tripacer Lightning
G-MBMG	Rotec Rally 2B
G-MBMT	Tri-Flyer Lightning
G-MBOF	Pakes Jackdaw
G-MBOH	MEA Mistral Trainer
G-MBPB	Pterodactyl Ptraveler
G-MBPG	Tri-Flyer Typhoon
G-MBPJ	Centrair Moto-Delta
G-MBPU	Hiway Demon
G-MBPX	Eurowing Goldwing
G-MBPY	Tripacer Gryphon
G-MBRB	Electraflyer Eagle
G-MBRD	American Eagle 215B
G-MBRH	Ultraflight Mirage
G-MBRS	American Eagle 215B
G-MBST	Gemini Sprint
G-MBSX	Ultraflight Mirage
G-MBTF	Gemini Sprint
G-MBTH	Whittaker MW-4
G-MBTJ	Tripacer Typhoon
G-MBTW	Aerodyne Vector 600
G-MBUE	MBA Tiger Cub 440
G-MBUZ	Wheeler Scout
G-MBVS	Skytrike Super Scorpion
G-MBWG	Huntair Pathfinder
G-MBYI	Ultraflight Lazair
G-MBYL	Huntair Pathfinder
G-MBYM	Eipper Quicksilver MX
G-MBZH	Eurowing Goldwing
G-MBZO	Tri-Flyer Striker
G-MBZV	American Eagle 215B
G-MCAI	Robinson R44
G-MCAP	Cameron C-80
G-MCCF	Thruster T600N
G-MCCY	Yakovlev Yak-52
G-MCEL	Pegasus Quantum
G-MCJL	Pegasus Quantum
G-MCMC	SOCATA TBM-700
G-MCMS	Aero Designs Pulsar XP
G-MCOX	Fuji FA.200-180AO
G-MCOY	Lindstrand LBL 77A
G-MCOY	Flight Design CT2K
G-MCXV	Colomban MC-15 Cri-Cri
G-MDAC	Piper PA-28-181 Archer
G-MDAY	Cessna 170B
G-MDBC	Pegasus Quantum
G-MDBD	Airbus A330-243
G-MDCA	Piper PA-34-220T Seneca
G-MDDT	Robinson R44
G-MDGE	Robinson R22B
G-MDJN	Beech 95-B55 Baron
G-MDKD	Robinson R22B
G-MDPI	Agusta 109A-II
G-MDPY	Robinson R44
G-MEAH	Piper PA-28R-200
G-MED	Airbus A321-231
G-MED	Airbus A321-231
G-MEDE	Airbus A320-232
G-MEDF	Airbus A321-231
G-MEDG	Airbus A321-231
G-MEDH	Airbus A320-232
G-MEDJ	Airbus A321-231
G-MEDK	Airbus A320-232
G-MEDL	Airbus A321-231
G-MEDM	Airbus A321-231
G-MEDS	Agusta A109E Power
G-MEEK	Enstrom 480
G-MEET	LearJet 40
G-MEGA	Piper PA-28R-201T
G-MEGG	Europa XS
G-MEGN	Beech B200 Super King Air
G-MELT	Reims F172H
G-MELV	MS.894E Minerva
G-MEME	Piper PA-28R-201
G-MEOW	CFM Shadow SA
G-MEPU	Rotorsport UK MT-03
G-MERC	Colt 56A
G-MERE	Lindstrand LBL-77A
G-MERF	Grob 115A
G-MERL	Piper PA-28RT-201
G-METH	Cameron C-90
G-MEUP	Cameron A-120
G-MFAC	Reims F172H
G-MFEF	Reims FR172J Rocket
G-MFHI	Europa
G-MFHT	Robinson R22B

☐ G-MFLI	Cameron V-90	
☐ G-MFLY	Mainair Rapier	
☐ G-MFMF	Bell 206B Jet Ranger	
☐ G-MFMM	Scheibe SF25C Falke	
☐ G-MGAA	Quad City Challenger	
☐ G-MGAG	Aviasud Mistral	
☐ G-MGAN	Robinson R44	
☐ G-MGCA	Jabiru UL	
☐ G-MGCB	Pegasus XL-Q	
☐ G-MGCK	Whittaker MW-6	
☐ G-MGDL	Pegasus Quantum	
☐ G-MGEC	Rans S6 Coyote II	
☐ G-MGEF	Pegasus Quantum	
☐ G-MGFK	Pegasus Quantum	
☐ G-MGGG	Pegasus Quantum	
☐ G-MGGT	CFM Shadow SA-M	
☐ G-MGGV	Pegasus Quantum	
☐ G-MGMC	Pegasus Quantum	
☐ G-MGMM	Piper PA-18-150	
☐ G-MGND	Rans S6 Coyote II	
☐ G-MGOD	Medway Raven X	
☐ G-MGOO	Renegade Spirit UK	
☐ G-MGPA	Ikarus C42 Cyclone	
☐ G-MGPD	Pegasus XL-R	
☐ G-MGPH	CFM Shadow SA-M	
☐ G-MGRH	Quad City Challenger	
☐ G-MGTG	Pegasus Quantum	
☐ G-MGTR	Huntwing Experience	
☐ G-MGTV	Thruster T600N	
☐ G-MGTW	CFM Shadow DD	
☐ G-MGUN	Pegasus AX2000	
☐ G-MGUY	CFM Shadow CD	
☐ G-MGWH	Thruster T300	
☐ G-MGWI	Robinson R44	
☐ G-MGYB	Embraer EMB135BJ	
☐ G-MHCB	Enstrom 280C	
☐ G-MHCD	Enstrom 280C-UK	
☐ G-MHCE	Enstrom F-28A	
☐ G-MHCF	Enstrom 280C-UK	
☐ G-MHCG	Enstrom 280C-UK	
☐ G-MHCI	Enstrom 280C	
☐ G-MHCJ	Enstrom F-28C	
☐ G-MHCK	Enstrom 280FX	
☐ G-MHCL	Enstrom 280C	
☐ G-MHCM	Enstrom 280FX	
☐ G-MHGS	GlaStar	
☐ G-MHJK	Diamond DA42 Twin Star	
☐ G-MHMR	Pegasus Quantum	
☐ G-MHRV	Van's RV-6A	
☐ G-MICH	Robinson R22B	
☐ G-MICI	Cessna 182S Skylane	
☐ G-MICK	Reims F172N	
☐ G-MICY	Everett Gyroplane	
☐ G-MIDC	Airbus A321-231	
☐ G-MIDD	Piper PA-28-140 Cherokee	
☐ G-MIDG	Bushby-Long Midget	
☐ G-MIDJ	Airbus A321-231	
☐ G-MIDK	Airbus A321-231	
☐ G-MIDL	Airbus A321-231	
☐ G-MIDM	Airbus A321-231	
☐ G-MIDO	Airbus A320-232	
☐ G-MIDP	Airbus A320-232	
☐ G-MIDR	Airbus A320-232	
☐ G-MIDS	Airbus A320-232	
☐ G-MIDT	Airbus A320-232	
☐ G-MIDU	Airbus A320-232	
☐ G-MIDV	Airbus A320-232	
☐ G-MIDW	Airbus A320-232	
☐ G-MIDX	Airbus A320-232	
☐ G-MIDY	Airbus A320-232	
☐ G-MIDZ	Airbus A320-232	
☐ G-MIFF	Robin DR.400-180 Regent	
☐ G-MIGG	WSK Lim-5	
☐ G-MIII	Extra EA300/L	
☐ G-MIKE	Brookland Hornet	
☐ G-MIKI	Rans S6 Coyote II (N)	
☐ G-MIKS	Robinson R44	
☐ G-MILA	Reims F172N	
☐ G-MILD	Scheibe SF25C Falke	
☐ G-MILE	Cameron V-77	
☐ G-MILI	Bell 206B Jet Ranger	
☐ G-MILN	Cessna 182Q Skylane	
☐ G-MILY	Grumman AA-5A Cheetah	
☐ G-MIMA	BAe 146-200	
☐ G-MIME	Europa	
☐ G-MIND	Cessna 404	
☐ G-MINN	Lindstrand LBL-80A	
☐ G-MINS	Nicollier HN700 Menestrel	
☐ G-MINT	Pitts S-1S Special	
☐ G-MIOO	Miles M.100 Student	
☐ G-MIRA	Jabiru SP-340	
☐ G-MISH	Cessna 182R Skylane	
☐ G-MITE	Raj Hamsa X'Air	
☐ G-MITS	Cameron N-77	
☐ G-MIWS	Cessna 310R	
☐ G-MJAE	American Eagle	
☐ G-MJAJ	Eurowing Goldwing	
☐ G-MJAM	Eipper Quicksilver MX	
☐ G-MJAN	Skytrike Highlander	
☐ G-MJAV	Hiway Demon	
☐ G-MJAY	Eurowing Goldwing	
☐ G-MJAZ	Ultravector 627	
☐ G-MJBK	Swallow B	
☐ G-MJBL	American Eagle	
☐ G-MJBS	UAS Storm Buggy	
☐ G-MJBV	American Eagle 215B	
☐ G-MJBZ	Huntair Pathfinder I	
☐ G-MJCE	Puma Sprint X	
☐ G-MJCU	Tarjani Typhoon	
☐ G-MJDE	Huntair Pathfinder I	
☐ G-MJDJ	Skytrike Demon	
☐ G-MJDP	Eurowing Goldwing	
☐ G-MJDR	Skytrike Demon	
☐ G-MJDW	Eipper Quicksilver MX	
☐ G-MJEB	Puma Sprint	
☐ G-MJEE	Tri-Flyer Typhoon	
☐ G-MJEO	American Eagle 215B	
☐ G-MJER	Tripacer Striker	
☐ G-MJFB	Tripacer Striker	
☐ G-MJFM	Huntair Pathfinder I	
☐ G-MJFX	Skyhook TR.1/Sabre	
☐ G-MJFZ	Skytrike Demon	
☐ G-MJHC	Tripacer Lightning	
☐ G-MJHR	Tri-Flyer Lightning	
☐ G-MJHV	Skytrike Demon	
☐ G-MJIA	Tripacer Striker	
☐ G-MJIC	Tripacer Striker	
☐ G-MJIF	Tri-Flyer Striker	
☐ G-MJJA	Huntair Pathfinder I	
☐ G-MJKB	Striplin Sky Ranger	
☐ G-MJKF	Hiway Demon	
☐ G-MJKO	Farnell Trike Gyr	
☐ G-MJKX	Skyrider Phantom	
☐ G-MJMD	Skytrike Demon	
☐ G-MJMN	Tri-Flyer Striker	
☐ G-MJMR	Tri-Flyer Typhoon	
☐ G-MJMS	Skytrike Demon	
☐ G-MJNM	American Eagle 430B	
☐ G-MJNO	Eagle Amphibian	
☐ G-MJNU	Skyhook/Cutlass	
☐ G-MJNY	Skyhook TR.1/Sabre	
☐ G-MJOC	Huntair Pathfinder I	
☐ G-MJOE	Eurowing Goldwing	
☐ G-MJPA	Rotec Rally 2B	
☐ G-MJPB	Manuel Ladybird	
☐ G-MJPE	Skytrike Demon	
☐ G-MJPV	Eipper Quicksilver MX	
☐ G-MJRL	Eurowing Goldwing	
☐ G-MJRO	Eurowing Goldwing	
☐ G-MJRR	Striplin Sky Ranger	
☐ G-MJRS	Eurowing Goldwing	
☐ G-MJRU	MBA Tiger Cub 440	
☐ G-MJRV	Eurowing Goldwing	
☐ G-MJSE	Skyrider Phantom	
☐ G-MJSF	Skyrider Phantom	
☐ G-MJSL	Dragon 200	
☐ G-MJSO	Skytrike Demon	
☐ G-MJSP	Romain Tiger Cub	
☐ G-MJST	Pterodactyl Ptraveler	
☐ G-MJSY	Eurowing Goldwing	
☐ G-MJSZ	Harker DH Wasp	
☐ G-MJTC	Tri-Flyer Typhoon	
☐ G-MJTE	Skyrider Phantom	
☐ G-MJTM	S.A.L. Pipistrelle	
☐ G-MJTP	Tri-Flyer Sealander	
☐ G-MJTR	Southdown Puma	
☐ G-MJTX	Skyrider Phantom	
☐ G-MJTZ	Skyrider Phantom	
☐ G-MJUC	MBA Tiger Cub 440	
☐ G-MJUR	Skyrider Phantom	
☐ G-MJUU	Eurowing Goldwing	
☐ G-MJUV	Huntair Pathfinder I	
☐ G-MJUW	MBA Tiger Cub 440	
☐ G-MJUX	Skyrider Phantom	
☐ G-MJVE	Hybred 44XL	
☐ G-MJVF	CFM Shadow CD	
☐ G-MJVN	Puma Striker	
☐ G-MJVP	Eipper Quicksilver MXII	
☐ G-MJVU	Eipper Quicksilver MXII	
☐ G-MJVX	Skyrider Phantom	
☐ G-MJVY	Dragon 150	
☐ G-MJWB	Eurowing Goldwing	
☐ G-MJWF	MBA Tiger Cub 440	
☐ G-MJWK	Huntair Pathfinder I	
☐ G-MJWW	MBA Tiger Cub 440	
☐ G-MJWZ	Panther XL	
☐ G-MJXY	Skytrike Demon	
☐ G-MJYD	MBA Tiger Cub 440	
☐ G-MJYP	Gemini Sprint	
☐ G-MJYV	Tri-Flyer Rapier	
☐ G-MJYW	Micro-Trike Gryphon	
☐ G-MJYX	Tri-Flyer Demon	
☐ G-MJZE	MBA Tiger Cub 440	
☐ G-MJZK	Puma Sprint	
☐ G-MJZU	Tri-Flyer Striker	
☐ G-MKAA	Boeing 747-2S4F	
☐ G-MKAK	Colt 77A	
☐ G-MKAS	Piper PA-28-140 Cherokee	
☐ G-MKIA	Spitfire I	
☐ G-MKSS	BAe 125-700B	
☐ G-MKVB	Spitfire LF.Vb	
☐ G-MKVI	DH.100 Vampire FB.6	
☐ G-MKXI	Spitfire PR.XI	
☐ G-MLAL	Jabiru J400	
☐ G-MLFF	Piper PA-23-250 Aztec E	
☐ G-MLGL	Colt 21A	
☐ G-MLHI	Maule MX-7-180	
☐ G-MLJL	Airbus A330-243	
☐ G-MLLA	SOCATA TB-200XL Tobago	
☐ G-MLLE	Robin DR.200A	
☐ G-MLSN	Hughes 369E	
☐ G-MLTY	Aerospatiale AS.365N2	
☐ G-MLWI	Thunder Ax7-77	
☐ G-MMAC	Dragon 200	
☐ G-MMAE	Dragon 200	
☐ G-MMAG	MBA Tiger Cub 440	
☐ G-MMAI	Dragon 150	
☐ G-MMAR	Gemini Sprint	
☐ G-MMAZ	Puma Sprint X	

☐ G-MMBL Ultrasports Puma DS	☐ G-MMPG Puma Sprint X	☐ G-MMZW Puma Sprint
☐ G-MMBN Eurowing Goldwing	☐ G-MMPH Puma Sprint X	☐ G-MNAC Gemini Flash
☐ G-MMBT MBA Tiger Cub 440	☐ G-MMPL Micro-Trike Striker	☐ G-MNAE Gemini Flash
☐ G-MMBU Eipper Quicksilver MXII	☐ G-MMPO Gemini Flash	☐ G-MNAI Panther XL-S
☐ G-MMBV Huntair Pathfinder I	☐ G-MMPU Tri-Flyer Typhoon	☐ G-MNAR Pegasus XL-R
☐ G-MMBY Panther XL	☐ G-MMPZ Teman Mono-Fly	☐ G-MNAV Puma Sprint
☐ G-MMBZ Solar Trike Typhoon	☐ G-MMRH Skytrike Demon	☐ G-MNAW Pegasus XL-R
☐ G-MMCB Huntair Pathfinder II	☐ G-MMRL Panther XL-S	☐ G-MNAX Pegasus XL-R
☐ G-MMCI Puma Sprint X	☐ G-MMRN Puma Sprint X	☐ G-MNAY Pegasus XL-R
☐ G-MMCN Skytrike Storm	☐ G-MMRP Gemini Sprint	☐ G-MNAZ Pegasus XL-R
☐ G-MMCV Skytrike Typhoon	☐ G-MMRT Southdown Raven X	☐ G-MNBA Pegasus XL-R
☐ G-MMCX MBA Tiger Cub 440	☐ G-MMRW Gemini Striker	☐ G-MNBB Pegasus XL-R
☐ G-MMCZ Tri-Flyer Striker	☐ G-MMSA Panther XL-S	☐ G-MNBC Pegasus XL-R
☐ G-MMDF Southdown Wild Cat	☐ G-MMSG Panther XL-S	☐ G-MNBD Gemini Flash
☐ G-MMDK Merlin Striker	☐ G-MMSH Panther XL-S	☐ G-MNBE Puma Sprint
☐ G-MMDN Gemini Striker	☐ G-MMSO Gemini Sprint	☐ G-MNBF Gemini Flash
☐ G-MMDP Gemini Sprint	☐ G-MMSP Gemini Flash	☐ G-MNBG Gemini Flash
☐ G-MMDR Huntair Pathfinder II	☐ G-MMTA Panther XL-S	☐ G-MNBI Pegasus XL-R
☐ G-MMEK Hybred 44XL	☐ G-MMTC Pegasus XL-R	☐ G-MNBM Puma Sprint
☐ G-MMFD Flexiform Striker Dual	☐ G-MMTD Tri-Flyer Demon	☐ G-MNBN Gemini Flash
☐ G-MMFE Tri-Flyer Sprint	☐ G-MMTG Puma Sprint	☐ G-MNBP Gemini Flash
☐ G-MMFG Micro-Trike Striker	☐ G-MMTJ Puma Sprint	☐ G-MNBS Gemini Flash
☐ G-MMFS MBA Tiger Cub 440	☐ G-MMTL Gemini Sprint	☐ G-MNBT Gemini Flash
☐ G-MMFV Gemini Striker	☐ G-MMTR Pegasus XL-R	☐ G-MNBV Gemini Flash
☐ G-MMFY Sims Striker	☐ G-MMTS Panther XL	☐ G-MNCA Skytrike Demon
☐ G-MMGF MBA Tiger Cub 440	☐ G-MMTV Eagle 215B Seaplane	☐ G-MNCF Gemini Flash
☐ G-MMGL MBA Tiger Cub 440	☐ G-MMTX Gemini Sprint	☐ G-MNCG Gemini Flash
☐ G-MMGS Panther XL	☐ G-MMTY Fisher Koala	☐ G-MNCI Puma Sprint
☐ G-MMGT Huntwing Avon	☐ G-MMTZ Eurowing Goldwing	☐ G-MNCJ Gemini Flash
☐ G-MMGU SMD Gazelle Sealander	☐ G-MMUA Puma Sprint	☐ G-MNCM CFM Shadow C
☐ G-MMGV Whittaker MW-5	☐ G-MMUH Tri-Flyer Sprint	☐ G-MNCO Eipper Quicksilver MXII
☐ G-MMHE Gemini Sprint	☐ G-MMUM MBA Tiger Cub 440	☐ G-MNCP Puma Sprint
☐ G-MMHK Skytrike Super Scorpion	☐ G-MMUO Gemini Flash	☐ G-MNCS Skyrider Phantom
☐ G-MMHL Skytrike Super Scorpion	☐ G-MMUR Skytrike Storm	☐ G-MNCV Hybred 44XL
☐ G-MMHN MBA Tiger Cub 440	☐ G-MMUV Puma Sprint	☐ G-MNDC Gemini Flash
☐ G-MMHS Flexiform Striker Dual	☐ G-MMUW Gemini Flash	☐ G-MNDD Mainair Scorcher
☐ G-MMIE MBA Tiger Cub 440	☐ G-MMUX Gemini Sprint	☐ G-MNDE Medway Half-Pint
☐ G-MMIL Eipper Quicksilver MXII	☐ G-MMVA Puma Sprint	☐ G-MNDF Gemini Flash
☐ G-MMIW Puma Sprint X	☐ G-MMVH Southdown Raven X	☐ G-MNDO Pegasus Flash
☐ G-MMIX MBA Tiger Cub 440	☐ G-MMVI Puma Sprint	☐ G-MNDU Midland Sirocco
☐ G-MMIZ Lightning Mk.II	☐ G-MMVS Skyhook Pixie Zeus	☐ G-MNDY Puma Sprint X
☐ G-MMJD Puma Sprint X	☐ G-MMVX Puma Sprint X	☐ G-MNEF Gemini Flash
☐ G-MMJF Panther XL-S	☐ G-MMVZ Puma Sprint	☐ G-MNEG Gemini Flash
☐ G-MMJG Tri-Flyer Striker	☐ G-MMWA Gemini Flash	☐ G-MNEH Gemini Flash
☐ G-MMJT Gemini Sprint	☐ G-MMWC Eipper Quicksilver MXII	☐ G-MNEI Hybred 44XLR
☐ G-MMJV MBA Tiger Cub 440	☐ G-MMWG Tri-Flyer Striker	☐ G-MNEK Medway Half-Pint
☐ G-MMJX Teman Mono-Fly	☐ G-MMWL Eurowing Goldwing	☐ G-MNER CFM Shadow CD
☐ G-MMKA Panther XL	☐ G-MMWS Tripacer Striker	☐ G-MNET Gemini Flash
☐ G-MMKE Birdman Chinook	☐ G-MMWX Puma Sprint	☐ G-MNEV Gemini Flash
☐ G-MMKG Hybred 44XL	☐ G-MMXD Gemini Flash	☐ G-MNEY Gemini Flash
☐ G-MMKL Gemini Flash	☐ G-MMXJ Gemini Flash	☐ G-MNFB Puma Sprint
☐ G-MMKM Gemini Striker	☐ G-MMXO Puma Sprint	☐ G-MNFF Gemini Flash
☐ G-MMKP MBA Tiger Cub 440	☐ G-MMXU Gemini Sprint	☐ G-MNFG Puma Sprint
☐ G-MMKR Tri-Flyer Lightning	☐ G-MMXV Gemini Flash	☐ G-MNFL AMF Chevvron
☐ G-MMKV Puma Sprint X	☐ G-MMXW Gemini Striker	☐ G-MNFM Gemini Flash
☐ G-MMKX Skyrider Phantom	☐ G-MMYA Pegasus XL-R	☐ G-MNFN Gemini Flash
☐ G-MMLE Eurowing Goldwing	☐ G-MMYF Puma Sprint	☐ G-MNFP Gemini Flash
☐ G-MMLH Skytrike Demon	☐ G-MMYL Cyclone 70-130SX	☐ G-MNGD Tripacer Typhoon
☐ G-MMMG Eipper Quicksilver MXL	☐ G-MMYN Panther XL-R	☐ G-MNGG Pegasus XL-R
☐ G-MMMH Hadland Striker	☐ G-MMYO Puma Sprint	☐ G-MNGK Gemini Flash
☐ G-MMML Dragon 150	☐ G-MMYT Puma Sprint	☐ G-MNGM Gemini Flash
☐ G-MMMN Panther XL-S	☐ G-MMYU Puma Sprint	☐ G-MNGT Gemini Flash
☐ G-MMNA Eipper Quicksilver MXII	☐ G-MMYV Tri-Flyer Striker	☐ G-MNGU Gemini Flash
☐ G-MMNB Eipper Quicksilver MX	☐ G-MMYY Puma Sprint	☐ G-MNGW Gemini Flash
☐ G-MMNC Eipper Quicksilver MX	☐ G-MMZA Gemini Flash	☐ G-MNGX Puma Sprint
☐ G-MMNH Dragon 150	☐ G-MMZF Gemini Flash	☐ G-MNHD Pegasus XL-R
☐ G-MMNN Sherry Buzzard	☐ G-MMZG Panther XL-S	☐ G-MNHE Pegasus XL-R
☐ G-MMNS Mitchell Super Wing	☐ G-MMZI Medway Half-Pint	☐ G-MNHF Pegasus XL-R
☐ G-MMNT Flexiform Strike Solo	☐ G-MMZJ Gemini Flash	☐ G-MNHH Pegasus XL-R
☐ G-MMOB Gemini Sprint	☐ G-MMZK Gemini Flash	☐ G-MNHI Pegasus XL-R
☐ G-MMOH Pegasus XL-R	☐ G-MMZM Gemini Flash	☐ G-MNHJ Pegasus XL-R
☐ G-MMOK Panther XL-S	☐ G-MMZN Gemini Flash	☐ G-MNHK Pegasus XL-R
☐ G-MMOW Mainair Gemini Flash	☐ G-MMZV Gemini Flash	☐ G-MNHL Pegasus XL-R

☐ G-MNHM	Pegasus XL-R	
☐ G-MNHN	Pegasus XL-R	
☐ G-MNHR	Pegasus XL-R	
☐ G-MNHS	Pegasus XL-R	
☐ G-MNHT	Pegasus XL-R	
☐ G-MNIA	Gemini Flash	
☐ G-MNID	Gemini Flash	
☐ G-MNIE	Gemini Flash	
☐ G-MNIF	Gemini Flash	
☐ G-MNIG	Gemini Flash	
☐ G-MNIH	Gemini Flash	
☐ G-MNII	Gemini Flash	
☐ G-MNIK	Pegasus Photon	
☐ G-MNIL	Puma Sprint	
☐ G-MNIM	Maxair Hummer	
☐ G-MNIS	CFM Shadow C	
☐ G-MNIT	Aerial Arts 130SX	
☐ G-MNIU	Pegasus Photon	
☐ G-MNIZ	Gemini Flash	
☐ G-MNJB	Southdown Raven X	
☐ G-MNJD	Tri-Flyer Sprint	
☐ G-MNJF	Dragon 150	
☐ G-MNJG	Gemini Sprint MS	
☐ G-MNJH	Pegasus Flash	
☐ G-MNJJ	Pegasus Flash	
☐ G-MNJL	Pegasus Flash	
☐ G-MNJN	Pegasus Flash	
☐ G-MNJO	Pegasus Flash	
☐ G-MNJR	Pegasus Flash	
☐ G-MNJT	Southdown Raven X	
☐ G-MNJU	Gemini Flash	
☐ G-MNJX	Hybred 44XL	
☐ G-MNKB	Pegasus Photon	
☐ G-MNKC	Pegasus Photon	
☐ G-MNKD	Pegasus Photon	
☐ G-MNKE	Pegasus Photon	
☐ G-MNKG	Pegasus Photon	
☐ G-MNKK	Pegasus Photon	
☐ G-MNKM	MBA Tiger Cub 440	
☐ G-MNKO	Pegasus XL-Q	
☐ G-MNKP	Pegasus Flash	
☐ G-MNKR	Pegasus Flash	
☐ G-MNKU	Puma Sprint	
☐ G-MNKV	Pegasus Flash	
☐ G-MNKW	Pegasus Flash	
☐ G-MNKX	Pegasus Flash	
☐ G-MNKZ	Southdown Raven X	
☐ G-MNLH	Romain Cobra	
☐ G-MNLI	Gemini Flash 2	
☐ G-MNLM	Southdown Raven X	
☐ G-MNLN	Southdown Raven X	
☐ G-MNLT	Southdown Raven X	
☐ G-MNLY	Gemini Flash	
☐ G-MNLZ	Southdown Raven X	
☐ G-MNMC	Gemini Flash	
☐ G-MNMD	Southdown Raven X	
☐ G-MNMG	Gemini Flash 2	
☐ G-MNMI	Gemini Flash 2	
☐ G-MNMK	Pegasus XL-R	
☐ G-MNML	Puma Sprint	
☐ G-MNMM	Aerotech MW.5K	
☐ G-MNMN	Hybred 44XLR	
☐ G-MNMU	Southdown Raven X	
☐ G-MNMV	Gemini Flash	
☐ G-MNMW	Whittaker MW-6	
☐ G-MNMY	Cyclone 70-110SX	
☐ G-MNNA	Southdown Raven X	
☐ G-MNNB	Southdown Raven X	
☐ G-MNNC	Southdown Raven X	
☐ G-MNNF	Gemini Flash 2	
☐ G-MNNG	Squires Photon	
☐ G-MNNI	Gemini Flash 2	
☐ G-MNNJ	Gemini Flash 2	
☐ G-MNNL	Gemini Flash 2	
☐ G-MNNM	Mainair Scorcher	
☐ G-MNNO	Southdown Raven X	
☐ G-MNNR	Gemini Flash 2	
☐ G-MNNS	Eurowing Goldwing	
☐ G-MNNY	Pegasus Flash	
☐ G-MNNZ	Pegasus Flash 2	
☐ G-MNPA	Pegasus Flash 2	
☐ G-MNPC	Gemini Flash 2	
☐ G-MNPG	Gemini Flash 2	
☐ G-MNPV	Mainair Scorcher	
☐ G-MNPY	Mainair Scorcher	
☐ G-MNPZ	Mainair Scorcher	
☐ G-MNRD	Ultraflight Lazair IIIE	
☐ G-MNRE	Mainair Scorcher	
☐ G-MNRI	Hornet Dual Raven	
☐ G-MNRK	Hornet Dual Raven	
☐ G-MNRM	Hornet Dual Raven	
☐ G-MNRP	Southdown Raven X	
☐ G-MNRS	Southdown Raven X	
☐ G-MNRT	Midland Sirocco	
☐ G-MNRW	Gemini Flash 2	
☐ G-MNRX	Gemini Flash 2	
☐ G-MNRZ	Mainair Scorcher	
☐ G-MNSA	Gemini Flash 2	
☐ G-MNSD	Tri-Flyer Typhoon	
☐ G-MNSH	Pegasus Flash 2	
☐ G-MNSI	Gemini Flash 2	
☐ G-MNSJ	Gemini Flash 2	
☐ G-MNSL	Southdown Raven X	
☐ G-MNSX	Southdown Raven X	
☐ G-MNSY	Southdown Raven X	
☐ G-MNTC	Southdown Raven X	
☐ G-MNTD	Aerial Arts Chaser	
☐ G-MNTE	Southdown Raven X	
☐ G-MNTI	Gemini Flash 2	
☐ G-MNTK	CFM Shadow CD	
☐ G-MNTM	Southdown Raven X	
☐ G-MNTN	Southdown Raven X	
☐ G-MNTP	CFM Shadow C	
☐ G-MNTT	Medway Half-Pint	
☐ G-MNTU	Gemini Flash 2	
☐ G-MNTV	Gemini Flash 2	
☐ G-MNTY	Southdown Raven X	
☐ G-MNTZ	Gemini Flash 2	
☐ G-MNUA	Gemini Flash 2	
☐ G-MNUD	Pegasus Flash 2	
☐ G-MNUE	Pegasus Flash 2	
☐ G-MNUF	Gemini Flash 2	
☐ G-MNUG	Gemini Flash 2	
☐ G-MNUI	Tri-Flyer Cutlass	
☐ G-MNUO	Gemini Flash 2	
☐ G-MNUR	Gemini Flash 2	
☐ G-MNUU	Southdown Raven X	
☐ G-MNUW	Southdown Raven X	
☐ G-MNUX	Pegasus XL-R	
☐ G-MNVB	Pegasus XL-R	
☐ G-MNVC	Pegasus XL-R	
☐ G-MNVE	Pegasus XL-R	
☐ G-MNVG	Pegasus Flash 2	
☐ G-MNVH	Pegasus Flash 2	
☐ G-MNVI	CFM Shadow C	
☐ G-MNVJ	CFM Shadow CD	
☐ G-MNVK	CFM Shadow CD	
☐ G-MNVL	Medway Half Pint	
☐ G-MNVN	Southdown Raven	
☐ G-MNVO	Hovey Whing-Ding	
☐ G-MNVP	Southdown Raven X	
☐ G-MNVT	Gemini Flash 2	
☐ G-MNVV	Gemini Flash 2	
☐ G-MNVW	Gemini Flash 2	
☐ G-MNVZ	Pegasus Photon	
☐ G-MNWG	Southdown Raven X	
☐ G-MNWI	Gemini Flash 2	
☐ G-MNWL	Arbiter Aerial Arts	
☐ G-MNWU	Pegasus Flash 2	
☐ G-MNWV	Pegasus Flash 2	
☐ G-MNWW	Pegasus XLTug	
☐ G-MNWY	CFM Shadow C	
☐ G-MNWZ	Gemini Flash 2	
☐ G-MNXB	Tri-Flyer Photon	
☐ G-MNXE	Southdown Raven X	
☐ G-MNXF	Puma Raven	
☐ G-MNXG	Southdown Raven X	
☐ G-MNXI	Southdown Raven X	
☐ G-MNXO	Hybred 44XLR	
☐ G-MNXP	Pegasus Flash 2	
☐ G-MNXS	Gemini Flash 2	
☐ G-MNXU	Gemini Flash 2	
☐ G-MNXX	CFM Shadow CD	
☐ G-MNXZ	Whittaker MW-5	
☐ G-MNYA	Pegasus Flash 2	
☐ G-MNYC	Pegasus XL-R	
☐ G-MNYD	Aerial Arts Chaser	
☐ G-MNYE	Aerial Arts Chaser	
☐ G-MNYF	Aerial Arts Chaser	
☐ G-MNYG	Southdown Raven	
☐ G-MNYJ	Gemini Flash 2	
☐ G-MNYK	Gemini Flash 2	
☐ G-MNYL	Southdown Raven X	
☐ G-MNYM	Southdown Raven X	
☐ G-MNYP	Southdown Raven X	
☐ G-MNYU	Pegasus XL-R	
☐ G-MNYW	Pegasus XL-R	
☐ G-MNYX	Pegasus XL-R	
☐ G-MNYZ	Pegasus Flash 2	
☐ G-MNZB	Gemini Flash 2	
☐ G-MNZC	Gemini Flash 2	
☐ G-MNZD	Gemini Flash 2	
☐ G-MNZF	Gemini Flash 2	
☐ G-MNZJ	CFM Shadow CD	
☐ G-MNZK	Pegasus XL-R	
☐ G-MNZP	CFM Shadow BD (mod)	
☐ G-MNZR	CFM Shadow BD	
☐ G-MNZS	Aerial Arts Alpha	
☐ G-MNZU	Eurowing Goldwing	
☐ G-MNZW	Southdown Raven X	
☐ G-MNZX	Southdown Raven X	
☐ G-MNZZ	CFM Shadow CD	
☐ G-MOAC	Beech F33A Bonanza	
☐ G-MOAN	Aeromot AMT-200S	
☐ G-MODE	Eurocopter EC120B	
☐ G-MOFB	Cameron O-120	
☐ G-MOFF	Cameron O-77	
☐ G-MOFZ	Cameron O-90	
☐ G-MOGI	Grumman AA-5A Cheetah	
☐ G-MOGY	Robinson R22B	
☐ G-MOHS	Piper PA-31-350 Chieftain	
☐ G-MOKE	Cameron V-77	
☐ G-MOLE	Taylor Titch	
☐ G-MOLI	Cameron A-250	
☐ G-MOLL	Piper PA-32T	
☐ G-MOMA	Thruster T600N	
☐ G-MOMO	Agusta 109E Power	
☐ G-MONB	Boeing 757-2T7	
☐ G-MONC	Boeing 757-2T7	
☐ G-MOND	Boeing 757-2T7	
☐ G-MONE	Boeing 757-2T7	
☐ G-MONI	Monnett Moni	
☐ G-MONJ	Boeing 757-2T7	
☐ G-MONK	Boeing 757-2T7	
☐ G-MONR	Airbus A300B4-605R	
☐ G-MONS	Airbus A300B4-605R	
☐ G-MONX	Airbus A320-212	
☐ G-MOOO	Learjet 40	
☐ G-MOOR	SOCATA TB-10 Tobago	

☐ G-MOOS	Percival Provost T1	
☐ G-MOSS	Beech D55 Baron	
☐ G-MOSY	Cameron O-84	
☐ G-MOTA	Bell 206B Jet Ranger	
☐ G-MOTH	DH.82A Tiger Moth	
☐ G-MOTI	Robin DR.500	
☐ G-MOTO	Piper PA-24-180 Comanche	
☐ G-MOTR	Enstrom 280C	
☐ G-MOUL	Maule M-6-235C	
☐ G-MOUN	Beech 200 Super King Air	
☐ G-MOUR	Folland Gnat T.1C	
☐ G-MOUT	Cessna 182T Skylane	
☐ G-MOVE	Piper PA-60-601P	
☐ G-MOVI	Piper PA-32R-301 SP	
☐ G-MOWG	Aeroprakt A22 Foxbat	
☐ G-MOZZ	Mudry CAP.10B	
☐ G-MPAA	Piper PA-28-181 Archer	
☐ G-MPAC	Pelican PL	
☐ G-MPBH	Reims FA152 Aerobat	
☐ G-MPBI	Cessna 310R	
☐ G-MPCD	Airbus A320-212	
☐ G-MPRL	Cessna 210M Centurion	
☐ G-MPSA	MBB BK.117C2	
☐ G-MPSB	MBB BK.117C2	
☐ G-MPSC	MBB BK.117C2	
☐ G-MPWI	Robin HR.100-210 Safari	
☐ G-MPWT	Piper PA-34-220T Seneca	
☐ G-MRAF	Aeroprakt A22 Foxbat	
☐ G-MRAJ	Hughes 369E	
☐ G-MRAM	Mignet HM-1000	
☐ G-MRED	Christavia Mk.1	
☐ G-MRJJ	P & M Quik	
☐ G-MRJK	Airbus A320-214	
☐ G-MRKI	Extra EA300	
☐ G-MRKS	Robinson R44	
☐ G-MRKT	Lindstrand LBL-90A	
☐ G-MRLL	North American P-51D	
☐ G-MRLN	Sky 240-24	
☐ G-MRMJ	Aerospatiale AS.365N3	
☐ G-MRMR	Piper PA-31-350 Chieftain	
☐ G-MROC	Pegasus Quantum	
☐ G-MROD	Van's RV-7A	
☐ G-MROY	Ikarus C42 Cyclone	
☐ G-MRRR	MDH 369E	
☐ G-MRSN	Robinson R22B	
☐ G-MRST	Piper PA-28R-201	
☐ G-MRTN	SOCATA TB-10 Tobago	
☐ G-MRTY	Cameron N-77	
☐ G-MRVL	Van's RV-7	
☐ G-MSAL	Morane MS.733	
☐ G-MSFC	Piper PA-38-112 Tomahawk	
☐ G-MSFT	Piper PA-28-161 Warrior	
☐ G-MSIX	Glaser-Dirks DG-800B	
☐ G-MSJF	Boeing 737-7Q8	
☐ G-MSKY	Ikarus C42 Cyclone	
☐ G-MSPT	Eurocopter EC135T2	
☐ G-MSPY	Pegasus Quantum	
☐ G-MSTC	Grumman AA-5A Cheetah	
☐ G-MSTG	North American P-51D	
☐ G-MSTR	Cameron Monster SS	
☐ G-MTAA	Pegasus XL-R	
☐ G-MTAB	Gemini Flash 2	
☐ G-MTAC	Gemini Flash 2	
☐ G-MTAE	Gemini Flash 2	
☐ G-MTAF	Gemini Flash 2	
☐ G-MTAG	Gemini Flash 2	
☐ G-MTAH	Gemini Flash 2	
☐ G-MTAI	Pegasus XL-R	
☐ G-MTAJ	Pegasus XL-R	
☐ G-MTAL	Pegasus Photon	
☐ G-MTAO	Pegasus XL-R	
☐ G-MTAP	Southdown Raven X	
☐ G-MTAR	Gemini Flash 2	
☐ G-MTAS	Whittaker MW-5C	
☐ G-MTAV	Pegasus XL-R	
☐ G-MTAW	Pegasus XL-R	
☐ G-MTAX	Pegasus XL-R	
☐ G-MTAY	Pegasus XL-R	
☐ G-MTAZ	Pegasus XL-R	
☐ G-MTBB	Southdown Raven X	
☐ G-MTBD	Gemini Flash 2	
☐ G-MTBE	CFM Shadow CD	
☐ G-MTBH	Gemini Flash 2	
☐ G-MTBJ	Gemini Flash 2	
☐ G-MTBK	Southdown Raven X	
☐ G-MTBL	Pegasus XL-R	
☐ G-MTBN	Southdown Raven X	
☐ G-MTBO	Southdown Raven X	
☐ G-MTBP	Aerotech MW-5B	
☐ G-MTBR	Aerotech MW-5B	
☐ G-MTBS	Aerotech MW-5B	
☐ G-MTBU	Pegasus XL-R	
☐ G-MTBW	Pegasus XL-R	
☐ G-MTBX	Gemini Flash 2	
☐ G-MTBY	Gemini Flash 2	
☐ G-MTBZ	Southdown Raven X	
☐ G-MTCA	CFM Shadow C	
☐ G-MTCE	Gemini Flash 2	
☐ G-MTCK	Pegasus Flash 2	
☐ G-MTCM	Southdown Raven X	
☐ G-MTCN	Pegasus XL-R	
☐ G-MTCO	Pegasus XL-R	
☐ G-MTCP	Aerial Arts Chaser	
☐ G-MTCR	Pegasus XL-R	
☐ G-MTCT	CFM Shadow CD	
☐ G-MTCU	Gemini Flash 2A	
☐ G-MTDD	Aerial Arts Chaser	
☐ G-MTDE	Aerial Arts Chaser	
☐ G-MTDF	Gemini Flash 2	
☐ G-MTDG	Gemini Flash 2	
☐ G-MTDI	Pegasus XL-R	
☐ G-MTDK	Aerotech MW-5B	
☐ G-MTDO	Eipper Quicksilver MXII	
☐ G-MTDR	Pegasus XL-R	
☐ G-MTDU	CFM Shadow CD	
☐ G-MTDW	Gemini Flash 2	
☐ G-MTDY	Gemini Flash 2	
☐ G-MTEC	Pegasus XL-R	
☐ G-MTEE	Pegasus XL-R	
☐ G-MTEI	Gemini Flash 2	
☐ G-MTEJ	Gemini Flash 2	
☐ G-MTEK	Gemini Flash 2	
☐ G-MTES	Pegasus XL-R	
☐ G-MTET	Pegasus XL-R	
☐ G-MTEU	Pegasus XL-R	
☐ G-MTEW	Pegasus XL-R	
☐ G-MTEX	Pegasus XL-R	
☐ G-MTEY	Gemini Flash 2	
☐ G-MTFA	Pegasus XL-R	
☐ G-MTFB	Pegasus XL-R	
☐ G-MTFC	Hybred 44XLR	
☐ G-MTFG	AMF Chevvron	
☐ G-MTFI	Gemini Flash 2	
☐ G-MTFK	Moult Trike Striker	
☐ G-MTFM	Pegasus XL-R	
☐ G-MTFN	Whittaker MW-5B	
☐ G-MTFP	Pegasus XL-R	
☐ G-MTFR	Pegasus XL-R	
☐ G-MTFT	Pegasus XL-R	
☐ G-MTFU	CFM Shadow CD	
☐ G-MTFZ	CFM Shadow CD	
☐ G-MTGA	Gemini Flash 2	
☐ G-MTGB	Thruster TST	
☐ G-MTGC	Thruster TST	
☐ G-MTGD	Thruster TST	
☐ G-MTGE	Thruster TST	
☐ G-MTGF	Thruster TST	
☐ G-MTGH	Gemini Flash 2	
☐ G-MTGJ	Pegasus XL-R	
☐ G-MTGK	Pegasus XL-R	
☐ G-MTGL	Pegasus XL-R	
☐ G-MTGM	Pegasus XL-R	
☐ G-MTGN	CFM Shadow B	
☐ G-MTGO	Gemini Flash 2A	
☐ G-MTGR	Thruster TST	
☐ G-MTGS	Thruster TST (mod)	
☐ G-MTGT	Thruster TST	
☐ G-MTGU	Thruster TST (mod)	
☐ G-MTGV	CFM Shadow CD	
☐ G-MTGW	CFM Shadow CD	
☐ G-MTGX	Hornet Dual Raven	
☐ G-MTHB	Aerotech MW-5B	
☐ G-MTHG	Pegasus XL-R	
☐ G-MTHH	Pegasus XL-R	
☐ G-MTHI	Pegasus XL-R	
☐ G-MTHJ	Pegasus XL-R	
☐ G-MTHN	Pegasus XL-R	
☐ G-MTHT	CFM Shadow CD	
☐ G-MTHV	CFM Shadow BD	
☐ G-MTHW	Gemini Flash 2	
☐ G-MTHZ	Gemini Flash 2A	
☐ G-MTIA	Gemini Flash 2A	
☐ G-MTIB	Gemini Flash 2A	
☐ G-MTIE	Pegasus XL-R	
☐ G-MTIH	Pegasus XL-R	
☐ G-MTIJ	Pegasus XL-R	
☐ G-MTIK	Southdown Raven X	
☐ G-MTIL	Gemini Flash 2A	
☐ G-MTIM	Gemini Flash 2A	
☐ G-MTIN	Gemini Flash 2A	
☐ G-MTIO	Pegasus XL-R	
☐ G-MTIP	Pegasus XL-R	
☐ G-MTIR	Pegasus XL-R	
☐ G-MTIS	Pegasus XL-R	
☐ G-MTIU	Pegasus XL-R	
☐ G-MTIV	Pegasus XL-R	
☐ G-MTIW	Pegasus XL-R	
☐ G-MTIX	Pegasus XL-R	
☐ G-MTIY	Pegasus XL-R	
☐ G-MTIZ	Pegasus XL-R	
☐ G-MTJA	Gemini Flash 2A	
☐ G-MTJB	Gemini Flash 2A	
☐ G-MTJC	Gemini Flash 2A	
☐ G-MTJD	Gemini Flash 2A	
☐ G-MTJE	Gemini Flash 2	
☐ G-MTJG	Hybred 44XLR	
☐ G-MTJH	Pegasus Flash	
☐ G-MTJL	Gemini Flash 2A	
☐ G-MTJS	Pegasus XL-Q	
☐ G-MTJT	Gemini Flash 2A	
☐ G-MTJV	Gemini Flash 2A	
☐ G-MTJW	Gemini Flash 2A	
☐ G-MTJX	Hornet Dual Raven	
☐ G-MTJZ	Gemini Flash 2A	
☐ G-MTKA	Thruster TST	
☐ G-MTKB	Thruster TST	
☐ G-MTKD	Thruster TST	
☐ G-MTKE	Thruster TST	
☐ G-MTKG	Pegasus XL-R	
☐ G-MTKH	Pegasus XL-R	
☐ G-MTKI	Pegasus XL-R	
☐ G-MTKN	Gemini Flash 2A	
☐ G-MTKR	CFM Shadow CD	
☐ G-MTKW	Gemini Flash 2A	
☐ G-MTKX	Gemini Flash 2A	
☐ G-MTKZ	Gemini Flash 2A	
☐ G-MTLB	Gemini Flash 2A	
☐ G-MTLC	Gemini Flash 2A	
☐ G-MTLG	Pegasus XL-R	

G-MTLI	Pegasus XL-R	
G-MTLJ	Pegasus XL-R	
G-MTLL	Gemini Flash 2A	
G-MTLM	Thruster TST	
G-MTLN	Thruster TST	
G-MTLT	Pegasus XL-R	
G-MTLV	Pegasus XL-R	
G-MTLX	Hybred 44XLR	
G-MTLY	Pegasus XL-R	
G-MTLZ	Whittaker MW-5	
G-MTMA	Gemini Flash 2A	
G-MTMC	Gemini Flash 2A	
G-MTME	Pegasus XL-R	
G-MTMF	Pegasus XL-R	
G-MTMG	Pegasus XL-R	
G-MTMI	Pegasus XL-R	
G-MTML	Gemini Flash 2A	
G-MTMO	Southdown Raven X	
G-MTMP	Hornet Dual Raven	
G-MTMR	Hornet Dual Raven	
G-MTMT	Gemini Flash 2A	
G-MTMV	Gemini Flash 2A	
G-MTMW	Gemini Flash 2A	
G-MTMX	CFM Shadow CD	
G-MTMY	CFM Shadow CD	
G-MTNC	Gemini Flash 2A	
G-MTNE	Hybred 44XLR	
G-MTNF	Hybred 44XLR	
G-MTNG	Gemini Flash 2A	
G-MTNH	Gemini Flash 2A	
G-MTNI	Gemini Flash 2A	
G-MTNJ	Gemini Flash 2A	
G-MTNK	Weedhopper JC-24B	
G-MTNL	Gemini Flash 2A	
G-MTNM	Gemini Flash 2A	
G-MTNO	Pegasus XL-Q	
G-MTNP	Pegasus XL-Q	
G-MTNR	Thruster TST (mod)	
G-MTNT	Gemini Flash 2A	
G-MTNU	Thruster TST	
G-MTNV	Thruster TST	
G-MTNY	Gemini Flash 2A	
G-MTOA	Pegasus XL-R	
G-MTOB	Pegasus XL-R	
G-MTOD	Pegasus XL-R	
G-MTOE	Pegasus XL-R	
G-MTOF	Pegasus XL-R	
G-MTOG	Pegasus XL-R	
G-MTOH	Pegasus XL-R	
G-MTOJ	Pegasus XL-R	
G-MTOK	Pegasus XL-R	
G-MTON	Pegasus XL-R	
G-MTOO	Pegasus XL-R	
G-MTOP	Pegasus XL-R	
G-MTOR	Pegasus XL-R	
G-MTOS	Pegasus XL-R	
G-MTOT	Pegasus XL-R	
G-MTOU	Pegasus XL-R	
G-MTOY	Pegasus XL-R	
G-MTOZ	Pegasus XL-R	
G-MTPA	Gemini Flash 2A	
G-MTPB	Gemini Flash 2A	
G-MTPC	Southdown Raven X	
G-MTPE	Pegasus XL-R	
G-MTPF	Pegasus XL-R	
G-MTPG	Pegasus XL-R	
G-MTPI	Pegasus XL-R	
G-MTPJ	Pegasus XL-R	
G-MTPK	Pegasus XL-R	
G-MTPL	Pegasus XL-R	
G-MTPM	Pegasus XL-R	
G-MTPP	Pegasus XL-R	
G-MTPR	Pegasus XL-R	
G-MTPS	Pegasus XL-Q	
G-MTPT	Thruster TST	
G-MTPU	Thruster TST	
G-MTPW	Thruster TST	
G-MTPX	Thruster TST	
G-MTPY	Thruster TST	
G-MTRA	Gemini Flash 2A	
G-MTRC	Midland Sirocco	
G-MTRL	Hornet Dual Raven	
G-MTRM	Pegasus XL-R	
G-MTRO	Pegasus XL-R	
G-MTRS	Pegasus XL-R	
G-MTRT	Southdown Raven X	
G-MTRV	Pegasus XL-Q	
G-MTRW	Southdown Raven X	
G-MTRX	Whittaker MW-5	
G-MTRZ	Gemini Flash 2A	
G-MTSC	Gemini Flash 2A	
G-MTSH	Thruster TST	
G-MTSJ	Thruster TST	
G-MTSK	Thruster TST	
G-MTSM	Thruster TST	
G-MTSN	Pegasus XL-R	
G-MTSP	Pegasus XL-R	
G-MTSR	Pegasus XL-R	
G-MTSS	Pegasus XL-R	
G-MTSY	Pegasus XL-R	
G-MTSZ	Pegasus XL-R	
G-MTTA	Pegasus XL-R	
G-MTTB	Pegasus XL-R	
G-MTTD	Pegasus XL-Q	
G-MTTE	Pegasus XL-Q	
G-MTTF	Whittaker MW-6	
G-MTTH	CFM Shadow BD	
G-MTTI	Gemini Flash 2A	
G-MTTM	Gemini Flash 2A	
G-MTTN	Skyrider Phantom	
G-MTTP	Gemini Flash 2A	
G-MTTR	Gemini Flash 2A	
G-MTTU	Pegasus XL-R	
G-MTTW	Geminis Flash 2A	
G-MTTX	Pegasus XL-Q	
G-MTTY	Pegasus XL-Q	
G-MTTZ	Pegasus XL-Q	
G-MTUA	Pegasus XL-R	
G-MTUB	Thruster TST	
G-MTUC	Thruster TST	
G-MTUD	Thruster TST	
G-MTUF	Thruster TST	
G-MTUI	Pegasus XL-R	
G-MTUJ	Pegasus XL-R	
G-MTUK	Pegasus XL-R	
G-MTUL	Pegasus XL-R	
G-MTUN	Pegasus XL-Q	
G-MTUP	Pegasus XL-Q	
G-MTUR	Pegasus XL-Q	
G-MTUS	Pegasus XL-Q	
G-MTUT	Pegasus XL-Q	
G-MTUU	Gemini Flash 2A	
G-MTUV	Gemini Flash 2A	
G-MTUX	Hybred 44XLR	
G-MTUY	Pegasus XL-Q	
G-MTVB	Pegasus XL-R	
G-MTVG	Mainair Mercury	
G-MTVH	Gemini Flash 2A	
G-MTVI	Gemini Flash 2A	
G-MTVJ	Gemini Flash 2A	
G-MTVK	Pegasus XL-R	
G-MTVL	Pegasus XL-R	
G-MTVM	Pegasus XL-R	
G-MTVN	Pegasus XL-R	
G-MTVO	Pegasus XL-R	
G-MTVP	Thruster TST	
G-MTVR	Thruster TST	
G-MTVS	Thruster TST	
G-MTVT	Thruster TST	
G-MTVV	Thruster TST	
G-MTVX	Pegasus XL-Q	
G-MTWB	Pegasus XL-R	
G-MTWC	Pegasus XL-R	
G-MTWD	Pegasus XL-R	
G-MTWF	Gemini Flash 2A	
G-MTWG	Gemini Flash 2A	
G-MTWH	CFM Shadow CD	
G-MTWK	CFM Shadow CD	
G-MTWL	CFM Shadow BD	
G-MTWR	Gemini Flash 2A	
G-MTWS	Gemini Flash 2A	
G-MTWX	Gemini Flash 2A	
G-MTWZ	Thruster TST	
G-MTXA	Thruster TST	
G-MTXB	Thruster TST	
G-MTXC	Thruster TST	
G-MTXD	Thruster TST	
G-MTXE	Hornet Dual Raven	
G-MTXI	Pegasus XL-Q	
G-MTXJ	Pegasus XL-Q	
G-MTXK	Pegasus XL-Q	
G-MTXL	Snowbird Mk.IV	
G-MTXM	Gemini Flash 2A	
G-MTXO	Whittaker MW-6	
G-MTXP	Gemini Flash 2A	
G-MTXR	CFM Shadow CD	
G-MTXS	Gemini Flash 2A	
G-MTXU	Snowbird Mk.IV	
G-MTXZ	Gemini Flash 2A	
G-MTYA	Pegasus XL-Q	
G-MTYC	Pegasus XL-Q	
G-MTYD	Pegasus XL-Q	
G-MTYE	Pegasus XL-Q	
G-MTYF	Pegasus XL-Q	
G-MTYH	Pegasus XL-Q	
G-MTYI	Pegasus XL-Q	
G-MTYL	Pegasus XL-Q	
G-MTYP	Pegasus XL-Q	
G-MTYR	Pegasus XL-Q	
G-MTYS	Pegasus XL-Q	
G-MTYT	Pegasus XL-Q	
G-MTYU	Pegasus XL-Q	
G-MTYV	Southdown Raven X	
G-MTYW	Southdown Raven X	
G-MTYX	Southdown Raven X	
G-MTYY	Pegasus XL-R	
G-MTZA	Thruster TST	
G-MTZB	Thruster TST	
G-MTZC	Thruster TST	
G-MTZD	Thruster TST	
G-MTZF	Thruster TST	
G-MTZG	Gemini Flash 2A	
G-MTZH	Gemini Flash 2A	
G-MTZJ	Pegasus XL-R	
G-MTZK	Pegasus XL-R	
G-MTZL	Gemini Flash 2A	
G-MTZM	Gemini Flash 2A	
G-MTZO	Gemini Flash 2A	
G-MTZP	Pegasus XL-Q	
G-MTZR	Pegasus XL-Q	
G-MTZS	Pegasus XL-Q	
G-MTZV	Gemini Flash 2A	
G-MTZW	Gemini Flash 2A	
G-MTZX	Gemini Flash 2A	
G-MTZY	Gemini Flash 2A	
G-MTZZ	Gemini Flash 2A	
G-MUCK	Lindstrand LBL-77A	
G-MUIR	Cameron V-65	
G-MULT	Beech 76 Duchess	

Reg	Type	Reg	Type	Reg	Type
G-MUMM	Colt 180A	G-MVDJ	Hybred 44XLR	G-MVHK	Thruster TST
G-MUMY	Van's RV-4	G-MVDK	Aerial Arts Chaser S	G-MVHL	Thruster TST
G-MUNI	Mooney M.20J	G-MVDL	Aerial Arts Chaser S	G-MVHP	Pegasus XL-Q
G-MURG	Van's RV-6	G-MVDT	Gemini Flash 2A	G-MVHR	Pegasus XL-Q
G-MURP	Aerospatiale AS.350B	G-MVDV	Pegasus XL-R	G-MVHS	Pegasus XL-Q
G-MURR	Whittaker MW-6	G-MVDW	Pegasus XL-R	G-MVHW	Pegasus XL-Q
G-MUSH	Robinson R44	G-MVDX	Pegasus XL-R	G-MVHY	Pegasus XL-Q
G-MUSO	Rutan LongEz	G-MVDY	Pegasus XL-R	G-MVHZ	Hornet Dual Raven
G-MUTE	Colt 31A	G-MVDZ	Pegasus XL-R	G-MVIB	Gemini Flash 2A
G-MUTZ	Jabiru J400	G-MVEC	Pegasus XL-R	G-MVIE	Aerial Arts Chaser S
G-MVAA	Gemini Flash 2A	G-MVED	Pegasus XL-R	G-MVIF	Hybred 44XLR
G-MVAB	Gemini Flash 2A	G-MVEE	Hybred 44XLR	G-MVIG	CFM Shadow B
G-MVAC	CFM Shadow CD	G-MVEF	Pegasus XL-R	G-MVIH	Gemini Flash 2A
G-MVAD	Gemini Flash	G-MVEG	Pegasus XL-R	G-MVIL	Snowbird Mk.IV
G-MVAF	Puma Sprint	G-MVEH	Gemini Flash 2A	G-MVIM	Snowbird Mk.IV
G-MVAG	Thruster TST	G-MVEI	CFM Shadow CD	G-MVIN	Snowbird Mk.IV
G-MVAH	Thruster TST	G-MVEJ	Gemini Flash 2A	G-MVIO	Snowbird Mk.IV
G-MVAI	Thruster TST	G-MVEK	Gemini Flash 2A	G-MVIP	AMF Chevvron
G-MVAJ	Thruster TST	G-MVEL	Gemini Flash 2A	G-MVIR	Thruster TST
G-MVAK	Thruster TST	G-MVEN	CFM Shadow CD	G-MVIT	Thruster TST
G-MVAL	Thruster TST	G-MVEO	Gemini Flash 2A	G-MVIU	Thruster TST
G-MVAM	CFM Shadow CD	G-MVER	Gemini Flash 2A	G-MVIV	Thruster TST
G-MVAN	CFM Shadow CD	G-MVES	Gemini Flash 2A	G-MVIX	Gemini Flash 2A
G-MVAO	Gemini Flash 2A	G-MVET	Gemini Flash 2A	G-MVIY	Gemini Flash 2A
G-MVAP	Gemini Flash 2A	G-MVEV	Gemini Flash 2A	G-MVIZ	Gemini Flash 2A
G-MVAR	Pegasus XL-R	G-MVEX	Pegasus XL-Q	G-MVJA	Gemini Flash 2A
G-MVAT	Pegasus XL-R	G-MVEZ	Pegasus XL-Q	G-MVJC	Gemini Flash 2A
G-MVAV	Pegasus XL-R	G-MVFA	Pegasus XL-Q	G-MVJD	Pegasus XL-R
G-MVAW	Pegasus XL-Q	G-MVFB	Pegasus XL-Q	G-MVJE	Gemini Flash 2A
G-MVAX	Pegasus XL-Q	G-MVFC	Pegasus XL-Q	G-MVJF	Aerial Arts Chaser S
G-MVAY	Pegasus XL-Q	G-MVFD	Pegasus XL-Q	G-MVJG	Aerial Arts Chaser S
G-MVBB	CFM Shadow BD	G-MVFE	Pegasus XL-Q	G-MVJH	Aerial Arts Chaser S
G-MVBC	Tri-Flyer 130SX	G-MVFF	Pegasus XL-Q	G-MVJI	Aerial Arts Chaser S
G-MVBD	Gemini Flash 2A	G-MVFH	CFM Shadow CD	G-MVJK	Aerial Arts Chaser S
G-MVBE	Mainair Scorcher	G-MVFJ	Thruster TST	G-MVJL	Gemini Flash 2A
G-MVBF	Gemini Flash 2A	G-MVFK	Thruster TST	G-MVJM	Microflight Spectrum
G-MVBG	Gemini Flash 2A	G-MVFL	Thruster TST	G-MVJN	Pegasus XL-Q
G-MVBI	Gemini Flash 2A	G-MVFM	Thruster TST	G-MVJO	Pegasus XL-Q
G-MVBK	Gemini Flash 2A	G-MVFN	Thruster TST	G-MVJP	Pegasus XL-Q
G-MVBL	Gemini Flash 2A	G-MVFO	Thruster TST	G-MVJR	Pegasus XL-Q
G-MVBM	Gemini Flash 2A	G-MVFP	Pegasus XL-R	G-MVJS	Pegasus XL-Q
G-MVBN	Gemini Flash 2A	G-MVFS	Pegasus XL-R	G-MVJT	Pegasus XL-Q
G-MVBO	Gemini Flash 2A	G-MVFT	Pegasus XL-R	G-MVJU	Pegasus XL-Q
G-MVBP	Thruster TST	G-MVFV	Pegasus XL-R	G-MVJW	Pegasus XL-Q
G-MVBT	Thruster TST	G-MVFW	Pegasus XL-R	G-MVKB	Hybred 44XLR
G-MVBY	Pegasus XL-R	G-MVFY	Pegasus XL-R	G-MVKC	Gemini Flash 2A
G-MVBZ	Pegasus XL-R	G-MVFZ	Pegasus XL-R	G-MVKF	Pegasus XL-R
G-MVCA	Pegasus XL-R	G-MVGA	Aerial Arts Chaser S	G-MVKH	Pegasus XL-R
G-MVCB	Pegasus XL-R	G-MVGB	Hybred 44XLR	G-MVKJ	Pegasus XL-R
G-MVCC	CFM Shadow CD	G-MVGC	AMF Chevvron	G-MVKK	Pegasus XL-R
G-MVCD	Hybred 44XLR	G-MVGD	AMF Chevvron	G-MVKL	Pegasus XL-R
G-MVCE	Gemini Flash 2A	G-MVGE	AMF Chevvron	G-MVKM	Pegasus XL-R
G-MVCF	Gemini Flash 2A	G-MVGF	Aerial Arts Chaser S	G-MVKN	Pegasus XL-Q
G-MVCI	Snowbird Mk.IV	G-MVGG	Aerial Arts Chaser S	G-MVKO	Pegasus XL-Q
G-MVCJ	Snowbird Mk.IV	G-MVGH	Aerial Arts Chaser S	G-MVKP	Pegasus XL-Q
G-MVCK	Cosmos Profil	G-MVGM	Gemini Flash 2A	G-MVKS	Pegasus XL-Q
G-MVCL	Pegasus XL-Q	G-MVGN	Pegasus XL-R	G-MVKT	Pegasus XL-Q
G-MVCM	Pegasus XL-Q	G-MVGO	Pegasus XL-R	G-MVKU	Pegasus XL-Q
G-MVCN	Pegasus XL-Q	G-MVGP	Pegasus XL-R	G-MVKV	Pegasus XL-Q
G-MVCP	Pegasus XL-Q	G-MVGU	Pegasus XL-Q	G-MVKW	Pegasus XL-Q
G-MVCR	Pegasus XL-Q	G-MVGW	Pegasus XL-Q	G-MVKZ	Aerial Arts Chaser S
G-MVCS	Pegasus XL-Q	G-MVGY	Hybred 44XLR	G-MVLA	Aerial Arts Chaser S
G-MVCT	Pegasus XL-Q	G-MVGZ	Ultraflight Lazair	G-MVLB	Aerial Arts Chaser S
G-MVCV	Pegasus XL-Q	G-MVHA	Aerial Arts Chaser S	G-MVLC	Aerial Arts Chaser S
G-MVCW	CFM Shadow BD	G-MVHB	Powerchute Raider	G-MVLD	Aerial Arts Chaser S
G-MVCY	Gemini Flash 2A	G-MVHC	Powerchute Raider	G-MVLE	Aerial Arts Chaser S
G-MVCZ	Gemini Flash 2A	G-MVHD	CFM Shadow CD	G-MVLF	Aerial Arts Chaser S
G-MVDA	Gemini Flash 2A	G-MVHE	Gemini Flash 2A	G-MVLG	Aerial Arts Chaser S
G-MVDD	Thruster TST	G-MVHF	Gemini Flash 2A	G-MVLJ	CFM Shadow CD
G-MVDE	Thruster TST	G-MVHG	Gemini Flash 2A	G-MVLL	Gemini Flash 2A
G-MVDF	Thruster TST	G-MVHH	Gemini Flash 2A	G-MVLP	CFM Shadow B
G-MVDG	Thruster TST	G-MVHI	Thruster TST	G-MVLR	Gemini Flash 2A
G-MVDH	Thruster TST	G-MVHJ	Thruster TST	G-MVLS	Aerial Arts Chaser S

Reg	Type	Reg	Type	Reg	Type
☐ G-MVLT	Aerial Arts Chaser S	☐ G-MVRD	Gemini Flash 2A	☐ G-MVXA	Whittaker MW-6
☐ G-MVLW	Aerial Arts Chaser S	☐ G-MVRF	Rotec Rally 2B	☐ G-MVXB	Gemini Flash 2A
☐ G-MVLX	Pegasus XL-Q	☐ G-MVRH	Pegasus XL-Q	☐ G-MVXC	Gemini Flash 2A
☐ G-MVLY	Pegasus XL-Q	☐ G-MVRI	Pegasus XL-Q	☐ G-MVXD	Hybred 44XLR
☐ G-MVMA	Pegasus XL-Q	☐ G-MVRJ	Pegasus XL-Q	☐ G-MVXE	Hybred 44XLR
☐ G-MVMC	Pegasus XL-Q	☐ G-MVRL	Aerial Arts Chaser S	☐ G-MVXI	Hybred 44XLR
☐ G-MVMG	Thruster TST	☐ G-MVRM	Gemini Flash 2A	☐ G-MVXJ	Hybred 44XLR
☐ G-MVMI	Thruster TST	☐ G-MVRO	CFM Shadow BD	☐ G-MVXL	Thruster TST
☐ G-MVMK	Hybred 44XLR	☐ G-MVRP	CFM Shadow CD	☐ G-MVXM	Hybred 44XLR
☐ G-MVML	Aerial Arts Chaser S	☐ G-MVRR	CFM Shadow CD	☐ G-MVXN	Aviasud Mistral
☐ G-MVMM	Aerial Arts Chaser S	☐ G-MVRT	CFM Shadow BD	☐ G-MVXR	Gemini Flash 2A
☐ G-MVMO	Gemini Flash 2A	☐ G-MVRU	Pegasus XL-Q	☐ G-MVXS	Gemini Flash 2A
☐ G-MVMR	Gemini Flash 2A	☐ G-MVRV	Powerchute Kestrel	☐ G-MVXV	Aviasud Mistral
☐ G-MVMT	Gemini Flash 2A	☐ G-MVRW	Pegasus XL-Q	☐ G-MVXX	AMF Chevvron
☐ G-MVMU	Gemini Flash 2A	☐ G-MVRX	Pegasus XL-Q	☐ G-MVYC	Pegasus XL-Q
☐ G-MVMV	Gemini Flash 2A	☐ G-MVRY	Hybred 44XLR	☐ G-MVYD	Pegasus XL-Q
☐ G-MVMW	Gemini Flash 2A	☐ G-MVRZ	Hybred 44XLR	☐ G-MVYE	Thruster TST
☐ G-MVMX	Gemini Flash 2A	☐ G-MVSB	Pegasus XL-Q	☐ G-MVYK	Hornet R-ZA
☐ G-MVMY	Gemini Flash 2A	☐ G-MVSD	Pegasus XL-Q	☐ G-MVYL	Hornet R-ZA
☐ G-MVMZ	Gemini Flash 2A	☐ G-MVSE	Pegasus XL-Q	☐ G-MVYN	Hornet R-ZA
☐ G-MVNA	Powerchute Raider	☐ G-MVSG	Aerial Arts Chaser S	☐ G-MVYP	Hybred 44XLR
☐ G-MVNB	Powerchute Raider	☐ G-MVSI	Hybred 44XLR	☐ G-MVYR	Hybred 44XLR
☐ G-MVNC	Powerchute Raider	☐ G-MVSJ	Aviasud Mistral	☐ G-MVYS	Gemini Flash 2A
☐ G-MVNK	Powerchute Raider	☐ G-MVSM	Midland Sirocco	☐ G-MVYT	Snowbird Mk.IV
☐ G-MVNL	Powerchute Raider	☐ G-MVSN	Gemini Flash 2A	☐ G-MVYU	Snowbird Mk.IV
☐ G-MVNM	Gemini Flash 2A	☐ G-MVSP	Gemini Flash 2A	☐ G-MVYV	Snowbird Mk.IV
☐ G-MVNN	Aerotech MW-5K	☐ G-MVST	Gemini Flash 2A	☐ G-MVYW	Snowbird Mk.IV
☐ G-MVNO	Aerotech MW-5K	☐ G-MVSV	Gemini Flash 2A	☐ G-MVYX	Snowbird Mk.IV
☐ G-MVNP	Aerotech MW-5K	☐ G-MVSW	Pegasus XL-Q	☐ G-MVYY	Aerial Arts Chaser S
☐ G-MVNR	Aerotech MW-5K	☐ G-MVSX	Pegasus XL-Q	☐ G-MVYZ	CFM Shadow BD
☐ G-MVNS	Aerotech MW-5K	☐ G-MVSY	Pegasus XL-Q	☐ G-MVZA	Thruster T300
☐ G-MVNT	Aerotech MW-5K	☐ G-MVSZ	Pegasus XL-Q	☐ G-MVZC	Thruster T300
☐ G-MVNU	Aerotech MW-5K	☐ G-MVTA	Pegasus XL-Q	☐ G-MVZD	Thruster T300
☐ G-MVNW	Gemini Flash 2A	☐ G-MVTC	Gemini Flash 2A	☐ G-MVZG	Thruster T300
☐ G-MVNX	Gemini Flash 2A	☐ G-MVTD	Whittaker MW-6	☐ G-MVZI	Thruster T300
☐ G-MVNY	Gemini Flash 2A	☐ G-MVTF	Aerial Arts Chaser S	☐ G-MVZJ	Pegasus XL-Q
☐ G-MVNZ	Gemini Flash 2A	☐ G-MVTI	Pegasus XL-Q	☐ G-MVZK	Quad City Challenger
☐ G-MVOB	Gemini Flash 2A	☐ G-MVTJ	Pegasus XL-Q	☐ G-MVZL	Pegasus XL-Q
☐ G-MVOD	Aerial Arts Chaser	☐ G-MVTK	Pegasus XL-Q	☐ G-MVZM	Aerial Arts Chaser S
☐ G-MVOF	Gemini Flash 2A	☐ G-MVTL	Aerial Arts Chaser S	☐ G-MVZO	Hybred 44XLR
☐ G-MVOH	CFM Shadow CD	☐ G-MVTM	Aerial Arts Chaser S	☐ G-MVZP	Renegade Spirit UK
☐ G-MVOJ	Snowbird Mk.IV	☐ G-MVUA	Gemini Flash 2A	☐ G-MVZS	Gemini Flash 2A
☐ G-MVOL	Snowbird Mk.IV	☐ G-MVUB	Thruster T300	☐ G-MVZT	Pegasus XL-Q
☐ G-MVON	Gemini Flash 2A	☐ G-MVUD	Hybred 44XLR	☐ G-MVZU	Pegasus XL-Q
☐ G-MVOO	AMF Chevvron	☐ G-MVUF	Pegasus XL-Q	☐ G-MVZV	Pegasus XL-Q
☐ G-MVOP	Aerial Arts Chaser S	☐ G-MVUG	Pegasus XL-Q	☐ G-MVZW	Hornet R-ZA
☐ G-MVOR	Gemini Flash 2A	☐ G-MVUI	Pegasus XL-Q	☐ G-MVZX	Renegade Spirit UK
☐ G-MVOT	Thruster TST	☐ G-MVUJ	Pegasus XL-Q	☐ G-MVZZ	AMF Chevvron
☐ G-MVOU	Thruster TST	☐ G-MVUK	Pegasus XL-Q	☐ G-MWAB	Gemini Flash 2A
☐ G-MVOV	Thruster TST	☐ G-MVUL	Pegasus XL-Q	☐ G-MWAC	Pegasus XL-Q
☐ G-MVOW	Thruster TST	☐ G-MVUM	Pegasus XL-Q	☐ G-MWAD	Pegasus XL-Q
☐ G-MVOX	Thruster TST	☐ G-MVUO	AMF Chevvron	☐ G-MWAE	CFM Shadow CD
☐ G-MVOY	Thruster TST	☐ G-MVUP	Aviasud Mistral	☐ G-MWAF	Pegasus XL-R
☐ G-MVPA	Gemini Flash 2A	☐ G-MVUR	Hornet RS-ZA	☐ G-MWAG	Pegasus XL-R
☐ G-MVPB	Gemini Flash 2A	☐ G-MVUS	Aerial Arts Chaser S	☐ G-MWAJ	Renegade Spirit UK
☐ G-MVPC	Gemini Flash 2A	☐ G-MVUU	Hornet R-ZA	☐ G-MWAL	Pegasus XL-Q
☐ G-MVPD	Gemini Flash 2A	☐ G-MVVH	Hybred 44XLR	☐ G-MWAN	Thruster T300
☐ G-MVPE	Gemini Flash 2A	☐ G-MVVI	Hybred 44XLR	☐ G-MWAP	Thruster T300
☐ G-MVPF	Hybred 44XLR	☐ G-MVVK	Pegasus XL-R	☐ G-MWAR	Pegasus XL-R
☐ G-MVPH	Whittaker MW-6S	☐ G-MVVN	Pegasus XL-Q	☐ G-MWAT	Pegasus XL-R
☐ G-MVPI	Gemini Flash 2A	☐ G-MVVO	Pegasus XL-Q	☐ G-MWAV	Pegasus XL-R
☐ G-MVPJ	Rans S5 Coyote	☐ G-MVVP	Pegasus XL-Q	☐ G-MWAW	Whittaker MW-6
☐ G-MVPK	CFM Shadow CD	☐ G-MVVR	Hybred 44XLR	☐ G-MWBJ	Medway Puma Sprint
☐ G-MVPL	Hybred 44XLR	☐ G-MVVT	CFM Shadow CD	☐ G-MWBK	Pegasus XL-Q
☐ G-MVPM	Whittaker MW-6T	☐ G-MVVU	Aerial Arts Chaser S	☐ G-MWBL	Pegasus XL-R
☐ G-MVPN	Whittaker MW-6	☐ G-MVVV	AMF Chevvron	☐ G-MWBO	Rans S4 Coyote
☐ G-MVPR	Pegasus XL-Q	☐ G-MVVZ	Powerchute Raider	☐ G-MWBP	Hornet R-ZA
☐ G-MVPS	Pegasus XL-Q	☐ G-MVWN	Thruster T300	☐ G-MWBR	Hornet R-ZA
☐ G-MVPX	Pegasus XL-Q	☐ G-MVWR	Thruster T300	☐ G-MWBS	Hornet R-ZA
☐ G-MVPY	Pegasus XL-Q	☐ G-MVWS	Thruster T300	☐ G-MWBU	Hornet R-ZA
☐ G-MVRA	Gemini Flash 2A	☐ G-MVWV	Hybred 44XLR	☐ G-MWBW	Hornet R-ZA
☐ G-MVRB	Gemini Flash	☐ G-MVWW	Aviasud Mistral	☐ G-MWBY	Hornet R-ZA
☐ G-MVRC	Gemini Flash	☐ G-MVWZ	Aviasud Mistral	☐ G-MWCB	Pegasus XL-Q

- G-MWCC Pegasus XL-R
- G-MWCE Gemini Flash 2A
- G-MWCF Pegasus XL-Q
- G-MWCG Microflight Spectrum
- G-MWCH Rans S6 Coyote II (N)
- G-MWCI Powerchute Kestrel
- G-MWCK Powerchute Kestrel
- G-MWCM Powerchute Kestrel
- G-MWCN Powerchute Kestrel
- G-MWCO Powerchute Kestrel
- G-MWCR Puma Sprint
- G-MWCS Powerchute Kestrel
- G-MWCU Pegasus XL-R
- G-MWCW Gemini Flash 2A
- G-MWCY Hybred 44XLR
- G-MWCZ Hybred 44XLR
- G-MWDB CFM Shadow CD
- G-MWDC Pegasus XL-R
- G-MWDD Pegasus XL-Q
- G-MWDE Hornet RS-ZA
- G-MWDI Hornet RS-ZA
- G-MWDJ Gemini Flash 2A
- G-MWDK Pegasus XL-Q
- G-MWDL Pegasus XL-Q
- G-MWDM Renegade Spirit UK
- G-MWDN CFM Shadow CD
- G-MWDP Thruster TST
- G-MWDS Thruster T300
- G-MWDZ Eipper Quicksilver MXL
- G-MWEE Pegasus XL-Q
- G-MWEF Pegasus XL-Q
- G-MWEG Pegasus XL-Q
- G-MWEH Pegasus XL-Q
- G-MWEK Whittaker MW-5
- G-MWEL Gemini Flash 2A
- G-MWEN CFM Shadow CD
- G-MWEO Whittaker MW-5
- G-MWEP Rans S4 Coyote
- G-MWER Pegasus XL-Q
- G-MWES Rans S4 Coyote
- G MWEY Hornet R-ZA
- G-MWEZ CFM Shadow CD
- G-MWFB CFM Shadow CD
- G-MWFC TEAM Minimax
- G-MWFD TEAM Minimax
- G-MWFF Rans S4 Coyote
- G-MWFG Powerchute Kestrel
- G-MWFI Powerchute Kestrel
- G-MWFL Powerchute Kestrel
- G-MWFS Pegasus XL-Q
- G-MWFT MBA Tiger Cub 440
- G-MWFU Quad City Challenger
- G-MWFV Quad City Challenger
- G-MWFW Rans S4 Coyote
- G-MWFX Quad City Challenger
- G-MWFY Quad City Challenger
- G-MWFZ Quad City Challenger
- G-MWGA Rans S5 Coyote
- G-MWGC Hybred 44XLR
- G-MWGG Gemini Flash 2A
- G-MWGI Aerotech MW-5B
- G-MWGJ Aerotech MW-5B
- G-MWGK Aerotech MW-5B
- G-MWGL Pegasus XL-Q
- G-MWGM Pegasus XL-Q
- G-MWGN Rans S4 Coyote
- G-MWGO Aerial Arts Chaser
- G-MWGR Pegasus XL-Q
- G-MWGU Powerchute Kestrel
- G-MWGV Powerchute Kestrel
- G-MWGW Powerchute Kestrel
- G-MWGZ Powerchute Kestrel
- G-MWHC Pegasus XL-Q

- G-MWHF Pegasus XL-Q
- G-MWHG Pegasus XL-Q
- G-MWHH TEAM Minimax
- G-MWHI Gemini Flash
- G-MWHL Pegasus XL-Q
- G-MWHM Whittaker MW-6S
- G-MWHO Gemini Flash 2A
- G-MWHP Rans S6 Coyote II (N)
- G-MWHR Gemini Flash 2A
- G-MWHT Pegasus Quasar
- G-MWHU Pegasus Quasar
- G-MWHX Pegasus XL-Q
- G-MWIA Gemini Flash 2A
- G-MWIB Aviasud Mistral
- G-MWIC Whittaker MW-5C
- G-MWIE Pegasus XL-Q
- G-MWIF Rans S6 Coyote II
- G-MWIG Gemini Flash 2A
- G-MWIH Gemini Flash
- G-MWIL Hybred 44XLR
- G-MWIM Pegasus Quasar
- G-MWIO Rans S4 Coyote
- G-MWIP Whittaker MW-6
- G-MWIR Pegasus XL-Q
- G-MWIS Pegasus XL-Q
- G-MWIU Pegasus Quasar
- G-MWIV Gemini Flash
- G-MWIW Pegasus Quasar
- G-MWIX Pegasus Quasar
- G-MWIY Pegasus Quasar
- G-MWIZ CFM Shadow CD
- G-MWJF CFM Shadow BD
- G-MWJG Pegasus XL-R
- G-MWJH Pegasus Quasar
- G-MWJI Pegasus Quasar
- G-MWJJ Pegasus Quasar
- G-MWJK Pegasus Quasar
- G-MWJN Pegasus XL-Q
- G-MWJP Hybred 44XLR
- G-MWJR Hybred 44XLR
- G-MWJS Pegasus Quasar
- G-MWJT Pegasus Quasar
- G-MWJV Pegasus Quasar
- G-MWJW Whittaker MW-5
- G-MWJX Puma Sprint
- G-MWJY Gemini Flash 2A
- G-MWKA Renegade Spirit UK
- G-MWKE Hornet RS-ZA
- G-MWKO Pegasus XL-Q
- G-MWKP Pegasus XL-Q
- G-MWKX Microflight Spectrum
- G-MWKY Pegasus XL-Q
- G-MWKZ Pegasus XL-Q
- G-MWLA Rans S4 Coyote
- G-MWLB Hybred 44XLR
- G-MWLD CFM Shadow CD
- G-MWLE Pegasus XL-R
- G-MWLF Pegasus XL-R
- G-MWLG Pegasus XL-R
- G-MWLH Pegasus Quasar
- G-MWLJ Pegasus Quasar
- G-MWLK Pegasus Quasar
- G-MWLL Pegasus XL-R
- G-MWLM Pegasus XL-Q
- G-MWLN Whittaker MW-6S
- G-MWLO Whittaker MW-6
- G-MWLP Gemini Flash
- G-MWLS Hybred 44XLR
- G-MWLT Gemini Flash 2A
- G-MWLU Pegasus XL-R
- G-MWLW TEAM Minimax
- G-MWLX Gemini Flash 2A
- G-MWLZ Rans S4 Coyote

- G-MWMB Powerchute Kestrel
- G-MWMC Powerchute Kestrel
- G-MWMD Powerchute Kestrel
- G-MWMG Powerchute Kestrel
- G-MWMH Powerchute Kestrel
- G-MWMI Pegasus Quasar
- G-MWMJ Pegasus Quasar
- G-MWMK Pegasus Quasar
- G-MWML Pegasus Quasar
- G-MWMM Gemini Flash 2A
- G-MWMN Pegasus XL-Q
- G-MWMO Pegasus XL-Q
- G-MWMP Pegasus XL-Q
- G-MWMR Pegasus XL-R
- G-MWMT Gemini Flash 2A
- G-MWMU CFM Shadow CD
- G-MWMV Pegasus XL-R
- G-MWMW Renegade Spirit UK
- G-MWMX Gemini Flash 2A
- G-MWMY Gemini Flash 2A
- G-MWMZ Pegasus XL-Q
- G-MWNA Pegasus XL-Q
- G-MWNB Pegasus XL-Q
- G-MWNC Pegasus XL-Q
- G-MWND Sherwood Ranger
- G-MWNE Gemini Flash 2A
- G-MWNF Renegade Spirit UK
- G-MWNG Pegasus XL-Q
- G-MWNK Pegasus Quasar
- G-MWNL Pegasus Quasar
- G-MWNO AMF Chevvron
- G-MWNP AMF Chevvron
- G-MWNR Renegade Spirit UK
- G-MWNS Gemini Flash 2A
- G-MWNT Gemini Flash 2A
- G-MWNU Gemini Flash 2A
- G-MWNV Powerchute Kestrel
- G-MWNX Powerchute Kestrel
- G-MWOC Powerchute Kestrel
- G-MWOD Powerchute Kestrel
- G-MWOE Powerchute Kestrel
- G-MWOF Microflight Spectrum
- G-MWOH Pegasus XL-R
- G-MWOI Pegasus XL-R
- G-MWOJ Gemini Flash 2A
- G-MWOK Gemini Flash 2A
- G-MWOM Pegasus Quasar
- G-MWON CFM Shadow CD
- G-MWOO Renegade Spirit UK
- G-MWOP Pegasus Quasar
- G-MWOR Pegasus XL-Q
- G-MWOV Whittaker MW-6
- G-MWOY Pegasus XL-Q
- G-MWPB Gemini Flash 2A
- G-MWPC Gemini Flash 2A
- G-MWPD Gemini Flash 2A
- G-MWPE Pegasus XL-Q
- G-MWPF Gemini Flash 2A
- G-MWPG Microflight Spectrum
- G-MWPH Microflight Spectrum
- G-MWPJ Pegasus XL-Q
- G-MWPK Pegasus XL-Q
- G-MWPN CFM Shadow CD
- G-MWPO Gemini Flash 2A
- G-MWPP CFM Shadow SA-M
- G-MWPR Whittaker MW-6
- G-MWPS Renegade Spirit UK
- G-MWPU Pegasus Quasar
- G-MWPW AMF Chevvron
- G-MWPX Pegasus XL-R
- G-MWPZ Renegade Spirit UK
- G-MWRB Gemini Flash 2A
- G-MWRC Gemini Flash 2A

☐ G-MWRD	Gemini Flash 2A
☐ G-MWRE	Gemini Flash 2A
☐ G-MWRF	Gemini Flash 2A
☐ G-MWRG	Gemini Flash 2A
☐ G-MWRH	Gemini Flash 2A
☐ G-MWRJ	Gemini Flash 2A
☐ G-MWRL	CFM Shadow CD
☐ G-MWRM	Hybred 44XLR
☐ G-MWRN	Pegasus XL-R
☐ G-MWRP	Pegasus XL-R
☐ G-MWRR	Gemini Flash 2A
☐ G-MWRS	Ultravia Super Pelican
☐ G-MWRT	Pegasus XL-R
☐ G-MWRU	Pegasus XL-R
☐ G-MWRV	Pegasus XL-R
☐ G-MWRW	Pegasus XL-Q
☐ G-MWRX	Pegasus XL-Q
☐ G-MWRY	CFM Shadow CD
☐ G-MWRZ	AMF Chevvron
☐ G-MWSA	TEAM Minimax
☐ G-MWSB	Gemini Flash 2A
☐ G-MWSC	Rans S6 Coyote II (N)
☐ G-MWSD	Pegasus XL-Q
☐ G-MWSE	Pegasus XL-R
☐ G-MWSF	Pegasus XL-R
☐ G-MWSH	Pegasus Quasar
☐ G-MWSI	Pegasus Quasar
☐ G-MWSJ	Pegasus XL-Q
☐ G-MWSK	Pegasus XL-Q
☐ G-MWSL	Gemini Flash 2A
☐ G-MWSM	Gemini Flash 2A
☐ G-MWSO	Pegasus XL-R
☐ G-MWSP	Pegasus XL-R
☐ G-MWSR	Pegasus XL-R
☐ G-MWSS	Hybred 44XLR
☐ G-MWST	Hybred 44XLR
☐ G-MWSU	Hybred 44XLR
☐ G-MWSW	Whittaker MW-6
☐ G-MWSX	Aerotech MW-5
☐ G-MWSY	Aerotech MW-5
☐ G-MWSZ	CFM Shadow CD
☐ G-MWTB	Pegasus XL-Q
☐ G-MWTC	Pegasus XL-Q
☐ G-MWTD	Microflight Spectrum
☐ G-MWTE	Microflight Spectrum
☐ G-MWTG	Gemini Flash 2A
☐ G-MWTH	Gemini Flash 2A
☐ G-MWTI	Pegasus XL-Q
☐ G-MWTJ	CFM Shadow CD
☐ G-MWTK	Pegasus XL-R
☐ G-MWTL	Pegasus XL-R
☐ G-MWTN	CFM Shadow CD
☐ G-MWTO	Gemini Flash 2A
☐ G-MWTP	CFM Shadow CD
☐ G-MWTR	Gemini Flash 2A
☐ G-MWTT	Rans S6 Coyote II (N)
☐ G-MWTU	Pegasus XL-R
☐ G-MWTY	Gemini Flash 2A
☐ G-MWTZ	Gemini Flash 2A
☐ G-MWUA	CFM Shadow CD
☐ G-MWUB	Pegasus XL-R
☐ G-MWUC	Pegasus XL-R
☐ G-MWUD	Pegasus XL-R
☐ G-MWUH	Renegade Spirit UK
☐ G-MWUI	AMF Chevvron
☐ G-MWUK	Rans S6 Coyote II (N)
☐ G-MWUL	Rans S6 Coyote II
☐ G-MWUN	Rans S6 Coyote II (N)
☐ G-MWUO	Pegasus XL-Q
☐ G-MWUR	Pegasus XL-R
☐ G-MWUS	Pegasus XL-R
☐ G-MWUU	Pegasus XL-R
☐ G-MWUV	Pegasus XL-R
☐ G-MWUX	Pegasus XL-Q
☐ G-MWUY	Pegasus XL-Q
☐ G-MWUZ	Pegasus XL-Q
☐ G-MWVA	Pegasus XL-Q
☐ G-MWVE	Pegasus XL-R
☐ G-MWVF	Pegasus XL-R
☐ G-MWVG	CFM Shadow CD
☐ G-MWVH	CFM Shadow CD
☐ G-MWVK	Mainair Mercury
☐ G-MWVL	Rans S6 Coyote II (N)
☐ G-MWVM	Pegasus Quasar
☐ G-MWVN	Gemini Flash 2A
☐ G-MWVO	Gemini Flash 2A
☐ G-MWVP	Renegade Spirit UK
☐ G-MWVR	Gemini Flash 2A
☐ G-MWVS	Gemini Flash 2A
☐ G-MWVT	Gemini Flash 2A
☐ G-MWVY	Gemini Flash 2A
☐ G-MWVZ	Gemini Flash 2A
☐ G-MWWB	Gemini Flash 2A
☐ G-MWWC	Gemini Flash 2A
☐ G-MWWD	Renegade Spirit UK
☐ G-MWWE	TEAM Minimax
☐ G-MWWG	Pegasus XL-Q
☐ G-MWWH	Pegasus XL-Q
☐ G-MWWI	Gemini Flash 2A
☐ G-MWWJ	Gemini Flash 2A
☐ G-MWWK	Gemini Flash 2A
☐ G-MWWL	Rans S6 Coyote II (N)
☐ G-MWWN	Gemini Flash 2A
☐ G-MWWP	Rans S4 Coyote
☐ G-MWWR	Microflight Spectrum
☐ G-MWWS	Thruster T300
☐ G-MWWV	Pegasus XL-Q
☐ G-MWWZ	Aerial Arts Chaser S
☐ G-MWXA	Gemini Flash 2A
☐ G-MWXB	Gemini Flash 2A
☐ G-MWXC	Gemini Flash 2A
☐ G-MWXF	Mainair Mercury
☐ G-MWXG	Pegasus Quasar
☐ G-MWXH	Pegasus Quasar
☐ G-MWXJ	Mainair Mercury
☐ G-MWXK	Mainair Mercury
☐ G-MWXL	Gemini Flash 2A
☐ G-MWXP	Pegasus XL-Q
☐ G-MWXR	Pegasus XL-Q
☐ G-MWXU	Gemini Flash 2A
☐ G-MWXV	Gemini Flash 2A
☐ G-MWXW	Aerial Arts Chaser S
☐ G-MWXX	Aerial Arts Chaser S
☐ G-MWXY	Aerial Arts Chaser S
☐ G-MWXZ	Aerial Arts Chaser S
☐ G-MWYA	Gemini Flash 2A
☐ G-MWYB	Pegasus XL-Q
☐ G-MWYC	Pegasus XL-Q
☐ G-MWYD	CFM Shadow C
☐ G-MWYE	Rans S6 Coyote II (N)
☐ G-MWYG	Gemini Flash 2A
☐ G-MWYH	Gemini Flash 2A
☐ G-MWYI	Pegasus Quasar
☐ G-MWYJ	Pegasus Quasar
☐ G-MWYL	Gemini Flash 2A
☐ G-MWYM	Aerial Arts Chaser S
☐ G-MWYN	Rans S6 Coyote II
☐ G-MWYS	Arrowflight Hawk
☐ G-MWYT	Gemini Flash 2A
☐ G-MWYU	Pegasus XL-Q
☐ G-MWYV	Gemini Flash 2A
☐ G-MWYY	Pegasus XL-Q
☐ G-MWYZ	Pegasus XL-Q
☐ G-MWZA	Mainair Mercury
☐ G-MWZB	AMF Chevvron
☐ G-MWZC	Gemini Flash 2A
☐ G-MWZD	Pegasus Quasar
☐ G-MWZE	Pegasus Quasar
☐ G-MWZF	Pegasus Quasar
☐ G-MWZG	Gemini Flash 2
☐ G-MWZI	Pegasus XL-R
☐ G-MWZJ	Pegasus XL-R
☐ G-MWZL	Gemini Flash 2A
☐ G-MWZM	TEAM Minimax
☐ G-MWZN	Gemini Flash 2A
☐ G-MWZO	Pegasus Quasar
☐ G-MWZP	Pegasus Quasar
☐ G-MWZR	Pegasus Quasar
☐ G-MWZS	Pegasus Quasar
☐ G-MWZT	Pegasus XL-R
☐ G-MWZU	Pegasus XL-R
☐ G-MWZV	Pegasus XL-R
☐ G-MWZW	Pegasus XL-R
☐ G-MWZY	Pegasus XL-R
☐ G-MWZZ	Pegasus XL-R
☐ G-MXVI	Spitfire LF.XVIe
☐ G-MYAB	Pegasus XL-R
☐ G-MYAC	Pegasus XL-Q
☐ G-MYAE	Pegasus XL-Q
☐ G-MYAF	Pegasus XL-Q
☐ G-MYAG	Quad City Challenger
☐ G-MYAH	Whittaker MW-5
☐ G-MYAI	Mainair Mercury
☐ G-MYAJ	Rans S6 Coyote II (T)
☐ G-MYAK	Pegasus Quasar
☐ G-MYAM	Renegade Spirit UK
☐ G-MYAN	MW-5K Seaplane
☐ G-MYAO	Gemini Flash 2A
☐ G-MYAP	Thruster T300
☐ G-MYAR	Thruster T300
☐ G-MYAS	Gemini Flash 2A
☐ G-MYAT	TEAM Minimax
☐ G-MYAU	Gemini Flash 2A
☐ G-MYAY	Microflight Spectrum
☐ G-MYAZ	Renegade Spirit UK
☐ G-MYBA	Rans S6 Coyote II
☐ G-MYBB	Maxair Drifter
☐ G-MYBC	CFM Shadow CD
☐ G-MYBD	Pegasus Quasar
☐ G-MYBE	Pegasus Quasar
☐ G-MYBF	Pegasus XL-Q
☐ G-MYBI	Rans S6 Coyote II (N)
☐ G-MYBJ	Gemini Flash 2A
☐ G-MYBL	CFM Shadow CD
☐ G-MYBM	TEAM Minimax
☐ G-MYBN	Skytrike Demon
☐ G-MYBO	Pegasus XL-R
☐ G-MYBP	Pegasus XL-R
☐ G-MYBS	Pegasus XL-Q
☐ G-MYBT	Pegasus Quasar
☐ G-MYBU	Aerial Arts Chaser S
☐ G-MYBV	Pegasus XL-Q
☐ G-MYBW	Pegasus XL-Q
☐ G-MYBY	Pegasus XL-Q
☐ G-MYBZ	Pegasus XL-Q
☐ G-MYCA	Whittaker MW-6T
☐ G-MYCB	Aerial Arts Chaser S
☐ G-MYCE	Pegasus Quasar
☐ G-MYCJ	Mercury
☐ G-MYCK	Gemini Flash 2A
☐ G-MYCL	Gemini Flash 2A
☐ G-MYCM	CFM Shadow CD
☐ G-MYCN	Mainair Mercury
☐ G-MYCO	Renegade Spirit UK
☐ G-MYCP	Whittaker MW-6
☐ G-MYCR	Gemini Flash 2A
☐ G-MYCS	Gemini Flash 2A
☐ G-MYCT	TEAM Minimax
☐ G-MYCU	Whittaker MW-6

☐ G-MYCV Mainair Mercury	☐ G-MYGV Pegasus XL-R	☐ G-MYLF Rans S6 Coyote II (N)
☐ G-MYCX Powerchute Kestrel	☐ G-MYGZ Gemini Flash 2A	☐ G-MYLG Gemini Flash 2A
☐ G-MYCY Powerchute Kestrel	☐ G-MYHF Gemini Flash 2A	☐ G-MYLH Pegasus Quantum
☐ G-MYCZ Powerchute Kestrel	☐ G-MYHG Cyclone AX3	☐ G-MYLI Pegasus Quantum
☐ G-MYDA Powerchute Kestrel	☐ G-MYHH Cyclone AX3	☐ G-MYLK Pegasus Quantum
☐ G-MYDC Mainair Mercury	☐ G-MYHI Rans S6 Coyote II (T)	☐ G-MYLL Pegasus Quantum
☐ G-MYDD CFM Shadow CD	☐ G-MYHJ Cyclone AX3	☐ G-MYLM Pegasus Quantum
☐ G-MYDE CFM Shadow CD	☐ G-MYHK Rans S6 Coyote II (N)	☐ G-MYLN Kolb Twinstar Mk.3
☐ G-MYDF TEAM Minimax	☐ G-MYHL Gemini Flash 2A	☐ G-MYLO Rans S6 Coyote II (N)
☐ G-MYDI Pegasus XL-R	☐ G-MYHM Cyclone AX3	☐ G-MYLP Kolb Twinstar Mk.3
☐ G-MYDJ Pegasus XL-R	☐ G-MYHN Gemini Flash 2A	☐ G-MYLR Gemini Flash 2A
☐ G-MYDK Rans S6 Coyote II (N)	☐ G-MYHP Rans S6 Coyote II (N)	☐ G-MYLS Mainair Mercury
☐ G-MYDM Whittaker MW-6S	☐ G-MYHR Cyclone AX3	☐ G-MYLT Mainair Blade
☐ G-MYDN Quad City Challenger	☐ G-MYHS Powerchute Kestrel	☐ G-MYLV CFM Shadow CD
☐ G-MYDO Rans S5 Coyote	☐ G-MYIA Quad City Challenger	☐ G-MYLW Rans S6 Coyote II (N)
☐ G-MYDP Kolb Twinstar Mk.3	☐ G-MYIE Whittaker MW-6S	☐ G-MYLX Medway Raven X
☐ G-MYDR Thruster T300	☐ G-MYIF CFM Shadow CD	☐ G-MYLY Medway Raven X
☐ G-MYDS Quad City Challenger	☐ G-MYIH Gemini Flash 2A	☐ G-MYLZ Pegasus Quantum
☐ G-MYDT Thruster T300	☐ G-MYII TEAM Minimax	☐ G-MYMB Pegasus Quantum
☐ G-MYDU Thruster T300	☐ G-MYIJ Cyclone AX3	☐ G-MYMC Pegasus Quantum
☐ G-MYDV Gemini Flash 2A	☐ G-MYIK Kolb Twinstar Mk.3	☐ G-MYME Cyclone AX3
☐ G-MYDW Whittaker MW-6	☐ G-MYIL Aerial Arts Chaser S	☐ G-MYMH Rans S6 Coyote II (N)
☐ G-MYDX Rans S6 Coyote II (N)	☐ G-MYIM Pegasus Quasar	☐ G-MYMJ Medway Raven X
☐ G-MYDZ Mignet HM-1000	☐ G-MYIN Pegasus Quasar	☐ G-MYMK Gemini Flash 2A
☐ G-MYEA Pegasus XL-Q	☐ G-MYIO Pegasus Quasar	☐ G-MYML Mainair Mercury
☐ G-MYEC Pegasus XL-Q	☐ G-MYIP CFM Shadow CD	☐ G-MYMM Air Creation Fun 18S
☐ G-MYED Pegasus XL-R	☐ G-MYIR Rans S6 Coyote II (N)	☐ G-MYMN Whittaker MW-6
☐ G-MYEF Whittaker MW-6	☐ G-MYIS Rans S6 Coyote II (N)	☐ G-MYMO Gemini Flash 2A
☐ G-MYEG Pegasus XL-R	☐ G-MYIT Aerial Arts Chaser S	☐ G-MYMP Rans S6 Coyote II (N)
☐ G-MYEH Pegasus XL-R	☐ G-MYIU Cyclone AX3	☐ G-MYMR Rans S6 Coyote II (N)
☐ G-MYEI Aerial Arts Chaser S	☐ G-MYIV Gemini Flash 2A	☐ G-MYMS Rans S6 Coyote II (N)
☐ G-MYEJ Aerial Arts Chaser S	☐ G-MYIX Quad City Challenger	☐ G-MYMV Gemini Flash 2A
☐ G-MYEK Pegasus Quasar	☐ G-MYIY Gemini Flash 2A	☐ G-MYMW Cyclone AX3
☐ G-MYEM Pegasus Quasar	☐ G-MYIZ TEAM Minimax	☐ G-MYMX Pegasus Quantum
☐ G-MYEN Pegasus Quasar	☐ G-MYJC Gemini Flash 2A	☐ G-MYMY Aerial Arts Chaser S
☐ G-MYEO Pegasus Quasar	☐ G-MYJD Rans S6 Coyote II (N)	☐ G-MYMZ Cyclone AX3
☐ G-MYEP CFM Shadow CD	☐ G-MYJF Thruster T300	☐ G-MYNA CFM Shadow C
☐ G-MYER Pegasus AX2000	☐ G-MYJG Thruster T300	☐ G-MYNB Pegasus Quantum
☐ G-MYES Rans S6 Coyote II (N)	☐ G-MYJJ Pegasus Quasar	☐ G-MYNC Mainair Mercury
☐ G-MYET Whittaker MW-6	☐ G-MYJK Pegasus Quasar	☐ G-MYND Gemini Flash 2A
☐ G-MYEU Gemini Flash 2A	☐ G-MYJM Gemini Flash 2A	☐ G-MYNE Rans S6 Coyote II (T)
☐ G-MYEV Whittaker MW-6	☐ G-MYJO Aerial Arts Chaser S	☐ G-MYNF Mainair Mercury
☐ G-MYEX Powerchute Kestrel	☐ G-MYJR Mainair Mercury	☐ G-MYNH Rans S6 Coyote II (T)
☐ G-MYFH Quad City Challenger	☐ G-MYJS Pegasus Quasar	☐ G-MYNI TEAM Minimax
☐ G-MYFI Cyclone AX3	☐ G-MYJT Pegasus Quasar	☐ G-MYNJ Mainair Mercury
☐ G-MYFK Pegasus Quasar	☐ G-MYJU Pegasus Quasar	☐ G-MYNK Pegasus Quantum
☐ G-MYFL Pegasus Quasar	☐ G-MYJW Aerial Arts Chaser S	☐ G-MYNL Pegasus Quantum
☐ G-MYFM Renegade Spirit UK	☐ G-MYJY Rans S6 Coyote II (N)	☐ G-MYNN Pegasus Quantum
☐ G-MYFN Rans S5 Coyote	☐ G-MYJZ Whittaker MW-5D	☐ G-MYNO Pegasus Quantum
☐ G-MYFO Aerial Arts Chaser S	☐ G-MYKA Cyclone AX3	☐ G-MYNP Pegasus Quantum
☐ G-MYFP Gemini Flash 2A	☐ G-MYKB Kolb Twinstar Mk.3	☐ G-MYNR Pegasus Quantum
☐ G-MYFR Gemini Flash 2A	☐ G-MYKC Gemini Flash 2A	☐ G-MYNS Pegasus Quantum
☐ G-MYFS Pegasus XL-R	☐ G-MYKD Aerial Arts Chaser S	☐ G-MYNT Pegasus Quantum
☐ G-MYFT Mainair Scorcher	☐ G-MYKE CFM Shadow BD	☐ G-MYNV Pegasus Quantum
☐ G-MYFU Gemini Flash 2A	☐ G-MYKF Cyclone AX3	☐ G-MYNX CFM Shadow SA-M
☐ G-MYFV Cyclone AX3	☐ G-MYKG Gemini Flash 2A	☐ G-MYNY Kolb Twinstar Mk.3
☐ G-MYFW Cyclone AX3	☐ G-MYKH Gemini Flash 2A	☐ G-MYNZ Pegasus Quantum
☐ G-MYFX Pegasus XL-Q	☐ G-MYKJ TEAM Minimax	☐ G-MYOA Rans S6 Coyote II (N)
☐ G-MYFY Cyclone AX3	☐ G-MYKL Medway Raven X	☐ G-MYOB Mainair Mercury
☐ G-MYFZ Cyclone AX3	☐ G-MYKN Rans S6 Coyote II (N)	☐ G-MYOF Mainair Mercury
☐ G-MYGD Cyclone AX3	☐ G-MYKO Whittaker MW-6S	☐ G-MYOG Kolb Twinstar Mk.3
☐ G-MYGE Whittaker MW-6	☐ G-MYKP Pegasus Quasar	☐ G-MYOH CFM Shadow CD
☐ G-MYGF TEAM Minimax	☐ G-MYKR Pegasus Quasar	☐ G-MYOI Rans S6 Coyote II (T)
☐ G-MYGH Rans S6 Coyote II	☐ G-MYKS Pegasus Quasar	☐ G-MYOL Air Creation Fun 18S
☐ G-MYGJ Mainair Mercury	☐ G-MYKT Cyclone AX3	☐ G-MYOM Gemini Flash 2A
☐ G-MYGK Aerial Arts Chaser S	☐ G-MYKV Gemini Flash 2A	☐ G-MYON CFM Shadow CD
☐ G-MYGM Quad City Challenger	☐ G-MYKX Mainair Mercury	☐ G-MYOO Kolb Twinstar Mk.3
☐ G-MYGN AMF Chevvron	☐ G-MYKY Mainair Mercury	☐ G-MYOR Kolb Twinstar Mk.3
☐ G-MYGO CFM Shadow CD	☐ G-MYKZ TEAM Minimax	☐ G-MYOS CFM Shadow CD
☐ G-MYGP Rans S6 Coyote II (T)	☐ G-MYLB TEAM Minimax	☐ G-MYOT Rans S6 Coyote II
☐ G-MYGR Rans S6 Coyote II (T)	☐ G-MYLC Pegasus Quantum	☐ G-MYOU Pegasus Quantum
☐ G-MYGT Pegasus XL-R	☐ G-MYLD Rans S6 Coyote II (T)	☐ G-MYOV Mainair Mercury
☐ G-MYGU Pegasus XL-R	☐ G-MYLE Pegasus Quantum	☐ G-MYOW Gemini Flash 2A

☐ G-MYOX	Mainair Mercury	
☐ G-MYOY	Cyclone AX3	
☐ G-MYOZ	Quad City Challenger	
☐ G-MYPA	Rans S6 Coyote II (T)	
☐ G-MYPC	Kolb Twinstar Mk.3	
☐ G-MYPD	Mainair Mercury	
☐ G-MYPE	Gemini Flash 2A	
☐ G-MYPG	Pegasus XL-Q	
☐ G-MYPH	Pegasus Quantum	
☐ G-MYPI	Pegasus Quantum	
☐ G-MYPJ	Rans S6 Coyote II (N)	
☐ G-MYPL	CFM Shadow CD	
☐ G-MYPM	Cyclone AX3	
☐ G-MYPN	Pegasus Quantum	
☐ G-MYPP	Whittaker MW-6S	
☐ G-MYPR	Cyclone AX3	
☐ G-MYPS	Whittaker MW-6S	
☐ G-MYPT	CFM Shadow CD	
☐ G-MYPV	Mainair Mercury	
☐ G-MYPW	Gemini Flash 2A	
☐ G-MYPX	Pegasus Quantum	
☐ G-MYPY	Pegasus Quantum	
☐ G-MYPZ	Quad City Challenger	
☐ G-MYRB	Whittaker MW-5	
☐ G-MYRC	Mainair Blade	
☐ G-MYRD	Mainair Blade	
☐ G-MYRE	Aerial Arts Chaser S	
☐ G-MYRF	Pegasus Quantum	
☐ G-MYRG	TEAM Minimax	
☐ G-MYRH	Quad City Challenger	
☐ G-MYRJ	Quad City Challenger	
☐ G-MYRK	Renegade Spirit UK	
☐ G-MYRL	TEAM Minimax	
☐ G-MYRM	Pegasus Quantum	
☐ G-MYRN	Pegasus Quantum	
☐ G-MYRO	Cyclone AX3	
☐ G-MYRP	Letov Sluka LK-2M	
☐ G-MYRR	Letov Sluka LK-2M	
☐ G-MYRS	Pegasus Quantum	
☐ G-MYRT	Pegasus Quantum	
☐ G-MYRU	Cyclone AX3	
☐ G-MYRV	Cyclone AX3	
☐ G-MYRW	Mainair Mercury	
☐ G-MYRY	Pegasus Quantum	
☐ G-MYRZ	Pegasus Quantum	
☐ G-MYSA	Aerial Arts Chaser S	
☐ G-MYSB	Pegasus Quantum	
☐ G-MYSC	Pegasus Quantum	
☐ G-MYSD	Quad City Challenger	
☐ G-MYSG	Mainair Mercury	
☐ G-MYSI	Mignet HM.14/93	
☐ G-MYSJ	Gemini Flash 2A	
☐ G-MYSK	TEAM Minimax	
☐ G-MYSL	Aviasud Mistral	
☐ G-MYSM	CFM Shadow CD	
☐ G-MYSO	Cyclone AX3	
☐ G-MYSP	Rans S6 Coyote II	
☐ G-MYSR	Pegasus Quantum	
☐ G-MYSU	Rans S6 Coyote II	
☐ G-MYSV	Aerial Arts Chaser S	
☐ G-MYSW	Pegasus Quantum	
☐ G-MYSX	Pegasus Quantum	
☐ G-MYSY	Pegasus Quantum	
☐ G-MYSZ	Mainair Mercury	
☐ G-MYTB	Mainair Mercury	
☐ G-MYTC	Pegasus XL-Q	
☐ G-MYTD	Mainair Blade	
☐ G-MYTE	Rans S6 Coyote II (N)	
☐ G-MYTG	Mainair Blade	
☐ G-MYTH	CFM Shadow CD	
☐ G-MYTI	Pegasus Quantum	
☐ G-MYTJ	Pegasus Quantum	
☐ G-MYTK	Mainair Mercury	
☐ G-MYTL	Mainair Blade
☐ G-MYTM	Cyclone AX3
☐ G-MYTN	Pegasus Quantum
☐ G-MYTO	Quad City Challenger
☐ G-MYTP	Arrowflight Hawk
☐ G-MYTT	Quad City Challenger
☐ G-MYTU	Mainair Blade
☐ G-MYTV	Hunt Wing Avon
☐ G-MYTX	Mainair Mercury
☐ G-MYTY	CFM Shadow SA-M
☐ G-MYTZ	Air Creation Fun 18S
☐ G-MYUA	Air Creation Fun 18S
☐ G-MYUB	Mainair Mercury
☐ G-MYUC	Mainair Blade
☐ G-MYUD	Mainair Mercury
☐ G-MYUE	Mainair Mercury
☐ G-MYUF	Renegade Spirit UK
☐ G-MYUH	Pegasus XL-Q
☐ G-MYUI	Cyclone AX3
☐ G-MYUK	Mainair Mercury
☐ G-MYUN	Mainair Blade
☐ G-MYUO	Pegasus Quantum
☐ G-MYUP	Letov Sluka LK-2M
☐ G-MYUR	Hunt Wing Avon
☐ G-MYUS	CFM Shadow CD
☐ G-MYUU	Pegasus Quantum
☐ G-MYUV	Pegasus Quantum
☐ G-MYUW	Mainair Mercury
☐ G-MYUZ	Rans S6 Coyote II (N)
☐ G-MYVA	Kolb Twinstar Mk.3
☐ G-MYVB	Mainair Blade
☐ G-MYVC	Pegasus Quantum
☐ G-MYVE	Mainair Blade
☐ G-MYVG	Letov Sluka LK-2M
☐ G-MYVH	Mainair Blade
☐ G-MYVI	Air Creation Fun 18S
☐ G-MYVJ	Pegasus Quantum
☐ G-MYVK	Pegasus Quantum
☐ G-MYVL	Mainair Mercury
☐ G-MYVM	Pegasus Quantum
☐ G-MYVN	Cyclone AX3
☐ G-MYVO	Mainair Blade
☐ G-MYVP	Rans S6 Coyote II (N)
☐ G-MYVR	Pegasus Quantum
☐ G-MYVS	Mainair Mercury
☐ G-MYVT	Letov Sluka LK-2M
☐ G-MYVV	Hybred 44XLR
☐ G-MYVY	Mainair Blade
☐ G-MYVZ	Mainair Blade
☐ G-MYWA	Mainair Mercury
☐ G-MYWC	Huntwing Avon
☐ G-MYWD	Thruster T600N
☐ G-MYWE	Thruster T600T
☐ G-MYWF	CFM Shadow CD
☐ G-MYWG	Pegasus Quantum
☐ G-MYWH	Huntwing Experience
☐ G-MYWI	Pegasus Quantum
☐ G-MYWJ	Pegasus Quantum
☐ G-MYWK	Pegasus Quantum
☐ G-MYWL	Pegasus Quantum
☐ G-MYWM	CFM Shadow CD
☐ G-MYWN	Aerial Arts Chaser S
☐ G-MYWO	Pegasus Quantum
☐ G-MYWP	Kolb Twinstar Mk.3
☐ G-MYWR	Pegasus Quantum
☐ G-MYWS	Aerial Arts Chaser S
☐ G-MYWT	Pegasus Quantum
☐ G-MYWU	Pegasus Quantum
☐ G-MYWV	Rans S4 Coyote
☐ G-MYWW	Pegasus Quantum
☐ G-MYWX	Pegasus Quantum
☐ G-MYWY	Pegasus Quantum
☐ G-MYWZ	Thruster TST

☐ G-MYXA	TEAM Minimax
☐ G-MYXB	Rans S6 Coyote II (N)
☐ G-MYXC	Quad City Challenger
☐ G-MYXD	Pegasus Quasar
☐ G-MYXE	Pegasus Quantum
☐ G-MYXF	Air Creation Fun 18S
☐ G-MYXG	Rans S6 Coyote II (N)
☐ G-MYXH	Pegasus AX3
☐ G-MYXI	Cook Aries 1
☐ G-MYXJ	Mainair Blade
☐ G-MYXK	Quad City Challenger
☐ G-MYXL	Mignet HM-1000
☐ G-MYXM	Mainair Blade
☐ G-MYXN	Mainair Blade
☐ G-MYXO	Letov Sluka LK-2M
☐ G-MYXP	Rans S6 Coyote II (T)
☐ G-MYXR	Renegade Spirit UK
☐ G-MYXS	Kolb Twinstar Mk.3
☐ G-MYXT	Pegasus Quantum
☐ G-MYXU	Thruster T300
☐ G-MYXV	Quad City Challenger
☐ G-MYXW	Pegasus Quantum
☐ G-MYXX	Pegasus Quantum
☐ G-MYXY	CFM Shadow CD
☐ G-MYXZ	Pegasus Quantum
☐ G-MYYA	Mainair Blade
☐ G-MYYB	Pegasus Quantum
☐ G-MYYC	Pegasus Quantum
☐ G-MYYD	Aerial Arts Chaser S
☐ G-MYYE	Hunt Wing Avon
☐ G-MYYF	Quad City Challenger
☐ G-MYYG	Mainair Blade
☐ G-MYYH	Mainair Blade
☐ G-MYYI	Pegasus Quantum
☐ G-MYYJ	Hunt Wing Avon
☐ G-MYYK	Pegasus Quantum
☐ G-MYYL	Cyclone AX3
☐ G-MYYN	Pegasus Quantum
☐ G-MYYP	AMF Chevvron
☐ G-MYYR	TEAM Minimax
☐ G-MYYS	TEAM Minimax
☐ G-MYYU	Mainair Mercury
☐ G-MYYV	Rans S6 Coyote II (N)
☐ G-MYYW	Mainair Blade
☐ G-MYYX	Pegasus Quantum
☐ G-MYYY	Mainair Blade
☐ G-MYYZ	Medway Raven X
☐ G-MYZA	Whittaker MW-6
☐ G-MYZB	Pegasus Quantum
☐ G-MYZC	Pegasus AX3
☐ G-MYZE	TEAM Minimax
☐ G-MYZF	Pegasus AX3
☐ G-MYZG	Pegasus AX3
☐ G-MYZJ	Pegasus Quantum
☐ G-MYZK	Pegasus Quantum
☐ G-MYZL	Pegasus Quantum
☐ G-MYZM	Pegasus Quantum
☐ G-MYZN	Whittaker MW-6S
☐ G-MYZO	Medway Raven X
☐ G-MYZP	CFM Shadow DD
☐ G-MYZR	Rans S6 Coyote II (N)
☐ G-MYZV	Rans S6 Coyote II (N)
☐ G-MYZY	Pegasus Quantum
☐ G-MZAA	Mainair Blade
☐ G-MZAB	Mainair Blade
☐ G-MZAC	Quad City Challenger
☐ G-MZAE	Mainair Blade
☐ G-MZAF	Mainair Blade
☐ G-MZAG	Mainair Blade
☐ G-MZAH	Rans S6 Coyote II (N)
☐ G-MZAJ	Mainair Blade
☐ G-MZAM	Mainair Blade
☐ G-MZAN	Pegasus Quantum

☐ G-MZAP	Mainair Blade
☐ G-MZAR	Mainair Blade
☐ G-MZAS	Mainair Blade
☐ G-MZAT	Mainair Blade
☐ G-MZAU	Mainair Blade
☐ G-MZAV	Mainair Blade
☐ G-MZAW	Pegasus Quantum
☐ G-MZAX	Pegasus Quantum
☐ G-MZAY	Mainair Blade
☐ G-MZAZ	Mainair Blade
☐ G-MZBA	Mainair Blade
☐ G-MZBB	Pegasus Quantum
☐ G-MZBC	Pegasus Quantum
☐ G-MZBD	Rans S6 Coyote II (N)
☐ G-MZBF	Letov Sluka LK-2M
☐ G-MZBG	Whittaker MW-6S
☐ G-MZBH	Rans S6 Coyote II (N)
☐ G-MZBI	Pegasus Quantum
☐ G-MZBK	Letov Sluka LK-2M
☐ G-MZBL	Mainair Blade
☐ G-MZBM	Pegasus Quantum
☐ G-MZBN	CFM Shadow CD
☐ G-MZBO	Pegasus Quantum
☐ G-MZBR	Southdown Raven X
☐ G-MZBS	CFM Shadow D
☐ G-MZBT	Pegasus Quantum
☐ G-MZBU	Rans S6 Coyote II (N)
☐ G-MZBV	Rans S6 Coyote II (N)
☐ G-MZBW	Quad City Challenger
☐ G-MZBX	Whittaker MW-6S
☐ G-MZBY	Pegasus Quantum
☐ G-MZBZ	Quad City Challenger
☐ G-MZCA	Rans S6 Coyote II (N)
☐ G-MZCB	Aerial Arts Chaser S
☐ G-MZCC	Mainair Blade
☐ G-MZCD	Mainair Blade
☐ G-MZCE	Mainair Blade
☐ G-MZCF	Mainair Blade
☐ G-MZCG	Mainair Blade
☐ G-MZCH	Whittaker MW-6S
☐ G-MZCI	Pegasus Quantum
☐ G-MZCJ	Pegasus Quantum
☐ G-MZCK	AMF Chevvron
☐ G-MZCM	Mainair Blade
☐ G-MZCN	Mainair Blade
☐ G-MZCO	Mainair Mercury
☐ G-MZCP	Pegasus XL-Q
☐ G-MZCR	Pegasus Quantum
☐ G-MZCS	TEAM Minimax
☐ G-MZCT	CFM Shadow CD
☐ G-MZCU	Mainair Blade
☐ G-MZCV	Pegasus Quantum
☐ G-MZCX	Hunt Wing Avon
☐ G-MZCY	Pegasus Quantum
☐ G-MZDA	Rans S6 Coyote II (N)
☐ G-MZDB	Pegasus Quantum
☐ G-MZDC	Pegasus Quantum
☐ G-MZDD	Pegasus Quantum
☐ G-MZDE	Pegasus Quantum
☐ G-MZDF	Mainair Blade
☐ G-MZDG	Rans S6 Coyote II (N)
☐ G-MZDH	Pegasus Quantum
☐ G-MZDJ	Medway Raven X
☐ G-MZDK	Mainair Blade
☐ G-MZDL	Whittaker MW-6S
☐ G-MZDM	Rans S6 Coyote II (N)
☐ G-MZDN	Pegasus Quantum
☐ G-MZDP	AMF Chevvron
☐ G-MZDR	Rans S6 Coyote II
☐ G-MZDS	Pegasus AX3
☐ G-MZDT	Mainair Blade
☐ G-MZDU	Pegasus Quantum
☐ G-MZDV	Pegasus Quantum
☐ G-MZDX	Letov Sluka LK-2M
☐ G-MZDY	Pegasus Quantum
☐ G-MZDZ	Hunt Wing Avon
☐ G-MZEA	Quad City Challenger
☐ G-MZEB	Mainair Blade
☐ G-MZEC	Pegasus Quantum
☐ G-MZED	Mainair Blade
☐ G-MZEE	Pegasus Quantum
☐ G-MZEG	Mainair Blade
☐ G-MZEH	Pegasus Quantum
☐ G-MZEJ	Mainair Blade
☐ G-MZEK	Mainair Mercury
☐ G-MZEL	Pegasus AX3
☐ G-MZEM	Pegasus Quantum
☐ G-MZEN	Rans S6 Coyote II (N)
☐ G-MZEO	Rans S6 Coyote II
☐ G-MZEP	Mainair Rapier
☐ G-MZER	Pegasus AX2000
☐ G-MZES	Letov Sluka LK-2M
☐ G-MZEU	Rans S6 Coyote II (N)
☐ G-MZEV	Mainair Rapier
☐ G-MZEW	Mainair Blade
☐ G-MZEX	Pegasus Quantum
☐ G-MZEY	Bantam B.22S
☐ G-MZEZ	Pegasus Quantum
☐ G-MZFA	Pegasus AX2000
☐ G-MZFB	Mainair Blade
☐ G-MZFC	Letov Sluka LK-2M
☐ G-MZFD	Mainair Rapier
☐ G-MZFE	Hunt Wing Avon
☐ G-MZFF	Hunt Wing Avon
☐ G-MZFG	Pegasus Quantum
☐ G-MZFH	AMF Chevvron
☐ G-MZFI	Lorimer Iolaire
☐ G-MZFK	Whittaker MW-6
☐ G-MZFL	Rans S6 Coyote II (N)
☐ G-MZFM	Pegasus Quantum
☐ G-MZFN	Rans S6 Coyote II
☐ G-MZFO	Thruster T600N
☐ G-MZFR	Thruster T600N
☐ G-MZFS	Mainair Blade
☐ G-MZFT	Pegasus Quantum
☐ G-MZFU	Thruster T600N
☐ G-MZFV	Pegasus Quantum
☐ G-MZFX	Pegasus AX2000
☐ G-MZFY	Rans S6 Coyote II (N)
☐ G-MZFZ	Mainair Blade
☐ G-MZGA	Pegasus AX2000
☐ G-MZGB	Pegasus AX2000
☐ G-MZGC	Pegasus AX2000
☐ G-MZGD	Rans S5 Coyote
☐ G-MZGF	Letov Sluka LK-2M
☐ G-MZGG	Pegasus Quantum
☐ G-MZGH	Hunt Wing Avon
☐ G-MZGI	Mainair Blade
☐ G-MZGJ	Kolb Twinstar Mk.3
☐ G-MZGK	Pegasus Quantum
☐ G-MZGL	Mainair Rapier
☐ G-MZGM	Pegasus AX2000
☐ G-MZGN	Pegasus Quantum
☐ G-MZGO	Pegasus Quantum
☐ G-MZGP	Pegasus AX2000
☐ G-MZGS	CFM Shadow DD
☐ G-MZGT	Tiger Light
☐ G-MZGU	Arrowflight Hawk
☐ G-MZGV	Pegasus Quantum
☐ G-MZGW	Mainair Blade
☐ G-MZGX	Thruster T600N
☐ G-MZGY	Thruster T600N
☐ G-MZGZ	Thruster T600N
☐ G-MZHA	Thruster T600T
☐ G-MZHB	Mainair Blade
☐ G-MZHC	Thruster T600T
☐ G-MZHD	Thruster T600T
☐ G-MZHE	Thruster T600N
☐ G-MZHF	Thruster T600N
☐ G-MZHG	Whittaker MW-6T
☐ G-MZHI	Pegasus Quantum
☐ G-MZHJ	Mainair Rapier
☐ G-MZHK	Pegasus Quantum
☐ G-MZHL	Mainair Rapier
☐ G-MZHM	TEAM Himax
☐ G-MZHN	Pegasus Quantum
☐ G-MZHO	Quad City Challenger
☐ G-MZHP	Pegasus Quantum
☐ G-MZHR	Pegasus AX2000
☐ G-MZHS	Thruster T600T
☐ G-MZHT	Whittaker MW-6
☐ G-MZHU	Thruster T600T
☐ G-MZHV	Thruster T600T
☐ G-MZHW	Thruster T600N
☐ G-MZHY	Thruster T600N
☐ G-MZIA	TEAM Himax
☐ G-MZIB	Pegasus Quantum
☐ G-MZIC	Pegasus Quantum
☐ G-MZID	Whittaker MW-6
☐ G-MZIE	Pegasus Quantum
☐ G-MZIF	Pegasus Quantum
☐ G-MZII	TEAM Minimax
☐ G-MZIJ	Pegasus Quantum
☐ G-MZIK	Pegasus Quantum
☐ G-MZIL	Mainair Rapier
☐ G-MZIM	Mainair Rapier
☐ G-MZIR	Mainair Blade
☐ G-MZIS	Mainair Blade
☐ G-MZIT	Mainair Blade
☐ G-MZIU	Pegasus Quantum
☐ G-MZIV	Pegasus AX2000
☐ G-MZIW	Mainair Blade
☐ G-MZIX	Mignet HM-1000
☐ G-MZIY	Rans S6 Coyote II (N)
☐ G-MZIZ	Renegade Spirit UK
☐ G-MZJA	Aviasud Mistral
☐ G-MZJB	Aviasud Mistral
☐ G-MZJD	Mainair Blade
☐ G-MZJE	Mainair Blade
☐ G-MZJF	Pegasus AX2000
☐ G-MZJG	Pegasus Quantum
☐ G-MZJH	Pegasus Quantum
☐ G-MZJI	Rans S6 Coyote II (N)
☐ G-MZJJ	Meridian Maverick
☐ G-MZJK	Mainair Blade
☐ G-MZJL	Pegasus AX2000
☐ G-MZJM	Rans S6 Coyote II (N)
☐ G-MZJN	Pegasus Quantum
☐ G-MZJO	Pegasus Quantum
☐ G-MZJP	Whittaker MW-6S
☐ G-MZJR	Pegasus AX2000
☐ G-MZJS	Meridian Maverick
☐ G-MZJT	Pegasus Quantum
☐ G-MZJV	Mainair Blade
☐ G-MZJW	Pegasus Quantum
☐ G-MZJX	Mainair Blade
☐ G-MZJY	Pegasus Quantum
☐ G-MZJZ	Mainair Blade
☐ G-MZKA	Pegasus Quantum
☐ G-MZKC	Pegasus AX2000
☐ G-MZKD	Pegasus Quantum
☐ G-MZKE	Rans S6 Coyote II
☐ G-MZKF	Pegasus Quantum
☐ G-MZKG	Mainair Blade
☐ G-MZKH	CFM Shadow DD
☐ G-MZKI	Mainair Rapier
☐ G-MZKJ	Mainair Blade
☐ G-MZKK	Mainair Blade
☐ G-MZKL	Pegasus Quantum

☐ G-MZKM	Mainair Blade	
☐ G-MZKN	Mainair Rapier	
☐ G-MZKR	Thruster T600N	
☐ G-MZKS	Thruster T600F	
☐ G-MZKT	Thruster T600T	
☐ G-MZKU	Thruster T600T	
☐ G-MZKV	Mainair Blade	
☐ G-MZKW	Quad City Challenger	
☐ G-MZKX	Pegasus Quantum	
☐ G-MZKY	Pegasus Quantum	
☐ G-MZKZ	Mainair Blade	
☐ G-MZLA	Pegasus Quantum	
☐ G-MZLC	Mainair Blade	
☐ G-MZLD	Pegasus Quantum	
☐ G-MZLE	Meridian Maverick	
☐ G-MZLF	Pegasus Quantum	
☐ G-MZLG	Rans S6 Coyote II (N)	
☐ G-MZLH	Pegasus Quantum	
☐ G-MZLI	Mignet HM.1000	
☐ G-MZLJ	Pegasus Quantum	
☐ G-MZLK	Tripacer Typhoon	
☐ G-MZLL	Rans S6 Coyote II	
☐ G-MZLM	Pegasus AX2000	
☐ G-MZLN	Pegasus Quantum	
☐ G-MZLP	CFM Shadow D	
☐ G-MZLR	Pegasus XL-Q	
☐ G-MZLS	Pegasus AX2000	
☐ G-MZLT	Pegasus Quantum	
☐ G-MZLU	Pegasus AX2000	
☐ G-MZLV	Pegasus Quantum	
☐ G-MZLW	Pegasus Quantum	
☐ G-MZLX	Bantam B.22S	
☐ G-MZLY	Letov Sluka LK-2M	
☐ G-MZLZ	Mainair Blade	
☐ G-MZMA	Pegasus Quasar	
☐ G-MZMB	Mainair Blade	
☐ G-MZMC	Pegasus Quantum	
☐ G-MZMD	Mainair Blade	
☐ G-MZME	Hybred 44XLR	
☐ G-MZMF	Pegasus Quantum	
☐ G-MZMG	Pegasus Quantum	
☐ G-MZMH	Pegasus Quantum	
☐ G-MZMJ	Mainair Blade	
☐ G-MZMK	AMF Chevvron	
☐ G-MZML	Mainair Blade	
☐ G-MZMM	Mainair Blade	
☐ G-MZMN	Pegasus Quantum	
☐ G-MZMO	TEAM Minimax	
☐ G-MZMP	Mainair Blade	
☐ G-MZMS	Rans S6 Coyote II (N)	
☐ G-MZMT	Pegasus Quantum	
☐ G-MZMU	Rans S6 Coyote II	
☐ G-MZMV	Mainair Blade	
☐ G-MZMW	Mignet HM-1000	
☐ G-MZMX	Pegasus AX2000	
☐ G-MZMY	Mainair Blade	
☐ G-MZMZ	Mainair Blade	
☐ G-MZNA	Quad City Challenger	
☐ G-MZNB	Pegasus Quantum	
☐ G-MZNC	Mainair Blade	
☐ G-MZND	Mainair Rapier	
☐ G-MZNE	Whittaker MW-6	
☐ G-MZNG	Pegasus Quantum	
☐ G-MZNH	CFM Shadow DD	
☐ G-MZNI	Mainair Blade	
☐ G-MZNJ	Mainair Blade	
☐ G-MZNL	Mainair Blade	
☐ G-MZNM	TEAM Minimax	
☐ G-MZNN	TEAM Minimax	
☐ G-MZNO	Mainair Blade	
☐ G-MZNP	Pegasus Quantum	
☐ G-MZNR	Pegasus Quantum	
☐ G-MZNS	Pegasus Quantum	

☐ G-MZNT	Pegasus Quantum	
☐ G-MZNU	Mainair Rapier	
☐ G-MZNV	Rans S6 Coyote II (N)	
☐ G-MZNX	Thruster T600N	
☐ G-MZNY	Thruster T600N	
☐ G-MZNZ	Letov Sluka LK-2M	
☐ G-MZOC	Mainair Blade	
☐ G-MZOD	Pegasus Quantum	
☐ G-MZOE	Pegasus AX2000	
☐ G-MZOF	Mainair Blade	
☐ G-MZOG	Pegasus Quantum	
☐ G-MZOH	Whittaker MW-5D	
☐ G-MZOI	Letov Sluka LK-2M	
☐ G-MZOJ	Pegasus Quantum	
☐ G-MZOK	Whittaker MW-6	
☐ G-MZOM	CFM Shadow DD	
☐ G-MZON	Mainair Rapier	
☐ G-MZOP	Mainair Blade	
☐ G-MZOR	Mainair Blade	
☐ G-MZOS	Pegasus Quantum	
☐ G-MZOV	Pegasus Quantum	
☐ G-MZOW	Pegasus Quantum	
☐ G-MZOX	Letov Sluka LK-2M	
☐ G-MZOY	TEAM Minimax	
☐ G-MZOZ	Rans S6 Coyote II (N)	
☐ G-MZPB	Mignet HM-1000	
☐ G-MZPD	Pegasus Quantum	
☐ G-MZPH	Mainair Blade	
☐ G-MZPJ	TEAM Minimax	
☐ G-MZPW	Pegasus Quasar	
☐ G-MZRC	Pegasus Quantum	
☐ G-MZRH	Pegasus Quantum	
☐ G-MZRM	Pegasus Quantum	
☐ G-MZRS	CFM Shadow CD	
☐ G-MZSC	Pegasus Quantum	
☐ G-MZSD	Mainair Blade	
☐ G-MZSM	Mainair Blade	
☐ G-MZTA	Mignet HM-1000	
☐ G-MZTS	Aerial Arts Chaser S	
☐ G-MZUB	Rans S6 Coyote II (N)	
☐ G-MZZT	Kolb Twinstar Mk.3	
☐ G-MZZY	Mainair Blade	
☐ G-NAAA	MBB Bo.105DBS/4	
☐ G-NAAB	MBB Bo.105DBS/4	
☐ G-NACA	Norman Freelance	
☐ G-NACI	Norman Freelance	
☐ G-NADS	TEAM Minimax	
☐ G-NANI	Robinson R44	
☐ G-NAPO	Pegasus Quantum	
☐ G-NAPP	Van's RV-7	
☐ G-NARG	Tanarg iXess 15-912S	
☐ G-NARO	Cassutt Racer	
☐ G-NATT	Rockwell 114A	
☐ G-NATX	Cameron O-65	
☐ G-NATY	Folland Gnat T.1	
☐ G-NBDD	Robin DR.400-180 Regent	
☐ G-NCFC	Piper PA-38-112 Tomahawk	
☐ G-NCFE	Piper PA-38-112 Tomahawk	
☐ G-NCUB	Piper J-3C-65 Cub	
☐ G-NDAA	MBB Bo.105DBS/4	
☐ G-NDGC	Grob 109	
☐ G-NDOL	Europa	
☐ G-NDOT	Thruster T600N	
☐ G-NDPA	Ikarus C42 Cyclone	
☐ G-NEAL	Piper PA-32-260	
☐ G-NEAT	Europa	
☐ G-NEAU	Eurocopter EC135T2	
☐ G-NEEL	Rotorway Exec 90	
☐ G-NEEN	Hughes 500N	
☐ G-NEGG	Acrosport 2	
☐ G-NEGS	Thunder Ax7-77	
☐ G-NEIL	Thunder Ax3	
☐ G-NELI	Piper PA-28R-180	

☐ G-NELY	MD Helicopters MD.600N	
☐ G-NEMO	Raj Hamsa X'Air	
☐ G-NEON	Piper PA-32-300	
☐ G-NERC	Piper PA-31-350 Chieftain	
☐ G-NESA	Europa XS	
☐ G-NESE	Tecnam P2002-JF	
☐ G-NESH	Robinson R44	
☐ G-NEST	Christen Eagle II	
☐ G-NESV	Eurocopter EC135T1	
☐ G-NESW	Piper PA-34-220T Seneca	
☐ G-NESY	Piper PA-18	
☐ G-NETB	Cirrus SR22	
☐ G-NETR	Aerospatiale AS.355F1	
☐ G-NETY	Piper PA-18-150	
☐ G-NEWR	Piper PA-31-350 Chieftain	
☐ G-NEWT	Beech 35A Bonanza	
☐ G-NEWZ	Bell 206B Jet Ranger	
☐ G-NFLA	BAe Jetstream 31	
☐ G-NFNF	Robin DR.400-180 Regent	
☐ G-NGRM	Spezio Tuholer	
☐ G-NHRH	Piper PA-28-140 Cherokee	
☐ G-NHRJ	Europa XS	
☐ G-NICC	EV-97 Eurostar	
☐ G-NICI	Robinson R44	
☐ G-NICK	Piper PA-18-95	
☐ G-NIDG	EV-97 Eurostar	
☐ G-NIEN	Van's RV-9A	
☐ G-NIFE	Stampe SV-4A	
☐ G-NIGC	Jabiru UL	
☐ G-NIGE	Luscombe 8E Silvaire	
☐ G-NIGL	Europa	
☐ G-NIGS	Thunder Ax7-65	
☐ G-NIJM	Piper PA-28R-180	
☐ G-NIKE	Piper PA-28-181 Archer	
☐ G-NIKK	Diamond Katana	
☐ G-NIKO	Airbus A321-211	
☐ G-NIMA	Kubicek BB30Z	
☐ G-NINA	Piper PA-28-161 Warrior	
☐ G-NINB	Piper PA-28-180 Cherokee	
☐ G-NINC	Piper PA-28-180 Cherokee	
☐ G-NINE	Murphy Renegade	
☐ G-NIOG	Robinson R44	
☐ G-NIOS	Piper PA-32R-301 SP	
☐ G-NIPA	Slingsby Nipper T66	
☐ G-NIPP	Slingsby Nipper T66	
☐ G-NIPR	Slingsby Nipper T66	
☐ G-NITA	Piper PA-28-180 Cherokee	
☐ G-NIVA	Eurocopter EC155B1	
☐ G-NJAG	Cessna 207	
☐ G-NJBA	Rotorway Exec 162F	
☐ G-NJIM	Piper PA-32R-301T	
☐ G-NJPW	P & M Quik GT450	
☐ G-NJSH	Robinson R22B	
☐ G-NJSP	Jabiru J430	
☐ G-NJTC	Aeroprakt A22 Foxbat	
☐ G-NLEE	Cessna 182Q Skylane	
☐ G-NLYB	Cameron N-105	
☐ G-NMAK	Airbus A319CJ	
☐ G-NMBG	Jabiru J400	
☐ G-NMEN	Aerospatiale AS.355N	
☐ G-NMID	Eurocopter EC135T2	
☐ G-NMOS	Cameron C-80	
☐ G-NNAC	Piper PA-18-135	
☐ G-NOBI	Spezio Tuholer Sport	
☐ G-NOCK	Reims FR182RG Skylane	
☐ G-NODE	Grumman AA-5B Tiger	
☐ G-NODY	American General AG-5B	
☐ G-NOIR	Bell 222	
☐ G-NOIZ	Yakovlev Yak-55M	
☐ G-NOMO	Cameron O-31	
☐ G-NONE	Dyn'Aero MCR-01	
☐ G-NONI	Grumman AA-5 Traveler	
☐ G-NOOK	Mainair Blade	

☐ G-NOOR	Rockwell 114B	
☐ G-NORA	Ikarus C42 Cyclone	
☐ G-NORB	Saturne A110K	
☐ G-NORD	Nord 854	
☐ G-NORT	Robinson R22	
☐ G-NOSE	Cessna 402B	
☐ G-NOSY	Robinson R44	
☐ G-NOTE	Piper PA-28-181 Archer	
☐ G-NOTS	Best Off Sky Ranger	
☐ G-NOTT	Nott ULD/2	
☐ G-NOTY	Westland Scout	
☐ G-NOWW	Mainair Blade	
☐ G-NPKJ	Van's RV-6	
☐ G-NPPL	Ikarus C42 Cyclone	
☐ G-NRDC	Norman NDN-6	
☐ G-NROY	Piper PA-32RT-300	
☐ G-NRRA	SIAI-Marchetti SF.260W	
☐ G-NRSC	Piper PA-23-250 Aztec E	
☐ G-NRYL	Mooney M.20R	
☐ G-NSBB	Ikarus C42 Cyclone	
☐ G-NSEW	Robinson R44	
☐ G-NSOF	Robin HR.200-120B	
☐ G-NSTG	Reims F150F	
☐ G-NSUK	Piper PA-34-220T Seneca	
☐ G-NTWK	Aerospatiale AS.355F2	
☐ G-NULA	Flight Design CT2K	
☐ G-NUTA	Christen Eagle II	
☐ G-NUTS	Cameron Mr Peanut SS	
☐ G-NUTT	P & M Quik	
☐ G-NUTY	Aerospatiale AS.350D	
☐ G-NVBF	Lindstrand LBL-210A	
☐ G-NVSA	DHC-8-311A	
☐ G-NVSB	DHC-8-311	
☐ G-NWAA	Eurocopter EC135 T2	
☐ G-NWAR	Agusta A109S Grand	
☐ G-NWPR	Cameron N-77	
☐ G-NWPS	Eurocopter EC135T1	
☐ G-NXUS	Nexus Mustang	
☐ G-NYLE	Robinson R44	
☐ G-NYMF	Piper PA-25-235 Pawnee	
☐ G-NYZS	Cessna 182G Skylane	
☐ G-NZGL	Cameron O-105	
☐ G-NZSS	Boeing Stearman E75	
☐ G-OAAA	Piper PA-28-161 Warrior	
☐ G-OABB	Jodel D.150 Mascaret	
☐ G-OABC	Colt 69A	
☐ G-OABO	Enstrom F-28A	
☐ G-OABR	American General AG-5B	
☐ G-OACA	Piper PA-44-180 Seminole	
☐ G-OACE	Valentin Taifun 17E	
☐ G-OACF	Robin DR.400-180 Regent	
☐ G-OACG	Piper PA-34-200T Seneca	
☐ G-OACI	MS.893E Rallye 180GT	
☐ G-OACP	DHC-1 Chipmunk	
☐ G-OADY	Beech 76 Duchess	
☐ G-OAER	Lindstrand LBL-105A	
☐ G-OAFT	Cessna 152	
☐ G-OAGI	FLS Sprint 160	
☐ G-OAHC	Beech F33C Bonanza	
☐ G-OAJB	Pegasus AX2000	
☐ G-OAJC	Robinson R44	
☐ G-OAJL	Ikarus C42 Cyclone	
☐ G-OAJS	Piper PA-39-160CR	
☐ G-OAKR	Cessna 172S Skyhawk	
☐ G-OAKW	Cessna 208B	
☐ G-OALD	SOCATA TB-20 Trinidad	
☐ G-OALH	Tecnam P92 Echo	
☐ G-OAMF	Pegasus Quantum	
☐ G-OAMG	Bell 206B Jet Ranger	
☐ G-OAMI	Bell 206B Jet Ranger	
☐ G-OAML	Cameron AML-105	
☐ G-OAMP	Reims F177RG	
☐ G-OANN	Zenair CH.601 HDS	
☐ G-OAPE	Cessna T303 Crusader	
☐ G-OAPR	Brantly B.2B	
☐ G-OAPW	Glaser-Dirks DG-400	
☐ G-OARA	Piper PA-28R-201T	
☐ G-OARC	Piper PA-28RT-201	
☐ G-OARG	Cameron C-80	
☐ G-OARI	Piper PA-28R-201	
☐ G-OARO	Piper PA-28R-201	
☐ G-OART	Piper PA-23-250 Aztec D	
☐ G-OARU	Piper PA-28R-201	
☐ G-OARV	ARV Super 2	
☐ G-OASH	Robinson R22B	
☐ G-OASJ	Thruster T600N	
☐ G-OASP	Aerospatiale AS.355F2	
☐ G-OASW	Schleicher ASW 27B	
☐ G-OATE	Pegasus Quantum	
☐ G-OATV	Cameron V-77	
☐ G-OAVA	Robinson R22	
☐ G-OAVB	Boeing 757-23A	
☐ G-OAWD	Aerospatiale AS.350B	
☐ G-OAWS	Cameron Colt 77A	
☐ G-OBAK	Piper PA-28R-201T	
☐ G-OBAL	Mooney M.20J	
☐ G-OBAM	Bell 206B Jet Ranger	
☐ G-OBAN	Jodel D.140B	
☐ G-OBAX	Thruster T600N	
☐ G-OBAZ	Best Off Skyranger	
☐ G-OBBC	Colt 90A	
☐ G-OBBO	Cessna 182S Skylane	
☐ G-OBBY	Robinson R44	
☐ G-OBCC	Cessna 560 Citation Ultra	
☐ G-OBDA	Diamond Katana	
☐ G-OBDM	Europa XS	
☐ G-OBDN	Piper PA-28-161 Warrior	
☐ G-OBEE	Stearman A75N-1	
☐ G-OBEI	SOCATA TB-200XL Tobago	
☐ G-OBEK	Agusta 109C	
☐ G-OBEN	Cessna 152	
☐ G-OBET	Sky 77-24	
☐ G-OBEV	Europa	
☐ G-OBFC	Piper PA-28-161 Warrior	
☐ G-OBFE	Sky 120-24	
☐ G-OBFS	Piper PA-28-161 Warrior	
☐ G-OBGC	SOCATA TB-20 Trinidad	
☐ G-OBHD	Short SD.360-200	
☐ G-OBIB	Colt 120A	
☐ G-OBIL	Robinson R22B	
☐ G-OBIO	Robinson R22B	
☐ G-OBJB	Lindstrand LBL-90A	
☐ G-OBJH	Colt 77A	
☐ G-OBJP	Pegasus Quantum	
☐ G-OBJT	Europa	
☐ G-OBLC	Beech 76 Duchess	
☐ G-OBLU	Cameron H-34	
☐ G-OBMI	Mainair Blade	
☐ G-OBMP	Boeing 737-3Q8	
☐ G-OBMS	Reims F172N	
☐ G-OBMW	Grumman AA-5 Traveler	
☐ G-OBNA	Piper PA-34-220T Seneca	
☐ G-OBNC	BN2B Islander	
☐ G-OBNW	Piper PA-31-350 Chieftain	
☐ G-OBRA	Cameron Z-315	
☐ G-OBRY	Cameron N-180	
☐ G-OBSM	Robinson R44	
☐ G-OBTS	Cameron C-80	
☐ G-OBUN	Cameron A-250	
☐ G-OBUU	Comper Swift Replica	
☐ G-OBUY	Colt 69A	
☐ G-OBWR	BAe ATP	
☐ G-OBYB	Boeing 767-304ER	
☐ G-OBYD	Boeing 767-304ER	
☐ G-OBYE	Boeing 767-304ER	
☐ G-OBYF	Boeing 767-304ER	
☐ G-OBYG	Boeing 767-304ER	
☐ G-OBYH	Boeing 767-304ER	
☐ G-OBYI	Boeing 767-304ER	
☐ G-OBYJ	Boeing 767-304ER	
☐ G-OBYT	Agusta Bell 206A	
☐ G-OCAD	Sequoia F.8L Falco	
☐ G-OCAM	Grumman AA-5A Cheetah	
☐ G-OCAR	Colt 77A	
☐ G-OCBI	Schweizer 269C-1	
☐ G-OCBS	Lindstrand LBL-210A	
☐ G-OCBT	Yakovlev Yak-52	
☐ G-OCCD	Diamond DA 40D Star	
☐ G-OCCE	Diamond DA 40D Star	
☐ G-OCCF	Diamond DA.40D Star	
☐ G-OCCG	Diamond DA.40D Star	
☐ G-OCCH	Diamond DA.40D Star	
☐ G-OCCK	Diamond DA.40D Star	
☐ G-OCCL	Diamond DA.40D Star	
☐ G-OCCM	Diamond DA.40D Star	
☐ G-OCCN	Diamond DA.40D Star	
☐ G-OCCO	Diamond DA.40D Star	
☐ G-OCCP	Diamond DA.40D Star	
☐ G-OCCR	Diamond DA.40D Star	
☐ G-OCCS	Diamond DA.40D Star	
☐ G-OCCT	Diamond DA.40D Star	
☐ G-OCCU	Diamond DA.40D Star	
☐ G-OCCW	Diamond DA42 Twin Star	
☐ G-OCCX	Diamond DA42 Twin Star	
☐ G-OCCY	Diamond DA42 Twin Star	
☐ G-OCCZ	Diamond DA42 Twin Star	
☐ G-OCDP	Flight Design CTSW	
☐ G-OCDW	Jabiru UL	
☐ G-OCFC	Robin R.2160	
☐ G-OCFD	Bell 206B Jet Ranger	
☐ G-OCFM	Piper PA-34-200 Seneca	
☐ G-OCHM	Robinson R44	
☐ G-OCIT	Cessna 208B	
☐ G-OCJK	Schweizer 269C	
☐ G-OCMM	Agusta 109A	
☐ G-OCMT	EV-97 Eurostar	
☐ G-OCON	Robinson R44	
☐ G-OCOV	Robinson R22B	
☐ G-OCPC	Reims FA152 Aerobat	
☐ G-OCRI	Colomban MC-15 Cri-Cri	
☐ G-OCSC	CL604 Challenger	
☐ G-OCSD	CL604 Challenger	
☐ G-OCST	Agusta Bell 206B	
☐ G-OCTI	Piper PA-32-260	
☐ G-OCTU	Piper PA-28-161 Warrior	
☐ G-OCUB	Piper J-3C-65 Cub	
☐ G-ODAC	Reims F152	
☐ G-ODAD	Colt 77A	
☐ G-ODAF	Lindstrand LBL-105A	
☐ G-ODAK	Piper PA-28-236 Dakota	
☐ G-ODAT	Aero L.29	
☐ G-ODAV	EV-97 Eurostar	
☐ G-ODAY	Cameron N-56	
☐ G-ODBN	Lindstrand Flowers SS	
☐ G-ODCC	Bell 206L Long Ranger	
☐ G-ODCS	Robinson R22B	
☐ G-ODDS	Pitts S-2A Special	
☐ G-ODDY	Lindstrand LBL-105A	
☐ G-ODEN	Piper PA-28-161 Warrior	
☐ G-ODGS	Jabiru UL	
☐ G-ODHB	Robinson R44	
☐ G-ODHG	Robinson R44	
☐ G-ODIN	Mudry CAP.10B	
☐ G-ODJB	Robinson R22B	
☐ G-ODJD	Raj Hamsa X'Air	
☐ G-ODJF	Lindstrand LBL 90B	
☐ G-ODJG	Europa	
☐ G-ODJH	Mooney M.20C	
☐ G-ODLY	Cessna 310J	

Registration	Type	Registration	Type	Registration	Type
G-ODMC	Aerospatiale AS.350B1	G-OGOS	Everett Gyroplane	G-OJRH	Robinson R44
G-ODMG	Aerospatiale AS.350B2	G-OGSA	Jabiru UL	G-OJRM	Cessna T182T
G-ODNH	Schweizer 269C-1	G-OGSS	Lindstrand LBL-120A	G-OJSA	BAe Jetstream 31
G-ODOC	Robinson R44	G-OGTS	Air Command 532 Elite	G-OJSH	Thruster T600N
G-ODOG	Piper PA-28R-200	G-OHAC	Reims F182Q Skylane	G-OJVA	Van's RV-6
G-ODOT	Robinson R22B	G-OHAL	Pietenpol Aircamper	G-OJVH	Reims F150H
G-ODPJ	VPM M16 Tandem	G-OHCP	Aerospatiale AS.355F1	G-OJVL	Van's RV-6
G-ODRY	EV-97 Eurostar	G-OHGC	Scheibe SF25C Falke	G-OJWS	Piper PA-28-161 Warrior
G-ODSK	Boeing 737-36Q	G-OHHI	Bell 206L Long Ranger	G-OKAG	Piper PA-28R-180
G-ODTW	Europa	G-OHIO	Dyn'Aero MCR-01	G-OKBT	Colt 25A
G-ODUD	Piper PA-28-181 Archer	G-OHKS	Pegasus Quantum	G-OKCC	Cameron N-90
G-ODVB	CFM Shadow DD	G-OHLI	Robinson R44	G-OKCP	Lindstrand Battery SS
G-OEAC	Mooney M.20J	G-OHMS	Aerospatiale AS.355F	G-OKED	Cessna 150L
G-OEAT	Robinson R22B	G-OHOV	Rotorway Exec 162F	G-OKEM	P & M Quik
G-OEBJ	Cessna 525	G-OHSA	Cameron N-77	G-OKEN	Piper PA-28-201T
G-OECM	Rockwell 114B	G-OHSL	Robinson R22B	G-OKER	Van's RV-7
G-OEDB	Piper PA-38-112 Tomahawk	G-OHVA	Mainair Blade	G-OKEV	Europa
G-OEDP	Cameron N-77	G-OHVR	Robinson R44	G-OKEY	Robinson R22B
G-OEGG	Cameron Egg-65 SS	G-OHWV	Raj Hamsa X'Air	G-OKIM	Best Off Sky Ranger
G-OEGL	Christen Eagle II	G-OHYE	Thruster T600N	G-OKIS	Tri-R Kis
G-OEJC	Robinson R44	G-OIBM	Rockwell 114	G-OKJW	Boeing 737-8Q8
G-OELD	Pegasus Quantum	G-OIBO	Piper PA-28-180 Cherokee	G-OKMA	Tri-R Kis
G-OELZ	Wassmer WA.52	G-OICO	Lindstrand LBL 42A	G-OKPW	Tri-R Kis
G-OEMT	MBB BK.117C-1	G-OIDW	Reims F150G	G-OKYA	Cameron V-77
G-OERR	Lindstrand LBL-60A	G-OIFM	Cameron Dude SS	G-OKYM	Piper PA-28-140 Cherokee
G-OERS	Cessna 172N Skyhawk	G-OIHC	Piper PA-32R-301	G-OLAU	Robinson R22B
G-OERX	Cameron O-65	G-OIIO	Robinson R22	G-OLAW	Lindstrand LBL-25A
G-OESY	Easy Raider J2.2(1)	G-OIMC	Cessna 152	G-OLCP	Aerospatiale AS.355N
G-OETI	Bell 206B Jet Ranger	G-OINK	Piper J-3C-65 Cub	G-OLDD	BAe 125-800B
G-OETV	Piper PA-31-350 Chieftain	G-OINV	BAe 146-300	G-OLDG	Cessna T182T
G-OEVA	Piper PA-32-260	G-OIOZ	Thunder Ax9-120	G-OLDH	Aerospatiale Gazelle
G-OEWD	Beech 390 Premier 1	G-OISO	Reims FRA150L Aerobat	G-OLDK	Learjet 45
G-OEYE	Rans S10 Sakota	G-OITV	Enstrom 280C	G-OLDM	Pegasus Quantum
G-OEZI	Easy Raider J2.2	G-OIZI	Europa XS	G-OLDN	Bell 206L Long Ranger
G-OEZY	Europa	G-OJAB	Jabiru SK	G-OLDP	P & M Quik
G-OFAA	Cameron Z-105	G-OJAC	Mooney M.20J	G-OLDT	Learjet 45
G-OFAS	Robinson R22B	G-OJAE	Hughes 269C	G-OLDW	Learjet 45XR
G-OFBJ	Thunder Ax7-77A	G-OJAG	Cessna 172S Skyhawk	G-OLEE	Reims F152
G-OFBU	Ikarus C42 Cyclone	G-OJAN	Robinson R22	G-OLEM	Jodel D.18
G-OFCH	Agusta Bell 206B	G-OJAS	Auster J1/U Workmaster	G-OLEO	Thunder Ax10-210
G-OFCM	Reims F172L	G-OJAV	BN2A-III Trislander	G-OLEZ	Piper J-3C
G-OFER	Piper PA-18-150	G-OJAZ	Robinson R44	G-OLFA	Aerospatiale AS.350B3
G-OFFA	Pietenpol Aircamper	G-OJBB	Enstrom 280FX	G-OLFB	Pegasus Quantum
G-OFFO	Extra EA.300/L	G-OJBM	Cameron N-90	G-OLFC	Piper PA-38-112 Tomahawk
G-OFIL	Robinson R44	G-OJBS	Cameron N-105	G-OLFO	Robinson R44
G-OFIT	SOCATA TB-10 Tobago	G-OJBW	Lindstrand Bottle SS	G-OLFT	Rockwell 114
G-OFLY	Cessna T210M	G-OJCW	Piper PA-32RT-300	G-OLGA	CFM Shadow SA-II
G-OFOA	BAe 146-100	G-OJDA	EAA Acrosport	G-OLJT	Gemini Flash 2A
G-OFOM	BAe 146-100	G-OJDC	Thunder Ax7-77	G-OLLI	Cameron Golly SS
G-OFOX	Denney Kitfox	G-OJDS	Ikarus C42 Cyclone	G-OLLS	Cessna T206H F/P
G-OFRB	Everett Gyroplane	G-OJEG	Airbus A321-231	G-OLMA	Partenavia P.68B
G-OFRY	Cessna 152	G-OJEH	Piper PA-28-181 Archer	G-OLNT	Aerospatiale AS365N1
G-OFST	Bell 206L Long Ranger	G-OJEN	Cameron V-77	G-OLOW	Robinson R44
G-OFTI	Piper PA-28-140 Cherokee	G-OJGT	Maule M-5-235C	G-OLRT	Robinson R22B
G-OGAN	Europa	G-OJHB	Colt Ice Cream SS	G-OLSF	Piper PA-28-161 Warrior
G-OGAR	PZL Ogar SZD45A	G-OJHL	Europa	G-OLTT	Pilatus PC-12/45
G-OGAY	Kubicek BB26	G-OJIB	Boeing 757-23A	G-OMAF	Dornier Do.228-200
G-OGAZ	Aerospatiale Gazelle	G-OJIL	Piper PA-31-350 Chieftain	G-OMAG	Cessna 182B Skylane
G-OGBD	Boeing 737-3L9	G-OJIM	Piper PA-28R-201T	G-OMAL	Thruster T600N
G-OGBE	Boeing 737-3L9	G-OJJB	Mooney M.20K	G-OMAP	Rockwell 685
G-OGCE	Bell 206L Long Ranger	G-OJJF	Druine Turbulent	G-OMAT	Piper PA-28-140 Cherokee
G-OGEA	Aerospatiale Gazelle	G-OJKM	Rans S7 Courier	G-OMAX	Brantly B.2B
G-OGEM	Piper PA-28-181 Archer	G-OJLH	TEAM Minimax	G-OMCC	Aerospatiale AS.350B
G-OGES	Enstrom 280FX	G-OJMB	Airbus A330-243	G-OMCD	Robinson R44
G-OGET	Piper PA-39-160CR	G-OJMC	Airbus A330-243	G-OMDB	Van's RV-6A
G-OGGY	Aviat A-1B Husky	G-OJMF	Enstrom 280FX	G-OMDD	Cameron Ax8-90
G-OGIL	Short SD.330-100	G-OJMR	Airbus A300B4-605R	G-OMDG	Diamond H.36
G-OGJM	Cameron C-80	G-OJMS	Cameron Z-90	G-OMDH	Hughes 369EE
G-OGJP	Hughes 369E	G-OJMW	Cessna 550 Citation II	G-OMDR	Agusta Bell 206B
G-OGJS	Puffer Cozy	G-OJNB	Lindstrand LBL-21A	G-OMEL	Robinson R44
G-OGKB	Aeromere F.8L Falco	G-OJOD	Jodel D.18	G-OMEN	Cameron Z-90
G-OGOA	Aerospatiale AS.350B	G-OJON	Taylor Titch	G-OMEX	Zenair CH.701 STOL
G-OGOH	Robinson R22B	G-OJPS	Bell 206B Jet Ranger	G-OMEZ	Zenair CH.601 HDS

G-OMFG	Cameron A-120	
G-OMGH	Robinson R44	
G-OMGI	Beech 200 Super King Air	
G-OMHC	Piper PA-28RT-201	
G-OMHD	Canberra PR.9	
G-OMHI	Mills MH-1	
G-OMHP	Jabiru UL	
G-OMIA	MS.893A Commodore	
G-OMIK	Europa	
G-OMIW	P & M Quik	
G-OMJC	Beech 390 Premier 1	
G-OMJT	Rutan LongEz	
G-OMKA	Robinson R44	
G-OMLC	EAA Acrosport	
G-OMLS	Bell 206B Jet Ranger	
G-OMMG	Robinson R22B	
G-OMMM	Colt 90A	
G-OMNI	Piper PA-28R-200	
G-OMOL	Maule MX-7-180C	
G-OMPW	P & M Quik	
G-OMRB	Cameron V-77	
G-OMRH	Cessna 550 Citation Bravo	
G-OMSS	Best Off Sky Ranger	
G-OMST	Piper PA-28-161 Warrior	
G-OMUM	Rockwell 114	
G-OMWE	Zenair CH.601HD	
G-OMYT	Airbus A330-243	
G-ONAF	Naval Aircraft N3N	
G-ONAL	Beech 200 Super King Air	
G-ONAV	Piper PA-31-310 Navajo	
G-ONCB	Lindstrand LBL-31A	
G-ONCL	Colt 77A	
G-ONCS	Tipsy Nipper 3B	
G-ONEP	Robinson R44	
G-ONER	Van's RV-8	
G-ONES	Slingsby T.67M	
G-ONET	Piper PA-28-180 Cherokee	
G-ONFL	Murphy Maverick	
G-ONGA	Robinson R44	
G-ONGC	Robin DR.400-180R	
G-ONHH	Ercoupe F1A	
G-ONIG	Murphy Elite	
G-ONIX	Cameron C-80	
G-ONJC	EMB-135BJ Legacy	
G-ONKA	Aeronca K	
G-ONMT	Robinson R22	
G-ONON	RAF 2000 GTX-SE	
G-ONPA	Piper PA-31-350 Chieftain	
G-ONSF	Piper PA-28R-201	
G-ONSO	Pitts S-1S Special	
G-ONTV	Agusta Bell 206B	
G-ONUN	Van's RV-6A	
G-ONUP	Enstrom F-28C	
G-ONYX	Bell 206B Jet Ranger	
G-OOAE	Airbus A321-211	
G-OOAF	Airbus A321-213	
G-OOAH	Airbus A321-211	
G-OOAN	Boeing 767-39HER	
G-OOAP	Airbus A320-214	
G-OOAR	Airbus A320-214	
G-OOAU	Airbus A320-214	
G-OOAV	Airbus A321-211	
G-OOAW	Airbus A320-214	
G-OOAX	Airbus A320-214	
G-OOBA	Boeing 757-28A	
G-OOBC	Boeing 757-28A	
G-OOBD	Boeing 757-28A	
G-OOBE	Boeing 757-28A	
G-OOBF	Boeing 757-28A	
G-OOBI	Boeing 757-2B7	
G-OOBJ	Boeing 757-236	
G-OOBK	Boeing 767-324ER	
G-OOBL	Boeing 767-324	

G-OOBM	Boeing 767-324ER	
G-OOCS	Hughes 369E	
G-OODE	Stampe SV-4C	
G-OODI	Pitts S-1D Special	
G-OODM	Cessna 525A CitationJet 2	
G-OODW	Piper PA-28-181 Archer	
G-OOER	Lindstrand LBL-25A	
G-OOFE	Thruster T600N	
G-OOFT	Piper PA-28-161 Warrior	
G-OOGA	Grumman GA-7 Cougar	
G-OOGI	Grumman GA-7 Cougar	
G-OOGL	Hughes 369E	
G-OOGO	Grumman GA-7 Cougar	
G-OOGS	Grumman GA-7 Cougar	
G-OOIO	Aerospatiale AS.350B3	
G-OOJC	Bensen B.8MR	
G-OOJP	Rockwell 114B	
G-OOLE	Cessna 172M Skyhawk	
G-OOLL	Tanarg iXess	
G-OOMF	Piper PA-18-150	
G-OONA	Robinson R44	
G-OONE	Mooney M.20J	
G-OONI	Thunder Ax7-77	
G-OONK	Cirrus SR22	
G-OONY	Piper PA-28-161 Warrior	
G-OOOB	Boeing 757-28A	
G-OOON	Piper PA-34-220T Seneca	
G-OOOX	Boeing 757-2YO	
G-OORV	Van's RV-6	
G-OOSE	Rutan VariEze	
G-OOSH	Zenair CH.601UL	
G-OOSI	Cessna 404	
G-OOSY	DH.82A Tiger Moth	
G-OOTB	SOCATA TB-20 Trinidad GT	
G-OOTC	Piper PA-28R-201T	
G-OOTT	Aerospatiale AS.350B3	
G-OOTW	Cameron Z-275	
G-OOUT	Colt SS	
G-OOXP	Aero Designs Pulsar XP	
G-OPAG	Piper PA-34-200 Seneca	
G-OPAM	Reims F152	
G-OPAT	Beech 76 Duchess	
G-OPAZ	Pazmany PL-2	
G-OPCG	Cessna 182T Skylane	
G-OPCS	Hughes 369C	
G-OPDS	Denney Kitfox	
G-OPEJ	TEAM Minimax	
G-OPEN	Bell 206B Jet Ranger	
G-OPEP	Piper PA-28R-201T	
G-OPET	Piper PA-28-181 Archer	
G-OPFA	Alpi Pioneer 300	
G-OPFR	Diamond DA42 Twin Star	
G-OPFT	Cessna 172R Skyhawk	
G-OPFW	HS.748-2A	
G-OPHT	Schleicher ASH 26E	
G-OPIC	Reims FRA150L Aerobat	
G-OPIK	Eiri PIK-20E	
G-OPIT	CFM Shadow SA	
G-OPJB	Boeing 757-23A	
G-OPJC	Cessna 152	
G-OPJD	Piper PA-28R-201T	
G-OPJH	Druine Condor	
G-OPJK	Europa	
G-OPJS	Pietenpol Aircamper	
G-OPKF	Cameron Bowler 90SS	
G-OPLC	DH.104 Dove 8	
G-OPME	Piper PA-23-250 Aztec D	
G-OPMT	Lindstrand LBL-105A	
G-OPNH	Glasair IIRG	
G-OPPL	Grumman AA-5A Cheetah	
G-OPRC	Europa XS	
G-OPSF	Piper PA-38-112 Tomahawk	
G-OPSL	Piper PA-32R-301 SP	

G-OPSS	Cirrus SR20	
G-OPST	Cessna 182R Skylane	
G-OPTF	Robinson R44	
G-OPTI	Piper PA-28-161 Warrior	
G-OPUB	Slingsby T.67M	
G-OPUP	Beagle B.121 Pup	
G-OPUS	Jabiru SK	
G-OPVM	Van's RV-9A	
G-OPWK	Grumman AA-5A Cheetah	
G-OPWS	Mooney M.20K	
G-OPYE	Cessna 172S Skyhawk	
G-ORAC	Cameron RAC Van SS	
G-ORAE	Van's RV-7	
G-ORAF	CFM Shadow SA	
G-ORAL	HS.748-2A	
G-ORAR	Piper PA-28-181 Archer	
G-ORAS	Clutton FRED II	
G-ORAY	Reims F182Q Skylane	
G-ORBK	Robinson R44	
G-ORBS	Mainair Blade	
G-ORCA	Van's RV-4	
G-ORCP	HS.748-2A	
G-ORCW	Shempp-Hirth Ventus	
G-ORDH	Eurocopter AS355N	
G-ORDS	Thruster T600N	
G-ORED	BN2T Islander	
G-OREV	Mini 500	
G-ORGY	Cameron Z-210	
G-ORHE	Cessna 500 Citation	
G-ORIG	Glaser-Dirks DG-800A	
G-ORIX	ARV Super 2	
G-ORJA	Beech B200 Super King Air	
G-ORJW	Laverda F.8L Falco	
G-ORMA	Aerospatiale A.355F1	
G-ORMB	Robinson R22B	
G-ORMG	Cessna 172R Skyhawk	
G-ORMW	Ikarus C42 Cyclone	
G-OROD	Piper PA-18-150	
G-OROS	Ikarus C42 Cyclone	
G-ORPC	Europa XS	
G-ORPR	Cameron O-77	
G-ORTH	Beech 65-E90 King Air	
G-ORUG	Thruster T600N	
G-ORVB	McCulloch J.2	
G-ORVG	Van's RV-6	
G-ORVR	Partenavia P.68B	
G-ORZA	Diamond DA42 Twin Star	
G-OSAT	Cameron Z-105	
G-OSAW	QAC Quickie Q2	
G-OSCC	Piper PA-32-300	
G-OSCH	Cessna 421C	
G-OSCO	TEAM Minimax	
G-OSDI	Beech 58 Baron	
G-OSEA	BN2B-26 Islander	
G-OSEE	Robinson R22B	
G-OSEP	Mainair Blade	
G-OSFA	Diamond H.36TC	
G-OSFS	Reims F177RG	
G-OSGB	Piper PA-31-350 Chieftain	
G-OSHL	Robinson R22B	
G-OSIC	Pitts S-1C Special	
G-OSII	Cessna 172N Skyhawk	
G-OSIS	Pitts S-1S Special	
G-OSIT	Pitts S-1T Special	
G-OSIX	Piper PA-32-260	
G-OSJF	Piper PA-23-250 Aztec F	
G-OSJL	Robinson R44	
G-OSJN	Europa XS	
G-OSKP	Enstrom 480	
G-OSKR	Best Off Sky Ranger	
G-OSKY	Cessna 172M Skyhawk	
G-OSLD	Europa XS	
G-OSLO	Schweizer 269C	

G-OSMD	Bell 206B Jet Ranger
G-OSMS	Robinson R22B
G-OSND	Reims FRA150M Aerobat
G-OSNI	Piper PA-23-250 Aztec C
G-OSOE	HS.748-2A
G-OSPD	EV-97 Eurostar
G-OSPK	Cessna 172S Skyhawk
G-OSPS	Piper PA-18-95
G-OSPY	Cirrus SR20
G-OSSA	Cessna TU206B
G-OSSF	Grumman AA-5A Cheetah
G-OSSI	Robinson R44
G-OSST	Colt 77A
G-OSTC	Grumman AA-5A Cheetah
G-OSTL	Ikarus C42 Cyclone
G-OSTU	Grumman AA-5A Cheetah
G-OSTY	Reims F150G
G-OSUP	Lindstrand LBL-90A
G-OSUS	Mooney M.20K
G-OSUT	Schiebe SF-25C
G-OSZA	Pitts S-2A Special
G-OSZB	Pitts S-2B Special
G-OTAL	ARV Super 2
G-OTAM	Cessna 172M Skyhawk
G-OTAN	Piper PA-18-135
G-OTBA	HS.748-2A
G-OTBY	Piper PA-32-300
G-OTCH	CFM Shadow SA
G-OTCV	Best Off Sky Ranger
G-OTCZ	Schempp-Hirth Ventus
G-OTDA	Boeing 737-31S
G-OTDI	Diamond DA.40D Star
G-OTEL	Thunder Ax8-90
G-OTFL	Eurocopter EC120B
G-OTFT	Piper PA-38-112 Tomahawk
G-OTGA	Piper PA-28R-201
G-OTHE	Enstrom 280C-UK
G-OTIB	Robin DR.400-180R
G-OTIG	Grumman FRA.5B Tiger
G-OTIM	Bensen B.8MV
G-OTJB	Robinson R44
G-OTJH	Pegasus Quantum
G-OTNA	Robinson R44
G-OTOE	Aeronca 7AC Champion
G-OTOO	Stolp SA.300
G-OTOY	Robinson R22B
G-OTRV	Van's RV-6
G-OTSP	Aerospatiale AS.355F1
G-OTTI	Cameron Otti SS
G-OTTO	Cameron Katalog SS
G-OTUG	Piper PA-18-150
G-OTUI	SOCATA TB-20 Trinidad
G-OTUN	EV-97 Eurostar
G-OTUP	Lindstrand LBL-180A
G-OTVI	Robinson R44
G-OTVR	Piper PA-34-220T Seneca
G-OTWO	Rutan Defiant
G-OTYE	EV-97 Eurostar
G-OTYP	Piper PA-28-180 Cherokee
G-OUCH	Cameron N-105
G-OUHI	Europa XS
G-OUIK	P & M Quik
G-OUMC	Lindstrand LBL-105A
G-OURO	Europa
G-OUVI	Cameron O-105
G-OVAA	Colt Jumbo SS
G-OVAG	Tipsy Nipper
G-OVAL	Ikarus C42 Cyclone
G-OVAX	Colt AS-80
G-OVBF	Cameron A-250
G-OVET	Cameron O-56
G-OVFM	Cessna 120
G-OVFR	Reims F172N
G-OVIA	Lindstrand LBL-105A
G-OVIC	Cameron A-250
G-OVID	Avid Flyer
G-OVII	Van's RV-7
G-OVIN	Rockwell 112TC
G-OVLA	Ikarus C42 Cyclone
G-OVMC	Reims F152
G-OVNR	Robinson R22B
G-OVOL	Best Off Sky Ranger
G-OVON	Piper PA-18-95
G-OWAC	Reims F152
G-OWAK	Reims F152
G-OWAL	Piper PA-34-220T Seneca
G-OWAP	Piper PA-28-161 Warrior
G-OWAR	Piper PA-28-161 Warrior
G-OWAZ	Pitts S-1C Special
G-OWCS	Cessna 182J Skylane
G-OWEL	Colt 105A
G-OWEN	K & S Jungster 1
G-OWET	Thurston TSC-1A2
G-OWFS	Cessna A152 Aerobat
G-OWGC	Slingsby T.61F
G-OWLC	Piper PA-31 Navajo
G-OWMC	Thruster T600N
G-OWND	Robinson R44
G-OWOW	Cessna 152
G-OWRD	Agusta A.109C
G-OWRT	Cessna 182G Skylane
G-OWST	Cessna 172S Skyhawk
G-OWWW	Europa
G-OWYE	Lindstrand LBL-240A
G-OWYN	Aviamilano F.14 Nibbio
G-OXBC	Cameron A-140
G-OXBY	Cameron N-90
G-OXKB	Cameron Jaguar SS
G-OXLB	Boeing 737-81Q
G-OXLC	Boeing 737-8BK
G-OXLS	Cessna 560 Citation XLS
G-OXOM	Piper PA-28-161 Warrior
G-OXTC	Piper PA-23-250 Aztec D
G-OXVI	Spitfire
G-OYAK	Yakovlev Yak-11C
G-OYES	Mainair Blade
G-OYIO	Robin DR.400 120
G-OYST	Agusta Bell 206B
G-OYTE	Rans S6 Coyote II
G-OZAR	Enstrom 480
G-OZBB	Airbus A320-212
G-OZBE	Airbus A321-231
G-OZBF	Airbus A321-231
G-OZBG	Airbus A321-231
G-OZBH	Airbus A321-231
G-OZBI	Airbus A321-231
G-OZBJ	Airbus A320-212
G-OZBK	Airbus A320-214
G-OZBL	Airbus A321-231
G-OZEE	Avid Speed Wing
G-OZEF	Europa XS
G-OZIE	Jabiru J400
G-OZOI	Cessna R182 Skylane RG
G-OZOO	Cessna 172N Skyhawk
G-OZRH	BAe 146-200
G-OZZI	Jabiru SK
G-OZZY	Robinson R22B2
G-PACE	Robin R.1180T Aiglon
G-PACL	Robinson R22B
G-PACT	Piper PA-28-181 Archer
G-PADD	Grumman AA-5A Cheetah
G-PADE	Reality Escapade
G-PADI	Cameron V-77
G-PAGS	Aerospatiale Gazelle
G-PAIZ	Piper PA-12 Super Cruiser
G-PALS	Enstrom 280C-UK
G-PARG	Pitts S-1C Special
G-PARI	Cessna 172RG Cutlass
G-PART	Partenavia P.68B
G-PASG	MBB Bo.105DBS/4
G-PASH	Aerospatiale AS.355F1
G-PASN	Enstrom F-28F
G-PASV	BN2B-21 Islander
G-PASX	MBB Bo.105DBS/4
G-PATF	Europa
G-PATG	Cameron O-90
G-PATN	SOCATA TB-10 Tobago
G-PATO	Zenair CH.601UL
G-PATP	Lindstrand LBL-77A
G-PATS	Europa
G-PATX	Lindstrand LBL-90A
G-PATZ	Europa
G-PAVL	Robin R.3000-120
G-PAWL	Piper PA-28-140 Cherokee
G-PAWN	Piper PA-25-260 Pawnee
G-PAWS	Grumman AA-5A Cheetah
G-PAXX	Piper PA-20-125 Pacer
G-PAYD	Robin DR.400-180 Regent
G-PAZY	Pazmany PL-4A
G-PBEE	Robinson R44
G-PBEK	Agusta 109A
G-PBEL	CFM Shadow DD
G-PBRL	Robinson R22B
G-PBUS	Jabiru SK
G-PBYA	PBY-5A Catalina
G-PBYY	Enstrom 280FX
G-PCAF	Pietenpol Aircamper
G-PCAM	BN2A-III Trislander
G-PCAT	SOCATA TB-10 Tobago
G-PCCC	Alpi Pioneer 300
G-PCDP	Zlin Z.526F
G-PCOP	Beech B200 Super King Air
G-PDGE	Eurocopter EC120B
G-PDGG	Sequoia F.8L Falco
G-PDGN	Aerospatiale AS.365N
G-PDGR	Aerospatiale AS.350B2
G-PDHJ	Cessna T182R
G-PDOC	Piper PA-44-180 Seminole
G-PDOG	Cessna L19E Bird Dog
G-PDSI	Cessna 172N Skyhawk
G-PEAK	Agusta Bell 206B
G-PECK	Piper PA-32-300 D
G-PEGA	Pegasus Quantum
G-PEGE	Best Off Sky Ranger
G-PEGG	Colt 90A
G-PEGI	Piper PA-34-200T Seneca
G-PEGY	Europa
G-PEJM	Piper PA-28-181 Archer
G-PEKT	SOCATA TB-20 Trinidad
G-PELS	Agusta Bell 206A
G-PEPA	Cessna 206H
G-PEPL	MD Helicopters MD.600N
G-PEPS	Robinson R44
G-PERC	Cameron N-90
G-PERE	Robinson R22B
G-PERZ	Bell 206B Jet Ranger
G-PEST	Hawker Tempest II
G-PETH	Piper PA-24-260 Comanche
G-PETR	Piper PA-28-140 Cherokee
G-PETS	Diamon DA 42 Twin Star
G-PFAA	EAA Biplane
G-PFAD	Wittman W.8 Tailwind
G-PFAF	Clutton FRED II
G-PFAG	Evans VP-1
G-PFAH	Evans VP-1
G-PFAL	Clutton FRED II
G-PFAO	Evans VP-1
G-PFAP	Phoenix Currie Wot
G-PFAR	Isaacs Fury II

☐ G-PFAT	Monnett Sonerai II
☐ G-PFAW	Evans VP-1
☐ G-PFAY	EAA Biplane
☐ G-PFCI	Piper PA-34-220T Seneca
☐ G-PFCL	Cessna 172S Skyhawk
☐ G-PFFN	Beech 200 Super King Air
☐ G-PFML	Robinson R44
☐ G-PFSL	Reims F152
☐ G-PGAC	Dyn'Aero MCR-01
☐ G-PGFG	Tecnam P92 Echo
☐ G-PGGY	Robinson R44
☐ G-PGHM	Air Creation Kiss 450
☐ G-PGSA	Thruster T600N
☐ G-PGSI	Robin R.2160
☐ G-PGUY	Sky 70-16
☐ G-PHAA	Reims F150M
☐ G-PHIL	Brookland Hornet
☐ G-PHLB	RAF 2000 GTX-SE
☐ G-PHLY	Reims FRA.150L
☐ G-PHML	American General AG-5B
☐ G-PHOR	Reims FRA150L Aerobat
☐ G-PHSI	Colt 90A
☐ G-PHTG	SOCATA TB-10 Tobago
☐ G-PHTO	Beech 390 Premier 1
☐ G-PHUN	Reims FRA150L Aerobat
☐ G-PHXS	Europa XS
☐ G-PHYL	Denney Kitfox
☐ G-PHYS	Jabiru SP-470
☐ G-PIAF	Thunder Ax6-65
☐ G-PIDG	Robinson R44
☐ G-PIEL	Piel Emeraude
☐ G-PIES	Thunder Ax7-77Z
☐ G-PIET	Pietenpol Aircamper
☐ G-PIGG	Lindstrand Flying Pig SS
☐ G-PIGI	EV-97 Eurostar
☐ G-PIGS	MS.892E Rallye 150GT
☐ G-PIGY	Short Skyvan
☐ G-PIIT	Pitts S-2
☐ G-PIIX	Cessna P210N Centurion
☐ G-PIKK	Piper PA-28-140 Cherokee
☐ G-PILE	Rotorway Exec 90
☐ G-PILL	Avid Flyer
☐ G-PIMM	UltraMagic M-77
☐ G-PINC	Cameron Z-90
☐ G-PING	Grumman AA-5A Cheetah
☐ G-PINT	Cameron Barrel SS
☐ G-PINX	Lindstrand Pink Panther
☐ G-PION	Alpi Pioneer 300
☐ G-PIPI	P & M Quik
☐ G-PIPR	Piper PA-18-95
☐ G-PIPS	Van's RV-4
☐ G-PIPY	Cameron Piper SS
☐ G-PIRO	Cameron TR-70
☐ G-PITS	Pitts S-2AE Special
☐ G-PITZ	Pitts S-2A Special
☐ G-PIXE	Colt 31A
☐ G-PIXI	Pegasus Quantum
☐ G-PIXL	Robinson R44
☐ G-PIXX	Robinson R44
☐ G-PIXY	Spitfire 26 replica
☐ G-PIZZ	Lindstrand LBL-105A
☐ G-PJCC	Piper PA-28-161 Warrior
☐ G-PJLO	Boeing 767-35EER
☐ G-PJMT	Neico Lancair 320
☐ G-PJNZ	Rockwell 114B
☐ G-PJSY	Van's RV-6
☐ G-PJTM	Reims FR172K Hawk XP
☐ G-PKPK	Schweizer 269C
☐ G-PKRG	Cessna 560 Citation XLS
☐ G-PLAC	Piper PA-31-350 Chieftain
☐ G-PLAD	Kolb Twinstar Mk.3
☐ G-PLAH	BAe Jetstream 31
☐ G-PLAJ	BAe Jetstream 31
☐ G-PLAL	Eurocopter EC135T2
☐ G-PLAN	Reims F150L
☐ G-PLAY	Robin R.2112 Alpha
☐ G-PLAZ	Rockwell 112
☐ G-PLBI	Cessna 172S Skyhawk
☐ G-PLEE	Cessna 182Q Skylane
☐ G-PLIV	Pazmany PL-4
☐ G-PLMB	Aerospatiale AS.350B2
☐ G-PLMH	Aerospatiale AS.350B2
☐ G-PLMI	Aerospatiale AS.365C1
☐ G-PLOD	Tecnam P92 Echo
☐ G-PLOW	Hughes 269
☐ G-PLPC	Schweizer 269C
☐ G-PLPM	Europa XS
☐ G-PLSA	Aero Designs Pulsar XP
☐ G-PLXI	BAe ATP
☐ G-PMAM	Cameron V-65
☐ G-PMAX	Piper PA-31-350 Chieftain
☐ G-PMNF	Spitfire HF.IX
☐ G-PNGC	Scleicher ASK 21
☐ G-PNIX	Reims FRA150L Aerobat
☐ G-POCO	Cessna 152
☐ G-POGO	Flight Design CT2K
☐ G-POLL	Best Off Sky Ranger
☐ G-POLY	Cameron N-77
☐ G-POND	Oldfield Baby Lakes
☐ G-POOH	Piper J-3C-65 Cub
☐ G-POOL	ARV Super 2
☐ G-POOP	Dyn'Aero MCR-01
☐ G-POPA	Beech A36 Bonanza
☐ G-POPE	Eiri PIK-20E
☐ G-POPI	SOCATA TB-10 Tobago
☐ G-POPP	Colt 105A
☐ G-POPS	Piper PA-34-220T Seneca
☐ G-POPW	Cessna 182S Skylane
☐ G-PORK	Grumman AA-5B Tiger
☐ G-PORT	Bell 206B Jet Ranger
☐ G-POSH	Colt 56A
☐ G-POWB	Beech 300 King Air
☐ G-POWL	Cessna 182R Skylane
☐ G-POZA	Reality Escapade
☐ G-PPLC	Cessna 560 Citation V
☐ G-PPLG	Rotorsport UK MT-03
☐ G-PPLL	Van's RV-7A
☐ G-PPPP	Denney Kitfox
☐ G-PPTS	Robinson R44
☐ G-PRAG	Brugger Colibri
☐ G-PRAH	Flight Design CT2K
☐ G-PREI	Beech 390 Premier 1
☐ G-PRET	Robinson R44
☐ G-PREY	Pereira Osprey 2
☐ G-PREZ	Robin DR.400-500
☐ G-PRII	Hawker Hunter PR.11
☐ G-PRIM	Piper PA-38-112 Tomahawk
☐ G-PRKR	CL604 Challenger
☐ G-PRLY	Jabiru SK
☐ G-PRNT	Cameron V-90
☐ G-PROB	Aerospatiale AS.350B2
☐ G-PROF	Lindstrand LBL-90A
☐ G-PROM	Aerospatiale AS.350B
☐ G-PROS	Van's RV-7A
☐ G-PROV	Jet Provost T.52A
☐ G-PROW	EV-97 Eurostar
☐ G-PRSI	Pegasus Quantum
☐ G-PRTT	Cameron N-31
☐ G-PRXI	Spitfire PR.XI
☐ G-PSAX	Lindstrand LBL-77B
☐ G-PSGC	Piper PA-25-260 Pawnee
☐ G-PSHR	Agusta Bell 206B
☐ G-PSKY	Best Off Sky Ranger
☐ G-PSNI	Eurocopter EC135
☐ G-PSON	Colt Cylinder One SS
☐ G-PSRT	Piper PA-28-151 Warrior
☐ G-PSST	Hawker Hunter F.58A
☐ G-PSUE	CFM Shadow CD
☐ G-PSUK	Thruster T600N
☐ G-PTAG	Europa
☐ G-PTAR	Best Off Sky Ranger
☐ G-PTDP	Bucker Bu.133C
☐ G-PTRE	SOCATA TB-20 Trinidad
☐ G-PTTS	Pitts S-2A Special
☐ G-PTWO	Pilatus P.2-05
☐ G-PTYE	Europa
☐ G-PUBS	Colt Beer Glass
☐ G-PUDL	Piper PA-18-150
☐ G-PUDS	Europa
☐ G-PUFF	Thunder Ax7-77
☐ G-PUFN	Cessna 340A
☐ G-PUGS	Cessna 182H Skylane
☐ G-PUKA	Jabiru J400
☐ G-PUMA	Aerospatiale AS.332L
☐ G-PUMB	Aerospatiale AS.332L
☐ G-PUMD	Aerospatiale AS.332L
☐ G-PUME	Aerospatiale AS.332L
☐ G-PUMH	Aerospatiale AS.332L
☐ G-PUMI	Aerospatiale AS.332L
☐ G-PUML	Aerospatiale AS.332L
☐ G-PUMN	Aerospatiale AS.332L2
☐ G-PUMO	Aerospatiale AS.332L2
☐ G-PUMS	Aerospatiale AS.332L2
☐ G-PUNK	Thunder Ax8-105
☐ G-PUPP	Beagle B.121 Pup 2
☐ G-PUPY	Europa XS
☐ G-PURL	Piper PA-32R-301 HP
☐ G-PURR	Grumman AA-5A Cheetah
☐ G-PURS	Rotorway Exec 152
☐ G-PUSH	Rutan LongEz
☐ G-PUSI	Cessna T303 Crusader
☐ G-PUSS	Cameron N-77
☐ G-PUSY	Sherwood Ranger
☐ G-PUTT	Cameron Golfball
☐ G-PVBF	Lindstrand LBL-260S
☐ G-PVCV	Robin DR400/140
☐ G-PVET	DHC-1 Chipmunk
☐ G-PVIP	Cessna 421C
☐ G-PVML	Robin DR400/140B
☐ G-PVPC	Pilatus PC-12/45
☐ G-PVST	Thruster T600N
☐ G-PWBE	DH.82A Tiger Moth
☐ G-PWIT	Bell 206L Long Ranger
☐ G-PWUL	Van's RV-6
☐ G-PYNE	Thruster T600N
☐ G-PYPE	Van's RV-7
☐ G-PYRO	Cameron N-65
☐ G-PZAZ	Piper PA-31-350 Chieftain
☐ G-PZIZ	Piper PA-31-350 Chieftain
☐ G-RABA	Reims FR172H Rocket
☐ G-RABS	Alpi Pioneer 300
☐ G-RACI	Beech 65-C90 King Air
☐ G-RACO	Piper PA-28R-200
☐ G-RACR	UltraMagic M-77
☐ G-RACY	Cessna 182S Skylane
☐ G-RADA	Soko P2 Kraguj
☐ G-RADI	Piper PA-28-181 Archer
☐ G-RADR	AD-4N Skyraider
☐ G-RAEM	Rutan LongEz
☐ G-RAES	Boeing 777-236
☐ G-RAFA	Grob 115A
☐ G-RAFB	Grob 115A
☐ G-RAFC	Robin R.2112 Alpha
☐ G-RAFE	Thunder Ax7-77
☐ G-RAFG	Slingsby T.67C
☐ G-RAFH	Thruster T600N
☐ G-RAFI	Jet Provost T.4
☐ G-RAFO	Beech B200 Super King Air
☐ G-RAFP	Beech B200 Super King Air

☐ G-RAFR	Best Off Sky Ranger	
☐ G-RAFS	Thruster T600N	
☐ G-RAFT	Rutan LongEz	
☐ G-RAFV	Avid Speed Wing	
☐ G-RAFW	Mooney M.20E	
☐ G-RAFZ	RAF 2000 GTX-SE	
☐ G-RAGE	Cassutt Racer IIIM	
☐ G-RAGS	Pietenpol Aircamper	
☐ G-RAGT	Piper PA-32-301FT	
☐ G-RAIG	Scottish Aviation Bulldog	
☐ G-RAIL	Colt 105A	
☐ G-RAIN	Maule M-5-235C	
☐ G-RAIX	CCF Harvard 4M	
☐ G-RAJA	Raj Hamsa X'Air	
☐ G-RALA	Robinson R44	
☐ G-RALD	Robinson R22B	
☐ G-RAMA	Cameron C-70	
☐ G-RAMI	Bell 206B Jet Ranger	
☐ G-RAMP	Piper J-3C-65 Cub	
☐ G-RAMS	Piper PA-32R-301 SP	
☐ G-RAMY	Bell 206B Jet Ranger	
☐ G-RANS	Rans S10 Sakota	
☐ G-RAPH	Cameron O-77	
☐ G-RAPI	Lindstrand LBL-105A	
☐ G-RAPP	Cameron H-34	
☐ G-RARB	Cessna 172N Skyhawk	
☐ G-RASA	Diamond DA42 Twin Star	
☐ G-RASC	Evans VP-2	
☐ G-RASH	Grob 109B	
☐ G-RATA	Robinson R22B	
☐ G-RATC	Van's RV-4	
☐ G-RATE	Grumman AA-5A Cheetah	
☐ G-RATH	Rotorway Exec 162F	
☐ G-RATI	Reims F172M	
☐ G-RATV	Piper PA-28R-201T	
☐ G-RATZ	Europa	
☐ G-RAVE	Gemini Raven X	
☐ G-RAVN	Robinson R44	
☐ G-RAWS	Rotorway Exec 162F	
☐ G-RAYA	Denney Kitfox	
☐ G-RAYE	Piper PA-32-260	
☐ G-RAYH	Zenair CH.701UL	
☐ G-RAYO	Lindstrand LBL-90A	
☐ G-RAYS	Zenair CH.250	
☐ G-RAYZ	Tecnam P2002EA Siera	
☐ G-RAZY	Piper PA-28-181 Archer	
☐ G-RAZZ	Maule MX-7-180	
☐ G-RBBB	Europa	
☐ G-RBCI	BN2A-III Trislander	
☐ G-RBJW	Europa XS	
☐ G-RBMV	Cameron O-31	
☐ G-RBOS	Colt AS-105	
☐ G-RBOW	Thunder Ax7-65	
☐ G-RBSN	Ikarus C42 Cyclone	
☐ G-RCED	Rockwell 114	
☐ G-RCEJ	BAe 125-800B	
☐ G-RCHY	EV-97 Eurostar	
☐ G-RCKT	Harmon Rocket II	
☐ G-RCMC	Murphy Renegade	
☐ G-RCMF	Cameron V-77	
☐ G-RCML	Sky 77-24	
☐ G-RCNB	Eurocopter EC120B	
☐ G-RCOM	Bell 206L Long Ranger	
☐ G-RCST	Jabiru J430	
☐ G-RDBS	Cessna 550 Citation II	
☐ G-RDCO	Jabiru J400	
☐ G-RDDT	Schempp-Hirth Duo Discus	
☐ G-RDEL	Robinson R44	
☐ G-RDHS	Europa XS	
☐ G-RDMV	Hawker 800XP	
☐ G-RDNS	Rans S6 Coyote II	
☐ G-RDWD	Robinson R44	
☐ G-READ	Colt 77A	
☐ G-REAL	Aerospatiale AS.350B2	
☐ G-REAN	Enstrom 480B	
☐ G-REAP	Pitts S-1S Special	
☐ G-REAR	Lindstrand LBL-69X	
☐ G-REAS	Van's RV-6A	
☐ G-REBA	RAF 2000 GTX-SE	
☐ G-REBB	Murphy Rebel	
☐ G-REBL	Hughes 269B	
☐ G-RECE	Cameron C-80	
☐ G-RECK	Piper PA-28-140 Cherokee	
☐ G-RECS	Piper PA-38-112 Tomahawk	
☐ G-REDB	Cessna 310Q	
☐ G-REDC	Pegasus Quantum	
☐ G-REDD	Cessna 310R	
☐ G-REDI	Robinson R44	
☐ G-REDJ	Aerospatiale AS.332L2	
☐ G-REDK	Aerospatiale AS.332L2	
☐ G-REDL	Aerospatiale AS.332L2	
☐ G-REDM	Aerospatiale AS.332L2	
☐ G-REDN	Aerospatiale AS.332L2	
☐ G-REDO	Aerospatiale AS.332L2	
☐ G-REDP	Aerospatiale AS.332L2	
☐ G-REDS	Cessna 560 Citation XL	
☐ G-REDX	Berkut	
☐ G-REDY	Robinson R22B	
☐ G-REDZ	Thruster T600N	
☐ G-REEC	Sequoia F.8L Falco	
☐ G-REED	Mainair Blade	
☐ G-REEF	Mainair Blade	
☐ G-REEM	Aerospatiale AS.355F1	
☐ G-REEN	Cessna 340	
☐ G-REES	Jodel D.140C	
☐ G-REET	Grumman AA-5B Tiger	
☐ G-REGE	Robinson R44	
☐ G-REJP	Europa XS	
☐ G-REKO	Pegasus Quasar	
☐ G-RENO	SOCATA TB-10 Tobago	
☐ G-REPH	Pegasus Quantum	
☐ G-RESG	Dyn'Aero MCR-01	
☐ G-REST	Beech 35P Bonanza	
☐ G-RETA	CASA I-131E	
☐ G-REUB	Embraer EMB-135BJ	
☐ G-REVO	Best Off Sky Ranger	
☐ G-REYS	Canadair CL-604	
☐ G-RFIO	Aeromot AMT-200	
☐ G-RFOX	Denney Kitfox	
☐ G-RFSB	Fournier RF5B	
☐ G-RFUN	Robinson R44	
☐ G-RGAP	Cessna 172S Skyhawk	
☐ G-RGEN	Cessna T337D	
☐ G-RGNT	Robinson R44	
☐ G-RGUS	Fairchild F.24A-46A	
☐ G-RHAM	Best Off Sky Ranger	
☐ G-RHCB	Schweizer 269C-1	
☐ G-RHHT	Piper PA-32RT-300	
☐ G-RHOP	BN2A-III Trislander	
☐ G-RHUM	ATR 42-300	
☐ G-RHYM	Piper PA-31 Navajo	
☐ G-RHYS	Rotorway Exec 90	
☐ G-RIAT	Robinson R22B2	
☐ G-RIBA	P & M Quik GT450	
☐ G-RIBZ	Enstrom 480B	
☐ G-RICK	Beech B55 Baron	
☐ G-RICO	American General AG-5B	
☐ G-RICS	Europa	
☐ G-RIDD	Robinson R22	
☐ G-RIDG	Van's RV-7A	
☐ G-RIDL	Robinson R22	
☐ G-RIEF	DG Flugzeugbau DG1000T	
☐ G-RIET	Diamond H.36	
☐ G-RIFB	Hughes 269C	
☐ G-RIFN	Mudry CAP.10B	
☐ G-RIGB	Thunder Ax7-77	
☐ G-RIGH	Piper PA-32R-301	
☐ G-RIGS	Piper PA-60-601P	
☐ G-RIHN	DR.107 One Design	
☐ G-RIIN	PZL Wilga 2000	
☐ G-RIKI	Mainair Blade	
☐ G-RIKS	Europa XS	
☐ G-RIKY	P & M Quik	
☐ G-RILA	Flight Design CTSW	
☐ G-RIMB	Lindstrand LBL-105A	
☐ G-RIME	Lindstrand LBL-25A	
☐ G-RIMM	Westland Wasp	
☐ G-RINN	Mainair Blade	
☐ G-RINO	Thunder Ax7-77	
☐ G-RINS	Rans S6 Coyote II	
☐ G-RINT	CFM Shadow SA	
☐ G-RISE	Cameron V-77	
☐ G-RISH	Rotorway Exec 162F	
☐ G-RISK	Hughes 369E	
☐ G-RIST	Cessna 310R	
☐ G-RISY	Van's RV-7A	
☐ G-RITT	P & M Quik	
☐ G-RIVE	Jodel D.150 Mascaret	
☐ G-RIVR	Thruster T600F	
☐ G-RIVT	Van's RV-6	
☐ G-RIXA	Piper J-3C-65 Cub	
☐ G-RIXS	Europa XS	
☐ G-RIXY	Cameron Z-77	
☐ G-RIZE	Cameron O-90	
☐ G-RIZI	Cameron N-90	
☐ G-RIZZ	Piper PA-28-161 Warrior	
☐ G-RJAH	Boeing Stearman D75N1	
☐ G-RJAM	Sequoia F.8L Falco	
☐ G-RJMS	Piper PA-28R-201	
☐ G-RJWW	Maule M-5-235C	
☐ G-RJWX	Europa XS	
☐ G-RJX	Embraer EMB-145MP	
☐ G-RJX	Embraer EMB-145MP	
☐ G-RJXA	Embraer EMB-145EP	
☐ G-RJXB	Embraer EMB-145EP	
☐ G-RJXC	Embraer EMB-145EP	
☐ G-RJXD	Embraer EMB-145EP	
☐ G-RJXE	Embraer EMB-145EP	
☐ G-RJXF	Embraer EMB-145EP	
☐ G-RJXG	Embraer EMB-145EP	
☐ G-RJXH	Embraer EMB-145EP	
☐ G-RJXI	Embraer EMB-145EP	
☐ G-RJXJ	Embraer EMB-135ER	
☐ G-RJXK	Embraer EMB-135ER	
☐ G-RJXL	Embraer EMB-145EP	
☐ G-RJXM	Embraer EMB-145EP	
☐ G-RJXN	Embraer EMB-145MP	
☐ G-RJXO	Embraer EMB-145MP	
☐ G-RKEL	Agusta Bell 206B	
☐ G-RKET	Taylor Titch	
☐ G-RLFI	Reims FA152 Aerobat	
☐ G-RLGG	Embraer EMB135BJ	
☐ G-RLMW	Tecnam P2002EA Siera	
☐ G-RLON	BN2A-III Trislander	
☐ G-RMAC	Europa	
☐ G-RMAN	Aero Designs Pulsar	
☐ G-RMAX	Cameron C-80	
☐ G-RMBM	Robinson R44	
☐ G-RMHE	Aerospool Dynamic WT9	
☐ G-RMIE	Bell 206B Jet Ranger	
☐ G-RMIT	Van's RV-4	
☐ G-RMMT	Europa XS	
☐ G-RMPY	EV-97 Eurostar	
☐ G-RMUG	Cameron Nescafe SS	
☐ G-RNAC	Yakovlev Yak-52	
☐ G-RNBW	Bell 206B Jet Ranger	
☐ G-RNCH	Piper PA-28-181 Archer	
☐ G-RNDD	Robin DR.400-500	
☐ G-RNGO	Robinson R22B	

☐ G-RNIE	Cameron Ball SS
☐ G-RNLI	Supermarine Walrus
☐ G-RNRM	Cessna A185F
☐ G-RNRS	Scottish Aviation Bulldog
☐ G-ROBD	Europa
☐ G-ROBN	Robin R.1180T Aiglon
☐ G-ROBT	Hawker Hurricane I
☐ G-ROCH	Cessna T303 Crusader
☐ G-ROCK	Thunder Ax7-77
☐ G-ROCR	Schweizer 269C
☐ G-RODC	Steen Skybolt
☐ G-RODD	Cessna 310R
☐ G-RODG	Jabiru UL
☐ G-RODI	Isaacs Fury
☐ G-ROGE	Robinson R44
☐ G-ROGY	Cameron C-60
☐ G-ROKT	Reims FR172E Rocket
☐ G-ROLF	Piper PA-32R-301 SP
☐ G-ROLL	Pitts S-2A Special
☐ G-ROLY	Reims F172N
☐ G-ROME	III Sky Arrow 650TC
☐ G-ROMP	Extra EA.230H
☐ G-ROMS	Lindstrand LBL-105G
☐ G-ROMW	Pegasus AX2000
☐ G-RONA	Europa
☐ G-ROND	Short SD.360-100
☐ G-RONG	Piper PA-28R-200
☐ G-RONI	Cameron V-77
☐ G-RONS	Robin DR.400-180 Regent
☐ G-RONW	Clutton FRED II
☐ G-ROOK	Reims F172P
☐ G-ROOV	Europa XS
☐ G-RORI	Folland Gnat T.1
☐ G-RORY	Piaggio P.149 D
☐ G-ROSI	Thunder Ax7-77
☐ G-ROSS	Practavia Pilot Sprite
☐ G-ROTF	Robinson R22B
☐ G-ROTI	Luscombe 8A Silvaire
☐ G-ROTR	Brantly B.2B
☐ G-ROTS	CFM Shadow SA
☐ G-ROUP	Reims F172M
☐ G-ROUS	Piper PA-34-200T Seneca
☐ G-ROUT	Robinson R22B
☐ G-ROVE	Piper PA-18-135
☐ G-ROVY	Robinson R22B
☐ G-ROWE	Reims F182P Skylane
☐ G-ROWI	Europa XS
☐ G-ROWL	Grumman AA-5B Tiger
☐ G-ROWN	Beech 200 Super King Air
☐ G-ROWR	Robinson R44
☐ G-ROWS	Piper PA-28-151 Warrior
☐ G-ROXY	Denney Kitfox
☐ G-ROYC	Jabiru UL-450
☐ G-ROZI	Robinson R44
☐ G-ROZY	Cameron R-36
☐ G-ROZZ	Ikarus C42 Cyclone
☐ G-RPAF	Europa XS
☐ G-RPBM	Cameron Z-210
☐ G-RPCC	Europa XS
☐ G-RPEZ	Rutan LongEz
☐ G-RPRV	Van's RV-9A
☐ G-RRCU	Robin DR.221 Dauphin
☐ G-RRFC	SOCATA TB-20 Trinidad
☐ G-RRGN	Spitfire PR.XIX
☐ G-RROB	Robinson R44
☐ G-RROD	Piper PA-30-160 B
☐ G-RROW	Lindstrand LBL 105A
☐ G-RRSR	Piper J-3C-65 Cub
☐ G-RRVX	Van's RV-10
☐ G-RSAF	Strikemaster Mk.80A
☐ G-RSKR	Piper PA-28-161 Warrior
☐ G-RSKY	Best Off Sky Ranger
☐ G-RSSF	Denney Kitfox
☐ G-RSUK	Autogyro Europe MT-03
☐ G-RSVP	Robinson R22B
☐ G-RSWO	Cessna 172R Skyhawk
☐ G-RSWW	Robinson R22B
☐ G-RTBI	Thunder Ax6-56
☐ G-RTMS	Rans S6 Coyote II
☐ G-RTMY	Ikarus C42 Cyclone
☐ G-RTRT	PZL Wilga 2000
☐ G-RTUG	Robin DR.400-180R
☐ G-RTWO	Robinson R44
☐ G-RTWW	Robinson R44
☐ G-RUBB	Grumman AA-5B Tiger
☐ G-RUBI	Thunder Ax7-77
☐ G-RUBN	Embraer EMB-135BJ
☐ G-RUBY	Piper PA-28R-201T
☐ G-RUDD	Cameron V-65
☐ G-RUES	Robin HR.100-210 Safari
☐ G-RUFF	Mainair Blade
☐ G-RUFS	Jabiru UL
☐ G-RUGS	Campbell Cricket
☐ G-RUIA	Reims F172N
☐ G-RULE	Robinson R44
☐ G-RUMI	Snowbird Mk.IV
☐ G-RUMM	Grumman F.8F-2P
☐ G-RUMN	Grumman AA-1A Trainer
☐ G-RUMT	Grumman F-7F-3P
☐ G-RUMW	Grumman FM-2
☐ G-RUNT	Cassutt Racer 3M
☐ G-RUSA	Pegasus Quantum
☐ G-RUSI	SOCATA TB-9 Tobago
☐ G-RUSL	Van's RV-6A
☐ G-RUVI	Zenair CH.601UL
☐ G-RUVY	Van's RV-9A
☐ G-RUZZ	Robinson R44
☐ G-RVAB	Van's RV-7
☐ G-RVAC	Van's RV-7
☐ G-RVAL	Van's RV-8
☐ G-RVAN	Van's RV-6
☐ G-RVAW	Van's RV-6
☐ G-RVBA	Van's RV-8A
☐ G-RVBC	Van's RV-6A
☐ G-RVBF	Cameron A-340
☐ G-RVCE	Van's RV-6A
☐ G-RVCG	Van's RV-6A
☐ G-RVCL	Van's RV-6
☐ G-RVDG	Van's RV-9A
☐ G-RVDJ	Van's RV-6
☐ G-RVDP	Van's RV-4
☐ G-RVDR	Van's RV-6A
☐ G-RVEE	Van's RV-6
☐ G-RVET	Van's RV-6
☐ G-RVGA	Van's RV-6A
☐ G-RVIA	Van's RV-6A
☐ G-RVIB	Van's RV-6
☐ G-RVIC	Van's RV-6A
☐ G-RVII	Van's RV-7
☐ G-RVIN	Van's RV-6
☐ G-RVIO	Van's RV-10
☐ G-RVIS	Van's RV-8
☐ G-RVIT	Van's RV-6
☐ G-RVIV	Van's RV-4
☐ G-RVIX	Van's RV-9A
☐ G-RVJM	Van's RV-6
☐ G-RVJO	Van's RV-9A
☐ G-RVJP	Van's RV-9A
☐ G-RVJW	Van's RV-4
☐ G-RVMB	Van's RV-9A
☐ G-RVMC	Van's RV-7
☐ G-RVMJ	Van's RV-4
☐ G-RVMT	Van's RV-6
☐ G-RVMZ	Van's RV-8
☐ G-RVNH	Van's RV-9A
☐ G-RVPH	Van's RV-8
☐ G-RVPL	Van's RV-8
☐ G-RVPM	Van's RV-4
☐ G-RVPW	Van's RV-6A
☐ G-RVRA	Piper PA-28-140 Cherokee
☐ G-RVRB	Piper PA-34-200T Seneca
☐ G-RVRC	Piper PA-23-250 Aztec E
☐ G-RVRD	Piper PA-23-250 Aztec E
☐ G-RVRE	Partenavia P.68B
☐ G-RVRF	Piper PA-38-112 Tomahawk
☐ G-RVRG	Piper PA-38-112 Tomahawk
☐ G-RVRH	Van's RV-3B
☐ G-RVRI	Cessna 172H Skyhawk
☐ G-RVRJ	Piper PA-23-250 Aztec E
☐ G-RVRK	Piper PA-38-112 Tomahawk
☐ G-RVRL	Piper PA-38-112 Tomahawk
☐ G-RVRM	Piper PA-38-112 Tomahawk
☐ G-RVRN	Piper PA-28-161 Warrior
☐ G-RVRO	Piper PA-38-112 Tomahawk
☐ G-RVRP	Van's RV-7
☐ G-RVRT	Piper PA-28-140 Cherokee
☐ G-RVRV	Van's RV-4
☐ G-RVRW	Piper PA-23-250 Aztec E
☐ G-RVSA	Van's RV-6A
☐ G-RVSD	Van's RV-9A
☐ G-RVSG	Van's RV-9A
☐ G-RVSH	Van's RV-6A
☐ G-RVSX	Van's RV-6
☐ G-RVUK	Van's RV-9A
☐ G-RVVI	Van's RV-6
☐ G-RWAY	Rotorway Exec
☐ G-RWEW	Robinson R44
☐ G-RWGW	Learjet 45
☐ G-RWHC	Cameron A-180
☐ G-RWIN	Rearwin 175
☐ G-RWLY	Europa XS
☐ G-RWMW	Zenair CH.601XL
☐ G-RWRW	UltraMagic M-77
☐ G-RWSS	Denney Kitfox
☐ G-RXUK	Lindstrand LBL-105A
☐ G-RXVH	Cessna 182T Skylane
☐ G-RYAL	Jabiru UL
☐ G-RYPH	Mainair Blade
☐ G-RYZZ	Robinson R44
☐ G-SAAA	Flight Design CTSW
☐ G-SAAB	Rockwell 112TC
☐ G-SAAM	Cessna T182
☐ G-SAAW	Boeing 737-8Q8
☐ G-SABA	Piper PA-28R-201T
☐ G-SABR	North American F-86A
☐ G-SACB	Reims F152
☐ G-SACD	Reims F172H
☐ G-SACH	GlaStar
☐ G-SACI	Piper PA-28-161 Warrior
☐ G-SACK	Robin R.2160
☐ G-SACO	Piper PA-28-161 Warrior
☐ G-SACR	Piper PA-28-161 Warrior
☐ G-SACS	Piper PA-28-161 Warrior
☐ G-SACT	Piper PA-28-161 Warrior
☐ G-SAFE	Cameron N-77
☐ G-SAFI	Piel Emeraude
☐ G-SAFR	SAAB 91D
☐ G-SAGA	Grob 109B
☐ G-SAGE	Luscombe 8A Silvaire
☐ G-SAHI	FLS Sprint 160
☐ G-SAIG	Robinson R44
☐ G-SAIX	Cameron N-77
☐ G-SAJA	Schempp-Hirth Discus
☐ G-SALA	Piper PA-32-300
☐ G-SALE	Cameron Z-90
☐ G-SALL	Reims F150L
☐ G-SAMG	Grob 109B
☐ G-SAMJ	Partenavia P.68B
☐ G-SAMM	Cessna 340A

☐ G-SAMP	Agusta A109E Power	☐ G-SEMR	Cessna T206H Stationair	☐ G-SIPA	SIPA 903
☐ G-SAMY	Europa	☐ G-SENA	Rutan LongEz	☐ G-SIRA	Embraer EMB-135BJ
☐ G-SAMZ	Cessna 150D	☐ G-SEND	Colt 90A	☐ G-SIRS	Cessna 560 Citation XL
☐ G-SAPM	SOCATA TB-20 Trinidad	☐ G-SENE	Piper PA-34-200T Seneca	☐ G-SISU	P & M Quik GT450
☐ G-SARA	Piper PA-28-181 Archer	☐ G-SENX	Piper PA-34-200T Seneca	☐ G-SITA	Pegasus Quantum
☐ G-SARH	Piper PA-28-161 Warrior	☐ G-SEPA	Aerospatiale AS.355N	☐ G-SIVJ	Aerospatiale Gazelle
☐ G-SARK	Strikemaster Mk.84	☐ G-SEPB	Aerospatiale AS.355N	☐ G-SIVN	MD Helicopters MD.500N
☐ G-SARM	Ikarus C42 Cyclone	☐ G-SEPC	Aerospatiale AS.355N	☐ G-SIVR	MD.900 Explorer
☐ G-SARO	Saro Skeeter AOP.12	☐ G-SEPT	Cameron N-105	☐ G-SIVW	Lake LA-250
☐ G-SARV	Van's RV-4	☐ G-SERC	Beech King Air 350	☐ G-SIXC	Douglas DC-6A/B
☐ G-SASA	Eurocopter EC135T1	☐ G-SERL	SOCATA TB-10 Tobago	☐ G-SIXD	Piper PA-32-300
☐ G-SASB	Eurocopter EC135T1	☐ G-SERV	Cameron N-105	☐ G-SIXS	Whittaker MW-6S
☐ G-SASC	Beech 200C Super King Air	☐ G-SETI	Sky 80-16	☐ G-SIXX	Colt 77A
☐ G-SASD	Beech 200C Super King Air	☐ G-SEVA	Replica Plans SE5A	☐ G-SIXY	Van's RV-6
☐ G-SASH	MD.900 Explorer	☐ G-SEVE	Cessna 172N Skyhawk	☐ G-SIZZ	Jabiru J400
☐ G-SATL	Cameron Sphere SS	☐ G-SEVN	Van's RV-7	☐ G-SJCH	BN2T-4S Islander
☐ G-SATN	Piper PA-25-260 Pawnee	☐ G-SEWP	Aerospatiale AS.355F2	☐ G-SJDI	Robinson R44
☐ G-SAUF	Colt 90A	☐ G-SEXE	Scheibe SF25C Falke	☐ G-SJEN	Ikarus C42 Cyclone
☐ G-SAUK	Rans S6ES Coyote II	☐ G-SEXI	Cessna 172M Skyhawk	☐ G-SJET	Boeing 767-216ER
☐ G-SAWI	Piper PA-32R-300T	☐ G-SEXX	Piper PA-28-161 Warrior	☐ G-SJKR	Lindstrand LBL-90A
☐ G-SAXC	Cameron N-105	☐ G-SFCJ	Cessna 525 CitationJet	☐ G-SJMC	Boeing 767-31K
☐ G-SAXN	Beech 200 Super King Air	☐ G-SFLY	Diamond DA.40 Star	☐ G-SKAN	Reims F172M
☐ G-SAYS	RAF 2000 GTX-SE	☐ G-SFOX	Rotorway Exec 90	☐ G-SKCI	Rutan VariEze
☐ G-SAZY	Jabiru J400	☐ G-SFPA	Reims F406	☐ G-SKEW	Mudry CAP.232
☐ G-SAZZ	Piel Emeraude	☐ G-SFPB	Reims F406	☐ G-SKIE	Steen Skybolt
☐ G-SBAE	Reims F172P	☐ G-SFRY	Thunder Ax7-77	☐ G-SKII	Agusta Bell 206B
☐ G-SBAR	Robinson R22B	☐ G-SFSL	Cameron Z-105	☐ G-SKKY	Cessna 172S Skyhawk
☐ G-SBHH	Schweizer 269C	☐ G-SFTA	Aerospatiale Gazelle	☐ G-SKNT	Pitts S-2A Special
☐ G-SBIZ	Cameron Z-90	☐ G-SFTZ	Slingsby T.67M	☐ G-SKOT	Cameron V-42
☐ G-SBKR	SOCATA TB-10 Tobago	☐ G-SGAS	Colt 77A	☐ G-SKPG	Best Off Sky Ranger
☐ G-SBLT	Steen Skybolt	☐ G-SGEC	Beech B200 Super King Air	☐ G-SKPH	Yakovlev Yak-50
☐ G-SBMM	Piper PA-28R-180	☐ G-SGEN	Ikarus C42 Cyclone	☐ G-SKRA	Best Off Sky Ranger
☐ G-SBMO	Robin R.2160	☐ G-SGSE	Piper PA-28-181 Archer	☐ G-SKRG	Best Off Sky Ranger
☐ G-SBRA	Robinson R44	☐ G-SHAA	Enstrom 280UK	☐ G-SKYC	Slingsby T.67M
☐ G-SBUS	BN2A-26 Islander	☐ G-SHAF	Robinson R44	☐ G-SKYE	Cessna TU206G
☐ G-SBUT	Robinson R22B	☐ G-SHAN	Robinson R44	☐ G-SKYF	SOCATA TB-10 Tobago
☐ G-SCBI	SOCATA TB-20 Trinidad	☐ G-SHAR	Cessna 182T Skylane	☐ G-SKYK	Cameron A-275
☐ G-SCFO	Cameron O-77	☐ G-SHAY	Piper PA-28R-201T	☐ G-SKYL	Cessna 182S Skylane
☐ G-SCHI	Aerospatiale AS.350B2	☐ G-SHCB	Schweizer 269C-1	☐ G-SKYN	Aerospatiale AS.355F1
☐ G-SCHO	Robinson R22B	☐ G-SHED	Piper PA-28-181 Archer	☐ G-SKYO	Slingsby T.67M
☐ G-SCII	Agusta A109C	☐ G-SHEZ	P & M Quik	☐ G-SKYR	Cameron A-180
☐ G-SCIP	SOCATA TB-20 Trinidad	☐ G-SHIM	CFM Shadow SA	☐ G-SKYT	III Sky Arrow 650TC
☐ G-SCLX	FLS Sprint 160	☐ G-SHOG	Colomban MC-15 Cri-Cri	☐ G-SKYU	Cameron A-210
☐ G-SCOI	Agusta 109E Power	☐ G-SHPP	Hughes 269A	☐ G-SKYV	Piper PA-28RT-201T
☐ G-SCOL	Gippsland GA-8 Airvan	☐ G-SHRK	Enstrom 280C-UK	☐ G-SKYW	Aerospatiale AS.355F1
☐ G-SCPD	Reality Escapade	☐ G-SHRT	Robinson R44	☐ G-SKYX	Cameron A-210
☐ G-SCPL	Piper PA-28-140 Cherokee	☐ G-SHSH	Europa	☐ G-SKYY	Cameron A-250
☐ G-SCTA	Westland Scout	☐ G-SHSP	Cessna 172S Skyhawk	☐ G-SLCE	Cameron C-80
☐ G-SCUB	Piper PA-18-135	☐ G-SHUF	Mainair Blade	☐ G-SLCT	Diamond DA42 Twin Star
☐ G-SCUD	Bensen B.8MR	☐ G-SHUG	Piper PA-28R-201T	☐ G-SLEA	Mudry CAP.10B
☐ G-SCUL	Rutan Cozy	☐ G-SHUU	Enstrom 280C-UK	☐ G-SLII	Cameron O-90
☐ G-SDCI	Bell 206B Jet Ranger	☐ G-SHUV	Woody Pusher	☐ G-SLIP	Easy Raider R100
☐ G-SDEV	DH.104 Dove 6	☐ G-SHWK	Cessna 172S Skyhawk	☐ G-SLMG	Diamond HK.36TTC
☐ G-SDFM	EV-97 Eurostar	☐ G-SIAI	SIAI-Marchetti SF.260W	☐ G-SLNW	Robinson R22B
☐ G-SDLW	Cameron O-105	☐ G-SIAL	Hawker Hunter F.58	☐ G-SLOK	Robinson R44
☐ G-SDOB	Tecnam P2002EA Siera	☐ G-SIAM	Cameron V-90	☐ G-SLTN	SOCATA TB-20 Trinidad
☐ G-SDOI	Aeroprakt A22 Foxbat	☐ G-SICA	BN-2B-20 Islander	☐ G-SLYN	Piper PA-28-161 Warrior
☐ G-SDOZ	Tecnam P92 Echo	☐ G-SICB	BN-2B-20 Islander	☐ G-SMAC	MD Helicopters MD.500N
☐ G-SEAI	Cessna U206G	☐ G-SIGN	Piper PA-39-160 CR	☐ G-SMAN	Airbus A330-242
☐ G-SEDO	Cameron N-105	☐ G-SIIB	Pitts S-2B Special	☐ G-SMAS	Strikemaster Mk.80A
☐ G-SEED	Piper J-3C-90 Cub	☐ G-SIID	Sukhoi Su-26	☐ G-SMBM	Pegasus Quantum
☐ G-SEEE	P & M Quik GT450	☐ G-SIIE	Pitts S-2B Special	☐ G-SMDH	Europa XS
☐ G-SEEK	Cessna T210M	☐ G-SIII	Extra EA300	☐ G-SMDJ	Aerospatiale AS.350B2
☐ G-SEFC	Boeing 737-7Q8	☐ G-SIIS	Pitts S-1S Special	☐ G-SMIG	Cameron O-65
☐ G-SEFI	Robinson R44	☐ G-SIJJ	North American P-51D	☐ G-SMJJ	Cessna 414A
☐ G-SEGA	Cameron Sonic SS	☐ G-SIJW	Scottish Aviation Bulldog	☐ G-SMKM	Cirrus SR20
☐ G-SEJW	Piper PA-28-161 Warrior	☐ G-SILS	Pietenpol Aircamper	☐ G-SMRS	Cessna 172F
☐ G-SELC	Diamond DA42 Twin Star	☐ G-SILY	Pegasus Quantum	☐ G-SMRT	Lindstrand LBL-260A
☐ G-SELF	Europa	☐ G-SIMI	Cameron A-315	☐ G-SMTC	Colt Hut SS
☐ G-SELL	Robin DR.400-180 Regent	☐ G-SIMM	Ikarus C42 Cyclone	☐ G-SMTH	Piper PA-28-140 Cherokee
☐ G-SELX	BN-2T Islander	☐ G-SIMP	Jabiru SP	☐ G-SMTJ	Airbus A321-211
☐ G-SELY	Agusta Bell 206B	☐ G-SIMS	Robinson R22B	☐ G-SNAK	Lindstrand LBL-105A
☐ G-SEMI	Piper PA-44-180 Seminole	☐ G-SIMY	Piper PA-32-300	☐ G-SNAP	Cameron V-77

☐ G-SNEV	CFM Shadow SA	
☐ G-SNIF	Cameron A-300	
☐ G-SNOG	Air Creation Kiss 400	
☐ G-SNOP	Europa	
☐ G-SNOW	Cameron V-77	
☐ G-SNOZ	Europa	
☐ G-SNUZ	Piper PA-28-161 Warrior	
☐ G-SOAR	Eiri PIK 20E	
☐ G-SOBI	Piper PA-28-181 Archer	
☐ G-SOCK	P & M Quik	
☐ G-SOCT	Yakovlev Yak-50	
☐ G-SOEI	HS.748-2A	
☐ G-SOFT	Thunder Ax7-77	
☐ G-SOHO	Diamond DA.40D Star	
☐ G-SOKO	Soko P2 Kraguj	
☐ G-SOLA	Starlite SL-1	
☐ G-SOLH	Bell 47G-5	
☐ G-SONA	SOCATA TB-9 Tampico	
☐ G-SOOC	Hughes 369HS	
☐ G-SOOM	Glaser-Dirks DG-500M	
☐ G-SOOS	Colt 21A	
☐ G-SOOT	Piper PA-28-180 Cherokee	
☐ G-SOOZ	Rans S6 Coyote II (N)	
☐ G-SOPH	Best Off Sky Ranger	
☐ G-SOPP	Enstrom 280FX	
☐ G-SORT	Cameron N-90	
☐ G-SOUL	Cessna 310R	
☐ G-SPHU	Eurocopter EC135T2	
☐ G-SOVA	Cessna 550 Citation II	
☐ G-SOVB	LearJet 45	
☐ G-SPAM	Avid Aerobat	
☐ G-SPAT	Aero AT-3 R100	
☐ G-SPDR	DH.115 Sea Vampire	
☐ G-SPEE	Robinson R22B	
☐ G-SPEL	Sky 220-24	
☐ G-SPEY	Agusta Bell 206B	
☐ G-SPFX	Rutan Cozy	
☐ G-SPHU	Eurocopter EC135T2	
☐ G-SPIN	Pitts S-2A Special	
☐ G-SPIT	Spitfire FR.XIVe	
☐ G-SPOG	Jodel DR.1050	
☐ G-SPOR	Beech 200 Super King Air	
☐ G-SPUR	Cessna 550 Citation II	
☐ G-SPYS	Robinson R44	
☐ G-SRAW	Alpi Pioneer 300	
☐ G-SRII	Easy Raider	
☐ G-SROE	Westland Scout	
☐ G-SRVA	Cirrus SR20	
☐ G-SRVO	Cameron N-90	
☐ G-SRWN	Piper PA-28-161 Warrior	
☐ G-SRYY	Europa XS	
☐ G-SRZO	Cirrus SR20	
☐ G-SSCL	Hughes 369E	
☐ G-SSEA	ATR 42-300	
☐ G-SSEX	Rotorway Exec 162F	
☐ G-SSIX	Rans S6 Coyote II (T)	
☐ G-SSJP	Robinson R44	
☐ G-SSKY	BN2A-2B Islander	
☐ G-SSLF	Lindstrand LBL-210A	
☐ G-SSSC	Sikorsky S-76C	
☐ G-SSSD	Sikorsky S-76C	
☐ G-SSSE	Sikorsky S-76C	
☐ G-SSTI	Cameron N-105	
☐ G-SSWE	Short SD.360-100	
☐ G-SSWM	Short SD.360-100	
☐ G-SSWO	Short SD.360-100	
☐ G-SSWR	Short SD.360-100	
☐ G-SSWV	Fournier RF5B	
☐ G-SSXX	Eurocopter EC135T2	
☐ G-STAA	Robinson R44	
☐ G-STAF	Van's RV-7A	
☐ G-STAT	Cessna U206F	
☐ G-STAV	Cameron O-84	
☐ G-STAY	Reims FR172K Hawk XP	
☐ G-STCH	Fiesler F156-A1 Storch	
☐ G-STDL	Phillips ST2 Speedtwin	
☐ G-STEA	Piper PA-28R-200	
☐ G-STEM	Stemme S-10V	
☐ G-STEN	Stemme S-10	
☐ G-STEP	Schweizer 269C	
☐ G-STER	Bell 206B Jet Ranger	
☐ G-STEV	Robin DR.221 Dauphin	
☐ G-STIG	Focke-Wulf FW.44J	
☐ G-STMP	Stampe SV-4A	
☐ G-STNS	Agusta 109A-II	
☐ G-STOB	Raytheon 400XP	
☐ G-STOK	Cameron 77B	
☐ G-STON	Eurocopter AS355N	
☐ G-STOO	Stolp SA.300 Too	
☐ G-STOP	Robinson R44	
☐ G-STOW	Cameron Wine Box	
☐ G-STPH	Robinson R44	
☐ G-STPI	Cameron A-210	
☐ G-STRF	Boeing 737-76N	
☐ G-STRG	Pegasus AX2000	
☐ G-STRH	Boeing 737-36N	
☐ G-STRI	Boeing 737-33A	
☐ G-STRJ	Boeing 737-33A	
☐ G-STRK	CFM Shadow SA-II	
☐ G-STRL	Aerospatiale AS.355N	
☐ G-STRM	Cameron N-90	
☐ G-STUA	Pitts S-2A Special	
☐ G-STUB	Pitts S-2B Special	
☐ G-STUE	Europa	
☐ G-STUY	Robinson R44	
☐ G-STWO	ARV Super 2	
☐ G-STYL	Pitts S-1S Special	
☐ G-SUCH	Cameron V-77	
☐ G-SUCK	Cameron Z-105	
☐ G-SUCT	Robinson R22	
☐ G-SUEB	Piper PA-28-181 Archer	
☐ G-SUEC	Piper PA-32-301XTC	
☐ G-SUED	Thunder Ax6-90	
☐ G-SUEY	Bell 206L Long Ranger	
☐ G-SUEZ	Agusta Bell 206B	
☐ G-SUFF	Eurocopter EC135T1	
☐ G-SUKI	Piper PA-38-112 Tomahawk	
☐ G-SUMX	Robinson R22B	
☐ G-SUMZ	Robinson R44	
☐ G-SUNN	Robinson R44	
☐ G-SUPA	Piper PA-18-150	
☐ G-SURG	Piper PA-30-160 B	
☐ G-SURY	Eurocopter EC135T2	
☐ G-SUSE	Europa XS	
☐ G-SUSI	Cameron V-77	
☐ G-SUSX	MD.900 Explorer	
☐ G-SUTD	Jabiru UL-D	
☐ G-SUTN	III Sky Arrow 650TC	
☐ G-SUZN	Piper PA-28-161 Warrior	
☐ G-SUZY	Taylor Monoplane	
☐ G-SVDG	Jabiru SK	
☐ G-SVEA	Piper PA-28-161 Warrior	
☐ G-SVET	Yakovlev Yak-50	
☐ G-SVIP	Cessna 421B	
☐ G-SVIV	Stampe SV-4C	
☐ G-SVPN	Piper PA-32R-301T	
☐ G-SVSB	Cessna 680 Sovereign	
☐ G-SWAT	Robinson R44	
☐ G-SWEE	Beech 95-B55 Baron	
☐ G-SWEL	Hughes 369HS	
☐ G-SWIS	DH.100 Vampire FB.6	
☐ G-SWLL	Aero AT-3	
☐ G-SWON	Pitts S-1S Special	
☐ G-SWOT	Phoenix Currie Wot	
☐ G-SWPR	Cameron N-56	
☐ G-SWWM	Aerospatiale Gazelle	
☐ G-SYDE	Piper PA-32R-301T	
☐ G-SYEL	Aero AT-3 R100	
☐ G-SYFW	WAR Focke-Wulf FW192	
☐ G-SYLJ	Embraer EMB-135BJ	
☐ G-SYPA	Aerospatiale AS.355F2	
☐ G-SYPS	MD.900 Explorer	
☐ G-SYUT	Air Craeation iXess	
☐ G-SYWL	Aero AT-3	
☐ G-TAAA	Cirrus SR20	
☐ G-TAAB	Cirrus SR22	
☐ G-TAAC	Cirrus SR20	
☐ G-TABI	Cirrus SR20	
☐ G-TABS	Embraer EMB-110P1	
☐ G-TACK	Grob 109B	
☐ G-TADC	Aeroprakt A22 Foxbat	
☐ G-TAFC	Maule M.7-235B	
☐ G-TAFF	CASA I-131E	
☐ G-TAFI	Bucker Bu.133C	
☐ G-TAGG	Eurocopter EC135T2	
☐ G-TAGH	Beech B200 Super King Air	
☐ G-TAGR	Europa XS	
☐ G-TAGT	Robinson R22B	
☐ G-TAIL	Cessna 150J	
☐ G-TAIR	Piper PA-34-200T Seneca	
☐ G-TAIT	Cessna 172R Skyhawk	
☐ G-TAJF	Lindstrand LBL-77A	
☐ G-TAKE	Aerospatiale AS.355F1	
☐ G-TAMA	Schweizer 333	
☐ G-TAMB	Schweizer 333	
☐ G-TAMC	Schweizer 333	
☐ G-TAMD	Schweizer 333	
☐ G-TAME	Schweizer 333	
☐ G-TAMF	Bell 206B Jet Ranger	
☐ G-TAMR	Cessna 172S Skyhawk	
☐ G-TAMS	Beech A23-24	
☐ G-TAMY	Cessna 421B	
☐ G-TANA	Air Creation iXess	
☐ G-TAND	Robinson R44	
☐ G-TANI	Grumman GA-7 Cougar	
☐ G-TANJ	Raj Hamsa X'Air	
☐ G-TANK	Cameron N-90	
☐ G-TANS	SOCATA TB-20 Trinidad	
☐ G-TANY	EAA Acrosport II	
☐ G-TAPE	Piper PA-23-250 Aztec D	
☐ G-TAPS	Piper PA-28RT-201T	
☐ G-TARG	Tanarg iXess	
☐ G-TARN	Pietenpol Aircamper	
☐ G-TART	Piper PA-28-236 Dakota	
☐ G-TASH	Cessna 172N Skyhawk	
☐ G-TASK	Cessna 404	
☐ G-TATS	Aerospatiale AS.350BA	
☐ G-TATT	GY-20 Minicab	
☐ G-TATY	Robinson R44	
☐ G-TAXI	Piper PA-23-250 Aztec E	
☐ G-TAYC	Gulfstream G550	
☐ G-TAYI	Grob 115	
☐ G-TAYS	Reims F152	
☐ G-TAZZ	DR.107 One Design	
☐ G-TBAE	BAe 146-200	
☐ G-TBAG	Murphy Renegade	
☐ G-TBAH	Bell 206B Jet Ranger	
☐ G-TBBC	Pegasus Quantum	
☐ G-TBEA	Cessna 525A CJ2	
☐ G-TBGL	Agusta 109A	
☐ G-TBGT	SOCATA TB-20 Trinidad	
☐ G-TBHH	Aerospatiale AS.355F	
☐ G-TBIC	BAe 146-200	
☐ G-TBIO	SOCATA TB-10 Tobago	
☐ G-TBJP	P & M Quik	
☐ G-TBLB	P & M Quik GT450	
☐ G-TBLY	Eurocopter EC120B	
☐ G-TBMW	Renegade Spirit UK	
☐ G-TBOK	SOCATA TB-10 Tobago	
☐ G-TBSV	SOCATA TB-20 Trinidad	

☐ G-TBTB	Robinson R44	☐ G-THEO	TEAM Minimax
☐ G-TBTN	SOCATA TB-10 Tobago	☐ G-THIN	Reims FR172E Rocket
☐ G-TBXX	SOCATA TB-20 Trinidad	☐ G-THLA	Robinson R22B
☐ G-TBZI	SOCATA TB-21 Trinidad TC	☐ G-THMB	Van's RV-9A
☐ G-TBZO	SOCATA TB-20 Trinidad	☐ G-THOA	Boeing 737-5L9
☐ G-TCAN	Colt 69A	☐ G-THOB	Boeing 737-5L9
☐ G-TCAP	BAe 125-800B	☐ G-THOC	Boeing 737-59D
☐ G-TCAS	Cameron Z-275	☐ G-THOD	Boeing 737-59D
☐ G-TCBA	Boeing 757-2Q8	☐ G-THOE	Boeing 737-3Q8
☐ G-TCEE	Hughes 369HS	☐ G-THOF	Boeing 737-3Q8
☐ G-TCMM	Agusta Bell 206B	☐ G-THOG	Boeing 737-31S
☐ G-TCNM	Tecnam P92 Echo	☐ G-THOH	Boeing 737-31S
☐ G-TCNY	P & M Quik	☐ G-THOI	Boeing 737-36Q
☐ G-TCOM	Piper PA-30-160 B	☐ G-THOJ	Boeing 737-36Q
☐ G-TCTC	Piper PA-28R-201T	☐ G-THOK	Boeing 737-36Q
☐ G-TCUB	Piper J-3C-65 Cub	☐ G-THOL	Boeing 737-36Q
☐ G-TCXA	Airbus A330-243	☐ G-THOM	Thunder Ax6-56
☐ G-TDFS	IMCO Callair A-9A	☐ G-THON	Boeing 737-36N
☐ G-TDOG	Scottish Aviation Bulldog	☐ G-THOS	Thunder Ax7-77
☐ G-TDRA	Cessna 172S Skyhawk	☐ G-THOT	Jabiru SK
☐ G-TDVB	Dyn'Aero MCR-01	☐ G-THRE	Cessna 182S Skylane
☐ G-TDYN	Aerospool Dynamic WT9	☐ G-THSL	Piper PA-28R-201
☐ G-TEAS	Tanarg iXess	☐ G-THZL	SOCATA TB-20 Trinidad
☐ G-TEBZ	Piper PA-28R-201	☐ G-TICH	Taylor Titch
☐ G-TECC	Aeronca 7AC Champion	☐ G-TIDS	Jodel D.150 Mascaret
☐ G-TECH	Rockwell 114	☐ G-TIGA	DH.82A Tiger Moth
☐ G-TECK	Cameron V-77	☐ G-TIGB	Aerospatiale AS.332L
☐ G-TECM	Tecnam P92 Echo	☐ G-TIGC	Aerospatiale AS.332L
☐ G-TECO	Tecnam P92 Echo	☐ G-TIGE	Aerospatiale AS.332L
☐ G-TECS	Tecnam P92 Echo	☐ G-TIGF	Aerospatiale AS.332L
☐ G-TECZ	Tecnam P92 Echo	☐ G-TIGG	Aerospatiale AS.332L
☐ G-TEDB	Reims F150L	☐ G-TIGJ	Aerospatiale AS.332L
☐ G-TEDF	Cameron N-90	☐ G-TIGO	Aerospatiale AS.332L
☐ G-TEDI	Best Off Sky Ranger	☐ G-TIGS	Aerospatiale AS.332L
☐ G-TEDS	SOCATA TB-10 Tobago	☐ G-TIGT	Aerospatiale AS.332L
☐ G-TEDW	Air Creation Kiss 450	☐ G-TIGV	Aerospatiale AS.332L
☐ G-TEFC	Piper PA-28-140 Cherokee	☐ G-TIII	Pitts S-2A Special
☐ G-TEHL	CFM Shadow SA-M	☐ G-TILE	Robinson R22B
☐ G-TELY	Agusta 109A	☐ G-TILI	Bell 206B Jet Ranger
☐ G-TEMB	Tecnam P2002EA Siera	☐ G-TIMB	Rutan VariEze
☐ G-TEMP	Piper PA-28-180 Cherokee	☐ G-TIMC	Robinson R44
☐ G-TEMT	Hawker Tempest II	☐ G-TIMG	Beagle A.61 Terrier
☐ G-TENG	Extra EA300/L	☐ G-TIMK	Piper PA-28-181 Archer
☐ G-TENS	Diamond Katana	☐ G-TIML	Cessna 172S Skyhawk
☐ G-TENT	Auster J/1N Alpha	☐ G-TIMM	Folland Gnat T.1
☐ G-TERN	Europa	☐ G-TIMP	Aeronca 7BCM Champion
☐ G-TERR	P & M Quik	☐ G-TIMS	Falconar F.12A
☐ G-TERY	Piper PA-28-181 Archer	☐ G-TIMY	Gardan GY-80-160
☐ G-TESI	Tecnam P2002EA Siera	☐ G-TINA	SOCATA TB-10 Tobago
☐ G-TEST	Piper PA-34-200 Seneca	☐ G-TING	Cameron O-120
☐ G-TETI	Cameron N-90	☐ G-TINK	Robinson R22B
☐ G-TEWS	Piper PA-28-140 Cherokee	☐ G-TINS	Cameron N-90
☐ G-TEXN	North American T-6G	☐ G-TINT	EV-97 Eurostar
☐ G-TEXS	Van's RV-6	☐ G-TINY	Zlin Z.526F
☐ G-TEXT	Robinson R44	☐ G-TIPS	Tipsy Nipper T.66
☐ G-TFCI	Reims FA152 Aerobat	☐ G-TIVS	Rans S6 Coyote II
☐ G-TFIN	Piper PA-32RT-300T	☐ G-TIVV	EV-97 Eurostar
☐ G-TFIX	Pegasus Quantum	☐ G-TJAL	Jabiru SPL-430
☐ G-TFLY	Air Creation Kiss 450	☐ G-TJAV	P & M Quik
☐ G-TFOG	Best Off Sky Ranger	☐ G-TJAY	Piper PA-22-135 Tri-Pacer
☐ G-TFOX	Denney Kitfox	☐ G-TKAY	Europa
☐ G-TFUN	Valentin Taifun 17E	☐ G-TKGR	Lindstrand Car SS
☐ G-TFYN	Piper PA-32RT-300	☐ G-TKIS	Tri-R Kis
☐ G-TGER	Grumman AA-5B Tiger	☐ G-TKNT	Agusta A109A-II
☐ G-TGGR	Eurocopter EC120B	☐ G-TKPZ	Cessna 310R
☐ G-TGRA	Agusta 109A	☐ G-TLDK	Piper PA-22-150 Tri-Pacer
☐ G-TGRD	Robinson R22B2	☐ G-TLEL	American Blimp A60+
☐ G-TGRE	Robinson R22A	☐ G-TLET	Piper PA-28-161 Warrior
☐ G-TGRS	Robinson R22B	☐ G-TMCB	Best Off Sky Ranger
☐ G-TGRZ	Bell 206B Jet Ranger	☐ G-TMCC	Cameron N-90
☐ G-THAT	Raj Hamsa X'Air	☐ G-TMKI	Percival Provost T1
☐ G-THEA	Boeing Stearman E75	☐ G-TMOL	SOCATA TB-20 Trinidad
☐ G-THEL	Robinson R44	☐ G-TMRA	Short SD.360-100

☐ G-TMRB	Short SD.360-200
☐ G-TMRO	Short SD.360
☐ G-TNRG	Tanarg Kitfox 15
☐ G-TNTN	Thunder Ax6-56
☐ G-TOAD	Jodel D.140
☐ G-TOAK	SOCATA TB-20 Trinidad
☐ G-TOBA	SOCATA TB-10 Tobago
☐ G-TOBI	Reims F172K
☐ G-TODE	Ruschmeyer RG90RG
☐ G-TOFT	Colt 90A
☐ G-TOGO	Van's RV-6
☐ G-TOHS	Cameron V-31
☐ G-TOIL	Enstrom 480B
☐ G-TOLL	Piper PA-28R-201
☐ G-TOLY	Robinson R22B
☐ G-TOMC	North American AT-6D
☐ G-TOMJ	Flight Design CT2K
☐ G-TOMM	Robinson R22B
☐ G-TOMS	Piper PA-38-112 Tomahawk
☐ G-TOMZ	Denney Kitfox
☐ G-TONN	P & M Quik
☐ G-TONS	Slingsby T.67M
☐ G-TOOL	Thunder Ax8-105
☐ G-TOOT	Dyn'Aero MCR-01
☐ G-TOPC	Aerospatiale AS.355F1
☐ G-TOPK	Europa
☐ G-TOPO	Piper PA-23-250 Aztec E
☐ G-TOPS	Aerospatiale AS.355F1
☐ G-TOPZ	Aerospatiale SA.342J
☐ G-TORC	Piper PA-28R-200
☐ G-TORK	Cameron Z-105
☐ G-TORN	Flight Design CTSW
☐ G-TORS	Robinson R22B
☐ G-TOSH	Robinson R22B
☐ G-TOTN	Cessna 210M Centurion
☐ G-TOTO	Reims F177RG
☐ G-TOUR	Robin R.2112 Alpha
☐ G-TOWS	Piper PA-25-260 Pawnee
☐ G-TOYA	Boeing 737-3Q8
☐ G-TOYB	Boeing 737-3Q8
☐ G-TOYC	Boeing 737-3Q8
☐ G-TOYD	Boeing 737-3Q8
☐ G-TOYE	Boeing 737-33A
☐ G-TOYF	Boeing 737-36N
☐ G-TOYG	Boeing 737-33R
☐ G-TOYH	Boeing 737-36N
☐ G-TOYZ	Bell 206B Jet Ranger
☐ G-TPSL	Cessna 182S Skylane
☐ G-TPWL	P & M Quik
☐ G-TRAC	Robinson R44
☐ G-TRAM	Pegasus Quantum
☐ G-TRAN	Beech 76 Duchess
☐ G-TRAT	Pilatus PC-12
☐ G-TRAV	Cameron A-210
☐ G-TRAX	Reims Cessna F172M
☐ G-TRBO	Schleicher ASW 28
☐ G-TRCW	Robinson R44
☐ G-TRCY	Robinson R44
☐ G-TREC	Cessna 421C
☐ G-TREE	Bell 206B Jet Ranger
☐ G-TREK	Jodel D.18
☐ G-TREX	Alpi Pioneer 300
☐ G-TRIB	Lindstrand LBL HS-110
☐ G-TRIC	DHC-1 Chipmunk
☐ G-TRIG	Cameron Z-90
☐ G-TRIM	Monnett Moni
☐ G-TRIN	SOCATA TB-20 Trinidad
☐ G-TRIO	Cessna 172M Skyhawk
☐ G-TRNT	Robinson R44
☐ G-TROP	Cessna 310R
☐ G-TROY	North American T-28A
☐ G-TRUD	Enstrom 480
☐ G-TRUE	Hughes 369E

☐ G-TRUK	Glasair IIRG	
☐ G-TRUX	Colt 77A	
☐ G-TRYK	Air Creation Kiss 400	
☐ G-TRYX	Enstrom 480B	
☐ G-TSDS	Piper PA-32R-301 SP	
☐ G-TSGJ	Piper PA-28-181 Archer	
☐ G-TSIX	North American AT-6C	
☐ G-TSKD	Raj Hamsa X'Air	
☐ G-TSKY	Beagle B.121 Pup 2	
☐ G-TSLC	Schweizer 269C-1	
☐ G-TSOB	Rans S6 Coyote II	
☐ G-TSOL	EAA Acrosport 1	
☐ G-TSUE	Europa	
☐ G-TSWI	Lindstrand LBL 90A	
☐ G-TTDD	Zenair CH.701	
☐ G-TTHC	Robinson R22B	
☐ G-TTIA	Airbus A321-231	
☐ G-TTIB	Airbus A321-231	
☐ G-TTIC	Airbus A321-231	
☐ G-TTID	Airbus A321-231	
☐ G-TTIE	Airbus A321-231	
☐ G-TTIF	Airbus A321-231	
☐ G-TTIG	Airbus A321-231	
☐ G-TTMB	Bell 206B Jet Ranger	
☐ G-TTOA	Airbus A320-232	
☐ G-TTOB	Airbus A320-232	
☐ G-TTOC	Airbus A320-232	
☐ G-TTOD	Airbus A320-232	
☐ G-TTOE	Airbus A320-232	
☐ G-TTOF	Airbus A320-232	
☐ G-TTOG	Airbus A320-232	
☐ G-TTOH	Airbus A320-232	
☐ G-TTOI	Airbus A320-232	
☐ G-TTOJ	Airbus A320-232	
☐ G-TTOY	CFM Shadow SA	
☐ G-TUBB	Jabiru UL-450	
☐ G-TUCK	Van's RV-8	
☐ G-TUDR	Cameron V-77	
☐ G-TUGG	Piper PA-18-180	
☐ G-TUGS	Piper PA-25-235 Pawnee	
☐ G-TUGY	Robin DR.400-180R	
☐ G-TULP	Lindstrand Tulips SS	
☐ G-TUNE	Robinson R22B	
☐ G-TURF	Reims F406	
☐ G-TURN	Steen Skybolt	
☐ G-TUSA	Pegasus Quantum	
☐ G-TUTU	Cameron O-105	
☐ G-TVAM	MBB Bo.105 DBS-4	
☐ G-TVBF	Lindstrand LBL-310A	
☐ G-TVCO	Gippsland GA-8 Airvan	
☐ G-TVEE	Hughes 369HS	
☐ G-TVII	Hawker Hunter T.7	
☐ G-TVIJ	CCF Harvard 4	
☐ G-TVIP	Cessna 404	
☐ G-TVTV	Cameron TV SS	
☐ G-TWEL	Piper PA-28-181 Archer	
☐ G-TWEY	Colt 69A	
☐ G-TWIN	Piper PA-44-180 Seminole	
☐ G-TWIZ	Rockwell 114	
☐ G-TWMC	Agusta A109E Power	
☐ G-TWOC	Schempp-Hirth Ventus	
☐ G-TWOT	Schempp-Hirth Discus	
☐ G-TWSR	Silence Twister	
☐ G-TWST	Silence Twister	
☐ G-TWTW	Kitfox Mk.2	
☐ G-TXSE	RAF 2000 GTX-SE	
☐ G-TYAK	Yakovlev Yak-52	
☐ G-TYCN	Agusta 109E Power	
☐ G-TYER	Robin DR.500	
☐ G-TYGA	Grumman AA-5B Tiger	
☐ G-TYGR	Best Off Sky Ranger	
☐ G-TYKE	Jabiru UL	
☐ G-TYMS	Cessna 172P Skyhawk	
☐ G-TYNE	SOCATA TB-20 Trinidad	
☐ G-TYRE	Reims F172M	
☐ G-TZEE	SOCATA TB-10 Tobago	
☐ G-TZII	Thorp T.211B	
☐ G-UACA	Best Off Sky Ranger	
☐ G-UAKE	North American P-51D	
☐ G-UANO	DHC-1 Chipmunk	
☐ G-UANT	Piper PA-28-140 Cherokee	
☐ G-UAPA	Robin DR.400-140B	
☐ G-UAPO	Ruschmeyer RG90RG	
☐ G-UAVA	Piper PA-30-160	
☐ G-UCCC	Cameron Sign SS	
☐ G-UDGE	Thruster T600N	
☐ G-UDOG	Scottish Aviation Bulldog	
☐ G-UFAW	Raj Hamsa X'Air	
☐ G-UFCB	Cessna 172S Skyhawk	
☐ G-UFCC	Cessna 172S Skyhawk	
☐ G-UFCD	Cessna 172S Skyhawk	
☐ G-UFCE	Cessna 172S Skyhawk	
☐ G-UFCF	Cessna 172S Skyhawk	
☐ G-UFCG	Cessna 172S Skyhawk	
☐ G-UFCH	Cessna 172S Skyhawk	
☐ G-UFLY	Reims F150H	
☐ G-UGLY	Aerospatiale Alouette II	
☐ G-UHIH	Bell UH-1H	
☐ G-UILD	Grob 109B	
☐ G-UILE	Neico Lancair 320	
☐ G-UILT	Cessna T303 Crusader	
☐ G-UINN	Stolp SA.300 Too	
☐ G-UIST	BAe Jetstream 31	
☐ G-UJAB	Jabiru UL	
☐ G-UJGK	Jabiru UL	
☐ G-UKAT	Aero AT-3	
☐ G-UKHP	BAe 146-300	
☐ G-UKOZ	Jabiru SK	
☐ G-UKUK	Head Ax8-105	
☐ G-ULAS	DHC-1 Chipmunk	
☐ G-ULES	Aerospatiale AS.355F2	
☐ G-ULHI	Scottish Aviation Bulldog	
☐ G-ULIA	Cameron V-77	
☐ G-ULLY	Thruster T600N	
☐ G-ULPS	Everett Gyroplane	
☐ G-ULSY	Ikarus C42 Cyclone	
☐ G-ULTR	Cameron A-105	
☐ G-UMMI	Piper PA-31-310 Navajo	
☐ G-UMMY	Best Off Sky Ranger	
☐ G-UNDD	Piper PA-23-250 Aztec E	
☐ G-UNER	Lindstrand LBL-90A	
☐ G-UNGE	Lindstrand LBL-90A	
☐ G-UNGO	Pietenpol Aircamper	
☐ G-UNIV	Montgomerie Gyro	
☐ G-UNIX	VPM M16 Tandem Trainer	
☐ G-UNYT	Robinson R22B	
☐ G-UPFS	Waco UPF-7	
☐ G-UPHI	Best Off Sky Ranger	
☐ G-UPHL	Cameron 80	
☐ G-UPPP	Colt 77A	
☐ G-UPPY	Cameron DP-80	
☐ G-UPTA	Best Off Sky Ranger	
☐ G-UPUP	Cameron V-77	
☐ G-UPUZ	Lindstrand LBL-120A	
☐ G-UROP	Beech 95-B55 Baron	
☐ G-URRR	Air Command 582	
☐ G-URUS	Maule MX-7-180B	
☐ G-USAM	Cameron Eagle SS	
☐ G-USIL	Thunder Ax7-77	
☐ G-USKE	Aviat A-1B Husky	
☐ G-USKY	Aviat A-1B Husky	
☐ G-USMC	Cameron USMC SS	
☐ G-USRV	Van's RV-6	
☐ G-USSI	Glasair III	
☐ G-USSR	Cameron Russian Doll	
☐ G-USSY	Piper PA-28-181 Archer	
☐ G-USTB	Agusta 109A	
☐ G-USTH	Agusta 109A-II	
☐ G-USTS	Agusta 109A-II	
☐ G-USTY	Clutton FRED II	
☐ G-UTSI	Rand KR-2	
☐ G-UTSY	Piper PA-28R-201	
☐ G-UTTS	Robinson R44	
☐ G-UTZI	Robinson R44	
☐ G-UURO	EV-97 Eurostar	
☐ G-UVBF	Lindstrand LBL-400A	
☐ G-UVIP	Cessna 421C	
☐ G-UVNR	Strikemaster	
☐ G-UZEL	Aerospatiale Gazelle	
☐ G-UZLE	Colt 77A	
☐ G-UZUP	EV-97 Eurostar	
☐ G-UZZL	Van's RV-7	
☐ G-UZZY	Enstrom 480	
☐ G-VAIR	Airbus A340-313X	
☐ G-VALS	Pietenpol Aircamper	
☐ G-VALV	Robinson R44	
☐ G-VALY	SOCATA TB-21 Trinidad GT	
☐ G-VALZ	Cameron N-120	
☐ G-VANA	Gippsland GA-8 Airvan	
☐ G-VANC	Gippsland GA-8 Airvan	
☐ G-VANN	Van's RV-7A	
☐ G-VANS	Van's RV-4	
☐ G-VANZ	Van's RV-6A	
☐ G-VARG	Varga Kachina	
☐ G-VART	Rotorway Exec	
☐ G-VASA	Piper PA-34-200 Seneca	
☐ G-VAST	Boeing 747-41R	
☐ G-VATL	Airbus A340-642	
☐ G-VBFA	UltraMagic N-250	
☐ G-VBFB	UltraMagic N-355	
☐ G-VBFC	UltraMagic N-250	
☐ G-VBFD	UltraMagic N-250	
☐ G-VBFE	UltraMagic N-355	
☐ G-VBFF	Lindstrand LBL 360A	
☐ G-VBIG	Boeing 747-4Q8	
☐ G-VBLU	Airbus A340-642	
☐ G-VBUG	Airbus A340-642	
☐ G-VBUS	Airbus A340-311	
☐ G-VCED	Airbus A320-231	
☐ G-VCIO	EAA Acrosport 2	
☐ G-VCML	Beech 58 Baron	
☐ G-VCXT	Schempp-Hirth Ventus	
☐ G-VDIR	Cessna T310R	
☐ G-VDOG	Cessna 305C Bird Dog	
☐ G-VECD	Robin R.1180T Aiglon	
☐ G-VECE	Robin R.2120U	
☐ G-VECG	Robin R.2160	
☐ G-VEIL	Airbus A340-642	
☐ G-VEIT	Robinson R44	
☐ G-VELA	SIAI-Marchetti S.205-22R	
☐ G-VELD	Airbus A340-313X	
☐ G-VENI	DH.112 Venom FB50	
☐ G-VENM	DH.112 Venom FB.1	
☐ G-VENT	Schempp-Hirth Ventus	
☐ G-VERA	Gardan Minicab	
☐ G-VERN	Piper PA-32-300	
☐ G-VETA	Hawker Hunter	
☐ G-VETS	Enstrom 280C-UK	
☐ G-VEYE	Robinson R22	
☐ G-VEZE	Rutan VariEze	
☐ G-VFAB	Boeing 747-4Q8	
☐ G-VFAR	Airbus A340-313X	
☐ G-VFIT	Airbus A340-642	
☐ G-VFIZ	Airbus A340-642	
☐ G-VFOX	Airbus A340-642	
☐ G-VFUN	Airbus A340-642	
☐ G-VGAG	Cirrus SR20	
☐ G-VGAL	Boeing 747-443	
☐ G-VGAS	Airbus A340-642	

Reg	Type	Reg	Type	Reg	Type
G-VGMC	Aerospatiale AS.355N	G-VMEG	Airbus A340-642	G-WACH	Reims FA152 Aerobat
G-VGOA	Airbus A340-642	G-VMFC	Piper PA-32R-301 SP	G-WACI	Beech 76 Duchess
G-VHOL	Airbus A340-311	G-VMJM	SOCATA TB-10 Tobago	G-WACJ	Beech 76 Duchess
G-VHOT	Boeing 747-4Q8	G-VMSL	Robinson R22B	G-WACL	Reims F172N
G-VIBA	Cameron DP-80	G-VNAP	Airbus 340-642	G-WACO	Waco UPF-7
G-VICC	Piper PA-28-161 Warrior	G-VNOM	DH.112 Venom FB50	G-WACT	Reims F152
G-VICE	Hughes 369E	G-VNON	Reality Escapade	G-WACU	Reims FA152 Aerobat
G-VICI	DH.112 Venom FB50	G-VNUS	Hughes 269C	G-WACW	Cessna 172P Skyhawk
G-VICM	Beech F33C Bonanza	G-VOAR	Piper PA-28-181 Archer	G-WACY	Reims F172P
G-VICS	Rockwell 114B	G-VODA	Cameron N-77	G-WADI	Piper PA-46-310P Malibu
G-VICT	Piper PA-31-310 Navajo	G-VOGE	Airbus A340-642	G-WADS	Robinson R22B
G-VIIA	Boeing 777-236	G-VOID	Piper PA-28RT-201	G-WAFU	Robinson R44
G-VIIB	Boeing 777-236	G-VOIP	Aerospatiale Gazelle	G-WAGG	Robinson R22B
G-VIIC	Boeing 777-236	G-VOLO	Alpi Pioneer 300	G-WAGN	Stinson 108-3 Voyager
G-VIID	Boeing 777-236	G-VONA	Sikorsky S-76A	G-WAGS	Robinson R44
G-VIIE	Boeing 777-236	G-VONB	Sikorsky S-76B	G-WAHL	QAC Quickie
G-VIIF	Boeing 777-236	G-VONC	Sikorsky S-76B	G-WAIN	Cessna 550 Citation II
G-VIIG	Boeing 777-236	G-VOND	Bell 222	G-WAIR	Piper PA-32-301
G-VIIH	Boeing 777-236	G-VONE	Aerospatiale AS.355N	G-WAIT	Cameron V-77
G-VIIJ	Boeing 777-236	G-VONF	Aerospatiale AS.355F1	G-WAKE	Mainair Blade
G-VIIK	Boeing 777-236	G-VONG	Aerospatiale AS.355F1	G-WAKY	Cyclone AX2000
G-VIIL	Boeing 777-236	G-VONH	Aerospatiale AS.355F1	G-WALI	Robinson R44
G-VIIM	Boeing 777-236	G-VONJ	Beech 390 Premier 1	G-WALY	Maule MX-7-180
G-VIIN	Boeing 777-236	G-VONK	Aerospatiale AS.355F1	G-WAMS	Piper PA-28R-201
G-VIIO	Boeing 777-236	G-VONS	Piper PA-32R-301T	G-WARA	Piper PA-28-161 Warrior
G-VIIP	Boeing 777-236	G-VOOM	Pitts S-1S Special	G-WARB	Piper PA-28-181 Archer
G-VIIR	Boeing 777-236	G-VPAT	Evans VP-1	G-WARD	Taylor Monoplane
G-VIIS	Boeing 777-236	G-VPCB	Evans VP-1	G-WARE	Piper PA-28-161 Warrior
G-VIIT	Boeing 777-236	G-VPSI	Cameron Z-1600	G-WARH	Piper PA-28-161 Warrior
G-VIIU	Boeing 777-236	G-VPSJ	Europa	G-WARK	Schweizer 269C
G-VIIV	Boeing 777-236	G-VRED	Airbus A340-642	G-WARO	Piper PA-28-161 Warrior
G-VIIW	Boeing 777-236	G-VROC	Boeing 747-41R	G-WARP	Cessna 182F Skylane
G-VIIX	Boeing 777-236	G-VROD	Aeroprakt A22 Foxbat	G-WARR	Piper PA-28-161 Warrior
G-VIIY	Boeing 777-236	G-VROE	Avro 652 Anson	G-WARS	Piper PA-28-161 Warrior
G-VIKE	Bellanca 17-30A	G-VROM	Boeing 747-443	G-WARU	Piper PA-28-161 Warrior
G-VIKY	Cameron A-120	G-VROS	Boeing 747-443	G-WARV	Piper PA-28-161 Warrior
G-VILA	Jabiru UL	G-VROY	Boeing 747-443	G-WARW	Piper PA-28-181 Archer
G-VILL	Lazer Z.200	G-VRST	Piper PA-46-310P Malibu	G-WARX	Piper PA-28-161 Warrior
G-VINH	Flight Design CTSW	G-VRTX	Enstrom 280FX	G-WARY	Piper PA-28-161 Warrior
G-VINO	Sky 90-24	G-VRVI	Cameron O-90	G-WARZ	Piper PA-28-161 Warrior
G-VIPA	Cessna 182S Skylane	G-VSEA	Airbus A340-311	G-WATR	Aviat A-1 Husky
G-VIPH	Agusta 109C	G-VSGE	Cameron O-105	G-WATV	Robinson R44
G-VIPI	BAe 125-800B	G-VSHY	Airbus A340-642	G-WAVA	Robin HR.200-120B
G-VIPP	Piper PA-31-350 Chieftain	G-VSSH	Airbus A340-642	G-WAVE	Grob 109B
G-VIPR	Eurocopter EC120B	G-VSUN	Airbus A340-313	G-WAVI	Robin HR.200-120B
G-VIPY	Piper PA-31-350 Chieftain	G-VTAL	Beech V35 Bonanza	G-WAVN	Robin HR.200-120B
G-VIPZ	Sikorsky S-61N	G-VTII	DH.115 Vampire T.11	G-WAVS	Piper PA-28-181 Archer
G-VITE	Robin R.1180T Aiglon	G-VTOL	Harrier T.52	G-WAVT	Robin R.2160i
G-VITL	Lindstrand LBL-105A	G-VTOP	Boeing 747-4Q8	G-WAVV	Robin HR200/120B
G-VIVA	Thunder Ax7-65	G-VTWO	Schempp-Hirth Ventus	G-WAVY	Grob 109B
G-VIVI	Taylor Titch	G-VUEA	Cessna 550 Citation II	G-WAZP	Best Off Sky Ranger
G-VIVM	Jet Provost T.5	G-VUEM	Cessna 501 Citation 1	G-WAZZ	Pitts S-1S Special
G-VIVO	Nicollier HN700 Menestrel	G-VUEZ	Cessna 550 Citation II	G-WBAT	Wombat Gyrocopter
G-VIVS	Piper PA-28-151 Warrior	G-VVBF	Colt 315A	G-WBEV	Cameron N-77
G-VIXN	DH Sea Vixen FAW.2	G-VVBK	Piper PA-34-200T Seneca	G-WBLY	P & M Quik
G-VIZA	Lindstrand LBL 260A	G-VVIP	Cessna 421C	G-WBMG	Cameron N-90
G-VIZZ	Sportavia RS.180	G-VVTV	Diamond DA42 Twin Star	G-WBTS	Falconar F-11-W200
G-VJAB	Jabiru UL	G-VVVV	Best Off Sky Ranger	G-WBVS	Diamond DA.40D Star
G-VJAM	Airbus A340-642	G-VVWW	Enstrom 280C	G-WCAO	Eurocopter EC135T1
G-VJIM	Colt Jumbo SS	G-VWEB	Airbus A340-642	G-WCAT	Colt Mitt SS
G-VKIT	Europa	G-VWIN	Airbus A340-642	G-WCCP	Beech 200 Super King Air
G-VKNA	Boeing 757-2YOER	G-VWKD	Airbus A340-642	G-WCEI	MS.894E Minerva
G-VKND	Boeing 757-225	G-VWOW	Boeing 747-41R	G-WCIN	Cessna 560 Citation XL
G-VKNG	Boeing 767-3Z9ER	G-VXLG	Boeing 747-41R	G-WCRD	Aerospatiale Gazelle
G-VKNH	Boeing 767-3YOER	G-VYGR	Colt 120A	G-WCUB	Piper PA-18-150
G-VKNI	Boeing 767-383ER	G-VYOU	Airbus A340-642	G-WDEB	Thunder Ax7-77
G-VKUP	Cameron Z-90	G-WAAC	Cameron N-56	G-WDEV	Aerospatiale Gazelle
G-VKVK	Aerospatiale AS.350B3	G-WAAN	MBB Bo.105D	G-WEBS	Champion 7ECA Citabria
G-VLCN	Avro Vulcan B.2	G-WAAS	MBB Bo.105DBS/4	G-WEEK	Best Off Sky Ranger
G-VLIP	Boeing 747-443	G-WACB	Reims F152	G-WEGO	Robinson R44
G-VLUV	Airbus A340-642	G-WACE	Reims F152	G-WELI	Cameron N-77
G-VMCG	Piper PA-38-112 Tomahawk	G-WACF	Cessna 152	G-WELL	Beech 65-E90 King Air
G-VMDE	Cessna P210N Centurion	G-WACG	Cessna 152	G-WELS	Cameron N-65

☐ G-WENA	Aerospatiale AS.355F1
☐ G-WEND	Piper PA-28RT-201
☐ G-WERY	SOCATA TB-20 Trinidad
☐ G-WESX	CFM Shadow SA
☐ G-WETI	Cameron N-31
☐ G-WFFW	Piper PA-28-161 Warrior
☐ G-WFLY	P & M Quik
☐ G-WFOX	Robinson R22B
☐ G-WGCS	Piper PA-18-95
☐ G-WGHB	Canadair T-33AN
☐ G-WGSC	Pilatus PC-6 B2-H4
☐ G-WHAM	Aerospatiale AS.350B3
☐ G-WHAT	Colt 77A
☐ G-WHEE	Pegasus Quantum
☐ G-WHEN	Tecnam P92 Echo
☐ G-WHIM	Colt 77A
☐ G-WHIN	Eurocopter EC135T2
☐ G-WHOG	CFM Shadow SA
☐ G-WHOO	Rotorway Exec
☐ G-WHOT	UltraMagic T-210
☐ G-WHRL	Schweizer 269C
☐ G-WHST	Aerospatiale AS.350B2
☐ G-WIBB	Jodel D.18
☐ G-WIBS	CASA I-131E
☐ G-WIDZ	Staaken Flitzer
☐ G-WIFE	Cessna R182 Skylane RG
☐ G-WIFI	Cameron Z-90
☐ G-WIIZ	Agusta Bell 206B
☐ G-WIKY	Cessna 208B
☐ G-WILD	Pitts S-1T Special
☐ G-WILG	PZL Wilga 35A
☐ G-WILT	Ikarus C42 Cyclone
☐ G-WIMP	Colt 56A
☐ G-WINA	Cessna 560 Citation XL
☐ G-WINI	Scottish Aviation Bulldog
☐ G-WINK	Grumman AA-5B Tiger
☐ G-WINS	Piper PA-32-300
☐ G-WIRE	Aerospatiale AS.355F1
☐ G-WIRL	Robinson R22B
☐ G-WISH	Lindstrand Cake SS
☐ G-WIXI	Mudry CAP.10B
☐ G-WIZA	Robinson R22B
☐ G-WIZD	Lindstrand LBL-180A
☐ G-WIZI	Enstrom 280FX
☐ G-WIZO	Piper PA-34-220T Seneca
☐ G-WIZR	Robinson R22B
☐ G-WIZS	P & M Quik
☐ G-WIZY	Robinson R22B
☐ G-WIZZ	Agusta Bell 206B
☐ G-WJAC	Cameron TR-70
☐ G-WJCJ	Eurocopter EC155
☐ G-WKRD	Aerospatiale AS.350B2
☐ G-WLAC	Piper PA-18-150
☐ G-WLDN	Robinson R44
☐ G-WLMS	Mainair Blade
☐ G-WLSN	Best Off Sky Ranger
☐ G-WLVE	Cameron Buddy 90SS
☐ G-WMAN	Aerospatiale Gazelle
☐ G-WMAO	Eurocopter EC135P2
☐ G-WMAS	Eurocopter EC135T1
☐ G-WMBT	Robinson R44
☐ G-WMID	MD.900 Explorer
☐ G-WMLT	Cessna 182Q Skylane
☐ G-WMPA	Aerospatiale AS.355F2
☐ G-WMTM	Grumman AA-5B Tiger
☐ G-WMWM	Robinson R44
☐ G-WNAA	Agusta 109E Power
☐ G-WNGS	Cameron N-105
☐ G-WNTR	Piper PA-28-161 Warrior
☐ G-WOCO	Waco YMF-F5C
☐ G-WOFM	Agusta A109E Power
☐ G-WOLF	Piper PA-28-140 Cherokee
☐ G-WOLV	Ikarus C42 Cyclone
☐ G-WOOD	Beech 95-A55 Baron
☐ G-WOOF	Enstrom 480
☐ G-WOOL	Colt 77A
☐ G-WORM	Thruster T600N
☐ G-WOWA	DHC-8-311
☐ G-WOWB	DHC-8-311
☐ G-WOWC	DHC-8-311
☐ G-WOWD	DHC-8-311
☐ G-WOWE	DHC-8-311
☐ G-WPAS	MD.900 Explorer
☐ G-WREN	Pitts S-2A Special
☐ G-WRFM	Enstrom 280C-UK
☐ G-WRIT	Colt 77A
☐ G-WRSY	Enstrom 480B
☐ G-WRWR	Robinson R22B
☐ G-WSEC	Enstrom F-28C
☐ G-WSKY	Enstrom 280C-UK
☐ G-WSSX	Ikarus C42 Cyclone
☐ G-WUFF	Europa
☐ G-WULF	WAR Focke-Wulf FW193
☐ G-WUSH	Eurocopter EC120B
☐ G-WVBF	Lindstrand LBL-210A
☐ G-WVIP	Beech B200 Super King Air
☐ G-WWAL	Piper PA-28R-180
☐ G-WWAY	Piper PA-28-181 Archer
☐ G-WWBB	Airbus A330-243
☐ G-WWBD	Airbus A330-243
☐ G-WWBM	Airbus A330-243
☐ G-WWIZ	Beech 58 Baron
☐ G-WYAT	CFM Shadow SA
☐ G-WYCH	Cameron Witch SS
☐ G-WYLE	Rans S6 Coyote II
☐ G-WYND	Wittman Tailwind
☐ G-WYNE	BAe 125-800B
☐ G-WYNT	Cameron N-56
☐ G-WYPA	MBB Bo.105DBS/4
☐ G-WYSP	Robinson R44
☐ G-WYVN	Glaser-Dirks DG-1000S
☐ G-WZOL	Sherwood Ranger
☐ G-WZRD	Eurocopter EC120B
☐ G-XALT	Piper PA-38-112 Tomahawk
☐ G-XARV	ARV Super 2
☐ G-XATS	Pitts S-2A Special
☐ G-XAVI	Piper PA-28-161 Warrior
☐ G-XAXA	BN2 Islander
☐ G-XAYR	Raj Hamsa X'Air
☐ G-XBCI	Bell 206B Jet Ranger
☐ G-XBOX	Bell 206B Jet Ranger
☐ G-XCCC	Extra EA300/L
☐ G-XCIT	Alpi Pioneer 300
☐ G-XCUB	Piper PA-18-150
☐ GXDWE	P & M Quik GT450
☐ G-XELA	Robinson R44
☐ G-XENA	Piper PA-28-161 Warrior
☐ G-XFLY	Mission M212-100
☐ G-XHOT	Cameron Z-105
☐ G-XIII	Van's RV-7
☐ G-XINE	Piper PA-28-161 Warrior
☐ G-XIOO	Raj Hamsa X'Air
☐ G-XKEN	Piper PA-34-200T Seneca
☐ G-XKKA	Diamond HK 36TTC
☐ G-XLAA	Boeing 737-8Q8
☐ G-XLAB	Boeing 737-8Q8
☐ G-XLAC	Boeing 737-81Q
☐ G-XLAC	Boeing 737-81Q
☐ G-XLAG	Boeing 737-86N
☐ G-XLAI	Boeing 737-8Q8
☐ G-XLAJ	Boeing 737-8Q8
☐ G-XLAK	Boeing 737-8FH
☐ G-XLAL	Boeing 737-8FH
☐ G-XLAM	Best Off Sky Ranger
☐ G-XLAN	Boeing 737-86N
☐ G-XLAO	Boeing 737-86N
☐ G-XLIV	Robinson R44	✓
☐ G-XLKF	Cessna T310Q
☐ G-XLLL	Aerospatiale AS.355F1
☐ G-XLMB	Cessna 560 Citation XL
☐ G-XLNT	Zenith CH.601XL
☐ G-XLTG	Cessna 182S Skylane
☐ G-XLXL	Robin DR.400-160 Major
☐ G-XMGO	Super Ximango
☐ G-XMII	Eurocopter EC135T1
☐ G-XOIL	Aerospatiale AS.355N
☐ G-XOXO	Extra EA.300/L
☐ G-XPBI	Letov Sluka LK-2M
☐ G-XPII	Cessna R172K Hawk XP
☐ G-XPSS	Short SD.360
☐ G-XPXP	Aero Designs Pulsar XP
☐ G-XRAF	Raj Hamsa X'Air
☐ G-XRAY	Rand KR-2
☐ G-XRED	Pitts S-1M Special
☐ G-XRLD	Cameron A-250
☐ G-XRVX	Van's RV-10
☐ G-XRXR	Raj Hamsa X'Air
☐ G-XSAM	Van's RV-9A
☐ G-XSDJ	Europa XS
☐ G-XSEA	Van's RV-8
☐ G-XSFT	Piper PA-23-250 Aztec F
☐ G-XSKY	Cameron N-77
☐ G-XTEE	AirBourne XT912
☐ G-XTEK	Robinson R44
☐ G-XTNI	AirBourne XT912-B
☐ G-XTNR	AirBourne XT912-B
☐ G-XTOR	BN2A-III Trislander
☐ G-XTRA	Extra EA230
☐ G-XTUN	Westland Bell 47G-3B1
☐ G-XVBF	Lindstrand LBL-330A
☐ G-XVOM	Van's RV-6
☐ G-XWEB	Best Off Sky Ranger
☐ G-XXEA	Sikorsky S-76C
☐ G-XXIV	Agusta Bell 206B
☐ G-XXRS	BD700 Global Express
☐ G-XXTR	Extra EA300/L
☐ G-XXVI	Sukhoi Su-26
☐ G-XYAK	Yakovlev Yak-52
☐ G-XYJY	Best Off Sky Ranger
☐ G-YAAK	Yakovlev Yak-50
☐ G-YACB	Robinson R22B2
☐ G-YAKA	Yakovlev Yak-50
☐ G-YAKB	Yakovlev Yak-50
☐ G-YAKC	Yakovlev Yak-52
☐ G-YAKH	Yakovlev Yak-52
☐ G-YAKI	Yakovlev Yak-52
☐ G-YAKK	Yakovlev Yak-50
☐ G-YAKM	Yakovlev Yak-50
☐ G-YAKN	Yakovlev Yak-52S
☐ G-YAKO	Yakovlev Yak-52
☐ G-YAKR	Yakovlev Yak-52
☐ G-YAKT	Yakovlev Yak-52
☐ G-YAKU	Yakovlev Yak-50
☐ G-YAKV	Yakovlev Yak-52
☐ G-YAKX	Yakovlev Yak-52
☐ G-YAKY	Yakovlev Yak-52
☐ G-YAKZ	Yakovlev Yak-50
☐ G-YANK	Piper PA-28-181 Archer
☐ G-YARR	Mainair Rapier
☐ G-YARV	ARV Super 2
☐ G-YAWW	Piper PA-28R-201T
☐ G-YBAA	Reims FR172J Rocket
☐ G-YCII	Yakovlev Yak-11C
☐ G-YCUB	Piper PA-18-150
☐ G-YEAH	Robinson R44
☐ G-YELL	Murphy Rebel
☐ G-YEOM	Piper PA-31-350 Chieftain
☐ G-YEWS	Rotorway Exec 152
☐ G-YFLY	VPM M16 Tandem

☐ G-YFUT	Yakovlev Yak-52		☐ G-ZAPH	Bell 206B Jet Ranger		☐ G-ZZZA	Boeing 777-236
☐ G-YFZT	Cessna 172S Skyhawk		☐ G-ZAPK	BAe 146-200QC		☐ G-ZZZB	Boeing 777-236
☐ G-YHPV	Cessna E310N		☐ G-ZAPM	Boeing 737-33A		☐ G-ZZZC	Boeing 777-236
☐ G-YIAN	Embraer EMB-135BJ		☐ G-ZAPN	BAe 146-200QC		☐ G-ZZZG	Alpi Pioneer 300
☐ G-YIII	Reims F150L		☐ G-ZAPO	BAe 146-200QC		☐ G-	
☐ G-YIIK	Robinson R44		☐ G-ZAPR	BAe 146-200QC		☐ G-	
☐ G-YIPI	Reims FR172K Hawk XP		☐ G-ZAPU	Boeing 757-2Y0		☐ G-	
☐ G-YJET	Bensen B.8MR		☐ G-ZAPV	Boeing 737-3YO		☐ G-	
☐ G-YKCT	Yakovlev Yak-52		☐ G-ZAPW	Boeing 737-3L9		☐ G-	
☐ G-YKSO	Yakovlev Yak-50		☐ G-ZAPX	Boeing 757-256		☐ G-	
☐ G-YKSS	Yakovlev Yak-55		☐ G-ZAPY	Robinson R22B		☐ G-	
☐ G-YKSZ	Yakovlev Yak-52		☐ G-ZAPZ	Boeing 737-33A		☐ G-	
☐ G-YKYK	Yakovlev Yak-52		☐ G-ZARI	Grumman AA-5B Tiger		☐ G-	
☐ G-YLYB	Cameron N-105		☐ G-ZARV	ARV Super 2		☐ G-	
☐ G-YMBO	Robinson R22M		☐ G-ZAVI	Ikarus C42 Cyclone		☐ G-	
☐ G-YMFC	Waco YMF		☐ G-ZAZA	Piper PA-18-95		☐ G-	
☐ G-YMMA	Boeing 777-236		☐ G-ZBED	Robinson R22B		☐ G-	
☐ G-YMMB	Boeing 777-236		☐ G-ZBLT	Cessna 182S Skylane		☐ G-	
☐ G-YMMC	Boeing 777-236		☐ G-ZEBO	Thunder Ax8-105		☐ G-	
☐ G-YMMD	Boeing 777-236		☐ G-ZEBY	Piper PA-28-140 Cherokee		☐ G-	
☐ G-YMME	Boeing 777-236		☐ G-ZEIN	Slingsby T.67M		☐ G-	
☐ G-YMMF	Boeing 777-236		☐ G-ZELE	Aerospatiale Gazelle		☐ G-	
☐ G-YMMG	Boeing 777-236		☐ G-ZENA	Zenair CH.701UL		☐ G-	
☐ G-YMMH	Boeing 777-236		☐ G-ZENI	Zenair CH.601HD		☐ G-	
☐ G-YMMI	Boeing 777-236		☐ G-ZENN	Schempp-Hirth Ventus		☐ G-	
☐ G-YMMJ	Boeing 777-236		☐ G-ZEPI	Colt GA-42		☐ G-	
☐ G-YMMK	Boeing 777-236		☐ G-ZERO	Grumman AA-5B Tiger		☐ G-	
☐ G-YMML	Boeing 777-236		☐ G-ZETA	Lindstrand LBL-105A		☐ G-	
☐ G-YMMM	Boeing 777-236		☐ G-ZEXL	Extra EA.300/L		☐ G-	
☐ G-YMMN	Boeing 777-236		☐ G-ZFLY	Robinson R22		☐ G-	
☐ G-YMMO	Boeing 777-236		☐ G-ZHKF	Reality Escapade		☐ G-	
☐ G-YMMP	Boeing 777-236		☐ G-ZHWH	Rotorway Exec		☐ G-	
☐ G-YNOT	Druine Condor		☐ G-ZIGI	Robin DR.400-180 Regent		☐ G-	
☐ G-YNYS	Cessna 172S Skyhawk		☐ G-ZIII	Pitts S-2B Special		☐ G-	
☐ G-YOGI	Robin DR.400-140B		☐ G-ZINT	Cameron Z-77		☐ G-	
☐ G-YORK	Reims F172M		☐ G-ZIPA	Rockwell 114A		☐ G-	
☐ G-YOTS	Yakovlev Yak-52		☐ G-ZIPI	Robin DR.400-180 Regent		☐ G-	
☐ G-YOXI	Zenair CH.601UL		☐ G-ZIPY	Wittman Tailwind		☐ G-	
☐ G-YOYO	Pitts S-1E Special		☐ G-ZITS	Aerospatiale AS.355F2		☐ G-	
☐ G-YPOL	MD.900 Explorer		☐ G-ZIZI	Cessna 525 CitationJet		☐ G-	
☐ G-YPSY	Andreasson BA4B		☐ G-ZLIN	Zlin Z.326		☐ G-	
☐ G-YRAF	RAF 2000 GTX-SE		☐ G-ZLLE	Aerospatiale Gazelle		☐ G-	
☐ G-YRIL	Luscombe 8E Silvaire		☐ G-ZLOJ	Beech A36 Bonanza		☐ G-	
☐ G-YROI	Air Command 532 Elite		☐ G-ZMAM	Piper PA-28-181 Archer		☐ G-	
☐ G-YROJ	RAF 2000 GTX-SE		☐ G-ZODI	Zenair CH.601UL		☐ G-	
☐ G-YROO	RAF 2000 GTX-SE		☐ G-ZODY	Zenair CH.601UL		☐ G-	
☐ G-YROS	Bensen B.8O-D		☐ G-ZOOL	Reims FA152 Aerobat		☐ G-	
☐ G-YROW	VPM M16 Tandem		☐ G-ZORO	Europa		☐ G-	
☐ G-YROX	Rotorsport UK MT-03		☐ G-ZOSA	Champion 7GCAA		☐ G-	
☐ G-YROY	Bensen B.8MR		☐ G-ZSKD	Cameron Z-90		☐ G-	
☐ G-YRUS	Jodel D.140E		☐ G-ZTED	Europa		☐ G-	
☐ G-YSMO	P & M Quik		☐ G-ZUMI	Van's RV-8		☐ G-	
☐ G-YSPY	Cessna 172Q Cutlass		☐ G-ZUMO	Pilatus PC-12		☐ G-	
☐ G-YSTT	Piper PA-32R-301		☐ G-ZVBF	Cameron A-400		☐ G-	
☐ G-YULL	Piper PA-28-180 Cherokee		☐ G-ZVKO	Edge 360		☐ G-	
☐ G-YUMM	Cameron N-90		☐ G-ZWAR	Eurocopter EC120B		☐ G-	
☐ G-YUPI	Cameron N-90		☐ G-ZXCL	Extra EA.300/L		☐ G-	
☐ G-YVBF	Lindstrand LBL-317S		☐ G-ZXEL	Extra EA.300/L		☐ G-	
☐ G-YVES	Alpi Pioneer 300		☐ G-ZXZX	Learjet 45		☐ G-	
☐ G-YVET	Cameron V-90		☐ G-ZYAK	Yakovlev Yak-52		☐ G-	
☐ G-YYAK	Yakovlev Yak-52		☐ G-ZZAJ	Schleicher ASH 26E		☐ G-	
☐ G-YYYY	Max Holste 1521C1		☐ G-ZZAP	Champion 8KCAB		☐ G-	
☐ G-YZYZ	Mainair Blade		☐ G-ZZDG	Cirrus SR20 G2		☐ G-	
☐ G-ZAAZ	Van's RV-8		☐ G-ZZEL	Aerospatiale Gazelle		☐ G-	
☐ G-ZABC	Sky 90-24		☐ G-ZZLE	Aerospatiale Gazelle		☐ G-	
☐ G-ZACE	Cessna 172S Skyhawk		☐ G-ZZOE	Eurocopter EC120B		☐ G-	
☐ G-ZACH	Robin DR.400-100		☐ G-ZZOW	Medway EclipseR		☐ G-	
☐ G-ZADA	Best Off Sky Ranger		☐ G-ZZSA	Eurocopter EC225LP		☐ G-	
☐ G-ZADY	Eurocopter EC120B		☐ G-ZZSB	Eurocopter EC225LP		☐ G-	
☐ G-ZAHN	Cessna 172S Skyhawk		☐ G-ZZSC	Eurocopter EC225LP		☐ G-	
☐ G-ZAIR	Zenair CH.601HD		☐ G-ZZSD	Eurocopter EC225LP		☐ G-	
☐ G-ZANG	Piper PA-28-140 Cherokee		☐ G-ZZSE	Eurocopter EC225LP		☐ G-	
☐ G-ZANY	Diamond DA.40D Star		☐ G-ZZXX	P & M Quik		☐ G-	

UK Aircraft bases & radio frequency guide

Presented here is an extract from the information available to all members in the ABIX on-line Based Aircraft database. The database was conceived by, and is maintained by, Dave Reid.

For each airfield in the database the following details are given. Name, Map ref (Lat/Long and OS map), location map and in the vast majority of cases an aerial photograph, together with a listing of aircraft based. If this list is opened further the details of a last noted date are shown. These dates are generated by members' reports for that field and these reports also update the database as a whole.

Members are encouraged to join the database and contribute to making the project grow. Please contact me at the email address on the main introduction page to set up your access.

Balloons are excluded from this listing. Although some are listed as based at airfields, they are rarely seen at those locations, most living at home with their owners.

The fleets of the many airlines are shown at the listed 'headquarters' base in most cases, except where otherwise shown.

PLEASE NOTE
The inclusion of any airfield in this section should not be taken as an indication of public access rights. You should always seek permission before entering any airfield. This listing in no way implies that any permission whatsoever has been granted.

I hope you find this listing of use, and I will welcome any feedback to the address at the start of the book.

Abbey Warren Farm, Bucknall, Lincoln

BSUA	MJDW	MYBD	MZOT
OAMF	REED		

Aberdeen
APP 119.050   TWR 118.1

AWMT	BCLD	BHBF	BHOH
BIBG	BKFN	BKZE	BKZG
BLPM	BLXR	BMDC	BSIZ
BSOZ	BUX	BUZD	BVKR
BWWI	BWZX	BZRS	CCYH
CDEA	CDEB	CDSV	CDTN
CHCF	CHCG	CHCH	CHCI
CHCK	CHCP	CLHD	DEFM
FLTA	FLTD	GNTZ	HAMR
ISSV	ISSW	JBKA	KAZA
KAZB	PUMA	PUMB	PUMD
PUME	PUMH	PUMI	PUML
PUMN	PUMO	PUMS	REDJ
REDK	REDL	REDM	REDN
RJXN	RJXO	ROOK	ROWN
SASC	SASD	SSSC	SSSD
SSSE	TBIC	TIGC	TIGE
TIGF	TIGG	TIGO	TIGS
TIGV	ZZSA	ZZSB	ZZSC
ZZSD			

Aboyne
A/G 130.100

BAHP	BCBJ	BFSD	BLRM
BXSP	BYHT	CCRA	KCIG
ORCW	TUGS		

Airfield Farm, Hardwick

AMVD	BPZE	BUTD	DEMH
EHBJ	ELMH	MRLL	MSTG

Alderney
APP 128.65   TWR 125.35

ANNG	BGXC	BXRG	DIKY
EGJA	ISLD	OACI	

Andreas, Isle of Man

AHAU	AVFU	BAEB	BIPA
BMFI	BOYR	BSYA	BXVM
BYJU	BYTV	CCJS	MZBV
MZHG			

Andrewsfield
A/G 130.550

ARDB	ARUY	ASIJ	ASRC
ASRW	ATAS	ATTV	ATWB
AVGK	AXCG	AYOZ	AYPS
BCDY	BKTV	BMXA	BNDO
BNGV	BNID	BRDB	BRVB
BRXF	BSFB	BTIK	BTUR
BVIE	BWEV	BXJM	BXSE
BXXK	BZDH	BZHE	CCIJ
GGLE	IKRK	JABU	JMTT
MASS	MWLA	OPTI	ORMG
OTAN	ROMP	RONG	SMRS
TEMP	YAKC		

Armshold Farm, Kingston, Cambridgeshire

BCCR	BDGB	BROP	BTKP
CBJP	CCMK	OCDP	RCKT

Arclid Green, Sandbach
APP 128.175

BYOT	BYOZ	CBJO	CBZB
CDDU	CDKM	CDWW	CEGW
LYNI	MNGT	MTWR	MVXC
MWAF	MWHO	MWPO	MWUV
MYIY	MYUB	MZAJ	MZDH
MZEK	MZKD	MZKZ	TPWL

Ashcroft Farm, Winsford
A/G 122.525

AXYU	AWOU	AXNP	BIDX
CBHU	LAZZ	MMBU	MTCU
OBMI	SUZY		

Askern

BRSP	MGCK	MMSO

Aston Down

BBOL	BXGZ	BZSP	CKHB
CKNK	FEFE	KDEY	

Audley End

AEOA	ANJD	ATTR	BCIH
BNPF	BRBC	BTOG	BTZD
MOTH	TSOB		

Badminton

ATHT	DIME

Bagby/Thirsk
APP 125.00   A/G 123.25

ANRP	ARLR	ASJY	ATGY
AVGZ	AVMD	AVZP	AWLA
AWUN	AXDV	AXHS	AXHT
AXPC	AYZU	BAVL	BDAP
BDGM	BFFY	BFGH	BIYU
BNDT	BPHL	BPJW	BRLR
BSPE	BVLT	BWUV	BYEK
BYME	BZDS	BZEN	CBMO
CDDP	CEEJ	DEND	DJET
GBUE	GBXS	IVII	JAME
LUNA	MNZJ	MTMY	MVEG
MVSE	MYED	NAPO	NNAC
OMLS	OPUB	SKYC	TAXI

Bakersfield, Northamptonshire

AHCN	CBGP	CBIV	CBXU
CDPA	CEDX	CMOR	IDOL
MGEC	OOXP		

Barkston Heath
APP 119.375   TWR 120.425

BWXA	BWXB	BWXC	BWXD
BWXE	BWXF	BWXG	BWXI
BWXK	BWXL	BWXM	BWXN
BWXO	BWXR	BWXS	BWXT
BWXU	BWXV	BWXW	BWXX
BWXY	BWXZ	FEWG	

Bann Foot, Lough Neagh

BDWA	BFHI	PFAL

Barton
A/G 122.700

AJEE	APUY	AREV	ARMR
ARVU	ASHX	ASMS	ATGO
AVER	AVFP	AVGI	AVSA
AVWT	AWJE	AWOF	AWPU
AWVA	AXJX	AYEF	AYGC
AYGX	AYSK	AZGF	AZGY
AZJY	BBKY	BBPY	BCPG
BDSL	BECF	BEIP	BEYW
BEZZ	BFHP	BFIG	BHAX
BHEK	BHRB	BIDG	BITM
BITO	BJXB	BKNA	BLTM
BMSA	BNHB	BNJD	BNKE
BOIL	BONG	BOPT	BOPU
BOYU	BPAI	BPVA	BRPY
BRWV	BRXS	BSUT	BTHP
BTRS	BTRT	BULM	BUZE
BUZN	BXLW	BXWP	BYFM
BYII	BZDD	BZGW	BZXT
CBHM	CBOR	CCEM	CCXZ
CDBA	CDCT	CDHE	CDKF
CDKO	CDMJ	CDMU	CDNW
CDOC	CDOM	CDRW	CDXM
CDZG	CEGZ	CEHV	CWIC
DAWG	FFAF	GCYC	GFEA
GFIA	GFIB	GFPA	GFSA
GMPH	GOTH	HALC	HDIX
HIZZ	HYST	IDWR	IIII
ISHA	JFWI	JLAT	KDIX

KNOX (continued)

KNOX	LACA	LACB	LADZ
LEGG	LYFA	MHCE	MNRZ
MVNX	MYYY	MZAF	MZFO
MZLG	MZMM	MZNY	OFOX
OGES	OUHI	PAWL	PFAD
PLAN	RACO	RATI	ROTS
SGSE	SKIE	SWEL	TAIR
TIMB	VETS	WIZI	YJET

Barton Ashes

AGXN	ALIJ	AYUJ	BFJJ
BMHL	BZOO	CCBA	CCBW
CCGR	CCZS	ECVB	MITE
MMAE	MRED	MYJD	MYSY
OPJH	SKAN	TEDI	

Baxby Manor, Husthwaite

AJIS	BXWK	BZIW	CBBO
CBZG	CBZT	CCBY	CCDO
CCGB	FLYF	IZIT	LYPG
MJMD	MJSZ	MMGL	MNBG
MTMP	MTSM	MTUD	MTXB
MTXD	MTYU	MVED	MVPB
MWYT	MZAB	MZJI	OJDS
OSEP	PROW	RAYH	SOOZ
SYUT	TIVV		

Baxterley/Charity Farm

ADPC	AKVP	ANKK	AOES
AOIR	BWHK	CORD	

Beccles
A/G 120.375

ASMY	ATHZ	AVZU	AZKZ
BAOP	BEIG	BEZK	BSKA
EFRY	EGAN	GTHM	KIPP

Beeches Farm, South Scarle

ARHZ	BICD	BPRA	BWYI
CDGI			

Belfast
APP 128.50   TWR 118.3

APXR	BAKH	BHYC	BKVT
BRME	BRTX	BSWR	BUUM
BXPM	CALL	CBRG	FCDB
IGLZ	IPAL	IPAX	JAJK
KENZ	KNAP	SEJW	

Belfast City

BBNT	CELY	JECM	JEDU
MGYB			

Bellarena

BKSP	BVYG	CKJJ	CKJN
RIET	TUGG		

Belle Vue Farm, Yarnscombe
A/G 123.575

BDEX	BUDT	BYOH	BZEL
MWIP	MWRY	OJJF	XPXP

Bembridge
A/G 123.250

ATRX	AVCN	AXZK	BDPN
BDVX	BDZI	BEDW	BEFI
BHGC	BWPX	BXRR	BXRS
BYCX	CBUI	CEIO	CEIP
CEIR	OBNC	SELX	SICA

Benson
APP 136.450   TWR 127.15

BDOD	ARRD	BEFA	BHDM
BNUL	BOCM	BYUV	BYVL
BYVP	BYVU	BYWA	BYXR
CHSU	ODPJ	ULAS	WACP

Benson's Farm, Laindon

AIDS	ARXP	BACL	CCGM
MVPK	OSCO		

Bere Farm, Warnford

AYJB	BSNF	IIYK

Beverley Linley Hill
A/G 123.050

BAIP	BAXV	BDJD	BGCM
BGSV	BIDH	BJUB	BTMR
HULL	IFLI	MYJY	MYYD

Bicester
A/G 129.975

ADRA	AKKH	ATJA	AYUP
BBCH	BKVC	BSDJ	BVYZ
BVZR	BXTO	CCZT	CDWZ
CFWW	CKKE	CTAA	DTUG
DTWO	EMJA	LABS	MYPS
OFFA	PAYD	RCMC	RTUG
SKYT	VKIT	ZLIN	

Bidford-on-Avon - Bickmarsh

AGYK	AKWS	ALWW	ARMG
AVOM	AXCM	AYBP	AYEH
BAPB	BEER	BGKC	BIRH
BTWI	BTZX	BVLV	BVPN
BVYP	BWBY	BYEL	CCVI
CKGD	CKGL	CKJE	CUBB
DURO	IOSI	KITS	LIDA
MWDM	NEGG	OBGC	PREZ

Biggin Hill
APP 129.400   TWR 134.8

ABNT	ABYA	AEOF	AEZJ
AKVZ	ALJF	APPL	ARJU
ARUG	ARYF	ASJL	ASKT
ASOH	ASSW	ATDN	ATJG
ATMY	ATOO	ATRW	ATXN
AVUD	AVWO	AXNX	AYPE
AYRM	AYSB	AZWY	BABK
BAJA	BAKJ	BAMS	BANX
BATR	BBIL	BBLH	BBTG
BEBE	BEUP	BEYZ	BFYC
BFZN	BGBR	BGFI	BGPH
BGRM	BGUB	BHBI	BHDU
BHIT	BHOR	BICG	BIMX
BKEW	BLKM	BLTY	BLZN
BMGG	BMIM	BMMM	BMTO
BNAJ	BNNZ	BNXT	BNZB
BOGG	BOGO	BOLU	BONR
BOOL	BOPX	BOZO	BPCR
BPWP	BPXJ	BRDG	BRVT
BSCN	BSFR	BSGT	BSKK
BSKL	BSPK	BSTE	BSVM
BSXA	BSZF	BTES	BTGZ
BTII	BTNH	BUSW	BWYG
BXGX	BXHH	BXWO	BYEA
BZEP	BZFR	CBEE	CBLZ
CBRL	CBSO	CBTN	CCPY
CCST	CDEO	CDYN	CEPT
COLL	DANT	DPHN	EMMY
EMSL	FARM	FCSP	GOLF

Biggin Hill (continued)

GOMO	HXTD	IANC	IFTE
IMBI	INIT	IPSY	IWDB
JAMA	JETI	JOYZ	LAKE
LARE	LDFM	LSFT	LUVY
MKSS	MOVE	MPAA	MVDY
NEWR	NJAG	OABR	OALD
OCBI	OFOA	OFOM	OIHC
OJAC	OJIM	OLDH	OMST
OPAG	ORTH	ORVG	OXTC
PJNZ	RCEJ	ROOV	SFCJ
SHPP	SOHO	TAMY	TKIS
TRIN	TWIZ	UTSI	VEZE
WARB	WARS	ZARI	ZOOL

Billericay

APBE	CBWJ	MWMI	NAPP
NJSP	ZZOW		

Birmingham
APP 118.05   TWR 118.3

BNEN	BNWY	BZAT	BZAU
BZAV	EMBH	JECK	JECL
JETO	JTNC	RENO	TOYC
VCED	WMID		

Blackacre Farm, Holt, Trowbridge

ATBL	LCGL	LOCH

Blackbushe
APP 125.250   TWR 122.300

ARLB	ARYI	ATEF	AVSF
BAAT	BBRC	BDFW	BEDG
BERI	BFIV	BFIY	BFLX
BICW	BLRI	BLTK	BLWV
BLXA	BMFP	BMTB	BMWR
BNJR	BNRK	BOJI	BOJK
BOMU	BOTI	BOWY	BPHI
BPTI	BSEU	BTFF	BWDT
BWLS	BWTA	BWTK	BWYM
BXLT	BYNA	BYOM	BZEA
BZEB	BZEE	CBBC	CBEK
CBGC	CBWD	CCAT	CCHT
CDTX	CLAC	DONS	ENTT
GOTO	HOOD	JJAN	LADI
LNYS	NODE	NOIR	NSUK
OBAK	OIBM	OJCW	OJIL
OLCP	OMUM	OOFT	OPPL
REDY	RIBZ	RICO	ROVY
RRFC	RUBB	RVSH	SIGN
TPSL	WJCJ	XXEA	

Blackpool - Squires Gate
APP 119.950   TWR 118.400

AIBW	ANWB	APTY	ARJS
ASNK	ATMJ	ATMW	AVUT
AVWG	AVYT	AWAJ	AXAB
AXUF	AYIM	AYNN	AYRG
AYUV	AZFR	AZIB	AZRD
AZUY	BAHX	BAJE	BAJN
BAJO	BASL	BBBK	BBKB
BCDJ	BCOO	BCWH	BDWY
BEJD	BELT	BFWE	BFZB
BGHM	BGMN	BGMO	BGPU
BHFI	BIUV	BIYX	BJKY
BJUC	BJWW	BJXA	BKXD
BLDK	BLLP	BLTF	BLUM
BLUN	BLWD	BLYE	BMKK
BNOJ	BNOM	BNOP	BNOZ
BNXV	BOER	BORJ	BORL
BORS	BPGZ	BPNJ	BPRN
BRBW	BRPE	BRPL	BRZS

BSEK BSHA BSSE BTEF
BTJA BUHO BULH BVDH
BVOU BVOV BVPR BWGF
BWHI BXIA BXOU BXTH
BYBR BZBU BZGB BZOZ
CCYG CYLS DACN DAKM
DPYE EEZS FOZZ GFNO
HMJB IMGL JANO JEMA
JEMB JEMC JEMD JJMX
JMAX JMXA KHOM LACI
MACA MAYO MICK NAAA
NWAA OAMP OBNW OJSA
OKEN OPFW ORAL ORCP
OSJF OSOE OTBA OTVR
OWFS OWRT OWST PLAH
PMAX RABA RACI REDD
SAMZ SBAE SOEI SUMX
TAIL TFUN UANT UFLY
UILT WMLT YMBO

Black Spring Farm, Castle Bytham
ARIH AWUB AXGR IIAC
OSLD PFAP SEED

Blue Tile Farm, Hindolveston, Norfolk
BYJD BYJO MYRP

Blue Tile Farm, Langham, Essex
AHBL AHVU ANEL BEWN
BUPG CIBO

Bodmin
APP 128.725   TWR 122.700
AKIB ARRY AXDC BACN
BCTK BCZM BDNO BECB
BGSA BKOA BMFZ BNSM
BPFM BRCT BRER BUAG
BWDP BXEZ BXOI BXWR
BYNK BZLV BZZD CBPR
CCKR CDJK FMGG IVOR
KDET MEME OCFC OPIC
OPIT YCUB YELL

Booker - Wycombe Air Park
TWR 126.550
AFVE AIST AISX AMPI
ANZT ARHM ARRZ ATBG
AVOZ AWFC AWMF AWXZ
AZRA BAMV BBHK BBII
BBMZ BCPU BGPN BGWM
BHDP BHLH BHSE BHUU
BIFA BILJ BJHB BLGH
BLWH BMCG BMIV BMLS
BNCR BNRY BODR BOMZ
BOSN BRWT BRZK BSAI
BSSX BSVG BTNA BTZE
BVGP BWTH BXDN BXGL
BXGO BXNG BXXN BYDK
BYEM BYHE BZXY CCFC
CDET CDVP CKGA CKJS
CKKH CKLA CKMM CURR
EGLL EGTB EHMM EROL
ERTI FEZZ GMAX HALP
HAPY HELN IIEI IIIT
IMIC ITII JBUZ JLEE
KUTU KYTE LARK MOVI
MRKI MXVI OASP OASW
ODAK ODIN ODOC OEAT
OMDH OMGH OPAT OPTF
ORBK OWAP PTTS RVVI
SAGA SALA SHUG SIAI

SPIN TBAH TIMC TOLY
UGLY USRV WACB WACE
WACF WACG WACH WACI
WACJ WACU WACY XATS
YFZT ZZAJ

Boscombe Down
APP 130.000   TWR 130.75
ACEJ AYYO BTEL BUUI
BYUJ BYUM BYVE BYXB
BYXJ BYXT SEVA

Bossington
ANKZ AOET BRGW BWYO

Bourn
A/G 124.350
ASAJ ASLH AVEN AXUA
BCUB BEKN BGBI BIWR
BIZE BIZF BKNI BKOT
BNSU BNSV BPIL BTGT
BUEF BUTG BYIM CCDK
CCFG CCGW CCZZ DASH
EDES GBJS GMKD HINZ
NCUB NEWS NIVA OTUI
RESG TFIN WIZS YBAA

Bournemouth - Hurn
APP 119.475   TWR 125.60
AGSH ASEO AVGE AWBC
AYND AZCL AZFM BAHO
BBNH BBTB BCJP BFOJ
BGLN BGOL BGRG BHJS
BJWI BLDV BNDE BNPH
BNUO BODX BOIX BOKY
BOSR BPKF BRFC BRHO
BRPU BSTP BTHJ BUXN
BWAF BWCS BWDV BWJW
BWOF BXMH BXPL BXTY
BXTZ BYBF BYDG BYHJ
BZAS BZGD BZLH BZNN
BZOY BZPJ BZRT BZXK
CBBF CBCY CBEL CBOT
CBUG CBZR CBZX CCWY
CDTK CEAC CEAE CEAF
CEAG CELM CELN CTCE
CTCF CVIX DHSS DHTT
DHUU DHVV DHWW DHXX
DHZZ DJAE DORN DUSK
ECJM ECON ELSE FAVC
FFRA FPIG FPLE FRAD
FRAF FRAH FRAI FRAJ
FRAK FRAO FRAP FRAT
FRBA GBFF GLTT GSYJ
HGPI HOPE HVIP IATU
IFIT IGIE IIZI IMEC
JADJ MAFE MAFF MAFI
MAPR MIGG MPWI MULT
NATY OBFC OLSF OMAF
PORK RHCB RIST SYDE
THOE THOF TRNT VENI
VICI VICT WWIZ ZERO
ZLOJ

Bourne Park, Hurstbourne Tarrant
AKVF ARLG BDEU BFDF
BFHR BHXK BWVI DOGG
MDAY

Braintree - Rayne Hall Farm
AHIP AROA ATVW AVPV
BCOI BMHS BOTO BPAB
BTSB BWFX BWXP CCFL
CCFM CCLX CCUL FRAN
HFCA JAMY MTNO MTNP
MVJG MVJS MYDS MYUP
MYUR

Bradleys Lawn, Heathfield
AKTH ARKS BAMR BOEH
BUWK BYBP

Branscombe
AOBH ASPV BEPC BGKO
BXRA BZFT CCPN FOXX
SAGE

Breighton
A/G 129.800
ABVE AEVS AEXF AGFT
AIXN AKAT AKSY AMAW
AOBG AOIS APVF AVPM
AXMT AYDV AYFC BAAD
BAHL BBCS BDTB BGAX
BGWO BICP BJAL BJZN
BMSE BSGF BSNN BSYG
BTWF BUTX BVEH BVGZ
BVXJ BWNK BYLL BZME
CBEI CBZK CDHI CDSJ
CDXE CUBJ DIZO ECUB
EJGO MZBH OELZ RASC
RODI RVDR TAFF TYAK
VANS WUFF

Brickhouse Farm, Frogland Cross
ADYS BANC BIVC BKHG
MMTY RAMP

Bristol - Filton
APP 122.725   TWR 132.350
AADND ALGT ASSS AWFB
BASJ BBXW BCCY BFZM
BKMI BSSW BYKP BZYD
JEAO RRGN SAPM WARE

Bristol - Lulsgate
APP 125.650   TWR 133.850
ATTI AYLA BABG BARP
BEWY BKBW BLYT BNKD
BOIZ BOSD BRTJ BRYU
BRYV BRYW BRYY BRYZ
BUYY BXSY BXTS CBXN
DIAT ELIS ERJA ERJB
ERJC ERJD ERJE ERJF
ERJG EZAA EZAC EZAZ
FEBY FILE GFCB KPAO
LECA MAIR MFMF OHMS
ROTF TEBZ YEOM

Brize Norton
APP 127.250   TWR 123.725
ATOI AYJP BDIE BNRG
BPAF BUKB BVVR BXIM
OJVH

Broadmeadow Farm, Hereford
BZGS BZWM CDKI CDVO
CDXP MNYL MTJS MTYR
MVGC MVHR MVJC MVKM
MVSX MVSZ MVYE MWIY

MWJH	MYEP	MYYE	MZAM
MVHW	MWSR	MYSZ	OUIK
UURO			

Brook Farm, Boylestone, Derbyshire

BHZU	BIJS	BXHJ	

Brook Farm, Pilling

BDAD	BROI	BYPO	BZMR
BZYM	CBFE	CBIC	CBVY
CBZS	CDIG	CEHI	MMXD
MTGV	MTVR	MVAD	MVAM
MVAO	MWDI	MWFD	MWHR
MWND	MWTJ	MYBM	MYOH
MYPJ	MYRL	MYSK	MZNC
MZNN	NIGC	WYAT	

Broomhil IFarm, West Calder

CCMD	CDNT	MYME	

Bruntingthorpe
A/G 122.825

BKFC	BKRN	BVLD	CPDA
ISKA	LUSC	SUMZ	TEDS
TOMC	VLCN		

Caernarfon - Llandwrog
A/G 122.250

AYPJ	BAGR	BAOJ	BNDW
BYCA	BYTU	CBDS	CBXJ
CCTT	CDCU	CGHM	HIJK
LION	MZGI	MZNB	PBYY
REEF	RUSI	TFIX	

Calton Moor

CBEM	CBPV	CHTG	MGND
MVUP	MWGG	MWNF	MYJO

Cambridge - Teversham
APP 123.600   *TWR 122.200*

AHIZ	ANDE	AOEI	AXMW
AYPH	AZGL	BAIG	BATN
BBZN	BFWB	BKMA	BKPD
BLST	BMFD	BOPH	BOYF
BXCG	BZNY	CBGZ	EFSM
EKYD	EMCA	FIRM	FLYS
HERC	HMMV	IDPH	IRPC
KEMY	LMLV	MATY	MBTW
NDOT	OPVM	OTYP	PGAC
RACY	RALA	RIKS	ROCH
RVJP	SBMM	SHWK	TILE
UFCB	UFCD	WRSY	ZADY
ZARV			

Cardiff - Rhoose
APP 126.625   *TWR 125.000*

ASUP	ATOL	AWMI	AZCZ
AZDJ	BBTY	BGRR	BGXB
BIJE	BJVV	BMDP	BNSY
BPWN	BRWR	BVMA	BXVA
CBLE	CBVB	CRIL	CWFB
EDGI	GALL	MEGN	MERL
OPET	PLAZ	SENX	

Cark-in-Cartmel

BEEG	CBDT		

Carlisle
APP 123.600   *A/G 123.600*

AVYM	BAKM	BFLZ	BGBG
BGSH	BJNN	BOIO	BRJV

BSEG	BTDW	BUNH	BWBI
BXDD	BZOF	CBDP	CCSK
CCWC	CDRH	CDRP	EJRS
FIFT	GAJB	GBRB	IFBP
JLIN	MAVI	MDKD	MVUD
MWPJ	MZDS	NJTC	OECM
PBUS	RNCH	SVPN	VIVS
XSFT	YROY		

Carr Farm, Thorney, Newark

AIKE	AJAS	AJXV	ANHU
ANHX	APTR	BXON	CBOA

Caunton - Knapthorpe Lodge

BOUN	BYFE	BYHV	BYJM
BYMI	BZLL	BZRR	BZWS
CBEX	CCAS	CDBY	CDOO
CDRR	MTWF	MVIT	MYAR
MYVH	MZFD	MZIV	MZJN

Challock

AZHD	AZMC	BFPS	BKTM
DUOT	MGMM		

Charlwood, Surrey

BLID	DACA	GACA	JETH
JETM	VIXN		

Charmy Down, Bath

MURR	MVLB	MWX	MWZM

Charterhall

AYCE	CCPS	CCPV	CZBE
UINN			

Chatteris - Lower Mount Pleasant Farm
A/G 129.900

BRJB	BTWZ	BWIL	CBFX
CCBG	CCKL	MNZR	MTBL
MTVN	MTYF	MVGO	MVHP
MVIP	MVZP	MWES	MWJN
MWMY	MWOO	MYKN	MZNP
MTSS			

Chavenage, Tetbury

BEVS	BSDI	MWFT	TUBB

Cheddington

AIJM	ATJT	BUSR	BWID

Cherry Tree Farm, Monewden

AZJN	BAAW	BCNX	BTON
BVVW	NZSS		

Cheyene Farm, Stonehaven

ARDT	BUZG	CDYU	MHGS

Chessington - Rushett Farm

AAOK	AIFZ	BAER	BAGT
BNPV	BROZ	BUYU	CDXR
DRSV	HAMP		

Chester
APP 123.35   *TWR 124.95*

ASIB	AXOZ	BBMJ	BGZF
BHKJ	BKIB	BLWP	BNJT
BODP	BPIK	BSDZ	BSLV
BSRP	BVHI	BVSP	BYMC
BZDI	BZGC	BZXA	CDJD
CLUX	EKWS	FZZA	GURU

Chilbolton
A/G 129.825

AAZG	BTCJ	BTJC	BXRZ
FORD	JABS	MNKZ	MTPT
MVJN	MVWZ	MVZC	MWJF
MYFZ	MZPH	PRIM	SIXS
WBTS	ZHKF		

Chiltern Park, Wallingford
A/G 134.025

MYDR	FROM	MFLY	MTHI
MWRC	MYLN	MZPB	

Chislet - Maypole Farm

AKUE	ASAX	ASFA	AXDI
AXGG	AZZV	BEVC	BIAC
BIBN	BKAM	BPLY	BRAR
BRXP	BUKH	CCAL	CDLL
CWBM	EXIT	MYWV	MZOX
PEGA	ZIII		

Church Farm, Askern

BZIP	CDZZ	MMWA	MTWS
MYDW	MYIZ		

Church Farm, Shotteswell

CBMZ	NIDG	RMPY	OTAL

Church Fenton
APP 126.500   *TWR 122.100*

BLES	BYVG	BYVI	BYVX
BYVZ	BYWO	BYWP	BYWS
BYWV	BYXE		

City of Derry

BASO	BSZI	BWWG	CBKY
FLOW	HMED	STEA	

Clacton
A/G 118.150

AKTN	BGWH	BIGJ	BIMM
BJTB	BKIJ	BNKP	BOHI
MWCI	OAHC		

Clench Common
A/G 129.825

BYNO	BZDB	CBHN	CCGI
CCVE	CCYE	CDTE	CDZJ
CDZK	CEDO	JABO	MGMC
MNRW	MTKA	MTPY	MTTY
MVAK	MVVO	MWUD	MWZF
MWZV	MZCP	MZFU	

Clipgate Farm, Denton

AXUC	BBNZ	BCUY	BETW
BFTX	BHKT	BIEO	BKJS
BKZT	BTBY	BWPE	BXUX
BZSZ	HALL	LAKI	MTSK
MYRO	OKED	ONUN	OROS

Cockerham - Tarn Farm

BUYF	BYJB	BYYN	BZAL
BZXX	CBHV	CBII	CBJT
CBWM	CCEH	CCHS	CCTM
CDAG	CDAY	CDGR	CDPE
CDWU	EDLY	ENVY	LYTB
MBIY	MGUN	MMBV	MMFG

KMRV	MHCI	MHCJ	OEDB
ONUP	OSKP	RULE	SHUU
UVNR	WOOF		

MMOW	MMTX	MNFP	MNMV
MNUE	MTEJ	MTFA	MTGA
MTJB	MTMT	MTZZ	MVBE
MVCI	MVCZ	MVWW	MVXS
MWBP	MWEY	MWKE	MWWE
MYPA	MYRD	MYVE	MYYV
MZEL	MZHT	MZIY	POLL
TFOG			

Coldharbour Farm, Willingham

AKUN	AYWH	BAFV	BJDF
BXMF	BZIV	CCNJ	JABB
MGDL	MWOH		

Colerne
APP 120.075 TWR 120.075

BYUH	BYVC	BYVN	BYWC
BYWE	BYWG	BYWI	BZDP
CBAN	KITI		

Coltishall
APP 125.900 TWR 122.100

AHHH	AYFV	BOOH	CDMA
EDGE	HIVE	IMCD	REDX

Comber, County Down

BVCT	MYAN	RSSF

Compton Abbas
VG 122.7

AGIV	ANOO	AOIL	APMH
ATHK	AVIN	AVJO	AWBU
AZCV	BAAF	BADM	BBCZ
BBKF	BCVG	BEYL	BFSY
BHPL	BJBW	BNNX	BPCK
BPOB	BPVE	BRBD	BRUB
BRUG	BSXC	BTIJ	BXAH
CBOY	CCYO	CDOK	DUST
CVIE	GERT	GRRR	HBBC
EUNG	LENA	MTLN	NLEE
OCDW	ONER	OONY	SVET
IML	YAKM	YAKN	YAKU
AKZ			

Coney Park, Leeds

OYC	BRVI	MRSN

Coningsby
PP 120.800 TWR 134.675

ISU	AMAU	AWIJ	BMSB
IUSO			

Cosford
PP 135.875 TWR 128.650

OUO	BHNO	BUJA	BYUF
YUK	BYVJ	BYVO	BYVY
YXF	BYXG	BYXL	BYXO
MAS			

Corn Wood Farm, Adversane

XZU	BYRO	MYOW	MZMW

Costock

ORN	EFOF	EMHH	MUSH
OJB	SCHO	WAGG	

Coventry - Baginton
PP 119.250 TWR 124.800

STM	AIDL	AKUJ	AMPY
IRA	AMSV	ANAF	APJB
PLO	APRS	APSA	ARYS

ASUS	AWEX	AWWE	AYJW
AZKS	BAHF	BBKG	BCPK
BCRT	BDCL	BDWP	BFLU
BOBA	BODY	BOFL	BOFM
BOLZ	BOMS	BOZR	BPBK
BPFL	BRFM	BRXW	BSEY
BTHI	BTOC	BTPH	BUKJ
BUWE	BVWC	BWFG	BXES
BXJA	BXOJ	BYEE	BYSE
CBBW	CBCA	CBCL	CBDK
CBSU	CDSX	CDZM	CLOS
COVA	COVB	COVD	DAZY
DCEA	DHDV	DHVM	DRFC
ETIN	EYES	FIJR	FIJV
FIND	FIZU	GAA	GAAF
GAFT	GBLR	HAFT	HANG
HART	HELV	HERM	HSLA
IOOX	IWRC	JAYI	JXTA
KAFT	LAFT	LOFB	LOFC
LOFD	LOFE	LOFF	LOFM
LOSM	MANH	NERC	NJIM
NOSE	OCOV	OGEM	OPSS
OVMC	PERZ	PLAJ	RHUM
SAMM	SBLT	SDEV	SIXC
SOUL	SVEA	TASK	THOA
THOB	THOD	THOG	THOH
THOJ	THOK	THOL	THON
WUSH	XKEN	XXTR	YMFC

Cranfield
APP 122.850 TWR 134.925

APVG	ARXH	ATHR	AVGD
AVGU	AVWI	AWFZ	AWOT
AXDW	AXIO	AZDE	AZLH
AZVG	BABH	BADJ	BBCI
BBKE	BBNI	BCCC	BCUO
BDOW	BEPY	BEUD	BEZI
BFSR	BGBN	BGGL	BGGM
BGGN	BGOG	BGON	BGRX
BHAR	BHFE	BHLX	BIFY
BJNZ	BLFI	BMSG	BMUT
BMVB	BNPM	BNPO	BNRP
BNTD	BODS	BOEW	BOEZ
BOUJ	BTGP	BTNT	BWFV
BWLF	BWWW	BXJJ	BYTE
BZLC	CBFP	CBRO	CCHA
CCHB	CCHC	CCHD	CCHF
CCHG	CCHK	CCLV	CCLW
CCMF	CCMR	COAI	DESL
DODR	DOOZ	DTCP	ECGC
EGTC	EMHK	EODE	ERIC
FDPS	FLYP	FOPP	GALA
GHRW	GUST	HASO	HONI
HRHI	IORG	IZZS	JENN
KNYT	KPTT	LAIN	LENX
LICK	LUCK	LUXE	MAPP
MILY	MOGI	MRKS	MRST
MWDZ	NFLA	NITA	NODY
OACA	OARI	OARO	OCCW
OCCX	OCCY	OCCZ	OLFC
OOGI	OPEP	PACE	SCHI
TWEL	TWIN	TZII	VANC
WIZA			

Cranwell
APP 119.375 TWR 125.050

BCKN	BIPN	BPNO	BUDA
BYHL	BYUB	BYUC	BYUE
BYUP	BYVA	BYVR	BYWB
BYWF	BYWK	BYWL	BYWU
BYWW	BYWY	BYWZ	BYXC

BYXD	BYXM	BYXN	BYXZ
BYYB	CKMW	RAFA	RAFB
RAFO	RAFP		

Craysmarsh Farm, Melksham

AJUE	BJAF	BUAB	BYLT
CBUZ	CCDL	CCEB	MCCF
MEOW	MYNT		

Croft Farm, Defford

AYTR	BARC	BJTP	BSFX
BTUS	BWPJ	BZUE	CCAE
CDXY	LAPN	MNNY	MNVL
MWMM	MYYZ	MZRS	WCUB

Crosland Moor
A/G 122.200

ARYH	ATDO	AVZV	BKKO
BOWP	BPMB	BSER	BXML
CCIO	GLUC	MWDJ	OSEA
RJMS	RUFF	WFLY	ZAIR

Crowfield
A/G 122.750

AWFF	BEOY	BIAH	BNJO
BPGH	BPWM	BSJU	BVVE
CBCP	CBMT	CCCN	CCID
CCNX	CEGH	DUDE	HILT
HIPE	IEJH	JJDC	VCIO

Crowland
A/G 129.975

ASNC	BDZA	BJYK	BLMW

Culdrose
APP 134.050 TWR 122.100

ATOD	BLLS	BYFL	HAJJ
UJGK	WEEK		

Cumbernauld
A/G 120.6

AWAT	AXIG	BBRX	BBTZ
BDBU	BDJV	BELF	BHAI
BHDR	BHRN	BIID	BJEE
BJEF	BJEJ	BLHJ	BLNJ
BMKG	BPCI	BPRJ	BRBY
BUBJ	BUTE	BVER	BVLG
BWLP	BXMZ	BXOF	BZMF
BZSD	CDUE	EGPG	FOLY
INKY	JSPC	JWFT	KAIR
LAMA	MNIU	MWXU	NETR
ORMB	PDGE	PIXI	PLMI
SELY	TBTN		

Dairy House Farm, Worleston

ASPF	FARR

Damyn's Hall, Upminster

AYBR	BHLT	BKHY	BLHW
BXDU	BYDV	CCXA	CCXB
CCXC	CDHO	DMWW	EERV
IZOD	MZHS	OURO	PPLL
UNYT	VINH		

Danehill

AXWT	BXWT	OWEN

Darley Moor

CDIU	MJYD	MVCJ	MVIN
MYUA	MZDG	WHEE	WLSN

Davidstow Moor
A/G 129.825

BUCG	BYID	BZFF	BZVR
CDBV	MJJA	MNGG	MNHE
MNHT	MNJN	MNNR	MNTV
MNUU	MNWV	MTES	MTPG
MTUC	MVEC	MVOT	MWAN
MWRZ	MWSX	MWSY	MWWK
MYOT	MYTL	MYVL	MZIR
MZIZ	RODG		

Deanland
A/G 129.725

AVKR	AWDO	AWFN	AXUK
BPEO	BRKY	BVSF	BWUN
BYFY	BYIJ	CBIP	CDMM
CECC	CEFM	MNZP	MWKA
MZKH	RARB	YSPY	

Deenethorpe
A/G 127.575

BDNW	BOHW	BOOX	BOVU
BWKT	BYKT	BZSM	CBYI
CCNW	CDVH	CHKN	EZAR
ICBM	KAZI	MNNC	MTAJ
MTAX	MTBK	MTPK	MTRM
MTUT	MTYA	MVAR	MVBF
MVCP	MVFA	MVFS	MVFV
MVGP	MVLF	MVRU	MVZJ
MWAW	MWCR	MWGR	MWIG
MWLT	MWNS	MWVA	MWWK
MWYY	MYEO	MYFU	MYLK
MYNJ	MYUD	MYWI	MZIL
MZJH	MZLF	MZMC	RCNB

Denford Manor, Hungerford

AAUP	AAZP	ACDA	AFGH
AMCM	APAM		

Denham
A/G 130.725

ASEP	ATHD	AVSB	AYAW
AZAB	BAEM	BASM	BFVS
BHCM	BIBA	BMLL	BMMK
BMTJ	BNHJ	BNSN	BOJS
BOLI	BOPA	BOXR	BPJR
BPJS	BRSE	BSDP	BSFP
BSJX	BSYI	BUFY	BURS
BURT	BWOH	CBTT	CBVZ
CCWJ	DAKO	DMCD	DNOP
FCKD	FEBE	FIBS	FIFI
GOTC	GWYN	HRNT	HUBB
HUNI	IJAG	JAMP	JANT
JEFA	JRED	JUIN	NSEW
OBFS	OBIO	OCTU	ODLY
ODMC	OJWS	OOGA	OTDI
OWAR	PATZ	PIXL	PIXX
PROB	PTWB	REEM	SHAN
SHAR	TAAA	TAAB	TIPS
TOPC	TOTO	XINE	XLTG
XOIL			

Deppers Bridge, Southam

MNMY	MNZS	MVGA	MVOD
MYWN			

Derby - Eggington
A/G 118.350

ACSP	ALTO	ARAX	ARFB
ARKN	ARWS	ASOK	AVLM
AVYK	AXIF	AXJI	AXJJ

AXPN	AXSC	AZCN	AZFA
AZTF	BAEY	BBJY	BCLW
BDBF	BETE	BGXR	BHAV
BHXA	BHZS	BITH	BJXZ
BKVF	BMEU	BNHK	BNMC
BNMD	BRND	BSUD	BSWH
BVLP	BYBD	BZBC	BZRA
CBME	CSMK	DACF	FIJJ
FNLY	GBFR	KWAX	ODAC
PTYE	RAYS	TRAX	

Dishforth
APP 130.100　　*TWR 122.100*

AOTF	AZBI	BARZ	BCCX
BUGZ	CKGK		

Doynton

BJEL	BTGG	BZUZ	CBYW
MGOD	MNZW	MRJJ	MTBO
MTSN	MTZF	MVDE	MWNU
MZDJ			

Draycott Farm, Chiseldon, Whiltshire

APAF	ASNW	BIAP	BKBF
BKDH	BKXR	BLFW	BRNX
BSGD	BSZD	BWOV	DOMS
JREE	MWPH	NOTY	TECM
TECS			

Droppingwell Farm, Bewdley

CCOO	MJUR	MJVX

Drummaird Farm, Bonnybank

MNKB	MYBC	MYSU	MNCM

Dundee - Riverside Park
APP 122.900　　*TWR 122.900*

AVXD	BNOF	BNON	BVHC
BVHE	BVHF	BVHG	CCET
MRAJ			

Dunkeswell
A/G 123.475

AHCR	AHVV	AICX	APZL
ATLT	AVSC	AVWR	AWVZ
AYEW	AYPT	BACE	BBGI
BETG	BFBY	BFEH	BFWD
BGSJ	BHNL	BHUG	BHXY
BIOU	BJFE	BJNF	BJNG
BKAY	BKPE	BMXC	BOLC
BPFC	BPFZ	BRHP	BRJA
BSHI	BTIV	BTKD	BUBT
BUDR	BVTA	BXRP	BYPG
BZOE	CBAX	CBBN	CBBP
CBDM	CBGD	CBKR	CBLF
CBPP	CBVC	CCGU	CDIL
CDIR	CDIZ	CDJC	CDOT
CEDC	CVAL	DENE	DLEE
DWEL	IXII	JODL	MGPA
MNKV	MNYM	MTNU	MVJF
MVOH	MVOR	MVOW	MWWS
MYBA	MYGT	MYMP	MYSC
MYWU	MZBW	MZBZ	MZCH
MZGV	NONE	OAJL	OFRY
OJAE	OLMA	OOSH	OSLO
OSTL	OVAL	PIPR	RJAM
RONW	RUVY	SILS	TBOK
THEO	VANA	VCML	

Dunsfold
APP 135.175　　*TWR 124.325*

ARXG	AXGS	BBPX	BDXJ
BGPA	BIMO	BITA	BKCV
BKDI	BRVG	BSNE	BUXJ
BWDF	BYLZ	EXPL	IANI
IIID	JJAB	LGEZ	MAUS
NWAR	PUDL	REAL	RVAL

Dunstable Downs

BCHT	BEUA	BJRP	BJRV
BLGS	BNXI	BVYM	CCLR
CKHD	CKHG	CKHP	CKKD
CKLC	CKLP	CKMG	CKNJ
CKNV	CKOI	IMOK	LGCA
LGCB	MSIX	TIMY	

Durham Tees Valley
APP 118.850　　*TWR 119.800*

ATRM	AVWL	AYSY	BBDL
BBSA	BCTF	BIXH	BKAS
BKWY	BLVI	BMJC	BOHT
BOLF	BPPS	BRDO	BRLO
BXHR	CBBT	CBBU	CFSA
EHXP	EWAW	FPLA	FPLB
FPLD	FRAL	FRAR	FRAS
FRAU	FRAW	GATE	JLCA
NAAS	NEAU	ONAL	OPFT
OSCH	SIMS	SOBI	WBVS
WYSP	YYAK		

Duxford
AFIS 122.075

AANM	ACAA	ACMN	AGJG
AGTO	AIYR	AKAZ	ANPE
ANRM	AOTR	APAO	ARUL
ASJV	ASTG	AWKO	AYGE
BCOU	BEDF	BGPB	BKGL
BLKZ	BOHO	BOMB	BPHZ
BPIV	BPTS	BPVO	BRAF
BRVE	BSKP	BSTM	BTCC
BTCD	BTXI	BUCM	BUOS
BURZ	BWUE	BWUH	BWUT
BWWK	BXCP	BXCV	BXDI
BXVI	BYNF	BZGK	BZGL
BZTF	BZXC	CBAB	CBLK
CBLS	CCCA	CCDR	CCKP
CCOM	CCVH	CCWB	CDVX
CDWH	DHCZ	FGID	GBAB
GBXF	GLAD	HURI	HURR
JPOT	LFVB	LFVC	MKVB
OISO	OXVI	PBYA	PMNF
PSIC	RAGE	RRSR	RUMM
RUMT	RUMW	RUNT	SABR
SBKR	TBRD	TROY	XYAK

Eaglescott
A/G 123.000

AJCP	AKRP	APWL	ARZW
AVNN	BAMB	BCBL	BGBF
BOLD	BOLG	BRHX	BTIL
BTKX	BXFG	BXGP	BYJP
BZHN	BZLZ	CCDU	CCEF
CCXP	CDNP	DADG	KFAN
KFOX	LEEN	LWNG	MVRJ
MYNV	MYZC	MZIK	MZJO
PAIZ	PION	RASH	

Earls Colne
A/G 122.425

AHSP	AOZL	ARHB	ATRI
ATTX	BAOB	BBDC	BCFR
BCHP	BDUM	BJDW	BKIT
BOFE	BOHS	BOLY	BOOG
BPCX	BRHA	BRPR	BSCV
BYSG	BZET	BZHF	CBSD
CBZF	CCIR	CCLP	DRZF
GCBC	GLIB	HFCL	ICCL
IRKB	LFIX	LOLA	MESS
OJRM	SHAY	SRZO	TZEE
WEBS			

Eastbach Farm, Coleford

AKXP	ASCM	BDAO	BDWE
BGXA	BJEV	BOLB	BRXE
BTFL	BUOL	CBWY	CCBK
MJBZ	MYRT		

East Barling, Essex

CBBM	IHOT	MYHP	MZHO
OJKM			

East Chinnock, Yeovil

ABEV	AOXN	FUEL

Easter Balgillo Farm, Finavon

BYXV	CBSZ	MTDK	MWNG

Easter Poldar Farm, Thornhill

BYRG	CBMJ	CCCG	CDTO
CWIK	MGTW	MNPG	MTJE
MWRN	MYZB	RIKI	RIKY
RYPH			

Easterton

BCSA	BTRU	BVLX

East Fortune
A/G 129.825

BJOE	BUKF	BYJK	BYZU
BZFC	BZUX	CBYO	CCEA
CCGK	CCPC	CCRT	CDWS
CEBD	MDBC	MMSP	MNEY
MTCA	MTHZ	MTIM	MTTM
MTXM	MVIX	MVLG	MVXR
MWLP	MWPD	MWTH	MWYL
MWZL	MYCJ	RIBA	

East Midlands - Castle Donington
APP 134.175 TWR 124.000

BAEZ	BAGB	BAPL	BDZU
BFJR	BGGO	BGGP	BHDD
BLZP	BMJD	BMPC	BMRD
BMRE	BNIW	BNUN	BOTG
BOUK	BPRY	BRGT	BVKB
BVKD	BVZE	BVZG	BVZH
BVZI	BWNT	BYZJ	CBIL
CDON	CECU	CLOW	COLA
MAA	FFWD	FNEY	ISPH
CBA	JCBC	JCBJ	JEMH
OVB	LVES	OBMP	OCSC
CSD	ODSK	OGBD	OGBE
IMC	RAZY	RJXA	RJXB
JXC	RJXD	RJXE	RJXF
JXG	RJXH	RJXI	RJXJ
JXK	RJXL	RJXM	TOYA
OYB	TOYD	TOYE	TOYF
OYG	TOYH	TOYI	TOYJ

East Winch

BBKI	BILL	BUXD	BYPU
CCYK	CUBN	DIWY	DOGE
LEMO	PUGS		

Eddsfield

ATML	BBIO	BIFO	BIWN
BKAO	BKTZ	BPNA	CBLP
CBRX	GCUF	GERY	MZEP
ROWS	THMB	VECD	

Edge Hill - Shenington

AHGW	AJON	AWBE	AZRK
BAJC	BJVC	BSTL	BTUA
MWJW	OFER	SIJW	

Edinburgh
APP 121.200 TWR 118.700

BDFY	BEHV	BMCI	BNGT
BNNU	BPFH	BSNG	BVCM
CJAD	CLAS	DRGS	EDCS
ROND	XPSS	BMXD	

Eggesford - Trenchard Farm
A/G 123.500

AIGD	AKVR	AMMS	AMUI
AOIY	AREI	ARNO	ARSL
ASMZ	AXCZ	AXMN	AXRR
AYPM	BCRK	BDFH	BFAX
BGKT	BGKZ	BKFR	BKVK
BRSO	BRWU	BXNN	CUBP

Elmsett - Poplar Hall Farm
A/G 130.9

AVLG	AWAZ	AZNL	AZVH
BDKW	BFRS	BIYW	BUBU
BXJB	BZML	SWEE	THOT

Elstree
A/G 122.400

ARYV	ASWL	ATPT	AVRU
AVWU	AWOE	AWTJ	AXRT
AXTJ	AZCP	AZDA	AZDG
BAIX	BARV	BCIJ	BCUH
BDLO	BDNU	BEVG	BFBB
BFDO	BFLI	BFSA	BFZO
BHDX	BHZK	BIKE	BJAJ
BJWH	BMIG	BMNL	BNRR
BNTT	BOFW	BOLT	BONS
BORH	BORI	BPSL	BPVN
BRBJ	BRRJ	BRRK	BSHP
BSYW	BTIM	BWGY	BWOI
BWOJ	BXHD	BYBI	BZJB
BZPG	BZVO	CCHE	CCWI
CEEN	CEEV	CEEY	CEEZ
CHUM	CLCG	CPMK	CYMA
DAVO	DONI	EDEN	EGEG
EGTR	ENTW	EXON	FLII
FNPT	GHKX	GIRY	GLED
IKAT	INDX	JAST	JATD
JBBZ	JESS	JUST	KCIN
KINE	LEAM	MASH	MOSS
MPBI	NOTE	OARC	OBNA
OCCE	OCCF	ODEN	OECH
OHCP	OLTT	ONAV	ONET
OOIO	OONA	OTIG	OWOW
OXOM	PEPS	PFCL	PHAA
PIIX	PURR	ROWL	RSVP
SKYW	SLTN	SUEB	TANI
TECH	TODE	TVEE	VICM
WARV	WOLF	ZMAM	

Emlyn's Field, Rhuallt

BRZW	BZER	MJMR	MMRP
MTRO	MTWG	MTZR	MVLR
MVYK	MWFS	MYRV	MZOP
MWAC			

Englefield

AORB	EIRE	MZOZ

Enniskillen, County Fermanagh
A/G 123.200

ATSL	AWKT	BBUG	BNMO
BXBP	BXGH	BXJW	CDCB
HARR	JOYT	KWIN	MWWV
OCON	TAFC	WIZY	

Enstone
A/G 129.875

AJJU	ALGA	ARDY	ATCD
ATIA	AWAC	AWBG	AWSP
AXPF	AYDZ	AYEJ	AYNA
BAMJ	BCEF	BDJP	BHJN
BJSZ	BLMG	BLMT	BMKF
BNFI	BOJW	BPJV	BPMW
BPMX	BSGJ	BSPA	BSSK
BTCE	BTUW	BUDC	BUGV
BUIP	BWAT	BWCV	BXCH
BXDH	BXJS	BXOY	BYBW
BYMB	BZKD	CBEH	CBGS
CBYE	CCMW	CCNG	CCXM
CMED	CPCD	CWVY	CXDZ
EMDM	EOFW	FALC	FARY
FINA	GGRR	GTGT	HEVN
JIMB	KWKI	LSKY	LULU
MARX	MMZG	MNDD	MTAY
MTYE	MVHI	MVKT	MVLX
MWVN	MYLE	MYNE	MYTY
MZDC	MZOD	MZOV	OHYE
OOMF	OSFA	RFIO	RVMB
SCBI	TCNY	TENS	UAVA

Eroll

AVID	ATCJ	BBCY	FOXG
MNAI	MTFN	MVVT	MWOK
MYYP			

Eshott
A/G 122.850

AVVC	AZWS	BACJ	BITE
BNIO	BRIY	BTDR	BTHN
BWVR	BYIZ	BZKF	BZLX
BZUH	BZXG	CBOK	CBWE
CBXF	CBYT	CCEG	CCKF
CCOK	CDAT	CDAX	CDOV
CDSH	CEEO	DCMI	DSKI
EDMC	JABZ	MMZF	MNKG
MNKO	MNTK	MNVZ	MTDI
MTJL	MTTX	MTUU	MTZY
MVPA	MVSN	MVUS	MWBL
MWKX	MWLJ	MWNA	MWPG
MWRG	MWRH	MYAY	MYDK
MYEI	MYLC	MYRE	MYXJ
MZED	MZEU	MZMA	MZOC
OYTE	RHAM	RTMS	TBBC
WACT			

Exeter
APP 128.975 TWR 119.800

ARLZ	ASII	ATSX	ATZS
AYII	AZJV	BAZT	BBKZ
BBZH	BCCJ	BCFF	BDLT

BERA	BFVU	BGFG	BGHP
BGVK	BHJI	BJCA	BJSV
BKGM	BKMX	BLLR	BMJO
BMOI	BOFC	BOJR	BPAS
BPZM	BRLI	BRYX	BSXZ
BTID	BUKX	BVGH	BWEG
BWFT	BWGM	BWGN	BXYO
BXYR	BYBL	BYNY	BZOL
CBAE	CDMX	CDSI	CDYK
CDYO	CEBU	CEFL	DAAT
DCPA	EGLT	ENCE	ETPS
FBEA	FBEB	FBEC	FBED
FIGA	FPSA	GAII	GAOM
HYAK	JEAU	JECN	JECO
JECP	JECR	JEDM	JEDN
JEDO	JEDP	JEDR	JEDT
JEDV	JEDW	JLRW	KEVB
KVIP	LSCM	MAFA	MAFB
NONI	ONES	OONK	OWAC
PIGI	PRII	PSST	PVCV
ROSS	SIAL	SOOT	TACK
TVII	TVIP	VETA	VIPP
VIPY	WACW	WARO	WARZ
WVIP	YOYO		

Fairoaks
AFIS 123.425

ARHW	AVNW	BAXS	BBRI
BDSB	BFBR	BFGD	BFMG
BGVN	BHAC	BHJF	BHWZ
BIOB	BJCW	BMKD	BOEN
BOKA	BOLV	BPIU	BPYR
BSBA	BTBC	BWGO	BWMI
BYDY	BYFR	BZLI	CBWB
CCYY	CHIP	DBOY	DORA
DSID	EMIL	EXEA	GASP
GDER	GJKK	HONG	HRYZ
INOW	JANN	JURG	KEEF
MCOX	NEON	OAMG	OOON
OPCG	RATV	SNUZ	STOR
STUK	SURY	TAPE	TAPS
TRUK	VECE	VECG	WOCO
ZAPH			

Farley Farm, Romsey

AKTI	AOHZ	ASHU	ASMA
BLPH	BRIJ	BUZH	BWCK
OGET			

Farnborough
APP 134.350   *TWR 122.500*

BBKX	BDDD	BMWE	BPPM
BVJT	CBHT	CDLT	DAEX
DAUF	DGET	ELNX	FBFI
FMAH	GHPG	GMAA	GMAB
GSSO	HAAM	IMAC	ITIH
JJSI	JMDW	LGAR	LGKO
LVLV	MABH	MAMH	MEET
OEWD	OMJC	PHTO	PRKR
REYS	SYLJ	VIPI	WCIN
XXRS	ZXZX		

Felthorpe
TWR 123.500

AIBR	ANFL	APKN	BXDG
CBAY	CBLL	CCRN	IKEV

Fenland
A/G 122.925

AFNI	AJAP	AMRF	AVHM
AWAX	AWST	AZIJ	BALH

BATJ	BCRB	BEZH	BGCY
BIHI	BIIK	BIOI	BIYY
BIZR	BLCW	BLVS	BORY
BOVT	BRBG	BRSW	BSME
BSUW	BSUZ	BSYV	BTLM
BTYI	BUKO	BXRC	CBBL
CCOR	CUPS	EDTO	ENII
HOLY	MWFL		

Feshiebridge

BZMM	KOFM	MZHA	

Fetterangus

BSTT	BVSB	MBFZ	MJWB
MMJV			

Field Farm, Oakley

BZAK	BZHG	BZLE	BZOU
BZUI	BZVK	BZWT	CBMS
MBRH	MMUR	MTCM	MVNU
MVUJ	MWTI	MWUO	MYBW
MYMW	ROYC		

Finmere

BDBH	BFAF	BUXK	BWMB
BZXM	CBET	GBEE	KAWA
MAIN	MISH	MNJU	MTJA
MVPR	MWYJ	MYIV	MZEZ
MZKK	SKRA	WLMS	

Fishburn
A/G 118.275

APYN	AYYX	BCXB	BGMT
BKFI	BKUR	BPXY	BTOT
BTXT	BVGF	BVMI	BWRR
BYIA	BZNW	BZWZ	CBJH
CCZA	CDBD	CDCP	CDLS
CDMF	CDPJ	DOGZ	EWES
HRLM	KEPP	MTTA	MVIU
MVPJ	MYLB	MZKE	NIEN
RATZ	RPRV	SIMP	UPTA

Fowel Hall Farm, Laddingford

AYME	BHHE	BXDY	CCOV
CDCI	TOPK		

Fowlmere
A/G 135.700

AZUM	BONC	BSII	BZHK
CBKC	CERT	DIXY	GURN
IKAP	JACS	KEMI	MAIK
OPWS	RIGH		

Franklyn's Field, Chewton Mendip

AJJT	AMIV	BSEF	MVZT
MWSC	PGFG	CDPH	MMHS

Frensham, Wilshanger

AXBW	OEZI

Full Sutton
A/G 132.325

AHUF	ASAU	ATLA	AVYL
AYCT	AYOW	BATV	BBDT
BBXB	BCPN	BDFZ	BEUI
BGWU	BHBZ	BILU	BKCL
BNSO	BOSM	BPUU	BVST
BWZA	BYOO	COLH	CONL
CVST	DFKI	EEJE	FLYA
JILL	JPAT	JWJW	MNXI
REDB	RJWW	ZEBY	ZIPA

Gallows Hill, Bovington Camp

ATMH	AYBG	OACE

Gamston
A/G 130.475

APXJ	ATMM	AVUG	AVVL
AWLP	AXKX	AXNS	BBEY
BBJI	BBJZ	BBYS	BDIG
BDTV	BEYO	BFPH	BGXS
BHEV	BIUW	BJVT	BMCN
BMSU	BNCO	BNPY	BODZ
BOIG	BOJM	BPTZ	BRDD
BTVX	BVAI	BVUV	BWFZ
BXLS	BXPI	BYSI	BYTI
BYZR	BZNK	CCKH	CCLC
CCZU	CDEJ	CDEL	CMSN
CTCD	DARA	EHMJ	FOFO
GUYS	HOLZ	HRPN	HUGS
ICON	JKMG	KDMA	KUBB
KWLI	LEOS	LIZA	LLMW
LYNC	MAMD	MOAN	MOLL
MOOR	MZEN	OCCD	OCCG
OCCH	OCCK	OCCL	OCCM
OCCN	OCCO	OCCP	OCCS
OCCT	OCCU	OJAZ	ORAY
ORJA	OWAL	PECK	PEPL
PETH	PLSA	RAMS	ROLY
SAAB	SERC	SGEC	STAA
TDFS	TEMT	WAGS	

Garston Farm, Marshfield

AZLF	BDIH	BMEH	BOZV
BPTA	BRJL	BSWB	BTMK
BUWL	BVAF	CCMM	CZCZ
JOLY	NINE	OLEM	TJAY

Gerpins Farm, Upminster

BYYX	DOZI	MJOC	MNXZ
MTGC	MTGR	MVYU	

Ginge, Wantage

MZKU	ORDS	RIVR

Glasgow/
APP 119.100   *TWR 118.800*

BAPI	BFZH	BGIG	BGIY
BNIM	BNVT	BSYZ	BVVK
BYUD	BYUR	BYVM	BZFP
CELR	EDCK	EZAT	EZAX
GNTB	GNTF	LGNA	LGNB
LGNC	LGND	LGNE	LGNF
LGNG	LGNH	LGNI	LGNJ
LGNK	OMGI	PCOP	

Glasgow City Heliport

SASA	SASB	SPHU

Glassonby

CBTD	CCNS	MMPZ	MVMO
MWLS	MWOV	MYBV	MZDF
MZJX			

Glenrothes
A/G 130.450

AANL	ANRF	AREH	BBTH
BFFE	BHDS	BHJK	BIOK
BITF	BKUE	BLAT	BURD
BVHD	BVUM	BWUB	CCIT
CDMT	CRAY	EIWT	FIFE
GBHI	GBLP	IDAY	LOST
MMYU	MZBB	MZBM	RLFI

TAYS TFCI WEND

Gloucester/Cheltenham/Staverton
APP 128.550 *TWR 122.900*
APIK ASRO ATSR AVJJ
AXEV AXVM AYWM AYZE
AZBE BEBU BEOH BEPF
BEZO BFEK BFOF BGBA
BGTJ BHCC BHFG BIMT
BIMZ BKCC BKGC BLGV
BMTR BOPC BOUP BOXT
BPKR BPMR BPON BRBB
BRBN BRBP BSGK BSOK
BSWC BSXB BTAW BTHV
BUIR BUPA BUUF BUZZ
BVMM BVSD BWLR BWNM
BXRV BYKO BZHU BZNE
BZRO CAHA CBRP CCFR
CCUO CHAV CZNE DAFY
DORS DUKY EELS EKIR
EKMN ESTA EWHT FORC
GEHP GFCA GFEY GFRD
GFRO GJCD GYMM HIVA
BFW IGHH IJBB JPSX
JPTT LNTY LUKY LUST
MAXI MDJN MEEK MLSN
MMCI NDAA OABO OASH
OGJP OJAN OJBB OJMW
OMNI ONPA OPFA ORIX
OTUG OTWO OVON OZAR
PASV PASX PWIT RAFT
RDBS REAN RNGO RYZZ
SAZZ SCPL SHED SRVA
TBGL TFYN TMOL TREX
TYRE UILE USKY WEGO
VIRL WIZO WMPA WYPA

Goodwood
AFIS 122.450
DXT ANEN AOFE APFU
RJH ARKJ ASCZ AWHY
ZBN AZSC BAWG BBIH
BMW BECT BEMB BFTT
GXO BHBT BHCZ BKII
MKR BNKH BNYB BOLO
PVI BPVW BPWI BRNV
SOG BTGJ BTRC BUCC
URI BVAC BXSG BXUC
YTB BZXB CBUK CCCR
ECY CFME CMOS COUP
PMS DMAC ELIT ELUT
LZY EOLD FLUX GBUN
OOD HOCK IANH IKBP
MD IZZZ KBPI LAOL
ARA LILY MATE MLLA
ACG OAMI OBBO OMDR
ODW ORAR OSUS PAWS
ART TIMP TOUR UNDD
ASA WELL WHAM

ransden Lodge
ETL BTOW CKFY CKGF

raveley Hall Farm, Graveley
BMT BGBE BVIK BZYN
BLA CBOM CCDZ CCLU
DLJ JSRV MMXU MTGH
VKK MVKZ MWYI MYDZ
VOL PBEL

Great Massingham
AHSS ARFH BLOS BRUN
BUNJ BVMD CBMP CDVL
FLAK RVPL

Great Yeldham Hall
BJML CBCZ MTGW

Griffins Farm, Temple Bruer
AJAM ARAZ BGEI BVFR
BVLF CBDJ MYSL SWOT

Grindale
ASVN ATCE STAT

Grove Farm, Needham
CBIB CCNH CCTV MNNM

Guernsey
APP 128.650 *TWR 119.950*
AVRZ BAJB BBHY BDTN
BDTO BEVT BGAJ BGTG
BLKY BPFN BSUF BWDA
BWDB BWLZ BXTN BYDF
BZIJ CDFF CIAS DAAZ
DISK DWPF EHLX FTSE
GFTA GFTB HMBJ HPSB
HPSF HPSL JOEY OCIT
OFCM OWLC PBEE PCAM
PUFN RBCI SMJJ SSEA
VICS XAVI XTOR ZIZI

Gunton Hall ,Somerton
BJGY BJVM

Guy Lane Farm, Waverton
BUXC BZTV CBVM MNUF
MTRA MYSG MZCV MZHB
RINN

Halesland
AVHY BTTZ KWAK

Halton
A/G 130.425
AOSK ASIY ATEX ATZM
AZGA BCXN BDPJ BHGJ
BIZI BNKI BSCZ BVTM
BXDM CBIN CHAR EDGA
FLKE ICRS MWDN MYZN
NADS NEWT OHAC PIET
PLIV RAFV RUMN SATN
WARR

Halwell
ASVG AXKJ BTDC CCHR
DIDY MBCL MTPF MYZE

Hampstead Norris
AFYD ANHK AYDI

Harringe Court, Sellindge, Folkestone
CCZO CDAZ MWLW MZIF

Haverfordwest - Withybush
A/G 122.200
ACZE AFZK ARRI ARXW
ASOC AVAR AVJF AVSD
AWVB AWXS AXXW AYLP
AYNJ AYPG AYRF AYRH
AZTK BAOH BAYO BBXK

BCHK BFOG BHZR BKCR
BKVB BMMI BMNV BMSF
BNAI BPPE BPWR BSPN
BSSB BSZB BTFE BUDO
BUYR BVRH BVYF BWJH
BYOJ BZJP CBRH CCGL
CDJM CECV FANL IMLI
IMPY IZZY JAES JFRV
KIRC MMVX MTJT MTXU
MVFW MVOX MVYT MWZR
MYUE MZGJ MZII OPAZ
PJTM REKO STAY TEDB
VERN WARP YROW

Hawksbridge Farm, Oxenhope
AWFW AYGA BWVV CDGG
CFWR ITON

Headcorn
A/G 122.0
ACDC ANJA APTZ APVZ
ARBZ ARGZ ARKP ARLK
ARMZ ARNZ ASKP ASTI
ATCC ATWJ AVEF AVIS
AWEF AXSM AXUB AZVJ
BAJZ BAMM BBYB BCID
BCXE BFIE BFJZ BFMR
BGHU BLYP BMCS BMLB
BMLX BNFV BNYL BOKX
BOMY BPLM BPZD BRNZ
BRXH BRZL BSAJ BSZG
BTDZ BTWY BURE BXHT
BZST BZWJ CBEG CBKF
CBMD CBOZ CDCE CEFP
EUSO GGHZ GGJK GUCK
ICOM LHCA MIDG PACT
PBRL PFSL PVML ROVE
SEXX SOCT SUCT SUPA
SUTN TBXX TOAD XXVI
YKSS

Headon Farm ,Retford
BYOS CBKM CBKN CBTM
CCDF CCRV CCTD CDKK
CDLR CDWP CDXN FEET
JAYS MGCB MTLJ MVHY
MWIH MWSP MYJW MYLL
MYND MZCG MZEO MZFS
MZKM

Henlow
TWR 121.100
ACUS ADHD AIYS AJVE
APAP ATUH ATVX AZZZ
BCGC BIGZ BJVJ BLUZ
BRUD BTBX BUHZ BYAV
BYLO BYSX BZRP CBGR
CCEK IFFR MNJT MYIN
OKIM RVGA RWIN SAHI
SAMG

Hendon
AAMX AANJ ABBB ABMR
AETA AFDX AGYX AITB
AIXA APUP ATVP AWAU
BEOX BFDE BIDW BLWM
EBIC EBJE OIOI OTHL
USTV

Henstridge - Lower Marsh
A/G 130.250

AHGZ	ALYG	ANEW	AWIF
AYPZ	AZVI	BCGB	BCOR
BFXR	BHBA	BJAO	BLLA
BLLB	BLLZ	BMOT	BSMN
BSRL	BTMP	BUEP	BVPX
BWAD	BWAH	BWUZ	BXCJ
BXHU	BXUA	CBCJ	CBSV
CCCE	CDGP	EYOR	FARO
HALJ	IRAF	MITT	NAAB
NUTA	OGAN	OOJC	SAZY
STOO	WHRL		

Hibaldstow

ANHR	ASDK	ATJV	BWCO
BXZB	BEOL		

High Cross, Ware

AXZD	BJUS	BJYN	HFBM
OPSF	OSJN	OWWW	ROLF

High Easter

BRKC	BUTF	NPKJ

Higher Barm Farm, Houghton

BTET	CRES	MNIZ	MVBL
MWHP	MYXC	MYXG	MZJK
MZMB	MZOH		

High Flatts Farm, Chester-le-Street

BJOT	BVJX

High Ham, Langport

BSEJ	BUEC	BZKS	BZWN

Hill Farm, Durley

AANV	ABDX	ABLS	ACNS
ADKM	AERV	AFDO	ALJL
AMIU	ARTH	ECDX	

Hinton-in-the-Hedges
A/G 119.450

ASOX	ASVP	ATMT	AVEX
AVOH	AYCC	AYRO	AZKW
BAIZ	BAPW	BCGJ	BCPD
BCTI	BEBG	BEYT	BFIU
BGMP	BGPI	BIZY	BKRH
BLTW	BMAO	BONU	BRGF
BSPI	BSYU	BTVW	BTXZ
BUFG	BUGW	BWWF	BZNX
CCOZ	CDDG	CDDK	CKKR
CSBM	CSIX	IIMT	SKYE
TESI			

Hook - Scotland Farm

AWKD	BRWA	BWFI	EMLE
LBUZ			

Horsford

CBGL	MAGG	SIIB

Hucknall
A/G 130.800

AEDB	AVRW	AXHV	BHRH
BJWT	BKPB	BPWD	BWFN
BXTD	CCOF	MTMR	MTTR
RRCU			

Humberside - Kirmington
APP 119.125   *TWR 124.900*

AWPJ	AXMA	AXSI	AZTS
BAFU	BAIW	BAXY	BBBC
BCRL	BEAC	BFCT	BGHJ
BIZM	BMAL	BPOM	BRWO
BSCE	BTEU	BTNC	BVTC
BWDR	BWSH	BXFU	BXFV
CBRJ	CDKB	CDYH	CDYI
DENZ	EEST	FMSG	FOSY
HPOL	IJYS	JPRO	LFSI
MAJA	MAJB	MAJC	MAJD
MAJE	MAJF	MAJG	MAJH
MAJI	MAJJ	MAJK	MAJL
MAJM	MAJN	MAJO	MAJP
MAJT	MAJU	MAJV	MAJW
MAJX	MAJY	MAJZ	OKYM
OOLE	PATN	RAMY	

Hunsdon
A/G 129

CBBZ	CBUF	BUX	CCIV
CCNP	CCRR	CCUF	CCWO
CJAY	COXY	MNKP	MTTD
MWDL	MWLH	MWLM	MYPW
MZFV	MZHN	MZLZ	MZNT
MZOW	WAZP	YZYZ	

Hunterston Farm, Stair

CCJW	CDJP	MWZE	MZFI

Husbands Bosworth
Launch Control 129.975

AVTV	AWGN	BBNA	BBSS
BCOY	BFAW	BHFR	BNED
BSIY	BUNC	BVTX	BVZZ
CDTZ	CKGX	CKKN	CKLB
CKLN	CKLY	CKMV	CKNR
CKNS	DUOX	GBGA	HBOS
TUGY			

Ince Blundell
A/G 129.825

BYKC	BYNM	BYRP	BYZS
BZFS	BZGZ	BZUN	CBAD
CBLW	CBVN	CBVR	CCJM
CCTP	CDBU	CDCG	CDFG
CDOA	CDUH	CFTJ	EEYE
GTSO	HARI	HIJN	HVAN
INCE	JOOL	MMAC	MMZD
MNBB	MNEH	MNIL	MNKC
MNUG	MTAG	MTGL	MTIO
MTJX	MTZW	MVIY	MVNW
MVPC	MVPI	MVUM	MWOJ
MWTY	MYAK	MYCK	MYEU
MYVA	MYYU	MZAP	MZAR
MZAT	MZCE	MZFF	MZGS
MZJA	MZJZ	MZKG	MZLC
MZLJ	MZME	MZOR	OLDP
OOLL	SCPD	VJAB	

Insch
TWR 129.825

AISS	AKTS	ARWR	AWUE
BDAG	BEZV	BSYH	BUOB-
BZOR	BZVA	BZVJ	CDOP
CEBZ	MTXK	MVCL	MVHZ
MVYY	MWTT	MWVH	MWXR
MYMX	MYNS	MYRS	MYVN
MZMF	MZMO		

Inverness
APP 122.600   *TWR 122.600*

ARNY	ASEU	ATBP	AZAW
AZWF	BCJO	BGKS	BHJO
BIIT	BKET	BLHS	BNHG
BRLP	BTCI	BTXG	BVJE
BWUP	BXET	BXZA	CEGT
DDIG	EXAM	FROH	HEMS
IFAB	INTS	JURA	LEAF
NTWK	OINV	PDGN	PLMB
PLMH	RICC	RICK	ROXY
THZL	TURF	UIST	

Jackrells Farm, Southwater

BAEE	BZEZ

Jenkin's Farm, Navestock

CCCP	CCXW	CDOZ	IVAR

Jericho Farm, Lambley

AZYS	BAHD	BHFK	FIII

Jersey
APP 120.300   *TWR 119.450*

AORG	AVLJ	AVUZ	AVWN
AWBN	AWPW	AYPU	AZRH
BAGG	BCBZ	BEDP	BFUB
BGTF	BGTT	BHTA	BIIP
BJPL	BJRG	BJTN	BJTY
BJUE	BJUU	BOET	BOXA
BOXC	BPDT	BTYC	BTYK
BWSG	CBPI	HROI	ISLB
ISLC	IYCO	JACA	JACB
JCAR	JCAS	JCIT	JJEN
LCOC	LLMC	OAPE	OSCC
OTBY	PFCI	POPS	REDS
RHOP	SMKM	SVSB	TABI
WAIN	XAXA	XLKF	XLMB

Jubilee Farm, Wisbec hSt. Mary

ARRE	BBGL	BWWN

Keevil

ARUV	BLMP	BMBJ	BSEL
BYEJ	BZPF	BZYG	CDFD
CKJP	CKMO		

Kemble
A/G 118.900

AHWJ	ARBE	ARJB	ASOI
BAGS	BCYM	BDXE	BDXF
BFDK	BGEW	BGNV	BHOZ
BHZT	BMGB	BMIO	BMIS
BOFY	BRIA	BTPN	BUDS
BUOD	BUXI	BVFA	BVMP
BVMT	BVUJ	BVVP	BVXR
BWAI	BWEB	BWGG	BWGK
BWNU	BWVS	BXAU	BXFI
BXKF	BXYT	BYFF	BYZZ
BZPB	BZPC	BZSE	BZSF
BZTH	CBGN	CBUJ	CCFW
CCGP	CCMZ	CDHU	CDLC
CDNC	CDOE	CDTU	CDXH
CEBR	CEFC	CEFW	CHPY
CSDJ	DGOD	EKKC	EZPZ
FFOX	FMKA	GANE	GREY
HACK	IIIS	IMUP	JEAJ
JEAV	JEBV	KEJY	MALA
MIME	MJWK	MTEC	MTLG
MTNK	MTSJ	MVFE	MWIO
MWMJ	MWMV	MYGD	MZCS

MZDM	MZJG	MZOI	NJPW
OMHD	OSIT	OSSF	OSTU
OZOO	PVET	RAIG	RJAH
RMAC	RNRS	RSWO	SAWI
TERR	ULHI	XSDJ	YAKB
YFLY			

Kidderminster

BYBK	BYBO	BYRV	CCKG
CDXG	MMKX	MTRT	MVCT
MWHT	MZAS	MZHL	MZND
XRXR			

Kidmore End, Reading

AGNJ	BRHW

Kimbolton

BDNX	CDDR	OVID	TOMZ

King's Farm, Thurrock

ATCX	ATNV	AWSL	AXHO
AYKW	BAIH	BBMB	BEBN
BIHD	BZMB	ENOA	MEAH
OSII	SIXD	ASUD	BZKL
KIMK	OFTI	WWAY	

Kington, Hereford

ASAA	MBAA	MBAB	MBKY
MBZV	MJAJ	MJSL	MMAG
MMHN	MTGB		

Kinloss

APP 119.350　　TWR 122.100

BKXO	BMUG	BROO	BSCP
CCSY	ETDC	MPBH	NOBI

Kintore

DEUX	HBMW	ONMT

Kirkbride

APP 123.600　　TWR 124.400

AYUT	BGIO	BHEM	BIPY
BORG	BRHL	BRUO	BSGS
BSZM	BUIG	BUPM	BUZL
BVMN	BVOH	BWJN	BXCL
BXDE	BYTS	BYZW	BZAO
BZIY	BZXL	CBFW	CBHB
CBNX	CBOU	CBPD	CBWW
CBXR	CBZL	CCCW	CCPE
CCXS	CDBE	CDGT	CEDP
CEEA	CEER	CEFH	GGCT
IIXX	MINS	MVEI	MVIL
MVYS	MVZZ	MWDC	MWNO
MZFL	RCHY	SELL	SIMY
VANN	YROS		

Kirknewton

ARZN	ATJC	BGRO	BRWP
BTZA	BVJN	BWYD	CBAP
CCVT	CCZM	CDGC	CEEG
EEZZ	MYZJ	OOJP	SDOI
SDOZ			

Kirkwall

BGVS	BJOP	BMFY	BPCA
CROY			

Kirton-in-Lindsey

BFEV	CKHC	DGIV

Kittyhawk Farm, Deanland

BOXJ	RECO	REEC

Lamb Holm Farm, Orkney

BXBC	BVKF	CDJL

Landmead Farm, Garford

ADWT	ANMY	ARNK	ASFK
BLIY	BOKH	BRAX	BTSM
BVWY	BYRH	CCTU	FLEX
HLCF	HOPY	MNTP	MTVP
MYVZ	PAXX		

Lasham

A/G 126.650

ADGP	ATRG	AVKD	AXJV
AXSF	BDIN	BJUD	BLJD
BMGR	BPIN	BSFF	BVVZ
BZLY	BZPH	CCHX	CCTK
CDOY	CKHM	CKHX	CKKM
CKKV	CKLV	CKML	CKNB
CKNC	CKNE	CKNF	CKOH
EGGS	HJSM	IIGI	JEDH
JIFI	KEPE	ORIG	PAWN
RHYM	RVIV	STEN	TOWS
TWOT	ZENN		

Leeds-Bradford

APP 123.750　　TWR 120.300

AVWD	AYCJ	BEUX	BEYV
BFFC	BFGL	BHSB	BMHT
BNYO	BODD	BOVK	BWEU
BXDT	BXGW	BXLY	BXOR
BYLH	CELA	CELB	CELC
CELD	CELE	CELF	CELG
CELJ	CELK	CELS	CELU
CELV	CELX	CELZ	EJEL
FIRS	FITZ	HERB	JACK
LSAA	LSAB	LSAC	LSAD
LSAE	LSAG	LSAH	LSAI
MOUN	MOUT	OADY	OLNT
ORDH	PASG	PROG	SASH
TRAN	TTHC		

Leeming

APP 123.300　　TWR 122.100

BRVL	BYVS	BYVV	BYWH
BYWT	BYXY	BYYA	

Lee-on-Solent

TWR 132.650

AAHI	AAJT	AALY	AAWO
AAYT	AFGZ	AGHY	AHPZ
AJGJ	AKTO	AODR	ASFL
ASVM	ATFD	ATIS	AXZF
AYLL	BAVH	BBVA	BCFO
BCLI	BDIJ	BDOL	BEBS
BIPV	BMDB	BNSZ	BNVE
BOZZ	BPJP	BPJU	BSAW
BTGU	BTLG	BTZB	BUJI
BUNB	BVNG	BYND	CBPC
CCHH	CECH	CEYE	CKHT
CKMC	CSNA	ERFS	GILT
LORD	LYAK	MAJR	MJTX
MMTL	MNDO	MVXD	MWLD
MYMB	MYOO	MYRH	MYXB
OSIX	OVFR	PNGC	PURL
RAIX	SJCH	TOBA	VIKE
WAHL	WNTR	YAAK	

Leicester (East)

A/G 122.125

AHLK	AMPG	AOCU	AOUP
APTU	ARDJ	ASHH	ASIL
ATLV	AWIR	AXBJ	AXIA
AXPB	AYWD	AZET	AZNO
AZRL	AZYF	BCAH	BFMK
BFNG	BGVB	BHEN	BHRP
BIJD	BKCE	BKCI	BKGW
BMCV	BNIK	BNNA	BNXE
BPBO	BPDV	BREY	BRFI
BRIH	BRPX	BSDH	BTAK
BUTZ	BVCS	BVOX	BYCZ
BYEZ	BYPH	BZFI	BZIG
BZPI	BZRV	CAPX	CBEF
CBSL	CCCB	CCVU	CHET
EFIR	EYAK	FLEA	FLIK
IIDY	IIIL	IIIV	JAWZ
JDEE	JEEP	JUGE	KARK
KEST	LEIC	LITZ	LOOP
MINT	MMNA	MTGS	MTLM
MVDK	MZHV	MZKJ	NICC
OCAD	OERS	OODI	ORBS
OSDI	PFFN	PITS	PJSY
RAFW	RAYA	SIIS	TOBI
TREK	WIBB		

Leuchars

APP 123.300　　TWR 122.100

AYHA	BYUG	BYUU	BYUW
BYUY	BYVB	BYVH	GBVX

Ley Farm, Chirk

ANFC	BWLY	CCNA	CWTD
MVBT	MYGF	MYIA	MZFN

Liskeard

A/G 129.900

BSML	CCUK	CEJS	CGRI
HDTV	JODI	OCST	ONTV
PBEK	TELY	TKNT	TMWC

Little Baddow - Retreat Farm

AYSH	BRXL	CCGA	MVCM

Little Gransden - Fullers Hill Farm

A/G 130.850

AELO	AGXV	AGYD	AIBX
ALWB	APYG	ARHC	ARMC
ATIR	ATVO	AWLO	AWSN
BABC	BBND	BCGS	BDFB
BECZ	BEVO	BHSS	BKBP
BKXA	BMET	BNHT	BOMP
BRPK	BSUE	BTRZ	BTUB
BULR	BWAC	BWIK	BWTO
BXFC	BYBZ	BZMY	CORA
HAMM	IUII	KYAK	MNZD
MVXA	MWJG	MZUB	OYAK
SKNT	TINY	TIVS	UPFS
VALS	XAYR	XYJY	

Little Robhurst Farm, Woodchurch

BMAY	BRBM	HAEC	TVIJ

Little Snoring

A/G 118.125

AWBS	BGKV	BIZK	BJCF
BKZV	BNNO	BONY	BPMU
BTEX	BTTD	BYHS	BYPE
BZHI	ETCW	GHZJ	HAFG
JABY	REDC		

Little Staughton
A/G 123.925

ARMO	ATSZ	ATUG	AXHA
BAHI	BIWW	BLAC	BRCM
BWYB	BYKB	CLUB	DENB
EIII	IIIE	ISFC	MTWK
MUTZ	TTDD		

Liverpool - John Lennon
APP 119.85   *TWR 126.350*

ARNJ	ARVT	AVCV	AVIA
AWFJ	AYPR	AYSX	BCSL
BDZC	BEWR	BFHU	BGVZ
BGXT	BHDE	BJND	BNMB
BNTP	BNTS	BOTH	BRHT
BRLG	BRUJ	BSDN	BSGL
BSRI	BTHA	BTJK	BTND
BUPC	BXDF	BXUY	BYBY
BYJF	BZXJ	CBCN	CBXK
CCTL	CCVG	CCXJ	CDTG
CHEZ	DFLY	DGWW	DNCS
EFAM	EGEE	EMMS	EZAY
EZBB	EZBG	EZDC	EZED
EZEJ	EZIS	EZIT	EZIY
EZMS	FARL	JETJ	JONH
JONI	LFSA	LFSD	LFSG
LFSH	LFSM	LFSN	NATT
OAWD	OLFT	ORVR	OTJB
PART	RVRB	RVRD	RVRE
RVRF	RVRG	RVRI	RVRJ
RVRK	RVRL	RVRM	RVRN
RVRO	RVRT	RVRW	SACB
SAMJ	SUKI	TABS	TSDS
WARW	YAWW		

London City
APP 132.700   *TWR 118.075*

BWIR	BWWT	BYHG	BYMK
BYML	BZOG	CFAA	FJET
LCYA			

London Colney

BYCL	BZGF	MGFK	MMGS
MMRL	MTSG	MVPS	MYCU
MYEF	PRAH		

London - Gatwick
APP 126.825   *TWR 121.800*

BNLC	BNLM	BNLP	BNLT
BNLV	BNYS	BOPB	CPER
DOCA	DOCB	DOCE	DOCF
DOCG	DOCH	DOCL	DOCN
DOCO	DOCS	DOCT	DOCU
DOCV	DOCW	DOCX	DOCY
DOCZ	EZAI	EZAK	EZAL
EZAM	EZAN	EZAO	EZAP
EZAS	EZAU	EZAV	EZAW
EZBA	EZBC	EZBD	EZBF
FJEA	FJEB	GBTA	GBTB
GFFA	GFFB	GFFE	GFFH
JEAK	JEAM	JEAS	JEAY
JEBA	JEBB	JEBC	JEBD
JEBE	JEBF	JEBG	JECE
JECF	JECG	JECH	JECI
JECJ	JEDI	JEDJ	JEDK
JEDL	LGTE	LGTF	LGTG
LGTH	LGTI	OAVB	OJIB
OOOB	OPJB	OXLB	OXLC
SJET	STRF	STRH	TTIA
TTIB	TTIC	TTID	TTIE
TTIF	TTIG	TTIH	TTII

TTIJ	TTOA	TTOB	TTOC
TTOD	TTOE	TTOF	TTOG
TTOH	TTOI	TTOJ	TTOK
VAEL	VAIR	VBIG	VBUS
VEIL	VFAB	VFAR	VGAL
VHOL	VHOT	VIIA	VIIB
VIIC	VIID	VIIE	VIIF
VIIG	VIIH	VIIJ	VIIK
VIIL	VIIO	VIIP	VIIR
VIIV	VIIW	VIIX	VIIY
VKNA	VKND	VKNG	VKNH
VKNI	VLIP	XLAA	XLAB
XLAC	XLAG	XLAI	XLAJ
XLAL			

London - Heathrow
APP 119.725   *TWR 118.5 or .7*

BNLA	BNLB	BNLD	BNLE
BNLF	BNLG	BNLH	BNLI
BNLJ	BNLK	BNLL	BNLN
BNLO	BNLR	BNLS	BNLU
BNLW	BNLX	BNLY	BNLZ
BNWA	BNWB	BNWC	BNWD
BNWH	BNWI	BNWM	BNWN
BNWO	BNWR	BNWS	BNWT
BNWU	BNWV	BNWW	BNWX
BNWZ	BPEC	BPED	BPEE
BPEI	BPEJ	BPEK	BUSB
BUSC	BUSE	BUSF	BUSG
BUSH	BUSI	BUSJ	BUSK
BYGA	BYGB	BYGC	BYGD
BYGE	BYGF	BYGG	BZHA
BZHB	BZHC	CIVA	CIVB
CIVC	CIVD	CIVE	CIVF
CIVG	CIVH	CIVI	CIVJ
CIVK	CIVL	CIVM	CIVN
CIVO	CIVP	CIVR	CIVS
CIVT	CIVU	CIVV	CIVW
CIVX	CIVY	CIVZ	CPEL
CPEM	CPEN	CPEO	CPES
CPET	DBCA	DBCB	DBCC
DBCD	DBCE	DBCF	DBCG
DBCH	DBCI	DBCJ	DBCK
EUOA	EUOB	EUOC	EUOD
EUOE	EUOF	EUOG	EUOH
EUOI	EUOJ	EUOK	EUOL
EUPA	EUPB	EUPC	EUPD
EUPE	EUPF	EUPG	EUPH
EUPJ	EUPK	EUPL	EUPM
EUPN	EUPO	EUPP	EUPR
EUPS	EUPT	EUPU	EUPV
EUPW	EUPX	EUPY	EUPZ
EUUA	EUUB	EUUC	EUUD
EUUE	EUUF	EUUG	EUUH
EUUI	EUUJ	EUUK	EUUL
EUUM	EUUN	EUUO	EUUP
EUUR	EUUS	EUUT	EUUU
EUXC	EUXD	EUXE	EUXF
EUXG	EUXH	EUXI	EUXJ
EUXK	EUXL	MIDC	MIDJ
MIDK	MIDL	MIDM	MIDO
MIDR	MIDS	MIDT	MIDU
MIDV	MIDW	MIDX	MIDY
MIDZ	RAES	VAST	VATL
VBLU	VEIL	VFIT	VFIZ
VFOX	VGAS	VGOA	VIIM
VIIN	VIIS	VIIT	VIIU
VMEG	YMMA	YMMB	YMMC
YMMD	YMME	YMMF	YMMG
YMMH	YMMI	YMMJ	YMMK
YMML	YMMM	YMMN	YMMO
YMMP	ZZZA	ZZZB	ZZZC

London - Stansted
APP 120.625   *TWR 123.800*

CDNK	CDSR	CDUI	CELP
CELW	EJAR	EJJB	EZAB
EZAD	EZAF	EZAG	
EZAJ	EZBE	EZEA	EZEB
EZEC	EZEF	EZEG	EZEK
EZEO	EZEP	EZET	EZEU
EZEV	EZEW	EZEZ	EZIA
EZIC	EZID	EZIE	EZIF
EZIG	EZIH	EZII	EZIJ
EZIK	EZIL	EZIM	EZIN
EZIO	EZIP	EZIR	EZIU
EZIV	EZIW	EZIX	EZIZ
EZMH	EZNC	EZNM	EZPG
EZSM	FULM	GSSA	GSSB
GSSC	HRDS	JETC	MOMO
OLDD	OLDG	OLDT	OLDW
ONJC	REUB	SAMP	SIRA
SIRS	SPUR	WINA	ZAPK
ZAPM	ZAPN	ZAPO	ZAPR
ZAPU	ZAPV	ZAPW	ZAPX
ZAPZ			

Long Marston - Stratford-upon-Avon
A/G 129.825

ATUD	BMSL	BSFY	BTRW
BXII	BXWH	BYRJ	BYZO
BZJZ	BZNC	BZYA	CBIS
CBMV	CBPU	CBXZ	CCDD
CCTZ	CCWU	CDFM	CDGH
CDUK	CEBH	CEEW	CEIV
HATZ	LDAH	LORT	MBHE
MJIR	MJKX	MMNB	MMUO
MNBN	MNEI	MNIA	MNNF
MTFZ	MTGO	MTPI	MTPX
MTTF	MTUI	MTVO	MTXE
MVAJ	MVAP	MVKS	MWEF
MWEG	MWIE	MWIM	MWRX
MWVE	MYAB	MYBZ	MYCR
MYDO	MYEA	MYMS	MYWJ
MYZV	MZAH	MZGO	MZGZ
MZJF	MZMS	MZNZ	ROZZ
STEV	YSMO		

Long Mynd

CKGV	CMGC	DDJF	KGAO
VENT			

Longside, Peterhead

BOWZ	BYNT	MWBO	MYAG
MYOZ	MYYF		

Long Stratton

GAZZ	USTH

Longwood Farm, Morestead

AAHY	APNT	ARTL	AYJY

Lotmead Farm, Wanborough

AOZH	BMYU	BOOD	BPHR

Lower Baads Farm, Peterculter

CDXB	RIAT	ZWAR

Lower Grounds Farm, Sherlowe

BZPM	NHRJ

Lower Upham Farm, Chiseldon
AYFF BFAK BREE BSHH
BZFK CBTK DUDZ GLHI
JESA MYNR MYYK MZKY
ODJD OJGT PVST RUFS
RVDP

Lower Wasing Farm, Brimpton
ARMN AVZW AWRY AWVF
BHYD BMVM BZYL CBYN
CCTW MYMH MZNV NFNF
SALL

Low Farm, South Walsham
AXLZ BCOB MNVG

Ludham
AVYS AWEV BCLU BFXF
CCYA JBSP JILS KEVI
LUDM RVPM

Luton
APP 129.550   *TWR 132.550*
BITY BJLY BRIF BRIG
BYAA BYAB BYAD BYAE
BYAF BYAH BYAI BYAJ
BYAK BYAL BYAN BYAO
BYAP BYAR BYAS BYAT
BYAU BYAW BYAX BYAY
CDCX CDZH CDZI CDZL
CPSH DAJB DIMB EOMA
EZAE EZBH EZJA EZJB
EZJC EZJF EZJG EZJH
EZJI EZJJ EZJK EZJL
EZJM EZJN EZJO EZJP
EZJR EZJS EZJT EZJU
EZJV EZJW EZJX EZJY
EZJZ EZKA EZKB EZKC
EZKD EZKE EZKF EZKG
MAJS MARA MONB MONC
MOND MONE MONJ MONK
MONR MONS MONX MPCD
MRJK NMAK OBAL OBYB
OBYD OBYE OBYF OBYG
OBYH OBYI OBYJ OJEG
OJMR OMAK OPFR OZBB
OZBE OZBF OZBG OZBH
OZBI OZBJ OZBK OZBL
SMAN TMRA

Luxter's Farm, Hambledon
AWJX BEWO BKOB BXBU
BZII

Lydd - Ferryfield
A/G 120.700
ARYK ASBY ASRK ATYS
AVNU AWTS BAKD BAMY
BDOT BHJU BIBW BIJV
BMLM BOUZ BSPG BTWX
BUCS BVJZ BVTO BWIA
BXVU BZAD CBAF CCHL
CDER CDJV EMAX EXEX
ILHS JPMA LYDB LYDC
LYDF NRRA OJAV OKPW
PIXS

yveden
AZMZ BXXI CKKB

Manchester
APP 135.000 / 118.575
TWR118.625 / 119.400
BCCF BCCK BCJM BCJN
BHLJ BIAR BIBX BJNH
BJTF BNSL BUVC BUVD
BXAR BXAS BXKA BXKB
BXKC BXKD BYTH BZAW
BZAX BZAY BZAZ CELH
CELI CPEP CRPH DAJC
DBLA DHJH EDNA EMBI
EMBJ FCLA FCLB FCLC
FCLD FCLE FCLF FCLG
FCLH FCLI FCLJ FCLK
FLTC GFFD GFFF GFFG
GFFI GFFJ GMPB GTDK
GTDL JDBC JMAA JMAB
JMCD JMCG JOEM LKTB
LUND MANS MDBD MLJL
MOOO NIKO OJMB OJMC
OOAN OOAP OOAR OOAU
OOAV OOAW OOAX OOBA
OOBC OOBD OOBE OOBF
OOBI OOBJ OOBK OOBL
OOBM OOBN OOBO OOOK
OOOX PJLO SJMC SLNW
SLOK SMTJ SOVA SOVB
TBIO TCBA TCXA WWBC
WWBM

Manor Farm, Dinton
AFGE AISA ARVZ ASHT
EHDS

Manor Farm, East Garston
ATJM BIXL BMJY TAFI

Manor Farm, Tongham
AZLE BUVR PCAF

Manston - Kent International
APP 126.350   *TWR 119.925*
BAPJ BCEN BFKH BGAB
BGPL BHED BHHG BJAG
BKPS BLVL BNGW BTAL
BTFG BVGS BXAB BXVZ
BZLP BZMO CBSN CBYX
CDYS CYRS DELF DERB
ERCO EYRE IBIG IZZI
LONE MAAX MVLY OETI
OHHI OSEE OTGA SUEY
SUEZ ZACE ZEIN

Manton - Elm Tree Park
CDCK CTSW TECZ

Mapperton Farm, Newton Peverill
BYTX CBLH FOXZ FXBT
MJCU MTWZ MVDL MVZG
MYCB OASJ

Marham
APP 124.100   *TWR 122.100*
BAEP BUDB CDIS CKLF
JAGS

Marley Hall, Ledbury
BPUM BYYT MYFM

MarshHill Farm, Aylesbury
AEXT BGPD BRCA

Melbourne - Melrose Farm
AWPY AXVK BPUG BTBL
BUWH BXIX

Membury
AHAG AHGD APZJ AWHX
AXXV BAEN BALG BAZC
BPZP CDBC IICX IIDI
IIXI KIMY LYDR MWZB

Mendlesham
ARBV BRPT BTZZ CCOY
JULE MTNT MVAI MVBB
MZGA WGHB

Meon
APMX BOOC BUOI BWYK

Meppershall - Standalone Farm
AIBH AMZT ANGK ATBX
AXGP AZSW BAFW BALI
BBZV BXPE BXTP CDXI
KUKI OCAM VMDE WOOD

Middle Pymore Farm, Bridport
BUKR MARO MVYN MWUL
MYIX RUSL

Middle Stoke, Isle of Grain
BMOK BYOR BYSS BZBP
BZYS CBMA CBMR CBTW
CBVE CCBU CCCI CCCU
CCDP CCEP CDWI KDCD
MNLT MNMN MNZX MTYW
MVNO MVXI MWBK MWSU
MYBB MYFI MYFV MYJU
MYPI MYRG MYWY MZFC
MZKS THAT

Middle Wallop
APP 126.700   *TWR 118.275*
ABOX APOI BONT BRHR
BUDL BUUA BUUB BUUC
BUUK BWXH SARO

Milfield
ATFR AXEO BJCI BUAC
CDPX CKMT CTUG MILD
TRBO

Mill Farm, Hughley, Much Wenlock
CCBJ CCXN MNKW MTFT

Mill Farm, Shifnal
AJES BYCJ BZRB BZYX
CBXC CCFA CCNB CLEE
GFOX ICWT LVPL MNCI
MNPV MTEW MTLL MTVT
MTXO MTXS MTZK MVBG
MVLS MVRL MWMT MWVM
MYGM MYKV MYRC

Mona
A/G 118.950
AWOA BHEG BILS BOGC
BSRK BUZM CCZY GFKY
JOST PRAG RVRA

Monkswell Farm, Horrabridge
MJTM	MMRH	MNCA	MTNR
MVNS			

Mount Airey Farm, South Cave
BTHE	BTRG	BZJM	EXLL
KATI	LFSC	PEKT	

Movenis
A/G 129.900
BOMN	DOTT	ETHY

Mullaghmore, Coleraine
AWLF	BOLL	BYCN	BYLJ
CDKH	MYIU	MYPM	MYZF
MZGU			

Nayland - Hill Farm
AHEC	APUW	ATLB	ATUF
AXHR	AYCO	AYUS	BCGH
BEIL	BIDO	BMWV	BPBB
BRXG	BSFV	BTTE	BUAA
BUYK	BWLJ	BZDR	VIVO

Netheravon
A/G 122.750
AGZZ	AHXE	ALRI	ARXU
AYRU	BDZD	BNGE	BNYM
BZAH	LEAP		

Nether Huntlywood Farm, Gordon
MNTI	MWUN	MZRM

Netherthorpe
TWR 123.275
AJIT	AJIU	ARJT	ASMW
AVHH	AWUJ	AXFN	AYEC
AYKL	AZEF	AZEW	AZHC
AZHU	AZUZ	BABE	BCOL
BDOG	BDWM	BFGG	BIUM
BIZG	BMBB	BMDS	BNSP
BNST	BOBV	BOBY	BOUE
BPEM	BPXA	BRNC	BRNK
BRNN	BUUJ	BUUX	BXEA
BXEB	BXYJ	CCSR	CCYS
CDZD	CEBF	EXTR	JBDH
JIMZ	KARA	KELS	KELZ
MVJU	OJON	OSIS	PHLY
PHOR	PHUN	PNIX	REAP
RIVT	RVPW	SEVE	SEVN
USTY	UZUP	WCEI	ZVKO

Newcastle
APP 124.375   TWR 119.700
ATEW	ATLM	AWBH	AXZM
AYMK	BAPV	BAWK	BHAY
BMUZ	BUIF	BVEZ	BXLO
BYYG	BZDU	BZTG	CCWM
FLPI	GLUG	ICAB	IKES
JARA	JBDB	KART	MOGY
NESV	NHRH	PDOC	REBB
RXVH	TYNE		

New Farm, Felton
AIEK	AKKB	BBAX	BMDE

New Farm House, Great Oakley
AHTE	ANIE	APAH	AROW
BCMD	BICE	BLDB	BZNO
CVMI	MWZS	VIVI	

Newnham, Baldock
BVFT	CCDM	MNNG	MTFM

Newton Bank Farm, Daresbury
CAIN	CBCF	CCLM	CCSD
CCXT	MNSH	MTWC	MVAB
MWLK	MYVT	SHUF	

Newtownards
A/G 128.300
AJIH	ANDP	ARCT	ARDS
AROO	AVFR	AVKK	AWLR
AYIT	AZCK	BAJR	BBHI
BBXL	BCBX	BFDC	BIDK
BMKC	BNKR	BNXU	BNZR
BOFX	BONO	BPJH	BSBZ
BTCR	BVAZ	BVJG	BWHY
BXVS	BZDM	BZEX	BZGX
BZJN	BZMC	BZNG	BZOI
BZPA	BZSG	BZUP	BZWB
CBDO	CBJM	CBVL	CBYJ
CBYY	CCCK	CCDG	CCEL
CCMP	CCNM	CCUD	CCWD
CDEW	CDHA	CDIP	CDUS
CEID	CEIG	CMXX	CTOY
EURX	EVEY	KYLE	LASN
LRSN	MCMS	MNPC	MNUA
MTBH	MTFI	MTKW	MTMA
MTSH	MVBP	MVMX	MVNA
MWPF	MWYG	MWZG	MYAM
MYCN	MYDN	MYJM	MYOM
MYSJ	MYWW	MZEM	MZIM
MZKN	MZLP	OELD	OLFB
ONYX	OPIK	OVNR	PYPE
TDRA	UFCE	UFCF	UFCG
UFCH	VDOG	WBLY	XTNI

North Coates
A/G 122.75
AKUW	ARCF	ASME	ASUB
AXTC	BIHX	BUVX	BYIS
BZGM	BZGN	CBCV	CCIF
CCZN	CDDI	CDSO	GTFC
INNY	MAXS	MJUX	MJYX
MNET	MTRV	MVMI	MWBR
MWFC	MWWL	MWWR	MYIR
ORUG	XPBI		

North Connel, Oban
A/G 118.050
BGGA	BVGI	BVVB	BWNI
ETIV	MVGH	MVWR	MYNN
OBAN	OMOL	TYKE	

North Denes Heliport
BLEZ	BVCX	CHCD	CHCT
DRNT			

Northfield Farm, Mavis Enderby
AHBM	AHSO	AIPV	CCBF

North Hill
BKVG	CDTH	CKHA	DSGC
KCHG	KEAM		

North Weald
A/G 123.525
AHUN	AKUM	AKUP	AOBU
ARFG	ARNP	AVNS	AVXF
AXPM	AXWA	BBMN	BCUS
BDXX	BEPV	BEWX	BFSC

BFXX	BGND	BHRO	BKOU
BLUV	BMPL	BNZM	BOPO
BOPR	BOYP	BPCL	BPTU
BRBH	BTMA	BVNU	BVPP
BVVS	BWGS	BWHU	BWOT
BWSV	BYCT	BYDE	BZWH
CBBA	CBCB	CBPM	CCKI
CCZX	CDTM	DCKK	EDRV
EENA	ELAM	FELL	FLSH
FRCE	FUNK	GEEP	GYAK
HRHS	HUEY	IPUP	JPTV
JYAK	KAEW	KANZ	KASX
KAXF	KAXT	KDOG	KITT
KNOT	KONG	MKXI	MOOS
ODAT	OEVA	PGSI	RADR
RAFI	REEN	REST	RIMM
RORI	SARK	SCLX	SPAT
TENG	TIMM	TRYX	TSKY
UKAT	VENM	VIVM	YAKK
YAKR	YCII	YKCT	YKSO
YKYK	YRIL		

Norwich
APP 119.350   TWR 124.250
ATEZ	ATVK	AWDP	AWNT
BABD	BBCC	BCRP	BFYA
BGLA	BGWJ	BHFC	BIEJ
BIIE	BJGX	BMTC	BNDR
BSLX	BSSC	BTAZ	BUCA
BXDS	BXNS	BXNT	CBBR
CBJJ	CBJK	CCVP	CDKA
CDOJ	CEBK	DEVL	EEGU
EYNL	FFRI	NCFE	OEMT
OETV	PPLC	TOPS	VELA
YAKO			

Nottingham - Tollerton
A/G 134.875
AJIW	AMTA	ATWA	AZBU
BBMR	BDSH	BFDI	BGBK
BGBW	BGGE	BGGI	BHGY
BHRC	BJUR	BMVL	BNRA
BNRX	BOLE	BPES	BPGU
BUUE	BVES	BVGO	BYJT
CBCR	CTRL	DMRS	DSPI
EDAV	FLAV	JONZ	LAOK
MSFC	OEAC	PERE	RCED
RMMT	RWAY	TIGA	

Nuthampstead
ASKL	AVOC	AWDR	AWWN
BUYS	TKAY		

Nympsfield
AWLZ	AXIW	AXJR	BGGD
CKGH	CKJV	CKNO	CKOD
NYMF	OPHT	OTCZ	TEMB

Oaksey Park - Cirencester
A/G 122.775
ADKK	ADMT	ADNE	AGXU
AKTR	AKXS	AMBB	APXT
ASAT	ATCL	ATZK	AVEU
AYGD	AYYT	AZBB	AZWB
BALF	BANB	BAPR	BDEH
BDFX	BHTC	BJBO	BPJH
BSDK	BUVA	BVAB	BVEP
BXID	BXWB	BYKJ	CLEA
CROL	EWME	IINI	OAKR
RIIN			

Old Buckenham
A/G 124.400

ADNZ	ARAT	AROY	AYAC
BAXJ	BERW	BHDZ	BMYC
BOHJ	BTEW	BUUD	BZWK
ELKA	ELLA	JWCM	NINA
NINB	NINC	OBEE	TAMS

Old Manor Farm, Anwick

BCOL	PDOG	SCUB

Old Sarum
A/G 123.200

ACDI	ANRN	AOTD	AXYK
AYHX	BAFL	BCUV	BCXJ
BDMS	BGVY	BHIY	BIHT
BJBX	BKJB	BSRX	BSVI
BSZW	BTFJ	BUJE	BULL
BUXX	BVSN	BVTD	BVZD
BXCW	BXTB	BYCV	BYHI
BYOG	BYRU	CBBB	CBGA
CBGI	CBPN	CBZM	CCWH
CDAA	CDCO	CDNA	CDSA
CECF	CECX	CLIF	DOME
DRAG	EGLS	EMER	EMLY
ERDA	FLYB	GORE	GPAG
GULP	HNGE	IMPX	IOIA
LORN	MACH	MACK	MBET
MMWC	MNZZ	MTBE	MTOE
MTXR	MVCF	MVLP	MVSD
MVVV	MWVG	MYLV	MYUS
MYXY	MZJT	NPPL	OFBU
OZEE	PILL	RMAN	ROBN
ROME	SARM	SGEN	SNEV
STUB	SVDG	TORC	WHEN
WHOG	WSSX	XTNR	ZODY

Old Warden
A/G 130.700

AAIN	AANG	AANH	AANI
AAPZ	AAYX	ABAG	ACSS
ACTF	ADEV	AEBB	AEEG
AENP	AEPH	AFTA	AFWT
AHKX	AHSA	AJRS	AKPF
AMRK	ANKT	AOKL	AOTK
ARSG	ASPP	AVYV	AWII
AXAN	AYEN	AZWT	BKTH
BNZC	BOCK	BSYF	BTBH
BWJM	BXIY	BYPY	BZSC
CAMM	EAGA	EBHX	EBIA
EBIR	EBJO	EBKY	EBLV
EBNV	EBWD	FOKK	GLSU
KAPW	KLEM	RETA	STCH
STIG	SWON		

Otherton, Cannock

BTAT	BTMX	BYKU	BZBX
BZEJ	BZHJ	CBDU	CBZN
CCOH	CHAD	FBAT	MBPG
MGAG	MJIA	MMYO	MNYJ
MTBJ	MTGU	MTNL	MTOB
MTRX	MVCY	MVET	MVJM
MVMT	MVMZ	MVTC	MWCG
MWHM	MWIA	MWIL	MWOF
MWRE	MWRR	MYBI	MYCP
MYFP	MYKA	MYPC	MYPR
MYTP	MYVR	MYYR	MZBU
MZEG	MZLI	MZLS	MZLT
MZMV	OEYE	PPPP	

Over Farm, Gloucester

BXVD	BZDC	BZWI	BZYU
CBJA	CCFZ	CCJT	CCMX
CCNE	CCZR	CDVZ	CEDL
CEHG	MNGM	MTHV	MTNH
MTYH	MYIL	MYMN	MYZA
MZBA	MZNJ		

Overseas

AAMY	ADKL	ADRH	AFAX
AGYY	AIYG	AJHS	AKDN
ALBD	ANXR	AOJR	APIH
APSR	ATTD	ATTM	BBMX
BBTS	BGJB	BGRT	BIKC
BIKF	BIKG	BIKI	BIKJ
BIKK	BIKM	BIKN	BIKO
BIKP	BIKS	BIKU	BIKV
BIKZ	BJXX	BKBB	BLTR
BLVB	BLXP	BMEG	BMRA
BMRB	BMRC	BMRF	BMRH
BMRJ	BNVZ	BRCI	BRDW
BRLV	BRXO	BSDS	BSLH
BTHH	BTOS	BTPA	BTPC
BTPE	BTPF	BTPG	BTPJ
BTUV	BUOR	BUVN	BVHT
BVKM	BVMU	BVVL	BWKG
BWVZ	BXHA	BXYG	BYNE
BYSJ	BYTG	BZPL	BZSY
BZUC	CBJZ	CBSR	CBSS
CBVK	CHLG	CIDD	CKEM
CKMI	CKMJ	CKMR	CVLH
DAKK	DHCC	DIIA	DIPM
EGNA	ELEN	FIGP	ILTS
IUAN	IVAN	JSAR	KWIK
LIPA	MANE	MANF	MIMA
MIRA	MKAA	MOAC	MWGU
MYWZ	MZDU	MZFG	MZJW
NANI	NOOR	NRYL	NYZS
OBWR	OJJB	OPNH	RIGS
STRI	STRJ	TIGT	TMRO
TRCW	TRCY	TRIC	UDOG
VCXT	WACO	WWBB	WWBD

Oxford - Kidlington
APP 125.325 *TWR 133.425*

AIIH	ATBI	AYEE	AZLN
BARG	BAWR	BBLU	BCGN
BCVY	BDUN	BEAG	BEJV
BFLH	BFNK	BGFT	BHFH
BHIC	BHYG	BHYP	BMDK
BOCG	BOSU	BOUL	BOUM
BOWE	BTGO	BTGV	BTRY
BTZP	BWTD	BXMY	BXTL
BYIK	BYJS	BYKN	BYKR
BYRY	BZIT	CBEW	CBFO
CBHY	CCTH	CDDA	CDDT
CDEH	CDNI	CECT	CEGF
CHEY	DATG	DMAH	DOVE
ELDR	EMID	EPED	FCED
FIAT	FOXM	FRYL	FWPW
GAFA	GOAC	GOJP	HCBI
HCSA	HGRB	HTRL	LENY
LINE	MPSA	MPSB	MPSC
OANI	OKAG	OODM	OSGB
OSPG	OSPY	PZAZ	PZIZ
ROUS	RUES	SHCB	SISU
SKYF	TBEA	USSI	VIPA
WHIN	WIRE	WMAO	WZRD

Oxton, Nottingham

CCAW	MTBD	MTOK	MVAA
MVSW	MWJJ	MWVT	MWYV
MZMJ	MZSM	MZZY	NOWW

Panshanger
A/G 120.250

AFSC	AZTW	BBDE	BCGI
BEEU	BEFF	BIDJ	BMJA
BMSD	BOOF	BUGG	BWPH
BZWG	CCZP	CDED	DJMM
EGLG	GROE	HELA	HISS
MANN	NUKA	OBSM	ODCS
OTFT			

Parham Park

AVPY	BAUC	BEOI	BPXB
BPZU	BYJH	DAWZ	DGCL
DIRK	GLID	IZII	RIEF

Park Farm, Eaton Bray

ATHU	BWWP	FIRZ	MWNR
MZMK	WAVE		

Parsonage Farm, Eastchurch

BTJB	FACE

Pent Farm, Postling

BREB	BRPH	BSYO	FLOR

Pepperbox, Salisbury

AWWP	BJBK	DYKE	EMSB

Perranporth - Trevellas
A/G 119.750

AOBO	ARLX	ARND	AVBS
BGIU	BMBZ	BYCS	BZTI
HHAV	IRIS	OMAG	PHML
ROUP	WACL		

Perth Scone
A/G 119.800

ADLY	AIRC	APXU	ARKM
AVFX	AVWV	BBKL	BBLS
BBSB	BCVH	BDKH	BFTG
BIXA	BKCW	BLWY	BMTA
BNJH	BOZS	BPLH	BRFB
BRWD	BSED	BSFE	BSMD
BSOU	BTSR	BUIL	BVPL
BXDA	BXIO	BYIP	BYPZ
BZOD	BZTN	CBKW	CBSP
CBVG	CBYD	CCEW	CCML
CCRI	CCWN	CCYJ	CDAO
CDBO	CDDF	CDFO	CDML
CDNF	CDSM	CECM	DABS
DEXP	DJCR	DNKS	EERH
EPTR	EYCO	FINZ	HACE
HIND	IASL	IFDM	IFLP
ISEH	KAMP	KRES	MTAE
MTML	MTNE	MTVG	MVGY
MVIE	MVMK	MWMS	MYKL
MYKP	MYMC	MYYN	MZBO
NESE	OANN	OMEZ	OVAG
PEGI	RUSA	RVEE	TANJ
TBTB	TINT	TOMJ	ZTED

Peterborough - Conington
A/G 129.725

BAGX	BEZF	BFKF	BFXS
BGAE	BGKU	BGNT	BIVA
BNJB	BOZI	BXAY	CDAC

CDSU DENC GCCL GDOG
MGAN OEZY PLOD POPW
RAFC WINI WMBT

Peterhead
BEJL BOWZ BYNT BYRE
EIKY MOLY MWBO MYAG
MYYF

Phoenix Farm, Lower Upham
APPN BFPP BRCV BWGJ
FLIT GRWW HDEW WALI

Pittrichie Farm, Whiterashes
AIJT APFV ATBS BDUY
BPRD BSPL BZUG MMGF
MNYU MWGA SAUK

Plymouth City - Roborough
APP 133.550   TWR 118.150
ARUZ ATBJ ATFM AYOY
AYPO BAII BCEA BFRI
BHOG BHXS BHZH BJVH
BNUY BSCW BSTO BTSJ
BUEG BUVO BXWA BYVF
BYVK BYWM BYXK BYXS
CDJW EMBX ENRM ISCA
KELV NCFC NVSA NVSB
SVIV TOLL WOWA WOWB
WOWC WOWD WOWE XSAM

Pocklington
A/G 130.100
ARGV AXED CKHR CKJA
CKJK CKKX OWGC

Popham
A/G 129.800
AFJB AIPR AIZU AKUR
ARHP ARML ARRX ATNL
ATOP AVNC AVRY AWOH
AWYJ AWYO AXBH AXJH
AXLS AYCF AYKD AYKT
AZEY BAEV BANW BASH
BAYP BBOH BCLL BCPJ
BCRR BCVB BDAI BGFF
BHMG BIAX BIUP BJBM
BJFM BKVP BLIT BPAW
BRBI BRDJ BRGG BRJK
BRKH BRTD BSLM BSTV
BTCH BTDE BTLB BUDI
BUIJ BULC BULO BUPB
BVBV BVVM BVZV BWMJ
BXCA BXGT BXJY CBNV
CBXH CCBC CCIC CCYB
CCYR CCZK CDEV CDHR
CDLW CDMS CDNY CDPZ
CDRO CDVI CEAN CIAO
CYRA ENGO EVLE LTFB
LZZY MTZD MTZL MVAH
MVDG MVFJ MVFZ MVIR
MVZW MYHH MYHM MYXF
MZFY MZJM MZLU NIGE
OSZB OVII PGSA RAFG
RVAC SAYS SDOB SHOG
TASH YAKI YAKX

Porthtowan - Trevissick Farm
ATIC AWFO

Portmoak
BFEB BFPA BODT BSTH
BSUO CKGB CKJM CKLD
INCA JCKT KAOM

Pound Green, Buttonoak, Bewdley
BYBO BYRV CCKG MMKX
MTRT MVCT MWHT MWJX
MZAS MZHL REGI XRXR

Prestwick
APP 120.550   TWR 118.150
ARGG ASAL ATDB ATOJ
ATOM ATZY AWUG AXSD
AZOT BDPA BDRD BDRJ
BFFW BFGX BFIN BHDW
BHZO BMYG BOAH BTFC
BUCT BVNS BWYE BWYH
BYLR CCVY ECGO EDCJ
FISH HVRD IARC KARI
MOUL OJHL OMJT TKPZ

Prospect Farm, Wollaston
ICMT MZCI MZCJ

Queach Farm, Bury St.Edmunds
AFIN BGLS BHMT BSWG

Quebec Farm, Knook, Warminster
APCC EFTE

Raby's Farm, Great Stukeley
AXNR BFAP BPAJ

Rathfriland, County Down
APUR BTKV MTKB

Rattlesden
AYUN BGGB CKJG CKMF
IVDM LAJT

Rayne Hall Farm, Rayne
A/G 125.500
AHIP AROA ATVW AVPV
BCOI BECN BMHS BOTO
BPAB BTSB BWFX BWXP
CCFM CCLX CCUL CSAV
FRAN HFCA MTNO MTNP
MVDF MVJG MVJS MYDS
MYUR

Rectory Farm, Abbotsley
ACMD AYLF BLPA

Redhill
TWR 119.600
ABNX ABWP AFPN AIUA
ALIW AMUF ANOH ARAN
ASMM ATBH ATKX AVEM
AVII AWES AYEV AZNK
BALZ BCBG BECA BFOE
BGFX BIDF BISZ BJWZ
BKPZ BLJO BLMA BLYD
BLZE BMKB BNYN BOAM
BOSO BPTE BPWS BSEP
BSMT BTBU BTHY BVDI
BWEF BWWB BXEC BXHF
BXLK BXPC BXPD BXZS
BXZY BYES BYPA BYZA
BZLA BZOB BZTA BZYE
BZYK CBFA CBHA CBRR

CBWZ CBXW CCGE CDJF
CDMG CDND CDTD CHAN
CONB DNHI DOIT EETG
EEUP ELTE EVTO FLYH
GZLE IICI ISHK KOOL
LHCB LHEL LOTA MDGE
MWUA MYCM MYOG MYSP
MZNH NARO NIKK ODNH
OFIL OJAS OLFA OODE
OPLC OROB OZZY PDHJ
RTMY SIVR SIVW SJDI
SKYN SOLH STUY TAKE
TIII TOMM USTB UZEL
WARD WENA XLIV ZITZ

Red House Farm, Preston Capes
MJSE MTHB RSKY

Redlands
BYON BYPB BYXW BYYY
CCDB CCII CDCM CDTA
MTCK MTCN MTIP MTYD
MVCV MVGU MVJT MVUK
MWDD MWPK MWPX MWZD
MYAS MYBT MYDT MYOY
MZCD MZMN OGSA REDZ

Rencomb
ACOJ AEML AESZ AGEG
AOJH BIXN BRTK ECAN
IOOI ISDN IVEL JGMN
KUUI NETY YAKV

Retreat Farm ,Little Baddow
AYSH MVCM

Reymerston Hall, Norfolk
ARRT ARZB ASDY ATHM
ATTB AVDG AVJV AVJW
AXAS AYVO BAHH BGGU
BGGV BGGW BLIK BMJX
BNDG SCAN VIEW

Retford - Headon Farm
BYTC BZAA BZVV CBKM
CBMM CCRV CCVA IZIT
MGCB MNSI MVHY MWIH
MWPO MWSP MYJW MYKC
MYXT MZKO

Rhigos
AWMD AWWI BARF BDDS
BHPS BHXD BKGB BVAW
RIDG

Rhosgoch
AYRT BADH BIIA BPIR
MWPZ

Ringmer
BFFP BUFR BVJK

Ripley, Derbyshire
BOUF LOYD MWMB

Rochdale
BZHY CBSM CEBM MTZV
MZCB

Roche, Cornwall
BZTC CWAL MVHK OHWV

Rochester
AFIS 122.250

AGLK	ARKK	AVKN	AXGZ
AXOJ	AYXU	AZDD	AZHI
AZKR	BBDP	BCCD	BCGM
BFBE	BFHV	BFXK	BGOJ
BHAJ	BHVV	BHZV	BIIB
BIJW	BLAM	BLLN	BLUX
BLZH	BMVA	BOGI	BOJZ
BOTV	BPOT	BPZA	BRGI
BRNE	BRSY	BSFA	BSLA
BTFS	BTHW	BUGB	BUKU
BVOA	BWNY	BYBJ	BYET
BYFA	BYIT	BZHP	BZKT
CBAL	CBGW	CBOS	CBRU
CBSH	CCIH	CCOC	CCSV
CCUA	CCVK	CDKP	CDMD
CDNM	CDUV	CDVN	CECG
CTKL	DDMV	DEAN	DENI
DIZY	DLOM	DSFT	EGHB
EMIN	ENRE	ESFT	FAIR
FEAB	FLOX	FRAG	HIRE
IBZS	IFLE	JAAB	JABE
MFHI	MTRW	MTXJ	MVJP
MVRW	MVSI	MVUB	MVZV
MWEE	MWFG	MYBS	MYZO
MYZY	MZAX	MZNS	NEMO
NORT	OOFE	OSPD	OWAK
PTRE	PTWO	RAVE	RGNT
RVET	SELF	SERL	SSCL
TADC	TGER	TRIO	TYGA
VMCG	XCCC	XLXL	ZIGI
ZIPI			

Roddige - Alrewas
A/G 129.825

BKTA	BZHO	BZWU	CDEN
MMZJ	MNCU	MNHK	MNHL
MTEE	MTGM	MTPJ	MTPM
MTPU	MTYI	MVDV	MVFT
MVJD	MVKH	MVTL	MVUR
MWDE	MWHL	MWKY	MWOI
MWRV	MWSE	MWVF	MWXW
MWZI	MWZU	MWZZ	MYEH
MYEM	MYFL	MYFW	MYMZ
MYNL	MYRY	MYSB	MYTJ
MYVC	MYXZ	MZMX	MZNG
MZRH	OLDM		

Romney Street Farm, Sevenoaks

AMKU	APJZ	ARRL

Ronaldsway IOM
APP 120.850   *TWR 118.900*

AFFD	ATRR	ATUL	AVKG
AWIT	AYPV	AZEG	BBEC
BGWW	BHLE	BSZU	BTAS
BXRH	BYHK	BZFN	CBWF
CCPW	CDSZ	CDUX	CITY
COZI	EMBC	EMBD	EMBE
EMBF	EMBG	EMBK	EMBL
EMBM	EMBN	EMBO	EMBP
EMBS	EMBT	EMBU	EMBV
EMBY	HRIO	LDWS	LEKT
LIDE	MABR	MFAC	MHCB
PETR	RNDD		

Rotary Farm, Hatch

AXRP	BTVE	DINT

Rothwell Lodge Farm, Kettering

AYUB	BBAY	BDCI	KIMB

Roughay Farm, Bishops Waltham

AKUK	APAJ	BBFL	BEDJ
BKFA	BRIK	BVCL	BWOR
BWVB	BXSV	CZAC	HJSS
NGRM	RAZZ		

Rufforth West

ARAW	ATSY	BJMR	BLCU
BLDG	BMLK	BTKB	BTWD
BUGT	BVNI	BYMF	BYMV
BZAF	BZSX	BZTR	BZUL
BZXV	CBDX	CBMB	CBUY
CCFT	CDYB	JAIR	JULL
KOKL	KOYY	LYND	MTEK
MTNI	MTTE	MTUK	MTYT
MTZX	MVRC	MVSB	MVST
MWSL	MWVL	MWZA	MWZY
MYKH	MYTX	MYYC	MZOE
MZRC	OHKS	RDNS	WAKY
XMGO			

Rush Green
A/G 122.350

AHAM	ANCS	APLU	AWVN
AZGZ	BOIA	BVPS	BZUY
JANS			

Rushmead Farm, South Wraxall

FLDG	MMML	MNJF	MTXC
MVZI			

Rydinghurst Farm, Cranleigh

AESB	AREX	BDEZ

Sackville Lodge, Riseley

ASLV	AVJK	AYEG	BAFT
BFZA	BHNP	BUOW	BVIN
BZEU	BZFB	BZJF	CBBH
CBTZ	CBVO	CBXA	CCZJ
DATH	KOLI	LOIS	MTSR
MURG	MWCC	MYIS	MZAW
MZFA	OAJB	RBBB	ROMW
SOPH			

Salisbury Hall, London Colney

ABLM	ADOT	AFOJ	AMXR
ANRX	AOJT	AOTI	AREA
ARYC	AVFH	AWJV	BBNC
BLKA	EBQP	VENM	VNOM

Saltby

BKVA	BNUX	BUHA	BUJX
BVKK	CKMA	CKNL	MNFL

Sandford Hall, Knockin

AVLO	BDVC	BMPY

Sandhill Farm, Shrivenham

AREO	BUFN	BXMV	BXUI

Sandown - Isle of Wight
A/G 123.500

AMVP	ANEZ	ATVS	ATXO
AVWJ	AWPN	AZKC	AZYU
BEUU	BEZR	BHMR	BHWY
BICS	BJDO	BNUV	BRDN
BRSF	BSZV	BTOO	BUND
BURH	BXAF	CDBZ	ELIZ
ESKY	FAMH	IOWA	MBJG

MOTO / ONAF

MOTO	MTZP	MZOS	NACI
ONAF	PRXI	ROCR	ZACH

Sandtoft
A/G 130.425

AOZP	ARCV	BAEO	BAEU
BAZS	BFEF	BGLG	BMOM
BOIY	BPII	BPVY	BROX
BSDO	BSMU	BSSF	BWGT
BYNP	BZJC	CBLT	CBOP
CCJO	CDFA	CEFJ	ERMO
FERN	JONY	JULZ	LENF
LINN	MEGA	MMMG	MVIM
MVKB	MWBS	MWFU	MWXJ
MWXK	MYVS	MZDK	OLJT
TAYI	TILI	TSIX	VARG

Sandy - Long Acre Farm

BVYK	BYHR	BYRS	BZMI
BZRJ	BZRY	CBEU	CBEV
CBUU	CBWI	CCDJ	CCWF
CDSW	CZMI	FFUN	KUPP
MGEF	MJAV	MNDU	MNFG
MTHT	MTZJ	MVAN	MVCD
MVDW	MVFN	MVKU	MVOP
MVPL	MWGM	MWHC	MWJY
MWLB	MWOR	MWXY	MWYC
MWZP	MYBU	MYFY	MYJS
MYKF	MYRF	MYSX	MYXD
MYYB	MZJY	MZLN	MZLX
MZOJ	PSUK	TBMW	WZOL

Scampton

BWFR	BWOU	HHAA	HHAB
HHAC	HHAE	HHAF	HPUX

Seething
A/G 122.600

AOSY	AVHL	AWTX	AYAT
BAIS	BANA	BAOS	BAUH
BCEP	BDBV	BJAV	BLRC
BOIV	BPIJ	BPWL	BSCS
BSOO	BWAP	BWTW	GCKI
GFLY	HUMH	MUNI	POPI

Seighford

ARBP	AZOA	AZYD	BNXL
BRRD			

Shacklewell Farm, Empingham

BANU	BKFZ	BTGM	IDII

Shawbury
APP 120.775   *TWR 122.100*

BIXV	BMID	ZZEL

Sheffield
APP 128.525

AYZI	BCKV	BFYM	BKAZ
BKBN	BNYK	BPOS	BRSJ
BRWX	BZVN	CCAH	CDYW
CEAW	CTCG	DLTR	FABI
FLIP	FLOP	HIEL	HMPH
HPAD	LENI	LFSJ	LFSK
LIMO	MOTR	OOGS	PASH
REDI	SYPS	TAMA	TAMB
TAMC	TAMD	TAME	

Shenington

AHGW	AJON	AWBE	AZRK
BAJC	BSTL	BTUA	OFER
SIJW			

Shenstone

AVMA	BUJV	BYFT	BYYC
CCVL	CCZD	CDBX	CDME
CDRM	IMAB	MGGG	MTTH
MVBZ	RONA		

Sherburn-in-Elmet
A/G 122.600

AIBY	ANON	ASAZ	ASMJ
ATHV	ATOU	AZFI	BARH
BBHF	BBJX	BBNJ	BDYD
BEHH	BEKO	BFAI	BFTC
BFTF	BFXW	BHEZ	BHIB
BHLW	BIOW	BKKZ	BKMB
BNOE	BNOH	BODB	BODC
BODE	BPXX	BPYO	BREU
BRJN	BRZX	BSDL	BSLT
BWZG	CBPY	CCTF	DECK
EKOS	FCUK	GDTU	GSPY
ICAS	IEYE	IIVI	IPKA
JMDI	LORC	NBDD	NOSY
OACF	OAJS	OBMS	OBMW
OLOW	OTVI	RONN	SABA
SACK	SACR	SACS	SACT
SKYL	STER	XIII	XTUN
YIII			

Shipdham
A/G 132.250

AHSD	ATOT	AVEH	AVUS
AVWA	AVZN	AYUM	BGRC
BGRI	BKHJ	BPIF	BRJC
BRPF	BUEK	BYBE	BZTX
CCCF	CCXK	FFTI	FIZZ
FTUO	JDIX	NIJM	OTAM
TINA			

Shobdon
A/G 123.500

ANFI	ANNE	AOIM	ARCS
ARVV	ATDA	ATON	ATOR
AWCP	AWMR	AXIX	AYXP
AZCU	AZRP	AZXD	BAHS
BAOU	BBJV	BDNG	BEZG
BFZT	BGTX	BHAA	BIXB
BJAP	BKMT	BLXO	BNGY
BNKC	BOAI	BOXV	BRPS
BSLU	BSRT	BTBG	BTIE
BTUG	BUEW	BUJB	BUYB
BVAH	BVIL	BVLW	BVMC
BVUT	BXJD	BYBA	BYCU
BYPF	BYTM	BZAM	BZXN
CAMB	CBIY	CBKG	CCDN
CCJA	CCPK	CDIF	CDNG
CDSB	CDSD	CDVU	CEBP
CJUD	CUTE	CXIP	DAND
DEBT	DINA	EGBS	FBRN
FTIM	IPSI	MABE	MNHF
MNVC	MTNC	MTNG	MTNM
MTOT	MVYD	MWCE	MWIX
MYLS	MYSA	MYVO	MZFR
NEAL	NUTY	OHSL	OJSH
OPME	OPUS	POCO	PSHR
SHIM	SPEE	SRAW	TDOG
TGRA	TGRD	TGRE	TGRS
TGRZ	UDGE	WARX	XBOX
XCIT			

Shoreham-by-Sea
APP 123.150　　　　　TWR 125.400

AKHP	AMNN	ANNI	ATXD
AVBT	AVKL	AWGD	AWLI
AWRK	AWSM	AWUZ	AXNN
AXTA	AYBD	AYCK	AZCB
BACP	BALN	BBAW	BBPO
BCCE	BCKT	BDCD	BFOV
BFPO	BFRV	BGHI	BGIB
BHIN	BHPZ	BIUY	BKRA
BLCG	BLIW	BLMR	BLPB
BMEX	BMIW	BMUO	BMYI
BNEL	BNKV	BNNR	BNNY
BNSI	BNYD	BOCL	BOHA
BOKB	BOTN	BOXH	BPAX
BPIZ	BPTG	BRBE	BRNT
BRRY	BSBW	BSLW	BSZT
BTGR	BTGS	BTJL	BTKT
BTYT	BUIK	BUJO	BUJP
BVHM	BVOK	BWAV	BWFH
BXEX	BXGM	BXXW	BXYM
BYKL	BYMD	BZDZ	BZEC
BZGA	CBGX	CCGH	CCPX
CCZG	CDDY	CDEK	CDJJ
CDMY	CDSF	CEGR	CROW
CUBY	CWFD	EDVL	EGAL
EKKL	ETAT	GDMW	GFCD
GOGS	HAIB	HANY	HHOG
IIEX	ITTI	JKMF	JKMH
LESZ	LOGO	MAIE	MALS
NEEN	NELY	OBEN	OFCH
OFST	OLEE	OOGL	OORV
OPST	OWYN	PHTG	RAIN
REBL	RINT	RSKR	RVCG
RVSX	SACD	SARA	SARH
SUSX	TBZO	TCMM	TEXN
TLET	TOGO	TROP	TRUD
UZZY	WARY	WIZR	WRWR
XARV	XENA	ZFLY	

Shotton Colliery, Peterlee

AZOE	BHWK	BVOS	BYIC
BZED	HALT	MNUX	MWWZ
MWZJ	MYBE	MYXN	MZIT

Sibson
A/G 122.300

ANSM	ARMA	ARVO	AZIK
BASP	BAXU	BDFJ	BEIA
BGMJ	BIOJ	BIRI	BNME
BOYB	BUPV	BXVK	BZFV
ELZN	ESSY	FAYE	NSOF
ODOG	ONSF	PDGG	PIGY
RGUS	RIZZ	RVUK	WREN
YOGI			

Siege Cross Farm, Thatcham

BCPH	BUCO	BVGY	CCCY
MTAS	MVKN	MYRJ	MZKW
PHYL			

Sittles Farm, Alrewas

AWPS	BMSC	BYSF	CBTO
CCDX	CCEJ	CCTO	CEIE
CHEB	MNBD	MROD	MVKC
MVLA	MVXB	MVXE	MWXB
MYAH	MYUZ	MZEW	MZFE
MZPJ	RVIA		

Sleap
A/G 122.450

AFRZ	ARID	ASVZ	ATKF
AVRS	AWIW	AXNJ	BADW
BAFA	BCHL	BFKB	BFZD
BFZU	BHAD	BILR	BJWX
BKAE	BKHD	BNKS	BOGK
BOIR	BOYI	BRHY	BRJT
BRUI	BSKW	BSOT	BTCA
BTUZ	BTZL	BUHR	BUKT
BVXE	BWMO	BXVO	BYZD
BZXZ	CBDG	CBOF	CCMI
CDAK	CDPV	CDVV	CHUG
CIFR	CROB	DAYS	ESCA
FOGI	HYLT	IYAK	LASS
LITE	LORR	MVOO	MWNP
MZFH	NEAT	NSTG	OPJK
OWAZ	PIPI	RDCO	REAS
RIDE	RJWX	SCIP	SEXE
SFLY	SHSP	SKYV	TANY
UROP			

Sorbie Farm, Kingsmuir

ATOZ	BEVB	BOOJ	BPPZ
BRFW	BRGO	BYPR	GNMG
OSSA	RNRM		

Southampton - Eastleigh
APP 128.850　　　　　TWR 118.200

BJDK	BJGM	BJRA	BOOE
BOUT	BYHM	CJAB	CJAG
CJAH	EMBW	JOAL	

Southend - Rochford
APP 130.775　　　　　TWR 127.725

AKUL	AOLK	ARUI	ATPN
ATTK	AVLI	AVNO	AVUU
AVWM	AVYR	AWTL	AWVE
AWYB	AXCA	AYAR	AZKE
AZOG	BACB	BBBN	BCIR
BEZC	BEZL	BGAF	BGLO
BHUJ	BIAY	BIEY	BKJW
BLPF	BLYK	BMLC	BMTS
BNFR	BNXD	BOFZ	BOHR
BOLW	BOTF	BPME	BPNT
BPVK	BSXI	BSZO	BVEV
BVGA	BVOB	CBFM	CCAV
CDLY	CDPF	CEDD	CNCN
CODE	CPFC	CTWW	EHUP
FAUX	FLTL	FLTZ	FLYI
FMAM	FSEU	GOBD	GROL
GUSS	HUFF	ICSG	JBIS
JBIZ	JEAW	JEET	JEMX
JIMH	LAOR	LAVE	LUSH
NELI	OBHD	OFLY	OLAU
OOTT	OVIN	OYST	POPA
RRVX	RVIX	SPOR	SSJP
STRE	THLA	THSL	TMRB
TSKD	ULES	UTSY	UVIP
VGAG	WYNE		

South Lodge Farm, Widmerpool

ASCC	AVLE	AVXY	TEWS

South Wraxall, Bradford-on-Avon

MMML	MNJF	MTGP	MTXC
MVZI			

Spanhoe

ANHS	ARRO	ARXB	ARYZ
ARZS	ASOM	AVHT	AVLC

AWSW AYDX BBXS BFNM
BKRK BLHN BMEA BRPZ
BRXN BVIS BVUG BWOX
BXKW CBJG CBVU CCOB
CDCS CDWF DAVD MSAL
MYDX MYSD MYTH

Spilsteads Farm, Sedlescombe
AWFT AXPG AYIJ BHRR
BTRF BXRB BZGY CDAI
CRIS

St Albans - Plaistows Farm
A/G 129.825
BYTA CBHK CCCD CCYM
CDNE CDRJ DARK DUGE
MBZH MGTG MMWX MNVK
MSPY MTFU MTLT MTMX
MTUV MVPF MWBU MWIZ
MWLE MYOU MYTI MYUI
MYUK MYWG MYWM MYXE
MZBS MZCT MZEE MZZT
OBAZ OESY PRSI TDVB
TEHL TNRG

St.Athan
TWR 118.125
BYSN BYUN BYUS BYUT
BYVW

St.Just
AWUX AWWU AWYX BDUL
BEUM BFHT BIHO BSDW
BUBN CBML EOLX MYNI
OCPC ROWE SBUS SSKY

St.Merryn
ARTZ AXPZ AXVN AZMJ
BMZS BVDJ CCIS GYRO
MICY MIKE PHIL

St.Michaels
BSEE BZUF CBJW CBLD
CBTE CCRW LUNE MMOB
MNFF MNTE MTAF MTIB
MTRZ MTTP MTXP MTZH
MVHF MVSV MWPB MWTO
MWYA MYRW MYTD MYUC
MYUW MYVB MZAV MZMY
YARR

Stancombe Farm, Askerswell
AYLV BGGC BWRC MYML

Stapleford
A/G 122.800
ATBW ATOA ATUI ATXM
AVCM AWEZ AZAJ AZOL
AZZO BBIA BBRA BCHM
BCKU BEHU BERY BEXO
BGAA BGVE BHEC BHGP
BHUP BHYR BHYX BIJB
BIJU BKCN BKHW BKLO
BLFZ BLVW BLWF BNJC
BNUS BNUT BOIC BOOI
BPRI BPRL BSVB BTGW
BTGX BTGY BTLP BTXK
BWOZ BXSR BXVB BXVY
BXWC BYCP BYHH BYMH
BYMJ BYOB BYYO CBKA
CBPK CBYU CCLJ CDAW

CDJT CHAS CHEM CHIK
CSCS DIGI DLDL EROM
EXEC FRYI FULL GAZI
HFCT HILO ISSY ITUG
JAKS JANA JENI KNOW
KSVB MOHS OCFM OPAM
OPJC ORMA OSTY PJCC
RROB SACI SACO SELC
SIID SLCT TEST WAMS
ZANY ZLLE ZYAK

Stoke Golding
AWGZ BWBZ GVPI PFAF
PRLY

Stoneacre Farm, Farthing Corner
ARNG AYGG BAKR BCYH
BFGK BJHK BLCI BNZL
BSNT

Stornoway
APP 123.500   TWR 123.500
ATNB BBHL BIMU BLAG
BLRL

Stour Row, Sturminster Newton
BWPS MNXX MTAW MZPW

Strathaven
BAGV BPGE CCSN DROP
BTJN BTWB BUPW BYEW
BYMT CCCM CCFB CCXL
FONZ HANS IMNY MBYI
MTGD MTGT MTUF MVZK
MWXA OPDS SJEN

Street Farm, Takeley
BUJZ BVOY BWUJ BYNH
BYNI BZBW BZES BZOM
BZXD CBWO CBZI CCFY
ESUS KENI RAWS WHOO

Streethay
AJAE APZX ATOH AYZK

Strubby
A/G 118.750
AYUR BFPM BGLZ BKVM
CKGU CKHH CKJL COCO
OMPW

Sturgate
A/G 130.300
ARRS AVZR AWVC AYYU
BDDG BGXD BHCP BIDI
BKWD BLHR BMJR BONW
BRIV BROR BRPV BSOE
BWII BWTC BXXT BYPN
BZEH GCAT IJOE JTCA
LUED MWVZ OBLC SPOG
TERY UAPO

Sumburgh
TWR 118.250
BCLC BDOC BRZZ REDO
REDP

Sutton Bank - Thirsk
BETM BFRY BJIV BSOM
BXSH BZEM CKGN CKJC
CKJH CKLW CKME CKND

IANB OSUT

Sutton Meadows - Argents Farm
BWSJ BYDZ CBDZ CCAB
CCWP CDPL DWMS INJA
MNGX MNJJ MNJS MNUD
MNYC MTIK MTIX MTIZ
MTYC MVCA MVLJ MVTI
MWOY MWSD MWSJ MWXG
MWXP MWZT MYHK MYTN
MYUO MZDY MZGN MZMT
OBJP PGHM RBSN TBJP
TFLY XWEB

Swanborough Farm ,Lewes
ADUR APVN ASMT AYTV
BFHH BHVF BLCT BZLK
CEEP CEGI MYMM OABB
TEXS

Swansea
A/G 119.700
AKTP BATW BAVR BFPZ
BIBT BKCX BOHH BOHU
BOMO BPWE BUTB BVVA
BWDS BXIF BXRF BXVX
BXYE BYLF BYZP BZAE
BZIM CCIZ CCYL CCYT
CDDE CDHM CDYC CDYT
CEBV ECBH GAME IANJ
JWDB KKER LAMS LFSB
LSWL MJAZ MVYV MWRB
RONS TOMS WAAS YFUT

Swanton Morley
BBXZ MVEL ORAF

Swinford
BYMU CBEN CCLS CDNH
JEZZ MJZU MMXO MNCV
MNJO MNLI MNWD MTAO
MTNJ MTSP MTSY MTZG
MVRH MVUI MWHF MWMN
MWUU MWVP MYIP MYNY
MYOF MYPV MYPX MYWL
MZLM NORA SMBM

Syerston
ATVF AWBJ BSSP BTUL
BTWE

Sywell
A/G 122.700
ADGT AGPK AKIN ALXZ
AMCK AMHF AMTV ANMO
ANNK ANTE AOJK APPM
ARAM ATIZ ATSI AVLB
AVLN AWYI AXDK AYIA
AZCT BAFG BAMU BAPX
BAXE BBMV BCST BETD
BIGK BIVF BKJF BMJM
BTBW BWOD BWZY BXOA
BYBU BYHP BZAP BZKJ
BZPZ BZWV BZWX BZXP
CBSX CCIY CCPA CCTI
CCUI CDFP CDWJ CDWK
CDWT CDWY CEAM CEDM
CEGJ CHPR CRLH CVIP
DHPM DIAM DJST ESLH
FORZ GEST HURN IGII
ISEL ISMO IXES JERS

JETZ KNIB KULA MAGZ
MALC MCEL MEDS MIII
MLLE MNRD MTTN MTWD
MVCS MVFD MVFO MVRP
MWGI MWHU MWJS MWOP
MWRT MWSI MWTD MWYZ
MYDP MYFO MYGO MYHR
MYOL MYPN MYVI MYWT
MYYL MZFX MZGG MZGK
MZIE MZIJ MZLW MZPD
NARG NJSH NOTS OAJC
OATE OCFD OCMT OEJC
OFFO OPJS OSHL OSKR
PIDG RATA RHHT RISK
SNOG SWLL SYEL SYWL
TANA TARG TIDS TMCB
UMMY UPHI VIPH WILG
WNAA XLAM XOXO ZEXL
ZXCL ZXEL

Talgarth
AZPA BSWL CKNG DLCB

Tandragee, Craigavon
CDIA CDKN CDNR CEAU
CEDR MGTV MVMG MYXU
MZBF

Tatenhill
A/G 124.075
APUZ ARBO ATNE ATXZ
AVGA AVRK AVRP AWBX
AXTL AYSD BBIF BBUE
BCVF BELP BFRR BGAG
BHRM BHVR BJOA BKVL
BMMP BMXJ BNCS BNFS
BNPZ BORO BPBG BRBX
BRUX BSBG BTXX BUPJ
BXAK BXTT BYDB BZVM
CDHC CTCL DDAY INDC
JAZZ JJPJ OMHC PARI
RUBY YANK

Thruxton
A/G 130.450
AOAA ARJV ARSU ARWB
ASUR BAAI BAKV BBDM
BDLY BEIS BFBU BFIB
BFZV BJST BKIS BKXP
BKZI BLMN BOCI BOTP
BRBK BTFT BUEX BXKL
BYRX CBOE CCBH CCBN
CCYX CDAF CDEF ESME
IEIO ILDA JAJB MILN
MSFT NRSC OFAS OPJD
OREV RROD SFTZ TRAC
UFCC URUS USSY YNOT

Tibenham - Airfield
AJKB AJTW AODT AVAW
AVVJ AZVL BUGL BYNS
DKDP KEMC NDGC OKIS
ONGC OTIB STEM

Tibenham - Priory Farm
A/G 118.325
AKVN ARFD ASSV BAVO
BCMT BGHY BHEL BHPK
BPML BULG BUPR CBXV
CCAN CCFO CCND CDDS
CDDX CDFU CDXU CEED

CRAB CUBE GPAS ILLE
MBYM MMLE MMUX MMWL
MNBP MNGK MNMI MTDW
MVIG MVVI MWMW MYAT
MYHN MYLW MYTO MZDX
MZES VILA WYLE

Tingwall
CDRY ORCA SICB

Top Farm, Croydon, Royston
A/G 130.850
APUE ATXA AWVG BCBR
BDAK BENJ BGSY BLDN
BNSG BPUA BTGD BVFZ
FALO GHOW UJAB

Tower Farm, Wollaston
BLHH BTFV MMWS MROC

Trehelig, Welshpool
ALWS AWTV BAHE BNEK
BWMK

Trenchard Lines, Upavon
BRBL BTWC CKGC LEES

Truleigh Manor Farm, Edburton
BBXY BTYY EWAN RMIT

Truro
A/G 129.800
BPFI BTOL CBFK HUTT
OGGY YIIK

Tunbridge Wells
APJO FYGJ

Turweston
A/G 122.175
ARYR ASIT AYAB AYJR
AZYA BACO BAXZ BENK
BFGS BHPY BJWO BKEK
BKGA BLRG BNCZ BNEE
BNNS BNVB BNYP BORK
BWMN BXOX BZTJ CBEZ
CDFE CEBE CSGT DNKN
ERRY FLCA LBDC NETB
OOTC PADD SURG TAAC
TENT TVCO

Upfield Farm, Whitson
BCLT BWWU BYCY CCKT
CWFA DTOY HOFC KSIR
MSKY MTXZ MWUX YVES
RYAL

Upper Harford Farm, Bourton-on-the-Water
BDWH BSVS BUDE

Usk
AVXA BJXK BLCV BPWK
CKJB

Valentine Farm, Odiham
AMSG AWLG BDKM

Valley Farm, Wlinwick
ARBS ASBA BAET BBJU
BVVN BOIB BTKA MMNS

Ventfield Farm, Oxfordshire
AKUO ATAU AWUL BKDX
BZJW CDJO HMPT OWET

Waddington
APP 127.350   *TWR 122.100*
AWUU AYFG AZLV BLAX
BMUD GNAA LNAA PSRT
ZANG

Wadswick Manor Farm, Corsham
CCAC KIMM PLAD

Waits Farm, Belchamp Walter
AKTK BKFK BMLT CBGH
CDVA IIIX

Walkeridge Farm, Overton
AFJA AOEX ASEB AYKS
BADV BSIF CDMZ MTZB
MVZA

Walney Island
ATFW BFUD BYEC BZHT
CDFY CDZT CKMZ

Walton Wood
ANZU BUTK BXYD DGHD
DRIV JWEB RFUN TINK

Warton
APP 129.525   *TWR 130.800*
AEBJ BGCO BLRA BWFM
BWWW LASU TBAE TCAP

Washington, West Sussex
BPVH MWUH

Watchford Farm
ADJJ ADPS AJAJ APYT
ARFV AVEY AVMB AVNZ
AXGV BAKN BAZM BGFJ
BHHX BJVS BRBV BTDT
BWHP BXMX BZND PFAA
REBA

Water Leisure Park, Skegness
AVDA AVPI AZEE BDTX
MJPV

Wathstones Farm, Newby Wiske
BBBW BWSI CBRC CBRD

Watnall
MNYA MWTK

Wellcross Grange, Slinfold
AVDV AZOU BBHJ BXSI

Wellesbourne Mountord
TWR 124.025
AJRE ARGY ARXT AVBG
AVIT AVLT AXXC AYMO
AYNF AYXS AZKO AZMD
AZSF BBMO BDBD BEVW
BGSW BHUI BKGT BLME
BLRF BMYD BNIV BNXX
BNZZ BOPD BOYV BPPF
BRXD BSCY BSLK BSMV
BSTR BTDN BTNE BUIH
BULJ BWNB BWNC BWND

BWVH BXSD BXYX BYKK
BZMH CDMH CEDG CEHK
DACC DCSG DEXT DMND
DWCE ETNT FLYT GHDC
GORF GOUP GYBO HKHM
JAVO JMKE LBMM LOYA
MASC MWFX NYLE OAKW
OIBO OMKA OSJL OSKY
OWND RALD RAVN RVRC
SBUT SSIX TCTC TORS
WAVI WAVS WAVV ZAPY

Welshpool - Trehelig
A/G 128.000
BAMC BERC BJYD BKXF
BOXU BPRM BWHF BYLS
CBKD CHAH CHZN MIWS
OONE TOYZ

Westfield Farm, Hailsham
AFYO BBPS BXZO MYWS

Weston Zoyland
BUKP BWYR BYYR BZBR
CCNR CCUR CCWZ CDAL
CDPD ELSI JAXS MNFB
MNHS MTGX MTIW MTIY
MTLZ MVCW MVDX MVFM
MVFY MVIV MVSY MWFY
MWJI MWLF MWUS MYGU
MYJG MYVK MYXP MYZG
MZBL MZDD MZHU MZJL
MZLV MZMG MZSD TUSA

Whaley Farm, New York, Lincoln
AWEP BPBJ FBWH TCUB

Whitehall Farm, Benington
ALOD AXCY BHOM BRRL
BZBZ

White House Farm, Southery
BZTY GPSF RCST UKOZ

White Waltham
A/G 122.600
ABDA ADKC AFGI AFZL
AHAN ALEH AMZU ANFM
ANLD AOBX AOJJ AREL
ARNL ARON ASMF ATOK
AVSI AVTP AWFP AWJY
AWSH AXOH AXSZ AYCG
AYIG AYRI AZFC AZOF
BAKW BBFD BBIX BCEY
BCRX BCWB BDEI BDJG
BEMW BEZP BHFJ BHYV
BHZE BICR BIHF BILI
BIPO BIRT BJKF BLMI
BNIP BNYZ BOBT BOSE
BPHW BPYN BPZB BPZY
BRDF BRDM BRNU BSPM
BSSA BTUM BUCH BUCK
BVVG BVWM BVXK BWVY
BXBK BXFE BXGV BXOZ
BXRT BXTI BXZM BYZY
BZBS BZDA BZIO BZMT
CBID CBRW CBUA CCJK
CCWA CCZV CDRU DUVL
ENNI GEHL GPMW HELE
HMPF IIIZ ISDB JEDS
MAXG MERF MLHI NIKE

NOIZ NROY OARA ODDS
OFIT OMIA OMIK OPUP
OSIC OSMD OSTC OTUN
PAVL PWBE RADI RIFN
SIII SKKY SKYO TSUE
TVAM UANO WARA WARU
WAZZ WLAC WWAL YAKH
YAKT YKSZ

Wick
TWR 119.700
AVIB AZKP BUHS CBKL
KOLB MYER MZLY OPYE
OVFM WERT

Wickenby
A/G 122.450
AHAL ARKG ASNI AWEM
AXHC BAIK BBFV BBTJ
BFTH BHWA BHWB BTNV
BTUK BXCT BYOV CCNU
CCUZ CCYZ CDDH CEEX
CSAV DASS IKUS JBRN
MWMU MWON MWPP MWTP
MWUC MZHW OMAL OOSI
PTAG SKEW SOKO SYFW
TJAL WORM XRED

Wickhambrook,Newmarket
MMJD MNRE MZGW

Wickwar
CBAS CCPF CCSX CCVR
MIKI MTOO MYBL MYEV

WilleyParkFarm,Caterham
BTIU KKES

Willingale
CBDY IJMC MCJL PAGS

Wing Farm, Longbridge Deverill
AYLC BMMV BZVB CDVK
MTKE MVOY MYVG OMHP
POZA UILD

Wishanger Farm, Frensham
ATAG AZEV BMWM BTSV
BVFM IDSL

Wittersham, Tenterden
CCVN CDXJ CECR

Wittering
TWR 125.525
AXTO CKMY SLEA

Wolverhampton
TWR 123.000
ARGO ATFF AVAX AWEL
AYZH AZID BAGN BAHJ
BAVB BBCA BBLM BFMX
BHVB BNMF BNTC BOGM
BOWO BOYL BPBM BPNI
BPYL BRBA BREP BRUM
BRXV BSIM BSNX BSYC
BTBA BTDV BTGH BTKL
BXAV BXTW BYJI BYSP
BYZM CCAU CCFP CDIY
CEGL CHAP CHER CJBC
DAAH FCAB FIGB FOLI

GMSI ILSE IOWE JUPP
KATT LACD LBRC OAAA
OBDA ODRY OIDW OKEV
OSMS PHYS RIBS SENE
SIVJ STNS TANS THRE
TIMK TREE WARH WOLV
YPSY YSTT ZZDG

Wombleton - Pickering
ATUB BDWX BSUX BUKZ
BYBX CBTB CBWX DISO
ENEE JERO KITH MMCZ
MNFM MNKE MVNT MWGK
MYPH MZGD OPRC PEGY
PIGS

Woodford
APP 120.700   TWR 120.700
BTZG BTZH BTZK BUWM
EASD PLXI

Woodvale
APP 121.000   TWR 119.750
BCVJ BSVH BTFO BVSS
BYUI BYUX BYUZ BYWD
BYWJ BYWN BYXA BYXI
BYXX CDAE FKNH JUDE
XMII

Wyton
A/G 134.050
BLPI BYUA BYUL BYUO
BYVD BYVT BYWR BYWX
BYXH BYXP CMBS FTIL
MTLX MWNK MYCL MYMJ
MZGF

Yatesbury
BWMF CBUS CCJD CDRG
CWMC MTOY MVKO MWAT
MYNK

Yaxham, Dereham
APVL MWIR

Yearby
APYB ASFR AZYY BOHV
BPAA BTMW CCLL OMMG
OOSE

Yeatsall Farm, Abbots Bromley
AKUI AOCR ARAS BAFP
BPGK BTBI BUAO HUEW

Yeovilton
APP 127.350   TWR 122.100
ALLF AVSP BARS BBRN
BEBZ BEXN BOIT BTIO
BUJM BWRA IIRG JPVA
OHGC OSAW RNAC

Yew Tree Farm, Lymm Dam
BLAF BWWZ DANA NDOL

NOTES

Current UK Military serials

Active aircraft including historic flights

☐ P7350	Spitfire IIA	
☐ AB910	Spitfire VB	
☐ KF183	Harvard IIB	
☐ LF363	Hurricane IIC	
☐ LS326	Swordfish II	
☐ MK356	Spitfire LF.IXC	
☐ MK673	Spitfire LF.XVIE	
☐ NF389	Swordfish III	
☐ PA474	Lancaster B.1	
☐ PM631	Spitfire PR XIX	
☐ PS915	Spitfire PR XIX	
☐ PZ865	Hurricane IIC	
☐ VR930	Sea Fury FB11	
☐ VZ345	Sea Fury T20S	
☐ WA638	Meteor T7	
☐ WB556	Chipmunk T.10	
☐ WB657	Chipmunk T.10	
☐ WD325	Chipmunk T.10	
☐ WG432	Chipmunk T.10	
☐ WG486	Chipmunk T.10	
☐ WK518	Chipmunk T.10	
☐ WK608	Chipmunk T.10	
☐ WK613	Chipmunk T.10	
☐ WK800	Meteor D16	
☐ WL419	Meteor T7	
☐ WV903	Sea Hawk FGA4	
☐ WV908	Sea Hawk FGA6	
☐ XP820	Beaver AL1	
☐ XR244	Auster AOP9	
☐ XR379	Alouette II AH2	
☐ XR807	VC10 C1K	
☐ XR808	VC10 C1K	
☐ XR810	VC10 C1K	
☐ XS596	Andover C1(PR)	
☐ XS606	Andover C1	
☐ XS646	Andover C1	
☐ XS709	Dominie T1	
☐ XS711	Dominie T1	
☐ XS712	Dominie T1	
☐ XS713	Dominie T1	
☐ XS727	Dominie T1	
☐ XS728	Dominie T1	
☐ XS730	Dominie T1	
☐ XS731	Dominie T1	
☐ XS736	Dominie T1	
☐ XS737	Dominie T1	
☐ XS739	Dominie T1	
☐ XS743	Basset CC1	
☐ XT131	Sioux AH1	
☐ XT626	Scout AH1	
☐ XV101	VC10 C1K	
☐ XV102	VC10 C1K	
☐ XV104	VC10 C1K	
☐ XV105	VC10 C1K	
☐ XV106	VC10 C1K	
☐ XV107	VC10 C1K	
☐ XV108	VC10 C1K	
☐ XV109	VC10 C1K	
☐ XV177	Hercules C3	
☐ XV184	Hercules C3	
☐ XV188	Hercules C3	
☐ XV196	Hercules C1	
☐ XV197	Hercules C3	
☐ XV199	Hercules C3	
☐ XV200	Hercules C1	
☐ XV202	Hercules C3	
☐ XV205	Hercules C1	
☐ XV209	Hercules C3	
☐ XV212	Hercules C3	
☐ XV214	Hercules C3	
☐ XV217	Hercules C3	
☐ XV220	Hercules C3	
☐ XV221	Hercules C3	
☐ XV226	Nimrod MR2	
☐ XV227	Nimrod MR2	
☐ XV229	Nimrod MR2	
☐ XV231	Nimrod MR2	
☐ XV232	Nimrod MR2	
☐ XV235	Nimrod MR2	
☐ XV236	Nimrod MR2	
☐ XV240	Nimrod MR2	
☐ XV241	Nimrod MR2	
☐ XV243	Nimrod MR2	
☐ XV244	Nimrod MR2	
☐ XV245	Nimrod MR2	
☐ XV246	Nimrod MR2	
☐ XV248	Nimrod MR2	
☐ XV249	Nimrod R1	
☐ XV250	Nimrod MR2	
☐ XV252	Nimrod MR2	
☐ XV254	Nimrod MR2	
☐ XV255	Nimrod MR2	
☐ XV260	Nimrod MR2	
☐ XV290	Hercules C3	
☐ XV294	Hercules C3	
☐ XV295	Hercules C1	
☐ XV299	Hercules C3	
☐ XV301	Hercules C3	
☐ XV302	Hercules C3	
☐ XV303	Hercules C3	
☐ XV304	Hercules C3	
☐ XV305	Hercules C3	
☐ XV307	Hercules C3	
☐ XV647	Sea King HU5	
☐ XV648	Sea King HU5	
☐ XV649	Sea King AEW2	
☐ XV651	Sea King HU5	
☐ XV653	Sea King HAS6	
☐ XV655	Sea King HAS6	
☐ XV656	Sea King AEW2	
☐ XV659	Sea King HAS6	
☐ XV660	Sea King HAS6	
☐ XV661	Sea King HU5	
☐ XV663	Sea King HAS6	
☐ XV664	Sea King AEW2	
☐ XV665	Sea King HAS6	
☐ XV666	Sea King HU5	
☐ XV670	Sea King HU5	
☐ XV671	Sea King AEW2	
☐ XV672	Sea King AEW7	
☐ XV673	Sea King HU5	
☐ XV675	Sea King HAS6	
☐ XV676	Sea King HAS6	
☐ XV677	Sea King HAS6	
☐ XV696	Sea King HAS6	
☐ XV697	Sea King HAS6	
☐ XV699	Sea King HU5	
☐ XV700	Sea King HAS6	
☐ XV701	Sea King HAS6	
☐ XV703	Sea King HAS6	
☐ XV706	Sea King HAS6	
☐ XV707	Sea King AEW7	
☐ XV708	Sea King HAS6	
☐ XV709	Sea King HAS6	
☐ XV711	Sea King HAS6	
☐ XV713	Sea King HAS6	
☐ XV714	Sea King AEW2	
☐ XW175	Harrier T4	
☐ XW198	Puma HC1	
☐ XW199	Puma HC1	
☐ XW201	Puma HC1	
☐ XW202	Puma HC1	
☐ XW204	Puma HC1	
☐ XW206	Puma HC1	
☐ XW207	Puma HC1	
☐ XW208	Puma HC1	
☐ XW209	Puma HC1	
☐ XW210	Puma HC1	
☐ XW211	Puma HC1	
☐ XW212	Puma HC1	
☐ XW213	Puma HC1	
☐ XW214	Puma HC1	
☐ XW216	Puma HC1	
☐ XW217	Puma HC1	
☐ XW218	Puma HC1	
☐ XW219	Puma HC1	
☐ XW220	Puma HC1	
☐ XW221	Puma HC1	
☐ XW222	Puma HC1	
☐ XW223	Puma HC1	
☐ XW224	Puma HC1	
☐ XW226	Puma HC1	
☐ XW227	Puma HC1	
☐ XW229	Puma HC1	
☐ XW231	Puma HC1	
☐ XW232	Puma HC1	
☐ XW234	Puma HC1	
☐ XW235	Puma HC1	
☐ XW236	Puma HC1	
☐ XW237	Puma HC1	
☐ XW241	SA330E Puma	
☐ XW664	Nimrod R1	
☐ XW665	Nimrod R1	
☐ XW846	Gazelle AH1	
☐ XW847	Gazelle AH1	
☐ XW848	Gazelle AH1	
☐ XW849	Gazelle AH1	
☐ XW851	Gazelle AH1	
☐ XW865	Gazelle AH1	
☐ XW897	Gazelle AH1	
☐ XW899	Gazelle AH1	
☐ XW904	Gazelle AH1	
☐ XW908	Gazelle AH1	
☐ XW909	Gazelle AH1	
☐ XW913	Gazelle AH1	
☐ XX112	Jaguar GR3	
☐ XX145	Jaguar T2A	
☐ XX154	Hawk T.1	
☐ XX156	Hawk T.1	
☐ XX157	Hawk T.1A	
☐ XX158	Hawk T.1A	
☐ XX159	Hawk T.1A	
☐ XX160	Hawk T.1	
☐ XX161	Hawk T.1W	
☐ XX162	Hawk T.1	
☐ XX165	Hawk T.1	
☐ XX167	Hawk T.1W	
☐ XX168	Hawk T.1	
☐ XX169	Hawk T.1	
☐ XX170	Hawk T.1	
☐ XX171	Hawk T.1	
☐ XX172	Hawk T.1	
☐ XX173	Hawk T.1	
☐ XX174	Hawk T.1	
☐ XX175	Hawk T.1	
☐ XX176	Hawk T.1W	
☐ XX177	Hawk T.1	

☐ XX178	Hawk T.1W	☐ XX290	Hawk T.1W	☐ XX418	Gazelle AH1
☐ XX179	Hawk T.1W	☐ XX292	Hawk T.1W	☐ XX419	Gazelle AH1
☐ XX181	Hawk T.1W	☐ XX294	Hawk T.1	☐ XX433	Gazelle AH1
☐ XX183	Hawk T.1	☐ XX295	Hawk T.1W	☐ XX435	Gazelle AH1
☐ XX184	Hawk T.1	☐ XX296	Hawk T.1	☐ XX437	Gazelle AH1
☐ XX185	Hawk T.1	☐ XX299	Hawk T.1W	☐ XX438	Gazelle AH1
☐ XX187	Hawk T.1A	☐ XX301	Hawk T.1A	☐ XX439	Gazelle AH1
☐ XX188	Hawk T.1A	☐ XX303	Hawk T.1A	☐ XX442	Gazelle AH1
☐ XX189	Hawk T.1A	☐ XX306	Hawk T.1A	☐ XX444	Gazelle AH1
☐ XX190	Hawk T.1A	☐ XX307	Hawk T.1	☐ XX445	Gazelle AH1
☐ XX191	Hawk T.1A	☐ XX308	Hawk T.1	☐ XX447	Gazelle AH1
☐ XX194	Hawk T.1A	☐ XX309	Hawk T.1	☐ XX448	Gazelle AH1
☐ XX195	Hawk T.1W	☐ XX310	Hawk T.1W	☐ XX449	Gazelle AH1
☐ XX196	Hawk T.1A	☐ XX311	Hawk T.1	☐ XX450	Gazelle AH1
☐ XX198	Hawk T.1A	☐ XX312	Hawk T.1W	☐ XX453	Gazelle AH1
☐ XX199	Hawk T.1A	☐ XX313	Hawk T.1W	☐ XX455	Gazelle AH1
☐ XX200	Hawk T.1A	☐ XX314	Hawk T.1W	☐ XX456	Gazelle AH1
☐ XX201	Hawk T.1A	☐ XX315	Hawk T.1A	☐ XX460	Gazelle AH1
☐ XX202	Hawk T.1A	☐ XX316	Hawk T.1A	☐ XX462	Gazelle AH1
☐ XX203	Hawk T.1A	☐ XX317	Hawk T.1A	☐ XX475	Jetstream T1
☐ XX204	Hawk T.1A	☐ XX318	Hawk T.1A	☐ XX476	Jetstream T1
☐ XX205	Hawk T.1A	☐ XX319	Hawk T.1A	☐ XX478	Jetstream T1
☐ XX217	Hawk T.1A	☐ XX320	Hawk T.1A	☐ XX481	Jetstream T1
☐ XX218	Hawk T.1A	☐ XX321	Hawk T.1A	☐ XX484	Jetstream T2
☐ XX219	Hawk T.1A	☐ XX322	Hawk T.1A	☐ XX486	Jetstream T2
☐ XX220	Hawk T.1A	☐ XX323	Hawk T.1A	☐ XX487	Jetstream T2
☐ XX221	Hawk T.1A	☐ XX324	Hawk T.1A	☐ XX488	Jetstream T2
☐ XX222	Hawk T.1A	☐ XX325	Hawk T.1A	☐ XX500	Jetstream T1
☐ XX224	Hawk T.1W	☐ XX326	Hawk T.1A	☐ XX723	Jaguar GR3A
☐ XX225	Hawk T.1	☐ XX327	Hawk T.1	☐ XX724	Jaguar GR3A
☐ XX226	Hawk T.1	☐ XX329	Hawk T.1A	☐ XX725	Jaguar GR3A
☐ XX227	Hawk T.1A	☐ XX330	Hawk T.1A	☐ XX729	Jaguar GR3
☐ XX228	Hawk T.1A	☐ XX331	Hawk T.1A	☐ XX738	Jaguar GR3
☐ XX230	Hawk T.1A	☐ XX332	Hawk T.1A	☐ XX748	Jaguar GR3A
☐ XX231	Hawk T.1W	☐ XX335	Hawk T.1A	☐ XX752	Jaguar GR3A
☐ XX232	Hawk T.1	☐ XX337	Hawk T.1A	☐ XX767	Jaguar GR3A
☐ XX233	Hawk T.1	☐ XX338	Hawk T.1W	☐ XX833	Jaguar T2B
☐ XX234	Hawk T.1	☐ XX339	Hawk T.1A	☐ XX835	Jaguar T4
☐ XX235	Hawk T.1W	☐ XX341	Hawk T.1Astra	☐ XX847	Jaguar T4
☐ XX236	Hawk T.1W	☐ XX342	Hawk T.1	☐ XX970	Jaguar GR3
☐ XX237	Hawk T.1	☐ XX345	Hawk T.1A	☐ XZ103	Jaguar GR3
☐ XX238	Hawk T.1	☐ XX346	Hawk T.1A	☐ XZ109	Jaguar GR3
☐ XX239	Hawk T.1W	☐ XX348	Hawk T.1A	☐ XZ112	Jaguar GR3A
☐ XX240	Hawk T.1	☐ XX349	Hawk T.1W	☐ XZ115	Jaguar GR3
☐ XX242	Hawk T.1	☐ XX350	Hawk T.1A	☐ XZ117	Jaguar GR3
☐ XX244	Hawk T.1	☐ XX351	Hawk T.1A	☐ XZ118	Jaguar GR3
☐ XX245	Hawk T.1	☐ XX371	Gazelle AH1	☐ XZ170	Lynx AH9
☐ XX247	Hawk T.1A	☐ XX372	Gazelle AH1	☐ XZ171	Lynx AH7
☐ XX248	Hawk T.1A	☐ XX375	Gazelle AH1	☐ XZ172	Lynx AH7
☐ XX250	Hawk T.1	☐ XX378	Gazelle AH1	☐ XZ173	Lynx AH7
☐ XX252	Hawk T.1A	☐ XX379	Gazelle AH1	☐ XZ174	Lynx AH7
☐ XX253	Hawk T.1A	☐ XX380	Gazelle AH1	☐ XZ175	Lynx AH7
☐ XX254	Hawk T.1A	☐ XX381	Gazelle AH1	☐ XZ176	Lynx AH7
☐ XX255	Hawk T.1A	☐ XX383	Gazelle AH1	☐ XZ177	Lynx AH7
☐ XX256	Hawk T.1A	☐ XX384	Gazelle AH1	☐ XZ178	Lynx AH7
☐ XX258	Hawk T.1A	☐ XX385	Gazelle AH1	☐ XZ179	Lynx AH7
☐ XX260	Hawk T.1A	☐ XX386	Gazelle AH1	☐ XZ180	Lynx AH7
☐ XX261	Hawk T.1A	☐ XX388	Gazelle AH1	☐ XZ181	Lynx AH7
☐ XX263	Hawk T.1A	☐ XX389	Gazelle AH1	☐ XZ182	Lynx AH7
☐ XX264	Hawk T.1A	☐ XX392	Gazelle AH1	☐ XZ183	Lynx AH7
☐ XX265	Hawk T.1A	☐ XX394	Gazelle AH1	☐ XZ184	Lynx AH7
☐ XX266	Hawk T.1A	☐ XX398	Gazelle AH1	☐ XZ185	Lynx AH7
☐ XX278	Hawk T.1A	☐ XX399	Gazelle AH1	☐ XZ187	Lynx AH7
☐ XX280	Hawk T.1A	☐ XX403	Gazelle AH1	☐ XZ190	Lynx AH7
☐ XX281	Hawk T.1A	☐ XX405	Gazelle AH1	☐ XZ191	Lynx AH7
☐ XX283	Hawk T.1W	☐ XX409	Gazelle AH1	☐ XZ192	Lynx AH7
☐ XX284	Hawk T.1A	☐ XX412	Gazelle AH1	☐ XZ193	Lynx AH7
☐ XX285	Hawk T.1A	☐ XX413	Gazelle AH1	☐ XZ194	Lynx AH7
☐ XX286	Hawk T.1A	☐ XX414	Gazelle AH1	☐ XZ195	Lynx AH7
☐ XX287	Hawk T.1A	☐ XX416	Gazelle AH1	☐ XZ196	Lynx AH7
☐ XX289	Hawk T.1A	☐ XX417	Gazelle AH1	☐ XZ197	Lynx AH7

☐ XZ198	Lynx AH7	☐ XZ335	Gazelle AH1	☐ XZ676	Lynx AH7
☐ XZ203	Lynx AH7	☐ XZ337	Gazelle AH1	☐ XZ677	Lynx AH7
☐ XZ205	Lynx AH7	☐ XZ338	Gazelle AH1	☐ XZ678	Lynx AH7
☐ XZ206	Lynx AH7	☐ XZ340	Gazelle AH1	☐ XZ679	Lynx AH7
☐ XZ207	Lynx AH7	☐ XZ341	Gazelle AH1	☐ XZ680	Lynx AH7
☐ XZ208	Lynx AH7	☐ XZ342	Gazelle AH1	☐ XZ689	Lynx HMA8
☐ XZ209	Lynx AH7	☐ XZ343	Gazelle AH1	☐ XZ690	Lynx HMA8
☐ XZ210	Lynx AH7	☐ XZ344	Gazelle AH1	☐ XZ691	Lynx HMA8
☐ XZ211	Lynx AH7	☐ XZ345	Gazelle AH1	☐ XZ692	Lynx HMA8
☐ XZ212	Lynx AH7	☐ XZ347	Gazelle AH1	☐ XZ693	Lynx HAS3S
☐ XZ214	Lynx AH7	☐ XZ349	Gazelle AH1	☐ XZ694	Lynx HAS3S
☐ XZ215	Lynx AH7	☐ XZ364	Jaguar GR3A	☐ XZ695	Lynx HMA8
☐ XZ216	Lynx AH7	☐ XZ391	Jaguar GR3	☐ XZ696	Lynx HAS3S
☐ XZ217	Lynx AH7	☐ XZ392	Jaguar GR3	☐ XZ697	Lynx HMA8
☐ XZ218	Lynx AH7	☐ XZ399	Jaguar GR3	☐ XZ698	Lynx HMA8
☐ XZ219	Lynx AH7	☐ XZ570	Sea King HAS5	☐ XZ699	Lynx HAS3S
☐ XZ220	Lynx AH7	☐ XZ574	Sea King HAS6	☐ XZ719	Lynx HMA8
☐ XZ221	Lynx AH7	☐ XZ575	Sea King HU5	☐ XZ720	Lynx HAS3S
☐ XZ222	Lynx AH7	☐ XZ576	Sea King HAS6	☐ XZ721	Lynx HMA8
☐ XZ228	Lynx HAS3S	☐ XZ578	Sea King HU5	☐ XZ722	Lynx HMA8
☐ XZ229	Lynx HAS3S	☐ XZ579	Sea King HAS6	☐ XZ723	Lynx HMA8
☐ XZ230	Lynx HAS3S	☐ XZ580	Sea King HAS6	☐ XZ725	Lynx HMA8
☐ XZ232	Lynx HAS3S	☐ XZ581	Sea King HAS6	☐ XZ726	Lynx HMA8
☐ XZ233	Lynx HAS3S	☐ XZ585	Sea King HAR3	☐ XZ727	Lynx HAS3S
☐ XZ234	Lynx HAS3S	☐ XZ586	Sea King HAR3	☐ XZ729	Lynx HMA8
☐ XZ235	Lynx HAS3S	☐ XZ587	Sea King HAR3	☐ XZ730	Lynx HAS3CTS
☐ XZ236	Lynx HMA8	☐ XZ588	Sea King HAR3	☐ XZ731	Lynx HMA8
☐ XZ237	Lynx HAS3S	☐ XZ589	Sea King HAR3	☐ XZ732	Lynx HMA8
☐ XZ238	Lynx HAS3S	☐ XZ590	Sea King HAR3	☐ XZ733	Lynx HAS3S
☐ XZ239	Lynx HAS3S	☐ XZ591	Sea King HAR3	☐ XZ735	Lynx HAS3S
☐ XZ245	Lynx HAS3S	☐ XZ592	Sea King HAR3	☐ XZ736	Lynx HMA8
☐ XZ246	Lynx HAS3S	☐ XZ593	Sea King HAR3	☐ XZ920	Sea King HU5
☐ XZ248	Lynx HAS3S	☐ XZ594	Sea King HAR3	☐ XZ921	Sea King HAS6
☐ XZ250	Lynx HAS3S	☐ XZ595	Sea King HAR3	☐ XZ922	Sea King HAS6
☐ XZ252	Lynx HAS3S	☐ XZ596	Sea King HAR3	☐ ZA105	Sea King HAR3
☐ XZ254	Lynx HAS3S	☐ XZ597	Sea King HAR3	☐ ZA110	Jetstream T2
☐ XZ255	Lynx HMA8	☐ XZ598	Sea King HAR3	☐ ZA111	Jetstream T2
☐ XZ257	Lynx HMA8	☐ XZ599	Sea King HAR3	☐ ZA126	Sea King HAS6
☐ XZ290	Gazelle AH1	☐ XZ605	Lynx AH7	☐ ZA127	Sea King HAS6
☐ XZ291	Gazelle AH1	☐ XZ606	Lynx AH7	☐ ZA128	Sea King HAS6
☐ XZ292	Gazelle AH1	☐ XZ607	Lynx AH7	☐ ZA129	Sea King HAS6
☐ XZ294	Gazelle AH1	☐ XZ608	Lynx AH7	☐ ZA130	Sea King HU5
☐ XZ295	Gazelle AH1	☐ XZ609	Lynx AH7	☐ ZA131	Sea King HAS6
☐ XZ296	Gazelle AH1	☐ XZ611	Lynx AH7	☐ ZA133	Sea King HAS6
☐ XZ298	Gazelle AH1	☐ XZ612	Lynx AH7	☐ ZA134	Sea King HU5
☐ XZ301	Gazelle AH1	☐ XZ615	Lynx AH7	☐ ZA135	Sea King HAS6
☐ XZ303	Gazelle AH1	☐ XZ616	Lynx AH7	☐ ZA137	Sea King HU5
☐ XZ304	Gazelle AH1	☐ XZ617	Lynx AH7	☐ ZA148	VC10 K3
☐ XZ307	Gazelle AH1	☐ XZ631	Tornado GR1	☐ ZA149	VC10 K3
☐ XZ308	Gazelle AH1	☐ XZ641	Lynx AH7	☐ ZA150	VC10 K3
☐ XZ309	Gazelle AH1	☐ XZ642	Lynx AH7	☐ ZA166	Sea King HU5
☐ XZ311	Gazelle AH1	☐ XZ643	Lynx AH7	☐ ZA167	Sea King HU5
☐ XZ312	Gazelle AH1	☐ XZ645	Lynx AH7	☐ ZA168	Sea King HAS6
☐ XZ313	Gazelle AH1	☐ XZ646	Lynx AH7	☐ ZA169	Sea King HAS6
☐ XZ314	Gazelle AH1	☐ XZ647	Lynx AH7	☐ ZA170	Sea King HU5
☐ XZ316	Gazelle AH1	☐ XZ648	Lynx AH7	☐ ZA291	Sea King HC4
☐ XZ317	Gazelle AH1	☐ XZ649	Lynx AH7	☐ ZA292	Sea King HC4
☐ XZ319	Gazelle AH1	☐ XZ651	Lynx AH7	☐ ZA293	Sea King HC4
☐ XZ320	Gazelle AH1	☐ XZ652	Lynx AH7	☐ ZA295	Sea King HC4
☐ XZ323	Gazelle AH1	☐ XZ653	Lynx AH7	☐ ZA296	Sea King HC4
☐ XZ324	Gazelle AH1	☐ XZ654	Lynx AH7	☐ ZA297	Sea King HC4
☐ XZ325	Gazelle AH1	☐ XZ655	Lynx AH7	☐ ZA298	Sea King HC4
☐ XZ326	Gazelle AH1	☐ XZ661	Lynx AH7	☐ ZA299	Sea King HC4
☐ XZ327	Gazelle AH1	☐ XZ663	Lynx AH7	☐ ZA310	Sea King HC4
☐ XZ328	Gazelle AH1	☐ XZ666	Lynx AH7	☐ ZA312	Sea King HC4
☐ XZ329	Gazelle AH1	☐ XZ669	Lynx AH7	☐ ZA313	Sea King HC4
☐ XZ330	Gazelle AH1	☐ XZ670	Lynx AH7	☐ ZA314	Sea King HC4
☐ XZ331	Gazelle AH1	☐ XZ672	Lynx AH7	☐ ZA319	Tornado GR1
☐ XZ332	Gazelle AH1	☐ XZ673	Lynx AH7	☐ ZA320	Tornado GR1
☐ XZ333	Gazelle AH1	☐ XZ674	Lynx AH7	☐ ZA322	Tornado GR1
☐ XZ334	Gazelle AH1	☐ XZ675	Lynx AH7	☐ ZA323	Tornado GR1

☐ ZA325	Tornado GR1	☐ ZA559	Tornado GR4	☐ ZA936	Puma HC1
☐ ZA326	Tornado GR1	☐ ZA560	Tornado GR1	☐ ZA937	Puma HC1
☐ ZA327	Tornado GR1	☐ ZA562	Tornado GR4	☐ ZA938	Puma HC1
☐ ZA328	Tornado GR1	☐ ZA563	Tornado GR4	☐ ZA939	Puma HC1
☐ ZA353	Tornado GR1	☐ ZA564	Tornado GR1	☐ ZA940	Puma HC1
☐ ZA354	Tornado GR1	☐ ZA585	Tornado GR4	☐ ZA947	Dakota C3
☐ ZA357	Tornado GR1	☐ ZA587	Tornado GR1	☐ ZB506	Sea King 4X
☐ ZA361	Tornado GR1	☐ ZA588	Tornado GR4	☐ ZB507	Sea King HC4
☐ ZA362	Tornado GR1	☐ ZA589	Tornado GR4	☐ ZB615	Jaguar T2A
☐ ZA365	Tornado GR4	☐ ZA591	Tornado GR4	☐ ZB665	Gazelle AH1
☐ ZA367	Tornado GR4	☐ ZA592	Tornado GR4	☐ ZB667	Gazelle AH1
☐ ZA369	Tornado GR4A	☐ ZA594	Tornado GR4	☐ ZB669	Gazelle AH1
☐ ZA370	Tornado GR1A	☐ ZA595	Tornado GR4	☐ ZB670	Gazelle AH1
☐ ZA371	Tornado GR4A	☐ ZA596	Tornado GR1	☐ ZB671	Gazelle AH1
☐ ZA372	Tornado GR1A	☐ ZA597	Tornado GR1	☐ ZB673	Gazelle AH1
☐ ZA373	Tornado GR4A	☐ ZA598	Tornado GR4	☐ ZB674	Gazelle AH1
☐ ZA374	Tornado GR1B	☐ ZA600	Tornado GR4	☐ ZB676	Gazelle AH1
☐ ZA375	Tornado GR1B	☐ ZA601	Tornado GR4	☐ ZB677	Gazelle AH1
☐ ZA393	Tornado GR1	☐ ZA602	Tornado GR1	☐ ZB679	Gazelle AH1
☐ ZA395	Tornado GR4A	☐ ZA604	Tornado GR4	☐ ZB682	Gazelle AH1
☐ ZA398	Tornado GR4A	☐ ZA606	Tornado GR4	☐ ZB683	Gazelle AH1
☐ ZA399	Tornado GR1B	☐ ZA607	Tornado GR4	☐ ZB684	Gazelle AH1
☐ ZA400	Tornado GR4A	☐ ZA608	Tornado GR4	☐ ZB686	Gazelle AH1
☐ ZA401	Tornado GR1A	☐ ZA609	Tornado GR4	☐ ZB688	Gazelle AH1
☐ ZA402	Tornado GR4A	☐ ZA611	Tornado GR4	☐ ZB689	Gazelle AH1
☐ ZA404	Tornado GR4A	☐ ZA612	Tornado GR1	☐ ZB690	Gazelle AH1
☐ ZA405	Tornado GR4A	☐ ZA613	Tornado GR1	☐ ZB691	Gazelle AH1
☐ ZA406	Tornado GR1	☐ ZA614	Tornado GR4	☐ ZB692	Gazelle AH1
☐ ZA407	Tornado GR1B	☐ ZA670	Chinook HC2	☐ ZB693	Gazelle AH1
☐ ZA409	Tornado GR1B	☐ ZA671	Chinook HC2	☐ ZD241	VC10 K4
☐ ZA410	Tornado GR4	☐ ZA673	Chinook HC2	☐ ZD242	VC10 K4
☐ ZA411	Tornado GR1B	☐ ZA674	Chinook HC2	☐ ZD249	Lynx HAS3S
☐ ZA412	Tornado GR1	☐ ZA675	Chinook HC2	☐ ZD250	Lynx HAS3S
☐ ZA446	Tornado GR1B	☐ ZA677	Chinook HC2	☐ ZD251	Lynx HAS3S
☐ ZA447	Tornado GR1B	☐ ZA679	Chinook HC2	☐ ZD252	Lynx HMA8
☐ ZA449	Tornado GR4	☐ ZA680	Chinook HC2	☐ ZD254	Lynx HAS3S
☐ ZA450	Tornado GR1B	☐ ZA681	Chinook HC2	☐ ZD255	Lynx HAS3S
☐ ZA452	Tornado GR1B	☐ ZA682	Chinook HC2	☐ ZD257	Lynx HMA8
☐ ZA453	Tornado GR1B	☐ ZA683	Chinook HC2	☐ ZD258	Lynx HMA8
☐ ZA455	Tornado GR1B	☐ ZA684	Chinook HC2	☐ ZD259	Lynx HMA8
☐ ZA456	Tornado GR4	☐ ZA704	Chinook HC2	☐ ZD260	Lynx HMA8
☐ ZA457	Tornado GR1B	☐ ZA705	Chinook HC2	☐ ZD261	Lynx HMA8
☐ ZA458	Tornado GR4	☐ ZA707	Chinook HC2	☐ ZD262	Lynx HMA8
☐ ZA459	Tornado GR1B	☐ ZA708	Chinook HC2	☐ ZD263	Lynx HAS3S
☐ ZA461	Tornado GR1B	☐ ZA709	Chinook HC2	☐ ZD264	Lynx HAS3S
☐ ZA462	Tornado GR1	☐ ZA710	Chinook HC2	☐ ZD265	Lynx HMA8
☐ ZA463	Tornado GR1	☐ ZA711	Chinook HC2	☐ ZD266	Lynx HMA8
☐ ZA465	Tornado GR1B	☐ ZA712	Chinook HC2	☐ ZD267	Lynx HMA8
☐ ZA469	Tornado GR1B	☐ ZA713	Chinook HC2	☐ ZD268	Lynx HMA8
☐ ZA470	Tornado GR4	☐ ZA714	Chinook HC2	☐ ZD272	Lynx AH7
☐ ZA472	Tornado GR1	☐ ZA718	Chinook HC2	☐ ZD273	Lynx AH7
☐ ZA473	Tornado GR1B	☐ ZA720	Chinook HC2	☐ ZD274	Lynx AH7
☐ ZA474	Tornado GR1B	☐ ZA726	Gazelle AH1	☐ ZD276	Lynx AH7
☐ ZA475	Tornado GR1B	☐ ZA728	Gazelle AH1	☐ ZD277	Lynx AH7
☐ ZA491	Tornado GR1B	☐ ZA729	Gazelle AH1	☐ ZD278	Lynx AH7
☐ ZA492	Tornado GR1B	☐ ZA730	Gazelle AH1	☐ ZD279	Lynx AH7
☐ ZA541	Tornado GR4	☐ ZA731	Gazelle AH1	☐ ZD280	Lynx AH7
☐ ZA542	Tornado GR4	☐ ZA733	Gazelle AH1	☐ ZD281	Lynx AH7
☐ ZA543	Tornado GR4	☐ ZA734	Gazelle AH1	☐ ZD282	Lynx AH7
☐ ZA544	Tornado GR4	☐ ZA735	Gazelle AH1	☐ ZD283	Lynx AH7
☐ ZA546	Tornado GR1	☐ ZA736	Gazelle AH1	☐ ZD284	Lynx AH7
☐ ZA547	Tornado GR4	☐ ZA766	Gazelle AH1	☐ ZD285	Lynx AH7
☐ ZA548	Tornado GR4	☐ ZA769	Gazelle AH1	☐ ZD318	Harrier GR7
☐ ZA549	Tornado GR4	☐ ZA771	Gazelle AH1	☐ ZD319	Harrier GR7
☐ ZA550	Tornado GR4	☐ ZA772	Gazelle AH1	☐ ZD320	Harrier GR7
☐ ZA551	Tornado GR4	☐ ZA773	Gazelle AH1	☐ ZD321	Harrier GR7
☐ ZA552	Tornado GR4	☐ ZA774	Gazelle AH1	☐ ZD322	Harrier GR7
☐ ZA553	Tornado GR4	☐ ZA775	Gazelle AH1	☐ ZD323	Harrier GR7
☐ ZA554	Tornado GR4	☐ ZA776	Gazelle AH1	☐ ZD327	Harrier GR7
☐ ZA556	Tornado GR4	☐ ZA934	Puma HC1	☐ ZD328	Harrier GR7
☐ ZA557	Tornado GR4	☐ ZA935	Puma HC1	☐ ZD329	Harrier GR7

☐	ZD330	Harrier GR7	☐	ZD720	Tornado GR1
☐	ZD346	Harrier GR7	☐	ZD739	Tornado GR1
☐	ZD347	Harrier GR7	☐	ZD740	Tornado GR4
☐	ZD348	Harrier GR7	☐	ZD741	Tornado GR1
☐	ZD351	Harrier GR7	☐	ZD742	Tornado GR4
☐	ZD352	Harrier GR7	☐	ZD743	Tornado GR1
☐	ZD353	Harrier GR7	☐	ZD744	Tornado GR1
☐	ZD354	Harrier GR7	☐	ZD745	Tornado GR4
☐	ZD375	Harrier GR9	☐	ZD746	Tornado GR4
☐	ZD376	Harrier GR7	☐	ZD747	Tornado GR1
☐	ZD378	Harrier GR7	☐	ZD748	Tornado GR4
☐	ZD379	Harrier GR7	☐	ZD749	Tornado GR1
☐	ZD380	Harrier GR7	☐	ZD788	Tornado GR1A
☐	ZD401	Harrier GR9	☐	ZD790	Tornado GR4
☐	ZD402	Harrier GR7	☐	ZD792	Tornado GR4
☐	ZD403	Harrier GR7	☐	ZD793	Tornado GR1
☐	ZD404	Harrier GR7	☐	ZD810	Tornado GR4
☐	ZD405	Harrier GR7	☐	ZD811	Tornado GR1
☐	ZD406	Harrier GR7	☐	ZD812	Tornado GR4
☐	ZD407	Harrier GR7	☐	ZD842	Tornado GR4
☐	ZD408	Harrier GR7	☐	ZD843	Tornado GR1
☐	ZD409	Harrier GR9	☐	ZD844	Tornado GR4
☐	ZD410	Harrier GR7	☐	ZD847	Tornado GR4
☐	ZD411	Harrier GR7	☐	ZD848	Tornado GR4
☐	ZD431	Harrier GR7	☐	ZD849	Tornado GR1
☐	ZD433	Harrier GR7	☐	ZD850	Tornado GR4
☐	ZD435	Harrier GR9	☐	ZD851	Tornado GR4
☐	ZD436	Harrier GR7	☐	ZD890	Tornado GR4
☐	ZD437	Harrier GR7	☐	ZD892	Tornado GR4
☐	ZD438	Harrier GR7	☐	ZD895	Tornado GR1A
☐	ZD461	Harrier GR7	☐	ZD948	Tristar KC1
☐	ZD463	Harrier GR7	☐	ZD949	Tristar K1
☐	ZD465	Harrier GR7	☐	ZD950	Tristar KC1
☐	ZD466	Harrier GR7	☐	ZD951	Tristar K1
☐	ZD467	Harrier GR7	☐	ZD952	Tristar KC1
☐	ZD468	Harrier GR7	☐	ZD953	Tristar KC1
☐	ZD469	Harrier GR7	☐	ZD980	Chinook HC2
☐	ZD470	Harrier GR7	☐	ZD981	Chinook HC2
☐	ZD476	Sea King HC4	☐	ZD982	Chinook HC2
☐	ZD477	Sea King HC4	☐	ZD983	Chinook HC2
☐	ZD478	Sea King HC4	☐	ZD984	Chinook HC2
☐	ZD479	Sea King HC4	☐	ZD993	Harrier T8
☐	ZD480	Sea King HC4	☐	ZD996	Tornado GR4A
☐	ZD559	Lynx AH5X	☐	ZE116	Tornado GR4A
☐	ZD560	Lynx AH7	☐	ZE156	Tornado F3
☐	ZD565	Lynx HMA8	☐	ZE157	Tornado F3
☐	ZD566	Lynx HMA8	☐	ZE158	Tornado F3
☐	ZD574	Chinook HC2	☐	ZE159	Tornado F3
☐	ZD575	Chinook HC2	☐	ZE160	Tornado F3
☐	ZD620	BAe 125 CC3	☐	ZE161	Tornado F3
☐	ZD621	BAe 125 CC3	☐	ZE162	Tornado F3
☐	ZD625	Sea King HC4	☐	ZE163	Tornado F3
☐	ZD626	Sea King HC4	☐	ZE164	Tornado F3
☐	ZD627	Sea King HC4	☐	ZE165	Tornado F3
☐	ZD630	Sea King HAS6	☐	ZE168	Tornado F3
☐	ZD633	Sea King HAS6	☐	ZE199	Tornado F3
☐	ZD634	Sea King HAS6	☐	ZE200	Tornado F3
☐	ZD636	Sea King AEW2	☐	ZE201	Tornado F3
☐	ZD637	Sea King HAS6	☐	ZE202	Tornado F3
☐	ZD703	BAe 125 CC3	☐	ZE203	Tornado F3
☐	ZD704	BAe 125 CC3	☐	ZE204	Tornado F3
☐	ZD707	Tornado GR4	☐	ZE206	Tornado F3
☐	ZD708	Tornado GR4	☐	ZE207	Tornado F3
☐	ZD709	Tornado GR4	☐	ZE208	Tornado F3
☐	ZD711	Tornado GR4	☐	ZE209	Tornado F3
☐	ZD712	Tornado GR1	☐	ZE250	Tornado F3
☐	ZD713	Tornado GR1	☐	ZE251	Tornado F3
☐	ZD714	Tornado GR4	☐	ZE253	Tornado F3
☐	ZD715	Tornado GR4	☐	ZE254	Tornado F3
☐	ZD716	Tornado GR1	☐	ZE255	Tornado F3
☐	ZD719	Tornado GR4	☐	ZE256	Tornado F3

☐	ZE257	Tornado F3
☐	ZE258	Tornado F3
☐	ZE287	Tornado F3
☐	ZE288	Tornado F3
☐	ZE289	Tornado F3
☐	ZE290	Tornado F3
☐	ZE292	Tornado F3
☐	ZE293	Tornado F3
☐	ZE294	Tornado F3
☐	ZE295	Tornado F3
☐	ZE338	Tornado F3
☐	ZE339	Tornado F3
☐	ZE340	Tornado F3
☐	ZE341	Tornado F3
☐	ZE342	Tornado F3
☐	ZE343	Tornado F3
☐	ZE368	Sea King HAR3
☐	ZE369	Sea King HAR3
☐	ZE370	Sea King HAR3
☐	ZE375	Lynx AH9
☐	ZE376	Lynx AH9
☐	ZE378	Lynx AH7
☐	ZE379	Lynx AH7
☐	ZE380	Lynx AH9
☐	ZE381	Lynx AH7
☐	ZE382	Lynx AH9
☐	ZE395	BAe 125 CC3
☐	ZE396	BAe 125 CC3
☐	ZE410	Agusta 109A
☐	ZE411	Agusta 109A
☐	ZE412	Agusta 109A
☐	ZE413	Agusta 109A
☐	ZE418	Sea King AEW2
☐	ZE420	Sea King AEW2
☐	ZE422	Sea King HAS6
☐	ZE425	Sea King HC4
☐	ZE426	Sea King HC4
☐	ZE427	Sea King HC4
☐	ZE428	Sea King HC4
☐	ZE432	BAC 111-479FU
☐	ZE433	BAC 111-479FU
☐	ZE438	Jetstream T3
☐	ZE439	Jetstream T3
☐	ZE440	Jetstream T3
☐	ZE441	Jetstream T3
☐	ZE449	Puma
☐	ZE495	Grob G103
☐	ZE496	Grob G103
☐	ZE498	Grob G103
☐	ZE499	Grob G103
☐	ZE501	Grob G103
☐	ZE502	Grob G103
☐	ZE503	Grob G103
☐	ZE504	Grob G103
☐	ZE520	Grob G103
☐	ZE521	Grob G103
☐	ZE522	Grob G103
☐	ZE524	Grob G103
☐	ZE526	Grob G103
☐	ZE527	Grob G103
☐	ZE528	Grob G103
☐	ZE529	Grob G103
☐	ZE530	Grob G103
☐	ZE531	Grob G103
☐	ZE532	Grob G103
☐	ZE533	Grob G103
☐	ZE534	Grob G103
☐	ZE550	Grob G103
☐	ZE551	Grob G103
☐	ZE552	Grob G103
☐	ZE553	Grob G103

☐ ZE554	Grob G103	☐ ZE735	Tornado F3	☐ ZF164	Tucano T1
☐ ZE555	Grob G103	☐ ZE736	Tornado F3	☐ ZF165	Tucano T1
☐ ZE557	Grob G103	☐ ZE737	Tornado F3	☐ ZF166	Tucano T1
☐ ZE558	Grob G103	☐ ZE755	Tornado F3	☐ ZF167	Tucano T1
☐ ZE559	Grob G103	☐ ZE756	Tornado F3	☐ ZF168	Tucano T1
☐ ZE560	Grob G103	☐ ZE757	Tornado F3	☐ ZF169	Tucano T1
☐ ZE561	Grob G103	☐ ZE758	Tornado F3	☐ ZF170	Tucano T1
☐ ZE562	Grob G103	☐ ZE760	Tornado F3	☐ ZF171	Tucano T1
☐ ZE563	Grob G103	☐ ZE761	Tornado F3	☐ ZF172	Tucano T1
☐ ZE564	Grob G103	☐ ZE763	Tornado F3	☐ ZF200	Tucano T1
☐ ZE584	Grob G103	☐ ZE764	Tornado F3	☐ ZF201	Tucano T1
☐ ZE585	Grob G103	☐ ZE785	Tornado F3	☐ ZF202	Tucano T1
☐ ZE586	Grob G103	☐ ZE786	Tornado F3	☐ ZF203	Tucano T1
☐ ZE587	Grob G103	☐ ZE787	Tornado F3	☐ ZF204	Tucano T1
☐ ZE590	Grob G103	☐ ZE788	Tornado F3	☐ ZF205	Tucano T1
☐ ZE591	Grob G103	☐ ZE790	Tornado F3	☐ ZF206	Tucano T1
☐ ZE592	Grob G103	☐ ZE791	Tornado F3	☐ ZF207	Tucano T1
☐ ZE593	Grob G103	☐ ZE793	Tornado F3	☐ ZF208	Tucano T1
☐ ZE594	Grob G103	☐ ZE794	Tornado F3	☐ ZF209	Tucano T1
☐ ZE595	Grob G103	☐ ZE808	Tornado F3	☐ ZF210	Tucano T1
☐ ZE600	Grob G103	☐ ZE810	Tornado F3	☐ ZF211	Tucano T1
☐ ZE601	Grob G103	☐ ZE831	Tornado F3	☐ ZF212	Tucano T1
☐ ZE602	Grob G103	☐ ZE832	Tornado F3	☐ ZF238	Tucano T1
☐ ZE603	Grob G103	☐ ZE834	Tornado F3	☐ ZF239	Tucano T1
☐ ZE604	Grob G103	☐ ZE835	Tornado F3	☐ ZF240	Tucano T1
☐ ZE605	Grob G103	☐ ZE837	Tornado F3	☐ ZF241	Tucano T1
☐ ZE606	Grob G103	☐ ZE838	Tornado F3	☐ ZF242	Tucano T1
☐ ZE607	Grob G103	☐ ZE839	Tornado F3	☐ ZF243	Tucano T1
☐ ZE608	Grob G103	☐ ZE887	Tornado F3	☐ ZF244	Tucano T1
☐ ZE609	Grob G103	☐ ZE888	Tornado F3	☐ ZF245	Tucano T1
☐ ZE610	Grob G103	☐ ZE889	Tornado F3	☐ ZF263	Tucano T1
☐ ZE611	Grob G103	☐ ZE907	Tornado F3	☐ ZF264	Tucano T1
☐ ZE613	Grob G103	☐ ZE908	Tornado F3	☐ ZF265	Tucano T1
☐ ZE614	Grob G103	☐ ZE936	Tornado F3	☐ ZF266	Tucano T1
☐ ZE625	Grob G103	☐ ZE941	Tornado F3	☐ ZF267	Tucano T1
☐ ZE626	Grob G103	☐ ZE942	Tornado F3	☐ ZF268	Tucano T1
☐ ZE627	Grob G103	☐ ZE961	Tornado F3	☐ ZF269	Tucano T1
☐ ZE628	Grob G103	☐ ZE963	Tornado F3	☐ ZF284	Tucano T1
☐ ZE630	Grob G103	☐ ZE964	Tornado F3	☐ ZF285	Tucano T1
☐ ZE631	Grob G103	☐ ZE965	Tornado F3	☐ ZF286	Tucano T1
☐ ZE632	Grob G103	☐ ZE966	Tornado F3	☐ ZF287	Tucano T1
☐ ZE633	Grob G103	☐ ZE967	Tornado F3	☐ ZF288	Tucano T1
☐ ZE635	Grob G103	☐ ZE968	Tornado F3	☐ ZF289	Tucano T1
☐ ZE636	Grob G103	☐ ZE969	Tornado F3	☐ ZF290	Tucano T1
☐ ZE637	Grob G103	☐ ZE982	Tornado F3	☐ ZF291	Tucano T1
☐ ZE650	Grob G103	☐ ZE983	Tornado F3	☐ ZF292	Tucano T1
☐ ZE651	Grob G103	☐ ZF116	Sea King HC4	☐ ZF293	Tucano T1
☐ ZE652	Grob G103	☐ ZF117	Sea King HC4	☐ ZF294	Tucano T1
☐ ZE653	Grob G103	☐ ZF118	Sea King HC4	☐ ZF295	Tucano T1
☐ ZE656	Grob G103	☐ ZF119	Sea King HC4	☐ ZF315	Tucano T1
☐ ZE657	Grob G103	☐ ZF120	Sea King HC4	☐ ZF317	Tucano T1
☐ ZE658	Grob G103	☐ ZF121	Sea King HC4	☐ ZF318	Tucano T1
☐ ZE659	Grob G103	☐ ZF122	Sea King HC4	☐ ZF319	Tucano T1
☐ ZE677	Grob G103	☐ ZF123	Sea King HC4	☐ ZF320	Tucano T1
☐ ZE678	Grob G103	☐ ZF124	Sea King HC4	☐ ZF338	Tucano T1
☐ ZE679	Grob G103	☐ ZF130	BAe 125 600	☐ ZF339	Tucano T1
☐ ZE680	Grob G103	☐ ZF135	Tucano T1	☐ ZF340	Tucano T1
☐ ZE681	Grob G103	☐ ZF136	Tucano T1	☐ ZF341	Tucano T1
☐ ZE682	Grob G103	☐ ZF137	Tucano T1	☐ ZF342	Tucano T1
☐ ZE683	Grob G103	☐ ZF138	Tucano T1	☐ ZF343	Tucano T1
☐ ZE684	Grob G103	☐ ZF139	Tucano T1	☐ ZF344	Tucano T1
☐ ZE685	Grob G103	☐ ZF140	Tucano T1	☐ ZF345	Tucano T1
☐ ZE686	Grob G103	☐ ZF141	Tucano T1	☐ ZF346	Tucano T1
☐ ZE700	BAe 146 CC2	☐ ZF142	Tucano T1	☐ ZF347	Tucano T1
☐ ZE701	BAe 146 CC2	☐ ZF143	Tucano T1	☐ ZF348	Tucano T1
☐ ZE704	Tristar C2	☐ ZF144	Tucano T1	☐ ZF349	Tucano T1
☐ ZE705	Tristar C2	☐ ZF145	Tucano T1	☐ ZF350	Tucano T1
☐ ZE706	Tristar C2A	☐ ZF160	Tucano T1	☐ ZF372	Tucano T1
☐ ZE728	Tornado F3	☐ ZF161	Tucano T1	☐ ZF373	Tucano T1
☐ ZE731	Tornado F3	☐ ZF162	Tucano T1	☐ ZF374	Tucano T1
☐ ZE734	Tornado F3	☐ ZF163	Tucano T1	☐ ZF375	Tucano T1

☐ ZF376	Tucano T1	
☐ ZF377	Tucano T1	
☐ ZF378	Tucano T1	
☐ ZF379	Tucano T1	
☐ ZF380	Tucano T1	
☐ ZF405	Tucano T1	
☐ ZF406	Tucano T1	
☐ ZF407	Tucano T1	
☐ ZF408	Tucano T1	
☐ ZF409	Tucano T1	
☐ ZF410	Tucano T1	
☐ ZF411	Tucano T1	
☐ ZF412	Tucano T1	
☐ ZF413	Tucano T1	
☐ ZF414	Tucano T1	
☐ ZF415	Tucano T1	
☐ ZF416	Tucano T1	
☐ ZF417	Tucano T1	
☐ ZF418	Tucano T1	
☐ ZF445	Tucano T1	
☐ ZF446	Tucano T1	
☐ ZF447	Tucano T1	
☐ ZF448	Tucano T1	
☐ ZF449	Tucano T1	
☐ ZF450	Tucano T1	
☐ ZF483	Tucano T1	
☐ ZF484	Tucano T1	
☐ ZF485	Tucano T1	
☐ ZF486	Tucano T1	
☐ ZF487	Tucano T1	
☐ ZF488	Tucano T1	
☐ ZF489	Tucano T1	
☐ ZF490	Tucano T1	
☐ ZF491	Tucano T1	
☐ ZF492	Tucano T1	
☐ ZF510	Tucano T1	
☐ ZF511	Tucano T1	
☐ ZF512	Tucano T1	
☐ ZF513	Tucano T1	
☐ ZF514	Tucano T1	
☐ ZF515	Tucano T1	
☐ ZF516	Tucano T1	
☐ ZF537	Lynx AH9	
☐ ZF538	Lynx AH9	
☐ ZF539	Lynx AH9	
☐ ZF540	Lynx AH9	
☐ ZF557	Lynx HMA8	
☐ ZF558	Lynx HMA8	
☐ ZF560	Lynx HMA8	
☐ ZF562	Lynx HMA8	
☐ ZF563	Lynx HMA8	
☐ ZF573	Islander CC2A	
☐ ZF622	PA31 Chieftain	
☐ ZG471	Harrier GR7	
☐ ZG472	Harrier GR7	
☐ ZG474	Harrier GR7	
☐ ZG477	Harrier GR7	
☐ ZG478	Harrier GR7	
☐ ZG479	Harrier GR7	
☐ ZG480	Harrier GR7	
☐ ZG500	Harrier GR7	
☐ ZG501	Harrier GR7	
☐ ZG502	Harrier GR7	
☐ ZG503	Harrier GR9	
☐ ZG504	Harrier GR9A	
☐ ZG505	Harrier GR7	
☐ ZG506	Harrier GR7	
☐ ZG507	Harrier GR9	
☐ ZG508	Harrier GR7	
☐ ZG509	Harrier GR7	
☐ ZG510	Harrier GR7	
☐ ZG511	Harrier GR9	
☐ ZG512	Harrier GR7	
☐ ZG530	Harrier GR9	
☐ ZG531	Harrier GR7	
☐ ZG705	Tornado GR4A	
☐ ZG706	Tornado GR1A	
☐ ZG707	Tornado GR4A	
☐ ZG709	Tornado GR4A	
☐ ZG712	Tornado GR4A	
☐ ZG713	Tornado GR4A	
☐ ZG714	Tornado GR4A	
☐ ZG726	Tornado GR4A	
☐ ZG727	Tornado GR1A	
☐ ZG728	Tornado F3	
☐ ZG729	Tornado GR4A	
☐ ZG731	Tornado F3	
☐ ZG732	Tornado F3	
☐ ZG734	Tornado F3	
☐ ZG750	Tornado GR4	
☐ ZG751	Tornado F3	
☐ ZG752	Tornado GR1	
☐ ZG753	Tornado F3	
☐ ZG754	Tornado GR1	
☐ ZG755	Tornado GR4	
☐ ZG756	Tornado GR4	
☐ ZG757	Tornado F3	
☐ ZG768	Tornado F3	
☐ ZG769	Tornado GR4	
☐ ZG770	Tornado F3	
☐ ZG771	Tornado GR4	
☐ ZG772	Tornado F3	
☐ ZG773	Tornado GR4	
☐ ZG774	Tornado F3	
☐ ZG775	Tornado GR4	
☐ ZG776	Tornado F3	
☐ ZG777	Tornado GR4	
☐ ZG778	Tornado F3	
☐ ZG779	Tornado GR4	
☐ ZG780	Tornado F3	
☐ ZG791	Tornado GR1	
☐ ZG792	Tornado GR4	
☐ ZG793	Tornado F3	
☐ ZG794	Tornado GR4	
☐ ZG795	Tornado F3	
☐ ZG796	Tornado F3	
☐ ZG797	Tornado F3	
☐ ZG798	Tornado F3	
☐ ZG799	Tornado F3	
☐ ZG816	Sea King HAS6	
☐ ZG817	Sea King HAS6	
☐ ZG818	Sea King HAS6	
☐ ZG819	Sea King HAS6	
☐ ZG820	Sea King HC4	
☐ ZG821	Sea King HC4	
☐ ZG822	Sea King HC4	
☐ ZG844	Islander AL1	
☐ ZG845	Islander AL1	
☐ ZG846	Islander AL1	
☐ ZG847	Islander AL1	
☐ ZG848	Islander AL1	
☐ ZG857	Harrier GR9	
☐ ZG858	Harrier GR9	
☐ ZG859	Harrier GR9	
☐ ZG860	Harrier GR7	
☐ ZG862	Harrier GR9	
☐ ZG884	Lynx AH9	
☐ ZG885	Lynx AH9	
☐ ZG886	Lynx AH9	
☐ ZG887	Lynx AH9	
☐ ZG888	Lynx AH9	
☐ ZG889	Lynx AH9	
☐ ZG914	Lynx AH9	
☐ ZG915	Lynx AH9	
☐ ZG916	Lynx AH9	
☐ ZG917	Lynx AH9	
☐ ZG918	Lynx AH9	
☐ ZG919	Lynx AH9	
☐ ZG920	Lynx AH9	
☐ ZG921	Lynx AH9	
☐ ZG923	Lynx AH9	
☐ ZG969	Pilatus PC9	
☐ ZG989	Islander AL1	
☐ ZG993	Islander AL1	
☐ ZG995	BN-2T-4S Defender	
☐ ZG996	BN-2T-4S Defender	
☐ ZG997	BN-2T-4S Defender	
☐ ZH101	Sentry AEW1	
☐ ZH102	Sentry AEW1	
☐ ZH103	Sentry AEW1	
☐ ZH104	Sentry AEW1	
☐ ZH105	Sentry AEW1	
☐ ZH106	Sentry AEW1	
☐ ZH107	Sentry AEW1	
☐ ZH115	Grob G109B	
☐ ZH116	Grob G109B	
☐ ZH117	Grob G109B	
☐ ZH118	Grob G109B	
☐ ZH119	Grob G109B	
☐ ZH120	Grob G109B	
☐ ZH121	Grob G109B	
☐ ZH122	Grob G109B	
☐ ZH123	Grob G109B	
☐ ZH124	Grob G109B	
☐ ZH125	Grob G109B	
☐ ZH126	Grob G109B	
☐ ZH127	Grob G109B	
☐ ZH128	Grob G109B	
☐ ZH129	Grob G109B	
☐ ZH144	Grob G109B	
☐ ZH145	Grob G109B	
☐ ZH146	Grob G109B	
☐ ZH147	Grob G109B	
☐ ZH148	Grob G109B	
☐ ZH184	Grob G109B	
☐ ZH185	Grob G109B	
☐ ZH186	Grob G109B	
☐ ZH187	Grob G109B	
☐ ZH188	Grob G109B	
☐ ZH189	Grob G109B	
☐ ZH190	Grob G109B	
☐ ZH191	Grob G109B	
☐ ZH192	Grob G109B	
☐ ZH193	Grob G109B	
☐ ZH194	Grob G109B	
☐ ZH195	Grob G109B	
☐ ZH196	Grob G109B	
☐ ZH197	Grob G109B	
☐ ZH200	Hawk 200	
☐ ZH205	Grob G109B	
☐ ZH206	Grob G109B	
☐ ZH207	Grob G109B	
☐ ZH208	Grob G109B	
☐ ZH209	Grob G109B	
☐ ZH211	Grob G109B	
☐ ZH247	Grob G109B	
☐ ZH248	Grob G109B	
☐ ZH249	Grob G109B	
☐ ZH257	Chinook CH47C	
☐ ZH263	Grob G109B	
☐ ZH264	Grob G109B	
☐ ZH265	Grob G109B	
☐ ZH266	Grob G109B	

☐ ZH267	Grob G109B	☐ ZH849	Merlin HM1	☐ ZJ133	Merlin HC3
☐ ZH268	Grob G109B	☐ ZH850	Merlin HM1	☐ ZJ134	Merlin HC3
☐ ZH269	Grob G109B	☐ ZH851	Merlin HM1	☐ ZJ135	Merlin HC3
☐ ZH270	Grob G109B	☐ ZH852	Merlin HM1	☐ ZJ136	Merlin HC3
☐ ZH271	Grob G109B	☐ ZH853	Merlin HM1	☐ ZJ137	Merlin HC3
☐ ZH272	Grob G109B	☐ ZH854	Merlin HM1	☐ ZJ138	Merlin HC3
☐ ZH278	Grob G109B	☐ ZH855	Merlin HM1	☐ ZJ164	Dauphin 2
☐ ZH279	Grob G109B	☐ ZH856	Merlin HM1	☐ ZJ165	Dauphin 2
☐ ZH536	Islander CC2	☐ ZH857	Merlin HM1	☐ ZJ166	Apache AH1
☐ ZH540	Sea King HAR3A	☐ ZH858	Merlin HM1	☐ ZJ167	Apache AH1
☐ ZH541	Sea King HAR3A	☐ ZH860	Merlin HM1	☐ ZJ168	Apache AH1
☐ ZH542	Sea King HAR3A	☐ ZH861	Merlin HM1	☐ ZJ169	Apache AH1
☐ ZH543	Sea King HAR3A	☐ ZH862	Merlin HM1	☐ ZJ170	Apache AH1
☐ ZH544	Sea King HAR3A	☐ ZH863	Merlin HM1	☐ ZJ171	Apache AH1
☐ ZH545	Sea King HAR3A	☐ ZH864	Merlin HM1	☐ ZJ172	Apache AH1
☐ ZH552	Tornado F3	☐ ZH865	Hercules C4	☐ ZJ173	Apache AH1
☐ ZH553	Tornado F3	☐ ZH866	Hercules C4	☐ ZJ174	Apache AH1
☐ ZH554	Tornado F3	☐ ZH867	Hercules C4	☐ ZJ175	Apache AH1
☐ ZH555	Tornado F3	☐ ZH868	Hercules C4	☐ ZJ176	Apache AH1
☐ ZH556	Tornado F3	☐ ZH869	Hercules C4	☐ ZJ177	Apache AH1
☐ ZH557	Tornado F3	☐ ZH870	Hercules C4	☐ ZJ178	Apache AH1
☐ ZH559	Tornado F3	☐ ZH871	Hercules C4	☐ ZJ179	Apache AH1
☐ ZH588	Eurofighter Typhoon	☐ ZH872	Hercules C4	☐ ZJ180	Apache AH1
☐ ZH590	Eurofighter Typhoon	☐ ZH873	Hercules C4	☐ ZJ181	Apache AH1
☐ ZH653	Harrier T10	☐ ZH874	Hercules C4	☐ ZJ182	Apache AH1
☐ ZH654	Harrier T10	☐ ZH875	Hercules C4	☐ ZJ183	Apache AH1
☐ ZH655	Harrier T10	☐ ZH877	Hercules C4	☐ ZJ184	Apache AH1
☐ ZH656	Harrier T10	☐ ZH878	Hercules C4	☐ ZJ185	Apache AH1
☐ ZH657	Harrier T10	☐ ZH879	Hercules C4	☐ ZJ186	Apache AH1
☐ ZH658	Harrier T10	☐ ZH880	Hercules C5	☐ ZJ187	Apache AH1
☐ ZH659	Harrier T10	☐ ZH881	Hercules C5	☐ ZJ188	Apache AH1
☐ ZH660	Harrier T10	☐ ZH882	Hercules C5	☐ ZJ189	Apache AH1
☐ ZH661	Harrier T10	☐ ZH883	Hercules C5	☐ ZJ190	Apache AH1
☐ ZH662	Harrier T10	☐ ZH884	Hercules C5	☐ ZJ191	Apache AH1
☐ ZH663	Harrier T10	☐ ZH885	Hercules C5	☐ ZJ192	Apache AH1
☐ ZH664	Harrier T10	☐ ZH886	Hercules C5	☐ ZJ193	Apache AH1
☐ ZH665	Harrier T10	☐ ZH887	Hercules C5	☐ ZJ194	Apache AH1
☐ ZH763	BAC 111-539GL	☐ ZH888	Hercules C5	☐ ZJ195	Apache AH1
☐ ZH775	Chinook HC2	☐ ZH889	Hercules C5	☐ ZJ196	Apache AH1
☐ ZH776	Chinook HC2	☐ ZH890	Grob G109B	☐ ZJ197	Apache AH1
☐ ZH777	Chinook HC2	☐ ZH891	Chinook HC2A	☐ ZJ198	Apache AH1
☐ ZH814	Bell 212	☐ ZH892	Chinook HC2A	☐ ZJ199	Apache AH1
☐ ZH815	Bell 212	☐ ZH893	Chinook HC2A	☐ ZJ200	Apache AH1
☐ ZH816	Bell 212	☐ ZH894	Chinook HC2A	☐ ZJ202	Apache AH1
☐ ZH821	Merlin HM1	☐ ZH895	Chinook HC2A	☐ ZJ203	Apache AH1
☐ ZH822	Merlin HM1	☐ ZH896	Chinook HC2A	☐ ZJ204	Apache AH1
☐ ZH823	Merlin HM1	☐ ZH897	Chinook HC3	☐ ZJ205	Apache AH1
☐ ZH824	Merlin HM1	☐ ZH898	Chinook HC3	☐ ZJ206	Apache AH1
☐ ZH825	Merlin HM1	☐ ZH899	Chinook HC3	☐ ZJ207	Apache AH1
☐ ZH826	Merlin HM1	☐ ZH900	Chinook HC3	☐ ZJ208	Apache AH1
☐ ZH827	Merlin HM1	☐ ZH901	Chinook HC3	☐ ZJ209	Apache AH1
☐ ZH828	Merlin HM1	☐ ZH902	Chinook HC3	☐ ZJ210	Apache AH1
☐ ZH829	Merlin HM1	☐ ZH903	Chinook HC3	☐ ZJ211	Apache AH1
☐ ZH830	Merlin HM1	☐ ZH904	Chinook HC3	☐ ZJ212	Apache AH1
☐ ZH831	Merlin HM1	☐ ZJ100	Hawk 102D	☐ ZJ213	Apache AH1
☐ ZH832	Merlin HM1	☐ ZJ117	Merlin HC3	☐ ZJ214	Apache AH1
☐ ZH833	Merlin HM1	☐ ZJ118	Merlin HC3	☐ ZJ215	Apache AH1
☐ ZH834	Merlin HM1	☐ ZJ119	Merlin HC3	☐ ZJ216	Apache AH1
☐ ZH835	Merlin HM1	☐ ZJ120	Merlin HC3	☐ ZJ217	Apache AH1
☐ ZH836	Merlin HM1	☐ ZJ121	Merlin HC3	☐ ZJ218	Apache AH1
☐ ZH837	Merlin HM1	☐ ZJ122	Merlin HC3	☐ ZJ219	Apache AH1
☐ ZH838	Merlin HM1	☐ ZJ123	Merlin HC3	☐ ZJ220	Apache AH1
☐ ZH839	Merlin HM1	☐ ZJ124	Merlin HC3	☐ ZJ221	Apache AH1
☐ ZH840	Merlin HM1	☐ ZJ125	Merlin HC3	☐ ZJ222	Apache AH1
☐ ZH841	Merlin HM1	☐ ZJ126	Merlin HC3	☐ ZJ223	Apache AH1
☐ ZH842	Merlin HM1	☐ ZJ127	Merlin HC3	☐ ZJ224	Apache AH1
☐ ZH843	Merlin HM1	☐ ZJ128	Merlin HC3	☐ ZJ225	Apache AH1
☐ ZH845	Merlin HM1	☐ ZJ129	Merlin HC3	☐ ZJ226	Apache AH1
☐ ZH846	Merlin HM1	☐ ZJ130	Merlin HC3	☐ ZJ227	Apache AH1
☐ ZH847	Merlin HM1	☐ ZJ131	Merlin HC3	☐ ZJ228	Apache AH1
☐ ZH848	Merlin HM1	☐ ZJ132	Merlin HC3	☐ ZJ229	Apache AH1

	Serial	Type
☐	ZJ230	Apache AH1
☐	ZJ231	Apache AH1
☐	ZJ232	Apache AH1
☐	ZJ233	Apache AH1
☐	ZJ234	Griffin HT1
☐	ZJ235	Griffin HT1
☐	ZJ236	Griffin HT1
☐	ZJ237	Griffin HT1
☐	ZJ238	Griffin HT1
☐	ZJ239	Griffin HT1
☐	ZJ240	Griffin HT1
☐	ZJ241	Griffin HT1
☐	ZJ242	Griffin HT1
☐	ZJ243	Squirrel HT2
☐	ZJ244	Squirrel HT2
☐	ZJ245	Squirrel HT2
☐	ZJ246	Squirrel HT2
☐	ZJ247	Squirrel HT2
☐	ZJ248	Squirrel HT2
☐	ZJ249	Squirrel HT2
☐	ZJ250	Squirrel HT2
☐	ZJ251	Squirrel HT2
☐	ZJ252	Squirrel HT2
☐	ZJ253	Squirrel HT2
☐	ZJ254	Squirrel HT2
☐	ZJ255	Squirrel HT1
☐	ZJ256	Squirrel HT1
☐	ZJ257	Squirrel HT1
☐	ZJ260	Squirrel HT1
☐	ZJ261	Squirrel HT1
☐	ZJ262	Squirrel HT1
☐	ZJ264	Squirrel HT1
☐	ZJ265	Squirrel HT1
☐	ZJ266	Squirrel HT1
☐	ZJ267	Squirrel HT1
☐	ZJ268	Squirrel HT1
☐	ZJ269	Squirrel HT1
☐	ZJ270	Squirrel HT1
☐	ZJ271	Squirrel HT1
☐	ZJ272	Squirrel HT1
☐	ZJ273	Squirrel HT1
☐	ZJ274	Squirrel HT1
☐	ZJ275	Squirrel HT1
☐	ZJ276	Squirrel HT1
☐	ZJ277	Squirrel HT1
☐	ZJ278	Squirrel HT1
☐	ZJ279	Squirrel HT1
☐	ZJ280	Squirrel HT1
☐	ZJ281	Phoenix UAV
☐	ZJ282	Phoenix UAV
☐	ZJ283	Phoenix UAV
☐	ZJ284	Phoenix UAV
☐	ZJ285	Phoenix UAV
☐	ZJ286	Phoenix UAV
☐	ZJ287	Phoenix UAV
☐	ZJ288	Phoenix UAV
☐	ZJ289	Phoenix UAV
☐	ZJ290	Phoenix UAV
☐	ZJ291	Phoenix UAV
☐	ZJ292	Phoenix UAV
☐	ZJ293	Phoenix UAV
☐	ZJ294	Phoenix UAV
☐	ZJ295	Phoenix UAV
☐	ZJ296	Phoenix UAV
☐	ZJ297	Phoenix UAV
☐	ZJ298	Phoenix UAV
☐	ZJ301	Phoenix UAV
☐	ZJ302	Phoenix UAV
☐	ZJ303	Phoenix UAV
☐	ZJ304	Phoenix UAV
☐	ZJ305	Phoenix UAV
☐	ZJ306	Phoenix UAV
☐	ZJ307	Phoenix UAV
☐	ZJ308	Phoenix UAV
☐	ZJ309	Phoenix UAV
☐	ZJ310	Phoenix UAV
☐	ZJ311	Phoenix UAV
☐	ZJ312	Phoenix UAV
☐	ZJ313	Phoenix UAV
☐	ZJ314	Phoenix UAV
☐	ZJ315	Phoenix UAV
☐	ZJ316	Phoenix UAV
☐	ZJ317	Phoenix UAV
☐	ZJ318	Phoenix UAV
☐	ZJ319	Phoenix UAV
☐	ZJ320	Phoenix UAV
☐	ZJ321	Phoenix UAV
☐	ZJ322	Phoenix UAV
☐	ZJ323	Phoenix UAV
☐	ZJ324	Phoenix UAV
☐	ZJ325	Phoenix UAV
☐	ZJ326	Phoenix UAV
☐	ZJ327	Phoenix UAV
☐	ZJ328	Phoenix UAV
☐	ZJ329	Phoenix UAV
☐	ZJ330	Phoenix UAV
☐	ZJ331	Phoenix UAV
☐	ZJ332	Phoenix UAV
☐	ZJ333	Phoenix UAV
☐	ZJ334	Phoenix UAV
☐	ZJ335	Phoenix UAV
☐	ZJ336	Phoenix UAV
☐	ZJ337	Phoenix UAV
☐	ZJ338	Phoenix UAV
☐	ZJ339	Phoenix UAV
☐	ZJ340	Phoenix UAV
☐	ZJ341	Phoenix UAV
☐	ZJ342	Phoenix UAV
☐	ZJ343	Phoenix UAV
☐	ZJ344	Phoenix UAV
☐	ZJ345	Phoenix UAV
☐	ZJ346	Phoenix UAV
☐	ZJ347	Phoenix UAV
☐	ZJ348	Phoenix UAV
☐	ZJ349	Phoenix UAV
☐	ZJ350	Phoenix UAV
☐	ZJ351	Phoenix UAV
☐	ZJ352	Phoenix UAV
☐	ZJ353	Phoenix UAV
☐	ZJ354	Phoenix UAV
☐	ZJ355	Phoenix UAV
☐	ZJ356	Phoenix UAV
☐	ZJ357	Phoenix UAV
☐	ZJ358	Phoenix UAV
☐	ZJ359	Phoenix UAV
☐	ZJ360	Phoenix UAV
☐	ZJ361	Phoenix UAV
☐	ZJ362	Phoenix UAV
☐	ZJ363	Phoenix UAV
☐	ZJ364	Phoenix UAV
☐	ZJ365	Phoenix UAV
☐	ZJ366	Phoenix UAV
☐	ZJ367	Phoenix UAV
☐	ZJ368	Phoenix UAV
☐	ZJ369	Phoenix UAV
☐	ZJ370	Phoenix UAV
☐	ZJ371	Phoenix UAV
☐	ZJ372	Phoenix UAV
☐	ZJ373	Phoenix UAV
☐	ZJ374	Phoenix UAV
☐	ZJ375	Phoenix UAV
☐	ZJ376	Phoenix UAV
☐	ZJ377	Phoenix UAV
☐	ZJ378	Phoenix UAV
☐	ZJ379	Phoenix UAV
☐	ZJ380	Phoenix UAV
☐	ZJ381	Phoenix UAV
☐	ZJ382	Phoenix UAV
☐	ZJ383	Phoenix UAV
☐	ZJ385	Phoenix UAV
☐	ZJ386	Phoenix UAV
☐	ZJ387	Phoenix UAV
☐	ZJ388	Phoenix UAV
☐	ZJ389	Phoenix UAV
☐	ZJ390	Phoenix UAV
☐	ZJ391	Phoenix UAV
☐	ZJ392	Phoenix UAV
☐	ZJ394	Phoenix UAV
☐	ZJ395	Phoenix UAV
☐	ZJ396	Phoenix UAV
☐	ZJ397	Phoenix UAV
☐	ZJ398	Phoenix UAV
☐	ZJ399	Phoenix UAV
☐	ZJ400	Phoenix UAV
☐	ZJ401	Phoenix UAV
☐	ZJ403	Phoenix UAV
☐	ZJ404	Phoenix UAV
☐	ZJ405	Phoenix UAV
☐	ZJ406	Phoenix UAV
☐	ZJ407	Phoenix UAV
☐	ZJ408	Phoenix UAV
☐	ZJ409	Phoenix UAV
☐	ZJ410	Phoenix UAV
☐	ZJ411	Phoenix UAV
☐	ZJ412	Phoenix UAV
☐	ZJ413	Phoenix UAV
☐	ZJ414	Phoenix UAV
☐	ZJ415	Phoenix UAV
☐	ZJ416	Phoenix UAV
☐	ZJ418	Phoenix UAV
☐	ZJ419	Phoenix UAV
☐	ZJ420	Phoenix UAV
☐	ZJ421	Phoenix UAV
☐	ZJ422	Phoenix UAV
☐	ZJ423	Phoenix UAV
☐	ZJ424	Phoenix UAV
☐	ZJ425	Phoenix UAV
☐	ZJ426	Phoenix UAV
☐	ZJ427	Phoenix UAV
☐	ZJ428	Phoenix UAV
☐	ZJ429	Phoenix UAV
☐	ZJ430	Phoenix UAV
☐	ZJ431	Phoenix UAV
☐	ZJ432	Phoenix UAV
☐	ZJ433	Phoenix UAV
☐	ZJ434	Phoenix UAV
☐	ZJ435	Phoenix UAV
☐	ZJ436	Phoenix UAV
☐	ZJ437	Phoenix UAV
☐	ZJ438	Phoenix UAV
☐	ZJ440	Phoenix UAV
☐	ZJ441	Phoenix UAV
☐	ZJ442	Phoenix UAV
☐	ZJ443	Phoenix UAV
☐	ZJ444	Phoenix UAV
☐	ZJ445	Phoenix UAV
☐	ZJ446	Phoenix UAV
☐	ZJ447	Phoenix UAV
☐	ZJ448	Phoenix UAV
☐	ZJ449	Phoenix UAV
☐	ZJ450	Phoenix UAV
☐	ZJ451	Phoenix UAV

☐ ZJ452	Phoenix UAV	☐ ZJ707	Griffin HT1	☐ ZK010	Hawk T2
☐ ZJ453	Phoenix UAV	☐ ZJ708	Griffin HT1	☐ ZK011	Hawk T2
☐ ZJ454	Phoenix UAV	☐ ZJ800	Eurofighter Typhoon T1	☐ ZK012	Hawk T2
☐ ZJ455	Phoenix UAV	☐ ZJ801	Eurofighter Typhoon T1	☐ ZK013	Hawk T2
☐ ZJ456	Phoenix UAV	☐ ZJ802	Eurofighter Typhoon T1	☐ ZK014	Hawk T2
☐ ZJ457	Phoenix UAV	☐ ZJ803	Eurofighter Typhoon T1	☐ ZK015	Hawk T2
☐ ZJ458	Phoenix UAV	☐ ZJ804	Eurofighter Typhoon T1	☐ ZK016	Hawk T2
☐ ZJ459	Phoenix UAV	☐ ZJ805	Eurofighter Typhoon T1	☐ ZK017	Hawk T2
☐ ZJ460	Phoenix UAV	☐ ZJ806	Eurofighter Typhoon T1	☐ ZK018	Hawk T2
☐ ZJ461	Phoenix UAV	☐ ZJ807	Eurofighter Typhoon T1	☐ ZK019	Hawk T2
☐ ZJ462	Phoenix UAV	☐ ZJ808	Eurofighter Typhoon T1	☐ ZK020	Hawk T2
☐ ZJ463	Phoenix UAV	☐ ZJ809	Eurofighter Typhoon T1	☐ ZK021	Hawk T2
☐ ZJ464	Phoenix UAV	☐ ZJ810	Eurofighter Typhoon T1	☐ ZK022	Hawk T2
☐ ZJ465	Phoenix UAV	☐ ZJ811	Eurofighter Typhoon T1	☐ ZK023	Hawk T2
☐ ZJ466	Phoenix UAV	☐ ZJ812	Eurofighter Typhoon T1	☐ ZK024	Hawk T2
☐ ZJ467	Phoenix UAV	☐ ZJ813	Eurofighter Typhoon T1	☐ ZK025	Hawk T2
☐ ZJ468	Phoenix UAV	☐ ZJ814	Eurofighter Typhoon T1	☐ ZK026	Hawk T2
☐ ZJ469	Phoenix UAV	☐ ZJ815	Eurofighter Typhoon T1	☐ ZK027	Hawk T2
☐ ZJ470	Phoenix UAV	☐ ZJ910	Eurofighter Typhoon F2	☐ ZK028	Hawk T2
☐ ZJ471	Phoenix UAV	☐ ZJ911	Eurofighter Typhoon F2	☐ ZK029	Hawk T2
☐ ZJ472	Phoenix UAV	☐ ZJ912	Eurofighter Typhoon F2	☐ ZK030	Hawk T2
☐ ZJ473	Phoenix UAV	☐ ZJ913	Eurofighter Typhoon F2	☐ ZK031	Hawk T2
☐ ZJ474	Phoenix UAV	☐ ZJ914	Eurofighter Typhoon F2	☐ ZK032	Hawk T2
☐ ZJ475	Phoenix UAV	☐ ZJ915	Eurofighter Typhoon F2	☐ ZK033	Hawk T2
☐ ZJ476	Phoenix UAV	☐ ZJ916	Eurofighter Typhoon F2	☐ ZK034	Hawk T2
☐ ZJ477	Phoenix UAV	☐ ZJ917	Eurofighter Typhoon F2	☐ ZK035	Hawk T2
☐ ZJ478	Phoenix UAV	☐ ZJ918	Eurofighter Typhoon F2	☐ ZK036	Hawk T2
☐ ZJ479	Phoenix UAV	☐ ZJ919	Eurofighter Typhoon F2	☐ ZK037	Hawk T2
☐ ZJ480	Phoenix UAV	☐ ZJ920	Eurofighter Typhoon F2	☐ ZK038	Hawk T2
☐ ZJ514	Nimrod MRA4	☐ ZJ921	Eurofighter Typhoon F2	☐ ZK039	Hawk T2
☐ ZJ515	Nimrod MRA4	☐ ZJ922	Eurofighter Typhoon F2	☐ ZK040	Hawk T2
☐ ZJ516	Nimrod MRA4	☐ ZJ923	Eurofighter Typhoon F2	☐ ZK041	Hawk T2
☐ ZJ517	Nimrod MRA4	☐ ZJ924	Eurofighter Typhoon F2	☐ ZK042	Hawk T2
☐ ZJ518	Nimrod MRA4	☐ ZJ925	Eurofighter Typhoon F2	☐ ZK043	Hawk T2
☐ ZJ519	Nimrod MRA4	☐ ZJ926	Eurofighter Typhoon F2	☐ ZK044	Hawk T2
☐ ZJ520	Nimrod MRA4	☐ ZJ927	Eurofighter Typhoon F2	☐ ZK450	Beech 200
☐ ZJ521	Nimrod MRA4	☐ ZJ928	Eurofighter Typhoon F2	☐ ZK451	Beech 200
☐ ZJ522	Nimrod MRA4	☐ ZJ929	Eurofighter Typhoon F2	☐ ZK452	Beech 200
☐ ZJ523	Nimrod MRA4	☐ ZJ930	Eurofighter Typhoon F2	☐ ZK453	Beech 200
☐ ZJ524	Nimrod MRA4	☐ ZJ931	Eurofighter Typhoon F2	☐ ZK454	Beech 200
☐ ZJ525	Nimrod MRA4	☐ ZJ932	Eurofighter Typhoon F2	☐ ZR321	Agusta A.109E
☐ ZJ526	Nimrod MRA4	☐ ZJ933	Eurofighter Typhoon F2	☐ ZR322	Agusta A.109E
☐ ZJ527	Nimrod MRA4	☐ ZJ934	Eurofighter Typhoon F2	☐ ZR323	Agusta A.109E
☐ ZJ528	Nimrod MRA4	☐ ZJ935	Eurofighter Typhoon F2	☐ ZZ171	C17A
☐ ZJ529	Nimrod MRA4	☐ ZJ936	Eurofighter Typhoon F2	☐ ZZ172	C17A
☐ ZJ530	Nimrod MRA4	☐ ZJ937	Eurofighter Typhoon F2	☐ ZZ173	C17A
☐ ZJ531	Nimrod MRA4	☐ ZJ938	Eurofighter Typhoon F2	☐ ZZ174	C17A
☐ ZJ627	Cranfield UAV	☐ ZJ939	Eurofighter Typhoon F2	☐ ZZ190	Hawker Hunter F58
☐ ZJ628	Cranfield UAV	☐ ZJ940	Eurofighter Typhoon F2	☐ ZZ191	Hawker Hunter F58
☐ ZJ629	Cranfield UAV	☐ ZJ941	Eurofighter Typhoon F2	☐ ZZ192	Grob G.103
☐ ZJ630	Cranfield UAV	☐ ZJ942	Eurofighter Typhoon F2		
☐ ZJ631	Cranfield UAV	☐ ZJ943	Eurofighter Typhoon F2		
☐ ZJ635	Twin Squirrel HCC1	☐ ZJ944	Eurofighter Typhoon F2		
☐ ZJ645	Alpha Jet	☐ ZJ954	SA.330H Puma		
☐ ZJ646	Alpha Jet	☐ ZJ955	SA.330H Puma		
☐ ZJ647	Alpha Jet	☐ ZJ956	SA.330H Puma		
☐ ZJ648	Alpha Jet	☐ ZJ957	SA.330H Puma		
☐ ZJ649	Alpha Jet	☐ ZJ958	SA.330H Puma		
☐ ZJ650	Alpha Jet	☐ ZJ959	SA.330H Puma		
☐ ZJ651	Alpha Jet	☐ ZJ960	Grob G109B		
☐ ZJ690	Global Express ASTOR	☐ ZJ961	Grob G109B		
☐ ZJ691	Global Express ASTOR	☐ ZJ962	Grob G109B		
☐ ZJ692	Global Express ASTOR	☐ ZJ963	Grob G109B		
☐ ZJ693	Global Express ASTOR	☐ ZJ964	Bell 212		
☐ ZJ694	Global Express ASTOR	☐ ZJ965	Bell 212		
☐ ZJ699	Eurofighter Typhoon	☐ ZJ966	Bell 212		
☐ ZJ700	Eurofighter Typhoon	☐ ZJ967	Grob G109B		
☐ ZJ703	Griffin HAR.2	☐ ZJ968	Grob G109B		
☐ ZJ704	Griffin HAR.2	☐ ZJ969	Bell 212		
☐ ZJ705	Griffin HAR.2	☐ ZJ989	EADS Eagle		
☐ ZJ706	Griffin HAR.2	☐ ZK005	Grob G109B		

NOTES

NOTES

Military / Civil cross reference

UK Markings

Mil	Code	Civil
1		G-BPVE
4		BAPC.11
12A		BAPC.2
14		BAPC.6
168		G-BFDE
304		BAPC.62
687		BAPC.181
1881		BAPC.122
2345		G-ATVP
2882		BAPC.234
3066		G-AETA
5964		BAPC.112
5964		G-BFVH
6232		BAPC.41
9917		G-EBKY
A485		BAPC.176
A1742		BAPC.38
A7317		BAPC.179
A8226		G-BIDW
B-415		BAPC.163
B595	W	G-BUOD
B1807	A7	G-EAVX
B2458	R	G-BPOB
B4863		BAPC.113
B5577	W	BAPC.59
B6401		G-AWYY
B7270		G-BFCZ
C1904	Z	G-PFAP
C3009	B	G-BFWD
C3011	S	G-SWOT
C4451		BAPC.210
C4912		BAPC.135
C4918		G-BWJM
C4988		G-BPLT
C4994		G-BLWM
C5430	V	G-CCXG
C9533	M	G-BUWE
D276	A	BAPC.208
D7889		G-AANM
D8096	D	G-AEPH
E449		G-EBJE
E2466		BAPC.165
E2939		G-ATXL
E8894		G-CDLI
F-141	G	G-SEVA
F235	B	G-BMDB
F904		G-EBIA
F938		G-EBIC
F-943		G-BIHF
F943		G-BKDT
F5447	N	G-BKER
F5459	Y	G-INNY
F5459	Y	BAPC.142
F5475	A	BAPC.250
F8010	Z	G-BDWJ
F8614		G-AWAU
H1968		BAPC.42
H3426		BAPC.68
H5199		G-ADEV
J7326		G-EBQP
J9941		G-ABMR
K-123		G-EACN
K-155		G-EAFN
K1786		G-AFTA
K1930		G-BKBB
K2048		G-BZNW
K2050		G-ASCM
K2059		G-PFAR
K2075		G-BEER
K2227		G-ABBB
K-2567		G-MOTH
K2572		G-AOZH
K-2585		G-ANKT
K2587		G-BJAP
K3241		G-AHSA
K3661	562	G-BURZ
K3731		G-RODI
K4232		SE-AZB
K4235		G-AHMJ
K-4259	71	G-ANMO
K5054		G-BRDV
K5054		BAPC.214
K5414	XV	G-AENP
K5673		BAPC.249
K5673		G-BZAS
K7271		BAPC.148
K7271		G-CCKV
K8203		G-BTVE
K8303	D	G-BWWN
K9926	JH-C	BAPC.217
L1070	XT-A	BAPC.227
L1679	JX-G	BAPC.241
L1710	AL-D	BAPC.219
L2301		G-AIZG
L6906		G-AKKY
L7005	PS-B	BAPC.281
L8353		G-AMMC
N248		BAPC.164
N500		G-BWRA
N1854		G-AIBE
N1977	8	G-BWMJ
N2532	GZ-H	BAPC.272
N3194	GR-Z	BAPC.220
N3289	DW-K	BAPC.65
N3313	KL-B	BAPC.69
N3317	AI-A	BAPC.268
N3788		G-AKPF
N4877	MK-V	G-AMDA
N5182		G-APUP
N5195		G-ABOX
N5199		G-BZND
N5492	B	BAPC.111
N6290		G-BOCK
N6452		G-BIAU
N-6466		G-ANKZ
N-6473		G-AOBO
N6720	VX	G-BYTN
N-6797		G-ANEH
N6847		G-APAL
N6965	FL-J	G-AJTW
N-9192	RCO-N	G-DHZF
N9389		G-ANJA
P641		BAPC.123
P2790		G-ORGI
P2793	SD-M	BAPC.236
P2902	DX-X	G-ROBT
P2921	GZ-L	BAPC.273
P2970	US-X	BAPC.291
P3059	SD-N	BAPC.64
P3208	SD-T	BAPC.63
P3679	GZ-K	BAPC.278
P3873	YO-H	BAPC.265
P6382	C	G-AJRS
P6775	YT-J	BAPC.299
P7350	XT-D	G-AWIJ
P8140	ZP-K	BAPC.71
P8448	UM-D	BAPC.225
R1914		G-AHUJ
R3821	UX-N	G-BPIV
R4115	LE-X	BAPC.267
R4118	UP-W	G-HUPW
R4959	59	G-ARAZ
R5136		G-APAP
R5172	FIJE	G-AOIS
R6690	PR-A	BAPC.254
S1287	5	G-BEYB
S1595		BAPC.156
S1579	571	G-BBVO
S1581	573	G-BWWK
T5672		G-ALRI
T-5854		G-ANKK
T-5879	RUC-W	G-AXBW
T6313		G-AHVU
T-6953		G-ANNI
T-7230		G-AFVE
T7245		G-ANEJ
T7281		G-ARTL
T7328		G-APPN
T7793		G-ANKV
T-7842		G-AMTF
T7909		G-ANON
T9707		G-AKKR
T9738		G-AKAT
T-7997		G-AHUF
V3388		G-AHTW
V6799	SD-X	BAPC.72
V7467	LE-D	BAPC.223
V7467	LE-D	BAPC.288
V9367	MA-B	G-AZWT
V9673	MA-J	G-LIZY
W2068	68	VH-ASM
W2718	AA5Y	G-RNLI
W5856	A2A	G-BMGC
W9385	YG-L	G-ADND
Z2033	N/275	G-ASTL
Z5140	HA-C	G-HURI
Z5252	GO-B	G-BWHA
Z7015	7-L	G-BKTH
Z7197		G-AKZN
AB196		G-CCGH
AB550	GE-P	BAPC.230
AB910	IR-G	G-AISU
AP507	KX-P	G-ACWP
AR213	PR-D	G-AIST
AR501	NN-A	G-AWII
AR614	DU-Z	G-BUWA
BB807		G-ADWO
BE421	XP-G	BAPC.205
BL924	AZ-G	BAPC.242
BM597	U-2	G-MKVB
BM631	XR-C	BAPC.269
BN230	FT-A	BAPC.218
BR600	SH-V	BAPC.222
BR600		BAPC.224
DE-208		G-AGYU
DE470	16	G-ANMY
DE623		G-ANFI
DE673		G-ADNZ
DE730		G-ANFW
DE992		G-AXXV
DF112		G-ANRM
DF128	RCO-U	G-AOJJ
DF155		G-ANFV
DR828	PB-1	N18V
EM720		G-AXAN
EN343		BAPC.226
EN398		BAPC.184

	Serial	Code	Reg		Serial	Code	Reg		Serial	Code	Reg
☐	EN526	SZ-G	BAPC.221	☐	RB412	DW-B	G-CEFC	☐	WD310	B	G-BWUN
☐	EP120	AE-A	G-LFVB	☐	RG333		G-AIEK	☐	WD331		G-BXDH
☐	FB226	MT-A	G-BDWM	☐	RM221		G-ANXR	☐	WD347		G-BBRV
☐	FE695	94	G-BTXI	☐	RN201		G-BSKP	☐	WD363		G-BCIH
☐	FE788		G-CTKL	☐	RR232		G-BRSF	☐	WD373	12	G-BXDI
☐	FE905		LN-BNM	☐	RT486	PF-A	G-AJGJ	☐	WD379	K	G-APLO
☐	FR886		G-BDMS	☐	RT610		G-AKWS	☐	WD390		G-BWNK
☐	FS628		G-AIZE	☐	RW386	NG-D	G-BXVI	☐	WD413		G-VROE
☐	FT375		G-BWUL	☐	SM845	GZ-J	G-BUOS	☐	WE569		G-ASAJ
☐	FT391		G-AZBN	☐	SM969	D-A	G-BRAF	☐	WE591	Y	G-ASAK
☐	FX301	FD-NQ	G-JUDI	☐	SX336	VL-105	G-KASX	☐	WF118		G-DACA
☐	FZ625		G-AMPO	☐	TA634	8K-K	G-AWJV	☐	WG308	8	G-BYHL
☐	HB275		G-BKGM	☐	TA719	6 T	G-ASKC	☐	WG316		G-BCAH
☐	HG691		G-AIYR	☐	TA805	FX-M	G-PMNF	☐	WG321	G	G-DHCC
☐	HH268		BAPC.261	☐	TB252	GW-H	G-XVIE	☐	WG348		G-BBMV
☐	HM580	KX-K	G-ACUU	☐	TD248	CR-S	G-OXVI	☐	WG350		G-BPAL
☐	HS503		BAPC.108	☐	TJ398		BAPC.70	☐	WG407	67	G-BWMX
☐	JF343*	JW-P	G-CCZP	☐	TJ534		G-AKSY	☐	WG422	16	G-BFAX
☐	JG891	T-B	G-LFVC	☐	TJ565		G-AMVD	☐	WG458	G	N458BG
☐	JV828		N423RS	☐	TJ569		G-AKOW	☐	WG465		G-BCEY
☐	KB889	NA-I	G-LANC	☐	TJ672	DT-S	G-ANIJ	☐	WG469	72	G-BWJY
☐	KD345	130	G-FGID	☐	TJ704	JA	G-ASCD	☐	WG472		G-AOTY
☐	KF584	RAI-X	G-RAIX	☐	TS423		N147DC	☐	WG719		G-BRMA
☐	KJ351		BAPC.80	☐	TS798		G-AGNV	☐	WJ358		G-ARYD
☐	KK116		G-AMPY	☐	TW439		G-ANRP	☐	WJ945	21	G-BEDV
☐	KL161	VO-B	N25644	☐	TW467		G-ANIE	☐	WK126	843	N2138J
☐	KZ321	JV-N	G-HURY	☐	TW511		G-APAF	☐	WK163		G-BVWC
☐	LB264		G-AIXA	☐	TW536	T-SV	G-BNGE	☐	WK436		G-VENM
☐	LB312		G-AHXE	☐	TW591		G-ARIH	☐	WK512	A	G-BXIM
☐	LB367		G-AHGZ	☐	TW641		G-ATDN	☐	WK514		G-BBMO
☐	LB375		G-AHGW	☐	VF512	PF-M	G-ARRX	☐	WK517		G-ULAS
☐	LB381		G-AHKO	☐	VF516		G-ASMZ	☐	WK522		G-BCOU
☐	LF789	R2-K	BAPC.186	☐	VF526	T	G-ARXU	☐	WK549		G-BTWF
☐	LF858		G-BLUZ	☐	VF581		G-ARSL	☐	WK577		G-BCYM
☐	LH291		BAPC 279	☐	VL348		G-AVVO	☐	WK585		G-BZGA
☐	LS326	L 2	G-AJVH	☐	VL349	V7-Q	G-AWSA	☐	WK586	V	G-BXGX
☐	LZ766		G-ALCK	☐	VM360		G-APHV	☐	WK590	69	G-BWVZ
☐	MAV467	R-O	BAPC.202	☐	VN799		G-CDSX	☐	WK609	93	G-BXDN
☐	MH415	FU-N	BAPC.209	☐	VP519		G-AVVR	☐	WK611		G-ARWB
☐	MH434	ZD-B	G-ASJV	☐	VP955		G-DVON	☐	WK622		G-BCZH
☐	MH486	FF-A	BAPC.206	☐	VP981		G-DHDV	☐	WK624	M	G-BWHI
☐	MJ627	9G-P	G-BMSB	☐	VR192		G-APIT	☐	WK628		G-BBMW
☐	MJ832	DN-Y	BAPC.229	☐	VR249	FA-EL	G-APIY	☐	WK630		G-BXDG
☐	MK732	3W-17	G-HVDM	☐	VR259	M	G-APJB	☐	WK633	B	G-BXEC
☐	MK805	SH-B	----------	☐	VS356		G-AOLU	☐	WK640	C	G-BWUV
☐	MK912	SH-L	G-BRRA	☐	VS623		G-AOKZ	☐	WK642		G-BXDP
☐	ML407	OU-V	G-LFIX	☐	VT871		G-DHXX	☐	WL626	P	G-BHDD
☐	MP425		G-AITB	☐	VV612		G-VENI	☐	WM167		G-LOSM
☐	MT438		G-AREI	☐	VX147		G-AVIL	☐	WP308	572	G-GACA
☐	MT928	ZX-M	G-BKMI	☐	VX927		G-ASYG	☐	WP788		G-BCHL
☐	MV268	JE-J	G-SPIT	☐	VZ345		D-CATA	☐	WP790	T	G-BBNC
☐	MV370		G-FXIV	☐	VZ638		G-JETM	☐	WP795	901	G-BVZZ
☐	MW763	HF-A	G-TEMT	☐	VZ728		G-AGOS	☐	WP800	2	G-BCXN
☐	NJ203		G-AKNP	☐	WB188		G-HUNT	☐	WP805		G-MAJR
☐	NJ633		G-AKXP	☐	WB188		G-BZPB	☐	WP808		G-BDEU
☐	NJ673		G-AOCR	☐	WB188		G-BZPC	☐	WP809	78	G-BVTX
☐	NJ695		G-AJXV	☐	WB533		G-DEVN	☐	WP833		G-BZDU
☐	NJ719		G-ANFU	☐	WB565	X	G-PVET	☐	WP840	9	G-BXDM
☐	NL750		G-AOBH	☐	WB569	R	G-BYSJ	☐	WP844		G-BWOX
☐	NL913		G-AOFR	☐	WB571	34	G-AOSF	☐	WP857	24	G-BDRJ
☐	NL985		G-BWIK	☐	WB585	M	G-AOSY	☐	WP859	E	G-BXCP
☐	NM181		G-AZGZ	☐	WB588	D	G-AOTD	☐	WP860	6	G-BXDA
☐	NP336		G-AGTB	☐	WB615	E	G-BXIA	☐	WP870	12	G-BCOI
☐	NS519		G-MOSI	☐	WB654	U	G-BXGO	☐	WP896		G-BWVY
☐	NX611	LE-C:DX-C	G-ASXX	☐	WB671	910	G-BWTG	☐	WP901		G-BWNT
☐	PL965	R	G-MKXI	☐	WB697	95	G-BXCT	☐	WP903		G-BCGC
☐	PL983	JV-F	G-PRXI	☐	WB702		G-AOFE	☐	WP925	C	G-BXHA
☐	PS853	C	G-RRGN	☐	WB711		G-APPM	☐	WP928	D	G-BXGM
☐	PT462	SW-A	G-CTIX	☐	WB726	E	G-AOSK	☐	WP929		G-BXCV
☐	PV303	ON-B	G-CCJL	☐	WD286		G-BBND	☐	WP930	J	G-BXHF
☐	PZ865	JX-E	G-AMAU	☐	WD292		G-BCRX	☐	WP971		G-ATHD

Serial	Code	Registration
WP983	B	G-BXNN
WP984	H	G-BWTO
WR360		G-DHSS
WR410		G-DHUU
WR421		G-DHTT
WR470		G-DHVM
WS774	4	G-ANSO
WT333		G-BVXC
WT722	878:VL	G-BWGN
WT723	866:VL	G-PRII
WV198	K	G-BJWY
WV318	D	G-FFOX
WV322	Y	G-BZSE
WV372	R	G-BXFI
WV499	G	G-BZRF
WV493	29:A-P	G-BDYG
WV740		G-BNPH
WV783		(G-ALSP)
WW421	P	G-BZRE
WW499	P-G	G-BZRF
WZ507	74	G-VTII
WZ584	K	G-BZRC
WZ589		G-DHZZ
WZ662		G-BKVK
WZ706		G-BURR
WZ847	F	G-CPMK
WZ868	H	G-ARMF
WZ872	E	G-BZGB
WZ879	X	G-BWUT
WZ882	K	G-BXGP
XA880		G-BVXR
XB259		G-AOAI
XD693	Z-Q	G-AOBU
XE489		G-JETH
XE601		G-ETPS
XE665	876:VL	G-BWGM
XE685	871:VL	G-GAII
XE689	864:VL	G-BWGK
XE897		G-DHVV
XE920	A	G-VMPR
XE956		G-OBLN
XF515	R	G-KAXF
XF597	AH	G-BKFW
XF603		G-KAPW
XF690		G-MOOS
XF785		G-ALBN
XF836		G-AWRY
XF868		G-BGSB
XF877	JX	G-AWVF
XF995		G-BZSF
XG160	U	G-BWAF
XG452		G-BRMB
XG547	T-S	G-HAPR
XG588		G-BAMH
XG775		G-DHWW
XH313	E	G-BZRD
XH558		G-VLCN
XJ348		G-AMXX
XJ389		G-AJJP
XJ398		G-BDBZ
XJ615		G-BWGL
XJ729		G-BVGE
XJ771		G-HELV
XK895	CU-19	G-SDEV
XK940		G-AYXT
XL426		G-VJET
XL502		G-BMYP
XL571	V	G-HNTR
XL573		G-BVGH
XL577	V	G-BXKF
XL587	Z	G-HPUX
XL602		G-BWFT
XL621		G-BNCX
XL714		G-AOGR
XL-716		G-AOIL
XL809		G-BLIX
XL812		G-SARO
XL954		G-BXES
XM223		G-BWWC
XM365		G-BXBH
XM424		G-BWDS
XM478		G-BXDL
XM479	54	G-BVEZ
XM496		G-BDUP
XM556		G-HELI
XM575		G-BLMC
XM655		G-VULC
XM685	PO:513	G-AYZJ
XM819		G-APXW
XN332	759	G-APNV
XN441		G-BGKT
XN459		G-BWOT
XN629	49	G-KNOT
XP254		G-ASCC
XP279		G-BWKK
XP355	A	G-BEBC
XP524	134	G-CVIX
XP672	3	G-RAFI
XP693		G-FSIX
XP772		G-DHCZ
XP907		G-SROE
XR240		G-BDFH
XR241		G-AXRR
XR246		G-AZBU
XR486		G-RWWW
XR537		G-NATY
XR538	1	G-RORI
XR592		G-AMWI
XR595	M	G-BWHU
XR673		G-BXLO
XR724		G-BTSY
XR773		G-OPIB
XR944		G-ATTB
XR991		G-MOUR
XR993		G-BVPP
XS111		G-TIMM
XS165	37	G-ASAZ
XS235		G-CPDA
XS451		G-LTNG
XS587		G-VIXN
XS765		G-BSET
XS770		G-HRHI
XT223		G-XTUN
XT420	606	G-CBUI
XT435	430	G-RIMM
XT634		G-BYRX
XT78?	(qv)	G-BMIR
XT787		G-KAXT
XT793	456	G-BZPP
XV130	R	G-BWJW
XV134	P	G-BWLX
XV137		G-CRUM
XV140	K	G-KAXL
XV268		G-BVER
XW289	73	G-JPVA
XW293	Z	G-BWCS
XW324	K	G-BWSG
XW325	E	G-BWGF
XW333		G-BVTC
XW354		G-JPTV
XW422		G-BWEB
XW423	14	G-BWUW
XW433		G-JPRO
XW635		G-AWSW
XW784	VL	G-BBRN
XW799		G-BXSL
XW854		G-CBSD
XW857		G-LEDR
XW858	C	G-DMSS
XW861	CU-52	G-BZFJ
XW898	G	G-CBXT
XX110		BAPC.169
XX226	74	BAPC.152
XX253		BAPC.171
XX406	P	G-CBSH
XX436	CU-39	G-ZZLE
XX467	86	G-TVII
XX513	10	G-CCMI
XX514		G-BWIB
XX515	4	G-CBBC
XX518	S	G-UDOG
XX521	H	G-CBEH
XX522	6	G-DAWG
XX524	4	G-DDOG
XX525	8	G-CBJJ
XX528	D	G-BZON
XX534	B	G-EDAV
XX537	C	G-CBCB
XX538	O	G-TDOG
XX543	F	G-CBAB
XX546	3	G-WINI
XX549	6	G-CBID
XX550	Z	G-CBBL
XX551	E	G-BZDP
XX554	9	G-BZMD
XX561	7	G-BZEP
XX611	7	G-CBDK
XX612	A03	G-BZXC
XX614	V	G-GGRR
XX619	T	G-CBBW
XX621	H	G-CBEF
XX622	B	G-CBGX
XX624	E	G-KDOG
XX625	1	G-CBBR
XX626	W:02	G-CDVV
XX628	9	G-CBFU
XX629	V	G-BZXZ
XX630	5	G-SIJW
XX631	W	G-BZXS
XX636	Y	G-CBFP
XX638		G-DOGG
XX658	3	G-BZPS
XX667	16	G-BZFN
XX668	I	G-CBAN
XX692	A	G-BZMH
XX693	7	G-BZML
XX694	E	G-CBBS
XX695	3	G-CBBT
XX698	9	G-BZME
XX699	F	G-CBCV
XX700	17	G-CBEK
XX702		G-CBCR
XX704		G-BCUV
XX707	4	G-CBDS
XX711	X	G-CBBU
XX713	2	G-CBJK
XX725	GU	BAPC.150
XX885		G-HHAA
XZ329		G-BZYD
XZ363	A	BAPC.151
XZ934	U	G-CBSI
ZA556		BAPC.155
ZA634	C	G-BUHA

☐ ZA652		G-BUDC
☐ ZB500		G-LYNX
☐ ZB627	A	G-CBSK
☐ ZB629		G-CBZL
☐ ZB647	40	G-CBSD
☐ ZF592		G-AWON
☐ ZH139	1	BAPC.191
☐ ZJ116		G-OIOI
☐ 8449M		G-ASWJ
☐	F	G-RUMW
☐	12	G-ARSG

UK 'B' Conditions markings

☐ G-17-3		G-AVNE
☐ G-29-1		G-APRJ
☐ U-0247		G-AGOY
☐ W-2		BAPC.85
☐ X-25		BAPC.274

Other markings

☐ SR-XP020		G-BZUG

Australia

☐ A2-4		VH-ALB
☐ A16-199	SF-R	G-BEOX
☐ A17-48		G-BPHR
☐ A21-14		G-AFOR
☐ A77-851		G-METE
☐ A81-17		G-AIMI
☐ A84-234		G-BURM
☐ N6-766		G-SPDR

Belgium

☐ 66		BAPC.19
☐ B-05		G-BDPP
☐ B-06		G-BDPU
☐ HD-75		G-AFDX
☐ T-24	UR-1	G-AMJD

Bolivia

☐ FAB-184		G-SIAI

Botswana

☐ OJ-1		G-BXFU
☐ OJ-8		G-BXFV

Burkino Faso

☐ BF8431	31	G-NRRA

Canada

☐ 622		N6699D
☐ RCAF 671		G-BNZC
☐ 920	QN-	CF-BXO
☐ 4188	-	G-ANOS
☐ 5429	Z	G-KAMM
☐ 16693	693	G-BLPG
☐ 18013	13	G-TRIC
☐ 18393		G-BCYK
☐ 20310	310	G-BSBG

China

☐	68	G-BVVG
☐ 50051		G-BAJJ
☐ 50055		G-BBWG
☐ 50258		G-ASDS
☐ HKG-6*		G-BPCL
☐ HKG-11*		G-BYRY
☐ HKG-13*		G-BXKW

Finland

☐ AV-57		G-EBNU

France

☐ 1 4513	S	G-BFYO
☐ 19		BAPC.136
☐ 20	315-SQ	G-BWGG
☐ 78		G-BIZK
☐ 124		G-BOSJ
☐ 143		G-MSAL
☐ 156		G-NIFE
☐ 157	1	G-AVEB
☐ 185	44-CA	G-BWLR
☐ 394		G-BIMO
☐ MS.824		G-AWBU
☐ 18-5395	CDG	G-CUBJ
☐ 51-7545	119	N14113
☐ 517692	142	G-TROY
☐ F-OTAN-6		G-BAYV

Germany

☐ 1		G-BWUE
☐ 1+4		G-BSLX
☐ 2+1	7334	G-SYFW
☐ 3		G-BAYV
☐ 4+--		G-AWHS
☐ 8+--		G-WULF
☐ -9		G-CCFW
☐ 14		BAPC.67
☐ 14		G-BSMD
☐ 17+TF		G-BZTJ
☐ 50 483	CW+BG	G-BXBD
☐ 97+04		G-APVF
☐ 99+32		G-BZGK
☐ 102/17		BAPC.88
☐ 152/17		G-ATJM
☐ 210/16		BAPC.56
☐ 403/17		G-CDXR
☐ 422/15		G-AVJO
☐ 425/17		BAPC.133
☐ 447/17		G-FOKK
☐ 450/17		G-BVGZ
☐ 694		BAPC.239
☐ 1227	DG+HO	G-FOKW
☐ 1480	6	BAPC.66
☐	C.L.1.1801/18	G-BNPV
☐	C.L.1.1803/18	G-BUYU
☐ 2292		BAPC.138
☐ 4477	GD+EG	G-RETA
☐ 5125/18		BAPC.110
☐ 6357	6	BAPC.74
☐ 7198/18		G-AANJ
☐ 10639	6 (Black)	G-USTV
☐ 191454		BAPC.271
☐ C19/15		BAPC.118
☐ D692		G-BVAW
☐ D-2692		G-STIG
☐ D5397/17		G-BFXL

☐ DR1/17		BAPC.139
☐	6G+ED	G-BZOB
☐	BU+CC	G-BUCC
☐	BU+CK	G-BUCK
☐	CC+43	G-CJCI
☐	CF+HF	EI-AUY
☐	DM+BK	G-BPHZ
☐	FI+S	G-BIRW
☐	GL+SU	G-GLSU
☐	KG+EM	G-ETME
☐	N8+AA	G-BFHD
☐	N9+AA	G-BECL
☐	NJ+C11	G-ATBG
☐	S4+A07	G-BWHP
☐	S5+B06	G-BSFB
☐	VK-NZ	G-BFHG

Hungary

☐ 503		G-BRAM

Ireland

☐ 161		G-CCCA
☐ 176		G-AMDD
☐ 177		G-BLIW

Israel

☐ 13		G-AHAY
☐ 171		G-AJMC

Italy

☐	W7	G-AGFT
☐ MM12822	20	G-FIST
☐ MM53211	ZI-4	BAPC.79
☐ MM52801	97-4	G-BBII

Japan

☐ 15-1585		BAPC.58
☐ 24		BAPC.83
☐ 997		BAPC.98

Netherlands

☐ 174	K	G-BEPV
☐ BI-005		G-BUVN
☐ A-12		G-APCU
☐ E-15		G-BIYU
☐ R-55		G-BLMI
☐ R-151		G-BIYR
☐ R-156		G-ROVE
☐ R-163		G-BIRH
☐ R-167		G-LION

North Korea

☐		G-BMZF

North Vietnam

☐ 1211		G-MIGG

Norway

☐ 423/427		G-AMRK
☐ 56321		G-BKPY

Oman

Serial	Code	Registration
417		G-RSAF
425		G-SOAF

Poland

Serial	Code	Registration
1018		G-ISKA

Portugal

Serial	Code	Registration
1365		G-DHPM
1373		G-CBJG
1377		G-BARS
1747		G-BGPB

Russia

Serial	Code	Registration
1 (White)		G-BZMY
1		G-YKSZ
07 (Yellow)		G-BMJY
9 (White)		G-OYAK
9		G-BVMU
10		G-BTZB
11 (Yellow)		G-YCII
26		G-BVXK
27 (Red)		G-YAKX
31 (Black)		G-YAKV
33 (Red)		G-YAKZ
36 (White)		G-IYAK
36 (White)		G-KYAK
39		G-XXVI
42 (White)		G-CBRU
48		G-CBSN
49		G-YAKU
50		G-CBRW
55		G-BVOK
61		G-YAKM
66		G-YAKN
139		G-BWOD
503		G-BRAM
893019	51	G-BZNT

Saudi Arabia

Serial	Code	Registration
1103		G-SMAS

South Africa

Serial	Code	Registration
92		G-BYCX

Spain

Serial	Code	Registration
E3B-153	781-75	G-BPTS
E3B-350	05-97	G-BHPL
E3B-369	781-32	G-BPDM
E3B-494	81-47	G-CDLC

Switzerland

Serial	Code	Registration
A-10		G-BECW
A-12		G-CCHY
A-50		G-CBCE
A-53		G-BZVS
A-57		G-BECT
A-125		G-BLKZ
A-806		G-BTLL
C-552		G-DORN
J-1167		G-MKVI
J-1573		G-VICI
J-1605		G-BLID
J-1758		G-BLSD
J-4021		G-HHAC
J-4031		G-BWFR
J-4058		G-HHAD
J-4072		G-HHAB
J-4081		G-HHAF
J-4090		G-SIAL
U-80		G-BUKK
U-95		G-BVGP
U-99		G-AXMT
U-110		G-PTWO
V-54		G-BVSD

U.S.A.

Serial	Code	Registration
1		G-BYPY
195700		G-OIDW
2538		N33870
7539	143	N63590
14		G-ISDN
17-6532	15	G-BSKS
18-0012		G-BLXT
18-2001		G-BIZV
112		G-BSWC
118		G-BSDS
169		N52485
1102	102	G-AZLE
1164		G-BKGL
14863		G-BGOR
16136	205	G-BRUJ
18263	822	N38940
111836	JZ-6	G-TSIX
111989		N33600
115042	TA-042	G-BGHU
115227		G-BKRA
115302	TP	G-BJTP
115353	A-373	G-AYPM
115684	VM	G-BKVM
124485	DF-A	G-BEDF
126603		G-BHWH
146289	2W	N99153
151632		G-BWGR
23		N49272
26		G-BAVO
27		G-AGYY
21714	201B	G-RUMM
24550	GP	G-PDOG
26922	AK 402	G-RADR
28521	TA-521	G-TVIJ
29261		G-CDET
☑ 212540	RD 40	G-BBHK
217786	25	CF-EQS
219993		NX793QG
226413	ZU-N	N47DD
228473		G-BLZW
231983	IY-G	F-BDRS
236657	D-72	G-BGSJ
237123		BAPC.157
238410	A-44	G-BHPK
243809		BAPC.185
252983		N66630
298177	R-8	N6438C
3		BAPC.140
Mar-23		G-BRHP
379		G-ILLE
3072	72	G-TEXN
3397	174	G-OBEE
30274		N203SA
31145	G-26	G-BBLH
31171		N7614C
31430		G-BHVV
31952		G-BRPR
314887		G-AJPI
☑ 315211	JB-Z	N1944A
315509	W7-S	G-BHUB
316250		G-AMJX
329405	A-23	G-BCOB
329417		G-BDHK
329471	F-44	G-BGXA
329601	D-44	G-AXHR
329854	R-44	G-BMKC
329934	B-72	G-BCPH
330238	A-24	G-LIVH
330485	C-44	G-AJES
343251	27	G-NZSS
41-33275	CE	G-BICE
42-17553	716	N1731B
42-35870	129	G-BWLJ
42-58678	IY	G-BRIY
42-78044		G-BRXL
42-84555	EP-H	G-ELMH
42-100766		6W-SAF
43	SC	G-AZSC
44		G-RJAH
44-9063		EI-ARS (2)
44-30861		N9089Z
44-42914		N31356
44-79609	S-44	G-BHXY
44-83184	7	G-RGUS
44-83868	N	N5237V
45-0951		G-BLFL
46-16130		G-BGCF
49		G-KITT
441		G-BTFG
4406	12	G-ONAF
40467	19	G-BTCC
46214	X-3	CF-KCG
413317	VF-B	N51RT
413573	B6-K	N6526D
413704	B7-H	G-BTCD
414419	LH-F	G-MSTG
433915		G-PBYA
436021		G-BWEZ
454467	J-44	G-BILI
454537	J-04	G-BFDL
461748	Y	G-BHDK
463209	WZ-S	BAPC.255
463864	HL-W	G-CBNM
472035		G-SIJJ
472216	HO-M	G-BIXL
472218	WZ-I	G-HAEC
472773	QP-M	G-CDHI
479744	49-M	G-BGPD
479766	63-D	G-BKHG
479781		G-AISS (2)
479897	JD	G-BOXJ
480015	M-44	G-AKIB
480133	B-44	G-BDCD
480173	H-57	G-RRSR
480321	H-44	G-FRAN
480480	E-44	G-BECN
480636	A-58	G-AXHP
480723	E5-J	G-BFZB
480752	E-39	G-BCXJ
480762		EI-BBV
493209	ANG	G-DDMV
5	146-11083	G-BNAI
51-11701	AAF258	G-BSZC
51-15319	A-319	G-FUZZ
54-2445	A-445	G-OTAN
54-2447		G-SCUB
54884	D-57-	N61787

☐ 56498		N44914
☐ 6-1042	7	G-BMZX
☐ 624	D-39	G-BVMH
☐ 669		G-CCXA
☐ 699		G-CCXB
☐ 72-21509	129	G-UHIH
☐ 7797		G-BFAF
☐ 85		G-BTBI
☐ 854		G-BTBH
☐ 855		N56421
☐ 897	E	G-BJEV
☐ 8178	FU-178	G-SABR
☐ 8242	FU-242	N196B
☐ 80105	19	G-CCBN
☐ 80425	4-WT	G-RUMT
☐ 90678	27	G-BRVG
☐ 92844	8	G-BXUL
☐ 93542	LTA-542	G-BRLV

Yugoslavia

| ☐ 30140 | | G-RADA |
| ☐ 30146 | | G-BSXD |

Unatributed

☐ 001		G-BYPY
☐ 52024	LK-A	G-HURR
☐ 442795		BAPC.199

UK Aviation Museums

This listing is a snapshot of what may be found in the larger museums and collections in the UK. The locations listed are those that offer regular public access.

Many of the entries are active aircraft and as such may not be present on any given day.

The listing is presented in alphabetical order by name.

Aeroventure
Doncaster, South Yorkshire

☐ G-AEJZ	Mignet H.M.14
☐ G-ALYB	Auster 5
☐ G-AOKO	Percival Prentice T.1
☐ G-APMY	Piper PA-23-160
☐ G-ARHX	D.H.104 Dove
☐ G-MJKP	Hiway Skytrike
☐ EI-JWN	Robinson R22
☐ N3188H	Aircoupe
☐ N4565L	Douglas DC-3
☐ K158	Austin Whippet replica
☐ WA662	Meteor T.7
☐ WB733	DHC-1 Chipmunk T.10
☐ WB969	Slingsby Sedbergh
☐ WE987	Slingsby Prefect TX.1
☐ WF122	Sea Prince T.1
☐ WX788	Venom NF.3
☐ WZ822	Slingsby Grasshopper
☐ XA870	Whirlwind HAS.1
☐ XD439	Vampire T.11
☐ XE317	Sycamore HR.14
☐ XE935	Vampire T.11
☐ XJ398	Whirlwind HAR.9
☐ XM350	Jet Provost T.3A
☐ XM561	Skeeter AOP.12
☐ XN386	Whirlwind HAR.9
☐ XP190	Scout AH.1
☐ XP706	Lightning F.3
☐ XS481	Wessex HU.5
☐ XS897	Lightning F.6
☐ XT242	Bell 473 Sioux
☐ XX411	Gazelle AH.1
☐ E-424	Hunter F.51

Airborne Forces Museum
Aldershot, Hampshire

☐ KP208	C47 Dakota

Battle of Britain Memorial Flight - Visitor Centre
RAF Coningsby, Lincolnshire

☐ P7350	Spitfire IIA
☐ AB910	Spitfire VB
☐ LF363	Hurricane IIC
☐ MK356	Spitfire IX
☐ PA474	Lancaster I
☐ PM631	Spitfire PR.XIX
☐ PS915	Spitfire PR.XIX
☐ PZ865	Hurricane II
☐ TE311	Spitfire XVI
☐ WG486	Chipmunk T.10
☐ WK518	Chipmunk T.10

☐ ZA947	Dakota III

Bouton Paul Aircraft Heritage Project
Wolverhampton, W.Midlands

☐ L7005	Defiant Replica
☐ PD585	Slingsby Cadet TX.1
☐ WN149	Balliol T.2
☐ WT877	Slingsby Cadet TX.3
☐ WZ755	Slingsby Grasshopper
☐ XR662	Jet Provost T.4

Bournemouth Aviation Museum
Hangar 600, Bournemouth Airport

☐ G-AGSH	DH.89A Dragon Rapide
☐ G-AZMF	BAC 111-530FX
☐ G-BEYF	H.P. Herald
☐ G-BKRL	Leopard
☐ G-BRNM	Leopard
☐ G-BWOF	Jet Provost T.5
☐ G-EWHH	Hunter F.58
☐ N7SY	Sea Prince T.1
☐ KF488	Harvard IIB
☐ WL505	Vampire FB.9
☐ WR421	Venom FB.50
☐ WS776	Meteor NF.14
☐ WW421	Provost T.1
☐ WZ589	Vampire T.11
☐ WZ798	Slingsby Grasshopper
☐ XE856	Vampire T.11
☐ XE920	Vampire T.11
☐ XG160	Hunter F.6A
☐ XR537	Gnat T.1
☐ XR954	Gnat T.1
☐ XT257	Wessex HAS.3
☐ XX897	Buccaneer S.2B
☐ C-552	EKW C-3605
☐ E-402	Hunter F.51

Brenzett Aeronautical Museum
Ivychurch Road, Romney Marsh, Kent

☐ WH657	Canberra B.2
☐ XK625	Vampire T.11

Bristol Aero Collection
Hangar A1, Kemble Airfield, Glos

☐ G-EASQ	Bristol Babe III (rep)
☐ G-ALBN	Bristol 173
☐ EL-WXA	Britannia 253
☐ RH746	Brigand TF.1
☐ XF785	Bristol 173
☐ XJ917	Sycamore HR.14
☐ XM496	Britannia 253
☐ XV798	Harrier GR.3
☐ A92-708	Jindivik 3

Bristol Industrial Museum
Bristol Docks

☐ XL829	Sycamore HR.14

British Aviation Heritage Collection
Bruntingthorpe, Leicestershire

☐ G-CPDA	Comet 4C
☐ F-BTGV	Super Guppy
☐ SX-OAD	Boeing 747-212B
☐ XH558	Vulvcan B.2

☐ XM715	Victor B.2
☐ XX894	Buccaneer S.2B
☐ XX900	Buccaneer S.2B
☐ XZ382	Jaguar GR.1
☐ 85	Mystere IVA
☐ 1018	PZL TS-11

Brooklands Museum
Weybridge, Surrey

☐ BAPC-187	Roe I biplane (Rep)
☐ BAPC-256	Demoiselle (Rep)
☐ BGA3922	Abbott-Baynes Scud
☐ G-EBED	Vickers 60 Viking (Rep)
☐ G-AACA	Avro 504K (Rep)
☐ G-ADRY	Mignet HM.14 (Rep)
☐ G-AEKV	Kronfeld Drone
☐ G-AGRU	Viking 1A
☐ G-APEP	V.953 Merchantman
☐ G-APIM	Viscount 806
☐ G-ASYD	BAC 111-475AM
☐ G-BBDG	Concorde 100
☐ G-BJHV	Voisin Scale Replica
☐ G-LOTI	Bleriot XI (Rep)
☐ G-MJPB	Ladybird Microlight
☐ G-VTOL	Harrier T.52
☐ A4O-AB	VC10
☐ B7270	Sopwith Camel F1 (Rep)
☐ F5475	R.A.F. S.E.5a (Rep)
☐ K5673	Hawker Fury I (Rep)
☐ N2980	Wellington IA
☐ Z2389	Hurricane IIA
☐ WF372	Varsity T.1
☐ XF314	Hunter F.51
☐ XL621	Hunter T.7
☐ XP984	Hawker P.1127
☐ E-421	Hunter F.51

Caernarfon Airworld Museum
Caernarfon Airport, Gwynedd

☐ G-AMLZ	Percival Prince
☐ G-MBEP	American Eagle 315
☐ G-MJSM	Weedhopper
☐ WM961	Sea Hawk FB.5
☐ WN499	Dragonfly HR.5
☐ WT694	Hunter F.1
☐ WV781	Sycamore HR.12
☐ XA282	Cadet TX.3
☐ XH837	Javelin FAW.7
☐ XJ726	Whirlwind HAR.10
☐ XK623	Vampire T.11
☐ XL618	Hunter T.7

Carpetbagger Aviation Museum
Harrington, Northamptonshire

☐ 42-12417	Harvard IIB

Charnwood Museum
Loughborough, Leicestershire

☐ G-AJRH	Auster J/1N Alpha

City of Norwich Aviation Museum
Horsham St Faith, Norfolk

☐ G-ASKK	H.P. Herald
☐ G-BHMY	Fokker F.27
☐ G-BTAZ	Evans VP-2
☐ G-OVNE	Cessna 401

☐ WK654	Meteor F.8
☐ XE683	Hunter F.51
☐ XG172	Hunter F.6A
☐ XM612	Vulcan B.2
☐ XP355	Whirlwind HAR.10
☐ XX109	Jaguar GR.1
☐ 121	Mystere IVA
☐ 16718	T-33A
☐ 53-686	Lightning F.53

Cranwell Aviation Heritage Centre
Sleaford, Lincolnshire

☐ XE946	Vampire T.11
☐ XP556	Jet Provost T.4

Croydon Airport Visitor Centre
Purley Way, Croydon

☐ G-AOXL	DH.114 Heron 2D
☐ T7793	DH.82A Tiger Moth

de Haviland Aircraft Heritage Centre
London Colney, Hertfordshire

☐ BAPC-216	DH.88 Comet
☐ BAPC-232	Horsa
☐ G-ABLM	Cierva C.24
☐ G-ADOT	DH.87B Hornet Moth
☐ G-AFOJ	DH.94 Moth Minor
☐ G-AKDW	DH.89 Dragon Rapide
☐ G-ANRX	DH.82A Tiger Moth
☐ G-AOTI	DH.114 Heron
☐ G-AREA	DH.104 Dove
☐ G-ARYC	DH.125
☐ G-AVFH	DH.121 Trident 2
☐ D-IFSB	DH.104 Dove 6
☐ F-BGNX	DH.106 Comet 1XB
☐ VP-FAK	DHC-3 Otter
☐ W4050	DH.98 Mosquito
☐ LF789	DH.82 Queen Bee
☐ TA122	DH.98 Mosquito FB.VI
☐ TA634	DH.98 Mosquito TT.35
☐ WM729	DH.100 Vampire NF.10
☐ WP790	DHC-1 Chipmunk
☐ WR539	DH.100 Vampire FB.4
☐ WX853	DH.112 Venom NF.3
☐ XG730	DH.112 Sea Venom
☐ XJ565	DH.110 Sea Vixen
☐ XJ772	DH.115 Vampire T.11
☐ J-1008	DH.100 Vampire FB.6
☐ J-1632	DH.100 Vampire FB.50
☐ J-1790	DH.100 Vampire FB.54

Dumfries & Galloway Aviation Museum
Heathhall Industrial Estate, Dumfries

☐ G-AWZJ	DH.121 Trident 3B
☐ G-MMIX	MBA Tiger Cub 440
☐ P7540	Spitfire 1
☐ WA576	Sycamore III
☐ WD386	DHC-1 Chipmunk
☐ WL375	Meteor T.7
☐ WT746	Hunter F.4
☐ XD547	Vampire T.11
☐ XP557	Jet Provost T.4
☐ 318	Mystere IV
☐ FT-36	Lockheed T-33
☐ 54-2163	F-100D Super Sabre
☐ 35075	SAAB Draken

IWM Duxford (All collections)
Duxford, Cambridgeshire

☐ G-AANM	Bristol F.2b Fighter
☐ G-ACAA	Bristol F.2b Fighter
☐ G-ACMN	DH.85
☐ G-ACUU	Cierva C.30A
☐ G-AFBS	Miles Magister
☐ G-AGJG	DH.89A Dragon Rapide
☐ G-AGTO	Auster J/1
☐ G-AHTW	Oxford I
☐ G-AIYR	DH.89A Dragon Rapide
☐ G-AKAZ	Piper J.3C-65
☐ G-AKIF	DH.89A Dragon Rapide
☐ G-ALDG	HP Hermes 4
☐ G-ALFU	DH.104 Dove 6
☐ G-ALWF	Viscount 701
☐ G-ALZO	Airspeed Ambassador
☐ G-ANPE	DH.82A Tiger Moth
☐ G-ANRM	DH.82A Tiger Moth
☐ G-ANTK	Avro York
☐ G-AOVT	Britannia 312
☐ G-APAO	DH.82A Tiger Moth
☐ G-APDB	DH.106 Comet 4
☐ G-APPM	DHC.1 Chipmunk
☐ G-APWJ	H.P. Herald
☐ G-ASGC	Super VC10
☐ G-ASTG	Nord 1002
☐ G-AVFB	Trident 2E
☐ G-AVMU	BAC-111
☐ G-AXDN	Concorde 101
☐ G-AXNW	Stampe SV-4C
☐ G-AYGE	Stampe SV-4C
☐ G-BEDF	B-17G
☐ G-BFYO	Spad XIII
☐ G-BGPB	Harvard IV
☐ G-BKGL	Beech 18
☐ G-BLKZ	Pilatus P.2
☐ G-BPHZ	Morane MS.505
☐ G-BPIV	Blenheim IV
☐ G-BSKP	Spitfire F.XIVe
☐ G-BTCC	Grumman Hellcat
☐ G-BTCD	P-51D Mustang
☐ G-BTXI	Harvard IIIB
☐ G-BUCJ	DHC.2 Beaver
☐ G-BUCM	Sea Fury FB.11
☐ G-BUOS	Spitfire FR.XVIIIe
☐ G-BWHI	DHC-1 Chipmunk T.10
☐ G-BWWK	Hawker Nimrod
☐ G-BXBD	Bucker Jungmann
☐ G-BXCV	DHC-1 Chipmunk T.10
☐ G-BXVI	Spitfire LF.XVIe
☐ G-BYNF	NA-64 Yale
☐ G-BYSJ	DHC-1 Chipmunk
☐ G-BZGA	DHC-1 Chipmunk
☐ G-BZGB	DHC-1 Chipmunk
☐ G-BZGK	OV-10B Bronco
☐ G-BZGL	OV-10B Bronco
☐ G-CBAB	Bulldog T.1
☐ G-CBLK	Hawker Hind
☐ G-CBNM	P-51D Mustang
☐ G-CCCA	Spitfire TR.9
☐ G-CCOM	Lysander IIIA
☐ G-CCVH	Curtiss H-75
☐ G-CCWB	Aero L-39ZA
☐ G-FGID	F1D Corsair
☐ G-GLAD	Gloster Gladiator
☐ G-HURI	Hurricane XIIB
☐ G-HURY	Hurricane IV
☐ G-LFVB	Spitfire V
☐ G-LFVC	Spitfire LF.Vc

☐ G-LIZY	Lysander IIIA
☐ G-MKVB	Spitfire VB
☐ G-MXVI	Spitfire LF.XVIe
☐ G-OXVI	Spitfire XVI
☐ G-PBYA	PBY-5 Canso
☐ G-PMNF	Spitfire HF.IX
☐ G-PSIC	P-51C Mustang
☐ G-RRSR	Piper J.3C-65
☐ G-RUMM	Grumman Bearcat
☐ G-RUMT	Grumman Tigercat
☐ G-RUMW	Grumman Wildcat
☐ G-SPIT	Spitfire XIVe
☐ G-TBRD	Lockheed T-33
☐ G-THUN	Republic P-47D
☐ G-TROY	T-28 Fennec
☐ G-USUK	Colt 2500A
☐ CF-EQS	Stearman A75N1
☐ CF-KCG	TBM Avenger
☐ EI-AUY	Morane MS.502
☐ F-BDRS	B-17G
☐ LN-AMY	AT-6 Harvard
☐ N47DD	P-47D Thunderbolt
☐ NX793QG	Bell P-39
☐ N7614C	B-25J
☐ N14113	T-28 Fennec
☐ FLARF2809	Polikarpov I-15
☐ SE-BRG	Firefly TT.1
☐ SE-CAU	Firefly TT.1
☐ E2581	Bristol F.2B
☐ F3556	R.E.8
☐ N4877	Anson I
☐ V9312	Lysander
☐ Z2315	Hurricane IIB
☐ KB889	Lancaster X
☐ LZ766	Percival Proctor
☐ MH434	Spitfire IX
☐ ML407	Spitfire T.9
☐ ML796	Sunderland MR.5
☐ NF370	Fairy Swordfish III
☐ PK624	Spitfire F.22
☐ TA719	Mosquito TT.35
☐ TG528	Hastings C.1A
☐ VN485	Spitfire 24
☐ WH725	Canberra B.2
☐ WJ945	Varsity T.1
☐ WK991	Meteor F.8
☐ WM969	Sea Hawk FB.5
☐ WZ590	Vampire T.11
☐ WZ979	DHC-1 Chipmunk T.10
☐ XE627	Hunter F.6
☐ XF708	Shackleton Mk.3
☐ XG613	Sea Venom FAW.21
☐ XG743	Sea Vampire T.22
☐ XG797	Gannet ECM.6
☐ XH648	Victor BK.1A
☐ XH897	Javelin FAW.9
☐ XJ824	Vulcan B.2
☐ XK936	Whirlwind HAS.7
☐ XM135	Lightning F.1A
☐ XN239	Slingsby Cadet TX.3
☐ XP281	Auster AOP.9
☐ XR222	TSR.2
☐ XS567	Wasp HAS.1
☐ XS576	DH.110 Sea Vixen
☐ XS863	Wessex HAS.1
☐ XT581	Northrop SD-1
☐ XV474	Phantom FGR.2
☐ XV865	Buccaneer S.2B
☐ XX108	Jaguar GR.1A
☐ XZ133	Harrier GR.3
☐ ZA465	Tornado GR.1

☐ ZE359	F-4J Phantom
☐ A-549	Pucara
☐ A19-144	Beaufighter XI
☐ UB425	Spitfire XI
☐ 18393	CF-100
☐ 9893	Bollingbroke IVT
☐ 501	MIG21
☐ 3794	MIG15
☐ 57	Mystere IVA
☐ 1190	Bf 109E
☐ 100143	Focke-Achgelis Fa330
☐ 96+21	MIL Mi-24
☐ 3685	Mitsubishi A6M Zero
☐ 6316	Junkers Ju 52/3mge
☐ 1133	BAC Strikemaster
☐ B2I-103	CASA 2.111B
☐ 43-15509	C-47A
☐ 44-61748	TB-29A
☐ 44-51228	B-24M
☐ 48-0178	F-86A Sabre
☐ 51-4286	Lockheed T-33A
☐ 54-2165	F-100D Super Sabre
☐ 56-0689	B-52D
☐ 56-6692	Lockheed U-2C
☐ 58-1822	F-105 Thunderchief
☐ 64-17962	Lockheed SR-71
☐ 67-0120	F-111E
☐ 72-21605	Bell UH-1H
☐ 76-0020	F-15
☐ 77-0259	Fairchild A-10A
☐ 252983	Schweizer T3A

East Midlands Aero Park
East Midlands Airport

☐ G-APES	Vanguard
☐ G-BEOZ	Argosy
☐ G-CSZB	Viscount 807
☐ G-FRJB	Britten Sheriff
☐ WH740	Canberra T.17
☐ WL626	Varsity T.1
☐ WM224	Meteor TT.20
☐ XD382	Vampire T.11
☐ XG588	Whirlwind 3
☐ XL569	Hunter T.7
☐ XM575	Vulcan B2
☐ XS876	Wessex HAS.1
☐ XT480	Wessex HU.5
☐ XT604	Wessex HC.2
☐ XV350	Buccaneer S.2B
☐ ZF558	Ligtning F.53

Farnborough Air Sciences Trust
Farnborough, Hampshire.

☐ G-AVMJ	BAC-111
☐ WV383	Hunter T.7
☐ WV795	Sea hawk FGA.6
☐ XN500	Jet Provost T.3A
☐ XP516	Gnat T.1
☐ XS420	Lightning T.5
☐ XW566	Jaguar B
☐ ZA195	Sea Harrier FA.2
☐ E-402	Hunter F.51
☐ 503	MiG21

Fenland Aviation Museum
3 Miles north of Wisbech

☐ XD434	Vampire T.11
☐ XM402	Jet Provost T.3

☐ XS459	Lightning T.5

Flambards Village
On the A3083 near RNAS Culdrose

☐ XG831	Gannet ECM.6
☐ XS887	Wessex HAS.1

Fleet Air Arm Museum
RNAS Yeovilton, Somerset
(Includes store)

☐ G-AZAZ	Bensen B.8M
☐ G-BFXL	Albatros D Va
☐ G-BGWZ	Eclipse Super Eagle
☐ G-BSST	Concorde
☐ B6401	Sopwith Camel Replica
☐ D5397	Albatros D.Va Replica
☐ L2301	Walrus I
☐ L2940	Blackburn Skua
☐ N1854	Fairey Fulmar
☐ N2078	Sopwith Baby
☐ N4389	Fairey Albacore
☐ N5378	Sea Gladiator
☐ N5419	Bristol Scout D Replica
☐ N5492	Sopwith Triplane Replica
☐ N6452	Sopwith Pup Replica
☐ P4139	Swordfish II
☐ S1287	Fairey Flycatcher
☐ Z2033	Fairey Firefly
☐ AL246	Martlet I
☐ DP872	Barracuda II
☐ EX976	AT-6D Harvard III
☐ KD431	Corsair IV
☐ KE209	Hellcat II
☐ LZ551	Sea Vampire 1
☐ SX137	Seafire F.17
☐ VH127	Fairey Firefly TT.4
☐ VR137	Wyvern TF.1
☐ VV106	Supermarine 510
☐ VX272	Hawker P.1052
☐ VX595	Dragonfly HR.5
☐ WA473	Attacker F.1
☐ WG774	BAC 221
☐ WJ231	Sea Fury FB.11
☐ WM292	Meteor TT.20
☐ WN493	Dragonfly HR.5
☐ WP313	Sea Prince T.1
☐ WS103	Meteor T.7
☐ WT121	Skyraider AEW.1
☐ WV106	Skyraider AEW.1
☐ WV856	Sea Hawk FGA.6
☐ WW138	Sea Venom FAW.22
☐ XA127	Sea Vampire T.22
☐ XA466	Gannet COD.4
☐ XA864	Whirlwind HAR.1
☐ XB446	Avenger ECM.6
☐ XB480	Hiller HT.1
☐ XD317	Scimitar F.1
☐ XG574	Whirlwind HAR.3
☐ XG594	Whirlwind HAS.7
☐ XJ481	Sea Vixen FAW.1
☐ XK488	Blackburn NA.39
☐ XL503	Gannet AEW.3
☐ XL580	Hunter T.8M
☐ XL853	Whirlwind HAS.7
☐ XN332	Saro P.531
☐ XN334	Saro P.531
☐ XN462	Jet Provost T.3A
☐ XN957	Buccaneer S.1
☐ XP142	Wessex HAS.3

☐ XP841	HP.115
☐ XP980	Hawker P.1127
☐ XS508	Wessex HU.5
☐ XS527	Wasp HAS.1
☐ XS590	Sea Vixen FAW.2
☐ XT176	Sioux AH.1
☐ XT427	Wasp HAS.1
☐ XT482	Wessex HU.5
☐ XT596	YF-4K Phantom
☐ XT769	Wessex HU.5
☐ XT778	Wasp HAS.1
☐ XV333	Buccaneer S.2B
☐ XW864	Gazelle HT.2
☐ XX411	Gazelle AH.1
☐ XZ493	Sea Harrier FRS.1
☐ XZ499	Sea Harrier FA.2
☐ 0729	Beech T-34C
☐ AE-422	Bell UH-1H
☐ 01420	MiG15
☐ 100545	Fa.330A-1
☐ 15-1585	Yokosuka Ohka 11
☐ 102/17	Fokker Dr I

Flying Aces Collection
Compton Abbas Airfield, Dorset

☐ G-AVJO	Fokker E.III Replica
☐ G-AWBU	Morana-Saulnier N Rep
☐ G-BAAF	ManninFlanders MF1 Replica
☐ G-BPOB	Sopwith Camel Replica
☐ G-BPVE	Bleriot XI Replica

Gatwick Aviation Museum
Charlwood, Surrey

☐ G-EGHB	Ercoupe 415D
☐ G-TURP	Gazelle 1
☐ VZ638	Meteor T.7
☐ WF118	Sea Prince T.1
☐ WH773	Canberra PR.7
☐ WP908	Sea Prince T.1
☐ WR974	Shackleton MR.3/3
☐ WR982	Shackleton MR.3/3
☐ WW442	Provost T.1
☐ XE489	Sea Hawk FB.5
☐ XJ587	Sea Vixen FAW.2
☐ XK885	Pembroke C.1
☐ XL591	Hunter T.7
☐ XL472	Gannet AEW.3
☐ XN923	Buccaneer S.1
☐ XP351	Whirlwind HAR.10
☐ XP398	Whirlwind HAR.10
☐ XV751	Harrier GR.3
☐ XX734	Jaguar GR.1
☐ ZF579	Lightning F.53
☐ E-430	Hunter F.51
☐ J-1605	Venom FB.50

Glasgow Museum of Transport
Glasgow city centre

☐ LA198	Spitfire F.21

The Helicopter Museum
Weston-super-Mare, Somerset

☐ G-ACWM	Cierva C.30A
☐ G-ALSX	Sycamore 3
☐ G-ANFH	Westland WS-55 srs 1
☐ G-AODA	Westland WS-55 srs 3

☐ G-AOZE	Widgeon 2
☐ G-ARVN	Servotec Grasshopper
☐ G-ASCT	Bensen B.8M
☐ G-ASHD	Brantly B2B
☐ G-ASTP	Hiller UH-12C
☐ G-ATBZ	Wessex 60
☐ G-ATKV	Westland WS-55 srs 3
☐ G-AVKE	Thruxton Gadfly
☐ G-AVNE	Wessex 60
☐ G-AWRP	Cierva Grasshopper
☐ G-AZYB	Bell 47H
☐ G-BAPS	Campbell Cougar
☐ G-BGHF	Westland WG.30
☐ G-BKGD	Westland WG.30
☐ G-ELEC	Westland WG.30
☐ G-HAUL	Westland WG.30
☐ G-LYNX	Lynx AH.1
☐ G-OAPR	Brantly B2B
☐ G-OTED	Robinson R22HP
☐ G-PASA	MBB Bo105D
☐ G-PASB	MBB Bo105D
☐ G-48-1	Sycamore III
☐ D-HMQV	Bolkow Bo102
☐ D-HOAY	Kamov Ka-26
☐ F-BMHC	SA.321F Super Frelon
☐ F-WQAP	Aerospatiale Dauphin
☐ N114WG	Westland WG.30
☐ OO-SHW	Bell 47H-1
☐ SP-SAY	Mil Mi-2
☐ 5N-ABW	Widgeon 2
☐ VZ962	Dragonfly HR.1
☐ WG719	Dragonfly HR.5
☐ XA862	Whirlwind HAR.1
☐ XD163	Whirlwind HAR.10
☐ XG452	Belvedere HC.1
☐ XG547	Sycamore HR.14
☐ XG596	Whirlwind HAS.7
☐ XK940	Whirlwind HAS.7
☐ XL811	Skeeter
☐ XM330	Wessex HAS.1
☐ XP165	Scout AH.1
☐ XP404	Whirlwind HAR.10
☐ XR486	Whirlwind HCC.12
☐ XR526	Wessex HC.2
☐ XS149	Wessex HAS.3
☐ XT190	Sioux AH.1
☐ XT443	Wasp HAS.1
☐ XT472	Wessex HU.5
☐ XV733	Wessex HCC.4
☐ XW839	Westland WG.13
☐ XX910	Lynx HAS.2
☐ ZE477	Lynx 3
☐ ZH647	EH.101
☐ 1005	PZL SM-2
☐ 96+26	Mil Mi-24D
☐ 2007	Mil Mi-1
☐ 09147	Mil Mi-4
☐ S-881	Sikorsky UH-19B
☐ S-886	Sikorsky UH-19B
☐ 108/CDL	Sud Djinn
☐ 51-16622	Piasecki HUP-3
☐ 66-16579	Bell UH-1H
☐ 67-16506	Hughes OH-6A
☐ 145872	Sikorsky CH-37C

Hooton Park Trust
Hooton Park, Cheshire

☐ G-AGPG	Avro XIX srs 2
☐ G-AJEB	Auster J/1N Alpha

The Imperial War Museum
Lambeth, South London

☐ 2699	RAF B.E.2c
☐ N6812	Sopwith 2F.1 Camel
☐ R6915	Spitfire 1
☐ 120235	Heinkel He 162A-1
☐ 477663	Fieseler Fi 103 V1
☐ 733682	Focke-Wulf Fw 190A-8
☐ 44-72258	North American P-51D

The Imperial War Museum North
Trafford Park, Manchester

☐ 159233	AV-8A

Lashenden Air Warfare Museum
Headcorn Airfield, Kent.

☐ BAPC-91	Fieseler Fi 103R-4
☐ WZ589	Vampire T.11
☐ XN380	Whirlwind HAS.7
☐ 84	Mystere IVA
☐ 100549	Focke-Achgelis Fa 330A1
☐ 56-3938	North American F-100F

Lincolnshire Aviation Heritage Centre
East Kirkby Airfield, Spilsby, Lincolnshire.

☐ AE436	Hampden
☐ MJ627	Spitfire Tr.IX
☐ NP294	Proctor IV
☐ NX611	Lancaster

Manchester Airport Viewing Park
Manchester Airport, Ringway.

☐ G-AWZK	Trident 3B
☐ G-BOAC	Concorde
☐ G-DMCA	Douglas DC-10-30
☐ G-IRJX	Avro RJX-100
☐ XD624	Vampire T.11

Midland Air Museum
Coventry Airport, Baginton, Coventry.

☐ BAPC-9	Humber Monoplane rep
☐ BAPC-126	Druine D.31 Turbulent
☐ BAPC-179	Sopwith Pup
☐ G-EBJG	Parnall Pixie III
☐ G-AEGV	H.M.14 Pou-Du-Ciel
☐ G-ALCU	DH.104 Dove 2
☐ G-AOKZ	Percival Prentice
☐ G-APJJ	Fairey Ultralight
☐ G-APRL	Argosy
☐ G-APWN	Whirlwind Srs 3
☐ G-ARYB	HS.125
☐ G-MJWH	Vortex 120
☐ EE531	Meteor F.4
☐ VF301	Vampire F.1
☐ VS623	Percival Prentice T.1
☐ VT935	Boulton Paul P.111A
☐ WF922	Canberra PR.3
☐ WS838	Meteor NF.14
☐ WV797	Sea Hawk FGA.6
☐ XA508	Gannett T.2
☐ XA699	Javelin FAW.5
☐ XD626	DH-115 Vampire T.11
☐ XE855	DH-115 Vampire T.11
☐ XF382	Hunter F.6A
☐ XG190	Hunter F.51

☐ XK741	Folland Gnat F.1
☐ XK789	Slingsby Grasshopper
☐ XL360	Vulcan B.2
☐ XN685	Sea Vixen FAW.2
☐ XR771	Lightning F.6
☐ ZE694	Sea Harrier FA2
☐ E-425	Hunter F.51
☐ 70	Mystere IVA
☐ 280020	Flettner Fl 282B Kolibri
☐ 408	PZL TS-11
☐ 959	MIG21 SPS
☐ 55-713	Lightning T.55
☐ 29640	SAAB J-29F
☐ 48-0242	F-86A Sabre
☐ 51-4419	Lockheed T-33
☐ 51-17473	Lockheed T-33
☐ 54-2174	F-100D Super Sabre
☐ 56-0312	TF-101 Voodoo
☐ 58-2062	DHC-2 Beaver
☐ 62-4535	Kaman HH-43B Huskie
☐ 63-7414	F-4C Phantom
☐ 63-7699	F-4C Phantom
☐ R-756	F-104G Starfighter
☐ 06 Red	MIL Mi-24D

Montrose Air Station Museum
North of Montrose on the A92

☐ XD542	Vampire T.11
☐ XE340	Sea Hawk FGA.5
☐ XE874	Vampire T.11
☐ XJ380	Sycamore HR.14
☐ XJ723	Whirlwind HAR.10

Muckleburgh Collection
Weybourne, Norfolk.

☐ WD686	Meteor NF.11
☐ XZ968	Harrier GR.3

Museum of Army Flying
Middle Wallop airfield, Hampshire

☐ BAPC-261	Hotspur
☐ G-APOI	Skeeter MK.8
☐ G-AXKS	Bell 47 G-4A
☐ G-OAAC	Airtour AH-77B
☐ P-5	Hafner Rotachute
☐ B-415	Hafner Rotabuggy replica
☐ N5195	Sopwith Pup
☐ T9707	Miles Magister
☐ KJ351	Airspeed Horsa
☐ TJ569	Auster 5
☐ TK777	Hamilcar
☐ WG432	DHC-1 Chipmunk
☐ WJ358	Auster 6
☐ WZ721	Auster AOP.9
☐ WZ772	Slingsby Grasshopper
☐ XG502	Sycamore HR.14
☐ XK776	ML Utility
☐ XL813	Skeeter AOP.12
☐ XM819	Edgar Percival E.P.9
☐ XP821	DHC-2 Beaver
☐ XP822	DHC-2 Beaver
☐ XP847	Scout AH.1
☐ XP910	Scout AH.1
☐ XR232	Alouette 2
☐ XT108	Agusta-Bell 47G Sioux
☐ XV127	Scout AH.1
☐ XX153	Lynx
☐ ZA737	Gazelle AH.1

☐ AE-409	Bell UH-1H
☐ 42-43809	Waco Hadrian
☐ 51-111989	Cessna L-19 Bird Dog
☐ 70-15990	Bell AH-1F

Museum of Artillery
Woolwich, Greater London

☐ XR271	Auster AOP.9

Museum of Berkshire Aviation
Woodley, Near Reading, Berkshire.

☐ G-APWA	Handley Page Herald
☐ G-MIOO	Miles M.100 Student
☐ L6906	Miles Magister
☐ DL349	Miles Master
☐ XG883	Gannett T.5
☐ XJ389	Fairey Jet Gyrodyne

Museum of Flight
East Fortune airfield, East Lothian

☐ BAPC-49	Pilcher Hawk
☐ BAPC-70	Auster AOP.5
☐ BAPC-160	Chargus 18/50
☐ BAPC-195	Birdman Moonraker
☐ BAPC-196	Southdown Sigma
☐ BAPC-197	Scotkites Cirrus
☐ BAPC-245	Electra Flyer Floater
☐ BAPC-246	Highway Clodbase
☐ W-2	Weir Autogiro
☐ G-ACVA	Kay Gyroplane
☐ G-ACYK	Spartan Cruiser
☐ G-AFJU	Miles Monarch
☐ G-AGBN	GAL 42 Cygnet
☐ G-AHKY	Miles M.18
☐ G-AMOG	Viscount 701
☐ G-ANOV	DH.104 Dove
☐ G-AOEL	DH.82A Tiger Moth
☐ G-ARCX	Meteor NF.14
☐ G-ASUG	Beech E.18S
☐ G-ATFG	Brantly B.2B
☐ G-ATOY	Piper PA-24-260
☐ G-AVPC	Druine Turbulent
☐ G-AXEH	Scottish Aviation Bulldog
☐ G-BBVF	Twin Pioneer
☐ G-BDFU	Dragonfly MPA
☐ G-BDIX	DH.106 Comet 4C
☐ G-BELF	BN-2 Islander
☐ G-BIRW	Morane-Saulnier MS.505
☐ G-BOAA	Concorde
☐ G-BVWK	Air & Space 18A
☐ G-BVWL	Air & Space 18A
☐ G-JSSD	BAe Jetstream 31
☐ G-MBJX	Hiway Super Scorpion
☐ G-MBPM	Eurowing Goldwing
☐ G-MMLI	Mainair Tri-Flyer
☐ VH-SNB	DH.84 Dragon
☐ V H-UQB	DH.80A Puss Moth
☐ RD220	Beaufighter TF.X
☐ TE462	Spitfire XVI
☐ VM360	Anson C.19
☐ WF259	Sea Hawk F.2
☐ WV493	Provost T.1
☐ WW145	Sea Venom FAW.22
☐ XA109	Sea VampirevT.22
☐ XA288	Slingsby Grasshopper
☐ XL762	Skeeter AOP.12
☐ XM597	Vulcan B2
☐ XN776	Lightning F.2A

☐ XT288	Buccaneer S.2B
☐ XV277	Harrier DB3
☐ ZE934	Tornado F.3T
☐ 9940	Bolingbroke IV
☐ 191659	Messerchmitt Me 163B-1
☐ 309	MI15
☐ 3677	MI15
☐ 155848	F4-S Phantom

Museum of Science & Industry in Manchester
Castlefield, Manchester

☐ BAPC-6	Roe Triplane replica
☐ BAPC-12	H.M.14 Flying Flea
☐ BAPC-98	Yokosuka MXY-7 Ohka
☐ BAPC-175	Volmer VJ.23
☐ BAPC-182	Wood Ornithopter
☐ G-EBZM	Avro Avian IIIa
☐ G-ABAA	Avro 504K
☐ G-ADAH	DH.89 Dragon Rapide
☐ G-APUD	Bensen B.7M
☐ G-AYTA	MS.880B Rallye
☐ G-MJXE	Mainair Tri-Flyer
☐ MT847	Spitfire FR.XIVe
☐ WG763	English Electric P.1A
☐ WP270	EoN Eton TX.1
☐ WR960	Shackleton AEW.2
☐ WT619	Hunter F.1
☐ WZ736	Avro 707A
☐ XG454	Belvedere HC.1
☐ XL824	Sycamore HR.14
☐ XS179	Jet Provost T.4

Newark Air Museum
Winthorpe Showground, Newark

☐ BAPC-43	H.M.14 Pou Du Ciel
☐ BAPC-183	Zurowski ZOP1
☐ G-AGOH	Auster J/1 Autocrat
☐ G-AHRI	DH.104 Dove I
☐ G-ANXB	DH.114 Heron 1B
☐ G-APVV	Mooney M.20A
☐ G-AXMB	Slingsby Cadet
☐ G-BFPZ	MS.880 Rallye
☐ G-BJAD	Clutton FRED
☐ G-BKPG	Luscombe P3 Rattler
☐ G-CCLT	Powerchute Kestrel
☐ G-MAZY	DH.82A Tiger Moth
☐ G-MBBZ	Vollmer VJ-24
☐ G-MBUE	MBA Tiger Cub 440
☐ G-MJCF	Hill Hummer
☐ G-MNRT	Sirocco
☐ VH-UTH	Monospar ST-12
☐ RA897	Slingsby Cadet TX.1
☐ TG517	Hastings T.5
☐ VL348	Avro Anson C.19
☐ VR249	Prentice T.1
☐ VZ608	Meteor FR.9
☐ VZ634	Meteor T.7
☐ WB624	DHC-1 Chipmunk T.10
☐ WF369	Varsity T.1
☐ WH791	Canberra PR.7
☐ WH904	Canberra T.19
☐ WK277	Swift FR.5
☐ WM913	Sea Hawk FB.3
☐ WR977	Shackleton MR.3
☐ WS692	Meteor NF.12
☐ WS739	Meteor NF.14
☐ WT651	Hunter F.1
☐ WT933	Sycamore HR.14

☐ WV606	Provost T.1
☐ WV787	Canberra B.8
☐ WW217	Sea Venom FAW.22
☐ WX905	Venom NF.3
☐ XA239	Slingsby Grasshopper
☐ XD593	Vampite T.11
☐ XH992	Javelin FAW.8
☐ XJ560	Sea Vixen FAW.2
☐ XL764	Skeeter AOP.12
☐ XM383	Jet Provost T.3A
☐ XM594	Vulcan B.2
☐ XM685	Whirlwind HAS.7
☐ XN964	Buccaneer S.1
☐ XP226	Gannett AEW.3
☐ XR534	Gnat T.1
☐ XS417	Lightning T.5
☐ XT200	Sioux AH.1
☐ XV728	Wessex HC.2
☐ XW276	Gazelle AH.1
☐ XX492	Jetstream T1
☐ XX634	Bulldog T.1
☐ ZA176	Sea Harrier FA2
☐ AR-107	SAAB Draken
☐ 51-9036	Lockheed T-33
☐ 3607	MI23ML
☐ 7006	MI27K
☐ 83	Mystere IV
☐ 37918	Viggen
☐ 56321	SAAB 91B Safir
☐ 54-2223	F-100D Super Sabre

Norfolk & Suffolk Aviation Museum
Flixton, Suffolk

☐ BAPC-71	Spitfire Replica
☐ BAPC-115	H.M.14 Pou-Du-Ciel
☐ BAPC-147	Bensen B.7 Gyroglider
☐ BAPC-239	Fokker D VIII Replica
☐ G-ANLW	Widgeon 2
☐ G-ASRF	Gowland Jenny Wren
☐ G-BABY	Taylor Titch
☐ G-BFIP	Wallbro Monoplane
☐ G-MJSU	MBA Tiger Cub 440
☐ G-MJVI	Lightwing Rooster
☐ G-MTFK	Moult Trike Striker
☐ N16676	Fairchild F.24
☐ N99153	North American T-28D
☐ VL349	Anson C.19
☐ VX580	Valetta C.2
☐ WF128	Sea Prince T.1
☐ WF643	Meteor F.8
☐ WH840	Canberra T.4
☐ WV605	Provost T.1
☐ XG254	Hunter FGA.9
☐ XG329	Lightning F.1
☐ XG518	Sycamore HR.14
☐ XH892	Javelin FAW.9R
☐ XJ482	Sea Vixen FAW.1
☐ XK624	Vampire T.11
☐ XN304	Whirlwind HAS.7
☐ XR485	Whirlwind HAR.10
☐ ZA175	Sea Harrier FA2
☐ A-528	Pucara
☐ 79	Mystere IVA
☐ 54-2196	F-100D Super Sabre
☐ 55-4433	Lockheed T-33

North East Aircraft Museum
Off the A19, Sunderland.

BAPC-96	Brown Helicopter
BAPC-119	Bensen B.7
BAPC-228	Olympus Hang Glider
G-ADVU	H.M.14 Pou-Du-Ciel
G-AFUG	Luton LA-4 Minor
G-APTW	Westland Widgeon
G-ARAD	Luton LA-4 Major
G-ASOL	Bell 47D
G-BAGJ	Gazelle
G-MBDL	Striplin Loneranger
G-OGIL	Short SD.330-100
G-SFTA	Westland Gazelle
TX213	Anson C.19
VV217	Vampire FB.5
WA577	Sycamore III
WB685	DHC-1 Chipmunk T.10
WG724	Dragonfly HR.5
WJ639	Canberra TT.18
WK198	Supermarine Swift F.4
WL181	Meteor F.8
WZ518	Vampire T.11
WZ767	Grasshopper TX.1
XG680	Sea Venom FAW.22
XL319	Vulcan B2A
XN258	Whirlwind HAR.9
XP627	Jet Provost T.4
XT148	Sioux AH.1
ZF594	Lightning F.53
A-522	Pucara
E-419	Hunter F.51
146	Mystere IVA
54439	Lockheed T-33
51-6171	F-100D Super Sabre
52-6541	F-84F Thunderstreak

RAF Manston History Museum
Manston Airport, Kent

LF751	Hurricane IIC
TB752	Spitfire XVI
VM791	Slingsby Cadet TX.3
WD646	Meteor TT.20
WP772	DHC-1 Chipmunk T.10
XA231	Slinsby Grasshopper
XJ727	Whirlwind HAR.10
XN380	Whirlwind HAS.7
XS482	Wessex HU.5

RAF Millom Museum
Haverigg, Cumbria

G-ADRX	Mignet HM.14
WD377	DHC-1 Chipmunk T.10
XK637	Vampire T.11
XM660	Whirlwind HAS.7
XN597	Jet Provost T.3

RAF Museum Cosford
RAF Cosford, Shropshire.

BAPC-82	Hawker 'Afgan' Hind
BAPC-94	Fieseler Fi 103 V1
BAPC-99	Yokosuka MXY-7 Ohka
G-AEEH	H.M.14 Pou-Du-Ciel
G-AFAP	CASA 352L
G-AGNV	York C.1
G-AIZE	Fairchild Argus
G-AJOV	Dragonfly

G-AOVF	Britannia 312
G-APAS	DH.106 Comet 1A
G-AVMO	BAC 111-510ED
G-BBYM	Handley Page Jetstream
G-EBMB	Hawker Cygnet
K9942	Spitfire F.1
AJ469	Ventura II
DG202	Gloster F9/40
KN645	C-47B Dakota
LF738	Hurricane IIC
RF398	Lincoln B.2
TA639	DH.98 Mosquito TT.35
TB675	Spitfire LF.XVIE
TG511	Hastings T.5
TX214	Anson C.19
VP952	DH.104 Devon C.2/2
VX461	DH.100 Vampire
VX573	Valetta C.2
WA634	Meteor T.7
WE600	Auster T.7 Antarctic
WE982	Slingsby Prefect TX.1
WG760	English Electric P.1A
WG768	Short SB.5
WG777	Fairey Delta 2
WK935	Meteor F.8 Prone
WL679	Varsity T.1
WL732	Sea Balliol T.21
WP912	DHC-1 Chipmunk
WS843	Meteor NF.14
WV562	Provost T.1
WV746	Pembroke C.1
WZ744	Avro 707C
XA564	Javelin FAW.1
XB812	Canadair Sabre 4
XD145	Saro SR.53
XD674	Jet Provost T.1
XD818	Valiant BK.1
XF926	Bristol 188
XG225	Hunter F.6A
XG337	Lightning F.1
XH171	Canberra PR.9
XH672	Victor K.2
XJ918	Sycamore HR.14
XK724	Gnat F.1
XL568	Hunter T.7
XL703	Pioneer CC.1
XL993	Twin Pioneer CC.1
XM351	Jet Provost T.3
XM555	Skeeter AOP.12
XM598	Vulcan B.2
XN714	Hunting H.126
XP411	Argosy
XR220	BAC TSR.2
XR371	Belfast C.1
XR525	Wessex HC.2
XR977	Gnat T.1
XS639	Andover E.3A
XS695	Kestrel FGA.1
XX496	Jetstream T1
XX765	Jaguar GR.1
XX946	Tornado
8469M	Focke-Achgelis Fa 330A1
8484M	Mitsubishi Ki-46 Dinah
A-515	Pucara
L-866	PBY-6A Catalina
7198/18	LVG C VI
191619	Messerschmit Me 163
420430	Messerschmit Me 410
475081	Fieseler Fi 156C Storch
44-13573	North American P-51D
74-0177	F-111F

204	SP-2H Neptune
01120	MI15bis
J-1704	Venom FB.4

RAF Museum Hendon
Hendon, North London.

BAPC-106	Bleriot XI
G-AAMX	DH.60GM Moth
168	Sopwith Tabloid replica
687	RAF B.E.2b
2345	Vickers FB.5 Gunbus rep
3066	Caudron G.III
E449	Avro 504K
F938	S.E.5a
A8226	Sopwith 1½ Strutter rep
C4994	Bristol M.1C replica
E2466	Bristol F.2B Fighter
F1010	Airco D.H.9A
F6314	Sopwith Camel
F8614	Vickers Vimy replica
J9941	Hawker Hart
K2227	Bristol Bulldog
K4232	Cierva C.30A
K4972	Hart IIA
K6035	Westland Wallace II
K8042	Gloster Gladiator II
L8756	Blenheim IV
N1671	Boulton Paul Defiant
N5182	Sopwith Pup Replica
N5912	Sopwith Triplane
N9899	Southampton I
P2617	Hurricane I
R5868	Avro Lancaster B.I
R9125	Lysander
T6296	D.H.82A Tiger Moth
W1048	Handley Page Halifax
W2068	Avro Anson I
X4590	Spitfire IA
Z7197	Percival Proctor III
BL614	Spitfire VB
DD931	Beaufort VIII
FE905	North American Harvard
FX760	Curtiss P-40
KK995	Sikorsky R-4B
KL216	P-47D Thunderbolt
KN751	B-24L Liberator
LB264	Auster 1
MF628	Wellington X
ML824	Short Sunderland V
MN235	Hawker Typhoon IB
MP425	Airspeed Oxford I
NV778	Tempest TT.5
PK724	Spitfire F.24
PR536	Hawker Tempest II
RD253	Beaufighter TF.X
TJ138	D.H.98 Mosquito B.35
WE139	Canberra PR.3
WH301	Meteor F.8
WP962	DHC-1 Chipmunk T.10
WV783	Sycamore HR.12
WZ791	Slingsby Grasshopper
XA302	Cadet TX.3
XG154	Hunter FGA.9
XG474	Belvedere HC.1
XL318	Vulcan B.2
XM555	Skeeter AOP.12
XP299	Whirlwind HAR.10
XS925	LIghtning F.6
XV424	Phantom FGR.2
XV732	Wessex HCC.4

☐ XW323	Jet Provost T.5A	
☐ XW547	Buccaneer S.2B	
☐ XW855	Gazelle HT.3	
☐ XZ997	Harrier GR.3	
☐ ZA457	Tornado GR.1	
☐ ZJ116	EH101 Merlin	
☐ 8476M	Kawasaki Ki-100	
☐ A2-4	Supermarine Seagull V	
☐ A16-199	Lockheed Hudson IV	
☐ 75	Hanriot HD-1	
☐ 920	Supermarine Stranraer	
☐ 8147/18	Fokker D VII	
☐ 4101	Messerschmit Bf 109E	
☐ 10639	Messerschmit Bf 109G2	
☐ 112372	Messerschmit Me 262	
☐ 120227	Heinkel He 162	
☐ 360043	Junkers Ju 88R-1	
☐ 494083	Junkers Ju 872	
☐ 584219	Focke-Wulf Fw 190F	
☐ 730301	Messerschmit Bf 110G	
☐ 3701152	Heinkel He 111H-2	
☐ MM.5071	Fiat CR.42	
☐ 853	Hunter FR.10	
☐ E3B-521	CASA 1.131	
☐ 34037	North American TB-25J	
☐ 44-13317	North American P-51D	
☐ 44-83868	B-17G Flying Fortress	

Real Airplane Museum
Breighton Airfield, East Yorkshire

☐ G-ABVE	Arrow Active II
☐ G-AEVS	Aeronca 100
☐ G-AEXF	Percival Mew Gull
☐ G-AKAT	Miles Hawk Trainer
☐ G-AMAW	Luton LA-4 Minor
☐ G-AOBG	Somers-Kendall SK.1
☐ G-AXEI	Ward Gnome
☐ G-AXMT	Bucker Bu.133
☐ G-BVGZ	Fokker Dr.1 Replica
☐ G-BWUE	Hispano HA-1112
☐ G-CBCE	CASA 1-131
☐ G-CDGU	Spitfire F.1
☐ G-CDHI	P.51D Mustanfg
☐ G-HURR	Hurricane XII
☐ G-MMUL	Ward Elf

Royal Engineers Museum
Chatham, Kent

☐ XT133	Sioux AH.1
☐ XZ964	Harrier GR.3

Science Museum, Kensington
Exhibition Road, London SW7

☐ BAPC-50	Roe Triplane
☐ BAPC-51	Vickers Vimy
☐ BAPC-52	Lilienthal Glider
☐ BAPC-53	Wright Flyer I replica
☐ BAPC-54	JAP-Harding Monoplane
☐ BAPC-55	Levavasseur Antoinette
☐ G-EBIB	RAF S.E.5a
☐ G-AAAH	D.H.60G Gipsy Moth
☐ G-ASSM	HS.125
☐ G-AWAW	Cessna 150F
☐ G-AZPH	Pitts S-1S Special
☐ N5171N	Lockheed 10A
☐ 304	Cody Biplane
☐ D7560	Avro 504K
☐ J8067	Westland-Hill Pterodactyl

☐ L1592	Hurricane I
☐ P9444	Spitfire IA
☐ S1595	Supermarine S.6B
☐ W4041/G	Gloster E.28/39
☐ AP507	Cierva C.30A
☐ XG900	Short SC.1
☐ XJ314	Rolls-Royce Flying Bedstead
☐ XN344	Skeeter AOP.12
☐ XP831	Hawker P.1127
☐ 210/16	Fokker E III
☐ 191316	Messerschmit Me 163B-1
☐ 442795	Fieseler Fi 103 V1

Science Museum, Wroughton
Wroughton Airfield, Near Swindon.

☐ G-AACN	H.P.39 Gugnunc
☐ G-ACIT	D.H.84 Dragon
☐ G-AEHM	H.M.14 Pou-du-Ciel
☐ G-ALXT	D.H.89A Dragon Rapide
☐ G-APWY	Piaggio P.166
☐ G-APYD	D.H.106 Comet 4B
☐ G-AVZB	LET Z.37 Cmelak
☐ G-AWZM	H.S.121 Trident 3
☐ G-BGLB	Bede BD-5B
☐ G-MMCB	Huntair Pathfinder II
☐ N18E	Boeing 247D
☐ N7777G	Constellation
☐ NC16701	Douglas Dc-3A
☐ VP975	D.H.104 Devon
☐ XP505	Gnat T.1

Second World War Aircraft Preservation Society
Lasham Airfield, Hampshire

☐ VH-FDT	DHA Drover 1
☐ 4X-FNA	Meteor NF.13
☐ VR192	Prentice T.1
☐ WF137	Sea Prince C.1
☐ WH291	Meteor F.8
☐ WV798	Sea Hawk FGA.6
☐ XK418	Auster AOP.9
☐ XM833	Wessex HAS.3
☐ E-423	Hunter F.51
☐ 22+35	F-104G Starfighter

Shoreham Airport Historical Association
Shoreham Airport, West Sussex

☐ WZ820	Slingsby Grasshopper

The Shuttleworth Collection
Bigglewade Airfield, Bedfordshire

☐ BAPC-2	Bristol Boxkite replica
☐ BAPC-3	Bleriot XI
☐ BAPC-4	Deperdussin Monoplane
☐ G-EBHX	D.H.53
☐ G-EBIR	D.H.51
☐ G-EBJO	ANEC II
☐ G-EBLV	D.H.60 Cirrus Moth
☐ G-EBNV	English Electric Wren
☐ G-EBWD	D.H.60X Hermes Moth
☐ G-AAIN	Parnall Elf II
☐ G-AANI	Blackburn Monoplane
☐ G-AANM	Bristol F.2B
☐ G-AAPZ	Desoutter I
☐ G-AAYX	Southern Martlet

☐ G-ABAG	D.H.60G Gipsy Moth
☐ G-ABXL	Granger Archaeopteryx
☐ G-ACSS	D.H.88 Comet Racer
☐ G-ACTF	Comper Swift
☐ G-AEBB	H.M.14 Pou-du Ciel
☐ G-AEEG	Miles M.3A Falcon
☐ G-AEXF	Percival Mew Gull
☐ G-AKKH	Gemini
☐ G-AMRK	Gloster Gladiator
☐ G-AOKL	Percival Prentice
☐ G-AOTK	Druine Turbi
☐ G-ARSG	Roe Triplane replica
☐ G-BKBB	Hawker Fury replica
☐ G-BNZC	DHC-1 Chipmunk T.22
☐ G-BSYF	Luscombe L.8
☐ G-CAMM	Hawker Cygnet
☐ G-KAPW	Provost T.1
☐ F904	RAF S.E.5a
☐ C4918	Bristol M.1C replica
☐ D8096	Bristol F.2B
☐ H5199	Avro 504K
☐ K1786	Hawker Tomtit
☐ K3215	Avro Tutor
☐ K5414	Hawker Hind
☐ N6101	Sopwith Pup
☐ N6290	Sopwith Triplane replica
☐ P6382	Miles M.14A Magister
☐ T6818	D.H.82A Tiger Moth
☐ V1075	Miles M.14A Magister
☐ Z7015	Sea Hurricane IIB
☐ V9441	Westland Lysander
☐ AR501	Spitfire VC

Snibston Discovery Park
Coalville Leicestershire

☐ G-AFTN	Taylorcraft Plus C2
☐ G-AIJK	Auster J/4
☐ VZ728	Desford Trainer
☐ XP280	Auster AOP.9

Solent Sky
Southampton, Hampshire

☐ BAPC-164	Wight Quadruplane rep
☐ G-ALZE	Britten-Norman BN-1F
☐ VH-BRC	Short Sandringham IV
☐ N248	Supermarine S.6A
☐ C4451	Avro 504J replica
☐ W2718	Walrus I
☐ BB807	D.H.82A Tiger Moth
☐ PK683	Spitfire 24
☐ TG263	Saro SR.A/1
☐ WM571	Sea Venom FAW.22
☐ WZ753	Slingsby Grasshopper
☐ XD332	Scimitar F.1
☐ XD596	Vampire T.11
☐ XF114	Swift F.7
☐ XJ581	Sea Vixen FAW.2
☐ XK740	Gnat F.1
☐ XL770	Skeeter AOP.12
☐ XN246	Slingsby Cadet TX.3
☐ U-1215	Vampire T.11

Solway Aviation Museum
Carlisle Airport, Crosby-on-Eden.

☐ G-APLG	Auster J/5L
☐ WE188	Canberra T.4
☐ WP314	Sea Prince T.1
☐ WS832	Meteor NF.14

☐ WV198   Whirlwind HAR.21
☐ WZ515   Vampire T.11
☐ WZ784   Slingsby Grasshopper
☐ XJ823   Vulcan B.2
☐ XV406   Phantom FGR.2
☐ ZF583   Lightning F.53

Stondon Transport Museum
Chichester, West Sussex

☐ G-ADRG   Mignet HM.14
☐ G-AXOM   Penn-Smith Gyroplane
☐ XN341   Skeeter AOP.12

Tangmere Military Aviation Museum
Chichester, West Sussex

☐ L1679   Hurricane I replica
☐ BL924   Spitfire V replica
☐ EE549   Meteor F.4
☐ WA879   Meteor F.8
☐ WB188   Hunter F.3
☐ WK281   Swift FR.5
☐ WP190   Hunter F.5
☐ XJ580   Sea Vixen FAW.2
☐ XN299   Whirlwind HAS.7
☐ XS511   Wessex HU.5
☐ XV408   Phantom FGR.2
☐ ZF578   Lightning F.53
☐ 19252   Lockheed T-33

Tank Museum
Bovingdon, Dorset

☐ TK718   Hamilcar 1
☐ XM564   Skeeter AOP.12

ThinkTank Museum
Birmingham City Centre

☐ P3395   Hurricane IV
☐ ML427   Spitfire IX

Ulster Aviation Society
Langford Lodge airfield, near Crumlin

☐ G-BDBS   Short SD330
☐ G-BTUC   Shorts Tucano
☐ G-MJWS   Eurowing Goldwing
☐ G-RENT   Robinson R.22B
☐ EI-BAG   Cessna 172A
☐ EI-BUO   Aero Composite Sea
              Hawker
☐ JV482   Grumman Wildcat
☐ WN108   Sea Hawk FB.5
☐ WZ549   Vampire T.11
☐ XV361   Buccaneer S.2B

Ulster Folk and Transport Museum
Holywood, County Down

☐ XG905   Short SC.1

Wellesbourne Wartime Museum
Wellesbourne Mountford Airfield,
Warwickshire

☐ RA-01378   Yakovlev Yak-52
☐ WV679   Provost T.1
☐ XK590   Vampire T.11
☐ XM655   Vulcan B.2

World Naval Base
Chatham Dockyard, Kent

☐ WG751   Dragonfly HR.3

Yorkshire Air Museum
Elvington Airfield, South-East of York

☐ BAPC-28   Wright Flyer replica
☐ BAPC-41   RAF B.E.2c replica
☐ BAPC-76   H.M.14 Pou-du-Ciel
☐ BAPC-157   Waco Hadrian
☐ BAPC-240   Bf-109G replica
☐ BAPC-254   Spitfire replica
☐ BAPC-265   Hurricane I replica
☐ G-AFFI   Mignet HM.14
☐ G-AMYJ   Douglas DC-3
☐ G-ASCD   Beagle Terrier 2
☐ G-AVPN   HPR-7 Herald
☐ G-MJRA   Mainair Demon 175
☐ G-MVIM   Noble Hardman Snowbird
☐ G-TFRB   Sport Elite Gyroplane
☐ F943   RAF S.E.5a replica
☐ H1968   Avro 504K replica
☐ FK338   Fairchild Argus
☐ HJ711   Mosquito NF.II
☐ LV907   HP Halifax II
☐ RA854   Kirby Cadet TX.1
☐ VV901   Avro Anson T.21
☐ WH846   Canberra T.4
☐ WH991   Dragonfly HR.5
☐ WK864   Meteor F.8
☐ WS788   Meteor NF.14
☐ XH278   Vampire T.11
☐ XH767   Javelin FAW.9
☐ XJ398   Whirlwind HAR.10
☐ XL231   Victor K.2
☐ XL571   Hunter T.7
☐ XN974   Buccaneer S.2A
☐ XP345   Whirlwind HAR.10
☐ XP640   Jet Provost T.4
☐ XS903   Lightning F.6
☐ XV748   Harrier GR.3
☐ XX901   Buccaneer S.2B
☐ XZ631   Tornado T
☐ ZA354   Tornado GR.1
☐ 538   Mirage IIIE
☐ 21417   Lockheed T-33
☐ N-268   Hunter FGA.78
☐ 237123   WACO Hadrian

Ireland current civil aircraft

Reg	Type
☐ EI-ABI	DH.84 Dragon
☐ EI-ADV	Piper PA-12 Super Cruiser
☐ EI-AFE	Piper J-3C-65 Cub
☐ EI-AFF	B.A. Swallow 2
☐ EI-AGD	Taylorcraft Plus D
☐ EI-AGJ	Auster J/1 Autocrat
☐ EI-AHI	DH.82A Tiger Moth
☐ EI-AKM	Piper J-3C-65 Cub
☐ EI-ALH	Taylorcraft Plus D
☐ EI-ALP	Avro Cadet Mk.1
☐ EI-ALU	Avro Cadet Mk.1
☐ EI-AMF	Taylorcraft Plus D
☐ EI-AMK	Auster J/1 Autocrat
☐ EI-AMY	Auster J/1N Alpha
☐ EI-ANA	Taylorcraft Plus D
☐ EI-ANT	Aeronca 7ECA Citabria
☐ EI-ANY	Piper PA-18-95
☐ EI-AOB	Piper PA-28-140 Cherokee
☐ EI-AOP	DH.82A Tiger Moth
☐ EI-APS	Schleicher ASK-14
☐ EI-ARW	Jodel DR.1050
☐ EI-ASR	McCandless M.4
☐ EI-AST	Reims F150H
☐ EI-ASU	Beagle A.61 Terrier
☐ EI-ATJ	Beagle B.121 Pup
☐ EI-ATS	MS.880B Rallye
☐ EI-AUE	MS.880 Rallye
☐ EI-AUG	MS.894A Minerva
☐ EI-AUM	Auster J/1 Autocrat
☐ EI-AUO	Reims FA150K Aerobat
☐ EI-AUS	Auster J/5F Aiglet Trainer
☐ EI-AUT	Ercoupe F1A
☐ EI-AUY	Morane MS.502 Criquet
☐ EI-AVM	Reims F150L
☐ EI-AWD	Piper PA-22-160 Tri-Pacer
☐ EI-AWH	Cessna 210J Centurion
☐ EI-AWP	DH.82A Tiger Moth
☐ EI-AWR	MFI-9
☐ EI-AWU	MS.880B Rallye
☐ EI-AYA	MS.880B Rallye
☐ EI-AYB	Gardan GY-80
☐ EI-AYF	Reims FRA150L Aerobat
☐ EI-AYI	MS.880B Rallye
☐ EI-AYK	Reims F172M
☐ EI-AYN	BN2A-8 Islander
☐ EI-AYO	Douglas DC-3
☐ EI-AYR	Schleicher ASK-16
☐ EI-AYT	MS.894A Minerva
☐ EI-AYV	MS.892A Commodore
☐ EI-AYY	Evans VP-1
☐ EI-BAJ	Stampe SV-4C
☐ EI-BAT	Reims F150L
☐ EI-BAV	Piper PA-22-108 Colt
☐ EI-BBC	Piper PA-28-180 Cherokee
☐ EI-BBD	Evans VP-1
☐ EI-BBE	Aeronca 7FC Tri-Traveler
☐ EI-BBI	MS.892E Rallye 150GT
☐ EI-BBJ	MS.880B Rallye
☐ EI-BBO	MS.893E Rallye 180GT
☐ EI-BBV	Piper J-3C-65 Cub
☐ EI-BCE	BN2A-26 Islander
☐ EI-BCF	Bensen B.8M
☐ EI-BCJ	Sequoia F.8L Falco
☐ EI-BCK	Reims F172N
☐ EI-BCL	Cessna 182P Skylane
☐ EI-BCM	Piper J-3C-65D Cub
☐ EI-BCN	Piper J-3C-65D Cub
☐ EI-BCO	Piper J-3C-65 Cub
☐ EI-BCP	Druine Condor
☐ EI-BCS	MS.880B Rallye
☐ EI-BCU	MS.880B Rallye
☐ EI-BCW	MS.880B Rallye
☐ EI-BDH	MS.880B Rallye
☐ EI-BDK	MS.880B Rallye
☐ EI-BDL	Evans VP-2
☐ EI-BDP	Cessna 182P Skylane
☐ EI-BDR	Piper PA-28-180 Cherokee
☐ EI-BEA	MS.880B Rallye
☐ EI-BEN	Piper J-3C-65E Cub
☐ EI-BEP	MS.892A Commodore
☐ EI-BFE	Reims F150G
☐ EI-BFF	Beech A23-24
☐ EI-BFI	MS.880B Rallye
☐ EI-BFO	Piper J-3C-90 Cub
☐ EI-BFP	MS.880B Rallye
☐ EI-BFR	MS.880B Rallye
☐ EI-BGA	MS.880B Rallye
☐ EI-BGB	MS.880B Rallye
☐ EI-BGC	MS.880B Rallye
☐ EI-BGD	MS.880B Rallye
☐ EI-BGJ	Reims F152
☐ EI-BGS	MS.893E Rallye 180GT
☐ EI-BGT	Colt Ax-7-77A
☐ EI-BGU	MS.880B Rallye
☐ EI-BHC	Reims F177RG
☐ EI-BHF	MS.892A Commodore
☐ EI-BHI	Bell 206B Jet Ranger
☐ EI-BHM	Reims F337E
☐ EI-BHN	MS.893A Commodore
☐ EI-BHP	MS.893A Commodore
☐ EI-BHT	Beech 77 Skipper
☐ EI-BHV	Aeronca 7EC Traveler
☐ EI-BHW	Reims F150F
☐ EI-BHY	MS.892E Rallye 150GT
☐ EI-BIB	Reims F152
☐ EI-BID	Piper PA-18-95
☐ EI-BIG	Zlin Z.526
☐ EI-BIJ	Agusta Bell 206B
☐ EI-BIK	Piper PA-18-180
☐ EI-BIM	MS.880B Rallye
☐ EI-BIO	Piper J-3C-65E Cub
☐ EI-BIR	Reims F172M
☐ EI-BIS	Robin R.1180T Aiglon
☐ EI-BIT	MS.887 Rallye
☐ EI-BIW	MS.880B Rallye
☐ EI-BJB	Aeronca 7DC Champion
☐ EI-BJJ	Aeronca 15AC Sedan
☐ EI-BJK	MS.880B Rallye
☐ EI-BJM	Cessna A152 Aerobat
☐ EI-BJO	Cessna R172K Hawk XP
☐ EI-BJT	Piper PA-38-112 Tomahawk
☐ EI-BKC	Aeronca 15AC Sedan
☐ EI-BKE	MS.885 Super Rallye
☐ EI-BKF	Reims F172H
☐ EI-BKK	Taylor Monoplane
☐ EI-BKN	MS.880B Rallye
☐ EI-BKU	MS.892A Commodore
☐ EI-BLB	Stampe SV-4C
☐ EI-BLD	MBB Bo.105CB
☐ EI-BLN	Eipper Quicksilver MX
☐ EI-BMA	MS.880B Rallye
☐ EI-BMB	MS.880B Rallye
☐ EI-BMF	Laverda F.8L Falco
☐ EI-BMH	MS.880B Rallye
☐ EI-BMI	SOCATA TB-9 Tampico
☐ EI-BMJ	MS.880B Rallye
☐ EI-BMM	Reims F152
☐ EI-BMN	Reims F152
☐ EI-BMU	Monnett Sonerai
☐ EI-BMW	Hiway Skytrike
☐ EI-BNF	Eurowing Goldwing
☐ EI-BNH	Hiway Skytrike
☐ EI-BNK	Cessna U206F
☐ EI-BNL	Rand KR-2
☐ EI-BNP	Rotorway Scorpion
☐ EI-BNT	Cvjetkovic CA-65
☐ EI-BNU	MS.880B Rallye
☐ EI-BOE	SOCATA TB-10 Tobago
☐ EI-BOV	Rand KR-2
☐ EI-BPE	Viking Dragonfly
☐ EI-BPL	Reims F172K
☐ EI-BPO	Southdown Puma
☐ EI-BPP	Eipper Quicksilver MX
☐ EI-BPU	Hiway Skytrike
☐ EI-BRS	Cessna P172D Skyhawk
☐ EI-BRU	Evans VP-1
☐ EI-BRV	Hiway Skytrike
☐ EI-BSB	Jodel D.112
☐ EI-BSC	Reims F172N
☐ EI-BSG	Bensen B.8O
☐ EI-BSK	SOCATA TB-9 Tampico
☐ EI-BSL	Piper PA-34-220T Seneca
☐ EI-BSO	Piper PA-28-140 Cherokee
☐ EI-BSW	Pegasus XL-R
☐ EI-BSX	Piper J-3C-65 Cub
☐ EI-BTX	MD82
☐ EI-BTY	MD82
☐ EI-BUA	Cessna 172M Skyhawk
☐ EI-BUC	Jodel D.9 Bebe
☐ EI-BUF	Cessna 210N Centurion
☐ EI-BUG	Gardan ST-10 Diplomat
☐ EI-BUH	Lake LA-4
☐ EI-BUJ	MS.889A Minerva
☐ EI-BUL	Aerotech MW-5
☐ EI-BUN	Beech 76 Duchess
☐ EI-BUT	MS.893A Commodore
☐ EI-BVJ	AMF Chevvron
☐ EI-BVK	Piper PA-38-112 Tomahawk
☐ EI-BVT	Evans VP-2
☐ EI-BVY	Zenair CH.200
☐ EI-BWH	Partenavia P.68
☐ EI-BXL	Polaris F1B
☐ EI-BXO	Fouga CM-170
☐ EI-BXT	Druine Condor
☐ EI-BYA	Thruster TST
☐ EI-BYD	Cessna 150J
☐ EI-BYF	Cessna 150M
☐ EI-BYG	SOCATA TB-9 Tampico
☐ EI-BYJ	Bell 206B Jet Ranger
☐ EI-BYL	Zenith CH.250
☐ EI-BYO	ATR 42-312
☐ EI-BYR	Bell 206L Long Ranger
☐ EI-BYX	Aeronca 7GC Sky-Trac
☐ EI-BYY	Piper J-3C-85 Cub
☐ EI-BZN	Boeing 737-3Y0
☐ EI-CAC	Grob 115A
☐ EI-CAD	Grob 115A
☐ EI-CAE	Grob 115A
☐ EI-CAN	Aerotech MW-5
☐ EI-CAP	Cessna R182 Skylane RG
☐ EI-CAU	AMF Chevvron
☐ EI-CAW	Bell 206B Jet Ranger
☐ EI-CAX	Cessna P210N Centurion
☐ EI-CAY	Mooney M.20C
☐ EI-CBK	ATR 42-312
☐ EI-CBQ	Boeing 737-3YO
☐ EI-CBR	MD83
☐ EI-CBS	MD83
☐ EI-CBY	MD83
☐ EI-CBZ	MD83
☐ EI-CCC	MD83
☐ EI-CCD	Grob 115A
☐ EI-CCE	MD83
☐ EI-CCF	Aeronca 11AC Chief
☐ EI-CCJ	Cessna 152
☐ EI-CCK	Cessna 152

Reg	Type		Reg	Type		Reg	Type
☐ EI-CCL	Cessna 152		☐ EI-CKU	Pegasus XL-R		☐ EI-CSJ	Boeing 737-8AS
☐ EI-CCM	Cessna 152		☐ EI-CLA	Diamond Katana		☐ EI-CSK	BAe 146-200
☐ EI-CCO	Piper PA-44-180 Seminole		☐ EI-CLL	Aerotech MW-6S		☐ EI-CSL	BAe 146-200
☐ EI-CCV	Cessna R172K Hawk XP		☐ EI-CLQ	Reims F172N		☐ EI-CSM	Boeing 737-8AS
☐ EI-CDD	Boeing 737-548		☐ EI-CLW	Boeing 737-3Y0		☐ EI-CSN	Boeing 737-8AS
☐ EI-CDE	Boeing 737-548		☐ EI-CLZ	Boeing 737-3Y0		☐ EI-CSO	Boeing 737-8AS
☐ EI-CDF	Boeing 737-548		☐ EI-CMB	Piper PA-28-140 Cherokee		☐ EI-CSP	Boeing 737-8AS
☐ EI-CDG	Boeing 737-548		☐ EI-CMK	Eurowing Goldwing		☐ EI-CSQ	Boeing 737-8AS
☐ EI-CDH	Boeing 737-548		☐ EI-CML	Cessna 150M		☐ EI-CSR	Boeing 737-8AS
☐ EI-CDP	Cessna 182L Skylane		☐ EI-CMN	Piper PA-12 Super Cruiser		☐ EI-CSS	Boeing 737-8AS
☐ EI-CDV	Cessna 150G		☐ EI-CMR	Rutan LongEz		☐ EI-CST	Boeing 737-8AS
☐ EI-CDX	Cessna 210K Centurion		☐ EI-CMS	BAe 146-200		☐ EI-CSU	Boeing 737-36E
☐ EI-CDY	MD83		☐ EI-CMT	Piper PA-34-200T Seneca		☐ EI-CSV	Boeing 737-8AS
☐ EI-CEG	MS.893E Rallye 180GT		☐ EI-CMU	Mainair Mercury		☐ EI-CSW	Boeing 737-8AS
☐ EI-CEN	Thruster T300		☐ EI-CMV	Cessna 150L		☐ EI-CSX	Boeing 737-8AS
☐ EI-CEP	MD83		☐ EI-CMW	Rotorway Exec 152		☐ EI-CSY	Boeing 737-8AS
☐ EI-CEQ	MD83		☐ EI-CMY	BAe 146-200		☐ EI-CSZ	Boeing 737-8AS
☐ EI-CER	MD83		☐ EI-CNA	Letov LK-2M Sluka		☐ EI-CTA	Boeing 737-8AS
☐ EI-CES	Taylorcraft BC-65		☐ EI-CNB	BAe 146-200		☐ EI-CTB	Boeing 737-8AS
☐ EI-CEY	Boeing 757-2Y0		☐ EI-CNC	TEAM Minimax		☐ EI-CTC	Medway EclipseR
☐ EI-CEZ	Boeing 757-2Y0		☐ EI-CNG	Air & Space 18A		☐ EI-CTG	Glasair RG
☐ EI-CFE	Robinson R22B		☐ EI-CNJ	BAe 146-RJ85		☐ EI-CTI	Reims FRA150L Aerobat
☐ EI-CFF	Piper PA-12 Super Cruiser		☐ EI-CNL	Sikorsky S-61N		☐ EI-CTL	Aerotech MW-5B
☐ EI-CFG	Piel Emeraude		☐ EI-CNQ	BAe 146-200		☐ EI-CTT	Piper PA-28-161 Warrior
☐ EI-CFH	Piper PA-12 Super Cruiser		☐ EI-CNU	Pegasus Quantum		☐ EI-CUA	Boeing 737-4K5
☐ EI-CFN	Cessna 172P Skyhawk		☐ EI-COG	Gyroscopic Gyroplane		☐ EI-CUD	Boeing 737-4Q8
☐ EI-CFO	Piper J-3C-65 Cub		☐ EI-COH	Boeing 737-430		☐ EI-CUE	Cameron N-105
☐ EI-CFP	Cessna 172P Skyhawk		☐ EI-COI	Boeing 737-430		☐ EI-CUG	Bell 206B Jet Ranger
☐ EI-CFX	Robinson R22B		☐ EI-COJ	Boeing 737-430		☐ EI-CUJ	Cessna 172N Skyhawk
☐ EI-CFY	Cessna 172N Skyhawk		☐ EI-COK	Boeing 737-430		☐ EI-CUM	Airbus A320-232
☐ EI-CFZ	MD83		☐ EI-COO	Carlson Sparrow II		☐ EI-CUN	Boeing 737-4K5
☐ EI-CGB	TEAM Minimax		☐ EI-COP	Reims F150L		☐ EI-CUP	Cessna 335
☐ EI-CGC	Stinson 108-3 Voyager		☐ EI-COQ	BAe 146-RJ70		☐ EI-CUS	Agusta Bell 206B
☐ EI-CGD	Cessna 172M Skyhawk		☐ EI-COY	Piper J-3C-65 Cub		☐ EI-CUT	Maule MX-7-180A
☐ EI-CGF	Luton Minor		☐ EI-COZ	Piper PA-28-140 Cherokee		☐ EI-CUW	BN2B-20 Islander
☐ EI-CGG	Ercoupe 415C		☐ EI-CPC	Airbus A321-211		☐ EI-CVA	Airbus A320-214
☐ EI-CGH	Cessna 210N Centurion		☐ EI-CPD	Airbus A321-211		☐ EI-CVB	Airbus A320-214
☐ EI-CGM	Pegasus XL-R		☐ EI-CPE	Airbus A321-211		☐ EI-CVC	Airbus A320-214
☐ EI-CGN	Pegasus XL-R		☐ EI-CPF	Airbus A321-211		☐ EI-CVD	Airbus A320-214
☐ EI-CGP	Piper PA-28-140 Cherokee		☐ EI-CPG	Airbus A321-211		☐ EI-CVL	Ercoupe 415CD
☐ EI-CGQ	Aerospatiale AS.350B		☐ EI-CPH	Airbus A321-211		☐ EI-CVM	Schweizer 269C
☐ EI-CGT	Cessna 152		☐ EI-CPI	Rutan LongEz		☐ EI-CVO	Boeing 737-4S3
☐ EI-CGU	Robinson R22		☐ EI-CPJ	BAe 146-RJ70		☐ EI-CVR	ATR 42-300
☐ EI-CGV	Piper J-5A Cub Cruiser		☐ EI-CPK	BAe 146-RJ70		☐ EI-CVS	ATR 42-310
☐ EI-CGX	Cessna 340		☐ EI-CPN	Auster J/4 Archer		☐ EI-CVW	Bensen B.8M
☐ EI-CHH	Boeing 737-317		☐ EI-CPO	Robinson R22B		☐ EI-CVX	Bensen B.8M
☐ EI-CHK	Piper J-3C-65 Cub		☐ EI-CPP	Piper J-3C-65 Cub		☐ EI-CVY	Brock KB-2
☐ EI-CHR	CFM Shadow BD		☐ EI-CPT	ATR 42-312		☐ EI-CWA	BAe 146-200
☐ EI-CHS	Cessna 172M Skyhawk		☐ EI-CPX	III Sky Arrow 650T		☐ EI-CWB	BAe 146-200
☐ EI-CHT	Pegasus XL-R		☐ EI-CRD	Boeing 767-31B		☐ EI-CWC	BAe 146-200
☐ EI-CHV	Agusta 109A		☐ EI-CRE	MD83		☐ EI-CWD	BAe 146-200
☐ EI-CIA	MS.880B Rallye		☐ EI-CRF	Boeing 767-31B		☐ EI-CWE	Boeing 737-42C
☐ EI-CIF	Piper PA-28-180 Cherokee		☐ EI-CRG	Robin DR.400-180R		☐ EI-CWF	Boeing 737-42C
☐ EI-CIG	Piper PA-18A-150		☐ EI-CRH	MD83		☐ EI-CWH	Agusta 109E Power
☐ EI-CIJ	Cessna 340		☐ EI-CRJ	MD83		☐ EI-CWL	Robinson R22B2
☐ EI-CIM	Avid Speed Wing		☐ EI-CRK	Airbus A330-301		☐ EI-CWR	Robinson R22B2
☐ EI-CIN	Cessna 150K		☐ EI-CRL	Boeing 767-343ER		☐ EI-CWW	Boeing 737-4Y0
☐ EI-CIR	Cessna 551 Citation IISP		☐ EI-CRM	Boeing 767-343		☐ EI-CWX	Boeing 737-4Y0
☐ EI-CIV	Piper PA-28-140 Cherokee		☐ EI-CRO	Boeing 767-3Q8ER		☐ EI-CWY	Boeing 737-4Y0
☐ EI-CIW	MD82		☐ EI-CRU	Cessna 152		☐ EI-CXC	Raj Hamsa X'Air
☐ EI-CIZ	Steen Skybolt		☐ EI-CRV	Diamond H.36		☐ EI-CXI	Boeing 737-46Q
☐ EI-CJJ	Slingsby Motor Tutor		☐ EI-CRW	MD83		☐ EI-CXJ	Boeing 737-4Q8
☐ EI-CJR	Stampe SV-4A		☐ EI-CRX	SOCATA TB-9 Tampico		☐ EI-CXK	Boeing 737-4S3
☐ EI-CJS	Jodel D.120A Paris-Nice		☐ EI-CRZ	Boeing 737-36E		☐ EI-CXL	Boeing 737-46N
☐ EI-CJT	Slingsby Motor Cadet		☐ EI-CSA	Boeing 737-8AS		☐ EI-CXM	Boeing 737-4Q8
☐ EI-CJV	ULF Moskito		☐ EI-CSB	Boeing 737-8AS		☐ EI-CXN	Boeing 737-329
☐ EI-CJZ	Aerotech MW-6S		☐ EI-CSC	Boeing 737-8AS		☐ EI-CXO	Boeing 767-3G5
☐ EI-CKF	Hunt Wing/Avon Trike		☐ EI-CSD	Boeing 737-8AS		☐ EI-CXR	Boeing 737-329
☐ EI-CKH	Piper PA-18-95		☐ EI-CSE	Boeing 737-8AS		☐ EI-CXS	Sikorsky S-61N
☐ EI-CKI	Thruster TST		☐ EI-CSF	Boeing 737-8AS		☐ EI-CXV	Boeing 737-8CX
☐ EI-CKM	MD83		☐ EI-CSG	Boeing 737-8AS		☐ EI-CXY	EV-97 Eurostar
☐ EI-CKN	Aerotech MW-6S		☐ EI-CSH	Boeing 737-8AS		☐ EI-CXZ	Boeing 767-216ER
☐ EI-CKT	Gemini Flash		☐ EI-CSI	Boeing 737-8AS		☐ EI-CZA	ATEC Zephyr 2000

Reg	Type	Reg	Type	Reg	Type
EI-CZC	CFM Shadow SA-II	EI-DDC	Reims F172M	EI-DGP	Urban Air Lambada
EI-CZD	Boeing 767-216ER	EI-DDD	Aeronca 7AC Champion	EI-DGQ	
EI-CZG	Boeing 737-4Q8	EI-DDE	BAe 146-200	EI-DGR	Urban Air Lambada
EI-CZK	Boeing 737-4Y0	EI-DDG		EI-DGS	ATEC Zephyr 2000
EI-CZL	Schweizer 269C-1	EI-DDH	Boeing 777-243ER	EI-DGT	Urban Air Lambada
EI-CZM	Robinson R44	EI-DDI	Hughes 269C-1	EI-DGV	ATEC Zephyr 2000
EI-CZN	Sikorsky S-61N	EI-DDJ	Raj Hamsa X'Air	EI-DGW	Cameron Z-90
EI-CZO	BAe 146-200	EI-DDK	Boeing 737-4S3	EI-DGX	Cessna 152
EI-CZP	Schweizer 269C-1	EI-DDL		EI-DGY	Urban Air Lambada
EI-DAA	Airbus A330-200	EI-DDM		EI-DGZ	Boeing 737-86N
EI-DAC	Boeing 737-8AS	EI-DDO	Montgomerie Merlin	EI-DHA	Boeing 737-8AS
EI-DAD	Boeing 737-8AS	EI-DDP	Puma Sprint	EI-DHB	Boeing 737-8AS
EI-DAE	Boeing 737-8AS	EI-DDQ		EI-DHC	Boeing 737-8AS
EI-DAF	Boeing 737-8AS	EI-DDR	Bensen B.8V	EI-DHD	Boeing 737-8AS
EI-DAG	Boeing 737-8AS	EI-DDW	Boeing 767-3S1	EI-DHE	Boeing 737-8AS
EI-DAH	Boeing 737-8AS	EI-DDX	Cessna 172S Skyhawk	EI-DHF	Boeing 737-8AS
EI-DAI	Boeing 737-8AS	EI-DDY	Boeing 737-4Y0	EI-DHG	Boeing 737-8AS
EI-DAJ	Boeing 737-8AS	EI-DDZ	Piper PA-28-181 Archer	EI-DHH	Boeing 737-8AS
EI-DAK	Boeing 737-8AS	EI-DEA	Airbus A320-214	EI-DHI	Boeing 737-8AS
EI-DAL	Boeing 737-8AS	EI-DEB	Airbus A320-214	EI-DHJ	Boeing 737-8AS
EI-DAM	Boeing 737-8AS	EI-DEC	Airbus A320-214	EI-DHK	Boeing 737-8AS
EI-DAN	Boeing 737-8AS	EI-DEE	Airbus A320-214	EI-DHM	Boeing 737-8AS
EI-DAO	Boeing 737-8AS	EI-DEF	Airbus A320-214	EI-DHN	Boeing 737-8AS
EI-DAP	Boeing 737-8AS	EI-DEG	Airbus A320-214	EI-DHO	Boeing 737-8AS
EI-DAR	Boeing 737-8AS	EI-DEH	Airbus A320-214	EI-DHP	Boeing 737-8AS
EI-DAS	Boeing 737-8AS	EI-DEI	Airbus A320-214	EI-DHQ	
EI-DAT	Boeing 737-8AS	EI-DEJ	Airbus A320-214	EI-DHR	Boeing 737-8AS
EI-DAV	Boeing 737-8AS	EI-DEK	Airbus A320-214	EI-DHS	Boeing 737-8AS
EI-DAW	Boeing 737-8AS	EI-DEL	Airbus A320-214	EI-DHT	Boeing 737-8AS
EI-DAX	Boeing 737-8AS	EI-DEM	Airbus A320-214	EI-DHU	Boeing 737-8AS
EI-DAY	Boeing 737-8AS	EI-DEN	Airbus A320-214	EI-DHV	Boeing 737-8AS
EI-DAZ	Boeing 737-8AS	EI-DEO	Airbus A320-214	EI-DHW	Boeing 737-8AS
EI-DBF	Boeing 767-3Q8ER	EI-DEP	Airbus A320-214	EI-DHX	Boeing 737-8AS
EI-DBG	Boeing 767-3Q8	EI-DER	Airbus A320-214	EI-DHY	Boeing 737-8AS
EI-DBH	CFM Streak Shadow	EI-DES	Airbus A320-214	EI-DHZ	Boeing 737-8AS
EI-DBI	Raj Hamsa X'Air	EI-DET	Airbus A320-214	EI-DIA	Pegasus XL-Q
EI-DBJ	Huntwing Pegasus XL	EI-DEU		EI-DIB	Air Creation Kiss
EI-DBK	Boeing 777-243ER	EI-DEW	BAe 146-300	EI-DIC	
EI-DBL	Boeing 777-243ER	EI-DEX	BAe 146-300	EI-DID	
EI-DBM	Boeing 777-243ER	EI-DEY	Airbus A319-112	EI-DIE	
EI-DBN	Bell 407	EI-DEZ	Airbus A319-112	EI-DIF	
EI-DBO	Air Creation Kiss 400	EI-DFA	Airbus A319-112	EI-DII	
EI-DBP	Boeing 767-35H	EI-DFB	Fokker F.28-100	EI-DIJ	Airbus A320-212
EI-DBU	Boeing 767-37E	EI-DFC	Fokker F.28-100	EI-DIK	
EI-DBV	Raj Hamsa X'Air	EI-DFD	Boeing 737-4S3	EI-DIQ	
EI-DBW	Boeing 767-201	EI-DFE	Boeing 737-4S3	EI-DIR	Airbus A330-202
EI-DBX	Magni M-18 Spartan	EI-DFF	Boeing 737-4S3	EI-DIY	Van's RV-4
EI-DCA	Raj Hamsa X'Air	EI-DFG	Embraer EMB-170LR	EI-DIZ	Airbus A320-232
EI-DCB	Boeing 737-8AS	EI-DFH	Embraer EMB-170LR	EI-DJA	
EI-DCC	Boeing 737-8AS	EI-DFI	Embraer EMB-170LR	EI-DJB	
EI-DCD	Boeing 737-8AS	EI-DFJ	Embraer EMB-170LR	EI-DJC	
EI-DCE	Boeing 737-8AS	EI-DFK	Embraer EMB-170LR	EI-DJD	
EI-DCF	Boeing 737-8AS	EI-DFL	Embraer EMB-170LR	EI-DJE	
EI-DCG	Boeing 737-8AS	EI-DFM	EV-97 Eurostar	EI-DJF	
EI-DCH	Boeing 737-8AS	EI-DFN	Airbus A320-211	EI-DJG	
EI-DCI	Boeing 737-8AS	EI-DFO	Airbus A320-211	EI-DJH	Airbus A320-232
EI-DCJ	Boeing 737-8AS	EI-DFP	Airbus A319-112	EI-DJI	Airbus A320-232
EI-DCK	Boeing 737-8AS	EI-DFQ		EI-DJJ	BAe 146-200
EI-DCL	Boeing 737-8AS	EI-DFR		EI-DJK	
EI-DCM	Boeing 737-8AS	EI-DFS	Boeing 767-33AER	EI-DJL	
EI-DCN	Boeing 737-8AS	EI-DFV	Airbus A320-233	EI-DJM	
EI-DCO	Boeing 737-8AS	EI-DFW	Robinson R44	EI-DJO	Agusta 109E Power
EI-DCP	Boeing 737-8AS	EI-DFX	Air Creation Kiss 400	EI-DJP	
EI-DCR	Boeing 737-8AS	EI-DFY	Raj Hamsa X'Air	EI-DJQ	
EI-DCS	Boeing 737-8AS	EI-DGA	Urban Air Lambada	EI-DJR	Boeing 737-3YO
EI-DCT	Boeing 737-8AS	EI-DGD	Boeing 737-430	EI-DJR	
EI-DCV	Boeing 737-8AS	EI-DGG	Raj Hamsa X'Air	EI-DJS	Boeing 737-3YO
EI-DCW	Boeing 737-8AS	EI-DGH	Raj Hamsa X'Air	EI-DJU	Boeing 737-86N
EI-DCX	Boeing 737-8AS	EI-DGI	ICP MXP-740 Savannah	EI-DJV	
EI-DCY	Boeing 737-8AS	EI-DGJ	Raj Hamsa X'Air	EI-DJW	Robinson R44
EI-DCZ	Boeing 737-8AS	EI-DGK	Raj Hamsa X'Air	EI-DJX	Howell Sidney Twinstarr
EI-DDA	Robinson R44	EI-DGL	Boeing 737-46J	EI-DJY	Grob 115
EI-DDB	Eurocopter EC120B	EI-DGO		EI-DJZ	

EI-DKA	
EI-DKB	ICP MXP-740 Savannah
EI-DKC	Pegasus Quasar
EI-DKD	Boeing 737-86N
EI-DKE	Air Creation Kiss
EI-DKI	Robinson R22B
EI-DKJ	Thruster T600N
EI-DKK	Raj Hamsa X'Air
EI-DKL	Boeing 757-231
EI-DKM	Agusta Bell 206B
EI-DKN	ELA Aviacion ELA-07
EI-DKQ	
EI-DKT	Raj Hamsa X'Air
EI-DKU	Air Creation Kiss
EI-DKV	Boeing 737-505
EI-DKW	EV-97 Eurostar
EI-DKY	Raj Hamsa X'Air
EI-DKZ	Reality Escapade
EI-DLA	
EI-DLB	Boeing 737-8AS
EI-DLC	Boeing 737-8AS
EI-DLD	Boeing 737-8AS
EI-DLE	Boeing 737-8AS
EI-DLF	Boeing 737-8AS
EI-DLG	Boeing 737-8AS
EI-DLH	
EI-DLI	
EI-DLJ	
EI-DLK	
EI-DLL	Boeing 737-8AS
EI-DLM	Boeing 737-8AS
EI-DLN	Boeing 737-8AS
EI-DLO	Boeing 737-8AS
EI-DLR	Boeing 737-8AS
EI-DLS	Boeing 737-8AS
EI-DLT	Boeing 737-8AS
EI-DLU	Boeing 737-8AS
EI-DLV	Boeing 737-8AS
EI-DLW	Boeing 737-8AS
EI-DLX	Boeing 737-8AS
EI-DLY	Boeing 737-8AS
EI-DLZ	Boeing 737-8AS
EI-DMA	
EI-DMB	Best Off SkyRanger
EI-DMC	Schweizer 269C-1
EI-DMG	Cessna 441
EI-DMH	Boeing 767-260ER
EI-DMI	
EI-DMJ	Boeing 767-306ER
EI-DMK	BAe 146-200
EI-DML	Bell 206B Jet Ranger
EI-DMM	
EI-DMN	
EI-DMP	Boeing 767-2Q8
EI-DMR	Boeing 737-436
EI-DMS	Robinson R22B
EI-DMT	Agusta 109C
EI-DMU	
EI-DMX	Boeing 737-753
EI-DMY	
EI-DMZ	
EI-DNA	
EI-DNB	
EI-DNC	
EI-DND	Boeing 737-86N
EI-DNE	
EI-DNF	
EI-DNG	
EI-DNH	
EI-DNI	
EI-DNJ	BAe 146-200
EI-DNL	Bensen B.8M
EI-DNM	
EI-DNN	
EI-DNO	
EI-DNP	Airbus A320-212
EI-DNR	
EI-DNS	Boeing 737-329
EI-DNT	Boeing 737-329
EI-DNU	
EI-DNV	Schweizer 269C-1
EI-DNW	
EI-DNX	Boeing 737-31S
EI-DNY	Boeing 737-3TO
EI-DNZ	Boeing 737-3TO
EI-DOA	
EI-DOB	
EI-DOD	Airbus A320-231
EI-DOE	Airbus A320-211
EI-DOF	Boeing 767-306ER
EI-DOG	
EI-DOH	Boeing 737-31S
EI-DOI	EV-97 Eurostar
EI-DOJ	Schweizer 269C-1
EI-DOK	
EI-DOL	
EI-DOM	Boeing 737-3G7
EI-DON	Boeing 737-3YO
EI-DOO	Boeing 737-35B
EI-DOP	Airbus A320-232
EI-DOR	Boeing 737-4YO
EI-DOS	Boeing 737-49R
EI-DOT	CRJ900
EI-DOU	CRJ900
EI-DOV	Boeing 737-48E
EI-DOW	Mainair Blade
EI-DOX	Pegasus XL-R
EI-DOY	PZL Koliber 150A
EI-DPA	Boeing 737-8AS
EI-DPB	Boeing 737-8AS
EI-DPC	Boeing 737-8AS
EI-DPD	Boeing 737-8AS
EI-DPE	Boeing 737-8AS
EI-DPF	Boeing 737-8AS
EI-DPG	Boeing 737-8AS
EI-DPH	Boeing 737-8AS
EI-DPI	Boeing 737-8AS
EI-DPJ	Boeing 737-8AS
EI-DPK	Boeing 737-8AS
EI-DPL	Boeing 737-8AS
EI-DPM	Boeing 737-8AS
EI-DPN	Boeing 737-8AS
EI-DPO	Boeing 737-8AS
EI-DPP	Boeing 737-8AS
EI-DPR	Boeing 737-8AS
EI-DPS	Boeing 737-8AS
EI-DPT	Boeing 737-8AS
EI-DPU	
EI-DPV	Boeing 737-8AS
EI-DPW	
EI-DPX	
EI-DPY	
EI-DPZ	
EI-DRA	Boeing 737-852
EI-DRB	Boeing 737-852
EI-DRC	Boeing 737-852
EI-DRD	Boeing 737-852
EI-DRE	Boeing 737-752
EI-DRF	
EI-DRG	Airbus A320-231
EI-DRH	Mainair Blade
EI-DRI	Canadair CRJ900
EI-DRJ	Canadair CRJ900
EI-DRK	Canadair CRJ900
EI-DRL	Raj Hamsa X'Air
EI-DRM	Urban Air Samba
EI-DRN	Robinson R44
EI-DRO	Tecnam P.2002JF
EI-DRP	
EI-DRR	Boeing 737-347
EI-DRT	Air Creation Tanarg
EI-DRU	Tecnam P92 Echo
EI-DRV	
EI-DRW	EV-97 Eurostar
EI-DRX	Raj Hamsa X'Air
EI-DSA	Airbus A320-216
EI-DSB	Airbus A320-216
EI-DSC	Airbus A320-216
EI-DSD	
EI-DSE	
EI-DSF	
EI-DSG	
EI-DSH	
EI-DSI	
EI-DSJ	
EI-DSK	
EI-DSL	
EI-DSM	
EI-DSN	
EI-DSO	
EI-DSP	
EI-DSR	
EI-DSS	
EI-DST	
EI-DSU	
EI-DSV	
EI-DSW	
EI-DSX	
EI-DSY	
EI-DSZ	
EI-DTA	
EI-DTB	
EI-DTC	
EI-DTD	
EI-DTE	
EI-DTF	
EI-DTG	
EI-DTH	
EI-DTI	
EI-DTJ	
EI-DTK	
EI-DTL	
EI-DTM	
EI-DTN	
EI-DTO	
EI-DTP	Boeing 737-347
EI-DTR	Robinson R44
EI-DTS	Piper PA-18-150
EI-DTT	ELA Aviacion ELA-07
EI-DTU	Boeing 737-5YO
EI-DTV	Boeing 737-5YO
EI-DTW	Boeing 737-5YO
EI-DTX	Boeing 737-5Q8
EI-DTY	Boeing 737-3M8
EI-DTZ	
EI-DUA	Boeing 757-256
EI-DUB	Airbus A330-301
EI-DUC	Boeing 757-256
EI-DUD	
EI-DUE	Boeing 757-256
EI-DUF	
EI-DUG	
EI-DUH	Piel CP.1310 Emeraude
EI-DUI	
EI-DUJ	
EI-DUK	Canadair CRJ900
EI-DUL	
EI-DUM	Canadair CRJ900
EI-DUN	Agusta 109E Power

☐ EI-DUO	
☐ EI-DUP	
☐ EI-DUR	
☐ EI-DUS	Boeing 737-3M8
☐ EI-DUT	
☐ EI-DUU	Canadair CRJ900
☐ EI-DUV	
☐ EI-DUW	ABS Aerolight Xenon
☐ EI-DUX	Canadair CRJ900
☐ EI-DUY	Canadair CRJ900
☐ EI-DUZ	
☐ EI-DVA	
☐ EI-DVB	Airbus 330-322
☐ EI-DVC	
☐ EI-DVD	Airbus A319-113
☐ EI-DVE	Airbus A320-214
☐ EI-DVF	Airbus A320-214
☐ EI-DVG	
☐ EI-DVH	
☐ EI-DVI	
☐ EI-DVJ	
☐ EI-DVK	
☐ EI-DVL	
☐ EI-DVM	
☐ EI-DVN	
☐ EI-DVO	
☐ EI-DVP	
☐ EI-DVR	
☐ EI-DVS	
☐ EI-DVT	
☐ EI-DVU	
☐ EI-DVV	
☐ EI-DVW	
☐ EI-DVX	
☐ EI-DVY	
☐ EI-DVZ	
☐ EI-DWA	
☐ EI-DWB	
☐ EI-DWC	
☐ EI-DWD	
☐ EI-DWE	
☐ EI-DWF	
☐ EI-DWG	
☐ EI-DWH	
☐ EI-DWI	
☐ EI-DWJ	
☐ EI-DWK	
☐ EI-DWL	
☐ EI-DWM	
☐ EI-DWN	
☐ EI-DWO	
☐ EI-DWP	
☐ EI-DWQ	
☐ EI-DWR	
☐ EI-DWS	
☐ EI-DWT	
☐ EI-DWU	
☐ EI-DWV	
☐ EI-DWW	
☐ EI-DWX	
☐ EI-DWY	
☐ EI-DWZ	
☐ EI-DXA	Ikarus C42 Cyclone
☐ EI-EBJ	Robinson R44
☐ EI-ECA	Agusta 109A
☐ EI-EDR	Piper PA-28R-200
☐ EI-EGG	Robinson R44
☐ EI-EGR	Robinson R44
☐ EI-EHB	Robinson R22B
☐ EI-EHC	Robinson R22B
☐ EI-EHD	Robinson R22B
☐ EI-EHE	Robinson R22B
☐ EI-EHG	Robinson R22B

☐ EI-EJR	Robinson R44
☐ EI-EMG	Robinson R22B
☐ EI-EUR	Eurocopter EC120B
☐ EI-EWR	Airbus A330-202
☐ EI-EXC	Robinson R44
☐ EI-EXG	Robinson R22B
☐ EI-FAR	Robinson R44
☐ EI-FBG	Reims F182Q Skylane
☐ EI-FXA	ATR 42-310
☐ EI-FXB	ATR 42-310
☐ EI-FXC	ATR 42-310
☐ EI-FXD	ATR 42-310
☐ EI-FXF	ATR 42-310
☐ EI-FXG	ATR 72-202
☐ EI-FXH	ATR 72-202
☐ EI-FXI	ATR 72-202
☐ EI-GAN	Bell 407
☐ EI-GAV	Robinson R22B
☐ EI-GBA	Boeing 767-266ER
☐ EI-GDL	Gulfstream 550
☐ EI-GER	Maule MX7-180A
☐ EI-GFC	SOCATA TB-9 Tampico
☐ EI-GKL	Robinson R22B
☐ EI-GPT	Robinson R22B
☐ EI-GPZ	Robinson R44
☐ EI-GSE	Reims F172M
☐ EI-GSM	Cessna 182S Skylane
☐ EI-GTY	Robinson R22B
☐ EI-GWT	Agusta 206B
☐ EI-GWY	Cessna 172R Skyhawk
☐ EI-HAM	Avid Flier
☐ EI-HAZ	Robinson R44
☐ EI-HCS	Grob 109B
☐ EI-HER	Bell 206B Jet Ranger
☐ EI-HHH	Agusta A109E Power
☐ EI-HOK	Eurocopter EC130B4
☐ EI-HXM	Bell 206B Jet Ranger
☐ EI-IAN	Pilatus PC-6/B2-H4
☐ EI-IAW	Learjet 60
☐ EI-IGA	Boeing 757-230
☐ EI-IGB	Boeing 757-230
☐ EI-IGC	Boeing 757-230
☐ EI-IHL	Aerospatiale AS.350B1
☐ EI-ING	Reims F172P
☐ EI-IPC	BN2 Islander
☐ EI-IRE	Canadair CL-604
☐ EI-IRV	Aerospatiale AS.350B
☐ EI-IZO	Eurocopter EC120B
☐ EI-JAC	Bell 206B Jet Ranger
☐ EI-JAL	Robinson R44
☐ EI-JAR	Robinson R44
☐ EI-JBC	Agusta 109A
☐ EI-JFA	Agusta 109S
☐ EI-JFD	Robinson R44
☐ EI-JFK	Airbus A330-301
☐ EI-JIM	Urban Air Samba XLA
☐ EI-JIV	Lockheed L-100
☐ EI-JON	Agusta 109E Power
☐ EI-JWM	Robinson R22B
☐ EI-KDH	Piper PA-28-181 Archer
☐ EI-KEV	Raj Hamsa X'Air
☐ EI-KEY	Robinson R44
☐ EI-KHL	Robinson R44
☐ EI-KHR	Robinson R22B
☐ EI-KJC	Hawker 850XP
☐ EI-LAF	Bell 206B Jet Ranger
☐ EI-LAJ	Robinson R44
☐ EI-LAL	Agusta 109E Power
☐ EI-LAX	Airbus A330-202
☐ EI-LIT	MBB Bo.105S
☐ EI-LKS	Eurocopter EC135T
☐ EI-LNX	Eurocopter EC130
☐ EI-LOC	Robinson R44

☐ EI-LTA	Boeing 757-23N
☐ EI-LTO	Boeing 757-23N
☐ EI-LTU	Boeing 757-23N
☐ EI-LTY	Boeing 757-23N
☐ EI-MAG	Robinson R22B
☐ EI-MAX	Learjet 31A
☐ EI-MCC	Robinson R44
☐ EI-MCF	Cessna 172R Skyhawk
☐ EI-MCP	Agusta A109C
☐ EI-MED	Agusta A109S Grand
☐ EI-MEJ	Bell 206B Jet Ranger
☐ EI-MEL	Agusta 109C
☐ EI-MEN	Agusta A109G Grand
☐ EI-MER	Bell 206B Jet Ranger
☐ EI-MES	Sikorsky S-61N
☐ EI-MIK	Eurocopter EC120B
☐ EI-MIP	Aerospatiale AS.365N
☐ EI-MIT	Agusta 109E Power
☐ EI-MJR	Robinson R44
☐ EI-MLN	Agusta 109E Power
☐ EI-MOR	Robinson R44
☐ EI-MUL	Robinson R44
☐ EI-MVK	Robinson R44
☐ EI-NBD	Robinson R44
☐ EI-NFW	Cessna 172S Skyhawk
☐ EI-NPG	Agusta A.109E Power
☐ EI-NVL	Jora
☐ EI-NZO	Eurocopter EC120B
☐ EI-OBJ	Robinson R22B
☐ EI-ODD	Bell 206B Jet Ranger
☐ EI-OFM	Reims F172N
☐ EI-ORD	Airbus A330-301
☐ EI-OZA	Airbus A300B4-103
☐ EI-OZB	Airbus A300B4-103
☐ EI-OZC	Airbus A300B4-103
☐ EI-PAT	BAe 146-200
☐ EI-PCI	Bell 206B Jet Ranger
☐ EI-PEC	Robinson R44
☐ EI-PEL	Agusta A.109E Power
☐ EI-PJD	Aerospatiale AS.350B2
☐ EI-PJW	Eurocopter EC120B
☐ EI-PKS	Bell 206B Jet Ranger
☐ EI-PMI	Agusta Bell 206B
☐ EI-POD	Cessna 177B Cardinal
☐ EI-POP	Cameron Z-90
☐ EI-PRI	Bell 206B Jet Ranger
☐ EI-RAV	Robinson R44
☐ EI-RCG	Sikorsky S-61N
☐ EI-REA	ATR 72-201
☐ EI-REB	ATR 72-201
☐ EI-RED	ATR 72-202
☐ EI-REE	ATR 72-202
☐ EI-REF	ATR 72-202
☐ EI-REG	ATR 72-202
☐ EI-REJ	ATR 72-201
☐ EI-REX	Learjet 60
☐ EI-RHM	Bell 407
☐ EI-RJA	BAe 146-RJ85
☐ EI-RJB	BAe 146-RJ85
☐ EI-RJC	BAe 146-RJ85
☐ EI-RJD	BAe 146-RJ85
☐ EI-RJE	BAe 146-RJ85
☐ EI-RJF	BAe 146-RJ85
☐ EI-RJG	BAe 146-RJ85
☐ EI-RJH	BAe 146-RJ85
☐ EI-RJI	BAe 146-RJ85
☐ EI-RJJ	BAe 146-RJ85
☐ EI-RJK	BAe 146-RJ85
☐ EI-RJL	BAe 146-RJ85
☐ EI-RJM	BAe 146-RJ85
☐ EI-RJN	BAe 146-RJ85
☐ EI-RJO	BAe 146-RJ85
☐ EI-RJP	BAe 146-RJ85

☐ EI-RJR	BAe 146-RJ85	☐
☐ EI-RJS	BAe 146-RJ85	☐
☐ EI-RJT	BAe 146-RJ85	☐
☐ EI-RJU	BAe 146-RJ85	☐
☐ EI-RJV	BAe 146-RJ85	☐
☐ EI-RJW	BAe 146-RJ85	☐
☐ EI-RJX	BAe 146-RJ85	☐
☐ EI-RMC	Bell 206B Jet Ranger	☐
☐ EI-RMH	Bell 407	☐
☐ EI-ROB	Robin R.1180TD Aiglon	☐
☐ EI-RON	Robinson R44	☐
☐ EI-SAC	Cessna 172P Skyhawk	☐
☐ EI-SAM	Extra EA300/200	☐
☐ EI-SAR	Sikorsky S-61N	☐
☐ EI-SAT	Steen Skybolt	☐
☐ EI-SBM	Agusta 109E Power	☐
☐ EI-SBP	Cessna T206H	☐
☐ EI-SEA	Searey	☐
☐ EI-SGF	Robinson R44	☐
☐ EI-SGN	Robinson R44	☐
☐ EI-SKG	Robin DR.400 135CDi	☐
☐ EI-SKL	Robin DR.400 135CDi	☐
☐ EI-SKR	Piper PA-44-180	☐
☐ EI-SKS	Robin R.2160	☐
☐ EI-SKT	Piper PA-44-180 Seminole	☐
☐ EI-SKU	Piper PA-28RT-201	☐
☐ EI-SKV	Robin R.2160	☐
☐ EI-SKW	Piper PA-28-161 Warrior	☐
☐ EI-SLA	ATR 42-310	☐
☐ EI-SLB	ATR 42-310	☐
☐ EI-SLC	ATR 42-310	☐
☐ EI-SLD	ATR 42-310	☐
☐ EI-SLE	ATR 42-310	☐
☐ EI-SLF	ATR 72-201F	☐
☐ EI-SLG	ATR 72-201F	☐
☐ EI-SLH	ATR 72-201F	☐
☐ EI-SMB	Short SD.360	☐
☐ EI-SMK	Zenair CH.701	☐
☐ EI-SNJ	Bell 407	☐
☐ EI-SQG	Agusta 109E Power	☐
☐ EI-STR	Bell 430	☐
☐ EI-STT	Cessna 172M Skyhawk	☐
☐ EI-SUB	Robinson R44	☐
☐ EI-SWD	Robinson R44	☐
☐ EI-TAB	Airbus A320-233	☐
☐ EI-TAC	Airbus A320-233	☐
☐ EI-TAG	Airbus A320-233	☐
☐ EI-TBM	SOCATA TBM-700	☐
☐ EI-TGF	Robinson R22B	☐
☐ EI-TIP	Bell 430	☐
☐ EI-TKI	Robinson R22B	☐
☐ EI-TMH	Robinson R44	☐
☐ EI-TON	Raj Hamsa X'Air	☐
☐ EI-TOY	Robinson R44	☐
☐ EI-TWO	Agusta 109E Power	☐
☐ EI-UFO	Piper PA-22-150 Tri-Pacer	☐
☐ EI-UNI	Robinson R44	☐
☐ EI-UPA	MD-11F	☐
☐ EI-UPE	MD-11F	☐
☐ EI-UPI	MD-11F	☐
☐ EI-UPO	MD-11F	☐
☐ EI-UPU	MD-11F	☐
☐ EI-WAC	Piper PA-23-250 Aztec E	☐
☐ EI-WAV	Bell 430	☐
☐ EI-WJN	BAe 125-700A	☐
☐ EI-WMN	Piper PA-23-250 Aztec E	☐
O EI-WOW	Eurocopter EC130B4	☐
☐ EI-WRN	Piper PA-28-151 Warrior	☐
☐ EI-XLA	Urban Air Samba XLA	☐
☐ EI-YBZ	Robinson R44	☐

Ireland Aircraft bases guide

Abbeyshrule
A/G 122.600

ATK	AVM	AWP	AWR
AYB	AYF	AYT	BCM
BFI	BGD	BGU	BPP
BPU	BSV	BUF	BXT
CGH	COT	COY	CPN
CUJ	DBX	DGA	DGP
DGR	DGY	DKC	DRM
NVL	SAM	XLA	SAT
G-ATMC	BUZA	BVPD	

Birr
A/G 122.950

AST	BAV	CJS	CMN
DKW	KEV	TON	

Clonbulloge

CDP	COM	DBJ	DKT
IAN	IPC		

Connemare - Inveran

AYN	BCE	CUW

Coonagh
A/G 129.900

AYA	BFP	BYX	CIZ
DDD	DNW	DOY	DRW

Cork
APP 119.100   TWR 119.3

BWH	CGP	CMT	COZ
DFW	DJY	DRN	ECA
EHE	HAZ	JAR	JON
MIP	MOR		
G-AVIC	CDFS	TAIT	

Dublin
APP 119.550   TWR 118.600

ABI	BYO	BYR	CBK
CCJ	CCL	CGQ	CMB
CPC	CPD	CPE	CPF
CPG	CPH	CPT	CRK
CSA	CSB	CSC	CSD
CSE	CSF	CSG	CSH
CSI	CSJ	CSM	CSN
CSO	CSP	CSQ	CSR
CSS	CST	CSV	CSW
CSX	CSY	CSZ	CTA
CTB	CUG	CVA	CVB
CVC	CVD	CVR	CVS
DAA	DAC	DAD	DAE
DAF	DAG	DAH	DAI
DAJ	DAK	DAL	DAM
DAN	DAO	DAP	DAR
DAS	DAT	DAV	DAW
DAX	DAY	DAZ	DCB
DCC	DCD	DCE	DCF
DCG	DCH	DCI	DCJ
DCK	DCL	DCM	DCN
DCO	DCP	DCR	DCS
DCT	DCV	DCW	DCX
DCY	DCZ	DEA	DEB
DEC	DEE	DEF	DEG
DEH	DEI	DEJ	DEK
DEL	DEM	DEN	DEO
DEP	DER	DES	DET
DHA	DHB	DHC	DHD
DHE	DHF	DHG	DHH
DHI	DHJ	DHK	DHM
DHN	DHO	DHP	DHR
DHS	DHT	DHV	DHW
DHX	DHY	DHZ	DJO
DJZ	DLB	DLC	DLD
DLE	DLF	DLG	DLH
DLI	DLJ	DLK	DLL
DLM	DLN	DLO	DLR
DLS	DLT	DLV	DLW
DLX	DLY	DLZ	DMK
DMT	DPA	DPB	DPC
DPD	DPE	DPF	DPG
DPH	DPI	DPJ	DPK
DPL	DPM	DPN	DPO
DPP	DPR	DPS	DPT
DPV	DUB	DUN	DUO
DUZ	DVE	DVF	EDR
EUR	EWR	GAN	ING
IRE	JFK	JIV	LAX
MCC	MES	MLN	ODD
OFM	ORD	PCI	POP
REA	REB	RED	REE
REJ	REX	RHM	RJK
RJL	SBP	SLA	SLB
SLC	SLD	SLE	SLF
SLG	SLH	SNJ	TIP
TWO			
G-JAKI	LJRM	OZRH	

Dublin - Knocksedan

BYJ	CHV	JBC	MEL

Farranfore

AUO	CUP	DMA

Galway
TWR 122.500

BYY	JFD	LAJ	LAL
LOC	MUL	REF	REG
REH	REI	RON	SWD

Gorey

ANT	CJJ	HCS

Gowan Grange

APS	BIK
G-AVOO	KOHF

Granard

DCA	DGG	DGJ

Hacketstown

BBO	BFV	BHN	CAY
CTL	DIA		

Kilkenny
A/G 122.900 / 130.400

AUE	BBI	BCS	DRO

Kilrush

ANY	AYR	AYY	BBV
BCN	BDL	BYL	CCF
CFF	CKH	CTL	CVW
DBI	DDR	DKE	DKJ
DKN	DOW	DTT	ELL
G-AGVN	ASCU	AVSE	AVZX
AWMN	BEMY	BMZX	BOOW
BSHK	BWKJ	BXDP	BXZT
BYFD	CCBR	CWOT	IVAL
JACO	KELL	MTKD	MTXL
MYDM	MYXK	RVIB	

Letterkenny

CXC	DDJ	DGK	
G-BUGJ	MBYK	MJBT	MMOG
MMPR	MYMR		

Oranmore Helipad

CZM	EBJ	EMG	GKL
GTY	IRV	MAG	MIK
MJR	PJW	RAV	TGF

Overseas

ARM	AUG	AUY	AVB
CBR	CCC	CEY	CEZ
CFZ	CHH	CIJ	CIR
CIW	CKM	CLW	CLZ
CMS	CMY	CNB	CNQ
COH	COI	COJ	COK
COQ	CPJ	CPK	CRD
CRE	CRF	CRH	CRJ
CRL	CRM	CRO	CRW
CRZ	CSK	CSL	CSU
CUA	CUD	CUM	CUN
CVO	CWA	CWB	CWC
CWD	CWE	CWF	CWW
CWX	CXI	CXJ	CXL
CXM	CXO	CXV	CZG
CZH	CZK	CZO	DBK
DBL	DBM	DBP	DDE
DDH	DDW	DDY	DEW
DEX	DEY	DEZ	DFA
DFD	DFE	DFF	DFG
DFH	DFI	DFJ	DFK
DFL	DFN	DFO	DFP
DFS	DGD	DJH	DJI
DJJ	DJR	DJS	DKD
DKL	DKV	DMJ	DMM
DMP	DMR	DMZ	DNA
DNJ	DNP	DNX	DNY
DNZ	DOF	DOH	DOK
DOL	DOM	DOP	DOS
DOT	DOU	DOV	DRG
DRI	DRJ	DRK	DRR
DTP	DTV	DTW	DTX
DTY	DUA	DUC	DUD
DUE	DUS	GAA	GBA
IGA	IGB	IGC	LTA
LTO	LTU	LTY	PAT
RJA	RJB	RJC	RJD
RJE	RJF	RJG	RJH
RJI	RJJ	RJN	RJO
RJP	RJR	RJS	RJT
RJU	RJV	RJW	RJX
SMB	UPA	UPE	UPI
UPO	UPU		

Rathcoole

AWH	CAU

Seven Parks Farm, Balbriggan

AGJ	ALP	AUM

Shannon
APP 121.400   TWR 118.700

BPL	DOR	GDL	IAW
LKS	LNX	RCG	RMC
WAC	WAV	WJN	WMN

Sligo
TWR 122.100

BBC	BGJ	CXS	SAC
SEA			
G-BTSP	BWJY	BXLR	BZXS
CDJU	HENT		

Thurles

BUC	CFX	CIA	CVL
HER			

Trim
A/G 123.300

AYK	BAJ	BFO	BVK
CUT	DDC	GER	POD
STT	UFO		
G-CBRF	MWHX	MZIB	

Waterford
TWR 129.850

AOB	ATJ	BDR	BRS
BSO	CDX	CGD	CIF
CIV	CMR	CNG	CNL
CPI	CRG	CRV	CZN
DDX	DJM	DMG	GFC
GWY	ROB	SAR	SKP
SKR	SKU	WRN	
G-BBZF	BEXW	BYXU	MLFF

Weston
A/G 122.400

BAT	BBJ	BCK	BCU
BEA	BEN	BHC	BRU
BSC	BSK	BSL	BUA
BUG	BUH	BUN	BUT
BYG	CAC	CAD	CAE
CAP	CAX	CCD	CDV
CFN	CFP	CFY	CGG
CHM	CIG	CIM	CIN
CLA	CML	CMV	CPO
CWR	CZP	DDA	DDB
DDI	DDZ	DGX	DIF
DJW	DKI	DKM	DMC
DMS	DNU	DOJ	EGG
FBG	GAV	GSE	GSM
GWT	HHH	IHL	JAC
KDH	KHL	KHR	LAF
LIT	MEN	MVK	PJD
SKG	SKL	SKS	SKT
SKV	SKW	TBM	TMH
TOY	UNI	YLG	
G-AYJA	BHVC	BSZC	BTVV
BZGH	MAYE	MCCY	OSPS
SEAI	SWAT	THEA	UTTS

Current Ireland Military serials |

**Active aircraft including historic
flights and museum exhibits**

- ☐ 34   Miles M.14 Magister
- ☐ 141 Avro Anson
- ☐ 164 DHC-1 Chipmunk
- ☐ 168 DHC-1 Chipmunk
- ☐ 169 DHC-1 Chipmunk
- ☐ 172 DHC-1 Chipmunk
- ☐ 183 Provost T.51
- ☐ 184 Provost T.51
- ☐ 187 DH115 Vampire T55
- ☐ 191 DH115 Vampire T55
- ☐ 192 DH115 Vampire T55
- ☐ 193 DH115 Vampire T55
- ☐ 195 Alouette III
- ☐ 196 Alouette III
- ☐ 197 Alouette III
- ☐ 198 DH115 Vampire T11
- ☐ 199 DHC-1 Chipmunk
- ☐ 202 Alouette III
- ☐ 203 Reims FR.172H
- ☐ 205 Reims FR.172H
- ☐ 206 Reims FR.172H
- ☐ 207 Reims FR.172H
- ☐ 208 Reims FR.172H
- ☐ 209 Reims FR.172H
- ☐ 210 Reims FR.172H
- ☐ 211 Alouette III
- ☐ 212 Alouette III
- ☐ 213 Alouette III
- ☐ 214 Alouette III
- ☐ 215 Fouga CM.170R
- ☐ 216 Fouga CM.170R
- ☐ 217 Fouga CM.170R
- ☐ 218 Fouga CM.170R
- ☐ 219 Fouga CM.170R
- ☐ 220 Fouga CM.170R
- ☐ 221 Fouga CM.170R
- ☐ 237 SA.342L Gazelle
- ☐ 240 Beech 200 King Air
- ☐ 241 SA.342L Gazelle
- ☐ 244 SA.365F Dauphin
- ☐ 245 SA.365F Dauphin
- ☐ 246 SA.365F Dauphin
- ☐ 247 SA.365F Dauphin
- ☐ 251 Gulfstream 4
- ☐ 252 CASA 235 MPA
- ☐ 253 CASA 235 MPA
- ☐ 254 BN-2T Islander
- ☐ 255 AS.355N2
- ☐ 256 Eurocopter EC135 T1
- ☐ 258 Lear Jet 45
- ☐ 260 Pilatus PC-9M
- ☐ 261 Pilatus PC-9M
- ☐ 262 Pilatus PC-9M
- ☐ 263 Pilatus PC-9M
- ☐ 264 Pilatus PC-9M
- ☐ 265 Pilatus PC-9M
- ☐ 266 Pilatus PC-9M
- ☐ 267 Pilatus PC-9M
- ☐ 270 Eurocopter EC135T2
- ☐ 271 Eurocopter EC135T2
- ☐ 274 AW139
- ☐ 275 AW139
- ☐ 280 AW139
- ☐ 281 AW139

NOTES

Foreign Registered aircraft based in the U.K & Ireland

Note : Aircraft marked with an * are either not airworthy or are stored.

☐ A6-ESH	Airbus A319-133X
☐ A6-HEH	Boeing 737-8AJ
☐ A6-HRS	Boeing 737-7EO
☐ A6-MRM	Boeing 737-8EC
☐ C-FQIP	Lake LA-4-200 Buccaneer
☐ C-GWJO*	Boeing 737-2A3
☐ CS-ARI	Robin HR.100/210 Safari
☐ D-ASDB	VFW-Fokker VFW-614
☐ D-CALM	Dornier Do 228-101
☐ D-EAAW	Bolkow Bo209-160RV
☐ D-EAGC	Cessna F172H
☐ D-EAOB	Piper PA-28-181 Archer II
☐ D-EAPF	Robin DR.400/180R
☐ D-EAWW	Piper PA-28R-201 Arrow III
☐ D-EBLI	Bölkow Bö.207
☐ D-EBLO*	Bölkow Bö.207
☐ D-EBWE	Piper PA-28-235 Cherokee
☐ D-EBWS	Cessna T210N Centurion II
☐ D-EBXR	Reims FR172K Hawk XP
☐ D-ECFE	Oberlerchner JOB 15-150
☐ D-ECGI	Bölkow Bö.208C Junior
☐ D-EDEL	Piper PA-32-300
☐ D-EDEQ	Beech B24R Sierra 200
☐ D-EDNA	Bölkow Bö.208C Junior
☐ D-EDYQ	Piper PA-32-260
☐ D-EEAH	Bölkow Bo.208C Junior
☐ D-EEHW	Cessna P210N Centurion
☐ D-EEPI	Wassmer WA.54 Atlantic
☐ D-EEVY	Cessna 170A
☐ D-EFFA	Ruschmeyer R90-230RG
☐ D-EFJG	Bölkow Bo.209-160RV
☐ D-EFQE	Bölkow Bo.207
☐ D-EFQR	Robin DR.400/180 Regent
☐ D-EFTI	Bölkow Bö.207
☐ D-EFVS	Wassmer WA.52 Europa
☐ D-EFZC	SIAI-Marchetti S.208
☐ D-EFZO	Cessna F172F
☐ D-EGDC	Grumman AA-5B Tiger
☐ D-EGEU*	Piper PA-22-108 Colt
☐ D-EGKE	SOCATA Rallye 180TS
☐ D-EGLW*	Piper PA-38-112 Tomahawk
☐ D-EGVA	Piper PA-28R-200 Arrow II
☐ D-EGVY	Piper PA-28-161 Warrior III
☐ D-EGXC	Piper PA-28R-201 Arrow
☐ D-EHJL	Piaggio FWP.149
☐ D-EHKY	Bölkow Bö 207
☐ D-EHLA	Bölkow Bö.207
☐ D-EHOP	Bolkow Bo.207
☐ D-EHUQ	Bölkow Bö.207
☐ D-EHYX*	Bölkow Bö.207
☐ D-EIAL	Piper PA-28-161 Warrior II
☐ D-EIAR	CEA DR.250/160 Capitaine
☐ D-EIIP	Reims F182Q Skylane
☐ D-EIKR	Robin DR.400/180 Regent
☐ D-EIVF	PZL-110 Koliber 150
☐ D-EJBI	Bölkow Bö.207
☐ D-EJLY	Cessna 182K Skylane
☐ D-EKDN	Beech A36 Bonanza
☐ D-EKHW	Piper PA-28RT-201T Arrow
☐ D-EKJD	Reims FR172J Rocket
☐ D-EMLS	Cessna T210L Centurion

☐ D-EMUH	Bölkow Bö.208C Junior
☐ D-EMZC	Reims FR172G Rocket
☐ D-ENTO	American General AG-5B
☐ D-EOMK	Robin DR.400/180 Regent
☐ D-ETTO	Extra EA.300/L
☐ D-EWAT	Commander 114B
☐ D-EXCC *	Piper PA-46-350P Malibu
☐ D-EXGC	Extra EA.200
☐ D-FBPS	Cessan 208B Caravan
☐ D-FLOH	Cessna 208B Caravan
☐ D-GPEZ*	Piper PA-30 C
☐ D-HCKV	Agusta A109A-II
☐ D-IBPN	Beech 58P Baron
☐ D-KGLM	Grob G.109B
☐ D-KIFF	SFS-31 Milan
☐ D-KMDP	Fournier RF-3
☐ D-KOOL	Schleicher ASH 25EB 28
☐ D-MBRG	Aerostyle Breezer
☐ D-MDMM	Impulse 100
☐ D-MVMM	WDL Fascination
☐ EC-CFA*	Boeing 727-256
☐ EC-DDX*	Boeing 727-256A
☐ EC-EP6	ELA Aviacion ELA-07
☐ EL-AKJ*	Boeing 707-321C
☐ EL-AKL*	Boeing 707-351C
☐ ES-YLK*	Aero L-29A Delfin
☐ F-BBSO*	Taylorcraft Auster 5
☐ F-BGCJ*	DH.82A Tiger Moth
☐ F-BGNR*	Vickers 708 Viscount
☐ F-BMCY*	Potez 840
☐ F-BMHM	Piper J-3C-65 Cub
☐ F-BRHN	Bölkow Bö.208C Junior
☐ F-BROC	CEA DR.360 Chevalier
☐ F-BSPQ	Robin DR.300/120 Prince
☐ F-BTKO	Robin HR.100/210 Safari
☐ F-GCTU	Piper PA-38-112 Tomahawk
☐ F-GFGH	SOCATA Rallye 235E
☐ F-GFLD*	Beech C90 King Air
☐ F-GFOR	Robin ATL
☐ F-GIBU	Aérospatiale SA.342J
☐ F-GJPB *	SOCATA TB-9 Tampico
☐ F-GJQI	Robin ATL L
☐ F-GKKI	Avions Mudry CAP.231EX
☐ F-GKMZ	Mudry CAP.232
☐ F-GLAO	SOCATA TB-9 Tampico
☐ F-GMHH*	Robin HR.100/210 Safari
☐ F-GODZ	Pilatus PC-6/340 Porter
☐ F-GOTC	Mudry CAP.232
☐ F-GOXD	Robin DR400/180RP
☐ F-GSGZ	Mudry CAP.232
☐ F-GXDB	Mudry CAP.232
☐ F-GXFP	Sud Aviation SA.318C
☐ F-GYRO	Mudry CAP.232
☐ F-JITM	Funk FK-14 Polaris
☐ F-PAGD*	Auster V J/1 Autocrat
☐ F-PYOY	Heintz Zenith 100
☐ 21YV	Dyn'Aero MCR-01
☐ 31WI	Farrington Twinstarr
☐ 95MR	Power Assist Swift
☐ HA-ACL	Dornier Do.28D-2
☐ HA-ACO	Dornier Do.28D-2
☐ HA-HUA	Yakovlev Yak-18T
☐ HA-HUB	Yakovlev Yak-12M
☐ HA-HUD	Sukhoi Su-29
☐ HA-IDL	Sud Aviation Alouette II
☐ HA-JAB	Yakovlev Yak-18T
☐ HA-JAC	Yakovlev Yak-18T

☐ HA-LAQ	LET L-410UVP-E4
☐ HA-LFM	Aérospatiale SA.341G
☐ HA-LFZ	Sud SA318C Alouette II
☐ HA-MKE	WSK-PZL Antonov An-2R
☐ HA-MKF	Antonov An-2
☐ HA-PPY	SOKO SO341 Gazelle
☐ HA-VOC	Dornier Do.28D-2
☐ HA-YAB	Yakovlev Yak-18T
☐ HA-YAD	Yakovlev Yak-18T
☐ HA-YAE	Yakovlev Yak-18T
☐ HA-YAF	Yakovlev Yak-18T
☐ HA-YAG	Yakovlev Yak-18T
☐ HA-YAH	Technoavia Yak-18T
☐ HA-YAJ	Yakovlev Yak-18T
☐ HA-YAK	Yakovlev Yak-18T
☐ HA-YAM	Yakovlev Yak-18T
☐ HA-YAN	Yakovlev Yak-18T
☐ HA-YAO	Sukhoi Su-29
☐ HA-YAP	Yakovlev Yak-18T
☐ HA-YAR	Sukhoi Su-29
☐ HA-YAU	Yakovlev Yak-18T
☐ HA-YAV	Yakovlev Yak-18T
☐ HA-YAW	Sukhoi Su-29
☐ HA-YAZ	Yakovlev Yak-18T
☐ HA-YDF	Technoavia SMG-92 Finist
☐ HA-YFC	LET L-410-FG
☐ HB-DFT	Mooney M.20J
☐ HB-ITF	Gulfstream IV
☐ HB-IVR	Canadair CL604 Challenger
☐ HB-OBP *	Piper J-3C-65 Cub
☐ HS-TFG	Rockwell 690B
☐ HZ-AB3	Boeing 727-2U5AR
☐ HZ-ARK	Gulfstream G-550
☐ HZ-OFC4	Dassault Falcon 900EX
☐ HZ-SJP3	Canadair CL604 Challenger
☐ I-6351	Tecnam P.92 Echo
☐ I-6929	Aeropro Eurofox
☐ I-EIXM*	Piper PA-18-135 Super Cub
☐ I-LELF	SIAI-Marchetti SF.260C
☐ I-TERB	BAe BAe.146-200
☐ I-TERK	BAe BAe.146-200
☐ I-TERV	BAe BAe.146-200
☐ I-TOMI*	Nardi FN.305D
☐ LN-AMY	North American AT-6D
☐ LN-KKA*	Fokker F.27-050
☐ LV-AZF	Boeing 747-267B
☐ LV-RIE	Nord 1002 Pingouin
☐ LV-WTY	McDonnell-Douglas MD-81
☐ LX-FTA	Dassault Falcon 900C
☐ LX-POO *	Raytheon RB390 Premier
☐ LX-TLB	Douglas DC-8-62F
☐ LX-TRE	Tecnam P2002JF Sierra
☐ LY-AFO	Antonov An-2R
☐ LY-AHD	Yakovlev Yak-12
☐ LY-ALT	Yakovlev Yak-52
☐ LY-BIG	Antonov An-2T
☐ LY-MHC	Antonov An-2R
☐ N1FD	SOCATA TB-200 Tobago
☐ N1FY	Cessna 421C Golden Eagle
☐ N2CL	Piper PA-28RT-201T Arrow
☐ N2FU	Learjet 31
☐ N2NF	Boeing 707-321C
☐ N2NR	Agusta A109A-II
☐ N2RK	Lockheed L.188PF Electra

Reg.	Type	Reg.	Type	Reg.	Type
N3HK	Cessna 340 II	N50AY	Commander 114	N99ET	SOCATA TB-10 Tobago
N4HG	Lockheed L.188PF Electra	N50VC	Cessna 525 CJ1+	N100JS	Cessna 525B CJ3
N4VQ	Beech A36 Bonanza	N51AH	Piper PA-32R-301 SP	N101DW	Piper PA-32R-300
N5LL	Piper PA-31 Navajo C	N51ER	Champion 7GCAA	N101UK	Mooney M.20K
N6NE	Lockheed Jetstar 731	N51WF	Rockwell 690C	N105SK	Reims F150L
N7AG	Agusta A109A Mk.II	N55BN	Beech 95-B55 Baron	N108SR	Cirrus Design SR22
N8JX	Extra EA300/S	N55CJ	Cessna 525 CitationJet	N109AB	Agusta A109E Power
N8MZ	Piper PA-30 B	N55EN	Beech E55 Baron	N109AN	Agusta A109A-II
N8YG	Piper PA-32R-301T II TC	N57CR	Hiller UH-12C	N109AR	Agusta A109A
N9AY	Cessna 421C Golden Eagle	N57MT	Cessna T303 Crusader	N109MJ	Agusta A109E Power
N9FJ	Aérospatiale AS.350B-2	N58GT	Beech B58 Baron	N109TD	Agusta A109E Power
N9SZ	Cirrus Design SR22-GTS	N58YD	Beech 58 Baron	N109TF	Agusta A109A-II
N10MC	Cirrus Design SR22	N59GG	Beech C90A King Air	N109TK	Agusta A109C
N11FV	Cessna T303 Crusader	N59SD	McD Douglas MD.369E	N109WF	Agusta A109A-II
N12AB	Ruschmeyer R90-230RG	N59VT	Beech K35 Bonanza	N112JA	Commander 112TC-A
N12ZX	Mooney M.20J	N60B*	Rockwell 690A	N112SR	Cirrus Design SR22-GTS
N13DT	Robinson R44	N60GM	Cessna 421C Golden Eagle	N112WM	Piper PA-32-300
N13PF	Piper PA-39 C/R	N60LW	Cessna 550 Citation Bravo	N113AC	SOCATA TB-20 Trinidad GT
N14AF	Commander 112TC-A	N60NZ	Beech 60 Duke	N114ED	Commander 114B
N14EP	SOCATA TB-20 Trinidad GT	N61DE	Piper PA-32-300 Six	N115MD	Commander 114TC
N14HF	Maule MT-7-235	N61HB	Piper PA-34-220T Seneca	N115TB	Commander 114TC
N14MT	Cessna TR182 Skylane RG	N61MF *	Mooney M.20J	N116HS	Bell UH-1L
N15CK	Maule MX-7-235	N61PS	Pitts S-2B	N116WG	Westland WG-30-100
N17UK	Cirrus Design SR22	N64GG	Raytheon B300 King Air	N119BM	Agusta A119 Koala
N18GH	McD MD.520N	N64JG	Bell 206B-2 Jet Ranger	N120HH	Bell 407
N18V	Beech UC-43-BH Traveler	N64VB	Beech 58 Baron	N121EL*	Gates Learjet 25
N19GL	Brantly B.2B	N65JF	Piper PA-28-181 Archer II	N121HT	Cirrus Design SR22
N20AG	SOCATA TB-20 Trinidad	N65MJ	Beech 58P Baron	N121MT	Britten-Norman BN-2T
N20UK	Mooney M.20F Executive	N66DN	Bombardier Learjet 45	N122MG	Cirrus Design SR22-GTS
N21UH	UH-12C	N66SG	Bombardier Learjet 45	N122SM	Cessna 525A CJ2
N22CG	Cessna 441 Conquest II	N66SW*	Cessna 340	N123AX	Piper PA-32R-301 II HP
N22NN	Cessna 182P Skylane	N69LJ	Bombardier Learjet 60	N123DU	Piper PA-28-161 Warrior II
N23KY	Cessna P210N Centurion	N69LP	Piper PA-61P -601P	N123DV	Cirrus Design SR22
N25KB	Piper PA-24-250 Comanche	N70AA	Beech 70 Queen Air	N123SA	Piper PA-18-150 Super Cub
N25PR	Piper PA-30-160 B	N70QJ	Sikorsky S-76A	N123UK	Mooney M.20J
N25XZ	Cessna 182G	N70VB	Ted Smith Aerostar 600A	N125AV	Beech 58 Baron
N26HE	Cessna 421C Golden Eagle	N71VE	Rockwell 690A	N125MM	Rockwell Turbo 690C
N27BG	Cessna 340A	N71WZ	Piper PA-46-350P Malibu	N125ZZ	Hawker 800XP
N27MW	Beech B58 Baron	N73GR	Piper PA-28-181 Archer III	N127BU	Cessna 551 Citation II/SP
N28TE	Raytheon 58 Baron	N73MW	Beech B200 Super King Air	N129SC	Piper PA-32-300
N30NW	Piper PA-30-160	N74DC	Pitts S-2A Special	N131CD	Cirrus Design SR20
N31GN	Cessna 310R II	N74PM	Agusta A109C	N132CK	Cessna 421A
N31NB	Piper PA-31 Turbo Navajo	N75TC	Cessna 172N	N132LE	Piper PA-32-300
N31RB	Grumman-American AA-5B	N77YY	Piper PA-32R-301T II TC	N134TT	Cessna 305C Bird Dog
N32LE	Piper PA-31T SP	N78GG	Beech F33A Bonanza	N136SA	American General AG-5B
N33EW	Mitsubishi MU-2B-60	N78HB	Aviat A-1B Husky	N142TW	Beech 58 Baron
N33NW	SOCATA TB-20 Trinidad	N78XP	Reims FR172K Hawk XP II	N145DF	Cessna S550 Citation II
N34FA	SOCATA TB-20 Trinidad	N79AP	Beech 58P Baron	N145DR	Piper PA-34-220T Seneca
N34RF	Beech C90B King Air	N79EL	Beech 400A Beechjet	N147CD	Cirrus Design SR22
N35AD	Piper PA-30	N79HR	Lancair LC41-550FG	N147DC	Douglas C-47A-75-DL
N35AL(2)	Diamond DA 42 Twin Star	N80BA	Pitts S-1A	N147GT	Cirrus Design SR22-G2
N35SN	Beech 35-33 Debonair	N80HC	Beech 58 Baron	N147KA	Cirrus Design SR22-GTS
N36NB	Beech A36 Bonanza	N80JN	Mitsubishi MU-2J	N147LD	Cirrus Design SR22
N36SU	Beech A36 Bonanza	N84VK	Piper PA-24-180 Comanche	N147LK	Cirrus Design SR22-GTS
N36TH*	Canadair Silver Star Mk.3	N85LB	Cessna 340A II	N147VC	Cirrus Design SR22
N37EL	SOCATA TB-20 Trinidad	N85VK	Partenavia P.68C	N150JC	Beech A35 Bonanza
N37LW	Piper PA-23-250 Aztec	N88NA	Piper PA-32R-301T	N151CG	Cirrus Design SR22
N37US	Piper PA-34-200T Seneca II	N89WC	Sikorsky S-76B	N153H	Bell 222B
N37VB	Cessna 421C	N90BE	Mooney M.20K	N154DJ	Cessna T303 Crusader
N39SE	Diamond DA.40 Star	N90DE	McD Douglas MD.369E	N160SR	Cirrus Design SR22
N39TA	Beech B24R Sierra 200	N90FL	Beech C90 King Air	N160TR	Piper PA-31T Cheyenne II
N40EA	Bell 222	N90SA	Reims F172M	N170AZ	Cessna 170A
N40GD	Cirrus Design SR22	N90U	Piper PA-46-350P Malibu	N171JB	Piper PA-28R-180 Arrow
N40XR	Bombardier Learjet 40	N90YA	Cessna 425 Corsair	N172AM	Cessna 172M Skyhawk II
N41AK	Beech F90 King Air	N91ME	SOCATA TB-20 Trinidad	N173RG	Velocity 173RG
N41FT	Piper PA-39 Twin	N91TH	Agusta A109E Power	N176AF	Cessna 650 Citation III
N42FW	Beech E33 Bonanza	N94SA	Champion 7ECA Citabria	N177MA	Piper PA-46-350P Malibu
N43GG	Piper PA-34-200T Seneca II	N95D	Piper PA-34-220T Seneca	N177SA	Reims F177RG
N43SV	Boeing-Stearman PT-13D	N95TA	Piper PA-31 Turbo Navajo	N180BB	Cessna 180K
N46PJ	Cessna 551 Citaion II/SP	N96HC	Bell 206L-1 Long Ranger II	N180FN	Cessna 180K
N46PL	Piper PA-46-500TP Malibu	N96MR	Cessna 525B CJ3	N180LK	Piper PA-28-180 Cherokee
N48NS	Cessna 550 Citation Bravo	N96XW *	Twinstarr Gyrocopter	N181WW	Beagle B.206 Srs.1
N49BH	Aviat A-1B Husky	N97GP	SOCATA TB-20 Trinidad	N182GC	Reims F182Q Skylane II

☐	N184CD	Cirrus Design SR20	☐ N297CJ	SE.313B Alouette II	☐ N456MS	BD-700 Global 5000
☐	N187SA	Piper PA-28R-200 Arrow II	☐ N297GT	SOCATA TB-21 Trinidad	☐ N456PP	Beech C90A King Air
☐	N188S	Agusta A109A-II	☐ N297SR	Cirrus Design SR22-GTS	☐ N456TL	Reims FT337GP
☐	N189SA	Piper PA-31-325 Navajo	☐ N2989M	Piper PA-32-300 Six	☐ N458BG	DHC.1 Chipmunk 22
☐	N191ME	Cessna T206H Stationair	☐ N305RD	Mooney M20K	☐ N468DB	Beech G58 Baron
☐	N192JM	Mooney M.20R Ovation	☐ N305SE	Mooney M.20K	☐ N470RD	Cirrus Design SRV-G2
☐	N195NJ	Agusta A109E Power	☐ N309CJ	Cessna 525A CJ2+	☐ N473DC	Douglas C-47A Dakota III
☐	N199PS	Piper PA-34-220T Seneca	☐ N309LJ*	Learjet Inc Learjet 25	☐ N476D	Pilatus PC-12/45
☐	N200UP	Dassault Falcon 50	☐ N310QQ	Cessna 310Q	☐ N477KA	Bell 407
☐	N201W	Bell 47D-1	☐ N310WT	Cessna 310R II	☐ N480BB	Enstrom 480B
☐	N201YK	Mooney M.20J	☐ N313CF	Bell UH-1H Iroquois	☐ N480KP	Enstrom 480B
☐	N202AA	Cessna 421C Golden Eagle	☐ N320MR	Piper PA-30	☐ N482CD	Cirrus Design SR22-GTS
☐	N203CD	Cirrus Design SR20-G2	☐ N321KL	Mooney M.20J (201)	☐ N485ED	Piper PA-23-250 Aztec C
☐	N203SA	Piper AE-1 Cub Cruiser	☐ N322MC	MD Helicopters MD 369E	☐ N485LT	Hawker 800XP
☐	N206CF	Cessna TU206G Stationair	☐ N322RJ	Beech 60 Duke	☐ N497XP	Hawker 400XP
☐	N206HE	Bell 206B Jet Ranger	☐ N324JC	Cessna 500 Citation I	☐ N498YY	Cessna 525 CitationJet
☐	N208B	Cessna 208B Caravan	☐ N324JS	SOCATA TBM-700	☐ N499MS	Piper PA-28-181 Archer III
☐	N208EC	Cessna 208B Caravan	☐ N325SC	Aérospatiale AS.355F2	☐ N500AV	Piper PA-24-260 Comanche
☐	N208ER	Bell 206B Jet Ranger	☐ N326SC	Aérospatiale AS.355F4	☐ N500CS	Beech B200 Super King Air
☐	N208NJ	Cessna 208B Caravan	☐ N328BX	CL-604 Challenger	☐ N500LN	Howard 500
☐	N209DW	Lancair LC41-550FG	☐ N337UK	Reims F337G Skymaster	☐ N500RK	Hughes 369HS
☐	N209SA	Piper PA-22-108 Colt	☐ N338DB	Piper PA-46-500TP Malibu	☐ N500SY	McD MD.369E
☐	N210AD	Cessna 210G Centurion	☐ N340CD	Cirrus Design SR22	☐ N500TY	MD Helicopters MD.369E
☐	N210CP	Cessna 210M Centurion	☐ N340DW	Cessna 340A-II	☐ N500XV	Hughes 369D
☐	N210EU	Cessna T210L Centurion	☐ N340GJ	Cessna 340A	☐ N500ZW	Hughes 369D
☐	N210NM	Cessna 210K Centurion	☐ N340SC	Cessna 340	☐ N502DW	Mudry CAP.10B
☐	N212MZ	Mooney M.20F	☐ N340YP	Cessna 340A II	☐ N502TC	Piper PA-30
☐	N212W	Hiller UH-12A	☐ N343RR	Piper PA-46-500TP Malibu	☐ N503DW	Mudry CAP.10B
☐	N216GC	Piper PA-28R-200 Arrow B	☐ N345TB	SOCATA TB-20 Trinidad	☐ N510W	Bell 222B
☐	N218BA	Boeing 747-245F	☐ N346X	Maule M5-210C	☐ N511TC	Cessna 525 CitationJet
☐	N218SA	Piper PA-24-250 Comanche	☐ N350DG	Lancair LC42-550FG	☐ N515SC	Piper PA-32R-301T II TC
☐	N218Y	Cessna 310Q	☐ N350PB	Piper PA-31-350 Chieftain	☐ N517TS	Agusta A109E Power
☐	N220RJ	Cirrus Design SR22	☐ N350UK	Aérospatiale AS.350B	☐ N518XL	Liberty Aerospace XL-2
☐	N222ED	Cirrus Design SR22-G2	☐ N352CM	Piper PA-46-350P Malibu	☐ N519MC	Piper PA-28-140 Cruiser
☐	N222SW	Cirrus Design SR22-G2	☐ N352F	Farnborough F1C3 Kestrel	☐ N524SF	Cessna 525 CitationJet
☐	N222WX	Bell 222A	☐ N357J	Cessna 525A CJ2	☐ N525DB	Reims F172H
☐	N228CX	SOCATA TBM-700	☐ N357PS	Dassault Falcon 20F-5	☐ N525PM	Cessna 525A CJ2
☐	N228TM	Raytheon Hawker 800XP	☐ N359DW	Piper PA-30	☐ N527EW	Cessna 501 Citation 1
☐	N230FT	Piper PA-28-161 Cadet	☐ N364AB	Beech B36TC Bonanza	☐ N529M	Hawker 800XP
☐	N230MJ	Piper PA-30 B	☐ N369AN	Cessna 182S	☐ N531RM	Aviat Pitts S.2C
☐	N231CM	Piper PA-46-500TP Malibu	☐ N369SB	Robinson R.44 Raven II	☐ N535CE	Cessna 560 Citation Ultra
☐	N234RG	Pilatus PC-12/45	☐ N370SA	Piper PA-23-250 Aztec F	☐ N535TK	Maule MXT-7-180
☐	N235PF	Piper PA-28-235 Pathfinder	☐ N373DJ	Cessna 650 Citation III	☐ N550PD	Cessna 550 Citation Bravo
☐	N237MM	Mooney M.20F Executive	☐ N375SA	Piper PA-34-200T Seneca II	☐ N554RB	Beech E55 Baron
☐	N2401Z	Piper PA-23-250 Aztec F	☐ N380CA	Piper PA-32R-301T IITC	☐ N555GS	Agusta A109E Power
☐	N242ML	Cessna 525 CitationJet	☐ N382AS	Reims F182Q Skylane	☐ N555WA	MD Helicopters MD.900
☐	N243SA	Piper PA-22-108 Colt	☐ N382RW*	Spitfire LFXVIe	☐ N556MA *	Beagle B.121 Pup 1
☐	N245CB	Piper PA-34-220T Seneca	☐ N393N	Robinson R44 Raven	☐ N559C	Piper PA-34-220T Seneca
☐	N249SP	Cessna 210L Centurion	☐ N395TC	Commander 114TC	☐ N560TH	Cessna 560XL Citation
☐	N249SR	BAe BAe125 Srs 800A	☐ N400RG	Boeing 727-22	☐ N562RR	Piper PA-32-301FT 6x
☐	N250AC	Piper PA-31 Navajo C	☐ N400UK	Lancair LC41-550FG	☐ N565F	Aérospatiale SA.341G
☐	N250BW	Piper PA-23-250 Aztec C	☐ N400YY	Extra EA400	☐ N565G	SOCATA TB-20 Trinidad
☐	N250CC	Piper PA-24-250 Comanche	☐ N401JN	Cessna 401	☐ N573VE	Cirrus Design SR22
☐	N250JF	Neico Lancair 360	☐ N407AG	Bell 407	☐ N575GM	SOCATA TB-20 Trinidad
☐	N250MD	Piper PA-31 Turbo Navajo	☐ N407WD	Bell 407	☐ N582C	SOCATA TBM-700
☐	N250TB	Piper PA-23-250 Aztec D	☐ N409SA	Reims FR182 Skylane RG	☐ N588CD	Cirrus Design SR22-GTS
☐	N250TM	Beech 200 Super King Air	☐ N411BC	Piper PA-28-181 Archer III	☐ N590CD	Cirrus Design SR22-G2
☐	N250TP	Beech A36TP Bonanza	☐ N411DP	Commander 114B	☐ N591JM	Agusta A109C
☐	N252JP	Hughes 369E	☐ N414FZ	Cessna 414RAM	☐ N593CD	Cirrus Design SR22
☐	N257JM	SOCATA TBM-850	☐ N414MB	Pitts S-2A	☐ N598MT	CL-604 Challenger
☐	N257SA	Piper PA-32-300 Cherokee	☐ N418WS	Beech 58 Baron	☐ N601AR	Piper Aerostar 601P
☐	N258RP	Beech 58 Baron	☐ N421CA	Cessna 421C Golden Eagle	☐ N604FD	Eurocopter EC.155B
☐	N259SA	Cessna F172G	☐ N423RS	Consolidated PBY-5A	☐ N606AT	Cessna 650 Citation VI
☐	N260AP	SIAI-Marchetti SF.260D	☐ N425DR	Cessna 425 Conquest I	☐ N614AW *	BAe BAe 146 Srs300A
☐	N262J	SOCATA TBM-700	☐ N425HS	Cessna 425	☐ N620LH	Aérospatiale AS.355F2
☐	N276SA	Brantly B.2B	☐ N425RR	Rockwell 690A	☐ N629RS	Piper PA-44-180T Seminole
☐	N277CD	Cessna 210L Centurion	☐ N434A	Cirrus Design SR22-GTS	☐ N634SR	Cirrus Design SR22-GTS
☐	N277SA	Piper PA-28-140 Cherokee	☐ N438DD	Cessna 310D	☐ N637CG	Agusta A109C
☐	N278DB	Mooney M.20R Ovation	☐ N440GC	Piper PA-44-180T Seminole	☐ N638DB	Piper PA-46-350P Malibu
☐	N278SA	Cessna 177RG	☐ N442BJ	Reims F177RG	☐ N642P	Piper PA-31 Turbo Navajo
☐	N280SA	Maule MX-7-180	☐ N449J	Agusta A109E Power	☐ N646JR	Piper PA-32RT-300T Lance
☐	N289CW	Cessna T303 Crusader	☐ N449TA	Piper PA-31 Turbo Navajo	☐ N650DR	Cessna 650 Citation III
☐	N295S	Piper PA-46-350P Malibu	☐ N454CC	Bell UH-1E	☐ N652NR	Cessna 560 Citation Encore

Registration	Type	Registration	Type	Registration	Type
N652P	Piper PA-18-150 Super Cub	N816RL	Beech E90 King Air	N2086P	Piper PA-23 Apache
N656JM	Reims FR182 Skylane RG	N818MJ	Piper PA-23-250 Aztec B	N2105J*	Bell 222
N660WB	Pilatus PC-12/47	N818Y	Piper PA-30 B	N2121T	Gulfstream AA-5B Tiger
N661KK	Piper PA-28-181 Archer II	N820CD	Cirrus Design SR22	N2136E	Piper PA-28RT-201 Arrow I
N663CD	Cirrus Design SR22	N831M	Hiller UH-12B	N2195B	Piper PA-34-200T Seneca II
N665CH	Cessna 525 CitationJet	N834CD	Cirrus Design SR22	N2216X	Cessna 337 Skymaster
N666AW	Piper PA-31 Navajo C	N836TP	Beech A36TP Bonanza	N2273Q	Piper PA-28-181 Archer II
N666BM	Aviat Pitts S-1T	N840CD	Cirrus Design SR20-GTS	N2299L	Beech F33A Bonanza
N666GA	Gulfstream AA-5B Tiger	N840PN	Rockwell 690C	N2326Y	Beech 58P Baron
N669MM	Bellanca 8KCAB-180	N840TC	Rockwell 690C	N2341S	Beech B300 Super King Air
N671B	Raytheon A36 Bonanza	N841WS	Hawker 800XP	N2366D	Cessna 170B
N672LE	Eurocopter EC.155B1	N846MA	Cessna 560 Citation V	N2379C	Cessna R182 Skylane RG
N672P	Cessna 210D Centurion	N852CD	Cirrus Design SR22	N2405Y	Piper PA-28-181 Archer II
N674BW	Grumman AA-5A Cheetah	N852FT*	Boeing 747-122F	N2437B	Cessna 172S
N675BW	Beech V35B Bonanza	N866C	Cirrus Design SR22	N2454Y	Cessna 182S
N680GG	Cessna 680 Sovereign	N866LP	Piper PA-46-350P Malibu	N2480X	Piper PA-31T1 Cheyenne I
N681EW	Reims F182Q Skylane II	N877SW	Agusta A109A-II	N2500	Beech D.18S
N691J	Piper PA-28RT-201T Arrow	N882	SOCATA TB-20 Trinidad GT	N2548T	Navion Rangemaster
N696XX	McD Douglas MD.369E	N882JH	Maule M.7-235B	N2652P	Piper PA-22-135 Tri-Pacer
N700EL	SOCATA TBM-700	N883DP	Cessna R182Skylane RGII	N2742Y	Hughes 369HS
N700S	SOCATA TBM-700	N889VF	Cessna T303 Crusader	N2923N	Piper PA-32-300
N700VA	SOCATA TBM-700	N897US	Fokker F.28-0100	N2929W	Piper PA-28-151 Warrior
N700VB	SOCATA TBM-700	N898US	Fokker F.28-0100	N2943D	Piper PA-28RT-201 Arrow
N702AR	SOCATA TBM-700	N900CB	Cessna 421C Golden Eagle	N2967N	Piper PA-32-300 Six
N702MB	SOCATA TBM-700	N900NS	Falcon 900EX/EASy	N3023W	Beech V35B Bonanza
N707TJ	Boeing-Stearman A75N1	N900RK	Mooney M.20J	N3044B	Piper PA-34-200T Seneca II
N707XJ	Cessna 177A Cardinal	N900UK	Cirrus Design SR22	N3084F	Reims F150L
N708SP	Bombardier Learjet 45	N902JW	MD Helicopters MD.902	N3103L	Beech 200 Super King Air
N709AM	SOCATA TB-21 Trinidad	N908W	Sikorsky S-92	N3109X	Cessna 150F
N709AT	Agusta A109E Power	N909PS	Cessna 501 Citation I/SP	N3400W	Piper PA-32-260 Cherokee
N709EL	Beech 400A Beechjet	N911DN	Bell UH-1H Iroquois	N3586D	Piper PA-31-325 Navajo
N711TL	Piper PA-60 Aerostar 700P	N916CD	Cirrus Design SR22	N3596T	AeroCommander 500
N712DB	Beech 65-A90 King Air	N918Y	Piper PA-30	N3669D	Beech 60 Duke
N715BC	Beech A36 Bonanza	N937BP	Mooney M.20J	N3864	Ryan Navion B
N717HL	Beech 58P Baron	N950H	Dassault Falcon 50EX	N3922B	Boeing-Stearman E75
N719CD	Cirrus Design SR22	N951SF	Beech 56TC Baron	N4085E	Piper PA-18-150 Super Cub
N719EL	Hawker 400XP	N956CD	Cirrus Design SR22	N4102D	Reims FR182 Skylane RG
N720B	Bell 206L-1 LongRanger II	N959JB	Piper PA-23-250 Aztec F	N4168D	Piper PA-34-220T Seneca
N726RP	Cessna 525A CJ2	N971RJ	Piper PA-39 Twin C/R	N4173T	Cessna 320D Skyknight
N731	Boeing Stearman A75N-1	N973BB	Mitsubishi MU-2B-60	N4178W	Piper PA-32R-301T IITC
N735BZ	Cessna 182Q Skylane	N980HB	Rockwell 695	N4238C	Mudry CAP.10B
N735CX	Cessna 182Q Skylane II	N982CD	Cirrus Design SR22-GTS	N4305H	Mooney M.20J
N737M	Boeing 737-8EQ	N989Y	Piper PA-24-260 Comanche	N4337K	Cessna 150K
N737RM	Cessna T182T Skylane	N994K	Hughes 269A (TH-55A)	N4422P	Piper PA-23-160 Geronimo
N741CD	Cirrus Design SR22	N997JM	SOCATA TBM-700	N4514X	Piper PA-28-181 Archer II
N745HA	Agusta A109A-II	N999BE	Falcon 2000EX/EASy	N4575C	Grumman G.21A Goose
N747MM	Piper PA-28R-200 Arrow II	N999F	Beech F33A Bonanza	N4596N	Boeing-Stearman E75
N747WW	Piper PA-23-250 Aztec D	N999MH	Cessna 195B	N4599W	Commander 112TC
N748J	Avro 748 Srs.1	N999PD	Waco YMF-F5C	N4698W	Commander 112TC-A
N750GF	Cessna 750 Citation X	N999RL	Robinson R44 Raven II	N4712V	Stearman PT-13D Kaydet
N750NS	Cessna 750 Citation X	N1024L	Beech 60 Duke	N4770B	Cessna 152
N753RT	Hughes 369D	N1027G	Maule M.7-235B	N4779B*	Cessna 152
N753TW	Cirrus Design SR22-GTS	N1092H	Beech C90A King Air	N4806E	Douglas B-26C Invader
N761JU	Cessna T210M Centurion	N1298C	Cirrus Design SR20	N5000S	Beech 58 Baron
N766AM	Aérospatiale AS.355N	N1320S	Cessna 182P Skylane II	N5020A	Cessna T182T
N767CM	Beech A36 Bonanza	N1325M	Boeing Stearman E75	N5043X	Cessna 172C
N770RM	SOCATA TB-9 Tampico	N1329T	Cessna T182T Skylane	N5050	Klemm Kl.35D
N777FC	Dassault Falcon 200	N1344	Ryan PT-22-RY Recruit	N5052P	Piper PA-24-180 Comanche
N778MA	Cessna 525A CJ2	N1350J	Commander 112B	N5057V	Boeing-Stearman PT-13D
N780ND	Hiller UH-12C	N1376C	Lancair LC41-550FG	N5084V	Cirrus Design SR22-G2
N781CD	Cirrus Design SR20-G2	N1407J	Commander 112A	N5113S	Cessna 750 Citation X
N790BH	Cirrus Design SR20-G2	N1424C	Cessna 182T Skylane	N5120	Bell 430
N799CD	Cirrus Design SR22-GTS	N1551D	Cessna 190	N5240H	Piper PA-16 Clipper
N799JH	Piper PA-28RT-201T Arrow	N1554E	Cessna 172N	N5264Q	MD Helicopters MD.369E
N800BN	CL-604 Challenger	N1604K*	Luscombe 8A Silvaire	N5277T	Piper PA-32-260
N800C	Cirrus Design SR22	N1711G	Cessna 340	N5315V	Hiller UH-12C
N800FR	Raytheon Premier 1A	N1731B	Boeing A75N-1 Stearman	N5317V	Hiller UH-12C
N800HL	Bell 222	N1745M	Cessna 182P Skylane II	N5320N	Piper PA-46-500TP Malibu
N800UK	Raytheon Hawker 800XP	N1778X	Cessna 210L Centurion	N5336Z	Cirrus Design SR20
N800VM	Beech 76 Duchess	N1835W	Beech 95-B55 Baron	N5428C	Cessna 170A
N808NC	Gulfstream 695B	N1937Z	Cessna 172RG Cutlass RG	N5632R	Maule M-5-235C
N808VT	Piper PA-28R-201 Arrow III	N1944A	Douglas DC-3C-47A-80-DL	N5647S	Maule M-5-235C Rocket
N810BW	Cessna 402C	N2061K	Beech 58P Baron	N5730H	Piper PA-16 Clipper

Reg	Type
☐ N5736	Raytheon Hawker 800XP2
☐ N5834N*	Commander 114
☐ N5839P	Piper PA-24-180 Comanche
☐ N5880T	Westland WG-30-100
☐ N5900H	Piper PA-16 Clipper
☐ N5915V	Piper PA-28-161 Warrior II
☐ N6010Y	Commander 114B
☐ N6024V	Commander 114B
☐ N6039X	Commander 114B
☐ N6081F	Commander 114B
☐ N6088C	Commander 114B
☐ N6095A	Commander 114B
☐ N6130X	Maule M6-235C
☐ N6182G	Cessna 172N Skyhawk II
☐ N6302W	GAF N22B Nomad
☐ N6339U	Piper PA-28-236 Dakota
☐ N6438C	Stinson L-5C Sentinel
☐ N6498U	Cessna T303 Crusader
☐ N6593W	Cessna P210N Centurion
☐ N6601Y	Piper PA-23-250 Aztec C
☐ N6602Y	Piper PA-28-140 Cherokee
☐ N6632L	Beech C23 Musketeer
☐ N6819F	Cessna 150F
☐ N6830B	Piper PA-22-150 Tri-Pacer
☐ N6907E	Cessna 175A Skylark
☐ N6954J	Piper PA-32R-300 Lance
☐ N7027E	Hawker Tempest V
☐ N7070A	Cessna S550 Citation II
☐ N7098V	North American TF-51D
☐ N7148R	Beech B55 Baron
☐ N7172Z	Hughes 369C
☐ N7205T	Beech A36 Bonanza
☐ N7219L	Beech B55 Baron
☐ N7223Y	Beech 58 Baron
☐ N7238X	Piper PA-18-95 Super Cub
☐ N7242N	Agusta A109A-II
☐ N7251Y	Beech A36 Bonanza
☐ N7263S	Cessna 150H
☐ N7348P	Piper PA-24-250 Comanche
☐ N7374A	Cessna A150M Aerobat
☐ N7423V	Mooney M.20E Chapparal
☐ N7456P	Piper PA-24-250 Comanche
☐ N7640F	Piper PA-32R-300 Lance
☐ N775RG	Maule M5-210C
☐ N7801R	Bell 47G-5
☐ N7832P	Piper PA-24-250 Comanche
☐ N7976Y	Piper PA-30 B
☐ N8105Z	Piper PA-28RT-201T Arrow
☐ N8153E	Piper PA-28RT-201T Arrow
☐ N8159Q	Cirrus Design SR20
☐ N8225Y	Cessna 177RG Cardinal
☐ N8241Z	Piper PA-28-161 Warrior II
☐ N8258F	Beech B36TC Bonanza
☐ N8412B	Piper PA-28RT-201T Arrow
☐ N8523Y	Piper PA-30
☐ N8702K	Cessna 340A
☐ N8754J	Aviat A-1 Husky
☐ N8862V	Bellanca 17-31ATC
☐ N8911Y	Piper PA-39 C/R
☐ N8990F	Hughes 269C
☐ N9057F	Hughes 369HS
☐ N9070L	BAe BAe 146 Srs 300
☐ N9086L	BAe BAe 146 Srs 300
☐ N9089Z	North American TB-25N
☐ N9122N	Piper PA-46-310P Malibu
☐ N9123X	Piper PA-32R-301T SP
☐ N9146N	Cessna 401B
☐ N9275Y	Piper PA-46-310P Malibu
☐ N9325N	Piper PA-200 Arrow
☐ N9381P	Piper PA-24-260C
☐ N9533Y	Cessna T.210N Centurion
☐ N9606H *	Fairchild M-62A-4 Cornell
☐ N9727G	Cessna 180H
☐ N9861M	Maule M.4-210C
☐ N9870C	Cessna T303 Crusader
☐ N9950	Curtiss P-40N Warhawk
☐ N10053	Boeing Stearman A75N1
☐ N11824	Cessna 150L
☐ N13253	Cessna 172M Skyhawk
☐ N14113	North American T-28B
☐ N19753	Cessna 172L
☐ N21381	Piper PA-34-200 Seneca
☐ N23659	Beech B58 Baron
☐ N24136	Beech A36 Bonanza
☐ N24730*	Piper PA-38-112 Tomahawk
☐ N25644	North American B-25D
☐ N26634	Piper PA-24-250 Comanche
☐ N29566	Piper PA-28RT-201 Arrow
☐ N30593	Cessna 210L Centurion
☐ N31008	Piper PA-32R-301 IIHP
☐ N31356	Douglas DC-4-1009
☐ N32180	Bell 407
☐ N33514	Hiller UH-12B
☐ N33870	Fairchild M62A Cornell
☐ N36362	Cessna 180 Skywagon
☐ N36665	Beech A36 Bonanza
☐ N37172	Beech B300 Super King Air
☐ N38273	Piper PA-28R-201 Arrow III
☐ N38763	Hiller UH-12B
☐ N38940	Boeing-Stearman A75N1
☐ N38945	Piper PA-32R-300 Lance
☐ N39605	Piper PA-34-200T Seneca II
☐ N41098	Cessna 421B Golden Eagle
☐ N42527	Bell 407
☐ N44914	Douglas C-54D Skymaster
☐ N45458	Piper PA-18-150 Super Cub
☐ N45462	Piper PA-18-150 Super Cub
☐ N45477	Piper PA-18-150 Super Cub
☐ N45490	Piper PA-18-150 Super Cub
☐ N45507	Piper PA-18-150 Super Cub
☐ N45526	Piper PA-18-150 Super Cub
☐ N45531	Piper PA-18-150 Super Cub
☐ N45543	Piper PA-18-150 Super Cub
☐ N45552	Piper PA-18-150 Super Cub
☐ N47351*	Cessna 152
☐ N47494	Piper PA-28R-201 Arrow III
☐ N49272	Fairchild M.62 Cornell
☐ N50029	Cessna 172
☐ N52485	Boeing-Stearman A75N1
☐ N53103	Cessna 177RG Cardinal
☐ N54105	Cirrus Design SR22-G2
☐ N54211	Piper PA-23-250 Aztec E
☐ N54922	Boeing-Stearman A75N1
☐ N56421	Ryan PT-22-RY Recruit
☐ N56462	Maule M.6-235 Rocket
☐ N56608	Boeing-Stearman A75N1
☐ N56643	Maule M.5-180C
☐ N57783	Stinson L-5 Sentinel
☐ N58566	BT-15-VN Valiant
☐ N59269	Boeing Stearman A75L3
☐ N60256	Beech C35 Bonanza
☐ N60526	Beech E55 Baron
☐ N61787	Piper J-3C-65 Cub
☐ N61970	Piper PA-24-250 Comanche
☐ N62171	Hiller Felt UH-12C
☐ N62842	Boeing-Stearman PT-17
☐ N63590	Boeing-Stearman N2S-3
☐ N65200	Boeing-Stearman D75N1
☐ N65565	Stearman B75N1 Kaydet
☐ N67548	Cessna 152
☐ N68427	Boeing-Stearman A75N1
☐ N70844	Piper PA-23-250 Aztec D
☐ N71763	Cessna 180K
☐ N74189	Boeing Stearman PT-17
☐ N75048	Piper PA-28-181 Archer II
☐ N75822	Cessna 172N
☐ N76402*	Cessna 140
☐ N80364	Cessna 500 Citation I
☐ N80533	Cessna 172M Skyhawk
☐ N81188	Piper PA-28-236 Dakota
☐ N84142	Lake LA-250
☐ N84718	Piper PA-28R-201T Arrow
☐ N90704	Grumman AA-5A Cheetah
☐ N90724	Hiller UH-12C
☐ N91384	Rockwell 690A
☐ N92001	MD Helicopters MD.900
☐ N92562	Piper PA-46-350P Malibu
☐ N93938	Erco 415C
☐ N95409	Cessna 172R
☐ N96240	Beech D18S (3TM)
☐ N97121*	Embraer EMB-110P1
☐ N97821	Mooney M.20J
☐ NC1328	Fairchild F24R-46KS Argus
☐ NC16403*	Cessna C.34 Airmaster
☐ NC18028	Beech D17S Staggerwing
☐ NC2612	Stinson Junior R
☐ NC33884	Aeronca 65CA Chief
☐ NC4531H	Piper PA-15 Vagabond
☐ NX71MY	Vimy 19/94 Inc Vimy FB-27
☐ NX793QG	Bell P-39Q Aircobra
☐ OE-KKC	Diamond DA 40D Star
☐ OE-XBA	Agusta-Bell AB206B
☐ OK-DUA 14	Jora sro Jora
☐ OK-DUU 15	Urban Air Lambada
☐ OK-FUA 05	Urban Air Lambada
☐ OK-GUA 16	Urban Air Samba
☐ OK-GUA 19	Urban Air Samba
☐ OK-GUA 24	Urban Air Samba
☐ OK-GUA 27	Urban Air Samba
☐ OK-GUA 28	Urban Air Samba
☐ OK-IUA 69	TL-2000 Sting RG
☐ OK-JUA 03	Urban Air Samba XXL
☐ OK-KUA 16	Urban Air Samba XXL
☐ OK-KUA 26	Urban Air Samba
☐ OO-A95	CFM Shadow C-D
☐ OO-AJK	Nord 1203 Norecrin
☐ OO-DFS	Piper PA-18 Super Cub 95
☐ OO-DHN*	Boeing 727-31
☐ OO-DHR*	Boeing 727-35F
☐ OO-EII	Bucker Bu.133C
☐ OO-GCO	Grumman-American AA-5A
☐ OO-MEL*	Focke-Wulf FWP.149D
☐ OO-MHB*	Piper PA-28-236 Dakota
☐ OO-NAT	SOCATA MS.880B Rallye
☐ OO-RLD	Miles M.65 Gemini 1A
☐ OO-SDK	*Boeing 737-229C
☐ OO-WIO*	Reims FRA150L Aerobat
☐ OO-YIO*	Robin DR.400/120 Dauphin
☐ OY-BTZ	Piper PA-31-350 Navajo
☐ OY-DRS	Reims F172K
☐ OY-EGZ	Cessna F172H
☐ OY-HGB*	Hughes 369D
☐ OY-ILG	BD-700 Global Express
☐ OY-JRO	Beech 65-B90 King Air
☐ OY-JRR	DHC.2 Turbo Beaver III
☐ OY-MUB*	Short SD.3-30 Var.200
☐ OY-NMH	GAF N-24A Nomad
☐ OY-OCV	Bombardier Learjet 45
☐ OY-PBI	LET L-410UVP-E20
☐ P4-HEC	Eurocopter EC.155B
☐ P4-LJG	Cessna 750 Citation X
☐ PH-2S5 *	CFM Shadow Series CD
☐ PH-3P3	WDL Fascination D4BK

☐ PH-3W6	CZAW CH-601XL Zodiac	
☐ PH-DUC	Glasair IIRG-S	
☐ PH-NLK*	Piper PA-23-160 Apache	
☐ PH-PAB	Neico Lancair 360	
☐ PH-PWA	Van's RV-8	
☐ PH-TMH	Piper PA-38-112 Tomahawk	
☐ PH-TWR	Ken Brock KB-2 Gyroplane	
☐ PH-ZZY	SOCATA MS893E Rallye	
☐ PK-MTV	BAe ATP	
☐ RA-01274	Yakovlev Yak-55	
☐ RA-44476	Yakovlev Yak-50	
☐ RA-44515	Yakovlev Yak-52	
☐ FLARF01035	Yakovlev Yak-52	
☐ FLARF02089	Polikarpov I-15bis	
☐ S5-HPC*	Agusta A109A	
☐ SE-BRG*	Fairey Firefly TT.1	
☐ SE-DRB*	BAe BAe 146 Series 200	
☐ SE-EOS	Piper PA-28-180 Cherokee	
☐ SE-FCM	Piper PA-28-180 Cherokee	
☐ SE-GPU	Piper PA-28-161 Warrior II	
☐ SE-GVH	Piper PA-38-112 Tomahawk	
☐ SE-HXF*	Rotorway Scorpion	
☐ SE-IIV	Piper PA-24-260 Comanche	
☐ SE-IRI	Cessna A185F Skywagon	
☐ SE-KBU	Christen A-1 Husky	
☐ SE-UCF	Slingsby T.61F Venture	
☐ SP-CHD*	PZL-101A Gawron	
☐ ST-AHZ	Piper PA-31 Turbo Navajo	
☐ SX-122*	Glasflügel H303 Mosquito	
☐ SX-AJM	Piper PA-28R-200 Arrow II	
☐ SX-BFM*	Piper PA-31-350 Chieftain	
☐ SX-BNL	Embraer EMB.110P2	
☐ SX-HCF	Agusta A109A-II	
☐ TC-ALM*	Boeing 727-230	
☐ TF-ELL	Boeing 737-210C	
☐ UR-67439	LET L-410UVP Turbolet	
☐ VH-AHL	Hawker Siddeley HS.748	
☐ VH-AMQ	Hawker Siddeley HS.748	
☐ VH-AYS	Hawker Siddeley HS.748	
☐ VH-JRQ	Jabiru Aircraft Pty J160-C	
☐ VP-BAA	Boeing 727-51	
☐ VP-BAB	Boeing 727-76	
☐ VP-BAM	BD-700 Global 5000	
☐ VP-BAT	Boeing 747SP-21	
☐ VP-BBW	Boeing 737-7BJ	
☐ VP-BBX	Gulfstream G-550	
☐ VP-BCC	Canadair CL600-2B19	
☐ VP-BCI	Canadair CL-600-2B19	
☐ VP-BCT	Rockwell 695B	
☐ VP-BDL	Dassault Falcon 2000	
☐ VP-BEP	Gulfstream V	
☐ VP-BFC	Cessna 525A CJ2	
☐ VP-BGE	Cessna 500 Citation I	
☐ VP-BGN	Gulfstream G-550	
☐ VP-BGO	CL-604 Challenger	
☐ VP-BIE	CL601 Challenger 1A	
☐ VP-BJA	CL-604 Challenger	
☐ VP-BKH	Gulfstream IV	
☐ VP-BKI	Gulfstream IVSP	
☐ VP-BKK	HS.125 Srs.400A/731	
☐ VP-BKQ	Bell 430	

☐ VP-BKZ	Gulfstream V	
☐ VP-BLA	Gulfstream G-550	
☐ VP-BLR	Gulfstream G-550	
☐ VP-BLS	Pilatus PC-XII	
☐ VP-BMP	Dassault Falcon 50EX	
☐ VP-BMZ	Rockwell Turbo 690D	
☐ VP-BNK	Hawker 800XP	
☐ VP-BNL	Gulfstream V	
☐ VP-BNM	Sikorsky S-76B	
☐ VP-BNO	Gulfstream G-550	
☐ VP-BNZ	Boeing 737-7HD	
☐ VP-BOW	BD-700 Global Express	
☐ VP-BPS*	Consolidated Catalina	
☐ VP-BUL	Aerospatiale AS.365N2	
☐ VP-BUS	Gulfstream IV	
☐ VP-BWR	Boeing 737-79T	
☐ VP-CAP	Canadair CL-604 Challenger	
☐ VP-CAT	501 Citation 1	
☐ VP-CBM	Cessna 550 Citation II	
☐ VP-CBX	Gulfstream Gulfstream V	
☐ VP-CCO	Cessna 550 Citation II	
☐ VP-CEB	BD700 Global Express	
☐ VP-CED	Cessna 550 Citation Bravo	
☐ VP-CFS	Hawker 800XP	
☐ VP-CFT	CL-601-3A Challenger	
☐ VP-CGE	Cessna 650 Citation VII	
☐ VP-CGL	Cessna 550 Citation Bravo	
☐ VP-CHU	CL-604 Challenger	
☐ VP-CIC	CL601 Challenger	
☐ VP-CJP	CL-601-3A Challenger	
☐ VP-CJR	Cessna 550 Citation II	
☐ VP-CKA	Boeing 727-82	
☐ VP-CLD	Cessna 550 Citation II	
☐ VP-CLV	BD-100 Challenger 300	
☐ VP-CMD	Falcon 2000EX/EASy	
☐ VP-CME	Boeing 767-231ER	
☐ VP-CMR	Gulfstream IV	
☐ VP-CNF	Cessna 525 CitationJet	
☐ VP-COD	Hawker 850XP	
☐ VP-COM	Cessna 500 Citation I	
☐ VP-COU	BD-700 Global Express	
☐ VP-CPT	BAe BAe 125 Srs.1000B	
☐ VP-CRB	Bombardier Learjet 60	
☐ VP-CSF	Gulfstream IV	
☐ VP-CSN	Cessna 560 Citation Ultra	
☐ VR-BEB*	BAC One-Eleven 527FK	
☐ VT-UBG	Hawker Siddeley HS.125	
☐ XB-RIY	Stearman N2S-3 Kaydet	
☐ YL-CBJ*	Yakovlev Yak-52	
☐ YL-LEU*	WSK-PZL Antonov An-2R	
☐ YL-LEV*	WSK-PZL Antonov An-2R	
☐ YL-LEW*	WSK-PZL Antonov An-2R	
☐ YL-LEX*	WSK-PZL Antonov An-2R	
☐ YL-LEY*	WSK-PZL Antonov An-2R	
☐ YL-LEZ*	WSK-PZL Antonov An-2R	
☐ YL-LFA*	WSK-PZL Antonov An-2R	
☐ YL-LFB*	WSK-PZL Antonov An-2R	
☐ YL-LFC*	WSK-PZL Antonov An-2R	
☐ YL-LFD*	WSK-PZL Antonov An-2R	
☐ YL-LHN*	Mil Mi-2	
☐ YL-LHO*	Mil Mi-2	
☐ YL-PAG*	Aero L-29A Delfin	
☐ YU-DLG	UTVA 66	
☐ YU-HEH	Soko SA.341G Gazelle	
☐ YU-HEI	Soko SA.341G Gazelle	
☐ YU-HES	Aérospatiale SA.342J	
☐ YU-HET	Aérospatiale SA.342	

☐ YU-HEV	Aérospatiale SA.342J	
☐ YU-HEW	Aérospatiale SA.341G	
☐ YU-HEY	Aérospatiale SA.341G	
☐ YU-PJB	Aérospatiale SA.341G	
☐ YU-YAB	SOKO G-2A Galeb	
☐ ZK-AGM*	DH.83 Fox Moth	
☐ ZK-BMI*	Auster B.8 Agricola Srs.1	
☐ ZK-CCU*	Auster B.8 Agricola	
☐ ZK-JQK	Pacific PAC 750XL	
☐ ZK-KAY	Pacific PAC 750XL	
☐ ZS-MBI	Commander 114	
☐ ZS-MRU	Douglas DC-3	
☐ ZS-ODJ	Hawker Siddeley HS.748	
☐ ZU-DCX *	Chayair Sycamore Mk 1	
☐ 4X-BJO*	Bell 206L-1 Long Ranger	
☐ 5N-AAN*	BAe BAe 125 Srs.F3B/RA	
☐ 5N-AGV	Gulfstream II	
☐ 5N-AJT*	Bell 212	
☐ 5N-AJU*	Bell 212	
☐ 5N-AJV*	Bell 212	
☐ 5N-AJW*	Bell 212	
☐ 5N-BHN*	Bell 212	
☐ 5N-HHH*	BAC One-Eleven 401AK	
☐ 7Q-YDF	Piper J3C-65 Cub	
☐ 9G-BOB	Westland Wessex HC.2	
☐ 9G-MKA	Douglas DC-8F-55	
☐ 9J-RBC	Piper PA-28-140 Cherokee	
☐ 9L-LSA	Sud Aviation SA330L Puma	
☐ 9L-LSG	Sud Aviation SA330F Puma	
☐ 9M-BCR	Dassault Falcon 20C	

NOTES

NOTES

TRY OUR COMPANIONS TO UKQR 2007 . . .

AIRLINE FLEETS – AFQR 2007

Around 220 A5-size pages listing the fleets of all the operators you are likely to see with jet and turbine equipment at any of the world's major airports, down to Jetstream/Beech 1900 size.   *Price £7.95 (or £6.95 to Air-Britain members)*

BUSINESS JETS & TURBOPROPS – BizQR 2007

Now 144 A5-size pages giving the registrations and types of all current business jets and business turboprops worldwide, together with serials and types of all those in current military service.Also includes latest US register reservations for all business types to January 2007.
Price £7.95 (or £6.95 to Air-Britain members)

. . . AND THEIR BIG BROTHERS

BUSINESS JETS INTERNATIONAL 2007

The only publication that gives full production lists for all biz-jets in c/n order with details of all regns/serials carried, model numbers and fates, plus a 48,000+ index of biz-jet regns, now in its 22nd edition at around 450 pages. Available June.

AIRLINE FLEETS 2007

800+ pages of around 3000 fleet lists with many extra features, including jet and turboprop airliners in non-airline use. Now in its 36th edition, this is the indispensable companion for the serious airline enthusiast. Available March/April.

UK/IRELAND CIVIL REGISTERS 2007

The 43rd annual edition of our longest-running title lists all current G- and EI- allocations, plus overseas-registered aircraft based in the British Isles, an alphabetical index by type, military-civil marks de-code, museum aircraft, plus full BGA and microlight details. Weighing in at around 600 pages, this is the UK civil aircraft register bible. Available March/April.

EUROPEAN REGISTERS HANDBOOK 2007

With over 650 A4 pages, the 22nd edition contains the current civil aircraft registers of 42 European countries from the Atlantic to the borders of Russia. The only such publication wlth full previous identities, ERH includes balloons, gliders and microlights. Available May.

For full details and prices of these and scores of other Air-Britain books, visit our web-site on **www.air-britain.co.uk**

AIR-BRITAIN MEMBERSHIP
Join on-line at www.air-britain.co.uk

Air-Britain was founded in 1948 and today has 4,000 current members including over 700 from outside the United Kingdom.

Air-Britain News (monthly – average 160 A5 pages) continuously updates this annual publication and all our other annual publications. For January-December 2007 the cost is £43 (UK), £52 (Europe), £58 (Rest of the World). This includes all the benefits listed below. If you join during the year you may pay a pro-rata subscription covering the balance of the year (if back magazines to January are not required). *Join now for two years 2007-2008 and save £5 off the total.*

Membership of 'Air-Britain' includes the following benefits:

▲ A quarterly house magazine, AIR-BRITAIN AVIATION WORLD, illustrated in colour and black & white, containing 48 pages of news, features and photographs.

▲ Three additional magazines (NEWS, AEROMILITARIA, ARCHIVE) available on subscription in any combination. All rates include the basic membership cost and benefits, and also offer a substantial saving on the cover prices of the magazines.

▲ Discounts on 'Air-Britain' Books. We publish 10-20 books per annum.

▲ Access to ab-ix, the 'Air-Britain' e-mail Information Exchange Service.

▲ Access to an on-line database of UK airfield residents.

▲ Access to Local Branches and the Specialist Information Service.

▲ Access to Air-Britain Trips

▲ Access to black & white and colour photograph libraries

▲ An annual Fly-In

▲ An annual Aircraft Recognition Contest

You can join Air-Britain direct from this advert on-line at **www.air-britain.co.uk**, where full details of the magazines and membership subscription rates are given. Membership normally runs January-December, but a number of alternative options are available to get new members started with a subscription.

Alternatively, you can contact us for a membership pack containing samples of our magazines, subscription rates, and a book list. Write to Air-Britain Membership Enquiries, 1 Rose Cottages, 17⁹ Penn Road, Hazlemere, High Wycombe, Bucks, HP15 7NE, UK. Tel 44 (0)1394 450767. E-mail: Barry.Collman@air-britain.co.uk.